Your Road Map to

BackOffice Expertise

Once you have mastered the basics of Windows NT Server and know how to create a new domain, or integrate your servers into existing networks, you are ready to add one or more of BackOffice's server-based applications.

Many organizations use BackOffice components to provide key functionality to their networks. This volume covers important BackOffice components, including:

- Exchange Server 5.0
- SQL Server 6.5
- Systems Management Server (SMS) 1.2
- SNA Server 3.0

It also includes information on security and software development in a BackOffice environment.

Learn How to Build an Enterprise E-Mail and Groupware Platform Using Exchange Server

This system offers many features including the ability to provide UseNet newsgroups or online discussion groups using **public folders**. You can deliver this functionality in **I-net** environments using standard Web browser-based clients.

Learn SQL Server—One of the Most Widely Used BackOffice Family Members

This relational database management system includes the ability to replicate data to other database servers and utilities for **integrating database information with Web pages**. Microsoft has also provided important tools for developers including the **Distributed Transaction Coordinator (DTC)** and **Microsoft Transaction Server (MTS)**, formerly known as Viper. Add these to your toolkit if you support computing solutions that use database technologies.

Explore the Power and Versatility of SMS

You may want to use SMS to **install** and **configure software**, **manage computer inventories**, and **diagnose hardware and network problems**. If you have a sound understanding of this product, you have added a powerful and versatile tool to your repertoire.

Learn the Synergistic Benefits of SNA Server

In host-based environments, or one of the many organizations that still run important systems on an **IBM mainframe**, SNA Server can provide synergistic benefits by linking the host with network-based clients and servers. Though somewhat specialized, this tool is vital in such environments.

Need the BackOffice Basics? Try Volume I

You may also want to explore *Special Edition Using Microsoft BackOffice, Volume I* (ISBN: 0-7897-1142-7), which covers (among other topics):

- The basics of BackOffice system architectures
- How to set up Windows NT servers
- Remote dial-up access
- Networking protocols

It also covers some of the newest BackOffice components, which form a complete set of **Internet** tools and applications that will allow you to create state-of-the-art Web servers for communicating and interacting with members of your organization and its constituents.

Special Edition

USING
MICROSOFT
BACKOFFICE,
VOLUME II

Written by Donald M. Benage and
Gregory A. Sullivan with

Azam A. Mirza • Larry D. Millett • David O'Leary
Kevin D. Runnels • J. Brad Rhodes • Robert S. Black • Allen Carson
Stephen E. Hayes • Michael W. Lichtenberg • Fred Sebestyen
Jeffrey J. Thurston • David Williams • Gary P. Dzurny • Tim Darby
Daniel Garcia • James D. Marshbank • Joseph P. Lengyel
Sherman D. Cassidy • Robert Bruce Thompson

Special Edition Using Microsoft BackOffice, Volume II

Library of Congress Catalog No.: 97-65020

ISBN: 0-7897-1130-3

99 98 97   6 5 4 3 2 1

Interpretation of the printing code: the rightmost double-digit number is the year of the book's printing; the rightmost single-digit number, the number of the book's printing. For example, a printing code of 97-1 shows that the first printing of the book occurred in 1997.

Screen reproductions in this book were created using Collage Plus from Inner Media, Inc., Hollis, NH.

Contents at a Glance

Volume I

Volume II

Table of Contents

VI | Exchange Server

VII SQL Server

VIII | SNA Server

IX | Systems Management Server (SMS)

42   Preparing for SMS   1445

Credits

PRESIDENT
Roland Elgey

PUBLISHER
Stacy Hiquet

DIRECTOR OF MARKETING
Lynn E. Zingraf

PUBLISHING MANAGER
Fred Slone

SENIOR TITLE MANAGER
Bryan Gambrel

EDITORIAL SERVICES DIRECTOR
Elizabeth Keaffaber

MANAGING EDITOR
Sandy Doell

ACQUISITIONS EDITOR
Jeff Riley

PRODUCT DEVELOPMENT SPECIALIST
Russ Jacobs

PRODUCTION EDITOR
Maureen A. McDaniel

COPY EDITORS
Christopher Nelson
Matthew B. Cox
Patrick Kanouse

PRODUCT MARKETING MANAGER
Kristine R. Ankney

ASSISTANT PRODUCT MARKETING MANAGERS
Karen Hagen
Christy M. Miller

STRATEGIC MARKETING MANAGER
Barry Pruett

TECHNICAL EDITOR
Joel Goodling

TECHNICAL SUPPORT SPECIALIST
Nadeem Muhammed

SOFTWARE SPECIALIST
Brandon K. Penticuff

ACQUISITIONS COORDINATOR
Carmen Krikorian

SOFTWARE RELATIONS COORDINATOR
Susan D. Gallagher

EDITORIAL ASSISTANT
Andrea Duvall

BOOK DESIGNER
Ruth Harvey

COVER DESIGNER
Dan Armstrong

PRODUCTION TEAM
Michael Beaty
Bryan Flores
Jessica Ford
Brian Grossman
Heather Howell
Tony McDonald
Angela Perry
Sossity Smith
Lisa Stumpf

INDEXERS
Ginny Bess
Charlotte Clapp

Composed in *Century Old Style* and *ITC Franklin Gothic* by Que Corporation.

About the Authors

Donald M. Benage

To my wife Diane, my son Andy, and my friends Bob and Steve—thanks for your love and support.

Donald M. Benage is an acknowledged information systems professional and Microsoft Certified Systems Engineer with more than 17 years experience applying leading technologies to complex business solutions. He has provided architecture strategy and technology assessments—as well as detailed systems and network designs—to numerous corporations in many different industries. This, coupled with his vast experience as a network administrator, has uniquely qualified him to work information technology issues with major corporate clients from initial design through implementation, culminating in a valuable transfer of his proactive network management disciplines to client personnel.

Donald began his career as the personal computer burst into the market. He has since achieved vast experience incorporating knowledge in management of computer support operations, hands-on software and hardware evaluation, design of strategic systems for practical implementation, and network administration. Specific Microsoft product expertise was further enhanced by his employment with Microsoft Corporation for more than four years, leaving their ranks as a senior systems engineer to pursue other challenges.

Donald is a frequent speaker in industry seminars and forums dedicated to understanding software development strategies and tools. As a Director with G. A. Sullivan, he manages the day-to-day operations of the Technology Center, its research and development facility. Donald continues in a career filled with recognition for excellence in technical ability and client service.

Gregory A. Sullivan

To my beautiful wife Christine, thanks for allowing me into your heart and your family. To my sister Kari and her husband Troy, thanks for giving us Shane—I know he will make us all proud.

Gregory A. Sullivan, founder and president of G. A. Sullivan, has been an early proponent of many significant advances in software development and, over the years, has amassed an impressive array of credentials.

Motivated by his enthusiasm for the personal computer revolution and how he believed it would ultimately impact the business community, Gregory started G. A. Sullivan in 1982 shortly after receiving his Bachelor's degree in Systems Science and Mathematics from Washington University School of Engineering and Applied Science in St. Louis, Missouri. By taking the simple computer tools available then, he applied them in support of his personal commitment to the short- and long-term success of his clients. As the personal computer revolution exploded into the business community, he focused his energies on rapidly emerging new technologies.

Gregory's recognized participation in the early design and development of new technology advances were critical to establishing and maintaining an industry leadership role. He successfully established formal relationships and partnership agreements with technology leaders such as Microsoft. Additionally, he has established numerous personal affiliations with leading technical forums and organizations. Gregory is a charter member of the Client-Server Round Table and an active member of the Association for Computing Machinery (ACM), the Institute of Electrical and Electronics Engineers (IEEE), and Tau Beta Pi. He is a member of the Washington University School of Engineering and Applied Science National Council, past President of the Alumni Advisory Council, and co-sponsor of the Stifel Jens Scholarship.

Gregory frequently addresses audiences on the topics of software, its application to information technology, and the advancement of the software development profession. By enthusiastically embracing such leadership opportunities within the industry, he has developed a widespread reputation and has positioned G. A. Sullivan as a premier software development and information technology service organization.

Azam A. Mirza

To my lovely wife for her understanding and patience; to my parents for giving me the education, dedication, and work ethic; and to my brother and sisters for providing the moments of laughter that helped me to accomplish my goals. Thank you all for being there.

Azam A. Mirza, a Microsoft Certified Systems Engineer specializing in client-server software development and distributed systems architecture, is a strong proponent of utilizing the Internet to help businesses meet today's challenges while positioning them to better compete in tomorrow's complex business environments. Azam holds a B.S. in Computer Science from Washington University in St. Louis, Missouri, and an M.S. in Engineering Management from the University of Missouri-Rolla. He is an expert in the design, development, implementation, and support of client-server applications in numerous operating system environments and on various hardware platforms. He has extensive software development experience in major software development languages and is well qualified in the field of Internet/intranet technologies. Azam routinely serves as the technical lead analyst and designer for an array of complex system development efforts across a wide range of industry disciplines.

His vast experience with the Internet graphical user interface applications design and development, coupled with his astute awareness of de facto standards and widely accepted guidelines for software development, has uniquely qualified him to author numerous standards documents on the consistent development of distributed applications. Azam has published a white paper on the emerging role the Internet is playing in the corporate world, "Intranets and the Internet: An I-Net Introduction." He has also authored a white paper on the Microsoft Active Platform, "Using Active Platform to Enhance Your Web Site." As a consultant for G. A. Sullivan, Azam significantly influences the direction business clients take in applying advanced solutions to their most complex business challenges.

Larry D. Millett

To the further adventures of Mr. Peanut and the Mighty Cosmo!

Larry D. Millett has an M.S. degree in Computer Science from Washington University in St. Louis, Missouri, and a B.A. degree in Philosophy from Harvard University. He has over ten years experience with microcomputer networks including consulting, training, and software development for clients nationwide. He is a member of ACM and a Microsoft Certified Professional. Previous publications include Que's *Special Edition Using Microsoft BackOffice,* white papers, technical articles, and commercial software.

As a G. A. Sullivan consultant, Larry provides technical leadership for distributed, multiplatform software projects. He lives in St. Louis with his wife and two sons, and can be reached by e-mail at **larrym@gasullivan.com.**

David O'Leary

Thanks to my brother Matt and Patrick Barlow for late-night proofreading and insight. Thanks to my parents for everything.

David O'Leary is a senior consultant with G. A. Sullivan specializing in object-oriented analysis, design, and programming. David, who holds a B.S. in Computer Science from Loyola University in New Orleans, Louisiana, gained his intimate knowledge of RAS through his involvement in many client-server and replication-based remote access applications.

Kevin D. Runnels

My work on this book is dedicated to my father, Gary Frederick Runnels (1939-1996), as well as to my grandparents, Mildred and Dealing Runnels.

Kevin D. Runnels is a Microsoft Certified Solution Developer with more than ten years experience in microcomputer programming, networking, and project management. Kevin has developed numerous systems for the accounting and financial services vertical markets and is a strong proponent of using computers as tools to expand business opportunities and markets as well as for traditional transaction processing. He is an expert in the design and development of client-server applications and distributed computing, especially in the Windows NT environment.

Kevin resides in the St. Louis area and has a B.S. in Business Administration from Southeast Missouri State University and an award in accounting from the University of California, Los Angeles. As a consultant for G. A. Sullivan, Kevin continues to leverage his practical business knowledge with his considerable technical expertise to solve complex business problems and to develop new business opportunities for clients nationwide.

J. Brad Rhodes

A special thanks to my wife Renee who has always been loving and patient. Thanks to my daughter Allison for always being a source of inspiration.

J. Brad Rhodes is an experienced developer of client-server systems with an emphasis on systems architecture. Challenged by his involvement in large and medium business solutions, Brad has acquired a thorough understanding of client-server systems development. He has spent the past nine years designing and implementing client-server systems with a special emphasis on open systems technology. His leadership has helped many companies adopt new technologies including relational database management systems, distributed systems, and object-oriented programming and design.

This experience has lead Brad to the position of Vice-President of Technology at Hamilton and Sullivan, a leading provider of client-server solutions for the banking and financial industry. At Hamilton and Sullivan, Brad oversees the development of next generation retail and commercial banking solutions.

Brad holds a B.S in Electrical Engineering from Southern Illinois University at Edwardsville, Illinois, and has nearly completed an M.S. in Electrical Engineering from Washington University in St. Louis, Missouri. Mr. Rhodes is also a Microsoft Certified System Engineer. He lives in the St. Louis area with his wife Renee and daughter Allison.

Robert S. Black

To Mom and Dad for your love, support, and understanding.

Robert S. Black is a graduate of Washington University in St. Louis, Missouri, where he earned a B.S. in both Computer Science and System Science and Engineering. He currently develops software for client-server applications as a software consultant at G. A. Sullivan.

Allen Carson

I dedicate this effort to my parents for putting up with me then, and to my wife Sharon for putting up with me now.

Allen Carson began his career 15 years ago, having spent the majority of those years developing different types of real-time control software. During that time, he participated in several international design projects which produced high-quality medical imaging products that have been distributed throughout the world.

Since joining G. A. Sullivan in 1994, Allen has contributed to numerous client-server software projects. His areas of expertise include database design, OLE server implementation, and GUI design and implementation in Visual C++ working in Windows NT and OS/2 environments. He also provided technical assistance for Que's *Special Edition Using Microsoft BackOffice.*

Allen received a B.E. in Electrical Engineering from Vanderbilt University in Nashville, Tennessee. He continuously pursues educational opportunities to remain current with emerging trends in technology. In preparation for this edition, he received a Certificate Of Excellence in the Official Microsoft Curriculum course, "Managing Webs and Web Content with MS FrontPage." In addition, he has contributed to the development of several Web sites.

Allen and his wife, Sharon Jaffe, reside in the St. Louis area where he is a consultant for G. A. Sullivan.

Stephen E. Hays

To my wife Laura and my children Doug, Sara, and Tom. Thank you for your loving support and understanding. Your encouragement has greatly helped with this project as it does with so many.

Stephen E. Hays is a Microsoft Certified Professional with over 13 years experience in the microcomputer industry. He is involved in all aspects of application development; Internet technology; voice, data, and video network integration; and wide area network implementations. He is responsible for technical review and implementation of the information systems at G. A. Sullivan.

Steve is a point man in hardware and software vendor relationships and partnerships for G. A. Sullivan with involvement in new product review, beta programs, and product implementation.

Steve, a native of St. Louis, resides with his wife Laura and three children, Doug, Sara, and Tom.

Michael W. Lichtenberg

To my wife Kate for all of your love and support.

Michael W. Lichtenberg, a Microsoft Certified Professional and PowerBuilder Certified Developer, holds a B.S. in Computer Science from Washington University in St. Louis, Missouri. He has five years experience in applications programming, focused primarily on client-server business solutions.

Mike's experience in developing client-server applications ranges from single-user solutions created using Xbase programming tools, to advanced solutions created using the most advanced application programming tools and back-end database systems. In various engagements, he has designed and implemented business solutions for a variety of industries, including retail, healthcare, and travel. He has applied his knowledge of application design and development to create business solutions using Microsoft Exchange Client.

Mike works as a consultant for G. A. Sullivan, and resides in Kirkwood, Missouri with his wife Kate.

Fred Sebestyen

Thanks to my wife Nancy for your love and support and my children Sarah and Jacob for your daily inspiration.

Fred Sebestyen earned his B.S. degree in Information Systems Management from Southwest Missouri State University in Springfield, Missouri. After graduation in 1983, he began his career with a local systems integrator in Springfield designing and implementing PC solutions for a variety of businesses.

Relocating back to his home in St. Louis, Fred worked for many years in the defense industry for a major defense contractor implementing and maintaining manufacturing systems. As a consultant, he worked on various classified projects for the defense industry using state-of-the-art technologies.

Advancing his career, he worked at the national service center of a major life insurance company in St. Louis. He established a solid background in information systems for the insurance industry performing many tasks ranging from application development in the DB/2 and IMS mainframe environment to providing technical support and maintenance for PC networks. Fred was also responsible for establishing the initial Web presence for this employer.

His expertise is in problem analysis and resolution using the latest and most appropriate technologies. Fred has maintained a close watch on new and emerging technologies throughout his career. With over 13 years experience in the computer industry, he has a solid background implementing PC networks and PC-based technologies. With the explosion of the World Wide Web, he has brought his knowledge and experience in the industry to the Web, developing Web sites and Web-based applications for a number of clients.

Fred is a consultant with G. S. Sullivan and resides in St. Louis with his wife Nancy and their two children Jacob and Sarah.

Jeffrey J. Thurston

It is to his family that Jeff wishes to dedicate his work and his life, none of which would be possible without their love, support, and patience.

Jeffrey J. Thurston is a Microsoft Certified Professional with more than 12 years of experience in the use and development of systems for microcomputers. Through his experiences with Novell NetWare, Microsoft Windows for Workgroups, and Microsoft Windows NT, he has developed a formidable knowledge of networking principles. Combined with experience in the languages of C and C++, BASIC, and Pascal, he has developed a broad knowledge base, allowing for a big-picture perspective on microcomputer solutions.

Jeff's most recent project involved a sophisticated client-server solution which included a custom SQL Server to Microsoft Access replicated database component. Development included the use of Microsoft Visual C++, Microsoft Visual Basic, Microsoft SQL Server, Windows 95, and Windows NT. Jeff routinely works with virtually all of the Microsoft development tools and operating systems to provide sophisticated solutions to the clients of G. A. Sullivan.

Jeff resides in the St. Louis area with his wife of 12 years, Joy, and their two sons Jonathan and Jeremy.

David Williams

To my wife Wendy and daughter Jennie—your love and understanding have always helped me through. You make everything worthwhile. To Mom and Dad, you taught me the principles by which I have always strived to live. Thank you.

David Williams has been involved in the design and development of leading-edge software systems for the past eight years. These systems range from scientific and engineering applications to information systems based on Internet technologies. He has had extensive development experience in VMS and UNIX as well as MS-DOS, Windows, and Windows NT. He is well-versed with the various TCP/IP protocols, and is a strong advocate for the use of object-oriented technologies in software design and development.

David holds a B.S. in Electrical Engineering from Purdue University in West Lafayette, Indiana and an M.S. in Electrical Engineering from Washington University in St. Louis, Missouri. He currently resides in the St. Louis area with his wife Wendy and daughter Jennifer.

Gary P. Dzurny

To my parents, who have always encouraged me in the things I have chosen to do. Thank you for all of your hard work and support.

Gary P. Dzurny has been programming for over 15 years concentrating mainly in the area of real-time data acquisition and analysis applications. Before arriving in St. Louis, Gary spent several years working as a Senior Software Engineer on the U.S. Army's Kwajalein Missile Range in the Republic of the Marshall Islands providing software and hardware support to a variety of range instrumentation systems including radar, optical tracking, and telemetry systems. It was here that he gained much experience with synchronous and asynchronous communication protocols. Prior to this, Gary was involved in anti-satellite and smart munitions studies.

More recently, he has been involved with developing a client-server-based reporting application used by a consortium comprised of the world's largest travel companies. Gary, who holds a B.S. in Engineering Physics from Murray State University, resides in the St. Louis area with his fiancée Amy and three children, Sydney, Christian, and Kirby. As a consultant for G. A. Sullivan and a microcomputer enthusiast, he is continuously working at keeping abreast of the current information processing and methodology trends.

Tim Darby

To my mother, Alice Darby.

Tim Darby has 15 years experience in information systems design and integration. He is knowledgeable in many areas of computing, including network management, network design, software development, and operating systems. For the past seven years, he has been involved in all aspects of network planning and integration on large client-server projects, including the Automated Patent System for the U. S. Patent Office. He specializes in Windows NT server-based solutions with SMS as the management platform. He is a Microsoft Certified Systems Engineer employed with Integra Technology International, Inc. He holds a B.S. in Electrical Engineering from Rice University.

Daniel Garcia

Daniel Garcia is a consultant at ConnectOS Corporation, which provides consulting and training for Microsoft Technologies and Web hosting. Daniel is a Microsoft Certified Systems Engineer. His specialties include Microsoft Windows NT Workstation, Microsoft Windows NT Server, Microsoft Internet Information Server, and Microsoft SNA Server. Daniel has experience with a wide range of computer systems, including mainframe, AS/400, VAX, Linux, Macintosh, and Wintel. He can be reached at **dgarcia@connectos.com**.

James D. Marshbank

To my wife Debbie, my mother Irene, and my sister Sandy Durham, thanks for all your love and encouragement. I am so blessed by God having made you a part of my life.

James D. Marshbank is a recognized information systems expert and Microsoft Certified Professional with more than 26 years experience in the management of computer facilities and operations, installation projects, software development projects, and major integration plans. Taking advantage of a strong technical and business background, he regularly participates in advanced technical research and authoring on a wide variety of subjects and projects in diverse forms. His vast experience in the mainframe and personal computer environments has allowed him to address specific technologies for interfacing these two environments and to explore strategies for supporting client enterprise networking needs.

Jim holds a B.S. in Applied Science from Miami University in Oxford, Ohio, and an M.A. in Business Management from Webster University in St. Louis, Missouri. He has been a long-standing advocate of applying advanced technologies to systems designed to achieve enterprise business goals. He is knowledgeable in the leading client-server environments and is an expert in analyzing client needs, determining solutions to those needs, and providing management of the software development and hardware integration projects to implement those solutions.

Jim and his wife Debbie reside in the St. Louis area where Jim, as a senior consultant for G. A. Sullivan, eagerly pursues opportunities to advance information technologies in solving intricate business problems.

Joseph P. Lengyel

Dedicated to the administrative staff at G. A. Sullivan.

Joseph P. Lengyel began his career ten years ago as a teacher. He is a well-qualified educator, experienced in teaching business and computer curriculums. With a B.S. in Business Administration from Fontbonne College in St. Louis, Missouri and upon completing an M.S. in Computer Information Systems from Colorado State University in Fort Collins, Colorado, he began pursuing a dual career in teaching and applying technology to business applications.

Joe's technical experience includes contributions in all aspects of the development effort with particular emphasis on Windows NT Server-based applications. These experiences range from participation in business process reengineering engagements and designing detail object and data models, to development tool evaluation and the practical application of technology through various development efforts.

Joe, who resides in the St. Louis area with his wife Rosalie, is a consultant for G. A. Sullivan. He continues to maintain a presence in teaching, capitalizing on first-hand experience in industry and his technical leadership roles in the effective use of information technology.

Sherman D. Cassidy

For my wife Liz, your love and support mean more than you know. For my daughter Irene, you make my life worth living.

Sherman D. Cassidy has an accomplished professional career including ten years in various information systems roles. Sherman's experience ranges from project management and technical leadership to hands-on participation in numerous development efforts.

He is knowledgeable in the leading operating system environments, major microcomputer programming languages, and database management systems. Sherman has particular expertise in all aspects of client-server software applications development. He is a Microsoft Certified Professional and has many acknowledged achievements including expertise in relational database design utilizing Microsoft SQL Server.

Sherman holds a B.S. in Business Administration from the University of Missouri-St. Louis. In addition to his technical background, he has formally taught computer curriculum and authored many diverse forms of articles, newsletters, training materials, and documents associated with systems development.

Sherman, his wife Liz, and daughter Irene reside in the St. Louis area where he is a consultant for G. A. Sullivan.

Robert Bruce Thompson

Robert Bruce Thompson is president of Triad Technology Group, Inc., a network consulting firm in Winston-Salem, North Carolina. He has 24 years experience in programming, systems analysis, microcomputers, data communications, and network administration. Bob is certified by Novell as a Master CNE, by IBM in Advanced Connectivity, by AT&T in Network Systems Design, and is now working on his Microsft CSE. He holds an M.B.A. from Wake Forest University. Bob specializes in network systems design, branch office networking, and the application of technology to the needs of small businesses. He's the lead author for Que's *Windows NT Workstation 4.0 Internet and Networking Handbook*, and a contributing author for Que's *Upgrading and Repairing Networks*. You can reach him via Internet mail at **rbt@ttgnet.com**.

Acknowledgments

A book of this size is necessarily an undertaking involving the stringent efforts of many people. We would like to thank all the authors, editors, and their families for the hard work and support they contributed. To the many people at Microsoft who helped us along the way, our sincere thanks. To all the people at Que whose professionalism and effort made this book possible, thank you. And to the many other people, friends, and customers of G. A. Sullivan who pitched in with assistance, we extend our sincere gratitude. Thank you all for your help.

In addition, we would like to thank the following people for their special efforts: Joe Ernst, Janine Harrison, Roxanne Hutson, Jim Marshbank, Bill Richardson, and Todd Warren.

We'd Like to Hear from You!

As part of our continuing effort to produce books of the highest possible quality, Que would like to hear your comments. To stay competitive, we *really* want you, as a computer book reader and user, to let us know what you like or dislike most about this book or other Que products.

You can mail comments, ideas, or suggestions for improving future editions to the address below, or send us a fax at (317) 581-4663. Our staff and authors are available for questions and comments through our Internet site at **http://www.quecorp.com** and Macmillan Computer Publishing also has a forum on CompuServe (type **GO QUEBOOKS** at any prompt).

In addition to exploring our forum, please feel free to contact me personally to discuss your opinions of this book: I'm **74671,3710** on CompuServe and **jriley@que.mcp.com** on the Internet.

Thanks in advance—your comments will help us to continue publishing the best books available on new computer technologies in today's market.

Jeff Riley
Acquisitions Editor
Que Corporation
201 W. 103rd Street
Indianapolis, Indiana 46290
USA

N O T E Although we cannot provide general technical support, we're happy to help you resolve problems you encounter related to our books, disks, or other products. If you need such assistance, please contact our Tech Support department at 800-545-5914 ext. 3833.

To order other Que or Macmillan Computer Publishing books or products, please call our Customer Service department at 800-835-3202 ext. 666.

Introduction

Special Edition Using Microsoft BackOffice, a book written by professionals for professionals, is about the Microsoft BackOffice family of products. This book is authored by a team of senior information system consultants and software engineers, all of whom apply their talents for G. A. Sullivan, a premier software development consulting company and Microsoft Solution Provider based in St. Louis, Missouri. *Special Edition Using Microsoft BackOffice* is designed to guide you through the complex implementation and administration issues associated with BackOffice. As such, it primarily focuses on how to prepare for, install, configure, and administer the various BackOffice products.

One of the most alluring features of this book is its up-to-date information. The authors worked hard to produce a time-critical, technically complete "how-to" book that offers in-depth coverage of the more important elements of the BackOffice family, including the following newest products of BackOffice:

- Exchange Server 5.0
- Microsoft Transaction Server (MTS)
- Active Server Pages
- Content Replication System
- Index Server
- SMS 1.2
- SNA Server 3.0

This book provides thorough coverage of these BackOffice products and includes sufficient Notes, Tips, and Cautions to ensure that you can implement and administer even the most troublesome features and elements of the individual applications.

Microsoft BackOffice, an integrated suite of server-based products that operates under control of the Windows NT Server operating system, is patterned after the success of Microsoft Office, a suite of client-based personal productivity tools designed for the client side of the client-server environment. BackOffice, designed for the server side of the client-server environment, significantly improves network administrator productivity in much the same way that Microsoft Office improves personal productivity. BackOffice was designed to be portable so that it operates on a variety of hardware platforms, and extensible so that new services can easily be added and existing services easily enhanced. Scalability is also a design feature. BackOffice needed to be stable in a growth environment where expansion of application scope could be offset by increasing the hardware's computing capability through additional processors.

Another design goal of BackOffice is that it comply with major open computer standards. Indeed, the BackOffice products do this, in addition to supporting the most popular network protocols. Consistency is also an important design consideration for BackOffice. The various products of BackOffice have a consistent graphical user interface, a consistent set of administrative tools, and a consistent applications programming interface. BackOffice is also designed to be easily integrated with other information system components, applications, and technologies. As such, BackOffice products integrate well with the Internet, UNIX, NetWare, other networks, and desktop computers.

A critical design goal is that BackOffice address the need to control access to and usage of services and resources. BackOffice does an excellent job of this. Primarily through the use of the Windows NT Server operating system—under which the other BackOffice products must operate—abundant security features and tools are available to secure transmissions, control access, and assign authorizations. Attaining a secure BackOffice environment, however, requires not only that these tools and features simply be available, but that they also be applied intelligently, that management of them be disciplined, and that appropriate controls be established.

Who Should Use This Book?

This book is aimed at administrators (of networks, systems, Web servers, databases, file servers, and so on) who are responsible for deploying the BackOffice suite, information systems managers faced with migration issues, and software developers who develop applications and interfaces used with the BackOffice family. The readers of this book will learn how to install, configure, and use BackOffice family components. This book provides excellent advice for administrators who have the task of implementing the BackOffice suite in a client-server environment. It also provides good advice for managers on how to use BackOffice to improve their business footing and leverage their automated information systems to maximize return on investment. Not only will managers learn what to do with BackOffice, they will also find out how to do it and, most importantly, why they should.

With the variety of material presented in *Special Edition Using Microsoft BackOffice*—coupled with its high quality of content, up-to-date material, level of detail, and easy to follow "how-to" format—this will be the all-encompassing book you will quickly come to depend on to supply answers to your BackOffice installation and administration questions. Although each of the products that make up the BackOffice suite is given a separate part within the book, special attention is paid to integration issues and techniques. Additionally, significant portions of the book are devoted to providing background material to enhance your understanding of critical concepts, and advanced topics explain how to really be effective with BackOffice in the enterprise.

How This Book Is Organized

This book is organized in a logical sequence starting in Part I and ending in Part X. Each part generally provides an overview of the BackOffice product, presents detailed instructions on how to install and configure the product, and then covers how the server administrator should use the product on a daily basis. Many parts include chapters explaining related technologies or advanced features of the product.

Volume I

Part I—Exploring Microsoft BackOffice
Part I gives an in-depth discussion of BackOffice and how it fits into an enterprise environment.

Chapter 1, "An Inside Look at BackOffice," describes the products that make up BackOffice and provides an overview of various process models, including the I-net process model. It also describes the role of BackOffice in this Internet-enabled, client-server world; describes how BackOffice moves you beyond client-server; and discusses the added value BackOffice offers to your computing enterprise.

Chapter 2, "Characteristics of BackOffice," details the BackOffice design goals, the role of BackOffice as a network operating system, and the services provided by BackOffice. The chapter concludes with a discussion of why BackOffice is a solid platform for the future and why it is important to you as an administrator, manager, developer, or user.

Chapter 3, "Planning for BackOffice," describes the various steps you should take prior to installing BackOffice. Some of these actions include building the network, establishing the administration team, analyzing the organizational requirements, preparing the facility, establishing policies and procedures, and licensing BackOffice.

Chapter 4, "Enterprise Planning and Implementation," discusses the most important considerations facing an administrator who is involved in creating an enterprise network and setting up servers to operate in such an environment. The chapter attempts to enhance your understanding of how computers on a large network are organized, the basics of network protocols, and Windows NT security.

Part II—Windows NT Server: Installation and Administration

Part II focuses on the base operating system, Windows NT Server, upon which all the other BackOffice products must run. The Windows NT Server part establishes a logical progression of chapters that is paralleled throughout the other parts of the book.

Chapter 5, "Implementing Windows NT Server," covers the installation and use of Windows NT Server. It includes a detailed, step-by-step procedure for installing Windows NT Server. This chapter also describes such related activities as partitioning hard disk space, exploiting the last known good feature, creating the Emergency Repair Disk, logging on and off the server, shutting down and restarting the server, connecting to the network from client workstations, and using Windows NT security.

Chapter 6, "Advanced Windows NT Server Configuration," provides details on using advanced capabilities and features of the operating system such as drive mirroring, and the use of RAID technology to build large disk arrays supporting error detection and recovery.

Chapter 7, "Administering Windows NT Server," outlines the network administrator's server management tasks. It includes a survey of the tools that come with Windows NT Server and discusses typical administrative tasks such as creating user accounts, sharing resources, and changing permissions.

Chapter 8, "Windows NT Server Directory Services," describes the directory services provided by Windows NT including the creation and management of domains, and the major domain models used to organize servers and networks. It also discusses the future of Windows NT directory services.

Part III—Windows NT Server: Enterprise Connectivity

Part III continues with advanced coverage of Windows NT Server. It includes information on using TCP/IP protocols, how to configure and use the remote dial-up component of Windows NT—the Remote Access Service (RAS)—and how to integrate Windows NT with NetWare and UNIX. It also details the protocols and products used to create Wide Area Networks (WANs) and support dial-up connectivity to the network.

Chapter 9, "Using TCP/IP with Windows NT Server," describes the Transmission Control Protocol/Internet Protocol, a network protocol and related applications that have gained wide acceptance and use on the Internet as well as on private networks. The chapter includes a brief tutorial on TCP/IP to help you understand some of the terminology and why things are done the way they are. The use of the Point-to-Point Tunneling Protocol (PPTP) to create Virtual Private Networks (VPNs) is discussed.

Chapter 10, "Name Resolution With TCP/IP," examines the mechanisms used to convert a friendly computer name into a computer's machine address. This basic network service is provided by both Domain Name System (DNS) and Windows Internet Naming System (WINS). The operation of these systems is described.

Chapter 11, "An Inside Look at Remote Access Service (RAS)," examines the basic capabilities of RAS, how to select hardware for dial-up access, and how RAS security is implemented.

Chapter 12, "Implementing Remote Access Service (RAS)," describes how to install and configure RAS using the various protocols available, and how to use the Remote Access administration tool.

Chapter 13, "Implementing Dial-Up Networking Clients," describes how to use RAS with different client configurations. It also shows how to use multilink channel aggregation to combine more than one modem or leased line for greater bandwidth and improved throughput.

Chapter 14, "Windows Integration with NetWare and UNIX," examines the use of Windows NT Server in heterogenous networks with several different operating systems. Novell NetWare issues (including NDS integration) and UNIX interoperability are both given particular attention.

Chapter 15, "Wide Area Network Technologies," describes WANs in more detail, including the strategies required for building WANs, the communication services used to provide WAN connectivity, and protocols.

Part IV—Implementing Intranet and Internet Technologies

After the base operating system—Windows NT Server—is covered, Part IV focuses on the newest additions to the BackOffice product suite, the Internet related products. You learn how this group of products can be used to build servers that allow your organization to have a presence on the Internet, or to create intranets that use Internet tools to deliver information internally.

Chapter 16, "The BackOffice I-Net Toolbox," describes the features of Internet Information Server (IIS) and Microsoft's overall strategy for Internet products. It also discusses third-party add-on products from other vendors.

Chapter 17, "I-Net Tools and Techniques," provides a brief introduction to the Internet and how it has changed the way people think of information technology. It also provides a basic understanding of what it means to your organization to embrace the Internet, and surveys how BackOffice can make your excursion into the Internet world a success.

Chapter 18, "Building a Web with Internet Information Server (IIS)," covers installing and configuring IIS. The use of the Internet Service Manager to control I-net servers is described in detail.

Chapter 19, "Web Browsers," provides an overview of the client-side of the Web—the browser. The two most widely used browsers, Netscape Navigator and Microsoft Internet Explorer, are both described.

Chapter 20, "Using Microsoft FrontPage 97," provides a detailed guide to creating and publishing Web pages with Microsoft's user-friendly Web editior—FrontPage 97. Web server administration and management are also discussed.

Part V—Advanced I-Net Development

Part V covers advanced Internet and intranet (I-net) technologies and products including how to build Web sites that incorporate database information to provide dynamic updates and a survey of Internet security techniques.

Chapter 21, "Implementing Index Server and the Content Replication System," describes two new BackOffice components that can play an important role in Web server management. Index Server provides powerful search capabilities to users who visit your Web site. CRS allows you to quickly and securely move Web content from server to server, across the Internet or within your own site, at prescheduled times.

Chapter 22, "Implementing Microsoft Proxy Server," details the steps required to set up and manage a proxy server to control access to the Internet and provide enhanced access to your user community.

Chapter 23, "Using Active Platform to Enhance Your Web Site," discusses the very latest Microsoft tools to build state-of-the-art Web sites. The components of Active Platform, and its use of ActiveX technology, are described in detail.

Chapter 24, "Dynamic Content with IIS Using dbWeb and IDC," describes two tools that can be used to include database information in your Web pages. The products discussed allow you to build dynamic pages that provide the specific information your Web users want.

Chapter 25, "Implementing Internet Security," outlines the rapidly changing field of Internet security. Several major technologies and tools are discussed, including Microsoft's Internet Security Framework.

Volume II

Part VI—Exchange Server

Part VI is devoted to the latest version of Microsoft Exchange Server—version 5.0. It describes how to set up the groupware and messaging subsystem of BackOffice, surveys the features of Exchange Server including integration with the Internet, and provides an overview of the various Exchange Server elements. It also describes how to install and configure Exchange Server, and how to install the client software to manage your personal messaging and scheduling needs. In addition, it describes how to implement, use, and replicate public folders, and how to install and use the advanced security features that complement the security already provided by Windows NT.

Chapter 26, "An Inside Look at Exchange Server," explores the capabilities of Exchange Server. Discussion focuses on what Exchange Server really is and what you should do with it.

The chapter also surveys the features of Exchange Server and provides an overview of the various Exchange Server elements.

Chapter 27, "Implementing Exchange Server," looks at how to size your server, install Exchange Server using the Exchange Setup program, use the Exchange Administrator program to configure your site and set up the mailboxes, and use the Exchange Server security features.

Chapter 28, "Using Exchange Client Applications," explores the client applications that come with Exchange Server, describes how to install the client software and use it to manage your personal messaging and scheduling needs, surveys the features of the Exchange Client that are particularly suited for remote users, and discusses the newest client application—Outlook.

Chapter 29, "Distributing Information with Exchange Server," explores the techniques used to create public folders, discusses the basics of implementing and using public folders, describes how to replicate them to other servers to balance the user load and make best use of available network bandwidth, and details how to replicate directory information across all servers in your organization. Internet integration techniques are also discussed.

Chapter 30, "Document Management with Exchange Server," describes how Exchange Server can be used to manage the flow of, storage of, and access to documents of many types. The creation of public folder applications is also discussed.

Chapter 31, "Exchange Server Advanced Topics," details how to install and use the Advanced Security features that complement the security already provided by Windows NT, how to install and use connectors for sending and receiving messages with Microsoft Mail (PC) users and the vast community attached to the Internet, and how to migrate mailboxes from a Microsoft Mail system.

Part VII—SQL Server

In-depth coverage of SQL Server 6.5 comes in Part VII. Included in the SQL Server chapters are discussions on relational database management systems, the role of the database administrator, designing databases, SQL Server management tools, selecting appropriate server hardware, recommended installation options, using SQL Enterprise Manager, proactively monitoring SQL Server, data replication, and the new Distributed Transaction Coordinator. The use of the Distributed Transaction Coordinator (DTC) and Microsoft Transaction Server (MTS) to build distributed applications has been added to this edition.

Chapter 32, "An Inside Look at Relational Databases," provides background information on SQL Server, relational database management systems (RDBMS), the role of the database administrator (DBA), and designing databases. This background information will form a critical foundation as you install SQL Server, create databases, and begin to use SQL Server as an important product for building client-server applications.

Chapter 33, "An Inside Look at SQL Server," describes the basic SQL Server environment, and explores the tools provided to manage SQL Server.

Chapter 34, "Building Your SQL Server," provides guidance on selecting appropriate server hardware; describes how SQL Server allocates and uses disk storage; discusses the installation options you must decide on for your installation to be a success; and details procedures for installing SQL Server, defining devices, defining databases, defining various database objects, and using the SQL Enterprise Manager to create login IDs and user names.

Chapter 35, "Maintaining SQL Server," discusses the various things you need to know to keep SQL Server running properly. Included in the discussion are some techniques for monitoring the health of SQL Server and some proactive steps you can take to ensure that no problems arise. Procedures for importing and exporting data are also discussed.

Chapter 36, "SQL Server Data Replication," explores the reasons data replication is becoming a widely used feature of SQL Server, and how to set up and manage this important capability.

Chapter 37, "Data Warehousing with SQL Server," describes the growing use of SQL Server to build a data warehouse of information that can be queried for analysis and review.

Chapter 38, "An Inside Look at Distributed Transaction Coordinator (DTC) and Microsoft Transaction Server (MTS)," describes two important tools for building distributed applications. The Distributed Transaction Coordinator (DTC), which is included with SQL Server, is described. Then MTS, a new product which was code-named Viper, is described. Although these advanced topics are not required for every SQL Server installation, they can be powerful additions to your SQL Server Administrator knowledge base.

Part VIII—SNA Server

Part VIII launches you into a thorough discussion of the BackOffice product designed to provide personal computer access to IBM mainframes or AS/400 minicomputers—SNA Server. You learn what the IBM System Network Architecture (SNA) is, how SNA Server integrates with the SNA network structure, the critical preinstallation actions that need to be taken when preparing for SNA Server, how to install and configure SNA Server, and the role of the SNA Server administrator in managing the SNA network.

Chapter 39, "SNA Server Preparation and Installation," provides an overview of IBM's SNA and Microsoft's SNA Server to include a brief survey of some of its more important features. It then acquaints you with the recommended installation preparation actions and details the steps necessary to install SNA Server using SNA Server Setup. Finally, the chapter outlines some common post-installation uses of SNA Server Setup.

Chapter 40, "Building SNA Server," covers the concepts and procedures for configuring the SNA Server and also for configuring the SNA Server-to-host connections. It includes detailed step-by-step procedures for configuring Synchronous Data Link (SDLC), 802.2, X.25, and Channel connections. It also explores the concepts and procedures necessary to configure logical units (LUs), group the LUs into pools, assign LU pools to users and groups, and configure downstream connections.

Chapter 41, "The Role of the SNA Server Administrator," explores the SNA Server Explorer features in detail and, where appropriate, outlines the step-by-step procedures necessary to perform specific tasks associated with them. Features covered include managing connectivity-to-host computer resources, managing access to SNA Server and host resources, and diagnosing problems.

Part IX—Systems Management Server (SMS)

The last product of BackOffice, Systems Management Server (SMS), is covered in Part IX. This part enhances your understanding of what SMS is and why it is needed; provides details on remote application installation, metering, and hardware and software inventory management; and explores the key features of Microsoft SMS and how they can be used to address systems management requirements for an enterprise-wide network. This part also describes how to set up SMS on your network and use it to become more productive as an administrator, some of the more advanced features of SMS and how to automate the process of software distribution and installation, and some techniques for monitoring and troubleshooting SMS.

Chapter 42, "Preparing for SMS," discusses what is meant by the term *systems management*, explores the key features of Microsoft SMS, and describes how this product can be used to address systems management requirements for an enterprise-wide network. It also surveys the various roles servers play in an SMS environment and the work they perform.

Chapter 43, "Implementing SMS," describes how to set up SMS on your network and use it to make you more productive as an administrator. Detailed information is provided to help you set up a primary site server for your central site, install other primary site servers and secondary site servers, and implement the site relationships. It also discusses procedures for adding logon servers and clients to a site and provides an overview of the basics of defining packages and jobs.

Chapter 44, "The Role of the SMS Administrator," describes some of the more advanced features of SMS and how to automate the process of software distribution and installation. SMS Security is reviewed, as well as accessing SMS from remote locations using dial-up lines. The Help Desk features of SMS are explored, and the Network Monitor protocol analysis tool is examined. Some techniques for monitoring and troubleshooting SMS are also discussed.

Chapter 45, "SMS Advanced Topics," describes some expert techniques to complement the routine tools that have already been described. The use of the Network Monitor to analyze network traffic is discussed, as well as third-party product integration.

Part X—Applying Microsoft BackOffice Technology

Part X deals with the practical perspective of using BackOffice to get work done. Discussion includes valuable information on evaluating your organization's needs and implementing a security system that meets those needs. Real-world application scenarios are examined to aid information systems managers and administrators in understanding what BackOffice means to application development and deployment. The concept of *proactive* versus *reactive* network administration is also examined. You learn how to develop aggressive network and server management approaches that usually prevent problems from occurring; but when problems do occur, mitigate their severity and correct them before the user community feels any significant impact.

Chapter 46, "Implementing Real-World Security," provides an overview of the field of security, recommends an approach to evaluating your organization's needs, and describes how to implement a system that meets your requirements. It discusses certain types of products and concepts from a broad perspective rather than from a detailed one because products will change and a targeted focus may invite overlooking other important security areas that may be weak.

Chapter 47, "Building BackOffice Applications," examines how BackOffice is applied to real-world situations. It is intended to aid information systems managers and administrators in understanding what BackOffice means to application development and deployment and, with the help of some application scenarios, highlights some important aspects of BackOffice with respect to application implementation.

Chapter 48, "Proactive Network Administration," discusses how to aggressively work as a network administrator to avoid problems. It helps you to develop an approach to network and server management that will catch most problems before the user community has felt any significant impact.

Appendixes

Appendix A, "SNA Server Preparation Forms," provides blank copies of forms that are useful in gathering and organizing SNA Server installation planning data.

Conventions Used In This Book

This book assumes that you are already familiar with the graphical user interface used in Windows-based applications. As such, no attempt has been made to describe "how" to select or choose various options in the dialog boxes discussed throughout this book. Instead, the terms *click*, *select*, *choose*, *highlight*, *activate*, *disable*, and *turn off/on* have been used to describe the process of positioning the cursor over a dialog box element (radio button, check box, command button, drop-down list arrow, and so on) and clicking a mouse button.

Those familiar with using the keyboard to select various dialog box options may relate this selection process to keystrokes instead of mouse clicks. Either method is equally acceptable.

Several type and font conventions are used in this book to help make reading it easier:

- *Italic type* is used to emphasize the author's points or to introduce new terms.
- Screen messages, code listings, and command samples appear in monospace typeface.
- URLs, newsgroups, Internet addresses, and anything you are asked to type appears in **boldface**.
- Keyboard hotkeys are indicated with underlining. For example, if you see the command Tools, Options, pressing Alt and T causes the Tools menu to appear.

At times, you may be required to press keyboard keys in selected combinations to activate a command or cause a selected display window to appear. When these situations occur, you see the key combinations described in a couple of different ways. When two or more keys need to be depressed simultaneously, a plus sign (+) is used to combine the keys. For example, if the

Alt and Tab keys need to be pressed simultaneously, you would see the annotation Alt+Tab. Likewise, if the Ctrl and Y keys need to be pressed simultaneously, it would be annotated Ctrl+Y. When keys need to be depressed in a certain sequence with no intervening actions, a comma (,) is used as a separator.

 T I P Tips present short advice on a quick or often overlooked procedure.

N O T E Notes provide additional information that may help you avoid problems, or offer advice that relates to the topic. ▪

CAUTION

Cautions warn you about potential problems that a procedure may cause, unexpected results, and mistakes to avoid.

▶ **See** these cross-references for more information on a particular topic.

Sidebar

Longer discussions not integral to the flow of the chapter are set aside as sidebars. Look for these sidebars to find out even more information.

 TROUBLESHOOTING

What is a troubleshooting section? Troubleshooting sections anticipate common problems in the form of a question. The response provides you with practical suggestions for solving these problems.

Exchange Server

CHAPTER 26

An Inside Look at Exchange Server

by Don Benage

Exchange Server is often thought of as the electronic mail (e-mail) component of Microsoft BackOffice. This is an accurate description as far as it goes—Exchange Server is an outstanding e-mail product. But Exchange Server offers more than just e-mail. It is a general purpose messaging and information delivery product that facilitates the exchange of information among groups of people and the development of groupware applications.

In this chapter, you explore the capabilities of Exchange Server. You learn about its features and investigate some of the benefits it can provide your organization. Exchange Server is a rich product with a great deal of functionality. You can start by using Exchange Server for e-mail, but to fully exploit its capacity, you will have to research its information sharing capabilities and leverage its programmable forms. ■

Components of Exchange Server

Learn about the components that make up Exchange Server, both on client computers and servers.

Features of Exchange Server

Find out what this product is capable of providing your organization. Learn about its advanced features that go well beyond basic e-mail.

Features of the Exchange Client

Explore the features of the Exchange Client and the capabilities it provides including e-mail and groupware applications.

Features of Schedule+

Learn about how Schedule+ can help you manage your personal schedule, plan meetings with colleagues, manage contact information, and track your To Do list.

Features of Outlook

Explore the features of Outlook, the new integrated personal organizer and e-mail client that is provided with Office 97.

What Is Exchange Server?

Microsoft Exchange Server is a collection of software applications, some client-based and some server-based, that cooperate to provide information-sharing facilities to groups of people and entire organizations. On the server, it comprises both standard and optional components. The standard server components include

- **Directory of users.** Contains information to facilitate e-mail delivery and other general information that can be customized to fit an organization's needs.
- **Information store.** Houses both public and private *folders* containing messages and other information types.
- **Message transfer agent (MTA).** Responsible for exchanging information in the system with other Exchange Servers and working in cooperation with other components called *connectors*, which exchange mail with foreign messaging systems (a term frequently used to describe other e-mail systems, including PC-based systems and those run on larger mini-computers or mainframes).
- **System attendant.** A multipurpose utility that enables you to monitor Exchange Server activities; generates e-mail addresses for new users; and provides a range of status checking, logging, and maintenance services.

The optional server components include the following:

- **Directory synchronization component.** Responsible for synchronizing directory information between Exchange Server and mail systems that use the Microsoft Mail 3.*x* directory synchronization protocol.
- **Key management component.** Enables the use of digital signatures and message encryption (encoding a message for protection and authentication).
- **X.400 Connector.** Works with the MTA to transfer messages among Exchange Servers and connects to other X.400-compatible messaging systems.
- **Internet connector.** Allows Exchange Server users to trade messages with Internet users.
- **Microsoft Mail connector.** Allows the interchange of messages with Microsoft Mail users.
- **Schedule+ Free/Busy connector.** Allows users of Schedule+, the Microsoft group scheduling application, to exchange times when users are busy and available with earlier versions of Schedule+.

These components work together as a cohesive unit. Most users will not be aware that the server-based services providing Exchange Server's functionality are not a single program. The relationship of the components in an Exchange Server system is shown in Figure 26.1. This diagram loosely represents the interaction among components.

FIG. 26.1
This diagram depicts the Microsoft Exchange components. It does not attempt to provide a comprehensive picture of all component intercommunication.

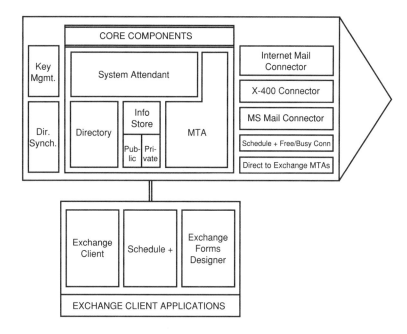

A number of client components also work together to provide comprehensive messaging services for desktop computer users. The client components include the following:

- **Exchange Client.** The primary component that helps users manage their mailboxes, compose and send e-mail, and use custom forms to exchange special types of information.

- **Schedule+ client.** Component that displays user and group schedules, assists with scheduling resources like conference rooms or special equipment, and assists with project and task management.

- **Exchange Forms Designer.** Allows organizations to create custom forms that facilitate the capturing, routing, and sharing of special types of information.

All these components, both client and server, are explored in more detail in the pages ahead. The important point here is the cooperation among components to manage and deliver information. In this respect, Exchange Server is similar to other BackOffice applications, especially SMS, which also uses a collection of components to deliver *packages* (usually new application software like Microsoft Excel) to desktop computers. However, the client components of Exchange Server are richer and more comprehensive, and the type of information being managed is different.

Exchange Server is one of the newest components of Microsoft BackOffice. Along with the Internet Information Server and other recently introduced Internet products like Proxy Server, it rounds out the collection of BackOffice components to form a remarkably powerful and flexible product. In its latest release, Exchange Server has gained many I-Net integration features and groupware enhancements for an even greater ability to provide many types of information to many types of clients.

Part
VI

Ch
26

Surveying Features in Microsoft Exchange Server

In addition to exploring the components of Exchange Server in detail, this Part VI, "Exchange Server," thoroughly examines the capabilities of this product. To give you a taste of the things you can do with Exchange Server, a few quick examples are presented here to whet your appetite. The procedures for implementing these capabilities are provided in upcoming chapters (see the section "From Here" at the end of this chapter).

Electronic Mail—Just the Beginning

Most users first use Exchange Server to send and receive e-mail, manage their e-mail mailbox, and use its address book to look up other e-mail users. E-mail messages created with the Exchange Client can contain rich text, including bullets, colored text, different fonts, and other formatting. You can assign different priorities to your messages and ask Exchange Server to provide *delivery receipts* and *read receipts* to notify you that your messages have been delivered or read by their recipients.

You can address e-mail to individual users or to *distribution lists* that specify a group of recipients. You can choose distribution lists from the address book on the server or create them as personal distribution lists. You can *carbon copy (CC)* additional recipients who should receive this message, and *blind carbon copy (BCC)* other recipients without the people appearing on the To: line or CC: line of the message being aware. You can send messages to other users in your organization or anywhere in the world with the appropriate connectors.

The Exchange Client's user interface is shown in Figure 26.2. Visible in the left pane of the Viewer window are a personal mailbox, access to an Administrator's mailbox, a local copy of sample applications provided with Exchange Server, and shared public folders.

Exchange Server is an enhanced replacement for Microsoft Mail version 3.*x*. For existing Microsoft Mail users, it is possible to use both products side-by-side during a migration period, as you gradually move users to Exchange Server.

Information Sharing with Public Folders

As the organization, and the administrative team, becomes more familiar with Exchange Server, the capability to share information in *public folders* can be exploited to share information among users in a variety of creative ways (see Figure 26.3). Two examples that are straightforward to implement are *bulletin boards* and *discussion databases*. By creating a public folder and setting its properties, you can control the form of the folder contents, who is authorized to access and modify the information, and how it is viewed.

You also can create *replicas* of the public folder, providing multiple copies of the folder to balance the access load among servers. And, you can reduce network bandwidth utilization by placing replicas in proximity to groups of users. Exchange Server automatically merges the changes made to various replicas at regularly scheduled intervals that you control, keeping their contents synchronized.

FIG. 26.2
The Exchange Client user interface shows the optional use of Microsoft Word as the editor for creating and reading e-mail messages.

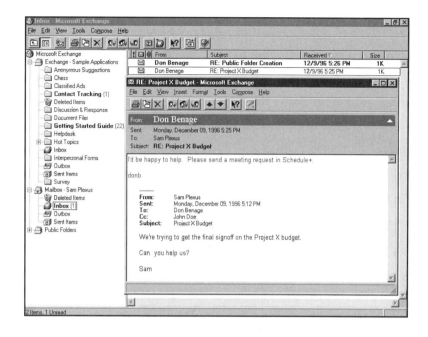

FIG. 26.3
An Exchange Client viewing a shared public folder. A custom form for making Help Desk requests, one of the sample forms provided with Exchange Server, is open in the foreground.

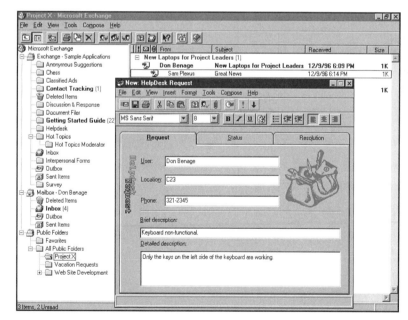

Part
VI

Ch
26

Using Custom Forms to Build Applications

Developers and advanced users, especially those with some experience using Visual Basic, can take advantage of the *electronic forms* capability to implement powerful and creative applications. These forms can use *controls*, the mechanisms that computer users are accustomed to manipulating in dialog boxes (see Figure 26.4). The controls may be buttons, simple text boxes, drop-down list boxes, or check boxes; or they may be more elaborate controls such as a fuel gauge or calendar control. Completed forms can be posted in a public folder, routed to a distribution list, or sent to a specific server for a particular action—updating a database, for example.

FIG. 26.4

A custom form being created with the Exchange Forms Designer.

Main window toolbar

Forms Designer toolbox

Forms Designer main window

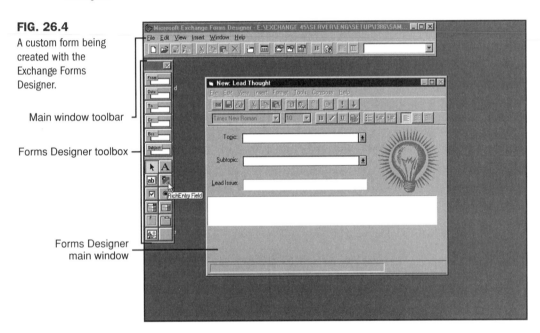

Using these forms and a little imagination can yield significant information management capabilities. An example included with Exchange Server, although admittedly somewhat frivolous, hints at the possibilities. It is a chess application that uses a form designed to resemble a chess board. It can be used to make chess moves and send them back and forth between users. This shows how highly customized these forms can be and the automatic routing that can be designated.

Group Scheduling

The Schedule+ group scheduling program has been available since 1993. Older versions have been included in Windows for Workgroups and are also available separately. Now, Microsoft has enhanced it and bundled it with the Exchange Client.

Schedule+ allows users to enter their own appointments on their personal calendar, as illustrated in Figure 26.5. They can set permissions to allow other users access to their schedule with varying degrees of authority. As appointments are entered, they can be marked private so that other users know only that you are busy but not see the contents of the appointment. Users also can enter recurring appointments—the second Thursday of every month, for example.

FIG. 26.5

The Schedule+ user interface is depicted in this figure. Some simple changes to the display have been made by selecting Tools, Options from the menu or direct manipulation with the mouse.

Events button

Right-click for Tab Gallery

Drag left or right

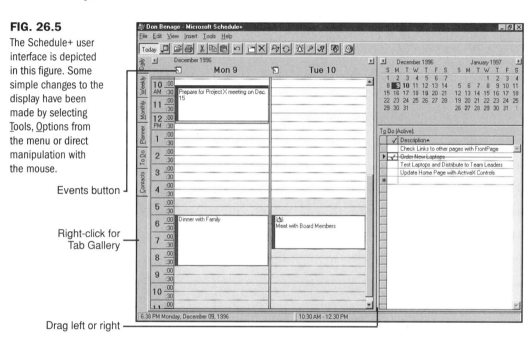

Using the Planner tab, you can schedule a meeting or event involving a group of people and even consult schedules for resources such as conference rooms or projection equipment. You can use the Planner to ensure that all mandatory attendees will be available for the scheduled time, automatically compose a meeting request e-mail for the event, and track responses to the request. In addition, you can enter information about projects and tasks for which you are responsible, drag and drop them onto your daily calendar to schedule them, and track partial completion of lengthy projects.

Integration with Other Systems

The use of electronic messaging as a component of a custom application is growing. The messaging infrastructure frequently extends beyond the high-speed LAN or WAN to include users who connect to the network from remote locations, or who interact with the organization only by e-mail through a public service provider or the Internet. The capability to create applications that use messaging as a transport mechanism extends the reach of the organization's information systems.

It is possible, for example, to create a sales support system that allows traveling or remote salespeople to e-mail a request for information on a product or its availability at the end of one day and receive an answer via e-mail early the next morning. SQL Server supports integration with e-mail through the SQL Mail feature. Using the messaging system to route information for validation and approval also can be an integral part of a custom application.

New Features in Exchange Server 5.0

Exchange Server 5.0 supports many new features. In particular, integration with the World Wide Web (WWW) and other I-net technologies plays an important part in the additions made to this version. There is also support for a growing number of standards and protocols.

The primary new features of Exchange Server 5.0 are listed as follows:

- Web browsers can now send and receive mail, access public folders, and use other information that has been published on an Exchange server.
- Post Office Protocol 3 (POP3) client support has been added to the server, allowing users to access their mailbox using popular Internet Mail client software from Microsoft, Netscape, and others.
- An Internet News Service has been added that provides the capability to support UseNet newsgroups with your Exchange Server.
- Support for the Lightweight Directory Access Protocol (LDAP) when accessing the directory information in Exchange Server.
- A new connector for cc:Mail which allows Exchange Server post offices to exchange mail with cc:Mail post offices. This can be used as part of a migration strategy, or simply to allow the two systems to interoperate.
- New Source Extractors have been added for Novell GroupWise and Collabra Share. Using these extractors you can easily migrate user accounts, mailboxes, and other information from these systems.
- Schedule+ client software for the Macintosh has been added to the Exchange Server support for that platform.

In addition to this list of features, the product has received overall tuning and bug-fixing attention, as you would expect with any new release. Finally, while it is not a feature of Exchange Server itself, Microsoft has added an important new Exchange Server client component to Microsoft Office. This new client is called *Outlook*, and it includes e-mail, scheduling, browsing for resources, journalizing daily activities, and many other capabilities into a single, integrated package. For more information about Outlook, see Chapter 28, "Using Exchange Client Applications."

Understanding the Server Components of Exchange Server

The server-based components of Exchange Server are primarily implemented as Windows NT *services*. As you have learned, these are a special type of application that runs unattended, with no input from the user. Services can be started, stopped, paused, or told to continue using the Services icon in the Control Panel or the Server Manager supplied with Windows NT. Most services can be configured by using an administration tool that comes with the product being used.

Some of the services have accompanying databases. For example, the Microsoft Exchange Directory service and the Microsoft Exchange Information Store service are both associated with a database. These respective databases contain the information managed by the services. As you see in upcoming sections, these databases can be shared, distributed databases in multiserver Exchange sites. There are also entries made in the Registry for each service. All Exchange Server services can be configured using the Exchange Administrator program.

▶ **See** "A Flexible Set of Services," **p. 54**

▶ **See** "Replicating Directory Information," **p. 996**

▶ **See** "Replicating Public Folders," **p. 1015**

Exchange Administrator

The Exchange Administrator tool can run on Windows NT Server or Windows NT Workstation. In version 5.0 of Exchange Server, the Exchange Administrator is not available for Windows, Windows for Workgroups, or Windows 95. A Windows 95 version may be available in the future. With the appropriate permissions, you can use this tool to configure and manage all the Exchange servers at the site you are currently logged on to and view the servers at other sites (see Figure 26.6).

FIG. 26.6
The Exchange Administrator is shown in this figure. The G. A. Sullivan organization has two sites—GAS-STL-EXHIBIT and GAS-NY-EXHIBIT. A properties dialog box is visible in the forefront.

Organization

Sites

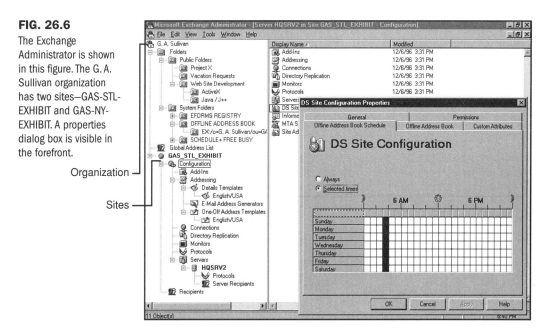

Part
VI

Ch

26

After you have installed Exchange Server, you use this tool to configure the server components, create mailboxes (or import mailboxes from another mail system), and perform other setup and configuration tasks. Monitoring utilities in this program also enables you to observe the status of Exchange servers and watch for potential problems. Detailed procedures for starting and using the Exchange Administrator are provided in upcoming sections. The remainder of this section provides an overview of the display and the way in which this utility is used.

Like several other tools and utilities provided by Microsoft, the Exchange Administrator display is divided into two *panes*. The left pane displays a hierarchy of *containers*. This display represents the contents of the *directory*, which is made up of all the objects in the Exchange Server *organization*. The right pane displays the contents of the container that is currently selected in the left pane. For example, if the Recipients object is selected in the left pane, the mailboxes (and other recipient objects such as distribution lists) that can be used as the target of a message display in the right pane.

N O T E   There is a slight difference in the behavior of this tool and that of the File Manager, another commonly used tool that has a two-pane display. When you open a folder in the File Manager, you always see the contents of that folder in the right pane because the folder is *selected*. The Exchange Administrator is more like the Windows 95 Explorer, another tool with a two-pane display, because it allows you to click plus/minus controls to the left of folders to open and close the folder without selecting it. If you want to display the contents of a folder you have opened with the plus control, you must select the folder with a single mouse click. The contents of the folder then display in the right pane. If you are familiar with the Explorer, this will be very natural. Users who are more familiar with the File Manager sometimes are confused by this behavior at first.   ■

Property Sheets

If you double-click an object in the contents pane, you will open the *property sheet* for that object. Property sheets are tabbed dialog boxes that allow you to view and modify values that represent the nature of the object and settings that control its behavior. Property sheets are used in other Microsoft products, but they are used more extensively and uniformly in Exchange Server. This can be a real advantage for the Exchange administrator. If you learn and understand the architecture of Exchange Server—what each component does and the way the components work together—it is fairly straightforward to find and adjust a component that needs to be modified.

In general, the changes that you make on property sheets are immediately applied when you click the Apply or OK button on the property sheet. There are some exceptions, however, that require you to stop and restart one of the services before the changes take effect. You are notified by an information box when this is the case.

The Directory

The *directory* is composed of two principal parts—the directory service and a corresponding database. The directory database, which is also called the Exchange database (EDB), is one of the two primary databases managed by Exchange Server (the Information Store is the other). It is located in the file DIR.EDB. The directory stores information about Exchange Server users and the components of the system itself. The Exchange Server directory is based on the X.500 specification established by the International Organization for Standards (ISO).

The directory service (DS) is one of the core components of Exchange Server and must be running for Exchange Server to function. Some of the optional components, such as connectors, can be temporarily shut down without affecting the overall operation of Exchange Server. The DS is responsible for maintaining the integrity of the EDB, participating in directory replication and providing directory information to Exchange clients and the Administrator program. Other services, such as the MTA and the System Attendant, use the configuration and routing information stored in the directory.

Information in the directory is used to build the *Global Address List (GAL)*, part of the address book used by clients. (The Personal Address Book for a user, stored in a file with an extension of PAB is also a component of the address book.) Information from the directory also is used to create the Offline Address Book, which is rebuilt at scheduled intervals based on the GAL or some subset of the directory.

When you start the Exchange Administrator program, the left pane of the window displays the directory for the server you are viewing. If you highlight one of the objects, the directory information for that object displays in the right pane. The directory stores different information for different types of objects. There are user-definable properties for recipient objects that you can use to customize the directory to better suit your organization's needs.

You can set up one Exchange server, or many, depending on the size of your organization and its geographic layout. If you use multiple servers, changes made to the directory on one Exchange server will be *replicated*, or copied, to the other Exchange servers in that site. Replication within a site, also called *intrasite replication*, happens automatically. Replication with other sites, *intersite replication*, can be configured to occur automatically on a schedule you establish and control.

Exchange Server can participate in Microsoft Mail 3.*x* directory synchronization protocol. If your organization uses Microsoft Mail and wants to run both systems side-by-side, you can install an optional component called the *Directory Synchronization Agent*. Synchronization with Microsoft Mail 3.*x* directories is not automatic and requires one server to be configured as the *master server* while others are configured as *requestor servers*. An Exchange Server can be either a server or requestor in a Microsoft Mail 3.*x* directory synchronization scenario. The native Exchange Server directory synchronization uses a different architecture known as *multimaster*, in which any server can initiate the replication of directory information.

▶ **See** "Replicating Directory Information," **p. 996**

Part

VI

Ch

26

The Message Transfer Agent (MTA)

In a system designed for managing messages, it should be no surprise that the *Message Transfer Agent (MTA)* is a critical component. You can think of the MTA as a postal worker who delivers the mail. The MTA works in conjunction with the MTAs on other Exchange servers to move messages from one post office to another. It also interacts with any connectors installed on your server to route messages addressed to recipients on foreign mail systems somewhere outside your organization.

The MTA uses information from the directory to find a recipient's address and then consults a routing table to determine if the recipient is on the same system, in the same site, at another site within the organization, or on a foreign mail system. By defining *address spaces*, you establish the addresses that the MTA will recognize and provide the information needed to create routing tables for each server. Messages that are addressed to recipients on the same server are treated as a special case and delivered directly by the information store.

The Information Store

The second primary database managed by Exchange Server (in addition to the directory database, EDB) is the *information store*. This is the repository for all public folders and messages stored on the server. It is divided into two separate files. The first file, PRIV.EDB, is the private information store that contains users' messages. The second file, PUB.EDB, contains public folders. These files are limited in size to 16 gigabytes (G) each, per server. The information store uses a transaction log, much like SQL Server, to maintain the integrity of information and ensure recoverability in the event of a system failure.

Like the directory, the information store also includes an active, server-based process, the *information store service*. This service cooperates with the other services in Exchange Server—the directory, the MTA, and the system attendant—to provide its features to users. In addition to interfacing with other services, the information store service is responsible for a number of tasks.

The information store is responsible for delivering messages to recipients that share the same *home server*. For messages sent to recipients on the same Exchange Server, the information store directly handles the delivery, without involving the MTA. If the recipients are not on the same server, it passes the message to the MTA, which may in turn pass the message to MTAs on other servers or one or more connectors.

The information store service updates the transaction log and the information store with new information. As information is inserted and deleted, this service also performs defragmentation of the database files to provide contiguous disk space for individual messages, a well-known performance improvement feature. It does not, however, compact the disk space used by the database files as messages are deleted. You can use a command-line utility, EDBUTIL, to reclaim unused space in the database files left by deleted messages and defragmentation.

The information store implements a feature called *single-instance storage*. As much as possible, a message addressed to multiple recipients is stored only once, and each recipient receives a pointer to the message rather than a copy of the message itself. This also is done with *attachments*, operating system files included in a message. To take maximum advantage of single-instance storage, you should group people who exchange many messages together on the same home server. This is a natural arrangement anyway and gives Exchange Server more opportunities to save space using this feature.

The System Attendant

The *system attendant* is another Windows NT service that performs routine maintenance chores on an Exchange Server. You might think of the system attendant as the manager of the post office, checking on other services and ensuring the accuracy of message delivery. It is responsible for the following tasks:

- As new recipients are added to a server, the system attendant generates the e-mail addresses used to address messages to those recipients. By default, Exchange Server generates three types of addresses: Microsoft Mail, SMTP (Internet), and X.400. If you have installed connectors to other e-mail systems, it generates an appropriate address for those systems, as well.

- The system attendant creates routing tables (and usually regenerates them once a day) that tell Exchange Server where to deliver messages with particular address types. For example, if the Internet Connector is installed on another server in your site, the routing table for your home server indicates that outgoing messages with an SMTP address type should be routed to the server with the connector first and then on to the Internet.

- The system attendant provides a number of monitoring and diagnostic services. For example, it gathers information on the performance of other services and provides it to monitoring tools. It also checks the links between servers, verifies the accuracy of directory replication information, and repairs inconsistent information.

Recipients

Any potential target of a message (or custom form, as you learn later) is known as a *recipient*. This includes not only user mailboxes and distribution lists, but also public folders. An e-mail address defined in the Exchange Server directory, but referencing a user's mailbox on another system, is called a *custom recipient*. Such a mailbox might be at another company, an organization such as a university, or an online service like CompuServe, America Online, or the Microsoft Network.

The directory has a *recipients container* that holds the definitions and properties of all the various types of recipients for the Exchange Server system. If you have the necessary access privileges, you can expand the recipients container in the Exchange Administrator and view the recipients defined on a particular system. As a normal user of Exchange Server, you can use the address book, which usually contains a Global Address List, a comprehensive list of all recipients. The contents of the address book are controlled by the administrators of the Exchange Server system.

Part

VI

Ch

26

In addition to individual custom recipients defined by an Exchange administrator, the address book may contain lists of recipients from other mail systems that are participating in a directory-synchronization process. Directory synchronization, frequently referred to as *dir synch*, automatically updates the directory information on one system with any changes made to the directory on another, and vice versa. This is a common situation in organizations that have an e-mail system running on a mainframe or mini-computer and another PC-based e-mail system. It also can be useful during a migration period, so that users on a new system can continue to exchange messages with users on the old system.

Mailboxes

Several components play a role in the storage of a user's messages. Each Exchange Server user has a designated mailbox, which is located on the user's *home server* in a *private information store*. All incoming messages are first transferred into the user's mailbox. Users may create a *personal folder file* (with a PST extension) on their computer's disk drive or on their private directory on a server, if they have such a directory. Incoming messages are still stored temporarily in the private store on the home server and then transferred to the personal folder file when the user connects to the server.

Users also can create an *offline folder file* (with an OST extension), which is a convenient alternative to a personal folder file for remote users. Public folders and personal folders that the user desires to have available offline are copied into the offline folder file and can be synchronized (or updated) regularly when connected to the network. The information is then available later when the user is disconnected from the network.

> **CAUTION**
>
> Personal files can be password protected. It is a good idea to protect personal files, especially if they contain sensitive information. This is even more important for laptop users because the risk of loss or theft is increased. Users should be cautioned, however, that if they forget their password, a new folder file must be created and the information in their old files is lost. This is different from their mailboxes on the server. If the user forgets the password for his or her mailbox, it can be reset (but not viewed) by an administrator.

A *schedule file* (with an SCD extension) contains the user's schedule information. This file, like the personal folder file, is stored on the user's own computer or a private area on a file server. A corresponding hidden file on the user's home server contains a copy of the user's schedule information to enable other users to view the schedule if they have access permissions. Another hidden file also contains free and busy information. This enables other users to see when someone might be available even if they aren't allowed to view the actual contents of the schedule. It is also possible to deny access to free/busy information.

In addition to the elements just described for storing messages and schedule information, there are several elements that enable identifying users and addressing messages. Exchange Server administrators define the contents of the address book, which is kept on servers. In addition to the Global Address List, administrators can define custom address lists. An Offline

Address Book also is designated. By default the Offline Address Book contains the entire Recipients container from the local site. Remote users can download a copy of the Offline Address Book to their local hard disk so that they can address messages when they are not connected to the network.

Users also have a *Personal Address Book* (stored in a file with a PAB extension), which can contain custom addresses and distribution lists the user defines. For convenience, users also can add any addresses from other lists to their Personal Address Book to make them easier to find quickly. Finally, one or more *profiles* can be created to specify the services the Exchange Client will use and the user's preferences.

Personal Folder File

Users can create personal folders to organize their own messages. When creating a profile, users can indicate whether new messages should be delivered to their mailbox (on the server) or delivered directly to the Inbox in their personal folder files whenever they launch the Exchange Client. If messages are delivered to their mailbox, users can still file individual messages in personal folders that they have created.

Users also can use the Inbox Assistant to create rules that will automatically file messages in folders. For example, you can define a rule that places messages from your manager in a folder called Manager, or any messages marked high-priority in a folder called Urgent. You also can create folders within folders, forming a hierarchical storage system. Folders can have names that include spaces and other special characters. Folders appear in the left pane of the client program's window. Folders are opened and closed using the plus/minus controls to the left of the folder in question.

Offline Folder File

The *offline folder file* is a powerful and easy to use mechanism allowing remote e-mail users, or users who travel with a laptop computer, to manage their access to information when they aren't connected to the network. First, users simply designate which folders from their mailbox on the server and which public folders should be available offline. Then, they select an option to synchronize offline folders with the online versions on the server(s). When that process is completed, they can disconnect from the network and continue to work as though they were connected, working with copies of the folders they designated on their own computer. When they reconnect again at a later time, they simply resynchronize, and all changes—both those made by the user to the offline folders and those made by other users to the online versions—are updated in all folders.

Public Folders

Public folders are one of the richest elements of Exchange Server. You can create public folders to serve many different purposes. You can design public folders to hold certain types of information and to display information in different views. Views can be assigned by an administrator and shared among many users. Personal views also can be defined by each user for his or her own use.

Part
VI
Ch
26

Public folders are stored on servers in the public information store. As users read the messages in a public folder, the *read status* is tracked *per user*. In other words, Exchange Server tracks who has read a message and who has not. A user running the Exchange Client program who is viewing the public folder will see the names of messages that he has not read appear in boldface type and messages that he has read in normal type. Another user viewing the same folder would see his own read status reflected through the use of boldface and normal type.

Exchange Server supports the capability to *replicate* public folders from one server to one or more additional servers. Although it is possible to have all users connect to a single server for a public folder, it may be wise to have multiple copies of heavily used public folders to distribute the workload among several servers. In addition, if your network includes more than one geographic location with slower network links between them, you may want to replicate public folder information during off-peak hours and let users connect to a local replica, thereby reducing bandwidth utilization during peak periods.

Public folders use a multiple-master architecture. When information in a public folder changes, it is replicated to all other servers that have been designated to contain a replica of that folder. Changes are replicated using e-mail messages. Exchange administrators can control when replication occurs and set limits on the size of messages that may be transmitted to control the impact of replication on the network.

Any and all of the replicas can be changed at any time. Therefore, at any given instant, the replicas of an active public folder will not be identical. They will be very similar, of course, with only recently updated information being different. If changes are made to two replicated copies of the same piece of information on different servers, the administrator of the public folder will be notified with a message indicating that a conflict must be resolved. No information is discarded by Exchange Server in this situation.

Distribution Lists

If a group of recipients is frequently used as a target for the same messages, you can create a distribution list that contains each recipient in the group. This list allows users to address messages to a single recipient, which represents the entire list with a single entry. The distribution list can contain individual mailbox names, custom recipients from other systems, public folders, or even other distribution lists. Take care to avoid nesting distribution lists too deeply, to avoid inadvertently sending multiple copies of a message to some recipients. Distribution lists can be defined by administrators and stored on the server. Individual users also can create their own distribution lists and keep them in their Personal Address Books.

Connectors

The Enterprise Edition of Exchange Server includes enhanced gateways, called connectors, which replace some of Microsoft's existing gateway products. However, Exchange Server maintains compatibility with the existing, DOS-based gateways. The new connectors are implemented as Windows NT-based services. They are the Internet Mail Service, the Microsoft Mail (PC) Connector, the Microsoft Mail (AppleTalk) Connector, the Schedule+ Free/Busy Connector, and the X.400 Connector. There is also a *site connector*, which is the easiest and most efficient way to connect one Exchange Server site to another. You can also use the Internet Mail Service or the X.400 Connector to connect sites on your own private network if you want.

Use of the Internet has exploded in the last few years. In addition to its original purpose of sharing research and information among universities, government agencies, and other organizations, the Internet has become a widely used method for exchanging e-mail messages. Messages are exchanged on the Internet using SMTP, the Simple Mail Transfer Protocol. This protocol defines the form of messages and the requirements for Internet hosts. The Internet Mail Service can send messages, receive messages, or both.

Messages that contain only text are easily transmitted over the Internet. However, messages increasingly contain elements in binary format, such as special formatting instructions or attachments. Some of the components that make up the Internet were not designed to transmit binary files. For these messages to pass through the Internet without being corrupted, they must be modified. The Internet Mail Service supports two mechanisms for handling this issue: Multipurpose Internet Mail Extensions (MIME) and UUEncode/UUDecode. The Internet Mail Service can automatically convert outgoing messages using the method you specify and convert incoming messages of either type.

Microsoft has offered two e-mail products in the past: Microsoft Mail for PC Networks and Microsoft Mail for AppleTalk Networks. Although the client and server components were different for these two products, they both supported Macintosh and IBM-compatible PC clients, and the two systems could be connected with a component called the Microsoft Mail Connector. Microsoft Mail for PC Networks was the focus of development efforts and included many advanced features including directory synchronization. This process kept the directories on all post offices (servers) synchronized with each other, a feature that Exchange Server also offers but implements differently.

▶ **See** "Replicating Directory Information," **p. 996**

▶ **See** "Setting Up a Site Connector," **p. 998**

Connectors are available for both of the older versions of Microsoft Mail so that existing users can coexist and exchange messages during a migration period, removing the need to upgrade all users at once. In addition to the connectors, migration tools are available that allow administrators to import and export directory information from one system to the other and to move users' mailboxes and existing folders and messages from the old system to Exchange Server. In addition, an Exchange Server can act as the directory server for the Microsoft Mail version 3.*x* directory-synchronization process, enabling the use of an Exchange Server system as a backbone connecting several older Microsoft Mail post offices.

An X.400 connector is also available for Exchange Server. This connector has been designed to communicate with other messaging systems that adhere to the X.400 standard as defined by the International Telecommunications Union (ITU). The ITU is a division of the United Nations and was formerly called the International Telegraph and Telephone Consultative Committee

Part

VI

Ch

26

(CCITT). This body has published versions of the X.400 recommendations at four-year intervals in 1984, 1988, and 1992. Exchange Server can exchange messages with systems that have implemented the 1984 and 1988 recommendations.

If your organization already has an existing X.400 messaging system in place, the Exchange Server MTA can exchange messages with the MTAs on other X.400 systems. In addition, Exchange servers can act as an X.400 backbone themselves by functioning as relay MTAs, which may eliminate the need for a public X.400 network provider. The X.400 Connector can be configured to use these networking protocols:

- TCP/IP
- TPO/X.25
- TP4/CLNP

The X.400 recommendations specify various components of a message called *bodyparts*. These components may be the text of a message, an attachment of some type, or other elements. A message also includes *header* information describing the sender, the recipient(s), and other information. Exchange Server supports *P1 envelopes* as described in the recommendations. It also supports P2 and P22 content if the message complies with the 1984 or 1988 recommendations, respectively. Message components that do not comply with the recommendations, or simply don't fit the categories currently defined, are *encapsulated* using the Transport Neutral Encapsulation Format (TNEF). And in situations where X.400 communications are used between Exchange Server sites, the native format used internally by the information store known as MDBEF is used to increase efficiency. This format is never used when communicating with other X.400 systems.

Finally, a Schedule+ Free/Busy Connector allows Exchange Server to exchange information with older Schedule+ users. Old Schedule+ clients will not be able to view the schedule of a user with the new Schedule+ (version 7.0), but they at least can see when the user is busy and available and send a meeting request. This is another feature that is an important part of a temporary coexistence and migration strategy.

Understanding Client Components

In addition to the many server components you have been learning about, the Exchange Client components play an important part in providing ease of use and functionality in Exchange Server. As you have already learned, the three main client components are the Exchange Client, Schedule+, and the Microsoft Forms Designer. This section explores these components in more detail and gives you an overview of the features available. Currently, client software is available for the following operating systems:

- MS-DOS
- Windows 3.1
- Windows for Workgroups
- Windows NT Workstation

■ Windows NT Server

■ Windows 95

The Windows NT client software is available for four CPU architectures (Intel, Alpha, MIPS, and PowerPC).

Exchange Client

The primary client component is, of course, the Exchange Client. This program represents the culmination of Microsoft's efforts to create a powerful, easy-to-use e-mail application that also supports information sharing among members of a workgroup or an entire organization. The Exchange Client contains many advanced features, including:

■ Support for profiles to allow multiple users to share the same computer, or one user to use more than one messaging system (see Figure 26.7).

FIG. 26.7

This dialog box shows the process of editing a user profile on the Windows 95 Exchange Client.

■ A toolbar to make it easy and fast to activate frequently used commands.

■ A graphical display using color, animated icons, and hierarchical folder controls to simplify message management.

■ Support for drag-and-drop operations. For example, you can drag an icon representing a message from your Inbox to a personal folder you created to file the message in your own personal filing system. You also can drag files from programs like the File Manager or the Windows 95 Explorer directly into the body of a message to include that file as an attachment.

■ The Inbox Assistant, an automated agent, filters messages based on criteria you define and stores them in your personal folders. Click the Add Rule button to bring up the Edit Rule dialog box (see Figure 26.8). The Inbox Assistant has other features to streamline message management, as well.

■ Support for remote e-mail users. Previous versions of Microsoft Mail required a separate client application to take full advantage of remote features. The standard client now supports remote features like downloading message headers first and then selectively

Part
VI

Ch
26

downloading only those messages you need most, or those that are small enough for practical download over a modem connection (see Figure 26.9).

FIG. 26.8

Use the Edit Rule dialog box to define a message filter for the Inbox Assistant.

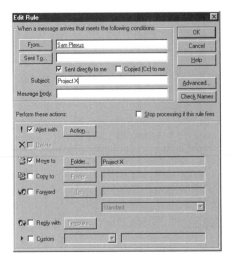

FIG. 26.9

The Remote Mail window is shown here being used to selectively download certain messages.

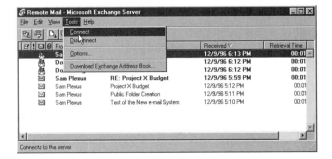

- Support for rich text such as bold, italics, different fonts, and colored text in messages.
- Support for OLE objects to be included in messages. These objects can appear as an icon, be represented by a Windows metafile, or appear as a native OLE object of the appropriate type.
- The capability to use Microsoft Word as your e-mail editor.

This list is just a sample of the features included in the Exchange Client. Detailed procedures for using this application are provided in Chapter 28, "Using Exchange Client Applications."

The Exchange Client uses a dual-pane window to show folders in the left pane and messages in the right pane. The left pane display can be turned off if the user prefers. The left pane contains the default folders (Inbox, Outbox, Sent Mail, and Deleted) and any folders you have created. When a folder is selected, the messages (or forms, files, and so on) that are in that folder are shown in the right pane.

Views can be defined that specify the columns that should be displayed for a particular folder. For example, a view could be defined that displays the sender's name, the subject, and the first part of the message body. Administrators can create views for public folders that are stored on the server. Users can use a predefined view, or they can create their own custom views.

Composing a new message can be initiated with a toolbar button or a menu selection. Users can address messages using the full Global Address List from the server, custom address lists defined by an administrator, or addresses they have defined themselves in their Personal Address Book. Users also can create their own distribution lists that contain recipients they frequently want to send the same information.

▶ **See** "Using Public Folders," **p. 1007**

Schedule+

Exchange Server includes an updated version of Schedule+, the group scheduling program. The new version contains many enhancements, including features common in Personal Information Managers, or PIMs. Here is a sample of the features provided by Schedule+:

■ Displays your personal schedule in a daily, weekly, or monthly format (see Figure 26.10). You can create custom views for your schedule by selecting options.

FIG. 26.10

Schedule+ is shown displaying a weekly schedule. Other tabs for additional windows are visible at the left of the display.

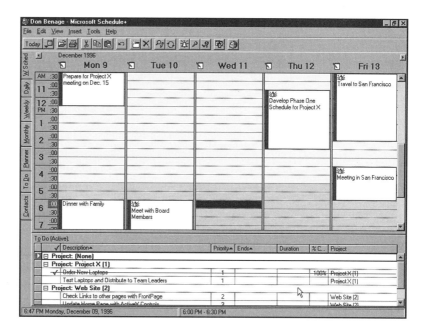

Part **VI**

Ch **26**

■ Uses a tabbed display window for easy movement from one display to another. You can add tabs to those shown by default to access other views of particular interest.

■ Displays a *Planner* page that shows a user's free and busy times. One or more additional recipients can be selected and their free/busy times overlaid on the display in different colors to simplify the process of finding a time when several people are available. In addition to users, schedules can be created for resources such as conference rooms and special equipment. Then the Planner can be used to schedule a time when the users and needed resources are available (see Figure 26.11).

FIG. 26.11

The Planner page in Schedule+ can be used to schedule a meeting.

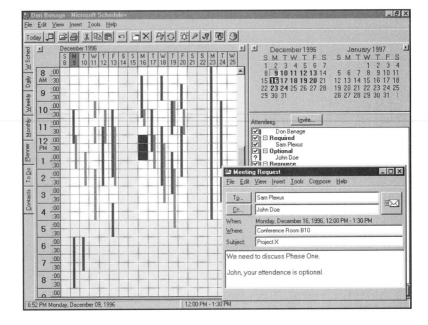

- Stores detailed information on a user's contacts, including addresses, phone numbers, birthdays, and notes.
- Stores a To Do list that can be sorted by project, priority, or other criteria (see Figure 26.12). The list includes columns for estimated effort, percentage complete, duration, and others.

FIG. 26.12

A sample To Do list is shown here with various projects and prioritized tasks for a particular user.

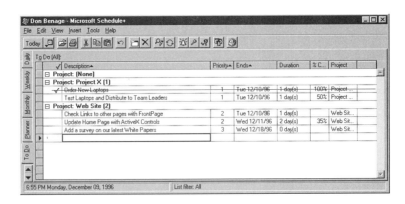

■ Includes a series of dialog boxes and several wizards that guide the user through Stephen Covey's *Seven Habits of Highly Effective People*. These dialogs boxes record the user's personal mission statement, the various roles they are called upon to perform in their personal and professional lives (for example, student, parent, engineer), and goals (both short-term and long-term) for each role (see Figure 26.13). The short-term goals are added to the To Do list, and may be placed on the daily or weekly schedule by dragging and dropping.

FIG. 26.13

The Seven Habits Wizard guides a user through the process of creating a personal mission statement.

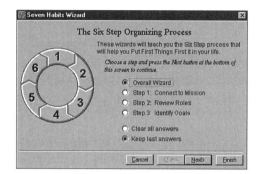

The Schedule+ tool works with e-mail to schedule meetings. A meeting request created in the Planner window generates e-mail messages to each of the invited recipients and tracks yes and no replies in a list window showing checks and Xs to indicate the various responses. It is also possible to integrate Schedule+ with the Microsoft Project application for advanced project management capabilities. The Microsoft Office Developer's Kit has information on programmatic interfaces to Microsoft Project and other useful information on developing integrated applications.

Part
VI

Ch
26

Outlook

Microsoft has included a new, integrated information management tool called Outlook in Microsoft Office 97. It offers some of the same features as Schedule+, but it is more of a personal schedule management tool (rather than group scheduling) and includes some additional capabilities that Schedule+ doesn't have. Schedule+ is still available and will probably still be preferred by some users, especially those who have a strong need for group scheduling. Outlook is available only for 32-bit Windows platforms (Windows 95 and Windows NT). Here is a sample of the features provided by this powerful new application:

■ Provides an elegant e-mail client with a variety of views available (see Figure 26.14). In addition, you can define custom views and flag messages for later action.

■ Displays your personal schedule in a daily, weekly, or monthly format (see Figure 26.15).

FIG. 26.14

This is the standard e-mail view shown by default when starting Outlook. The Office Assistant, an automated assistant that provides how-to advice and suggestions, is visible at the lower right.

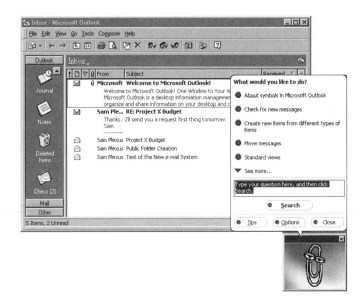

FIG. 26.15

This is the weekly schedule display provided by Outlook.

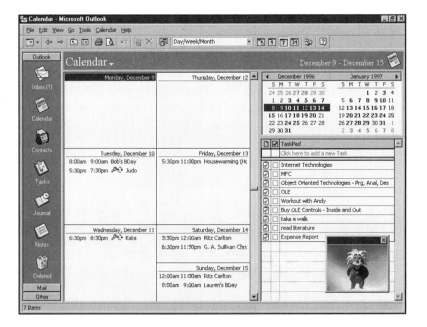

■ Uses the *Outlook bar* with a number of icon groups for easy movement from one display to another. The Outlook bar is visible at the left of the screen in all of the Outlook figures.

■ Displays a *Journal* page that shows when you completed selected tasks, sent or received e-mail from selected individuals, or other important activities that you want to track (see Figure 26.16).

FIG. 26.16
The Journal page in Outlook can be used to track your activities.

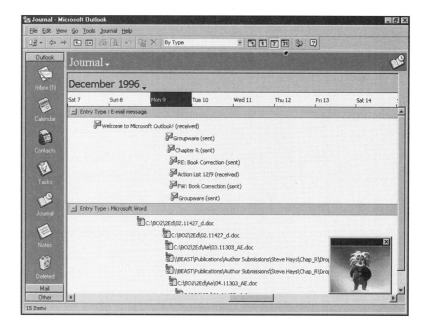

■ Stores detailed information on contacts, including addresses, phone numbers, birthdays, and notes.

■ Stores a To Do list that can be sorted by project, priority, or other criteria.

■ Allows you to enter ad hoc notes (similar to "Post-it™" Notes) as displayed in Figure 26.17.

FIG. 26.17
Some sample Notes are shown in this figure.

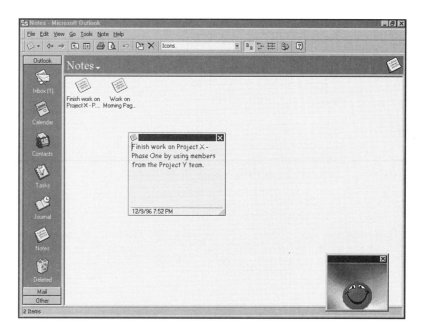

■ In addition to personal schedule and contact management, Outlook also allows you to browse for information on your computer (see Figure 26.18).

FIG. 26.18

Outlook helps you to file and locate information stored on your computer.

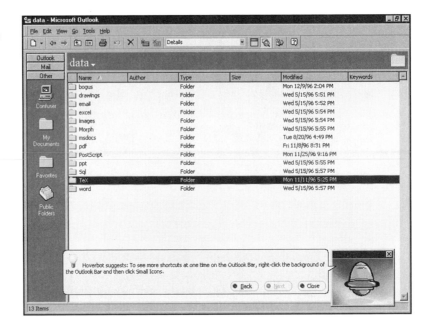

■ Outlook also provides access to public folders on an Exchange Server (see Figure 26.19).

FIG. 26.19

This figure depicts a public folder devoted to Object Oriented Technology. A number of ongoing discussions are visible in the pane on the right side of the window.

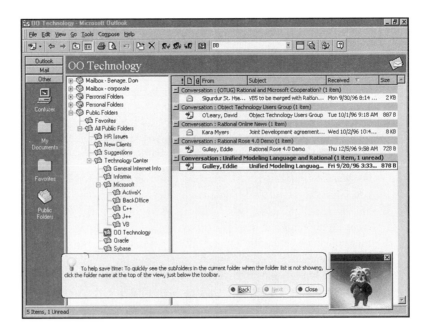

Outlook is a powerful blend of personal information management and activity tracking. It can be used as a task planner with the capability to delegate work and track progress on assigned tasks. For many people, this will be the best all-around tool for electronic mail and daily personal management.

Exchange Forms Designer

The Exchange Forms Designer is not a client application in the same sense that Schedule+ and the Exchange Client are client applications. It is a development tool that allows administrators or advanced users to create custom forms. Using the Forms Designer, you can lay out the appearance of the form, add the elements you want to appear on the form (including text, graphics, and other controls), create custom Help for the form, and generate Visual Basic code for the form. A set of templates is included to make it easier to create common types of forms. For example, there is a template for a send form, which you can use as the basis for forms that are used to send information from one user to other recipients. There is even a Form Template wizard that guides users through the process of selecting an appropriate template and setting some of the properties for the form to match the needs expressed.

The two basic types of forms are *send forms* and *post forms*. You've just learned the purpose of send forms. Post forms are used for posting information in a folder for subsequent viewing. They are most commonly used in conjunction with a public folder. Each form can contain one or two windows. One-window forms are used when the same window can be used to enter and send (or post) the information, and then subsequently to open and view the information. If the characteristics of the form used to enter information need to be different from the window used for subsequent viewing, a two-window form is more suitable.

After the basic form has been generated with the Forms wizard, you can set properties for the various elements on the form to further customize its appearance and behavior. Properties can be set for the entire form, for a particular window, or for individual fields. You also can add controls and Visual Basic code to create forms with highly customized behavior. See the *Application Designer's Guide* provided with the Exchange Server documentation for more information on creating custom forms with the Exchange Forms Designer.

▶ **See** "Creating a Custom Form," **p. 1053**

Part

VI

Ch

26

Understanding Organizations, Sites, and Domains

The word "organization" has a special meaning in the context of an Exchange Server discussion. Throughout this book, "organization" is generally used in its traditional connotation—a collection of people and resources such as a corporate entity or educational institution with some common purpose or goal. An Exchange Server organization is the largest entity describing a collection of servers and related clients that share a directory of objects and addresses. When "organization" is used in Exchange Server chapters, it should be obvious from the context which type of organization is meant. In some cases, either definition is applicable and some ambiguity does not affect the meaning of the sentence.

Organizations are divided into *sites*. A site is a collection of servers that share common configuration elements and are connected to each other with high-speed communications links. Usually a site is geographically located on a single LAN, although with (expensive) high-speed WAN links, a logical *site* could actually extend over a large geographic area. The connectivity and exchange of information among servers on the same site is easy to configure. The synchronization of directory information (mailboxes, distribution lists, custom recipients, and configuration information for various objects in the system) is done automatically between the servers in a site. To connect two sites, you must configure an explicit connector and define processes to share directory information.

▶ **See** "Replicating Directory Information," **p. 996**

Windows NT Domains provide the security context that all Exchange Server objects depend on. Windows NT security is the basis for all permissions that are assigned and the audit and monitoring features offered by Exchange Server. It is not necessary to create a one-to-one mapping between sites and domains. You could, for example, use a single Windows NT domain for your entire organization and still decide to use multiple logical sites (perhaps one per department) for your Exchange Server system. Conversely, a single Exchange Server site might span multiple Windows NT domains. Remember that domains are designed to provide security for shared resources on the network. Exchange Server sites are designed to facilitate the transmission and sharing of information. The two structures may or may not coincide.

Organizing Your Enterprise

Although you can certainly use Exchange Server to handle messaging for a small- to medium-sized organization or department, it has been designed with the power and features to handle the needs of the largest organizations. You can add processors and other equipment to a single server (assuming that the computer you have selected supports these additions), and Windows NT and Exchange Server will take advantage of the additional capability provided by these additions. You also can increase the power of your Exchange Server system by adding more computers. The architecture of an Exchange Server system allows you to implement services on a collection of machines that work together cooperatively to deliver the facilities provided by the system as a whole.

Careful planning is required for your Exchange Server system to work reliably and deliver the full functionality of which it is capable. If you are implementing more than one or two Exchange servers, you should take the time to study the *Concepts and Planning Guide* provided with the Exchange Server product. It provides a wealth of planning information that is beyond the scope of this book and can help you with designing medium to very large Exchange Server systems. This section provides some basic guidelines to aid your planning process and help to make your implementation successful.

Planning Your Site

A good first step when approaching any computer system implementation is to do some research and characterize the intended user community. What are the different tasks performed by these people? What information is required to perform those tasks? Is there information that would be helpful, but is not currently available? Create a table that lists groups of users and the applications they need. Review the features of Exchange Server and look for capabilities that closely match the needs of users. E-mail is a natural starting point with the product, but you also should explore the groupware capabilities provided by shared public folders with or without the use of custom forms.

Evaluate the physical network that will support your Exchange Server system. It is helpful to get a copy of any existing diagrams that document the network in use or to create such a diagram if none exist. Pay particular attention to slow links between locations, especially if there is a high degree of interaction between the people at those locations. Gather and review statistics on the current network bandwidth utilization and try to characterize the network's peak and off-peak periods.

When considering the question of how many servers, and how many users per server, be conservative in your estimates. It is useful to estimate the approximate number of messages per day that will be sent by users. Talk to a sample of people in each area of your organization. If they aren't sure, ask for a rough estimate—5, 50, 500? What kinds of messages will be sent? Will they frequently include large attachments or primarily be just text? This load-evaluation process, if done carefully and thoroughly, can be a tremendous help when estimating the number of servers required to meet the needs of your organization. Some rules of thumb are provided in the *Installation Manual* and the *Concepts and Planning Guide* provided with Exchange Server that can help you decide.

You should establish some conventions for naming entities in the Exchange Server system. Every element of the system will have a display name and a directory name. In general, you cannot change the directory name after the object is defined. The display name is used in the Exchange Administrator program's display, and the directory name is used in entries made into the Windows NT event log and various other log files that can be created. The scheme you define should make it easy to decide on a new name, and it should provide the capability to create unique names throughout the organization without having to always check for a conflict.

Part
VI

Ch
26

Geographic Considerations

An important part of the planning process as pointed out in the preceding discussion is the identification of slow links between groups of users. These are the potential bottlenecks in the flow of information, and you must take steps to avoid such an eventuality. Using the replication features provided with the product, you can mitigate slow links by locating *replicas*, or copies, of important information in the same local LAN segment with each group of users. A single copy of updated information will be sent to and from the replica as changes are made. Rather than many users each attaching to a folder on the side of a slow link, they will be able to attach to the replica on their own LAN segment.

Using these capabilities can have a dramatic effect on reducing the burden placed on networking equipment by increased network bandwidth utilization. By providing users with a local copy of information, you can realize enormous bandwidth savings. If you need to further manage the use of a slow link, you can schedule the updates made between replicas for off-peak hours when the effects of transmitting the information will have less of an impact on other network applications.

In addition, as you plan your system you should consider backup contingencies for system components that may fail. For example, the Dynamic RAS Connector may be a useful backup alternative to another connector in use over a WAN link. If the WAN link fails, and the standard connector can't be used, the Dynamic Remote Access Service (RAS) connector can provide a useful, perhaps slower, backup connection that will get the information transferred.

Functional Considerations

In addition to the geographic concerns, you need to consider functional concerns. For example, you should consider redundancy for the components that deliver any functionality considered "mission critical." If a groupware application created with Exchange Server is required for a department to do its job, then the design of the system should reflect that fact. It is less desirable, in such an environment, to place all users on one large server. There are advantages to using a small number of large computers to build your system, but there are disadvantages as well. The use of smaller computers in larger numbers may provide a better opportunity to distribute the workload and yield some built-in redundancy so that a single component failure won't put everyone out of commission.

From Here...

In this chapter, you were introduced to the components that make up Exchange Server. You learned about the various Windows NT Server services that comprise the server-based components and the client components that work together so that users can read their messages, manage their schedule, and exchange information of all types with other users in their organization.

Refer to the following chapters for related information:

- For information on setting up Exchange Server, see Chapter 27, "Implementing Exchange Server."

- For information on client software, see Chapter 28, "Using Exchange Client Applications."

- For information on creating public folders, replicating public folders, and managing directory information, see Chapter 29, "Distributing Information with Exchange Server."

- For information on managing documents and creating public folders applications, see Chapter 30, "Document Management with Exchange Server."

- For information on setting up connectors to foreign message systems and procedures for using Exchange Server's advanced security options, see Chapter 31, "Exchange Server Advanced Topics."

CHAPTER 27

Implementing Exchange Server

by Don Benage

In this chapter, you learn how to install Exchange Server and configure the most common options you may need to customize your installation. You learn procedures for running the Setup program and the accompanying Performance Optimizer, a companion utility that you run after setup is complete and anytime you make changes to the server. The Performance Optimizer fine-tunes the operating parameters of Exchange Server to take maximum advantage of the server's resources, such as memory and processing power. It also helps you to relocate various disk-based files to new locations if needed.

You also learn how to use the Exchange Administrator program to customize your site and the servers in the site. Procedures for configuring the *dead letter recipient*, the *Offline Address Book*, and the aging options for *tombstones* (objects that represent elements deleted from the directory) are all explained. You learn how to create recipients and their e-mail addresses. Procedures for setting up mailboxes for Exchange Server users are described, as well as the process for creating custom recipients so that Exchange Server users can send mail to users on other mail systems. You also learn how to create distribution lists. ■

How to install Exchange Server and configure common options

Learn how to run the Setup program to install Exchange Server.

How to use the Performance Optimizer to fine-tune your server

Look here to find out how to use the Performance Optimizer to tune your Exchange Server installation to take maximum advantage of your server's hardware.

How to use the Exchange Administrator to customize your site and your server

Look here to find out how you can use the Exchange Administrator program to customize your site, and the servers in your site, to best meet your needs.

How to create recipients— mailboxes, distribution lists, and custom recipients

The procedures for creating recipients are described, along with useful tips to make them more effective.

Sizing Your Server

Before actually setting up your first server, a little more planning is important to ensure that the machine you have selected is an appropriate candidate for an Exchange Server. This product places fairly heavy demands on the equipment if you have a large number of users that actively use the features of the product. The decisions you make, and any limits you set, can have a profound impact on the performance and usability of Exchange Server.

At the end of Chapter 26, "An Inside Look at Exchange Server," you learned how Exchange servers are grouped together in sites and how a collection of sites comprises an organization. You also learned how to undertake a planning process to evaluate user needs and plan for services to meet those needs. The information that you gather and determine during that planning process is an important component of the next step—sizing your server. As you make specific plans for hardware for your server(s), it is important that your choices reflect the needs of your user community. The following are some of the questions you should answer before deciding on a particular server:

- How many users will have mailboxes on this server?
- How active will they be in their use of Exchange Server?
- Will the average user send three messages a day or 50?
- How many messages will be addressed to multiple users on the same server?
- Will messages frequently include the use of special formatting or attachments?
- Does your organization use multimedia data types, including audio and video files?
- Will your organization use electronic forms to build groupware applications?
- Will your organization use public folders for bulletin boards or other shared information applications?

As mentioned earlier, Exchange Server can place significant demands on the server equipment. If you are setting up a single server for a small group of users (less than 20) and their use of the system will be light, the guidelines provided here are less important. It is a fact, however, that in most organizations the use of electronic messaging and related technologies experiences dramatic growth as users discover the features and capabilities of the system.

Exchange Server offers features that are particularly attractive in environments where it is difficult to meet with colleagues due to hectic schedules, travel demands, or other factors that make face-to-face meetings an infrequent alternative. In addition, if collaboration on documents, presentations, or other items that can be included as message attachments is common, your plans should allow for larger messages with attachments, even if this feature is not widely used in your current environment. This affects both the size of all information stores, server-based and client-based, and the network bandwidth utilization.

In large organizations with many servers, the decision on what hardware to buy is somewhat complicated by the fact that you may address the needs of your organization with a small number of servers with many users, or a large number of servers with fewer users. If you want to put 500 or more users on a single server, a computer with four Pentium processors, 256M of

RAM, and 8G of disk space would not be an unreasonable choice. With less than 100 users, a single processor, 32M of RAM, and 2G of disk space may be adequate. Even a relatively small organization may weigh the alternatives between one large server with all services including connectors, or reducing the size of the main server and moving one or more connectors to other computers.

By increasing the number of computers used, you increase the amount of work you must perform to install and configure equipment and software, but you reduce the number of users that are affected by a single machine failure. You also allow more flexibility in locating servers on the same physical LAN segment with the users whose mailboxes are on that server. This is an excellent way to reduce bandwidth use on large networks with routers or hubs that limit the scope of packet transmissions.

If you opt for fewer large servers, you will benefit from an overall reduction in network traffic because many messages will be addressed to users on the same server, and there will be less replication of directory and public folder information. This also leverages Exchange Server's *single instance storage* feature, which stores only a single instance of a message addressed to multiple users on the same server. It is generally easier to upgrade in this environment, and it simplifies replication of directory information and public folders. It does place increased demands on the network adapters used in the servers, as these become potential bottlenecks with a large number of users simultaneously accessing the same machine. The increased size of the information stores also affects the time required to perform backup and recovery operations. In addition, a large number of users will be affected by a server outage. You should strongly consider using fault tolerant devices and an uninterruptible power supply (UPS).

Of course, there is no single correct answer to these questions because they depend to some degree on the qualities and culture of the organization in question. However, some general guidelines can narrow the possibilities and streamline your selection process. Specific minimum requirements are provided on the product box and may change slightly as new versions are released in the future. The information provided here applies to the release of Exchange Server, version 4.5, a free upgrade to purchasers of BackOffice 2.5, which initially included Exchange Server 4.0. If you are using a later version, you should double-check the product package to be sure that there have not been any significant changes.

Microsoft recommends the following server hardware:

- Use at least a 90 MHz Pentium processor, or a RISC processor with equivalent processing power.

- To improve throughput, use multiple disk drives configured as a striped drive set.

- In addition to the disk space used by Windows NT Server, you need room for the Information Stores (both public and private) and the Directory Service.

- You also need to provide for a large Windows NT Server pagefile, especially if the server has a large amount of RAM. The recommended allowance for a pagefile is 100M plus an amount equal to the quantity of physical RAM.

N O T E   You can create a striped drive set using the Disk Administrator utility provided with Windows NT Server. This allows Windows NT to spread information across multiple hard disks, thereby improving the speed of information storage and retrieval.

With regard to disk space, you should generally be deciding how many gigabytes rather than how many megabytes, and remember that it is difficult to buy too much. The maximum space that Exchange Server can use is 16G per server, which is significantly less than Windows NT Server's theoretical limit.

A good strategy to adopt when choosing a server is to select a machine that you can upgrade later if additional power is needed. Most manufacturers offer models that have slots for additional adapters and support multiple disk controller cards and drives. Some models even allow you to add additional processors or connect a separate disk subsystem to add a large amount of disk storage capacity. Selecting a machine with a high degree of expandability can make it easier to respond to growth by avoiding the need to build a new server and move user mailboxes.

▶ **See** "Configuring Hard Disk Space," **p. 159**

Running Exchange Setup

You are now ready to install your server. In this section, you learn how to use the Setup program to install files and set up the server-based services that make up Exchange Server. You also learn how to use the Performance Optimizer, a utility much like the wizards included in many Microsoft products. The Performance Optimizer asks you a series of questions, analyzes the server, verifies or changes the location of files, and tunes various performance parameters to make best use of your equipment.

The Setup Program

To install Exchange Server, you must first install Windows NT Server. If you intend to install the Internet Connector on this server, you also must configure the server to use the TCP/IP protocol before installation. You should know what type of Windows NT domain model you are using and understand the implications of domain security. In addition, you should create a service account for use by the server-based services in Exchange Server. If you are using a master domain model, the service account should be created in the master domain.

To create a service account for use by Exchange Server, you must be an administrator for the domain containing the account. To create the account, follow these steps:

1. Start the User Manager for Domains utility. Choose File, Select Domain, and then choose the domain that will contain the new account.

2. Choose User, New User. The New User dialog box appears.

3. Enter the information required, including name, password, and so on.

4. Select the following options: User Cannot Change Password and Password Never Expires.

5. Deselect (or clear) the following options if they are selected: User Must Change Password at Next Logon and Account Disabled.

6. Click Add, and then Close.

For the installation to be successful, you need information from the planning process outlined in Chapter 26. Specifically, you need the following:

- Information about the naming conventions you have established for your organization, sites, and servers. You also need the actual name for this site and this server.

- The name and password for a Windows NT account that is a member of the local Administrators group on this server. By default the global Domain Admins group is added to the local Administrators group when a server is added to a domain.

- The name and password for the service account that you intend to use. The steps for creating a service account are described in the preceding series of steps.

You also should be sure that no "messaging-aware" applications are running. These applications can open Dynamic Link Libraries (DLLs) that need to be upgraded or replaced and prevent the Setup program from successfully completing. An example of such an application is the Schedule+ Reminder utility, which runs in the background and pops up to remind you of appointments. Although these applications are more commonly run on clients than servers, it is best to make sure that you won't have a problem of this type. The simplest way to ensure that this doesn't happen is to check the Startup group for any such applications and temporarily remove any that you find. Then log off and back on to the server. You may also want to temporarily stop any services that use messaging protocols such as MAPI (for example, a groupware service of some type).

To install Microsoft Exchange Server, follow this procedure:

1. Make sure that you are logged on with an account that is a member of the local Administrator's group on this computer. You can do this by running User Manager for Domains and double-clicking the Administrator's group. (If you can't open the group, you aren't logged on as an administrator.) Verify that the account you are using appears in the list of administrators.

N O T E The Domain Admins global group is a member of the Administrators local group by default. If you are logged on with a Domain Admin account, you should have the appropriate rights unless this default has been changed.

2. Insert the Exchange Server CD into the CD-ROM drive of your computer. Some Exchange Server packages, the Enterprise Edition for example, contain multiple CDs. Be sure that you are using the Server CD.

3. Using the Explorer, or a similar utility, find the directory that corresponds to the type of CPU architecture your computer has (Intel X86, Alpha, MIPS, PowerPC). Launch the SETUP.EXE program. The Welcome dialog box appears. Click OK. The Microsoft Exchange Server Setup dialog box appears (see Figure 27.1).

Part VI Ch 27

FIG. 27.1

The Microsoft Exchange Server Setup dialog box displays the choices for different possible installation types.

4. If you want to use a different disk drive or directory from the one selected by default, click Change Directory. Enter the location you prefer.

5. Click the button corresponding to the type of installation you want to perform—Typical, Complete/Custom, or Minimum. Step 6 is for the Complete/Custom selection. If you choose another selection, skip to step 7.

6. If you chose Complete/Custom, the Microsoft Exchange Server Setup – Complete/Custom dialog box appears (see Figure 27.2). Using this dialog box, you can select exactly those elements you want to install. You also can change the disk drive or directory if you find that there is not enough disk space on the previously selected drive. Select Microsoft Exchange Server and Microsoft Exchange Administrator and review the Space Required and Space Available displays. When you are satisfied that you have made the appropriate selections, click Continue.

FIG. 27.2

The Microsoft Exchange Server Setup Complete/Custom dialog appears when you click the Complete/Custom button. Use this dialog box to select the elements you want to install.

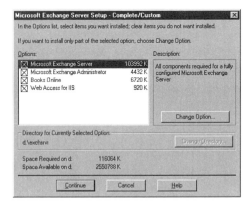

7. You should now be viewing the Choose Licensing Mode dialog box. Select the type of licensing you want to use—Per Server or Per Seat. Check the I Agree option button. Then click Continue. If you selected Per Server, be sure to enter the number of client

access licenses you have purchased in the Per Server dialog box. The Organization and Site dialog box appears (see Figure 27.3).

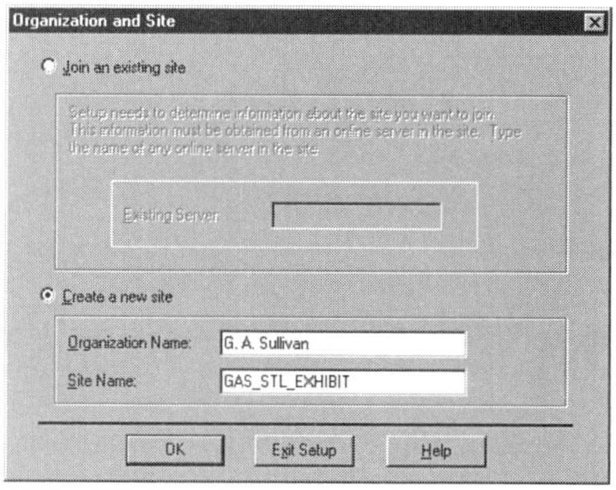

FIG. 27.3

Use the Organization and Site dialog box to either join an existing site or create a new site.

8. Click the appropriate option button. If you are joining an existing site, enter the site name in the text box provided. If you are creating a new site, enter your Organization Name and Site Name in the bottom half of the dialog box. Click OK.

9. When the verification dialog box appears, double-check the entries you made and then click OK if no corrections are needed. The Site Services Account dialog box appears (see Figure 27.4). If you are joining an existing site, the same service account that is in use on other servers will be used for this one, as well.

FIG. 27.4

Use the Site Services Account dialog box to indicate the account that should be used by all server-based services for Exchange Server.

Part
VI

Ch
27

10. Click Browse to select the service account. The Add User or Group dialog box appears (see Figure 27.5).

11. Select the account to use from the list of accounts in your domain. If you are using a master domain model, click the List Names From drop-down list box to select the master domain. Then choose the account. Click OK. You return to the Site Services Account dialog box.

12. Enter the Account Password in the appropriate text box and click OK.

13. A message box may appear indicating that additional rights have been granted to the service account (for example, the Log On as a Service right). Click OK. If you already granted the service account, the Log On as a Service right, this message does not appear.

FIG. 27.5

Select the service account to use from the list of accounts in your domain.

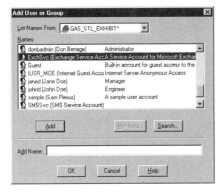

14. Click OK to complete the installation. The Setup program copies the files required for the options you specified and installs the services. When this process is complete, a dialog box appears asking if you want to run the Optimizer, as shown in Figure 27.6.

FIG. 27.6

This dialog box indicates that Exchange Server setup has successfully completed and asks if you want to run the Optimizer.

15. You can run the Optimizer now or at a later time. If you plan to add other elements to your server before using it, you may want to wait and run the Optimizer after you've installed all elements (for example, connectors).

Always run the Optimizer before placing an Exchange Server into production use. It performs important performance tuning and optimizations that can have a big impact on the performance of your server. If you want to run the Optimizer now, click Run Optimizer and proceed to the next section, "The Performance Optimizer," for instructions on completing this process. Otherwise, skip to the section titled "Using the Exchange Administrator Program to Configure Your Site" to continue.

T I P Setup installs approximately 45M of files that may not be needed on all servers. The online documentation takes up about 30M of space and is located in the file \EXCHSRVR\BIN\EXCHDOC.HLP by default. The sample applications, including the Getting Started public folder, require approximately 16M, and are located in the file \EXCHSRVR\SAMPAPPS\CLIENTS\SAMPAPPS.PST. You may want to delete these files from some servers in a multiserver site to conserve space.

▶ **See** "Understanding BackOffice Structures for Organizing Servers," **p. 104**

▶ **See** "Licensing BackOffice," **p. 89**

▶ **See** "Using Service Accounts," **p. 114**

The Performance Optimizer

For the first time, Microsoft has included a utility specifically designed to optimize the performance of a server-based application. Although the Setup programs for other components of BackOffice can adjust parameters in the Registry based on the type of installation you specify, and some components perform dynamic tuning of parameters, the Performance Optimizer is the first stand-alone utility designed for this purpose.

The Performance Optimizer is different from the very useful, general purpose Performance Monitor provided with Windows NT. The Optimizer measures a few specific server elements, such as the speed of disk drives and changes the configuration of Exchange Server. It is only used for Exchange Server, and it measures only the most important server elements. The Performance Monitor provides a vast amount of performance measurement information on virtually every aspect of server (and Windows NT Workstation) operation. It does not, however, directly make changes to the server's configuration.

You should run the Performance Optimizer at the following times:

- Immediately following the successful completion of the Setup program.

- Anytime you change the hardware configuration of your server, especially if you add memory, or additional disk storage components, because these are the elements that the Optimizer analyzes most carefully.

- Anytime you change the software configuration of a server. If you add a connector, for example, or make significant changes to the size of the Information Store by adding large public folders or importing lots of mailboxes during a migration, you should re-run the Optimizer.

- If you want to move files to a different physical disk, even if you haven't added new components, the Optimizer offers an easy way to perform this task.

- During performance-tuning operations. You can use the Optimizer, in conjunction with other Exchange Server components like Server Monitors, Link Monitors, and the Windows NT Performance Monitor, to do comprehensive performance analysis and tuning.

Part

VI

Ch

27

To run the Performance Optimizer, follow these steps:

1. If you are continuing with the Optimizer immediately after running Setup, skip to step 2. Otherwise, launch the Performance Optimizer from the Exchange Server program group. The Welcome dialog box appears, as shown in Figure 27.7.

2. If this is a production server with active users, you should wait until off-peak hours when a temporary outage affects the smallest number of users. If it is acceptable to stop all services now and continue with the optimization process, click Next. A dialog box appears with a number of questions for you to answer (see Figure 27.8).

FIG. 27.7

The Welcome dialog box for the Performance Optimizer warns you that all services must be stopped before it can continue.

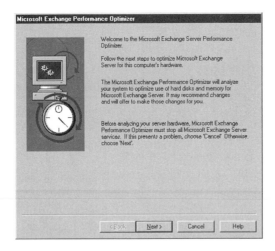

FIG. 27.8

This dialog box is used by the Performance Optimizer to gather information from you that it cannot automatically detect.

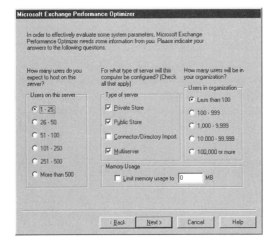

3. Answer the questions regarding the number of users on this server, in your entire organization, and the type of server you are optimizing. Click Next. After some tests are run, a dialog box appears suggesting the most desirable locations for various files (see Figure 27.9).

4. Based on the results of the Optimizer's tests, the best locations for various files will be suggested. You can override the choices made by the Optimizer by manually entering a path for any elements you want. Click Next.

5. A final dialog box appears indicating that you have successfully optimized your server (see Figure 27.10). When you click the Finish button, the Exchange Server services start with the new operating parameters in effect.

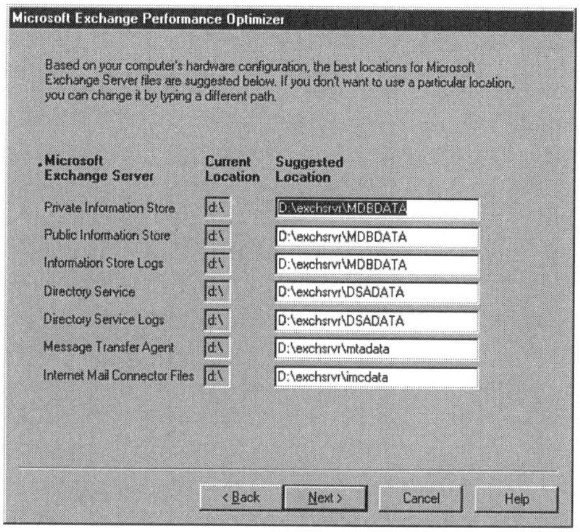

FIG. 27.9

This dialog box shows the recommended file locations based on the results of disk-speed tests.

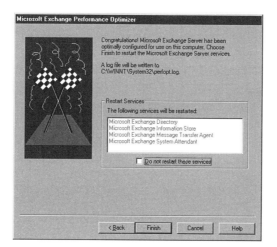

FIG. 27.10

This dialog box indicates the Performance Optimizer has successfully completed.

Using the Exchange Administrator Program to Configure Your Site

After running the Setup program and the Performance Optimizer, there are still some important steps you should take to finish configuring your server. You should complete some of these steps before adding user mailboxes to the server, and these are described first. Others are items that may change over the course of time and can be revisited at regular intervals to see if changing conditions warrant any new settings.

The first task you must complete, before any other work can be done, is to start the Exchange Administrator program. You can run this administrative utility on computers running Windows

Part
VI

Ch
27

NT Workstation or on the actual Exchange servers themselves. You cannot run it on computers running Windows 3.1, Windows for Workgroups, or Windows 95. Install the Administrator program on at least two different computers to make sure that it is available in the event of an emergency, or in case one of the machines is down.

To use the Exchange Administrator, you must be logged on with an account that has appropriate access rights. By default, the account that was logged on during setup and the service account used by Exchange Server services are both granted administrative privileges. You can grant privileges to other accounts using the Administrator program. Make sure that you are logged on with an appropriate account before you proceed.

To run the Exchange Administrator program, follow these steps:

1. Double-click the Exchange Administrator icon. By default, it is located in the Microsoft Exchange (Common) program group. The default path to the program is \EXCHSRVR\BIN\ADMIN.EXE. The Connect to Server dialog box appears (see Figure 27.11).

FIG. 27.11

The Connect to Server dialog box allows you to choose the server you want to administer.

2. Enter the name of the server. If you want, click Browse to browse your organization or a particular site. The Server Browser dialog box appears, as shown in Figure 27.12.

FIG. 27.12

The Server Browser dialog box displays your organization, sites, and servers.

3. Select the server you want to administer. Click OK to return to the Connect to Server dialog box.

4. Select the Set as Default check box if this is the server you will use most frequently. Click OK. The Microsoft Exchange Administrator display appears (see Figure 27.13).

N O T E   If appropriate access permissions have been granted to the account you are using, you can administer servers on the local site or servers on remote sites that are connected with LAN/WAN connections that support remote procedure call (RPC) communications. Some connection types are suitable for transferring e-mail messages but do not support RPCs. The Administrator program must be installed on a computer in such a site for administrative operations to be performed. ▨

FIG. 27.13

The Exchange Administrator program's dual-pane display shows the directory hierarchy in the left pane and the contents of the selected element (the Configuration container) in the right pane.

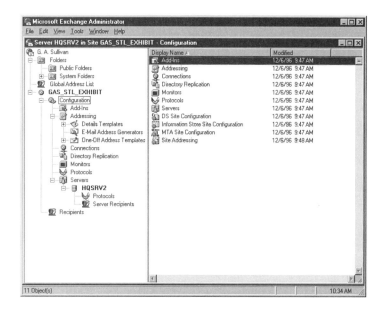

Some general notes about the Administrator program's display are in order. The program uses a dual-pane display. In the left pane, the *directory* for your entire organization is displayed in a hierarchical fashion, starting with the topmost organization elements, then sites and their elements, and then servers. Most of the individual objects in the left pane can contain other objects, and they are therefore called *containers*. The left pane is referred to as the *container area*. The right pane displays the contents of the currently selected container and is referred to as the *contents area*.

The Administrator program lets you modify servers and objects in a site only after you have connected to a server in that site. When you connect to a particular server, the Administrator program lets you modify other servers and objects in the same site as the server to which you connected. Other sites appear dimmed, and the information about these sites and objects is read-only. If you have appropriate rights and want to administer another site (which is connected over a network link with RPC support), you can connect to any server in that site. After connecting to one server at startup, you can connect to additional servers by choosing File, Connect to Server from the menu.

Most of the objects in the directory can be configured by setting properties on the *property page* for that object. The next few sections describe important options and properties that you should set before using Exchange Server.

Granting Administrative Permissions to Other Windows NT Accounts

When you installed Exchange Server and created your site, the account with which you were logged on was granted the role of Permissions Admin for the site container. This role gives that account rights to perform administrative functions including the capability to change permissions for various objects in the site. The first time you want to grant administrative permissions, you should log on with the installing account. Thereafter, any account that has been granted the Permissions Admin role for an object, the site object for example, can grant other accounts permissions or perform other administrative tasks.

Various roles are available (for example, Permissions Admin, View Only Admin, and User), depending on the object selected. In addition, you can create a custom role by selecting various rights on an ad hoc basis. As with other BackOffice components, it is a good practice to avoid giving a large group of people extensive administrative permissions. You should certainly have at least two administrators to back up each other in case of emergency, and in a large site or organization, it may be appropriate to delegate the administration of individual sites and servers to various individuals, with two "master" administrators. In general, however, people should be granted only the permissions they actually need.

Remember that permissions are inherited "downstream." That is, if an account is granted permissions on a container, the account has the same permissions on every object in that container. Therefore, objects that are lower in the hierarchy sometimes display a set of inherited permissions that are read-only and a set of permissions for the currently selected object. To change the inherited permissions, you must select the container object. For example, to grant permissions for an entire site, highlight the site container. If you want to grant permissions for some, but not all, of the servers in a site, set permissions on the server objects individually.

To grant administrative permissions to additional accounts, make sure that you have logged on with the account you used to install Exchange Server (or an account that has subsequently been granted Permissions Admin capabilities), and then follow these steps:

1. Start the Exchange Administrator if you have not already done so. Connect to a server in the site you want to administer.

2. To make the Permissions tab visible on all objects, choose Tools, Options from the menu.

3. Click the Permissions tab, and then select the check box Show Permissions page for all objects. Also select the check box Display Rights for Roles on Permissions Page. This shows you exactly which rights correspond to a given role. Click OK.

4. Highlight the object for which you want to grant permissions. Choose File, Properties to display the property pages for the object (see Figure 27.14).

5. Click the Permissions tab.

6. Depending on the level of the object, you may see a read-only box labeled Windows NT Accounts with Inherited Permissions. You cannot change this information except by opening the property pages for the appropriate container object from which these permissions are inherited. Look for the section labeled Windows NT Accounts with Permissions. You can highlight existing accounts and either change their role with the drop-down list, or delete them with the Remove button.

FIG. 27.14

The property pages for the GAS_STL_EXHIBIT site object allow you to set permissions for the entire site named GAS_STL_EXHIBIT.

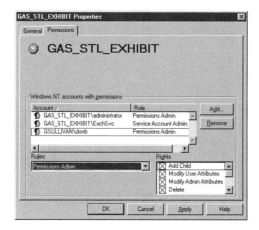

7. Click Add to grant permissions to a new account. The Windows NT Add Users and Groups dialog box appears. Select the users and groups that you want to grant a specific role and click OK.

8. Highlight the users one at a time and select the roles they should have from the drop-down list. You can scroll the Roles list to see exactly what permissions correspond to a particular role. The Help button supplies an explanation of the various rights if you want more detailed information. Click OK when you are finished.

Configuring Directory Service (DS) Site Options

As described earlier, the directory contains entries for virtually every object in your entire organization—servers, mailboxes, connectors, folders, and many others. Information from the directory is used to generate the Global Address List and the Offline Address Book. The directory is used by all other Exchange services as a source of information on the properties and configuration of the organization.

To view the property pages for the DS Site Configuration, follow these steps:

1. Start the Exchange Administrator if you have not already done so. Connect to a server that is in the site you want to administer.

2. In the container area (the left pane) of the display, find the site you want to administer. Click the plus sign to the left of the site name to expand the display if it is not already open. Select the Configuration container. In the contents area (the right pane), you should see the DS Site Configuration object.

3. Double-click the DS Site Configuration object to open the property pages (see Figure 27.15).

FIG. 27.15

The DS Site Configuration property page allows you to configure options for the Directory Service.

Setting Options for Tombstones In addition to adding new users and other new elements to the system, you occasionally need to remove various objects. Because the directory is distributed, potentially among many servers around the globe, there is no single place to delete the object. The information regarding its deletion must be propagated to all other repositories of directory information. This is done for you automatically.

When an item is deleted, a marker called a *tombstone* (indicating the operation has occurred) is placed in the directory. This marker is replicated to other servers in the organization so that they know to remove the deleted object from their copy of the directory. After a specified interval of time, the tombstone itself is removed during a process called *garbage collection*.

Two options are on the General property page for the DS Site Configuration that affect this behavior—Tombstone Lifetime (Days) and Garbage Collection Interval (Hours). It is important to set the tombstone lifetime to an interval long enough to be sure that it has propagated to all servers. On the other hand, allowing many deleted objects to reside in your directory is inefficient. You should, therefore, attempt to strike a balance. Take the longest time possible to reach your most distant servers and add an additional time period to allow for unexpected events such as a server down for repair. Do not set the tombstone lifetime too high, however, or you will waste space carrying them in your directory long after all servers have received the information.

N O T E By reviewing the settings controlling the replication of directory objects and doing some experimentation, you should be able to calculate a reasonable value for the tombstone lifetime. ▪

A similar balanced approach is appropriate for the Garbage Collection interval. When the lifetime has elapsed for a tombstone object, you want to get rid of it as quickly as possible. On the other hand, you don't want the garbage collection process running so frequently that it is affecting server performance and generally finding no new work that needs to be done.

To set options for tombstones and garbage collection, follow this procedure:

1. Open the DS Site Configuration property page (see the preceding procedure).
2. Select the General tab.
3. Enter values for the Tombstone Lifetime (Days) and the Garbage Collection Interval (Hours).
4. Click OK.

▶ **See** "Replicating Directory Information," **p. 996**

Offline Address Book   If you have remote users, for example people who connect to the network from home computers or traveling users with notebook computers, you will want to create an *Offline Address Book*. This address book can be downloaded to the local hard disk of a remote computer to avoid lengthy delays in accessing addressing information over slower remote links. You can create one Offline Address Book per site. The Offline Address Book is built from the contents of any recipients container in your site. You should usually use the Global Address List container because it contains all recipients from all sites in your organization.

You can select the server you want to use for generating and storing the Offline Address Book. A potentially good server might be an Exchange server that also supports the Remote Access Service (RAS). Because remote users connect directly to that server for network access, downloading the Offline Address Book from its disk storage might be marginally faster than another server on the network. The Offline Address Book is regenerated at regular intervals (every night by default) so that it includes new recipients and stays up to date.

To configure Offline Address Book properties, follow these steps:

1. Open the DS Site Configuration property page.
2. Select the Offline Address Book tab (see Figure 27.16).

FIG. 27.16

Use the Offline Address Book tab of the DS Site Configuration property sheet to specify the Offline Address Book server and the recipients container to be used to generate the Offline Address Book. There is also a button to manually generate a new Offline Address Book immediately.

Part
VI

Ch
27

3. Select the server you want to use to generate and store the Offline Address Book.

4. If you want to change the container used as the basis for the Offline Address Book, click Modify in the box labeled: Generate Data Files From the Address Book Container. By default, the entire recipients container is used. The Offline Address Book Container dialog box appears (see Figure 27.17).

FIG. 27.17

The Offline Address Book Container dialog box allows you to browse the contents of the directory and select the recipients container you want to use to generate the Offline Address Book.

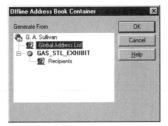

5. Use the plus control to expand the Recipients container. Select the container you want to use. Click OK to return to the Offline Address Book tab.

6. Click the Offline Address Book Schedule tab to modify the schedule for generating new versions of the Offline Address Book (see Figure 27.18).

FIG. 27.18

The Offline Address Book Schedule tab lets you specify a schedule for regular regeneration of the Offline Address Book.

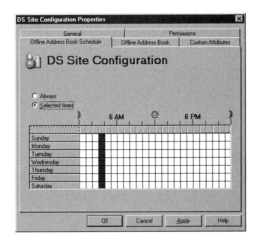

7. Select the times on the grid that correspond to the times you want to regenerate a new copy of the Offline Address Book. If you want the process to begin again immediately each time it finishes (to regenerate constantly, in other words), you can select the Always option button. This places an added burden on the server you selected for this task and is not usually necessary unless you have a great deal of turnover in your recipients list and need almost immediate access to new names. Click OK.

TIP Remember, remote users need to download a new copy of the Offline Address Book, which may take some time on a slow link, before they can benefit from a newly generated address book. You should assume most remote users will have an out-of-date address book, and remind help-line and support personnel to suggest downloading a new copy of the Offline Address Book if they can't find someone's e-mail address, especially new or transferred users.

Configuring Information Store Options

Several options impact the behavior of the information stores on the servers in your site. By selecting the Information Store Site Configuration object, you can configure all information stores on all servers in your site. You can change the display name of this object using the procedure described next. Even if the name has been changed, you should be able to recognize the object by its icon. If you cannot find the object through the following procedure, consult other administrators in this site for assistance in finding the new display name.

To view the property pages for the Information Store Site Configuration, follow these steps:

1. Start the Exchange Administrator if you have not already done so. Connect to a server that is in the site you want to administer.

2. In the container area (the left pane) of the display, find the site you want to administer. Click the plus sign to the left of the site name to expand the display if it is not already open. Select the Configuration container. In the contents area (the right pane) you should see the Information Store Site Configuration object.

3. Double-click the Information Store Site Configuration object to open the property pages (see Figure 27.19).

FIG. 27.19

Use the Information Store Site Configuration property page to configure options for the information stores on all servers in the site.

Part
VI

Ch
27

The steps required to change the options for the Information Store Site Configuration object are described in the next two sections, "Setting Top-Level Folder Permissions" and "Setting Properties for Storage Warnings."

Setting Top-Level Folder Permissions An important option to configure is the container that will contain public folders and the list of recipients who can create top-level folders. It is generally a good idea to limit the number of people who can create top-level folders. These folders appear at the highest level of the public folder hierarchy. When someone creates a new top-level folder, they can specify who has the capability to create other folders within that top-level folder. Having too many folders at the top level can make it difficult to find a folder you are looking for and limit the effective use of public folders. A small group of people is more likely to maintain a sensible structure that lends itself to appropriate usage.

By default, all users can create top-level folders. As soon as you make an entry in the Top Level Folder Creation tab of the Information Store Site Configuration property page, this default is cleared. Only those users listed in the All̲owed box can then create top-level folders. Users not listed, or those listed in the N̲ot Allowed box are denied. You need not explicitly list everyone who should be denied this capability in the N̲ot Allowed box. This list is provided so that if you enter one or more distribution lists in the Allowed box, you can explicitly override individual members of the distribution list.

> **CAUTION**
>
> Unless you make an entry in the Top Level Folder Creation dialog box, all users in the Global Address List are able to create top-level folders. This can lead to a disorganized layout for your public folder hierarchy and make it difficult for people to quickly find information. Top-level folders are most effective when a somewhat uniform naming scheme and organization are used. Some flexibility at lower levels may be appropriate.

To set permissions for creating top-level folders, follow this procedure:

1. Open the Information Store Site Configuration property page.
2. Select the Top Level Folder Creation tab (see Figure 27.20).

FIG. 27.20
The Top Level Folder Creation tab contains a list of those recipients allowed to create top-level folders and those who are explicitly denied the capability to do so.

3. First, specify those recipients who will be allowed this right in the All_owed to Create Top Level Folders box. Select the A_ll option button if you want everyone, except those explicitly listed in the _Not Allowed box (see step 4) to be able to create top-level folders. Alternatively, you can select the Li_st option button and specify those users who can create top-level folders. You can specify a distribution list if you want. Click _Modify button and select recipients from the Global Address List or any other recipients container.

4. Next, you can specify any recipients who should not be allowed to create top-level folders, even if they are a member of a distribution list that is allowed. You also can explicitly deny some recipients if you selected that A_ll users should be All_owed in step 3.

5. Click OK to register your changes.

Setting Properties for Storage Warnings   In the Information Store Site Configuration dialog box, you also can set options for storage warnings. In most sites, it is appropriate to set some limits on the amount of information that can be kept in mailboxes and public folders. You can set these limits using the Advanced property page for mailboxes and public folders. It is inevitable that sooner or later some of these limits will be exceeded. Exchange Server can automatically send warnings to mailbox owners or public folder contacts apprising them of the condition. You can specify the schedule for sending these warnings.

To set properties for storage warnings, follow these steps:

1. Open the Information Store Site Configuration property page.

2. Select the Storage Warnings tab (see Figure 27.21).

FIG. 27.21
The Storage Warnings tab enables you to specify the time period and frequency that warnings are sent for those recipients who have exceeded storage limits in the Information Store.

3. Select an option button to specify the frequency for sending storage warnings:

- Select _Never if you don't want to send any warnings.

- A_lways sends warnings every 15 minutes.

Part

VI

Ch

27

- • Selected Times causes storage warnings to be sent based on the schedule you indicate in the grid (see next step).

4. You can select specific times for each day of the week that storage warnings should be sent. By default, the grid shows one-hour intervals. Select the 15 Minute option button to cause the grid display to show 15-minute intervals if you want to have more control over when warnings are sent.

5. Click OK to register your changes.

Configuring Site Options for MTAs

Message Transer Agents (MTAs) can be thought of as the "postal workers" of the e-mail system. They are the active elements that actually moves messages from one location to another. There are several options you should consider changing for the MTAs on the servers in your site, which are discussed in the following sections. By selecting the MTA Site Configuration object, you can configure all MTAs on all servers in your site. The display name of this object can be changed using a procedure described in the following steps. Even if the name has been changed, you should be able to recognize the object by its icon. If you cannot find the object following the outlined procedure, consult other administrators in this site for assistance in finding the new display name.

To view the property pages for the Information Store Site Configuration dialog box, follow these steps:

1. Start the Exchange Administrator if you have not already done so. Connect to a server that is in the site you want to administer.

2. In the container area (the left pane) of the display, find the site you want to administer. Click the plus sign to the left of the site name to expand the display if it is not already open. Select the Configuration container. In the contents area (the right pane), you should see the MTA Site Configuration object.

3. Double-click the MTA Site Configuration object to open the property pages (see Figure 27.22).

FIG. 27.22
The MTA Site Configuration property pages provide control over the operation of the MTAs on all servers in the site.

The steps required to change the options for the MTA Site Configuration object are described in the next two sections, "The Dead Letter Recipient" and "Messaging Defaults."

The Dead Letter Recipient   If an MTA finds that a message is undeliverable, you either can have it delivered to a mailbox designated as the dead letter recipient or simply delete the message manually. When establishing new servers or when significant changes are made that affect addressing or message routing (for example, the addition of a new connector), it is a good idea to use a dead letter recipient to monitor possible delivery problems.

To designate a mailbox as the dead letter recipient, follow these steps:

1. Open the MTA Site Configuration property page (see the stepped procedure in the preceding section).
2. Select the General tab.
3. Click Modify in the Dead letter recipient box. Select a recipient from the Global Address List or any other recipient container.
4. Click OK to register your changes.

Messaging Defaults   You can control the behavior of the MTAs on your site by changing the messaging defaults. These properties specify how MTAs should respond to errors in transmission and how they should operate under normal circumstances. You can specify a checkpoint size, for example, that indicates how large a block of information should be transferred before a checkpoint is inserted. A checkpoint in this context, much like a checkpoint in SQL Server database terminology, causes the information transferred so far to be *committed*. That is, a specified block of information has been delivered correctly, and has been stored on non-volatile storage media such as a hard disk. If an error occurs after the checkpoint process completes, the transfer can resume from that point, rather than start over at the beginning. Setting a smaller checkpoint value may improve performance if you are using an unreliable or noisy connection. On a clean, high-speed link, a small checkpoint size is an impediment.

You should not change the values on this property page under normal circumstances. If you detect problems in message delivery that are not related to addressing issues (for example, the message was addressed to a recipient that doesn't exist), you can carefully experiment with changing these values. The Reset Default Values button restores all values to their original defaults. If you decide to attempt a tuning process on these values, select a particular element to change and then use logging, the Performance Monitor, and other diagnostic tools to see the results. Use a slow and deliberate approach rather than change many values at once. Some values are closely related, such as the checkpoint size and the window size, and may need to be adjusted simultaneously. The Help button displays information on the meaning of all these parameters.

To change the messaging defaults for MTAs in your site, follow this procedure:

1. Open the MTA Site Configuration property page (see earlier procedure).
2. Select the Messaging Defaults tab (see Figure 27.23).

Part
VI

Ch

27

FIG. 27.23

Use the Messaging Defaults tab of the MTA Site Configuration dialog box to control the behavior of MTAs in the site. This property page also can control how MTAs respond to error conditions.

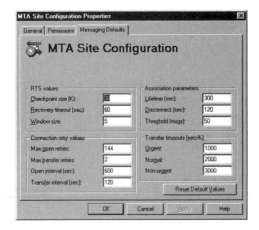

3. Change values as necessary. Click the Help button for additional information on the meaning and significance of the various parameters. Click OK when you are finished to register your changes.

Setting Up Site Addressing

Clearly some of the most important elements of a messaging system are those components that generate and manage e-mail addresses and calculate the appropriate routes to use when transferring messages. Exchange Server sets up default e-mail addresses automatically and uses these defaults to generate new e-mail addresses as recipients are added to the system. Although the default values may be correct, it is prudent to check the site addressing parameters before you add recipients so that they have correct address information from the start. You can regenerate e-mail addresses for recipients based on changed address defaults at a later time if necessary. You also can regenerate routing tables as needed. This is particularly important when new elements that affect routing, such as a new connector, are added to a site.

To review and modify site addressing properties, follow these steps:

1. Start the Exchange Administrator if you have not already done so. Connect to a server that is in the site you want to administer.

2. In the container area (the left pane) of the display, find the site you want to administer. Click the plus sign to the left of the site name to expand the display if it is not already open. Select the Configuration container. In the contents area (the right pane) you should see the Site Addressing object.

3. Double-click the Site Addressing object to open the property pages.

4. Select the General tab (see Figure 27.24).

5. On this property page, you can specify the server that will calculate the routing table for the site. This routing table then is replicated to all other servers in the site. Select the server you want to use in the Routing Calculation Server drop-down list.

FIG. 27.24

The General tab of the Site Addressing property page is primarily for specifying a server that is responsible for calculating the routing table for the site.

6. You also can select a check box to indicate that this Exchange Server site should Share Address Space with Other X.400 Systems. This is especially useful when there is a migration period, or when coexistence with another non-Microsoft X.400-based system is needed.

7. Select the Site Addressing tab (see Figure 27.25).

FIG. 27.25

The Site Addressing tab shows the partial e-mail addresses that will be used to generate actual addresses as new recipients are created.

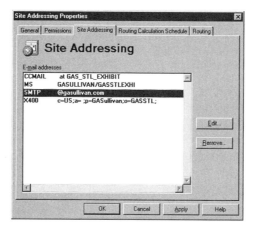

8. The Site Addressing tab shows the partial e-mail addresses that were generated from the organization and site names you specified during installation. If these names contain special characters that are not permitted in an address, or if there are other changes you need to make, highlight an address type and click Edit.

9. Change the partial address and click OK.

10. Now select the Routing Calculation Schedule tab (see Figure 27.26).

FIG. 27.26

The Routing Calculation Schedule tab is the place to specify when new routing tables should be built on a regular basis.

11. This property page works in much the same way as the storage warnings page does. Simply select an option button for Never, Always, or Selected Times:

- If you choose Selected Times, you should indicate on the schedule grid when this calculation should occur.

- The Always selection causes routing information to begin recalculation again as soon as it completes, adding a significant load to the routing calculation server you set on the General tab. This level of recalculation is overkill for most sites.

- The Never selection allows you to manually start the routing recalculation whenever you make changes that necessitate the task. This is done on the Routing tab.

Complete any changes you want to make on the Routing Calculation Schedule tab, and then click the Routing tab (see Figure 27.27).

FIG. 27.27

The Routing property page of the Site Addressing dialog box shows the routing table for a site.

12. The Routing table for the site is built using information from the Address Space property pages of any connectors or gateways installed in your site and those from connected sites. By selecting an entry and clicking Details, you can see the route, including various hops, that a message would take to reach a destination with a particular address type. You also can manually force a rebuild of the routing table by clicking the Recalculate Routing button.

13. Click OK when you have finished making changes to the Site Addressing property pages.

Using the Exchange Administrator Program to Configure Your Servers

You have learned how to set properties that apply globally to services throughout a site. Now you learn how to set properties for a specific server. In some cases, the properties are the same as the site properties you already set and simply provide a more granular level of control by allowing you to set the properties on individual servers to different values. Also, some properties must be set on a server-by-server basis and cannot be specified on a site level.

First, you learn how to set the properties of the *server object* itself, and then to change the properties of the various services running on that server—the Directory Service, the Information Stores (public and private), the System Attendant, and the MTA.

Setting Server Properties

Most of the time, you don't need to change the properties on the server object. You can use the Database Paths tab to specify where the various files used by Exchange Server should be located; however, this activity is best performed using the Performance Optimizer, which does actual speed testing to determine the best location for each element and then moves it to the appropriate place. The most likely change you might make to a server object's properties is to change logging levels or add a service to the list of monitored services. Both of these items can play a role in diagnosing problems with a particular server.

To view or modify the properties for the server object for a particular server, follow this procedure:

1. Start the Exchange Administrator if you have not already done so. Connect to a server that is in the site you want to administer.

2. In the container area (the left pane) of the display, find the site you want to administer. Click the plus sign to the left of the site name to expand the display if it is not already open. Click the plus sign to the left of the Configuration object to expand its display. You should see the Servers object. Click the plus sign to the left of the Servers object to expand its display.

3. Highlight the server object you want to view or modify. Choose File, Properties to open the property pages (see Figure 27.28).

Part
VI

Ch
27

> **NOTE** Double-clicking the server object does not open the property pages for the server. You must Choose File, Properties from the menu. ▪

FIG. 27.28

These are the property pages for the server named HQSRV2. They are used to set server-specific properties. Some properties of services, which have their own property pages, like the Information Store, are set elsewhere.

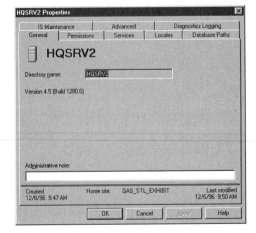

4. If you want to change the location of the various databases used by Exchange Server, click the Database Paths tab. As mentioned earlier, it is usually better to use the Performance Optimizer to change these items, but there may be a need that requires you to manually move one or more of these items. Highlight the item you want to move and click Modify. A dialog box appears that you can use to select the location for the object in question.

5. Click OK when you are satisfied with your selection.

 TIP You can change the database paths for a server only by logging on to that server directly. You cannot change the paths for a server you have connected to over the network.

6. A more common change that is made using these pages is a change in the logging levels. If you are troubleshooting some difficulty with this server, you can select elements of the server you want to watch closely and increase the logging level for that element. To change the logging levels for a server component, click the Diagnostics Logging tab (see Figure 27.29).

7. Highlight the service for which you want to change logging levels. In the box on the right of the dialog box, you see various categories of events that are associated with this service and the current levels that are set. Highlight one or more of the categories you want to change and then select the appropriate option button at the bottom of the dialog box to set the new logging level. Click Apply to register your changes.

8. Next, select the Services tab (see Figure 27.30).

FIG. 27.29

The Diagnostics Logging tab allows you to select an appropriate logging level for various components on the server.

FIG. 27.30

The Services tab of the server object property page shows the services installed on this server and those that will be monitored by a Server Monitor configured for this server.

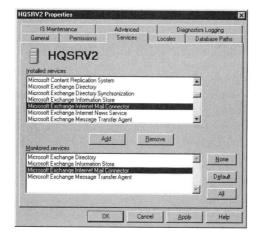

9. By default, the Directory Service, Information Store, and MTA are monitored. If you want to add any other services, highlight them in the list of Installed Services and click Add. You also can highlight services in the Monitored Services box and click Remove to remove them.

10. Next, click the Advanced tab (see Figure 27.31).

11. Under normal circumstances, the directory contains an entry for every mailbox and public folder contained in the private and public information stores, and there is not an entry for any recipient objects that do not have a corresponding place in the information stores. In other words, they are consistent; they agree with one another. If you ever need to restore the directory or an information store from a backup, the two may disagree with one another. Click the Adjust button to correct any inconsistencies.

FIG. 27.31

Use the Advanced tab to resolve inconsistencies between the Directory Service and the Information Store.

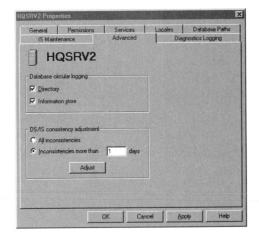

12. Click OK to save your changes.

Setting Properties for Exchange Services

You have seen how to make changes to the properties on the server object. You also have learned the "trick" to displaying the property pages for the server object—because double-clicking doesn't work, remember to choose <u>F</u>ile, <u>P</u>roperties. Now you learn how to set properties for the individual services on a server. The entire set of services is not described because you don't generally need to make changes to all these elements. Rather, the general procedure for finding and opening the property pages for specific services is given, and some examples of properties that bear special attention are listed.

One service, the Information Store, has two sets of property pages—one for each of its two components. The first is the Private Information Store and the second is, of course, the Public Information Store. The property pages for the Public Information Store are used regularly if you actively deploy public folders, one of the most useful features of Exchange Server. The process of creating public folders, setting their properties, and configuring replication is discussed in Chapter 29, "Distributing Information with Exchange Server."

N O T E   In addition to setting the diagnostic logging level for all services using the property pages for the server object as you learned earlier, you also can set diagnostic logging levels for a particular service by accessing its property pages using the following procedure. You can use either method, for example, to set logging levels for the MTA on the server HQSRV2. If you want to change logging levels for several services, the property pages for the server object is more efficient. ■

To set properties for a specific service on a server, the Directory Service for example, follow these steps:

1. Start the Exchange Administrator if you have not already done so. Connect to a server that is in the site you want to administer.

2. In the container area (the left pane) of the display, find the site you want to administer. Click the plus sign to the left of the site name to expand the display if it is not already open. Click the plus sign to the left of the Configuration object to expand its display. You should see the Servers object. Click the plus sign to the left of the Servers object to expand its display.

3. Highlight the server object whose service properties you want to view or modify. In the contents pane, you should see the services on that server listed. Double-click the service you want to view or modify. A dialog box similar to the one depicted in Figure 27.32 appears, depending on the service you select.

FIG. 27.32

You can uses the property pages for a service on a particular server to control the behavior of that service. This figure shows the property pages for the MTA on the server named HQSRV2.

4. You have already learned how to use tabbed property pages to change the properties for different elements. Using those same techniques, you can change the properties for any of the server-based services on a server. The list following this series of steps highlights some of the most useful tabs and properties that you may want to explore. Remember to take advantage of the Help button to find more information on particular settings.

5. After viewing and modifying the properties you want, click OK to close the tabbed dialog box and register your changes.

Some of the items you may want to consider viewing or changing:

- The General tab of the MTA property pages allows you to set a name and password for the MTA on that server. This is unnecessary for communications with other Microsoft Exchange Servers in the same site, which already use secure RPC communications links. It may be useful for communications with foreign X.400 systems or to provide additional security when communicating with Microsoft Exchange Servers at other sites.

- The General tab of the MTA property pages allows you to set limits on the size of messages to be processed by the MTA. This limit applies to all messages that the MTA processes. Messages that exceed this limit are returned to the sender as nondeliverable, with an indication the size was too large.

Part

VI

Ch

27

You can set limits on the size of messages allowed for a single recipient on the Advanced tab of the mailbox property pages for that recipient. If you have set size limits for the MTA, the more restrictive of the two values is used.

- The Queues tab of the MTA property pages allows you to view messages waiting to be delivered by the MTA on this server. There are separate queues for each connector and gateway, as well as each server in a site. You can view details on any message by clicking the Details button. With some queues, you can change the priority of a message (high-priority messages are delivered first).

- The General tab of the Private Information Store property pages allows you to set two limits on the amount of storage for individual mailboxes. If the Issue Warning limit is exceeded, a warning is sent at the interval specified in the Storage Warnings property page of the Information Store Site Configuration object, as described earlier. If the Prohibit Send limit is exceeded, users of this mailbox cannot send messages until they delete some of the information in their mailbox.

- The General tab of the Private Information Store property pages also allows you to specify another server in this site to contain all public folders created by users with mailboxes in this Private Information Store. This can be useful to separate the administration of these different types of information. Also, in a multiserver site, you can build one large server and make it a dedicated public folder server by deleting its Private Information Store. All remaining servers can then designate this server as the location for their public folders and delete their own Public Information Stores, which improves their efficiency.

As you have already seen, some of the property pages for the Directory Service and the MTA contain buttons that initiate a process (rather than opening a new dialog box, which allows you to change additional properties as most of the buttons do). The Information Stores and the System Attendant have no buttons of this type. Although some of these buttons have already been discussed, the following list includes them as a convenient reference:

- The Advanced tab of the server object property pages contains a button to Adjust Inconsistencies Between the Directory Service and the Information Store.

- The General tab of the Directory Service property pages contains an Update Now button to initiate directory synchronization between servers in the site. This is done automatically every five minutes. If you have made changes to the directory on a server and do not want to wait, you can use this button.

- The General tab of the Directory Service property pages also contains a Check Now button to initiate a knowledge consistency check. This updates the directory replication tables for the site by checking that all active servers in the site are represented with an entry in the directory. This happens automatically every three hours by default. If you make changes that affect directory replication and want to update the tables immediately, you can use this button.

- The General tab of the MTA property pages contains a Recalculate Routing button that causes the routing table for the server to be rebuilt. This is done automatically once a day, but can be forced with this button whenever a connector or gateway is added, changed, or removed.

▶ **See** "Replicating Directory Information," **p. 996**

Setting Up Recipients

Clearly one of the most important tasks you need to perform as an Exchange Server administrator is setting up recipients. These include not only standard mailboxes for users on this system, but also distribution lists, custom recipients from other messaging systems, and public folders. Public folders are covered in Chapter 29, "Distributing Information With Exchange Server," but this section teaches you how to create the other recipient types.

Before you actually create new recipients, you should review two items to be sure that they are set properly. These settings simplify the process, and ensuring they are correct now helps to avoid having to individually correct every newly created recipient later. You have already learned how to check the partial e-mail addresses used to generate e-mail addresses for new recipients. The Site Addressing property page for this task is located in the Configuration container for the site. Although you can change this later and regenerate new e-mail addresses for all your recipients, it is best to get it right before defining new recipients. See "Setting Up Site Addressing" earlier in this chapter.

You also should check the Auto-Naming options. These options allow you to define the manner in which default display names and aliases are created for new recipients. These options are not properties of a site or a server, but rather are defined for use by an administrator using the Exchange Administrator program on a particular computer. Any new recipients created using the Administrator program on that computer reflect the options that have been set. You can change the options at any time to reflect new defaults.

To define Auto-Naming options, follow this procedure:

1. Start the Exchange Administrator if you have not already done so. Connect to a server that is in the site you want to administer.
2. Choose Tools, Options from the menu. The Options dialog box appears (see Figure 27.33).
3. You can set options for Display Name Generation and Alias Name Generation. There are option buttons representing a variety of alternatives with examples of each one. Select the option button corresponding to the method you desire. You can, if you want, create a custom entry using the special character strings described in the bottom panel of the dialog box.
4. Click OK to register your changes.

You are now ready to create new recipients. This can be accomplished in a variety of ways, all of which lead to the same result. You can create a new recipient using the following tools:

■ The Exchange Server Administrator program

Part
VI

Ch
27

FIG. 27.33

The Options dialog box allows you to set Auto-Naming defaults and Permissions options for the Exchange Administrator running on the local computer.

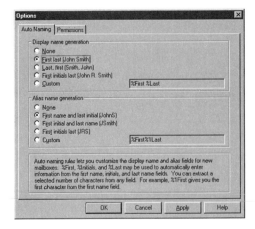

■ The Windows NT User Manager, which creates a new mailbox for a user at the same time you create a new Windows NT user ID

■ Various extraction, importing, and migration tools that are available to facilitate the creation of large numbers of users in a single operation

In this section, you learn how to use the Administrator program to create a mailbox for use by e-mail administrators and how to create a mailbox at the same time a user account is created with User Manager for Domains. You also learn how to extract a list of Windows NT users from a domain controller to create accounts for multiple users at once and how to create a template mailbox with address and phone information that can be copied as new recipients are created. Other extraction and migration tools are available, and Microsoft continues to work on new migration tools for additional foreign messaging systems. They are not covered in this book, but you can find more information on these tools in the *Microsoft Exchange Server Migration Guide*, part of the documentation available for Exchange Server.

Creating an Administrator's Mailbox

You may want to create a separate Administrator's mailbox. This can be used as a dead letter recipient and also can be a target for requests for help. The Windows NT accounts for several administrator's can be granted permissions to use the mailbox. Using the Inbox Assistant, or the Delivery Options tab described later, you can create a rule to forward messages directed at this mailbox to the personal mailbox of the administrator currently "on call." If the administrator does not want their personal mailbox cluttered up with e-mail administrator requests, they can simply create a profile for the Administrator's mailbox and open it directly. There is a great deal of flexibility in the use of the Exchange Client, which is explored in more detail in the next chapter. For now, the steps you should take to set up the simple scenario outlined earlier are described.

N O T E Although this is perhaps obvious, it may be worth noting that the property that allows a user to act as an administrator for Exchange Server is not the mailbox they are assigned, but the Windows NT account used to log on. For many administrative tasks, a user does not even need the use of a mailbox. Permissions to objects in the directory hierarchy are assigned to Windows NT accounts rather than mailboxes. ▩

To create an administrator's mailbox and grant permissions for several Windows NT accounts to share it, follow these steps:

1. Start the Exchange Administrator if you have not already done so. Connect to a server that is in the site you want to administer.

2. Highlight the recipients container in which you want to create the mailbox. You might use the site's default recipients container, for example, or the recipients container for a particular server.

3. Choose File, New Mailbox from the menu. The Properties dialog box for a new mailbox appears (see Figure 27.34).

FIG. 27.34

The Properties dialog box allows you to set up a new mailbox for one or more users. Normally, a single user is assigned to a mailbox, but it can be shared.

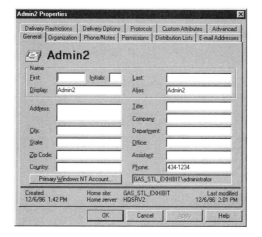

4. Enter appropriate information in the Name box. If this is a shared mailbox, you may want to skip the First, Initials, and Last boxes and simply enter a title such as Administrator in the Display and Alias boxes. The display name is used for the Exchange Administrator program's directory listing, and the address book seen by users. The alias name is used to create e-mail addresses for this mailbox.

5. Click Primary Windows NT Account and select an account to use this mailbox. For an Administrator's mailbox, you may want to have the Administrator account from the Windows NT domain, or the master domain, be the primary account for this mailbox. You can still give permissions to other accounts to use it on a regular basis, but you will have the Administrator account as a backup.

6. All other fields on the General tab are optional. Fill them in as appropriate and click the Organization tab (see Figure 27.35).

Part
VI

Ch
27

FIG. 27.35

Use the Organization tab to indicate the manager and direct reports of the user of this mailbox.

7. The Organization tab is less useful for generic mailboxes that are shared. You may want to indicate the manager responsible for e-mail administrators as a group. Click the Phone/Notes tab (see Figure 27.36).

FIG. 27.36

The Phone/Notes tab displays phone number information for this mailbox.

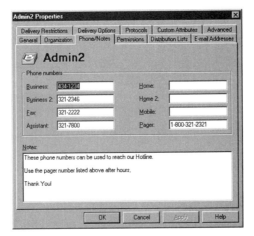

8. For a shared mailbox, you can indicate a shared *hotline* number, or pager that is passed to the person currently on call. This tab, along with the General, Organization, Distribution List Membership, and E-mail Addresses tabs, is visible in the Address Book on every client workstation. This is therefore a convenient way to distribute any phone numbers associated with e-mail administrators. Click the Permissions tab.

9. As you learned earlier in the section "Granting Administrative Permissions to Other Windows NT Accounts," you can grant permissions to any object in the directory. This property page functions in the same manner as other permissions pages. Click the Add button and add the Windows NT accounts of administrators who will share this account.

10. One additional option you may want to set is on the Delivery Options tab. Rather than using the Inbox Assistant to forward messages to the on-call administrator, you can set another mailbox as an alternate recipient. Select the Deliver Messages to Both Recipient and Alternate Recipient check box to keep a record of all messages received in this mailbox. If someone is the primary person on call for long periods of time, this may be a more efficient means of forwarding mail than the Inbox Assistant.

You may add this recipient to any appropriate distribution lists, but you should avoid using this as a personal mailbox. Each administrator should still have his or her own private mailbox and use this only for e-mail administration tasks.

11. The mailbox is now ready. Click OK to create the mailbox.

   ▶ **See** "Creating a User Profile," **p. 959**

   ▶ **See** "Using the Inbox Assistant to Manage Information," **p. 977**

Creating Mailboxes with the Exchange Administrator

To create a mailbox for a standard user, follow this procedure:

1. Start the Exchange Administrator if you have not already done so. Connect to a server that is in the site you want to administer.

2. Highlight the recipients container in which you want to create the mailbox. You might use the site's default recipients container, for example, or the recipients container for a particular server.

3. Choose File, New Mailbox. The Properties tabbed dialog for a new mailbox appears.

4. Enter appropriate information in the Name box. Fill in the First, Initials, and Last text boxes, and the Display and Alias boxes are generated according to the rules you specified in the Auto-Naming Options dialog box (see "Setting Up Recipients" earlier in this chapter). You can override either the display name or the alias name if you want. The display name is used for the Exchange Administrator program's directory listing and the Address Book seen by users. The alias name is used to create e-mail addresses for this mailbox.

5. Click the Primary Windows NT Account and select an account to use this mailbox.

6. All other fields on the General tab are optional. Fill them in as appropriate and click the Organization tab.

7. You can indicate the manager, and any people who report directly to the owner of this mailbox. Click the Phone/Notes tab.

8. Enter phone numbers and any notes that you want for the user of this mailbox. This tab, along with the General, Organization, Distribution List Membership, and E-mail Addresses tabs, is visible in the Address Book on every client workstation. This is, therefore, a convenient way to distribute any phone numbers associated with users. Click the Distribution Lists tab (see Figure 27.37).

Part
VI

Ch
27

FIG. 27.37

The Distribution Lists tab allows you to add a mailbox to one or more distribution lists and displays any lists of which you are currently a member.

9. Add this recipient to any appropriate distribution lists. Click Modify to open a dialog box for this purpose. You can select predefined distribution lists from any recipients container. Click the Advanced tab (see Figure 27.38).

FIG. 27.38

The Advanced tab allows you to set message size limits and storage limits for this mailbox.

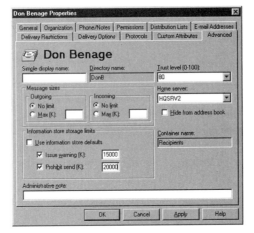

 T I P You can suppress a mailbox from displaying in the Address Book by making it a "hidden" mailbox using the Hide from Address Book check box on the Advanced tab of the recipient's dialog box. This is especially useful if service accounts or administrator accounts have associated mailboxes which should not be used by most users.

10. In the Message Sizes box, you can specify the maximum size of incoming or outgoing messages allowed by users of this mailbox. You also can set storage limits for this mailbox. If you don't want this mailbox to appear in the Address Book, you can select the Hide from Address Book check box.

N O T E You can set message size limits and storage limits for all mailboxes on a server using the MTA's General property page and the Private Information Store's General property page, as described earlier in this chapter in the section "Using the Exchange Administrator Program to Configure Your Servers." ▪

11. The mailbox is now ready. Click OK to create the mailbox.

Creating Mailboxes with User Manager for Domains

When you installed Exchange Server, the User Manager for Domains utility provided with Windows NT was updated to provide new capabilities. You can create mailboxes for new users at the same time their Windows NT account is created. If you want to do this as a default option, you can launch User Manager for Domains and choose Exchange, Options from the menu. Select the check box labeled Always Create an Exchange Mailbox when creating Windows NT accounts.

Once you have enabled this option, you can create a mailbox as you create a new user by following these steps:

1. Start the User Manager for Domains program. Notice that the Exchange menu option has been added to the program's menu bar. If this is not visible, you either need to log on to an Exchange Server machine, or install the Exchange Administrator on the computer you are using.

2. Choose User, New User from the menu. Enter appropriate account information in the New User dialog box. Click Add. The Connect to Server dialog box appears.

3. Enter the name of the Exchange Server that should contain this new mailbox. You can easily move mailboxes using the Advanced property page for a recipient in the Exchange Administrator program (or choose Tools, Move Mailbox) if you later need to move it.

4. A Properties dialog box appears. Fill in this dialog box exactly as you would when using the Exchange Administrator as described earlier in the section "Creating Mailboxes with the Exchange Administrator."

   ▶ **See** "User Manager for Domains," **p. 188**

Creating a Recipient Template for Use with Directory Import

If you are adding Exchange Server to an existing Windows NT domain or to another type of network that is supported with migration tools, you can automate the process of creating user accounts. You can extract the list of users defined on the network and use that list as the basis for a directory import process. The Exchange Server directory contains more detailed information than is provided on most networks, so you may want to use a *recipient template* to complete some of the information that is shared by a group of users. For example, if a large group of users shares the same address information or a common phone number (for a main switchboard), you can create a mailbox with only those fields that are common among the group completed. Then during the import process described in the next section, you can specify this mailbox as the recipient template.

Part VI
Ch
27

Create the mailbox following the standard procedures outlined earlier in the section "Creating Mailboxes with the Exchange Administrator." You need to complete the mandatory fields (Display and Alias) required by Exchange Server, but they will not be applied to new mailboxes when this mailbox is used as a template. Then complete those fields that are shared by many users such as the street address, city, state, and so on. Then proceed with the next section.

Using Directory Import to Create Mailboxes

As previously mentioned, Microsoft has created a variety of migration tools to facilitate the process of implementing Exchange Server, and new migration tools may be added in the future. Using these tools, you can extract the list of users that are defined for a network and use it to create new mailboxes. This section describes how to extract a list of users from a Windows NT domain and then use it as the basis for creating new mailboxes.

To extract a list of users from a Windows NT domain, follow these steps:

1. Start the Exchange Administrator if you have not already done so. Connect to a server that is in the site you want to administer.

2. Choose Tools, Extract Windows NT Account List. The Windows NT User Extraction dialog box appears (see Figure 27.39).

FIG. 27.39

The Windows NT User Extraction dialog box enables you to extract accounts from a Windows NT domain for subsequent use in the automated creation of mailboxes.

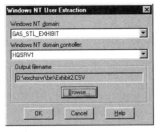

3. Select the name of the domain you want to extract user accounts from in the Windows NT Domain drop-down list. Select the primary domain controller, or a backup domain controller, in the Windows NT Domain Controller drop-down list.

4. Enter a fully qualified path name for the file you want to create, or click Browse and use the resulting dialog box to select a directory and create a file name.

5. Click OK. A dialog box appears that reports progress during the extraction. If you have a relatively small domain, this may appear only momentarily. Then the NT User Extractor Complete dialog box appears.

6. This dialog box provides an error status report, if any, on the extraction process. Click OK.

The file that results, which has a CSV extension by default, is a text file that you can read and modify with any text editor. The function and syntax of the various components are relatively obvious. The identifier ˜Server is replaced on import with the name of the server where the import operation is being performed and becomes the default home server for the newly created mailboxes. If you want to use a different home server, you can replace ˜Server with the name of an Exchange Server in your site before importing the list.

To do a directory import operation for automatically creating new mailboxes, follow these steps:

1. Start the Exchange Administrator if you have not already done so. Connect to a server that is in the site you want to administer.

2. Choose Tools, Directory Import. The Directory Import dialog box appears (see Figure 27.40).

FIG. 27.40

Use the Directory Import dialog box to specify the extraction file you want to import, a recipients template, and the recipients container for the new mailboxes.

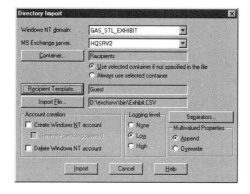

3. Click Import File and browse for the file you just created or any other appropriate import file you want to use. Click OK to return to the Directory Import dialog box.

4. Select the recipients container in which you want to create the new mailboxes. If you are using a recipients template as described in the earlier section "Creating a Recipient Template for Use with Directory Import," click Recipient Template and select the mailbox you want to use as a template from the Global Address List or other recipients container.

5. You shouldn't use the Account Creation box in the context described here. It is possible, however, to create a CSV file from another database, or even manually, and use it to create mailboxes and corresponding Windows NT accounts at the same time. In such a situation, you select the Create Windows NT Account check box.

6. Click Import. A dialog box appears that reports progress during the import operation. If you have a relatively small list of users, this may appear only momentarily. Then the Directory Import Complete dialog box appears.

7. This dialog box provides an error status report, if any, on the extraction process. Click OK.

The new mailboxes now appear in the Exchange Administrator display, in the contents area for the container in which they were created. They also are added to the Global Address List and now can be added to any distribution lists in which they should be included.

Part
VI

Ch
27

Setting Up Custom Recipients

Custom recipients are e-mail addresses that represent users on foreign messaging systems. They may have an e-mail address of several different types including an SMTP address (for an Internet user), an X.400 address, or a Microsoft Mail address. An Exchange administrator can add them to any recipients container in the directory, or users can add their own custom recipients to their Personal Address Books. A recipient needed by many people in a site is best added by an administrator.

To add a custom recipient to the directory, follow these steps:

1. Start the Exchange Administrator if you have not already done so. Connect to a server that is in the site you want to administer.

2. Highlight the recipients container in which you want to create the custom recipient. You might use the site's default recipients container, for example, or the recipients container for a particular server.

3. Choose File, New Custom Recipient from the menu. The New E-Mail Address dialog box appears (see Figure 27.41).

FIG. 27.41

The New E-Mail Address dialog box allows you to specify the type of e-mail address you want to create.

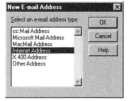

4. Select the type of e-mail address to use for the new custom recipient and click OK. An address template for the type of address you selected appears (see Figure 27.42).

FIG. 27.42

The Internet Address Properties dialog box is used to enter an Internet address, which is most commonly of the form **user@organization.com**.

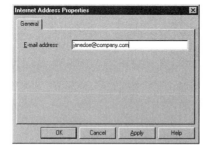

5. Enter the address for the custom recipient and click OK. A Properties dialog box appears with similar options as a normal mailbox.

6. There are some differences in the Advanced tab, and it is not associated with any particular Windows NT account. Complete any additional information you want. Click OK.

A custom recipient has a different icon than a standard mailbox, and there are a few differences in the property pages as noted in the preceding step 6. Other than these differences, they can be used very much like any other recipient. They can be included in distribution lists and appear in the Global Address List.

Creating Distribution Lists

When a group of recipients is frequently the target of the same information, the group can be put into a distribution list. The group then can be addressed with a single recipient name, rather than each individual recipient's having to be included in the To: or CC: line of a message. Like custom recipients, distribution lists can be created in the directory by an administrator, or personal distribution lists can be added to users' Personal Address Books.

To create a distribution list, follow these steps:

1. Start the Exchange Administrator if you have not already done so. Connect to a server that is in the site you want to administer.

2. Highlight the recipients container in which you want to create the distribution list. You might use the site's default recipients container, for example, or the recipients container for a particular server.

3. Choose File, New Distribution List from the menu. A Properties dialog box for the new distribution list appears (see Figure 27.43).

FIG. 27.43

The Properties dialog box for a distribution list is different from those used for new mailboxes or custom recipients. You use the properties in this dialog box to define the members and characteristics of the distribution list.

4. Enter a Display Name and Alias Name for the distribution list. These names serve the same function for distribution lists as they do for mailboxes, and they are required.

5. In the Owner box, you can click Modify to select a recipient to act as the owner of this address list.

Part
VI

Ch
27

T I P The owner of a distribution list is able to modify the members of the address list using the Exchange
Client program. Exchange administrators can modify the member list using the Exchange Administrator
program as you are doing now.

6. In the Members box, click M̲odify to select the members of this distribution list. The
   Distribution List dialog box appears (see Figure 27.44).

FIG. 27.44

The Distribution List
dialog box allows you to
select recipients from
any recipients container
or the Global Address
List to be included in
this distribution list.

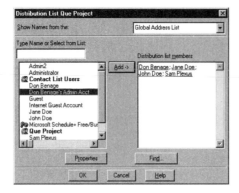

7. Highlight names in the list box on the left and click A̲dd to move them into the Distribution List M̲embers box on the right. You can highlight any recipient and click P̲roperties
   if you want to check a recipient for further identification, and you can use the Fin̲d button
   to search for recipients matching certain criteria in the specified address book.

8. The other tabs are similar to normal mailboxes with a few differences. In particular, the
   Advanced tab is different and allows you to specify Distribution List options you may
   want to consider. The Help button provides more information on what each of the
   options means.

9. The Distribution Lists tab allows you to make this distribution list a member of another
   distribution list, thereby *nesting* the lists. At times, this is appropriate. For example, you
   might have a distribution list for each department and include all of them in a distribution list for the entire organization. You should avoid nesting too deeply, however, or you
   may cause some recipients to receive multiple copies of messages.

10. When you have finished entering information into the property pages, click OK to create
    the distribution list.

From Here...

You have now learned how to set up Exchange Server, how to use the Performance Optimizer
to fine-tune your server, and how to use the Exchange Administrator to set important options
for your site and your servers. You learned how to change settings that affect the operation of
the Information Stores, MTAs, and Directory services running in your site. In addition, you
learned how to set up various types of recipients, from individual mailboxes to distribution lists.

Refer to the following chapters for related information:

- For information on using the Exchange Client and Schedule+, see Chapter 28, "Using Exchange Client Applications."
- For more on creating public folders, replicating public folders, and managing directory information, see Chapter 29, "Distributing Information with Exchange Server."
- To learn about document management, see Chapter 30, "Document Management with Exchange Server."
- For a discussion on setting up connectors to foreign message systems and procedures for using Exchange Server's advanced security options, see Chapter 31, "Exchange Server Advanced Topics."

CHAPTER 28

Using Exchange Client Applications

by Don Benage

In this chapter, you explore the client applications that come with Exchange Server. In addition to the e-mail client, which is usually referred to as the Exchange Client, there is a personal and group scheduling application called Schedule+. You also can use an exciting new component of Microsoft Exchange 5.0 called Outlook 97 as your Exchange client software. Outlook 97 is also an included component of Office 97. This product combines some features of both the Exchange Client and Schedule+ to create a personal information-management tool. This chapter shows you how to install client software and use it to manage your personal messaging and scheduling needs. You also learn about the features of the Exchange Client that are particularly suited for remote users. ■

How to use the Exchange Client to compose, read, and respond to e-mail

Learn basic tasks like how to create user profiles, send and receive e-mail, and manage various types of recipients.

How to use Schedule+ as a personal and group scheduling tool

Look here to find out how Schedule+ can help you manage your personal schedule, plan meetings, send and respond to meeting requests, manage information on personal and business contacts, and manage your To Do list.

How to use Outlook, the new Exchange client software, to manage e-mail, organize your personal schedule, and track your productivity

Learn the basic tasks using the latest e-mail client from Microsoft.

How to use the Remote Mail features of the Exchange Client

Learn the procedures for connecting to a remote network using the Windows NT Remote Access Service (RAS) and using the Exchange Client remotely.

Understanding Exchange Client

The client applications included with Exchange Server are receiving more detailed coverage in this book because they include many more features than the client software provided with other BackOffice components. In addition, the Exchange Client is used to create public folders, one of the most powerful features of Exchange Server. It is, therefore, an important part of the administrator's repertoire and should be understood thoroughly.

The Exchange Client is somewhat similar to the Exchange Inbox provided with Windows 95, but has been enhanced with additional features and improved performance and made available for additional platforms. Schedule+ was originally included with Windows for Workgroups and sold separately as an individual application. It is not included with Windows 95 but is included with Microsoft Office 95 (which also runs on Windows NT). Check with your software provider for details on upgrading existing copies of Microsoft Mail and Schedule+. Outlook, as mentioned previously, is part of Microsoft Office 97.

The Exchange Client is available for Windows 95, Windows NT (Workstation or Server), Windows for Workgroups, Windows 3.1, and MS-DOS. The features discussed in this chapter are available in the 32-bit versions of the Exchange Client for Windows 95 and Windows NT. The other versions are similar but include somewhat less functionality.

Installing Exchange Client Software

This section describes how to install the three main client components of Exchange Server:

- Outlook 97
- Exchange Client 5.0
- Schedule+ 7.5

If you are unsure which client components you want to use, review the client features overview provided in Chapter 26, "An Inside Look at Exchange Server."

▶ **See** "Understanding Client Components," **p. 896**

The Exchange Client CD contains both the Exchange Client program and Schedule+.

N O T E   There is more than one setup program on the Exchange Client CD. The setup program that you encounter first as you browse the CD (in `C:\Eng` for the English language version) is used to install *all* Exchange Client applications on a *server* for subsequent use during over-the-network installations. This is automatically done on Exchange Servers that are set up using the Exchange Server CD. The Client CD is used to set up additional file servers (or peer NT Workstations) as additional locations to access the client software. This might be useful, for example, to distribute the load during large installation projects. The share point that is created is called `\\<servername>\Exchange` by default. ■

The Client CD also includes individual client setup programs for each supported client. For example, in the `\Eng\WinNT\I386` subdirectory is a setup program to run directly on a

Windows NT Workstation system. You can install the Exchange Client or Schedule+ using this program. Outlook 97 is installed using its own CD.

Installing Outlook 97

To install Outlook 97, follow these steps:

1. Insert the Outlook 97 CD into your computer's CD-ROM drive, or connect to a shared network installation point (see the preceding Note). If you are using the CD on a computer running Windows 95 or Windows NT 4.x, the CD automatically starts using the Auto-Run feature. Click the Install Microsoft Outlook button in the opening dialog box.

   If you don't have an Auto-Run CD dialog box, find the SETUP program in the root directory of the CD and launch it.

2. A Welcome dialog box displays. It reminds you to shut down any other applications that may be running. Click Continue.

3. Next, you must select the folder into which you will install Outlook. Either accept the default location or click Change Folder if you want to select a different folder. When you have the correct folder selected, click OK to continue.

4. You may be prompted to register your software. If so, enter the appropriate Name, Organization, and CD key in the dialog boxes provided for that purpose.

5. When the installation type dialog box displays, select the type of installation you want to perform (Custom is described here):

   - Typical (approximately 32M)
   - Custom (maximum 39M)

6. After you click Custom, the Microsoft Outlook 97 Custom dialog box displays (see Figure 28.1).

FIG. 28.1

Use the Custom dialog box to select exactly which components and options you want to install.

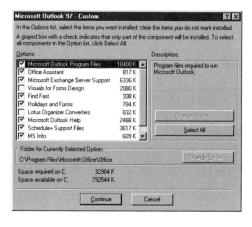

Part

VI

Ch

28

7. Select any of the optional components listed, and click the Change Option button to specify exactly the optional features for that component you want to install. Click the Continue button when you are finished.

8. A series of progress indicators and reminder dialog boxes display as the application is installed. When all files have been copied to your disk, and appropriate Registry entries have been made, a Restart Windows dialog box displays. Click the Restart Windows button to finish the installation.

   After Windows reboots, a success dialog box should display indicating that Outlook has been successfully installed.

In order to use Outlook (or any other Exchange client component), you must first define a *profile*. This is described in the next section "Creating a User Profile."

Installing Exchange Client 5.0

If you prefer the more traditional Exchange Client 5.0 to Outlook 97, the procedures for installing it are provided next. The Exchange Client doesn't include the personal management features of Outlook, but does a great job of managing e-mail and access to public folders. (Remember that you can use them both interchangeably, especially for administrators and support personnel.) You use the same procedure to install Schedule+.

To install the Exchange Client or Schedule+, follow these steps:

1. Locate the appropriate copy of SETUP.EXE for the particular client platform you are installing (e.g. the Windows NT Workstation client for an Intel processor is in the \Eng\WinNT\I386 folder). Launch the program.

2. A Welcome dialog box displays. It reminds you to shut down any other applications that may be running. Click Continue.

3. If any other version(s) of Microsoft Exchange have been installed on this system before, a new dialog box prompts you either to replace the older version or to select another folder in which to install the new version separately. Click Change Folder if needed. When you have the correct folder selected, click OK to continue.

4. You may be prompted to register your software. If so, enter the appropriate Name, Organization, and CD key in the dialog boxes provided for that purpose.

5. The installation type dialog box displays. Select the type of installation you want to perform (Custom is described here):
   - Typical
   - Custom
   - Laptop

6. After clicking Custom, the Microsoft Exchange Custom dialog box displays (see Figure 28.2).

FIG. 28.2

Use the Custom dialog box to select exactly which components and options you want to install.

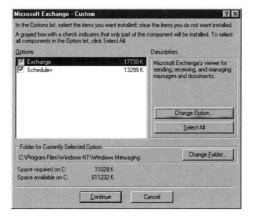

7. Select either Exchange or Schedule+ and click the Change Option button to choose the optional components you want to install. Click the Continue button when you are finished.

8. A series of progress indicators and reminder dialog boxes displays as the applications are installed. When all files have been copied to your disk, and appropriate Registry entries have been made, a success dialog box should display indicating that the client software has been successfully installed.

Before you can use Exchange client software, you need to create a user *profile* which is described in the next section.

Creating a User Profile

To use Outlook, the Exchange Client, or Schedule+, you must first create a *profile*. This is a collection of configuration information that tells the Exchange Client who you are and what services you will be using. On Windows 95 and Windows NT operating systems, this information is kept in the *Registry*, a hierarchical database of configuration data. (On older Windows versions and MS-DOS, this information is kept in a file with an INI extension.)

Creating a Profile

It would be difficult to describe all the possible options, and their combinations, that you can set in a profile. Two examples are presented in this chapter. The first example, presented in this section, is appropriate for local network access to an Exchange Server and illustrates the use of a Personal Address Book, a personal folder file, and an offline folder file. The second example, presented later in the chapter in the "Creating a Profile for Remote Access" section, describes a profile suitable for remote client access.

To create a user profile, follow this procedure:

1. Open the Control Panel.

Part
VI

Ch
28

2. Double-click the Mail and Fax icon. If any profiles have already been created on this computer, a Properties dialog box appears showing the properties of the current profile. If no profiles have been defined, you should see the General tab of the Mail and Fax dialog box. If so, skip to step 4.

3. Click the Show Profiles button. The General tab of the Mail and Fax dialog box appears (see Figure 28.3).

FIG. 28.3

The General tab of the Mail and Fax dialog box displays currently defined profiles. Using the Add button, you can define a new profile.

4. You can highlight an existing profile and click Properties to view the properties of existing profiles. To add a new profile, click Add. This launches the Microsoft Exchange Setup Wizard.

5. On the opening dialog box of the Wizard, you can choose between two option buttons: Use the Following Information Services, or Manually Configure Information Services. If you select the first option, the Wizard assists you in creating an appropriate profile. The manual method is explained here. Select the option button labeled Manually Configure Information Services. Click Next.

6. Enter a name for this profile. The name can include spaces, and it should indicate the user of the profile and give a brief description of the profile's purpose. For example, you could enter **John Doe as Administrator** or **Jane Doe with Remote**. Click Next, and a blank Properties dialog box appears, as shown in Figure 28.4.

7. You must select the services you will use with this profile. Click Add, and the Add Service to Profile dialog box appears.

N O T E   The word "services" in the Properties dialog box shown in Figure 28.4 does not refer to a Windows NT service as it has commonly been used in this book. It is used in a more general sense to refer to various providers of information such as a Microsoft Exchange server, a Microsoft Mail server, an online service, or even personal folders created on your local disk drive. ▨

8. Select Microsoft Exchange Server and click OK. A Microsoft Exchange Server dialog box appears. This dialog box allows you to specify the server you will use and other options. Enter the name of the home server for your mailbox and the mailbox name. You

can enter either the display name or the alias. To be sure that you have entered a correct name, click the Check Name button. If the name corresponds to an existing mailbox on the server you entered, both names will be underlined to signify a match.

FIG. 28.4

This Properties dialog box is used to configure a profile for a particular user with a defined set of services.

9. Select an option button in the When Starting box. If you are creating a profile for a notebook computer that is used while disconnected from the network or for a home computer, select Work Offline and use dial-up networking. For most computers in an office environment, select Connect with the Network. If you want to make this selection each time you start the Exchange Client, select the Choose the Connection Type When Starting check box. Click the Advanced tab (see Figure 28.5).

FIG. 28.5

The Advanced tab allows you to select additional mailboxes to open (provided that you have permissions) and set security options. You also can access offline folder file settings.

10. If you want to open any additional mailboxes for which this user has permissions, click Add and enter the name of the mailbox. You can specify encryption with a local network or dial-up connection to provide additional protection against unauthorized message capture and viewing. If you want to use the same logon ID for both network access and for your mailbox(es), select the Use Network Security During Logon check box.

11. The offline folder file is an important component of remote mail use. It is discussed in more detail later in this chapter along with the other two tabs, Dial-Up Networking and Remote Mail, in the "Creating a Profile for Remote Access" section. For now, it is useful

Part
VI

Ch
28

to create this file specifying a name other than the default if you want to use multiple profiles on this machine. Click the Offline Folder File Settings button; the Offline Folder File Settings dialog box appears (see Figure 28.6).

FIG. 28.6

The Offline Folder File Settings dialog box allows you to specify the location and name of your offline folder file. You also can specify encryption options and use buttons to compact your file or temporarily disable its use.

12. Enter a fully qualified file name, or use the Browse button to specify a location for the file. Offline folder files have an extension of OST (for *offline store*). The other options on this dialog box are described later in this chapter in the section "Creating a Profile for Remote Access."

T I P   It is a good idea to keep all files associated with Exchange Client in a single data folder (or subdirectory) for easy backups. A useful method is to create a folder, for example C:\data\email, and locate all files there. You may want to use the same identifier for the first part of each component's name and let the extension differentiate them. For example, the user Sam Plexus might create a profile that specified (and created) an offline folder file called SAMPLE.OST, a personal folder file called SAMPLE.PST, and a Personal Address Book stored in SAMPLE.PAB. Instructions for specifying the personal folder file and the Personal Address Book are given in the next two sections.

13. Click OK to return to the Microsoft Exchange Server dialog box. Then click OK again to return to the Properties dialog box for this profile. You have defined a profile to use Microsoft Exchange Server. You can stop now and use your profile, or define two additional and useful options. These are the personal folder file and the Personal Address Book.

14. Click OK to close the dialog box and finish, or continue with the next procedure.

N O T E   If you are completing the profile definition process for the first time, you must complete the Microsoft Exchange Setup Wizard by clicking the Finish button. Do *not* do this if you are continuing with the next process to create a Personal Address Book. ▪

Creating a Personal Address Book

A Personal Address Book is a useful place to store frequently used e-mail addresses. It is usually more convenient to find addresses in your Personal Address Book than to use the Global

Address List. In addition, you can create your own distribution lists and store them in your Personal Address Book.

To create a Personal Address Book, follow these steps:

1. If you are continuing from the last procedure, skip to step 5. If you are just beginning a profile modification, open the Control Panel.

2. Double-click the Mail and Fax icon. A Properties dialog box appears showing the properties of the current profile. If this is the profile you want to modify, skip to step 5. To choose a different profile, continue with step 3.

3. Click the Show Profiles button. The General tab of the Mail and Fax dialog box appears.

4. Highlight the profile to which you want to add a Personal Address Book, and click the Properties button to open its Properties dialog box.

5. You are now ready to add a Personal Address Book. Click Add. In the resulting Add Service to Profile dialog box, select Personal Address Book and click OK. The Personal Address Book dialog box appears, as shown in Figure 28.7.

FIG. 28.7

The Personal Address Book dialog box is used to specify the name and location of the Personal Address Book for this profile. You also can control the way in which names appear in the Personal Address Book.

6. Enter a fully qualified file name, or use the Browse button to specify a location for the file. Personal address book files have an extension of PAB. See the tip earlier in the chapter for suggestions on naming conventions. If you want, you can click the Notes tab and enter any explanatory text describing this address book, the profile it is used in, or any other information you feel would be useful.

7. Click OK to return to the Properties dialog box for this profile. You can stop now and use your profile, or continue with the next procedure to define a personal folder file. Click OK to close the dialog box and finish, or continue with the next procedure.

Part

VI

Ch

28

N O T E If you are completing the profile definition process for the first time, you must complete the Microsoft Exchange Setup Wizard by clicking the Finish button. Do not do this if you are continuing with the next process to create a personal folder file. ■

Creating a Personal Folder File

A personal folder file allows you to store messages and other information in a file on your local hard disk. You can encrypt this file and use a password to prevent unauthorized access. It is, therefore, a highly secure information store. Personal folder files also travel with you if you use a notebook computer although the offline folder file is the primary mechanism for making information available when you are not connected to the network, as you learn later in this chapter. See the section "Using Dial-Up Access to Exchange Server" in this chapter for more information.

To create a personal folder file, follow these steps:

1. If you are continuing from the preceding procedure, skip to step 5. If you are just beginning a profile modification, open the Control Panel.

2. Double-click the Mail and Fax icon. A Properties dialog box appears showing the properties of the current profile. If this is the profile you want to modify, skip to step 5. To choose a different profile, continue with step 3.

3. Click the Show Profiles button. The General tab of the Mail and Fax dialog box appears.

4. Highlight the profile to which you want to add a personal folder file, and click the Properties button to open its properties dialog box.

5. You are now ready to add a personal folder file. Click Add. In the resulting Add Service to Profile dialog box, select Personal Folders and click OK. The Create/Open Personal Folders File dialog box appears.

6. Use this dialog box to select a location for a personal folder file and enter a name in the File Name box. Click OK. The Create Microsoft Personal Folders dialog box appears (see Figure 28.8).

FIG. 28.8

Use this dialog box to specify security options for the personal folder file associated with this profile.

7. Select an encryption setting and create a password to protect this file if you want. You can leave the password blank and leave the file unencrypted if you are not concerned about security.

CAUTION

Users should be warned that if they forget the password to their personal folder file, there is *no way to unlock it*. Unlike a server-based password that an administrator can clear, the password for a personal store cannot be cleared by an administrator. If the file is password protected, and especially if it is encrypted, a forgotten password means a total loss of all information in the file.

8. Click OK to return to the Properties dialog box for this profile. Click OK to finish. If you are completing the profile definition process for the first time, complete the Microsoft Exchange Setup Wizard by clicking the Finish button. If you are editing an existing profile, ignore the last remark because there is no active wizard.

Creating a Profile for Another Mailbox

If more than one user will use the Exchange Client on a computer, you can create profiles for additional users that reference their mailboxes on their home servers. To create a profile for another user, log on with the user's account or another account (such as an administrator's account) that has access rights to the mailbox in question. Then, simply follow the procedures outlined earlier to add a new profile to those already defined on the computer. Specify the appropriate home server and mailbox when defining properties for Exchange Server or any other messaging service you want to use.

 If a user needs access to more than one Exchange Server mailbox (for example, an administrative mailbox), you can use two profiles to access them individually, or you can use one profile and specify additional mailboxes to be opened simultaneously with a single profile. This is selected on the Advanced tab of the Exchange Server properties dialog box, as outlined in step 10 of the procedure for creating a user profile in the section "Creating a Profile" earlier in the chapter.

Selecting the Profile You Want to Use

After you have defined multiple profiles, you need a way to specify which profile should be used with Exchange client software. You can set an option so that Outlook (or the Exchange Client) will ask you which profile to use each time it starts, or you can manually select a different profile using the Mail and Fax icon in the Control Panel. Both methods are outlined in this section.

To manually select a profile for use the next time you launch Outlook or the Exchange Client, follow this procedure:

1. Open the Control Panel.
2. Double-click the Mail and Fax icon. A Properties dialog box appears showing the properties of the current profile. If this is the profile you want to use, you are already done and can click OK to close the dialog box. To choose a different profile, continue with step 3.

Part
VI

Ch
28

3. Click the Show Profiles button. The General tab of the Mail and Fax dialog box appears.

4. Select a profile with the drop-down list labeled When Starting Microsoft Exchange, Use This Profile.

5. Click Close.

To set an option in Outlook (or in the Exchange Client) so that it prompts you to select a profile each time is starts, follow these steps:

1. Start Outlook. On a computer using the Windows 95 or Windows NT 4.0 graphical interface, you can double-click the Outlook icon that is added to the desktop during setup. On a computer using the Program Manager, double-click the Outlook icon in the Outlook program group.

2. Choose Tools, Options from menu. The Options dialog box Outlook appears (see Figure 28.9).

FIG. 28.9

This dialog box allows you to set options for Outlook. Most of these options affect only the user making the changes. They become part of the profile for that user.

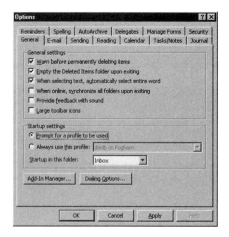

3. On the General tab, there is a box labeled Startup Settings. Select the Prompt for a Profile To Be Used option button.

4. Click OK to close the dialog box and register your selection.

N O T E   An identical procedure is followed in the Exchange Client program. The dialog box looks somewhat different, but the menu choices are the same. ■

Using Outlook

This section describes Outlook, the new information-management utility that combines e-mail and scheduling with capabilities for workgroup collaboration. Outlook is a combined tool that can be used as a replacement for the Exchange Client and Schedule+ (using Outlook's

Calendar features), or you can set up Outlook to use Schedule+ for scheduling. The main features of Outlook are the following:

- E-mail
- Contact management
- Task management
- Notes
- Calendar

The remainder of this section provides a quick introduction to the use of Outlook. To use Outlook, follow these steps:

1. Start Outlook. On Windows 95 and Windows NT 4.0 systems a Shortcut icon for Outlook is placed on the desktop during setup. For older versions of Windows, find the Outlook icon in a Program Manager group. The main Outlook window displays (see Figure 28.10).

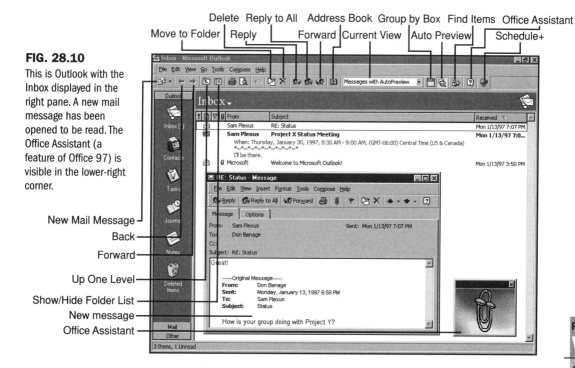

FIG. 28.10
This is Outlook with the Inbox displayed in the right pane. A new mail message has been opened to be read. The Office Assistant (a feature of Office 97) is visible in the lower-right corner.

2. You can customize the Outlook display quite a bit to suit your own working style and preferences. The default display includes a menu bar at the top, a toolbar just below the menu (refer to Figure 28.10), with the remainder of the screen divided into two primary panes. The left pane is used to select the item to view in the right pane, which provides a detailed view of the selected item in the left pane.

Part
VI

Ch
28

3. Make sure that the Outlook pane is displayed at the left of the screen. You can click the horizontal bars labeled Outlook, Mail, and Other to change the display in the left pane. By right-clicking in the left pane, you can change the view used to display the contents of this pane. Select the Inbox icon.

4. To read an e-mail message from your Inbox, double-click the icon or text representing the message in the right pane. Click the Close button when finished.

5. To create a new message, click the New Mail Message toolbar button, or choose Compose, New Mail Message from the menu. Click the Send button when finished composing and addressing your message.

6. Click the Contacts icon in the left pane of the display. The Contacts window displays on the right (see Figure 28.11).

FIG. 28.11

The Contacts window is used to manage information about personal and business contacts. Double-clicking a contact opens a window displaying detailed information about that contact as shown here.

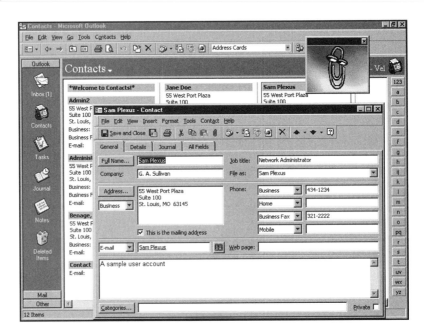

7. To create a new contact, click the New Contact toolbar button (the same one that was the New Mail Message button at the far left), or select Contacts, New Contact from the menu. Click the Save and Close button when finished entering information about your contact.

8. Click the Tasks icon in the left pane. The Tasks window displays (see Figure 28.12).

9. Click the New Task toolbar button to create a new task (the same one that was the New Mail Message button), or select Tasks, New Task from the menu. Click the Save and Close button when finished entering information about your task.

10. You also can keep ad hoc notes (similar to paper "sticky" notes) in Outlook. Click the Notes icon in the left panel. The Notes window displays (see Figure 28.13).

FIG. 28.12

The Tasks list helps you manage your things-to-do list.

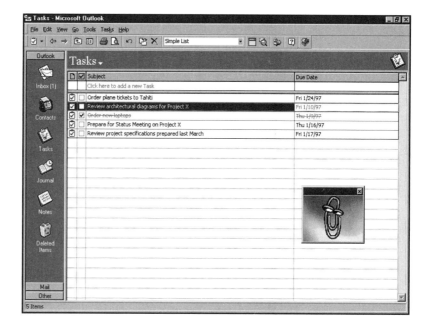

FIG. 28.13

Sample electronic sticky notes are shown in this figure, which depicts the Notes window in Outlook.

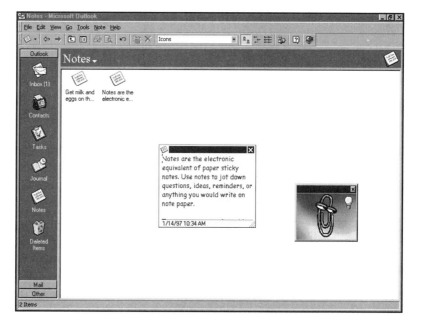

11. New notes are created in a manner similar to creating other new items—with the toolbar button or menu selection. Individual notes can be left open and will be visible even if Outlook is minimized or all other Outlook windows are closed.

12. In addition to viewing e-mail messages and other items of information, you can use Outlook to browse and work with your own computer and other computers on your network. Click the horizontal bar labeled Other in the left pane. Then click My Computer (see Figure 28.14).

FIG. 28.14

The right pane of the Outlook display shows a view of My Computer on a Windows NT Workstation (v4.0) system. The folder list was displayed by clicking the (D:) just below the toolbar.

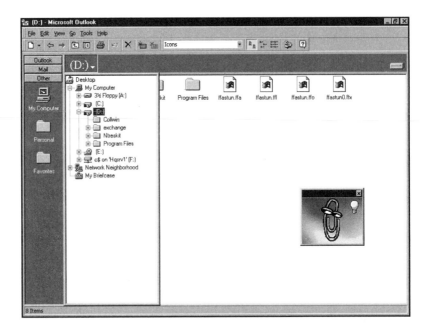

13. In addition to the personal management features you've already seen, Outlook supports collaboration with others in your organization in a number of ways. Two of them are shown here. Click the Calendar icon in the left pane. The Calendar window displays (see Figure 28.15).

14. You can request a meeting with other members of your organization. If they also are using Outlook, you can check their availability or view their schedule. To request a meeting, choose Calendar, New Meeting Request from the menu. The Meeting dialog box is shown in Figure 28.15. Click the Invite Others button to add attendees. Click the Send button when you are finished.

15. You also can delegate tasks and track progress automatically using Outlook. Click the Tasks icon in the left pane again. Select Tasks, New Task Request from the menu (see Figure 28.16).

16. Enter any pertinent information about the task request. Click the Send button when you are finished. As the recipient works on the task, they can send status reports which will automatically update the current status of this task.

FIG. 28.15

The Calendar feature of Outlook allows you to manage your own schedule, as well as schedule group meetings and view other people's schedules as shown here.

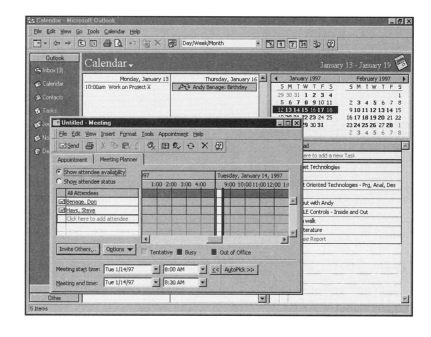

FIG. 28.16

This figure depicts a Task Request form requesting assistance from Steve Hays on Project X. It shows that 25% of this task is already complete.

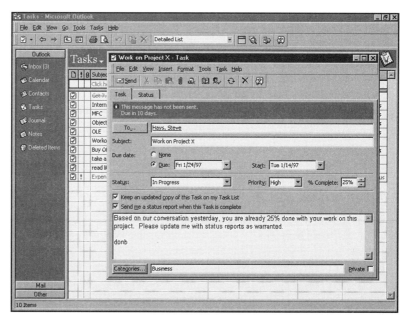

This section has provided a brief overview of Outlook. This product is very feature rich; it is worth exploring in more detail, or using the Office Assistant—the automated help application—to experiment with new features you want to use.

N O T E   The Office Assistant is an automated help facility that works much like a wizard; however, the Office Assistant makes use of an animated character to provide advice and assistance. You can select from among a number of different characters, with different personalities, or turn the assistant off completely if you prefer not to use it.

Using the Exchange Client

The Exchange Client is a traditional e-mail client application. It has some new features added with version 5.0 that continue to make this a fine e-mail client. As an alternative to Outlook, you can use the Exchange Client with the Schedule+ application described later in this chapter. In this section, you learn how to perform all the basic operations you need to open your mailbox, send and read messages, and use a few advanced techniques, all performed with the Exchange Client.

Starting the Exchange Client

Although you had your first lesson on starting the Exchange Client earlier in the chapter, a more complete set of steps is presented here. To start the Exchange Client, follow these steps:

1. On a computer using the Windows 95 graphical interface, double-click the Inbox icon on the desktop. On a computer using the Program Manager, double-click the Microsoft Exchange icon in the Microsoft Exchange program group.

2. If the Choose Profile dialog box appears, as it will if you have selected the option to prompt for a profile at startup, select the Profile Name you want to use and click OK.

3. Depending on your configuration, you also may need to respond to a dialog box asking whether you should Connect or Work Offline. Select the choice that reflects whether your computer is attached to the network and is able to connect to your Exchange Server.

4. In addition, you may need to enter a password for any personal folder files you have defined and password-protected for this profile.

Sending a Message

You have learned how to create profiles, which is the hardest part of using the Exchange Client. Now you learn how to use the Exchange Client to send a message, an activity you are likely to perform many times. This program contains many advanced features. This chapter only explores the basics and a few useful advanced features. You are encouraged to set up the Getting Started public folder to help new users of the system.

▶ **See** "Using Public Folders," **p. 1007**

To send a message, follow these steps:

1. Start the Exchange Client.

2. Depending on your configuration, you may need to respond to a dialog box asking whether you should Connect or Work Offline. You can select either option. If you compose messages while offline, they are delivered the next time you connect to the server.

3. Click the New Message button on the toolbar, or choose Compose, New Message from the menu. A new message form appears. The default New Message form is pictured in Figure 28.17.

FIG. 28.17

The New Message form is used to address and compose a message. If you have selected the option to use Microsoft Word as your editor, your New Message dialog box will have a different appearance. Click the To button to open the Address Book and select a recipient.

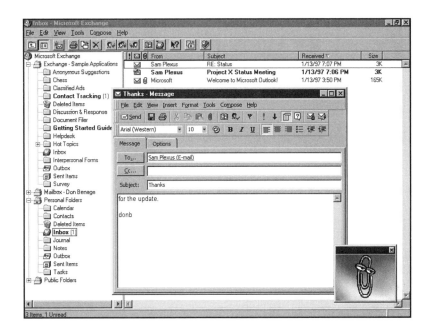

4. You also can set an option to use Microsoft Word as your e-mail editor, which changes the appearance of and options available on your New Message form. To do so, choose Compose, Wordmail Options from the menu. The basic features discussed here are available with either option.

 The WordMail option will only appear on the menu if you have installed the WordMail capability which is a component of Microsoft Word. You must use the setup program for Microsoft Word or Microsoft Office to add this component if you want to use Word for your e-mail editor.

5. Click the To button to open the Address Book and select a recipient. The Select Names dialog box appears (see Figure 28.18). Alternatively, you can manually enter a name in the To text box.

Part
VI

Ch
28

FIG. 28.18

You use the Address Book to find recipients and address messages.

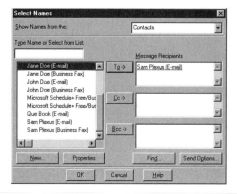

6. In the Address Book dialog box, select one or more names to send this message and click the To button. The names appear in the Message Recipients list. You can highlight any name and click the Properties button to view that recipient's properties pages for help in identifying ambiguous names.

7. If you want to send anyone a copy of this message, select those names and click the Cc button. You can also send a blind carbon copy using the Bcc button if you have enabled this option. Other recipients will be unaware that you have sent a copy of this message to anyone on the Bcc address line.

8. Click OK to return to the New Message form. Enter a Subject for the message. Then use the mouse or the Tab key to position your insertion point (cursor) in the body of the message.

9. Enter any text you want in the body of the message. You can use buttons on the toolbar to format your text with bold, italic, colors, and so on. Click the Send button to send your message.

Reading, Replying to, and Forwarding Messages

Now you learn the basic procedures needed to read your e-mail messages, reply to them, and forward messages to other recipients. A few useful options are discussed that may make this task easier and more productive.

To read and respond to e-mail messages, follow these steps:

1. Start the Exchange Client.

2. To read new messages, select an Inbox. Depending on your configuration, your messages may be delivered to the Inbox in your mailbox on the server, or they may be automatically transferred to the Inbox in your personal folders when you connect.

3. New messages appear in the right pane of the window. Double-click a message to open it. The message appears in its own window that can be manipulated individually (maximized, minimized, and so on).

Delivery options are set on the Delivery tab of the Options dialog box, which is opened by choosing Tools, Options from the menu.

4. On the toolbar of the message form are buttons representing several options. You can Reply to Sender, which sends a reply only to the sender. You can Reply to All, which sends a reply to everyone listed on the To and Cc lines. You also can Forward a message to someone who has not yet received a copy. Click one of these buttons to respond to the message.

5. A New Message form is created automatically for your response. The subject will be identical to the initial message with RE: or FW: added as a prefix to indicate it is a reply or forwarded message. On the Read tab of the Options dialog box, you can specify that a copy of the original should be included when you reply to a message. You also can indent the original message to distinguish it from your reply or comments.

6. Add any comments you want to include at the beginning of the message body. You also can intersperse comments within the body of the original text if appropriate.

7. Click the Send button to send your message.

Managing Recipients

One advantage of giving users a Personal Address Book is that it allows them to personally manage their own recipients file. In general, you do not want to allow all users to add custom recipients to a recipients container on the server. If a new recipient name will be widely used and belongs in the Global Address List or another recipients container, an administrator can create a custom recipient on the server using the Exchange Administrator program. For the ad hoc needs that occur in typical daily use, the Personal Address Book is an ideal mechanism to give users some level of autonomy, without cluttering the Global Address List.

Creating a Custom Recipient in Your Personal Address Book   To create a custom recipient in your Personal Address Book, follow these steps:

1. Start the Exchange Client.

2. Click the Address Book toolbar button, or choose Tools, Address Book from the menu.

3. Click the New Entry toolbar button, or select File, New Entry from the menu. The New Entry dialog box appears, as shown in Figure 28.19.

4. Select the type of address you will be creating. Click OK.

5. A Properties dialog box customized for the address type appears. Enter the information for the address you want to create. If you are unsure of some of the fields needed for a particular type of address, the Help button offers a description of each field and appropriate entries.

6. Click OK. If you don't see your new entry, make sure that the Personal Address Book is selected in the drop-down list labeled Show Names From The, which appears in the upper-right corner of the dialog box.

Part
VI

Ch
28

FIG. 28.19

This dialog box allows you to specify the type of address for a new recipient. You also can specify the address book in which you want to store this recipient.

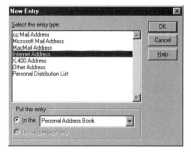

You now can use this address anytime you are addressing a message or form by selecting Personal Address Book in the drop-down list in the upper-right corner of the Address Book dialog box.

Creating a Personal Distribution List   Creating a personal distribution list is similar to creating a custom recipient. Personal distribution lists are stored in your Personal Address Book and provide the same benefits as distribution lists from the server—you can use a single recipient name to specify a group of recipients that are frequently the target of the same messages or forms.

To create a personal distribution list, follow these steps:

1. Start the Exchange Client.
2. Click the Address Book toolbar button, or choose Tools, Address Book from the menu.
3. Click the New Entry toolbar button, or choose File, New Entry from the menu. The New Entry dialog box appears.
4. Select Personal Distribution List and click OK. The New Personal Distribution List Properties dialog box appears, as shown in Figure 28.20.

FIG. 28.20

This dialog box allows you to create a personal distribution list. You also can enter notes describing the list or its contents.

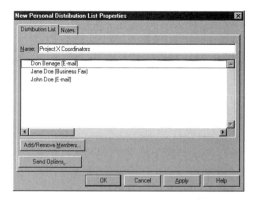

5. Click Add/Remove Members. An Edit New Personal Distribution List Members dialog box appears, which allows you to selectively add or remove members for the list. Select

the recipients you want to add to this distribution list and click the Members button. Click OK to return to the New Personal Distribution List Properties dialog box.

6. Click OK to return to the Address Book. If you don't see your new entry, make sure that the Personal Address Book is selected in the Show Names From The drop-down list, which appears in the upper-right corner of the Address Book dialog box.

Managing a Distribution List in the Directory   If you have been designated as the owner of a distribution list stored on the server, you can edit its membership from the Exchange Client. This is a convenient capability, and it allows administrators to delegate the management of some distribution lists to an appropriate manager or project leader.

To edit the contents of a server-based distribution list using the Exchange Client, follow these steps:

1. Start the Exchange Client.

2. Click the Address Book toolbar button, or choose Tools, Address Book from the menu.

3. Select Global Address List in the Show Names from the drop-down list.

4. Find the distribution list for which you are the designated owner and double-click its icon. A Properties dialog box for the distribution list appears.

5. You now can make changes to the membership of the distribution list by clicking the Modify Members button. You also can view, but not change, the other distribution lists this list is a member of (a nested list) and view the e-mail addresses for this distribution list.

6. Click OK.

Using the Inbox Assistant to Manage Information

One of the most useful features of the Exchange Client is the Inbox Assistant, a utility that allows users to leverage the processing power of the server. By setting options on a client computer, users can cause a server-based process to automatically filter their messages for certain criteria. Messages that have specific characteristics can be moved to a folder, automatically replied to, forwarded to another mailbox, or a variety of other options.

A few examples of the things you can do with the Inbox Assistant are presented in this section. Remember, this is a distinctly different capability from similar client-based features offered in the past on various e-mail packages. Client-based approaches to this situation require users to leave their computers connected to the network and actively logged on. Even with keyboard locking and other similar security measures, the client-based approach is much less powerful and requires several compromising concessions to be made.

To use the Inbox Assistant to automate message handling, follow these steps:

1. Start the Exchange Client.

2. Choose Tools, Inbox Assistant from the menu. The Inbox Assistant dialog box appears (see Figure 28.21).

Part

VI

Ch

28

FIG. 28.21

Use the Inbox Assistant dialog box to specify rules that control the behavior of a server-based process that can automate message handling.

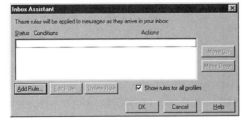

3. Click Add Rule. The Edit Rule dialog box appears, as shown in Figure 28.22.

FIG. 28.22

The Edit Rule dialog box allows you to specify detailed criteria for filtering messages and the actions that should be taken in the event of a match.

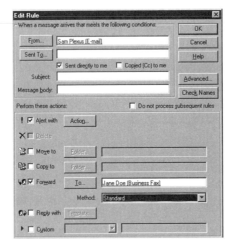

4. In the box at the top of the Edit Rule dialog box, specify any criteria you want to apply as a filter to incoming messages. For example, you might specify all messages from your boss or all managers in your organization. Using the Advanced button, you can specify messages whose size are within a certain range, that were sent within a range of dates, or that have attachments; or you can indicate that you will filter all messages that do not match the indicated criteria. You can even filter for use of a particular form.

5. In the box at the bottom of the Edit Rule dialog box, specify the actions that should be performed when a message meets the criteria stipulated. You can specify that an Alert box should notify you when a message matches and optionally play a sound file. Naturally, this option is useful only when you are actively connected. Other available options include moving or copying the message from your Inbox to a particular folder, or automatically replying and/or forwarding the message to another mailbox.

6. Click OK to activate the new rule. It is added to the list of rules shown in the Inbox Assistant dialog box. You may need to change the order in which your rules are applied to achieve the desired behavior if some of the filter criteria overlap. Use the Move Up and Move Down buttons in the Inbox Assistant dialog box to change the order in which rules are applied.

To use the Inbox Assistant to file messages automatically, follow these steps:

1. Click Add Rule. The Edit Rule dialog box appears.

2. In the box at the top of the Edit Rule dialog box, specify any criteria you want to apply as a filter to incoming messages.

3. In the box at the bottom of the Edit Rule dialog box, select the Move To check box and click the corresponding Folder button. If you want to leave the original in your Inbox and file a copy, select the Copy To check box and click its Folder button. In the resulting dialog box, select the folder where the matching messages or forms should be placed. Click OK to return to the Edit Rule dialog box.

4. Click OK to activate the new rule. It is added to the list of rules shown in the Inbox Assistant dialog box. You may need to change the order in which your rules are applied to achieve the desired behavior if some of the filter criteria overlap. Use the Move Up and Move Down buttons in the Inbox Assistant dialog box to change the order in which rules are applied.

Handling Messages While Out of the Office

The following example demonstrates the use of the Out of Office Assistant, another server-based process that can streamline communications when you must be away from your office for an extended period of time. To use the Out of Office Assistant, follow these steps:

1. Start the Exchange Client.

2. Choose Tools, Out of Office Assistant from the menu. The Out of Office Assistant dialog box appears (see Figure 28.23).

FIG. 28.23

This dialog box specifies the actions that should be taken with your messages when you are away from the office for an extended time period.

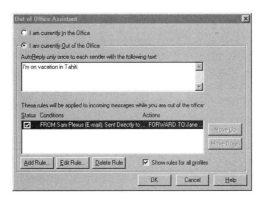

3. At the top of the Out of Office Assistant dialog box, the I Am Currently In the Office option button is used to disable this assistant when you return from your absence. It is selected by default. To enable the Out of Office Assistant, select the option button labeled I Am Currently Out of the Office.

Part
VI

Ch
28

4. Enter a short message that you want to use as a reply to anyone sending you a message. For example, you might indicate where you have gone, the nature of your absence, or the date and time when you expect to return. You also might indicate whether an assistant or colleague will receive forwarded messages that match certain criteria (see step 5). This information helps the sender take appropriate action if something needs immediate attention.

5. At the bottom of the dialog box, you can create rules using the same procedure you learned for the Inbox Assistant. These rules are applied to messages during your absence.

6. After ensuring that the correct option button is selected at the top of the dialog box and reviewing your message and the content and order of your rules, click OK to enable the Out of Office Assistant. If you are leaving for a long trip or vacation, it is wise to have a colleague test your procedures at least once before you leave.

You have learned the basic procedures for using the Exchange Client to send and receive e-mail messages and automate some of your message handling procedures. Next you learn about the personal and group scheduling product that acts as a companion to the Exchange Client—Schedule+.

Using Schedule+

In addition to helping you manage information with the Exchange Client, Schedule+ can help you manage your time. It also can automate the process of planning meetings and scheduling the use of resources such as conference rooms or projection equipment. You can use Schedule+ to view the schedules of your colleagues, provided that you have been given permission. Also included are a To Do list to help you organize your projects and a contact list to keep track of the people with whom you communicate.

The Seven Habits Wizard even helps you through the process of defining a personal mission statement and identifying the various roles you are called upon to fulfill and the goals you have for each of them. This process was created and refined by Steven Covey and described in his book *The Seven Habits of Highly Effective People*. The techniques outlined in this book and implemented in the Seven Habits Wizard have helped many people become more effective and make better use of their time.

Starting and Exiting from Schedule+

There is a special relationship between the Exchange client and Schedule+. Schedule+ shares the same profiles and startup procedures as the Exchange Client. If you start Schedule+, the message delivery components of Exchange will be active so that any meeting requests you want to send can be delivered. Although you may not have the Exchange Client interface open, message delivery still occurs as a background task. For example, if you specified that new messages should be delivered to a personal folder file with password protection, you are asked to enter that password when starting Schedule+, and incoming messages are placed in that file. If you start the Exchange Client before you exit from Schedule+, you do not need to enter any additional passwords.

You may start either application first. If one application is already running, starting the second one does not require profile selection or password entry. If both are running, choose File, Exit from the menu of one application to quit that application and leave the other running. Choosing File, Exit and Log Off saves your changes and exits both applications, closing the message delivery components, as well.

To start Schedule+, follow these steps:

1. On a computer using the Windows 95 graphical interface, use the Start button and select Schedule+ from the Programs menu. It also may appear as a button on the Microsoft Office shortcut bar if you are a Microsoft Office user. On a computer using the Program Manager, double-click the Schedule+ icon in the Microsoft Exchange program group.

2. If the Choose Profile dialog box appears, select the profile you want to use and click OK.

3. Depending on your configuration, you also may need to respond to a dialog box asking whether you should Connect or Work Offline. Select the choice that reflects whether your computer is attached to the network and able to connect to your Exchange Server.

4. In addition, you may need to enter a password for any personal folder files you have defined and password-protected for this profile.

Scheduling an Appointment

To place an appointment on your own schedule, follow these steps:

1. Start Schedule+. The Schedule+ window appears (see Figure 28.24).

2. Using the tabs at the left of the display, select the Daily view. You also can schedule appointments using a Weekly view if you prefer.

3. Click the Today button in the upper-left corner to display today's appointments. Select any other date by clicking it on the calendar in the upper-right corner, or by using the drop-down calendar control next to the Today button.

4. Scroll the daily schedule display until the time span you want to schedule is visible. Click and hold down the mouse button, dragging the highlight from the beginning to the end of the time span. The selected time appears in a pop-up tip window and in the right half of the status bar at the bottom of the window. Release the mouse button. If the wrong time period is highlighted, repeat the operation.

5. Click the Insert New Appointment toolbar button, or choose Insert, Appointment from the menu. The Appointment dialog box appears, as shown in Figure 28.25.

Part
VI

Ch
28

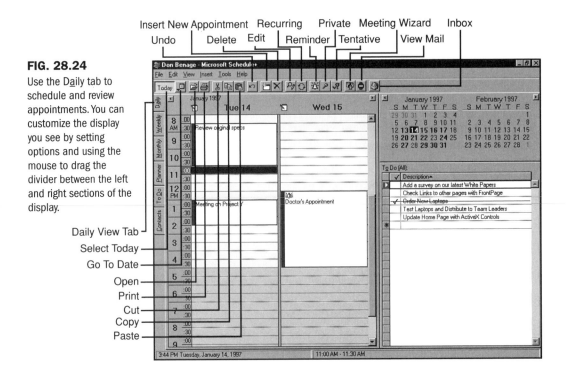

FIG. 28.24

Use the Daily tab to schedule and review appointments. You can customize the display you see by setting options and using the mouse to drag the divider between the left and right sections of the display.

Daily View Tab
Select Today
Go To Date
Open
Print
Cut
Copy
Paste

FIG. 28.25

Use the Appointment dialog box to enter the details for an appointment.

6. Complete the dialog box by entering a description. If you want, enter the location of the appointment in the Where box. If you click the Private button, other users will see that you have something scheduled at this time, but not be able to view the details of the appointment. If you click the Tentative button, the appointment appears with a gray background (by default—colors can be changed) to alert others that you may be available during this period. The Attendees and Planner tabs are explained later in this section.

7. Click OK to enter the appointment. If you need to make changes, you can edit the appointment by highlighting it with a single mouse click and choosing Edit, Edit Item from the menu. Alternatively, you can double-click the bar at the beginning of the appointment. To move the appointment, you can drag the bar at the beginning to a new start time, or drag the bar at the end of the appointment to change its length.

Most people have some events that recur—appointments that happen at the same time on a regular basis. Schedule+ makes it easy to place a recurring appointment on your schedule once a day, once a week, or at even more challenging intervals like the second Thursday of every month.

To create a recurring appointment on your own schedule, follow these steps:

1. Choose Insert, Recurring Appointment from the menu. The Appointment Series dialog box shown in Figure 28.26 appears.

FIG. 28.26
The When tab of the Appointment Series dialog box is used to enter the interval for a recurring appointment.

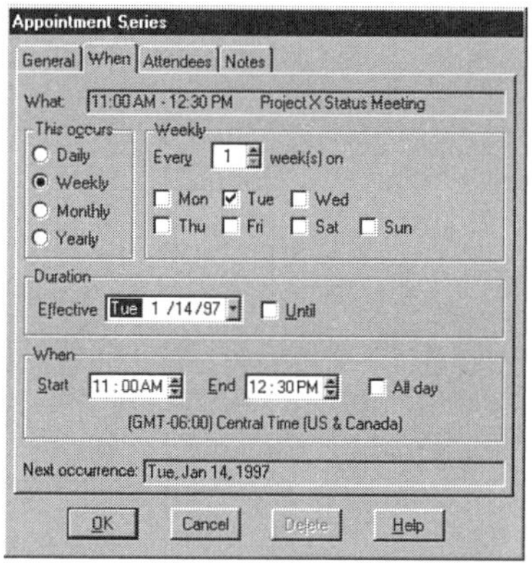

2. Enter the information on the General tab as you would for any appointment. Click the When tab.

3. Select the Daily, Weekly, Monthly, or Yearly option button. The box immediately to the right of these buttons changes to reflect your choice. You can then refine the interval selection further. You also can select a duration for this task. You can set a start date, and when you select the Until check box, you can set an end date, as well.

4. Select the time of day this appointment will take place in the When box. The Attendees tab is explained later in this section. Click OK.

Managing Meetings

You have seen some of Schedule+'s capabilities for personal scheduling. Now you learn how it can help you manage meetings and schedule appointments for groups of people. For individuals or resources such as conference rooms to be included in group scheduling activities, they must have a mailbox on the Exchange Server. If you create a mailbox for a conference room, for example, you can designate an owner for the mailbox and forward mail sent there to the

Part
VI

Ch
28

owner's own mailbox. You also can create a profile so that the owner opens both his personal mailbox and those of any resources he owns automatically when he starts the Exchange Client. The owner can be the final arbitrator of any conflicts regarding the resources schedule and can respond to meeting requests.

Opening Another User's Schedule   To open the schedule for another person or resource and to change access permissions for your own schedule, follow these steps:

1. Choose File, Open, and then select Other's Appointment Book from the resulting pop-up menu. The Open Other's Appointment Book dialog box appears.

2. Select a name from the Global Address List, or other recipients container, and click OK. If you have Read permission for the schedule, a new window opens and displays the schedule for your review.

3. To change the access permissions for your schedule, choose Tools, Set Access Permissions. The Set Access Permissions dialog box appears, as shown in Figure 28.27.

FIG. 28.27

Use this dialog box to set permissions for other users to view your schedule. You can designate different permissions for each user that will apply to different components of your schedule file.

4. You can specify different roles for each user and for a default that will apply to the components of your schedule. Set the default permissions you want most people to have.

5. Click Add and assign special roles to those people who should have more or less access than the default. Click OK when you are satisfied with your selections.

Using the Planner to Check Free and Busy Times and to Schedule Meetings   Although the capability to open another user's schedule is great if you want a meeting with that individual, when you are planning a meeting with a larger attendance, viewing individual schedules can be tedious. The Planner was designed to help find available time periods for groups of people. It allows you to specify the attendees for a meeting and then overlay all their schedules on a grid. Through the use of color-coding, you can tell when all required attendees and the necessary resources are available, and also when optional attendees are available. By selecting a particular time on the grid, individual attendees who are not available are indicated with a × next to their name in the list at the right.

To use the Planner to schedule a meeting, follow these steps:

1. Start Schedule+. Click the Planner tab, as shown in Figure 28.28.

FIG. 28.28

The Planner tab is useful for viewing the schedules of multiple people and resources at once. You also can use this tab to request a meeting.

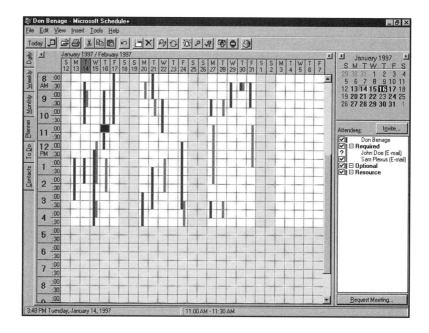

2. Use the arrow controls at the upper corners of the grid and the scroll bar at the right if you need to change the portion of the calendar that is visible. If you want to select a date several months in advance, you can use the drop-down calendar control adjacent to the Today button to move the grid to the approximate location you desire. When you are satisfied with the grid display, click the Invite button. The Select Attendees dialog box appears (see Figure 28.29).

FIG. 28.29

The Select Attendees dialog box allows you to specify the required and optional attendees and any resources that may be required.

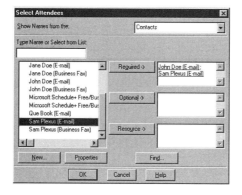

Part

VI

Ch

28

T I P The Invite button is useful even if you do not plan to actually send a meeting request at this time. It allows you to specify the schedules you want to overlay on the grid for further review.

3. Select the required recipients and optional attendees of the proposed meeting. Also, specify any scheduled resources that you may require. Click OK. The busy times of those selected display on the grid, and their names are listed at the right of the window.

N O T E Remember that for you to specify a resource, a mailbox and schedule file must be created for the resource, and an owner must be assigned to read and respond to meeting requests on behalf of the resource. ▨

4. Select a potential meeting time of the correct duration on the grid. Any attendees who are busy during that time are indicated with a × next to their name in the list at right.

5. You can experiment with different times and click the Invite button again to refine your list of attendees and time slot.

6. You also can use the Auto Pick feature to find a time. Select a block of time equivalent to the desired length of the meeting on the grid before you want the meeting to occur. Then choose Tools, Auto Pick. The first time of sufficient length during which all attendees are available will be highlighted. You can select Auto Pick repeatedly to continue reviewing available time slots.

7. When you are satisfied that you have the best possible time, click the Request Meeting button. This opens a Meeting Request form that you can complete and send to invite the attendees listed. As they respond to the meeting request, you can monitor their responses using a technique outlined in the following section.

Managing Meeting Requests   After you have sent a meeting request, the invited attendees will receive your request and respond. The meeting request form appears in their Inbox and contains buttons at the top to Accept, Decline, Tentatively Accept, and View Schedule. When they reply with one of the available options, their responses are returned to your Inbox where you can review them. You also can open the dialog box for the appointment and click the Attendees tab (see Figure 28.30). This displays the list of all invited attendees and shows their status. You also can click the Planner tab in the Appointment dialog box to see a miniature version of the larger planner window you used earlier to plan the meeting (see Figure 28.31).

FIG. 28.30

The Attendees tab of an appointment shows the responses made to a meeting request.

FIG. 28.31

The Planner tab shows a smaller version of the planner page used earlier to schedule a meeting. You can use it in much the same way as you do the planner page.

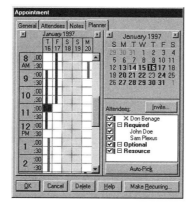

Entering Contact Information

Schedule+ also allows you to enter contact information, including business and personal addresses, phone numbers, reminders for birthdays and anniversaries, and notes. This information can be a valuable complement to the Address Book in Exchange Server. Although the Address Book stores much of the same information, it is usually inappropriate to enter someone in the Address Book if you do not want to send them e-mail. Doing so invites others to send e-mail, which would be undeliverable and cause confusion among users. The contact manager is a good place to keep track of personal and business contacts you don't exchange e-mail with.

Part
VI

Ch
28

To enter contact information in Schedule+, follow these steps:

1. Start Schedule+. Click the Contacts tab (see Figure 28.32).

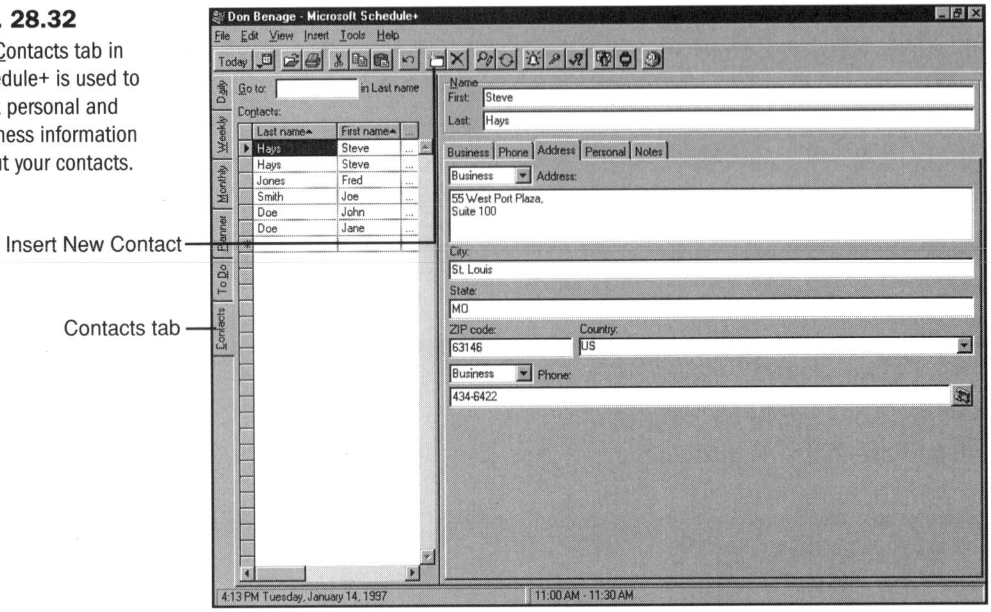

FIG. 28.32

The Contacts tab in Schedule+ is used to track personal and business information about your contacts.

Insert New Contact

Contacts tab

2. Click the Insert New Contact toolbar button, or choose Insert, Contact from the menu. A Contact dialog box appears.

3. Enter the information for this contact and click OK.

Creating a To Do List

Schedule+ also includes a To Do list, which allows you to enter information about tasks and organize them under project headings. You can specify an estimated effort, track progress by updating the % complete field, and enter the actual effort required. The To Do list appears alongside your schedule in the Daily view. You can use the mouse to drag and drop tasks onto your schedule to automatically enter them.

To enter a task in the To Do list, follow these steps:

1. Start Schedule+. Click the To Do tab (see Figure 28.33).

2. Choose Insert, Project. The Project dialog box appears. Enter a name for your project, and a default priority for tasks in this project. Click OK.

3. Highlight the project and click the Insert New Task button on the toolbar, or choose Insert, Task from the menu. A Task dialog box appears. Enter information about the task and click OK.

Alternatively, you can enter information directly in the spreadsheet-like grid display instead of using the Insert dialog boxes. Select a cell in the grid and then enter or edit information using the mouse or keyboard.

FIG. 28.33

The To Do tab allows you to enter task information and sort it by project or other criteria.

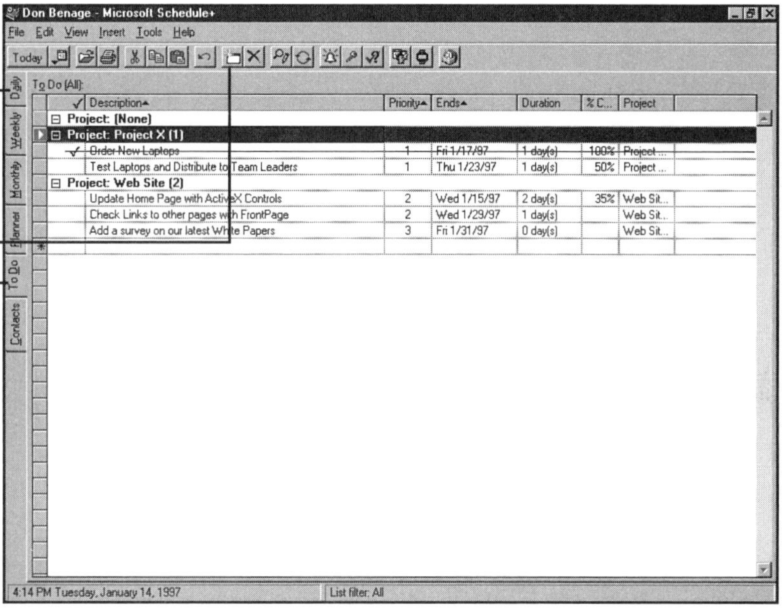

Daily tab

Insert New Task

To Do tab

4. Click the Daily tab. Your task should appear on the right of the schedule. Click the column headings of the To Do list with the right mouse button to access a context-sensitive pop-up menu that allows you to customize the columns you want to see.

5. Use the mouse to drag and drop a task directly onto your schedule. You can adjust the amount of time you want to spend by dragging the bar at the end of the task, just as you would adjust an appointment. You can change the start time by dragging the bar at the beginning of the appointment.

Now that you have been introduced to Schedule+, you learn how to use the remote mail features of the Exchange Client. These techniques are particularly important for notebook computer users or those who use a home computer to access the network.

Using Dial-Up Access to Exchange Server

The Exchange Client includes new features specially designed to meet the needs of remote users. Previous versions of Microsoft Mail required users to purchase a separate client to take full advantage of remote features, but this client could operate over the same connection type used for other networking functionality. The standard networking client could be used over a dial-up connection, but it did not always provide the most reliable results or full access to

Part
VI

Ch
28

remote features. The Exchange Client addresses these issues by providing a single client that operates over a local network connection or uses RAS to connect to the network over a dial-up phone line. It also provides a rich set of features for remote users.

Creating a Profile for Remote Access

Earlier in this chapter, you learned how to create profiles to specify different services and options for the Exchange Client. You may want to review that section, "Creating a User Profile," before you continue. In this section, you learn how to create a profile specifically tailored for remote use. If you will be defining the profile from a remote location, connect to the network first, as outlined in the following "Using the Remote Access Service" Section. You will need to be able to connect to the server in step 8 to ensure that your profile is properly defined.

To create a profile for remote access, follow these steps:

1. Open the Control Panel.

2. Double-click the Mail and Fax icon. If any profiles have already been created on this computer, a Properties dialog box appears showing the properties of the current profile. If no profiles have been defined, you should see the General tab of the Mail and Fax dialog box. If so, skip to step 4.

3. Click the Show Profiles button. The General tab of the Mail and Fax dialog box appears.

4. To add a new profile, click the Add button. This launches the Microsoft Exchange Setup Wizard.

5. In the opening dialog box of the Wizard, you can choose from two option buttons—Use the Following Information Services, or Manually Configure Information Services. If you select the first option, the Wizard assists you with creating an appropriate profile. The manual method is explained here. Select the option button labeled Manually Configure Information Services. Click Next.

6. Enter a name for this profile. The name can include spaces and should indicate the user of the profile and a brief description of the profile's purpose. For example, you could enter **John Doe as Remote User** or **Jane Doe with Traveling Laptop**. Click Next. A blank Properties dialog box appears.

7. Select the services you will use with this profile. Click Add. The Add Service to Profile dialog box appears.

8. Select Microsoft Exchange Server and click OK. A Microsoft Exchange Server dialog box appears. This dialog box allows you to specify the server you will use and other options. Enter the name of the home server for your mailbox and the mailbox name. You can enter either the display name or the alias. To be sure that you have entered a correct name, click the Check Name button. If the name corresponds to an existing mailbox on the server you entered, both names will be underlined to signify a match.

9. Select the Work Offline and Use Dial-Up Networking option button in the When starting box. If you want to make this selection each time you start the Exchange Client, select the check box labeled Choose the Connection Type When Starting. Click the Advanced tab.

10. If you want to open any additional mailboxes for which this user has permissions, click Add and enter the name of the mailbox. You can specify encryption with a local network or dial-up connection to provide additional protection against unauthorized message capture and viewing. If you want to use the same logon ID for both network access and for your mailbox(es), select the Use Network Security During Logon check box.

11. The offline folder file is an important component of remote mail use. It is useful to create this file specifying a name other than the default if you want to use multiple profiles on this machine. Click the Offline Folder File Settings button.

12. Enter a fully qualified file name, or use the Browse button to specify a location for the file. Offline folder files have an extension of OST (for offline store). Select an option button for the encryption setting. This helps to secure the information in your offline folder file if this computer should fall into the wrong hands.

13. You can use the buttons at the bottom of the Offline Folder File Settings dialog box to launch a process to compact your offline folder file and eliminate empty space left by deleted messages, or temporarily disable the use of the offline folder file. Click OK to close the Offline Folder File Settings dialog box. Then click the Dial-Up Networking tab (see Figure 28.34).

FIG. 28.34

The Dial-Up Networking tab specifies the RAS connection you want to use with this profile and your logon information.

14. Specify a connection to use with this profile, or select the option button at the bottom labeled Do Not Dial, Use Existing Connection, if you want to manually invoke the connection process yourself. Click the Remote Mail tab (see Figure 28.35).

15. On this tab, you can set up an automated connection and e-mail download. This can occur without your assistance while you are involved in another activity if you set it up carefully. In the Remote Mail Connections box, you can specify the mail to be transferred. The default is to transfer all mail. In the Scheduled Connections box, you can create a schedule for an automated mail transfer. Enter your selections.

16. Click OK to return to the Microsoft Exchange Server dialog box. Then click OK again to return to the Properties dialog box for this profile. You have defined a profile to use Microsoft Exchange Server. You can stop now and use your profile, or define two additional and useful options—the personal folder file and the Personal Address Book.

Part
VI

Ch
28

FIG. 28.35

The Remote Mail tab allows you to specify regularly scheduled connections that will be made automatically, without any assistance from a user. Specify connection information on the Dial-Up Networking tab.

17. Click OK to close the dialog box and finish, or see the "Creating a Personal Address Book" and "Creating a Personal Folder File" sections earlier in this chapter for procedures to create those services.

Using the Remote Access Service

To use the RAS client software, you must first configure a connection. This procedure varies with different operating systems and is not covered in this book. The steps required to use a RAS connection on a Windows 95 client are outlined in this section.

To use a RAS connection on a Windows 95 computer, follow these steps:

1. Double-click My Computer and then double-click the Dial-Up Networking folder. Double-click the connection you want to use. A Connect To dialog box for your connection appears, as shown in Figure 28.36.

FIG. 28.36

Use the Connect To dialog box to log on to your network from a remote location.

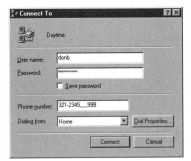

2. Enter your User name and Password and click the Connect button.

Your modem will dial the remote network and connect if there is an available modem (the line is not busy) and your account and password are correct.

After you have connected with RAS, you are operating as a fully functional network client, albeit with a slower link to the network. You can connect to any network resources for which you have access privileges, including shared directories and printers. In addition, you can now use the Exchange Client to connect to your mailbox.

Using Remote Mail Features in the Exchange Client

You have learned how to create a profile for remote mail and how to connect to a remote network using RAS. In this section, you learn the basics of the remote mail features in the Exchange Client. You can manually initiate a connection to the remote network, as outlined in the previous section, or you can let the Exchange Client initiate the connection when needed. This is controlled by the settings you made on the Dial-up Networking tab of your profile definition.

To use remote mail features, follow these steps:

1. Depending on the settings in your profile, you may need to manually connect to the network. If you specified Do Not Dial, Use Existing Connection on the Dial-Up Networking tab of your profile, connect to the network manually.

2. Start the Exchange Client.

3. If the Choose Profile dialog box appears, select the profile you want to use and click OK.

4. Depending on your configuration, you also may need to respond to a dialog box asking whether you should Connect or Work Offline. Select Work Offline.

5. When the client interface is presented, choose Tools, Remote Mail from the menu. A Remote Mail window appears (see Figure 28.37).

FIG. 28.37

The Remote Mail window has a toolbar and menu choices specially designed for remote mail use.

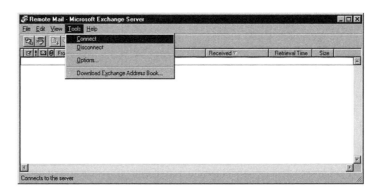

6. Click the Connect button on the remote mail toolbar, or choose Tools, Connect on the menu. A dialog box appears that you can use to specify the actions you want to take.

7. Select Update Headers. A progress indicator appears showing the progress of your connection (see Figure 28.38).

Part
VI

Ch
28

FIG. 28.38

A progress indicator shows the progress of message transfer over a remote connection.

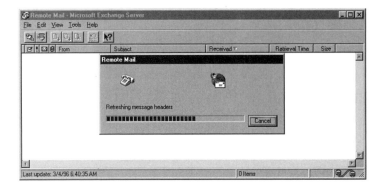

8. When the headers have been updated, you can review the messages in your mailbox on the server and select only those you want to read. You may prefer, for example, to wait until a later time to read large messages of over 250K. Select the messages you want to read and click the Mark to Retrieve toolbar button.

9. Click the Connect button again and select the option to Retrieve Marked Items. If you have any outgoing mail in your Outbox, select the option to Upload Messages.

10. Click OK. Your messages are transferred.

From Here...

You have now learned how to set up the Exchange Client software, how to use the Outlook Client, Exchange Client, and Schedule+ to manage your messaging and schedule, and how to use the remote mail features of the Exchange Client. In addition, you have learned how to set up a shared contact list that can be used by a group of people to complement the Exchange Server Address Book.

The following chapters contain information related to the information covered in this chapter:

■ For information on setting up Exchange Server, see Chapter 27, "Implementing Exchange Server."

■ For information on creating public folders, replicating public folders, and managing directory information, see Chapter 29, "Distributing Information with Exchange Server."

■ For information on using public folders to manage the flow and storage of documents, see Chapter 30, "Document Management with Exchange Server."

■ For information on setting up connectors to foreign message systems and procedures for using Exchange Server's advanced security options, see Chapter 31, "Exchange Server Advanced Topics."

Distributing Information with Exchange Server

by Don Benage

One of the most important features of Exchange Server is its scalability. This applies not only to the capability to add processors, memory, and additional disk components to a single server, but also to the capability to add additional servers. Exchange Server has been designed to allow a distributed system of many servers, each communicating with other servers and playing a role in the delivery of information to users.

In this chapter, you explore the techniques used to create public folders, a cornerstone of Exchange Server's information sharing capabilities. You learn the basics of implementing and using public folders and how to replicate them to other servers to balance the user load and make the best use of available network bandwidth. You also learn how to replicate directory information across all servers in your organization. ■

How to replicate directory information—within your site and with other sites

Learn how to keep directory information synchronized across all servers—within your site and throughout your organization.

How to use the Exchange Client to create and manage public folders

Look here to find out how to create public folders using the Exchange Client. Learn how to set permissions and properties for public folders with the Exchange Client and the Exchange Administrator.

How to replicate public folders to other servers and use public folders at other sites

Find out how to make public folders available on multiple servers to distribute the load and improve performance.

How to track messages and diagnose problems with Exchange Server

Look here to find the procedures for tracking messages as they flow through the system. Find out how to use link monitors, server monitors, and the Windows NT Performance Monitor to monitor the health of your Exchange Server site and diagnose problems.

Replicating Directory Information

As you have already learned, the directory is one of the core services that make up Exchange Server. It is made up of a Windows NT service and a corresponding database. This core component must run on every Exchange Server in your organization. The directory is used to build the address book and the Global Address List and provides information on the elements of the various sites and the entire organization to the other components of Exchange Server.

> **N O T E** The term *directory* can also be used to refer to the conceptual list of named objects that make up an Exchange Server site. The physical manifestation of this list consists of the directory information on all servers in the site, which may not always be exactly the same on all servers if new information has been added and not yet replicated. There is still, however, one conceptual "directory" for the site. Each Exchange Server will have its own Directory Service that implements the directory on that server, and replicates its information to other servers as described in this chapter. ▦

The architecture of the Exchange Server directory does not force all changes to the database to occur on a single server. If you want to add a new element such as a mailbox or custom recipient to the directory, you can do so at any server in the site. Exchange Server automatically processes the changes and updates all other servers within a site. This is known as *intrasite replication*. You do not need to take any action to make this process occur—it is the default behavior of Exchange Servers in a site. However, there is a method for forcing the servers within a site to synchronize their directories, a capability that is occasionally useful if you make an important change and do not want to wait for the normal processing interval (which is every five minutes).

You also can replicate directory information from one site to another. This is referred to as *intersite replication* and requires a little more work to set up, but is still a relatively straightforward process. For intersite replication, two servers, one from each site, are designated as *bridgehead servers* and configured to pass directory information between one another. This is done by creating and configuring a *directory-replication connector*, a special type of connector designed for this task. The directory changes are passed as standard e-mail messages.

Intrasite Replication

As was just mentioned, intrasite replication is automatic. No special configuration is required. A server whose directory has been changed notifies other servers in the local site that a change has occurred. They then request updated information from the changed server, which responds with the new information. This process occurs approximately every five minutes. You can force this process to begin if you want by using a button located on the General tab of the Directory Service dialog box for any one of the servers in the site.

To manually start a *directory-replication* process in the local site, follow these steps:

1. Start the Exchange Administrator if you have not already done so. Connect to a server that is in the site you want to administer.

2. In the container area (the left pane) of the display, find the site you want to administer. Click the plus sign to the left of the site name to expand the display if it is not already open. Click the plus sign to the left of the Configuration object to expand its display. You should see the Servers object. Click the plus sign to the left of the Servers object to expand its display.

3. Highlight the server object for one of the servers in the site. Any server can initiate intrasite directory replication, but if you know one of the servers carries a smaller workload due to its configuration, there may be a slight efficiency advantage in using it to launch this process.

4. In the contents pane, you should see the services on that server listed. Double-click the Directory Service. The dialog box for the Directory Service appears (see Figure 29.1).

FIG. 29.1

The General tab of the Directory Service for a particular server allows you to initiate intrasite directory replication.

5. Click the General tab. Two buttons are available. For this process, use the top button labeled Update Now, to update this directory from within this site.

6. Click the Update Now button. A dialog box provides a progress report on the update process, and then an information dialog box notifies you that the process has finished.

Intersite Replication

To configure intersite replication, you must create a *directory-replication* connector. The server on which the connector is created becomes the *local bridgehead server*. The server at the remote site with which it is paired is the *remote bridgehead server*. There can be only one such pairing between any two sites. You can use a single server in the local site to connect to more than one remote site, but you cannot have two connections between the same two sites. For example, a server in the site named EXTERNAL can connect to a server in the INTERNAL site and to a server in the CORPHQ site, but it cannot connect to *two* servers in the INTERNAL site because that would constitute two connections between the same two sites.

The process of configuring *directory-replication* connectors is simplified if the two sites are on the same LAN (or connected with a high-speed line capable of Remote Procedure Call (RPC) communications). Both the local and the remote bridgehead servers can be configured at the same time in a single process. If the two sites are not on the same LAN, an administrator from each site must set them up separately and make sure that the pair are configured properly to communicate with each other. If the sites are joined by a connection that is not active at all times, for example the Dynamic RAS connector, make sure that the schedule you establish for replicating intersite directory information corresponds to the availability of a connection between the sites.

Setting Up a Site Connector

You need to have some sort of message delivery connector between sites to replicate directory information. The *directory-replication* connector is not a general purpose connector that can function on its own. It requires that one of the other connectors be available to deliver messages. Several connectors are suitable for connecting two sites. The connectors that can function in this capacity that are currently available are presented in the following list. Additional connectors may be offered in the future by Microsoft or third-party vendors.

- Site connector
- Dynamic RAS connector
- X.400 connector
- Internet Mail Service

The simplest of these to implement and manage is the site connector. Although connectors are covered in more detail in Chapter 31, "Exchange Server Advanced Topics," the procedures for installing a site connector are provided here. This connector is suitable only for environments where two sites are on the same LAN and can communicate over a protocol that supports Remote Procedure Call (RPC) communications. If you have two sites that meet these criteria, the site connector is a good choice for a first site-to-site link. After you have linked two sites with a messaging connector, you can implement directory replication and public folder replication.

To implement a site connector, you configure one or multiple servers on each site as *messaging bridgehead servers*. Unlike the directory-replication connector, which requires that a single server be responsible for acting as a bridgehead server to the remote site, a site connector can use one or more servers in the site as messaging bridgehead servers. You can specify a particular server if you want to control which server must provide this additional messaging load, or you can indicate that any server in the site can be used. You also can control which servers in the remote site should be used as target servers and indicate a routing cost for each target server. This is nothing more than a number (from 0 to 100 with a default value of 1) that provides a relative indication of which servers are most able to handle incoming messages. Servers with a value of 0 are used first; those with 100 are used last; and two servers that have the same value receive roughly the same load. This mechanism effectively allows you to control the order in which target servers are selected.

Site connectors provide one-way message transfer. You may want to create a corresponding site connector *from* the remote site *to* the local site. Because these connectors require a LAN protocol capable of using RPC, you can use the Exchange Administrator to connect to both sites in separate windows at the same time, provided that you have granted permissions to each site for the same account. You need Admin permissions for the Configuration container (or at least the Connections container) to create the site connector. In addition, the service account in the local site (where the connector is being defined) must have the User role for the target servers or the Configuration container in the remote site. If it does not, you can use the Override tab (described in step 9 of the following steps) to enter an account name and password that do.

To complete this task, you need the following:

- You must have the name of a server in the remote site. It is preferable to have the names of all servers in the remote site and a ranking of their suitability as target servers for incoming messages.

- You must log on with an account that has administrative permissions for the Configuration container in the local site. If you plan to create a site connector for the remote site to connect to the local site, you need administrative permissions for the remote Configuration container, as well.

- If the Exchange service account for the local site does not have User role permissions for the servers or Configuration container at the remote site, you must have the name and password of an account that does to use on the Override tab. Again, if defining a second site connector at the remote site, the same condition applies with the sites reversed.

N O T E Site connectors use X.400 addressing to route messages to other sites. If you have not already done so, you should check that the X.400 address properties are correct. You can find them on the Site Addressing tab of the dialog box for the Site Addressing object in the Configuration container for each site. Make sure that only valid characters are used in the addresses that were generated by default during the Exchange Server installation. The Private Management Domain Name should be the same as your organization name or an abbreviated version using only characters that are valid in X.400 addresses.

To set up a site connector, follow these steps:

1. Start the Exchange Administrator if you have not already done so. Connect to a server that is in the site you want to administer.

2. In the container area (the left pane) of the display, find the site you want to administer. Click the plus sign to the left of the site name to expand the display if it is not already open. Click the plus sign to the left of the Configuration object to expand its display.

3. Highlight the Connections object. Choose File, New Other from the menu, and then choose Site Connector. The New Site Connector dialog box appears.

4. Enter the name of the server in the remote site to which you want to connect. Click OK. A Site Connector dialog box appears (see Figure 29.2).

FIG. 29.2

This Site Connector dialog box allows you to specify properties for a connection between two sites over a high-speed LAN connection capable of RPC communications.

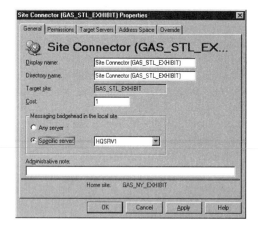

5. If you want, you can change the default <u>D</u>isplay Name and Directory <u>N</u>ame for this connector. The directory name is used in any messages written to the event log regarding this connector. The display name appears in the Exchange Administrator's display.

N O T E The only time you can change the directory name of an object is during its initial creation. If you want to change it later, you must delete the object and create a new one. While this achieves more or less the same effect as renaming the object, it can be disruptive to the flow of information through the Exchange Server environment and creates opportunities for errors. It is best to get it right the first time. ■

6. Enter a routing <u>C</u>ost for this connector. If multiple connections between two sites exist, the active connection with the lowest cost is used for message delivery. Therefore, if you have a large network with multiple connections between two sites, you can use this routing cost to help Exchange Server calculate the most efficient route. Connections over high-speed links should have low routing costs. As the speed of the link gets slower, you should use a higher routing cost. As long as a low-cost route is active, it is selected before the others. If it is temporarily out of commission due to maintenance or other causes, another route is used.

7. Select a Sp<u>e</u>cific Server to act as a messaging bridgehead between the two sites, or leave the default setting of Any Ser<u>v</u>er. Click the Target Servers tab (see Figure 29.3).

8. By default, all servers in the remote site are placed in the <u>T</u>arget Servers list. You can remove or add servers to the <u>T</u>arget Servers list for this connector at any time. The server you initially specified when creating the site connector is given a routing cost of 1 (a very low cost) by default. You can change the routing cost value for individual servers to reflect which are the most suitable as targets for incoming messages. The available server with the lowest cost is used. Click the Address Space tab (see Figure 29.4).

FIG. 29.3

The Target Servers tab of a Site Connector dialog box enables you to specify those servers in the target site to which messages are sent directly. Messages with destination addresses on other servers in the remote site are routed using intrasite connectivity.

FIG. 29.4

Use this tab to specify partial e-mail addresses to be used to build routing tables. The X.400 address of the remote site itself is entered automatically.

9. Enter partial addresses that will match the types of e-mail addresses that should be routed to the remote site over this site connector. For example, if the remote site contained the only Internet Mail Service for your organization, you would want all messages with SMTP addresses to be forwarded to that site. You would create a new Internet address with only an asterisk in the address field so that all messages with an SMTP address outside your organization would be routed to the remote site. Click the Override tab (see Figure 29.5).

10. If both sites are in the same Windows NT domain and both use the same Exchange service account, using the Override tab is unnecessary. If the two sites share the same master domain, you can enter a service account from the master domain in this dialog box. Otherwise, you should use the Exchange service account from the remote site. You will need to get this account information from an administrator for the remote site if you have not already done so. Enter the account ID (in the Windows NT Username text box), password, and domain name (if necessary). Click OK.

FIG. 29.5

You can use the Override tab to enter an account and password that will provide a security context for message transfer between two sites with no domain trust relationships.

11. A dialog box appears asking if a site connector should also be created in the remote site (see Figure 29.6). This is usually a good idea unless you have a specific reason to manually create the matching site connector in the other site. If you don't want to take advantage of this opportunity, click No to finish the process. Skip to step 13.

FIG. 29.6

This dialog box gives you the opportunity to create a remote site connector at this time.

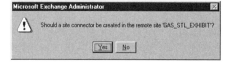

12. Otherwise, click the Yes button and complete the resulting dialog boxes for the remote site connector in the same manner prescribed above. Click the OK button when finished.

 TIP If you have Windows NT administrative privileges at the remote site, you can see the account ID (but not its password) by choosing Computer, Services from the menu in the Windows NT Server Manager. Highlight a Microsoft Exchange service—Directory, Information Store, Message Transfer Agent (MTA), or System Attendant—and click the Startup button.

13. If your account information and permissions were set correctly, you should have an operational site connector (or two if you chose to set up the remote site as well), usually in less than a minute. If you get an error message about your account permissions, use the Exchange Administrator to review or assign permissions on the remote site's Configuration container and try again (see Figure 29.7).

FIG. 29.7

In this figure you can see two sites, each with replicated directory information about the other site.

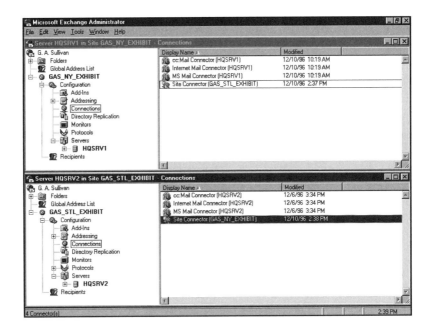

You may want to create a site connector from the remote site to the local site to enable bidirectional message transfer. Typically the flow of information between sites is not in only one direction. Each site has messages addressed to recipients in the other site, and so there must be a mechanism to move messages both ways. If you are planning to implement a directory-replication connector, or public folder replication, this is required.

▶ **See** "A Flexible Set of Services," **p. 54**

Setting Up Bridgehead Replication Servers

To create an intersite directory-replication connector between two sites on the same LAN, which simultaneously creates the local and the remote bridgehead servers, follow these steps:

1. Start the Exchange Administrator if you have not already done so. Connect to a server in the site you want to administer.

2. In the container area (the left pane) of the display, find the site you want to administer. Click the plus sign to the left of the site name to expand the display if it is not already open. Click the plus sign to the left of the Configuration object to expand its display. Highlight the Directory Replication object.

3. Choose File, New Other from the menu, and then select Directory Replication Connector. A New Directory Replication Connector dialog box appears, as shown in Figure 29.8.

FIG. 29.8

Use this dialog box to configure bridgehead servers for directory replication. If two sites are on the same LAN, you can configure the local and remote bridgehead servers at the same time.

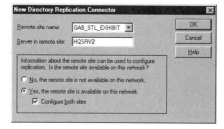

4. Select the Remote Site Name in the drop-down list, or enter its name directly. Enter the name of the Server in Remote Site you want to use as the only directory-replication bridgehead server to the local site.

5. Select an option button to indicate whether the remote site is on the same LAN as this site. If it is, you can create and configure a directory-replication connector on the remote site simultaneously. If the remote site is not on the same LAN, an administrator at the remote site needs to create a corresponding bridgehead server on the remote site, using the computer you have specified. Click OK. A Directory Replication Connector dialog box appears, as shown in Figure 29.9.

FIG. 29.9

This is the dialog box for the directory-replication connector being created. Both the local and remote bridgehead servers are specified on the General tab.

6. If necessary, change the selected bridgehead servers in the drop-down list boxes. If you want, you can change the Display Name and the Directory Name for this connector. As usual, after this connector is created, its directory name can no longer be changed. This is the name that will be used in messages written to the event log regarding this connection. Click the Schedule tab (see Figure 29.10).

7. You can modify the default schedule once every three hours if you want. If you select the Always option button, updates are sent every 15 minutes, and the schedule is ignored. Selecting Never disables directory replication. Click the Sites tab (see Figure 29.11).

FIG. 29.10

The Schedule tab allows you to specify the interval at which changes to directory information are transmitted to the remote site. The default schedule is every three hours.

FIG. 29.11

The Sites tab shows the Inbound Sites and Outbound Sites serviced by this directory-replication connector. It does not display this information until the creation of the connector is complete and directory replication has occurred at least once.

8. The Sites tab remains empty until the connector has been created and directory replication occurs. You can review this tab later to see the results. The remote site, also known as the *directly connected site*, should appear in the Inbound Sites list, along with any other sites with which it shares directory information through other directory-replication connectors.

9. When this dialog box has been filled in by the directory-replication process, you can select an inbound site and click the Request Now button. A Directory Update Type dialog box appears. You can then select to receive the changes since the last replication (Update Only New and Modified Items) or the entire directory of the selected site (Refresh All Items in the Directory).

CAUTION

Selecting the R̲efresh All Items in the Directory option button begins an operation that may take several hours and can negatively affect network traffic and processing times for the servers and network links involved. This activity is best done during off-peak hours.

10. Click OK to create your directory-replication connector(s). It may take some time before the changes are reflected in the display of the Exchange Administrator, depending on the schedule you specified. During this time, if you try to select an object that has not been completely replicated, you may get a message indicating that the recalculation of the directory hierarchy is not yet complete. Wait a few minutes and try again. If you want to manually request updated information go to step 11.

11. Because you have made a change that affects the directory, you can open the dialog box for the Directory Service on the local bridgehead server and use the C̲heck Now button to request a Knowledge Consistency check. This causes the Directory Service to discover the new site connection and request updated information. It will still take some time for the operation to complete, depending on the size of the directory at the remote site. When it is complete, you can recalculate routing tables using the General tab of the MTA to reflect the new information in the directory. This occurs automatically at the scheduled times if you do not initiate it manually.

When the directory-replication operation has finished, the remote site's directory information should appear in the Exchange Administrator's display when you connect to your local site. The reverse also is true—information from your site appears in the directory of the remote site. Figure 29.12 depicts the Exchange Administrator connected to two sites, GAS_STL_EXHIBIT and GAS_NY_EXHIBIT. In the display for the GAS_STL_EXHIBIT site, you can see the site connector to the GAS_NY_EXHIBIT site in the contents area for the highlighted Connections object. A similar site connector is defined in the GAS_NY_EXHIBIT site to connect to the GAS_STL_EXHIBIT. In the display for the GAS_NY_EXHIBIT site, the directory-replication connector is visible in the contents area of the highlighted Directory Replication object. Again, there is a corresponding connector in the GAS_STL_EXHIBIT site.

Remember, if your directory display does not update immediately, be patient. This process can take some time, especially the first time when all information must be sent. With large sites containing many directory items, the process can take hours. Before you start reconfiguring elements of the process, give the process some time to complete. You also can use techniques described later in this chapter in the "Monitoring Your Site" section to watch for signs of progress without dismantling the pieces.

FIG. 29.12

The Exchange Administrator showing two sites that have site connectors and directory-replication connectors linking them together.

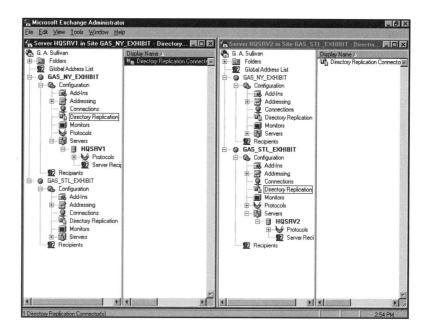

Part

VI

Ch

29

Using Public Folders

One of the most powerful features offered by Exchange Server is the capability to create and share *public folders*. They allow users to easily share information with other users by dragging a copy of a message into a public folder for others to view. Users also can compose (fill out) a *form* and post it in the public folder. Depending on the design of the folder, other users may be able to respond to this posting with a reply displayed directly beneath the original message and slightly indented. It is easy to create a bulletin board system to facilitate discussions of all types. The techniques for creating public folders and using forms within them are discussed later in this section.

A public folder created on one server can be made available to users with mailboxes on other servers in the site, or even in other sites. If the network links between the public folder server and clients are too slow, or the load placed on the server is too great due to high demand, the folder can be *replicated* to other public folder servers. This can distribute the load and provide high-speed access to a public folder server for all client workstations.

Folders can contain other folders. A folder at the highest level in the hierarchy is called a *top-level folder*. An important configuration detail is the designation of those users who can create top-level folders in the public folder hierarchy. Having too many top-level folders makes the hierarchy unwieldy, and it becomes difficult to find the items for which you are looking. Therefore, it makes sense to limit the number of people who can create top-level folders and to use the top level for broad categories that contain many other folders.

Public folders can be designed to use standard forms provided with Exchange Server for e-mail messages or posting messages in discussion forums. You also can use *custom forms* created with the Forms Designer, an application provided with Exchange Server. A variety of specialized forms are provided with the sample applications included with Exchange Server. You can copy and modify these forms to create a wide range of *groupware* applications. You can explicitly control which forms can be used in a public folder. For more information on creating custom forms, see *Microsoft Exchange Server Application Designer's Guide*, part of the documentation available for Exchange Server.

In addition to forms support, you can define *views*, which specify the columns, grouping, and sort order of the information displayed in a folder. You can create custom views and make them available to users of the public folder, or the users themselves can create personal views. Different views can be applied to the same folder to enhance the readability of the information being presented to the user.

You also can set permissions on a public folder to control access to its contents. Unlike other objects in the Exchange Server directory, which have access control based on Windows NT accounts, public folders control access based on mailboxes and distribution lists. There is still an indirect correspondence to the Windows NT logon ID, because any given mailbox has permissions for specific (usually one) Windows NT logon IDs. But when you grant permissions to use a public folder, you indicate specific mailboxes or the members of one or more distribution lists. You can assign roles to the users of a public folder such as *reviewer* (read-only access), *author* (read/write access to their own items), or *owner* (all rights in the folder, including the capability to delete information created by other users).

Creating Public Folders

There are many things you can do with public folders, especially with the addition of custom forms. This section presents a simple example to help you get started. After working through this example, you will have a basic understanding of the possibilities, and you can explore the additional capabilities offered by this element of Exchange Server in the *Application Designer's Guide*, which comes with Exchange Server.

In the example, you create a top-level folder called *Programming Tools Discussions*, and then a folder within that top-level folder called *Visual Basic Discussions*. This structure is to underscore the desirability of not cluttering the top level with too many folders. Then you create a view and set properties on the folder so that it can function as a discussion forum for issues regarding the Visual Basic programming language.

After following the example to create a public folder, you learn how to copy forms into the various libraries that can store them, and how to use forms in your public folders. Finally, in the next section you learn how to replicate public folders to other servers, including servers in another site. See Chapter 4, "Designing Microsoft Exchange Public Folders," in the *Application Designer's Guide*.

Creating a New Public Folder   To create a new public folder, follow these steps:

1. Start the Exchange Client.

2. Highlight the folder named All Public Folders. Choose File, New Folder from the menu. A New Folder dialog box appears.

3. Enter the name of your new folder. In the example, the folder name is **Project X**. Click OK, and the new folder appears.

4. Right-click the mouse pointer on the Project X folder. Select Properties from the resulting pop-up menu. A Properties dialog box appears (see Figure 29.13).

FIG. 29.13

This dialog box is for setting properties for the public folder named in its title bar. You can use it to control the views, forms, and permissions for the folder.

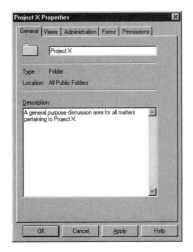

5. Enter a description for the folder on the General tab.

6. Click the Views tab. Using the option buttons, you can select either Personal Views or Folder Views. In the example, you create a folder view that is a modified version of the personal view called Group by Conversation Topic.

7. Select the Personal Views option button, and then the Group by Conversation Topic form in the list.

8. Click New. A New View dialog box appears with settings from the existing view.

9. Enter a name for the view (in this example, it is **Main View for Discussions**) and click the Folder Views option button.

10. Click the Columns button, and the Columns dialog box appears (see Figure 29.14).

11. Use the Add and Remove buttons to include Conversation Topic, Item Type, From, Subject, Item Text, and Received in the Show the Following list.

12. Use the Move Up and Move Down buttons to arrange the columns in the order they are listed, or as you want.

FIG. 29.14

The Columns dialog box allows you to specify the columns that should be included in a defined view. You can indicate their order and a column width for each.

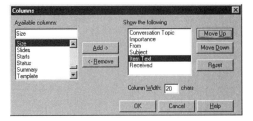

13. Highlight Item Text and enter **40** for the Column <u>W</u>idth. Click OK to return to the New View dialog box.

14. For the example, no other changes should be made. If you want to examine some of the possibilities that can be selected, however, click the <u>G</u>roup By, <u>S</u>ort, and <u>F</u>ilter buttons in the New View dialog box.

15. Click OK to return to the Properties dialog box for the folder. Click the Administration tab (see Figure 29.15).

FIG. 29.15

Use the Administration tab to set administrative options for a public folder. You can specify a default view for the folder and indicate to whom the folder will be made available (either All <u>u</u>sers with access permission, or <u>O</u>wners only).

16. Select the view you just created as the Initial <u>V</u>iew on Folder. While creating and testing a new form, it is a good idea to make it available only to the owners (namely you). When you have finished the form, you can make it available to all users with permissions. You can add another owner to the form if you want assistance with design or testing. This is done on the Permissions tab in step 12. Click the Forms tab.

17. On this tab, you can specify the forms that can be used with this folder. By clicking the <u>M</u>anage button, you can invoke the Forms Manager, which allows you to copy forms from the Organization Forms Library, another Folder Forms Library, or your Personal Forms Library into the Forms Library for this folder. (The use of forms is described in more detail in the "Using Forms With Your Folder" section later in this chapter.)

For this example, you use only the standard forms, so you should not add any to the list of forms associated with this folder. Click the option button labeled Forms Listed Above and the Standard Forms. Then click the Permissions tab (see Figure 29.16).

FIG. 29.16

Use the Permissions tab to specify who is allowed to use this folder and designate their privileges.

18. Use the Permissions tab to set default permissions for all users and to designate specific roles for individual users or distribution lists. Click OK to complete your new public folder.

> **N O T E** As an alternative, you can choose File, New Discussion Folder from the menu. This will automatically create a public folder that uses the "Unread by Conversation" view, which is an ideal view for generic discussion folders. You can achieve the same results by manually setting the same options; this menu choice just simplifies the task. ▓

It is a good idea to test your new folder before making it available to users. To test it, choose Compose, New Post in This Folder. A New Post form appears. You can complete the form and click the Post button at the far right (which looks like a push pin). Double-click the message you just posted and click the Post Reply in This Folder toolbar button. This opens a reply posting form, which is added to the folder indented under your original posting (see Figure 29.17).

When you are satisfied that it works, use the Administration tab on the Properties pages for the form to indicate that it should be made available to All Users with Access Permissions instead of Owners Only, by using the procedures you just learned (refer to step 16).

FIG. 29.17

This is a discussion-forum public folder being tested by the owner for the first time.

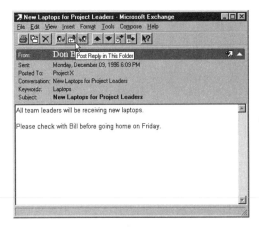

Using Forms with Your Folder   You can create custom forms with the Forms Designer, a development tool that is somewhat similar to using Visual Basic and offers a wizard to guide you through the initial design of a new form. You can use Visual Basic to automate and control the behavior of the created form. A variety of sample forms are included with the Forms Designer, and you can use them as the bases for additional forms development.

A sample personal folder file that demonstrates many of these forms, SAMPAPPS.PST, can be shared on a server so users can copy it to their local hard disks. They can then add it to their profile as an additional personal folder file and open it for experimentation. SAMPAPPS.PST requires approximately 17M of space to install. A read-me file included with the samples describes this process.

You can store forms in one of three places: the Organization Forms Library, another Folder Forms Library, or your Personal Forms Library. In this section, you learn how to create an Organization Forms Library using the Exchange Administrator and how to copy forms into the various libraries with the Forms Manager in the Exchange Client.

N O T E   The first time a particular user makes use of a new custom form, a copy of the form will be downloaded to the user's computer. It is a good idea to warn users about this potential delay so they understand this occurs only one time per form and don't become frustrated or disenchanted with the application. ▪

To create an Organization Forms Library, follow these steps:

1. Start the Exchange Administrator.

2. Choose Tools, Forms Administrator. The Organization Forms Library Administrator dialog box appears.

3. Click New, and the Create New Forms Library dialog box appears, as shown in Figure 29.18.

FIG. 29.18

This dialog box allows you to create language-specific forms libraries that are accessible to all users in the entire organization.

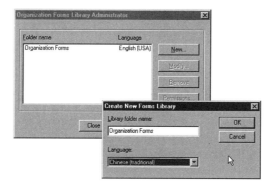

4. You can enter a name or use the default name of Organization Forms. Select the language for the library you want to create and click OK.

To copy forms into one of the forms libraries, follow these steps:

1. Start the Exchange Client.

2. Choose Tools, Options.

3. Then select the Exchange Server tab and click the Manage Forms button. The Forms Manager dialog box is shown in Figure 29.19.

FIG. 29.19

Use the Forms Manager dialog box to copy and install forms into one of the forms libraries.

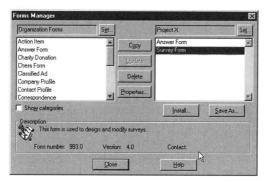

4. Click the Set button on the left half of the display and select the library that contains the form you want to copy. Select the library you want to copy into on the right half of the dialog box. Highlight the forms you want to copy in the list at the left and click Copy.

5. Close the Forms Manager. You now can use the form in this public folder.

T I P You also can highlight a folder whose form library contains a form you want to copy (one of the samples provided with Exchange Server, for example) and right-click the folder. Select Properties from the resulting pop-up menu. Click the Forms tab on the dialog box and then click the Manage button. The Forms Manager dialog box then appears. With this method, the library from which forms will be copied is selected on the right half of the display, and the Set button is gray indicating that you can't change this setting. Select the library you want to copy into on the left half of the dialog box and click Copy.

To use a special form in a folder, follow these steps:

1. Start the Exchange Client.

2. Highlight the folder you want to use. It must have properties that allow custom forms to be used for the next steps to work. Not all folders allow the use of custom forms. See step 17 of the procedure shown in the section "Creating a New Public Folder" earlier in this chapter for information on setting these properties.

3. If the folder has properties set to allow any form, you can select Compose, New Form and select a form you want to use from the Organization Forms Library.

4. If the folder has forms in its own library, there will be an additional choice on the bottom of the Compose menu to create a new form of this type.

5. Use the Compose menu in one of the ways described earlier and select a new form. Complete the form and click the Post button, or another activation control specific to the form. On some standard forms, the Post button pictures a push pin. On others, it appears as a toolbar button with an envelope in motion (like the Send button). A sample form is depicted in Figure 29.20.

FIG. 29.20
Here is a HelpDesk form being used in the Visual Basic Discussions folder created earlier.

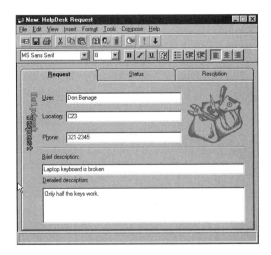

Replicating Public Folders

A public folder server is any server that contains a Public Information Store. A site can have one or more public folder servers, but there must be at least one public folder server per site. You can create a site without any private information stores, which would then be referred to as a *dedicated public folder site*. If a public folder is replicated to a particular server, only one replica of that particular folder is allowed per server. Each replica has the same status as all other replicas. Any replica can be changed, and the changes will eventually be replicated to all other copies of the folder at the scheduled replication times. At any particular moment in time, therefore, the various replicas may not be identical.

The entire public folder *hierarchy* showing all public folders available in a site, and the property information for those folders, is replicated to all public folder servers regardless of whether the server contains a replica of the actual public folder. Users do not need to know where a public folder is located to use it. When you remove the Private Information Store from a server, it becomes a *dedicated public folder server*. Creating such a server can be a useful way to manage the resources allocated to public folder usage.

On the General tab of the Private Information Store of each server (if it has a Private Information Store), you can designate which public folder server will be used by any mailboxes on that server. New public folders created by users of those mailboxes will be stored on the designated public folder server. The users also will access this server to receive the public folder hierarchy, which allows them to view all public folders in the organization for which they have been granted permissions.

Configuring Public Folder Replication

There are two dialog boxes that you can use to replicate public folders. You can either use the dialog box for the Public Information Store on the server to which you want to add the replica, or the dialog box for the public folder you want to replicate. In this section, you learn how to use the dialog box for the Public Information Store to add a replica to a server and then check the status of the replication process using the dialog box for the public folder itself.

To replicate a public folder, follow these steps:

1. Start the Exchange Administrator if you have not already done so. Connect to a server that is in the site you want to administer.

2. In the container area (the left pane) of the display, find the site you want to administer. Click the plus sign to the left of the site name to expand the display if it is not already open. Click the plus sign to the left of the Configuration object to expand its display. You should see the Servers object. Click the plus sign to the left of the Servers object to expand its display.

3. Highlight the server object for the server to which you want to add a replica. Double-click the Public Information Store object in the contents area. The dialog box for the Public Information Store appears, as shown in Figure 29.21.

FIG. 29.21

This dialog box allows you to set basic properties for the Public Information Store on a server and to configure replication of public folders.

4. On the General tab, you can set a storage limit for all public folders on this server. If a public folder exceeds this limit, the owner of the public folder will receive storage warnings at the scheduled intervals set on the Storage Warnings tab of the dialog box for the Information Store Site Configuration object. Click the Instances tab (see Figure 29.22).

FIG. 29.22

You use this tab to create an instance, or replica, of a public folder on the local server.

5. If the public folder you are replicating does not yet exist in the local site, select a site where it does exist in the Site drop-down list. If the folder is on another server in the local site, this step is unnecessary.

N O T E If the site to which you want to add the public folder does not appear in the list, you must set up some sort of connector between the sites and implement directory-replication connectors. See "Replicating Directory Information" earlier in this chapter. ■

6. Select the folder you want to replicate from the Public Folders list. Click Add to move that folder name into the list box labeled Folders on This Information Store. Click OK. The folder will be replicated to this server. This process may take some time, depending on the replication schedule, the message load on the system, and other factors. You can reopen the dialog box you were just using at a later time and click the Folder Replication Status and Public Folder Resources tabs to see the current status of the replication process. For an alternative status-checking method, see the next procedure.

To check the status of a particular public folder's replication and to see all the public folder servers that contain a replica, follow these steps:

1. Start the Exchange Administrator if you have not already done so. Connect to a server that is in the site you want to administer.

2. In the container area (the left pane) of the display, find the Folders object. Click the plus sign to the left of the Folders object to expand the display if it is not already open. Click the plus sign to the left of the Public Folders object to expand its display. You should see the top-level public folders. If the folder for which you want to check the status is not a top-level folder, continue to click the plus signs to the left of the folders that have them until you find the folder in question.

3. Highlight the folder name and choose File, Properties. A dialog box for the folder appears, as shown in Figure 29.23.

FIG. 29.23

Use this tabbed dialog box to configure and check the status of a particular public folder. An individual replication schedule can be set for this folder, and the location of all its replicas can be listed.

4. On the General tab, you can change the display name for the folder, set an age limit for messages and postings in all replicas, and click the Client Permissions button to set permissions. You also can set permissions by using the Exchange Client, as you learned when you created a public folder. Click the Replicas tab (see Figure 29.24).

FIG. 29.24

This tab shows all the replicas that have been created for this public folder. Servers in other sites are listed as `<site_name>/` `<server_name>`.

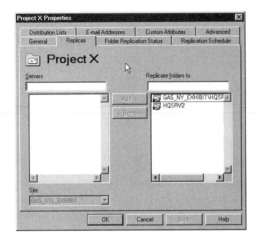

5. You can use the Replicas tab to create additional replicas of a folder or just to see where they already exist. Click the Folder Replication Status tab (see Figure 29.25).

FIG. 29.25

This tab is used to check the status of folder replication. You can use it to tell if the local folder has been modified since the last replication event left the folders "In Sync."

6. If enough time has elapsed for your folder to be replicated, the status of that event will be reflected in the Folder Replication Status tab.

You have learned how to create public folders and replicate them to other sites and servers. Now you learn some techniques to help resolve problems and monitor the health of your Exchange Server organization.

Network News

One of the most popular services provided by the Internet is network news. This service provides the capability for network users to conduct bulletin-board-style discussions. Multiple *threaded* conversations are presented and organized so you can read an entry and post a response that is (usually) indented beneath the original entry. This facilitates a large group of people discussing a topic in an orderly fashion. Anyone can get involved in an interesting thread if they have something to offer, or simply read the dialogue among others.

Exchange Server Newsgroup Support

Exchange Server 5.0 adds support for the Network News Transport Protocol (NNTP), the basic engine of network newsgroups. There are a number of features provided by this support:

- Exchange Server can accept a UseNet newsfeed from your Internet Service Provider (ISP) giving your user community local access to network news.

- Any NNTP newsreader software can access public folders (and other newsgroups) on an Exchange Server.

- Any Exchange client software (including the new Outlook client) can access both public folders and newsgroups on an Exchange Server providing more features than the typical newsreader software (e.g., customized views and offline operation with folder synchronization).

- A variety of security options are available including the standard Windows NT challenge/response protocol and clear-text authentication with the option to encrypt network traffic using the Secure Sockets Layer (SSL).

- A newsfeed wizard simplifies the setup of newsfeeds. Both *push* and *pull* type newsfeeds are supported. With a push feed, your ISP will automatically send you updates as necessary. Using a pull feed, you can schedule the times at which you wish to pull down the latest information from your ISP.

Public folders, a feature that has been provided by Exchange Server from its first release, can now be made available to client computers running any NNTP newsreader software. For example, you can use the Internet News add-on for Microsoft's Internet Explorer, or the network news support in Netscape Navigator. This extends the reach of public folders to users who are not running the Exchange Client or Outlook.

It also makes it possible for those who *are* using the Exchange Client or Outlook to enjoy the benefits of a full-featured client when reading newsgroups. Features like custom views and the capability to copy frequently accessed newsgroups (now equivalent to public folders) into the Favorites folder for offline use and subsequent synchronization are not available in most newsreader applications. Plus, these users can benefit from a single-user interface and application for both newsgroups and standard e-mail.

Setting Up the Internet News Service (INS)

You must contact your ISP in order to implement a UseNet newsfeed. Exchange Server supports both push-style and pull-style newsfeeds, but push feeds are the most commonly used. You need the following information from your ISP in order to set up your newsfeed:

- The host name of the NNTP server (for example, **news.microsoft.com** is the host name of Microsoft's primary NNTP server)
- Their UseNet site name, which is often the same as the host name
- An *active file* containing a list of the newsgroups that are available from the NNTP server

In addition, you must provide your ISP with some information to complete the process:

- The host name or IP address of your new Internet News server (the server running the Internet News Service)
- The type of transfer you want to implement, either push or pull
- A list of the newsgroups you want to support (if using a push feed)

If you provide your ISP with the host name of your news server, you need to be sure that it is listed in Domain Name Service (DNS). Windows NT Server 4.0 includes DNS support, which is discussed in Chapter 10, "Name Resolution with TCP/IP." Your ISP is undoubtedly running DNS on one of their servers. They must be able to resolve your host name to an IP address for the newsfeed to work.

The Internet News Service can automatically generate a list of newsgroups using wild-card patterns to specify which groups should be included and excluded. This list should be provided to the ISP if you are using a push feed.

To set up NNTP support, follow these steps:

1. Start the Exchange Administrator if you have not already done so. Connect to a server in the site you want to administer.

2. In the container area (the left pane) of the display, find the site you want to administer. Click the plus sign to the left of the site name to expand the display if it is not already open. Click the plus sign to the left of the Configuration object to expand its display.

3. Select the Connections object. Then choose File, New Other, Newsfeed from the menu. A Newsfeed Configuration Wizard dialog box displays (see Figure 29.26). Review the information on this dialog box (it is a summary of the same checklists provided at the beginning of this section). Click Next to continue.

4. The next dialog box (they are all titled Newsfeed Configuration Wizard) prompts you to enter the name of the server on which you will install this newsfeed (see Figure 29.27). You can enter the name directly, or use the drop-down list box to select it.

FIG. 29.26

This dialog box introduces the Wizard that will assist you as you enter the various properties of your newsfeed.

FIG. 29.27

This dialog box is used to enter the name of the server and the UseNet site name for this newsfeed, which is the same as the fully qualified domain name (FQDN) for the server.

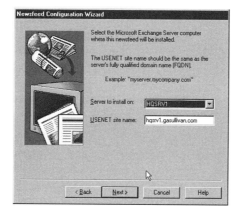

You also need to enter your UseNet site name. For example, an appropriate name for a news server at a company named G. A. Sullivan might be **news1.gasullivan.com**. Click Next to continue.

5. Next you will select the type of newsfeed you want to create (see Figure 29.28). Your newsfeed can be Inbound Only, Outbound Only, or both. Outbound feeds will propagate your own messages out to the rest of the Internet. Inbound feeds replicate messages from your ISP's UseNet site to your server(s). An inbound feed can be either a push or pull feed. Use the option labeled Accept Incoming Messages for a push feed (your ISP will "push" the messages to your site). Alternatively, you can Pull Incoming Messages. Click Next to continue.

FIG. 29.28

You can set up a variety of different newsfeed types using this wizard. Typical options are denoted as such.

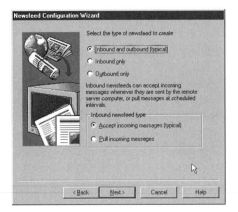

6. You can now select the type of connection you will use to connect to your ISP. This can be either a dial-up connection or a LAN connection, typically an ISDN or T1 connection. Click Next to continue.

   ▶ **See** "Configuring the Windows NT 4.0 Client," **p. 387**
   ▶ **See** "Networking Services," **p. 461**

7. Depending on the type of newsfeed you selected, you will be prompted to specify how frequently your news server will connect to the ISP. You can select times from 15 minutes to 24 hours. Click Next to continue.

8. Enter your ISP's UseNet site name (for example, **news.netprovider.net**). This is one of the required pieces of information listed at the beginning of the section. Click Next to continue.

9. Next, enter the names or IP addresses of any host computers that will provide an inbound newsfeed to this server. This is another bit of information provided by your ISP. If you are setting up a simple newsfeed with just a single inbound server, its name will probably be the same as the ISP's UseNet site name. Click Next to continue.

10. Depending on the security requirements imposed by your ISP, you may need to enter account and password information for the remote server providing your inbound newsfeed. If so, enter the information in the current dialog box displayed for that purpose. Click Next to continue.

11. The next dialog box informs you that the Wizard is now ready to install your INS. It also reminds you that you will need to select the newsgroups you want to include in your newsfeed after the INS is set up. Click Next to continue.

12. You will be prompted to enter the password for the service account being used for the INS (the same one being used for Exchange Server). Enter the Password, and click Next to continue.

13. You must now select an Internet News Administrator (see Figure 29.29). Click the Change button and select the account you want to be responsible for administering newsgroups. You can add other newsgroup administrators by assigning permissions to the public folders created to contain newsgroup messages. This is discussed earlier in the section "Using Public Folders."

FIG. 29.29

The Internet news administrator is given full permissions for the public folders that will be created to contain newsgroup messages.

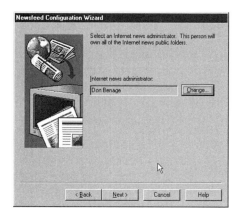

14. The final step is to provide the "active file," which contains the list of newsgroups you want to publish on your INS server (see Figure 29.30). This is provided by your ISP. Either specify the location, or click the option labeled "I don't have an active file. I'll get it later." Click Next to continue.

FIG. 29.30

The active file is just a list of newsgroups you want to provide on your INS server. It can be modified later if your preferences change.

15. INS setup is complete. The last dialog box reminds you that there will be a delay before newsgroup messages appear on your server. Click Finish.

Once you have configured your news server, you need to wait (probably an hour or more) for the newsfeed to go active and all the news to be downloaded. This will place a significant load on your network connection, and you may want to schedule this to occur only during the night. The Schedule tab of the Newsfeed Properties dialog box you used earlier to configure the Internet News Service allows you to specify when this activity should occur.

Diagnosing Problems

With almost any product that involves the complexity of a corporate messaging system, problems will occur. These may be due to human error, a component failure (such as a server crashing), or a software error. Exchange Server includes an impressive array of diagnostic and monitoring tools to help you manage your messaging system and resolve any issues that may arise. This section presents an overview of some of the techniques you can employ to troubleshoot Exchange Server.

Setting Up Message Tracking

The capability to track the progress of a message as it is transferred through the organization by the various elements of an Exchange Server system is a useful diagnostic aid. Exchange Server offers the capability to perform message tracking with the use of log files that you can enable for the elements of Exchange Server. By default, the message-tracking logs are turned off. Logging can have an impact on messaging throughput and should probably not be left on at all times for most sites. If you are experiencing difficulties, however, the message-tracking logs can be turned on, and as new problems arise you can use this additional information to follow the behavior of your system and see what is going wrong.

When you enable message tracking for an Exchange Server element, all similar elements on other servers in the site also are tracking enabled. You can enable message tracking on the Information Stores and the MTAs for a site by using the General tab of the dialog box for the Site Configuration object. Message tracking also can be enabled on MS Mail connectors and Internet Mail Services. You must enable tracking on each connector manually. After you have enabled message tracking, the services affected must be stopped and restarted on each server for tracking to begin. Clearly this is an activity that is best done during off-peak hours.

To enable message tracking on the Information Stores and MTAs for a site, follow these steps:

1. Start the Exchange Administrator if you have not already done so. Connect to a server that is in the site you want to administer.

2. In the container area (the left pane) of the display, find the site you want to administer. Click the plus sign to the left of the site name to expand the display if it is not already open. Select the Configuration container. In the contents area (the right pane) you should see the Information Store Site Configuration object.

3. Double-click the Information Store Site Configuration object to open its dialog box. Click the General tab, as shown in Figure 29.31.

FIG. 29.31

Using the General tab of the Information Store Site Configuration object, you can enable message tracking for all information stores in the site.

4. Click the Enable Message Tracking check box. Click OK to close the dialog box.

5. Double-click the MTA Site Configuration object to open its dialog box. Click the General tab.

6. Click the check box to Enable Message Tracking. Click OK to close the dialog box.

7. You must now stop and restart these services on all servers. The best tool for this task is the Windows NT Server Manager.

8. Start the Server Manager. Highlight a server and choose Computer, Services. The Services dialog box appears, as shown in Figure 29.32.

FIG. 29.32

Use the Services dialog box in Server Manager to stop and start services so that message tracking can begin. Although you can do this via the Control Panel Services icon, the Server Manager allows you to perform the task on multiple machines from a remote computer.

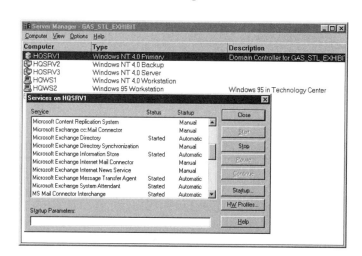

9. Highlight the Microsoft Exchange service you want to stop. Click Stop. When the service has stopped, click Start to restart the service and begin logging message-tracking information. You should stop and restart both the Information Store and the MTA if you want full message-tracking information.

After you have enabled message tracking, the information needed for this task will be captured in log files stored in the \EXCHSRVR\TRACKING.LOG directory. These files are created each day using Greenwich Mean Time (GMT). All the information in the files is date-and-time stamped using GMT. The logs contain information about the movement of messages through each component of an Exchange Server system. You can open them using a text editor such as Notepad, import them into a spreadsheet, or use them as input for the message-tracking tools provided with Exchange Server. Two of those tools, the Select Message to Track dialog box and the Message Tracking Center, are explored next.

Before you can track the progress of a message, you must first find at least one instance of its presence in the log files. This process is made easier with the use of the Select Message to Track dialog box, a tool created for just this purpose. After the message has been found, you can use the Message Tracking Center to track its progress through the system and view its path in a hierarchical display.

To find and track a message, follow these steps:

1. Start the Exchange Administrator. Connect to a server in the site you want to administer.

2. Choose Tools, Track Message. A Connect to Server dialog box appears. The ideal server to enter is the home server of the person or service that sent the message; however, you can start on any server in the site if you are unsure. Enter the name of a server and click OK. Two dialog boxes open: Message Tracking Center and Select Message to Track, as shown in Figure 29.33.

FIG. 29.33

These two dialog boxes work together to help you track messages. Use the Select Message to Track dialog box to help find the message somewhere in the system; then the Message Tracking Center dialog box finds and displays the other elements of the system that have handled the message.

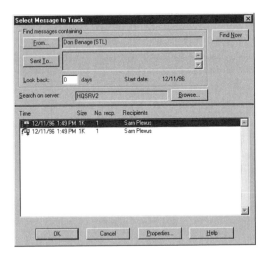

3. Enter the criteria (for example, sender's name, recipient's name, or number of days to check) for the message you want to track in the Select Message to Track dialog box. Then click Find Now. The messages that match the criteria are displayed in the list at the bottom of the dialog box. You can double-click a message to view its properties.

4. You can refine your criteria and search again, or select a message to track. When you are ready to track a message, highlight the message and click OK. The Select Message to Track dialog box closes, and the properties of the selected message are automatically entered into the Message Tracking Center.

5. Click the Track button, and the Message Tracking Center dialog box appears, as shown in Figure 29.34.

FIG. 29.34

Here the Message Tracking Center shows the tracking hierarchy of a message delivered in the local Private Information Store.

6. You can click Search to find another message to track, or click Advanced Search to enter criteria for an advanced search by message ID, for a message transferred into the local site from a foreign messaging system, or for a message generated by one of Exchange Server's services. Close the Message Tracking Center using the Control menu in the upper-left corner of the dialog box when you are finished.

Monitoring Your Site

Exchange Server provides a number of useful tools for monitoring the status of the system and its performance. These tools offer the possibility of proactive management that uncovers problems and corrects them before any impact—or at least any major impact—is noticed by users. To achieve this level of control, you must have a thorough understanding of the tools and their uses. This section introduces you to three of the most important monitoring tools available for Exchange Server:

- Windows NT Event Viewer
- Link monitors
- Server monitors

The Windows NT Performance Monitor also can play an important role in monitoring Exchange Server, in addition to its many other uses. It is covered in Chapter 48, "Proactive Network Administration."

▶ **See** "Using the Performance Monitor," **p. 1664**

Using the Windows NT Event Viewer   The Windows NT Event Viewer is often overlooked as a troubleshooting device when it should generally be the first place you look when there is any difficulty. Although its usefulness is more reactive than proactive, it is nonetheless important. Most actions taken by the Exchange Server system cause entries to be made in the event log, provided that you have set logging levels as described in this section. They appear in the Application log for the server. A sample of the type of message you will find is shown in Figure 29.35.

FIG. 29.35

The Windows NT Event Viewer is displaying the Application log. An Exchange Server event has been selected for viewing.

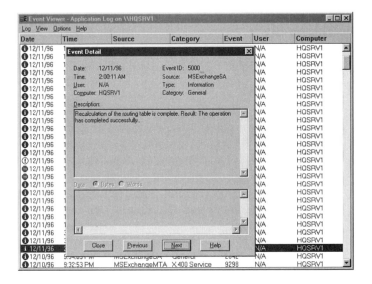

If there is a particular element of Exchange Server that you are concerned about, you can set a higher level of logging to provide additional detail for analysis. Under normal circumstances, only critical events are logged, but you can expand the level of logging provided for individual elements of Exchange Server. For example, Figure 29.36 shows the Diagnostics Logging tab for the Private Information Store on the server named INFOSRV2. As you can see, there is a very granular level of control, allowing you to set a higher logging level for only those aspects in which you are most interested.

FIG. 29.36

This tab is representative of the Diagnostics Logging tabs available on dialog boxes for the major services in Exchange Server. You can select individual areas of interest and set logging to a higher level so that more information is recorded in the Windows NT Application event log.

Part
VI

Ch
29

Creating Link Monitors   Link monitors allow you to make sure that messages are being delivered between your server and another location. They do this by *bouncing* a test message, called a *ping message*, from your server to one or more additional servers and back again. They also can bounce ping messages with foreign messaging systems (other e-mail systems besides Exchange Server, whether PC-based or run on a mainframe or mini-computer), although the setup is slightly more involved. These test messages are routed through the system just like other messages; however, they are delivered to the System Attendant on the server, which has been designed to receive and reply to ping messages.

The most reliable way to use link monitors with a foreign messaging system is to implement a utility program on the foreign system that serves the same receive-and-return function. An alternative is to allow the foreign system to return a Non-Delivery Report (NDR), which is a feature offered by most systems. You simply send a message to an address that you know is invalid and wait for the NDR. You should create a custom recipient for the invalid address that can then be used by the link monitor. It is a good idea to select the option to Hide from Address Book on the Advanced tab of the dialog box for the custom recipient to avoid having users send messages to this invalid address.

You define a link monitor by specifying the servers or custom recipients in other systems that will receive the ping messages. Then, when you start the monitor, you indicate the server that will send the messages. You can define specific actions that will occur if the return messages aren't received in a period you specify. An application can be run (to set off a beeper, for example), a mail message can be sent, or a Windows NT alert can be raised.

The actions that are triggered and the time limits for the message to make its round-trip journey are the same for all servers and recipients specified in a given link monitor. You can create additional link monitors with a variety of time limits and resultant actions. It is up to you, therefore, to group the targets of bounced messages with others requiring similar settings and to create additional monitors to meet special needs. It makes no sense, for example, to include a server on the local site that should be responding in less than five minutes in the same link monitor with a group of recipients halfway around the world on the Internet.

To create a new link monitor, follow these steps:

1. Start the Exchange Administrator. Connect to a server in the site you want to administer.

2. In the container area (the left pane) of the display, find the site you want to administer. Click the plus sign to the left of the site name to expand the display if it is not already open. Click the plus sign to the left of the Configuration object to expand its display.

3. Highlight the Monitors object. Select File, New Other, and then select Link Monitor. A blank Properties dialog box for a new link monitor appears (see Figure 29.37).

FIG. 29.37

The Properties dialog box for a link monitor allows you to define or modify a link monitor's characteristics.

4. On the General tab, enter a Display Name and a Directory Name for the link monitor (they can be the same). Select a location for the log file to be used by this monitor. This is not required, although highly recommended. If you do not specify a log file name, no information will be logged. Next, specify the intervals at which ping messages should be sent for Normal sites and Critical sites (those in which a warning or error condition has been detected).

5. The Permissions tab for link monitors functions in the same manner as those for other objects. You can assign permissions or roles for particular Windows NT accounts. Click the Notification tab (see Figure 29.38).

6. The Notification tab allows you to specify the actions to take if a round trip is not completed within the bounce message return time set on the Bounce tab, discussed later. You can specify multiple actions. Figure 29.38 depicts a new launch process being defined and a mail message action already defined. Click the Servers tab (see Figure 29.39).

7. Select the servers that you want to use as the targets for ping messages whenever this link monitor starts. Use the Site drop-down list to select servers at another site. As noted in the discussion at the beginning of this section, all the servers specified in a particular link monitor should provide roughly the same expected round trip for a bounced message to be effective. Click the Bounce tab (see Figure 29.40).

FIG. 29.38

This tab enables you to specify the actions to be taken if a ping message does not complete its round trip within the time allowed.

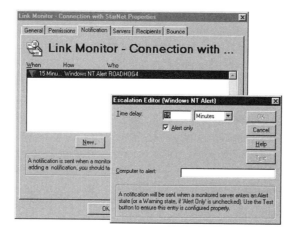

FIG. 29.39

Use the Servers tab to denote servers that will be the targets of ping messages when this link monitor starts. The server to send ping messages is specified as you start the monitor.

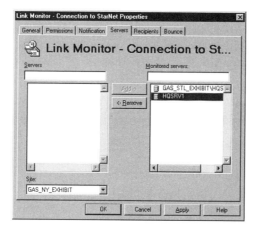

FIG. 29.40

This tab allows you to specify the bounced message return times that will cause a warning state and then an alert state to be entered.

8. You must set this tab carefully for the monitor to be meaningful. You should base your settings on the results of testing, especially if you are bouncing messages off foreign messaging systems. The value you enter should strike a balance between being so long that a problem could go unnoticed for an extensive period of time, and being so short that the monitor is too sensitive and indicates a problem even during routine heavy loads or other situations that cause only slight delays. Click OK to define your link monitor.

The next procedure shows you how to create a server monitor. The process is similar to creating a link monitor, and some of the tabs on the dialog box are discussed only briefly because of the similarities. The section following server-monitor creation shows you how to start and use link monitors and server monitors, and how you can combine them to provide a detailed look at the health of your system.

Creating Server Monitors   Server monitors work to ensure that the services that should be running on a server are still running. They do this through the use of RPC communications. A server monitor can only monitor the status of servers that are reachable by a high-speed communications link capable of supporting RPCs. A server monitor can detect when services have stopped and can also attempt to restart them. It is also possible to use a server monitor to synchronize the internal clocks of the servers being monitored, which can make the information used for message tracking and other data written in log files more meaningful.

Server monitors can operate on any Windows NT services running on a server, not just those used by Exchange Server. You can add a service to the list of those that should be monitored by using the Properties dialog box for the server itself. To access the Properties dialog box, highlight the server's object in the contents area of the Servers container and choose File, Properties.

To create a server monitor, follow this procedure:

1. Start the Exchange Administrator. Connect to a server in the site you want to administer.

2. In the container area (the left pane) of the display, find the site you want to administer. Click the plus sign to the left of the site name to expand the display if it is not already open. Click the plus sign to the left of the Configuration object to expand its display.

3. Highlight the Monitors object. Select File, New Other, and then select Server Monitor. A blank Properties dialog box for a new server monitor appears (see Figure 29.41).

4. On the General tab, enter a Display Name and a Directory Name for the server monitor (they can be the same). Select a location for the log file to be used by this monitor. This is not required, although highly recommended. If you do not specify a Log File name, no information will be logged. Next, specify the intervals at which the status of services on the servers will be checked for Normal sites and Critical sites (those in which a warning or error condition has been detected).

5. The Permissions, Notification, and Servers tabs all function in the same manner as those on a link monitor's dialog box. Please see steps 5–7 of the procedures for link monitors outlined in the preceding section for information about these tabs. Click the Actions tab (see Figure 29.42).

FIG. 29.41

This is the General tab of the dialog box for a server monitor. You use it to set the name, log file, and polling interval.

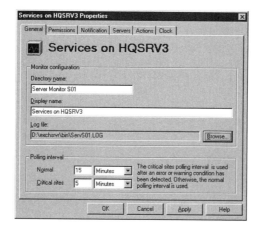

FIG. 29.42

Use the Actions tab to define an escalating set of actions to be taken if a server's services are found to be stopped. In addition to attempting to restart the services themselves, it is possible to attempt a shutdown and restart of the entire machine.

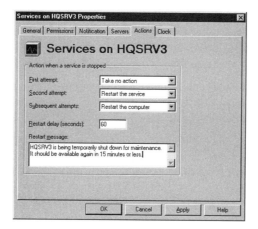

6. The Actions tab is used to specify the actions that should be taken when the services being monitored have stopped. You can specify Take No Action, Restart the Service, and Restart the Computer. Before a computer restart, you can enter a message that will be broadcast to warn users logged on to that computer of the impending shutdown; however, they will not see such a broadcast warning displayed unless they are running WinPopup, or a similar network message utility. Click the Clock tab (see Figure 29.43).

CAUTION

You should exercise care when using the Restart the Computer option. Other services may be running on a computer that have nothing to do with Exchange Server, and an automated restart with only 60 or even 180 seconds delay before the restart may have a negative impact on the other applications using that computer. This option is most useful for computers dedicated to a single purpose.

FIG. 29.43

The Clock tab lets you specify the allowable time differences between the computer running the monitor and the monitored servers. A warning or alert condition can be raised, or the clocks can be synchronized.

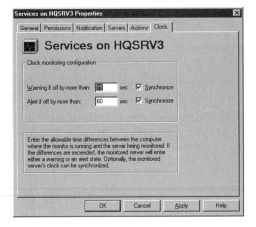

7. You can use the Clock tab to indicate the difference in time that will be allowed before setting a warning or alert condition, or optionally resynchronizing the clocks.

8. Click OK to create the new server monitor.

Using Server Monitors and Link Monitors You have learned how to create both link monitors and server monitors. Now you learn how to put them to use. Both of these diagnostic devices run inside the Exchange Administrator program. This implies that they must be run from within a logon session started with a particular account ID and password. A number of important consequences arise from this fact.

A server monitor can check the status of running services on a server with no particular security clearance, but to restart a service or synchronize the clocks on servers, the server monitor needs to run under an account context with sufficient permissions to perform those actions. Furthermore, this kind of proactive monitoring is needed 24 hours a day, seven days a week at many organizations. Because these aren't services that can run unattended without an account logging on, some means of automatically logging on to Windows NT and launching these monitors must be provided, or steps must be taken to avoid the computer being shut down or losing power and rebooting.

The *Administrator's Guide for Exchange Server* details the steps required to automatically log on to Windows NT and start these monitoring utilities. The security implications of a machine set up to automatically log on in an account context with sufficient privileges to stop and start services on servers and reset clocks is unsettling. At a *minimum*, such a machine should be provided with a screen saver with an extremely short timeout period that will lock the console, and it should be placed in an area with good physical security and regular human presence. Because a natural use for these monitors is to leave a graphic display visible so that an error condition might be noticed by a nearby operator, the use of a screen saver may be impossible. You might explore some method of locking the keyboard instead. An obvious place for such a machine is in a support center or operations room where the dangers mentioned earlier would be somewhat mitigated.

To start a server monitor and a link monitor, follow these steps:

1. Start the Exchange Administrator. Connect to a server in the site you want to administer.

2. In the container area (the left pane) of the display, find the site you want to administer. Click the plus sign to the left of the site name to expand the display if it is not already open. Click the plus sign to the left of the Configuration object to expand its display.

3. Highlight the Monitors object. In the contents area, highlight the monitor you want to start. If you are not sure which one you want to use, you can double-click the monitor objects to open their dialog boxes for more information. After highlighting the desired monitor, choose Tools, Start Monitor.

4. A Connect to Server dialog box appears. The server you enter here will be the server used to send ping messages for link monitors and to send RPC requests for service information for server monitors. The servers that will be the targets of those requests are defined in the monitor definitions on the Servers tab. Enter the name of a server, or use the Browse button to select a server, and click OK. A monitor window with the name of the selected monitor displayed in the title bar opens.

5. After a period of time, dependent on the definition of the monitor and the conditions of the network, the monitor will begin displaying the results of its first requests. At the interval you specified in the definition of the monitor, it resends either ping messages (link monitor) or RPC requests (server monitor). The display is automatically refreshed to reflect the results of this ongoing process. Summary results appear in tabular form, but you also can double-click a line item to open a Properties dialog box for more information (see Figure 29.44).

FIG. 29.44

Here the Exchange Administrator has an active link monitor and an active server monitor. A line item in the link monitor has been double-clicked to open a Properties dialog box for more information.

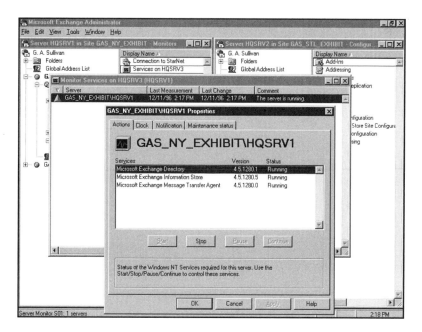

6. You can start more than one monitor at the same time. Simply highlight another monitor in the contents area of the Monitors object and choose Tools, Start Monitor. When you have started all the monitors you want, you can minimize the Server window you originally opened to present a less cluttered display.

From Here...

You have now learned how to replicate information throughout your site and across your organization. In addition, you have explored the methods for creating public folders with the Exchange Client and how to publish those folders for use on your network. You also have discovered the tools and techniques used to monitor the health of your Exchange Server system and how to diagnose potential problems.

See the following chapters for related information:

- For an overview of Exchange Server and to review basic information on this BackOffice Family component, see Chapter 26, "An Inside Look at Exchange Server."
- For information on setting up Exchange Server, see Chapter 27, "Implementing Exchange Server."
- For more on using the Exchange Client, see Chapter 28, "Using Exchange Client Applications."
- For information on setting up connectors to foreign message systems and procedures for using Exchange Server's advanced security options, see Chapter 31, "Exchange Server Advanced Topics."

CHAPTER 30

Document Management with Exchange Server

by Mike Lichtenberg

Microsoft Exchange Server provides much more than simply a messaging platform. There are many ways you can extend Exchange Server to provide powerful business solutions for your organization.

In the modern business world, the concept of a document has shifted from a printed, typed, or handwritten item to nearly any type of information, including e-mail messages, faxes, electronic reports, and even database query results. Microsoft Exchange Server provides a platform on which you can effectively manage all your company's documents, regardless of their format or where they reside.

In this chapter, you learn how *public folder applications* and *custom forms* provide unique ways to collect and view information with Exchange Server. ∎

Public folder applications

Learn how to create an Exchange Server public folder application and use it to organize documents created in Microsoft Word.

BackOffice integration

Learn how to integrate Exchange Server with SQL Server and the other BackOffice applications to provide business solutions for your organization.

Custom forms

Use the Exchange Forms Designer to build custom forms that can reduce administrative tasks in your organization.

Document routing

Learn how to fill out routing slips from within Microsoft Office applications and create Inbox rules to streamline your organization's workflow. Learn how to route documents and track messages.

The Basics of Document Management

Public folder applications provide repositories in which any type of document can be stored and accessed. Public folder replication allows data stored in public folders to be accessed by anyone in your organization. In addition, integration with Microsoft Office enables you to post documents directly into public folders. Custom forms allow standard company documents, such as expense reports, vacation requests, insurance claims, and so on, to be made available online for easy completion and submission. You also can use custom forms in conjunction with public folders to provide unique ways to view information.

As Figure 30.1 illustrates, you can use Exchange Server in conjunction with the entire suite of Microsoft Office and BackOffice applications to provide robust business solutions for managing documents and information. In this chapter, you see how integration with these applications allows data that is stored in a variety of external locations, including Word and Excel documents and SQL Server databases, to be made available in one central location. This chapter also shows you how to use Exchange Server to organize your documents based on characteristics of the documents themselves.

FIG. 30.1

This illustration shows how Exchange Server integrates with the entire suite of Microsoft Office and BackOffice applications.

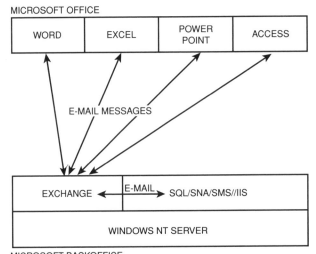

In addition to the business solutions you can build using public folders, custom forms, and application integration, third-party vendors have already produced a number of applications which leverage the services provided by Exchange Server. Some examples of third-party tools that have been, or can be, built on top of Exchange Server include the following:

- EDI applications
- Document management systems
- Integrated voice mail

■ Document publishing applications

■ Workflow applications

This chapter also explains the powerful document-routing capabilities provided by Exchange Server, which you can take advantage of to improve and streamline your business processes. Exchange Server integrates with Microsoft Office applications to provide routing slips that you can use to send documents to recipients in an ordered and controlled manner. Inbox Rules allow you to automate the movement of messages through Exchange Clients. Furthermore, you can request notifications to track the flow of messages throughout your organization.

Part
VI

Ch
30

Document Library

Microsoft Exchange Server provides an excellent platform on which to build an electronic document library. Your organization's library of electronic documents may include marketing literature, technical specifications, employee handbooks, training manuals, standard forms, and other business-related data. It is likely that all this information is stored in a variety of locations in your organization. You can use Exchange Server to provide a single location through which your users can store and access all the electronic documents in your organization. On the following pages, you see how to create public folder applications and custom forms to improve the collection, storage, organization, and presentation of your organization's documents. In addition, you see how you can integrate Exchange Server with the applications that make up Microsoft Office and BackOffice, providing more ways to access, organize, and present business data.

Folder applications are often used in conjunction with custom forms to provide a wide variety of document-management solutions. You can place any type of document you want into public folders and then use folder views to organize those documents into meaningful, easy-to-use formats, as shown in Figure 30.2. Folder permissions allow you to restrict access to documents to only the users you specify, and folder replication allows these users to be physically located anywhere in your organization. By combining custom forms with public folder applications, you can provide unique ways to manage documents and information, as Figure 30.3 shows. You also can use custom forms to create electronic documents that reduce the need for paper forms in your organization.

An excellent source of information about the types of folder applications and custom forms that you can create is the sample applications which ship with the Exchange Client software. Some of the applications that are included in the samples are the following:

■ **Contact Tracking.** Collects data in one place that relates to all facets of a client organization.

■ **Helpdesk.** Provides a tracking system for a customer-support organization.

■ **Classified Ads.** Supports an organization-wide bulletin board for the buying and selling of items.

■ **Survey.** Uses survey and answer forms to collect information from users.

FIG. 30.2

You can use public folder applications such as this one to store and organize data in useful and meaningful ways. In this illustration, the items contained in the Helpdesk public folder are organized by the persons assigned to the items.

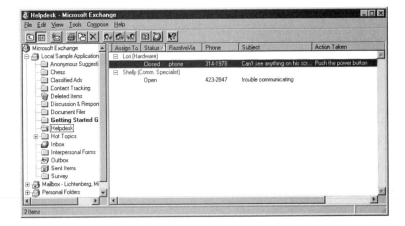

FIG. 30.3

Custom forms let you collect and display information in unique ways.

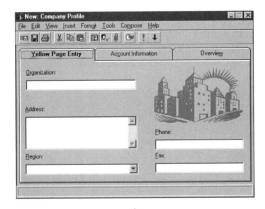

You can install the sample applications on any Exchange Client. They are installed in a series of personal folders, as shown in Figure 30.4. After they have been installed, you can examine them at your leisure and customize them to create new applications.

N O T E See the *Microsoft Exchange Application Designer's Guide* for more information about the Microsoft Exchange sample applications. ▪

In addition to the folder and form applications you can build, you can take advantage of the integration of Exchange Server with the suite of Microsoft Office and BackOffice applications to create powerful document-management solutions. Many of the Office and BackOffice applications provide direct integration with Exchange Server. For example, the SQL Mail agent of Microsoft SQL Server has the capability to directly populate Exchange Server public folders. Exchange Server can access properties of documents created using Microsoft Office applications. In addition, Exchange Server uses the standard Messaging Application Programming Interface (MAPI) to send messages. The use of MAPI allows Exchange Server to communicate with a wide variety of applications. Thus you can extend Exchange Server in almost any way you can imagine by taking advantage of the Visual Basic for Applications scripting language, which is built into the Office applications, or by creating custom solutions with Microsoft Visual Basic.

FIG. 30.4

When installed, the sample applications that ship with the Exchange Client are stored in the collection of personal folders shown here.

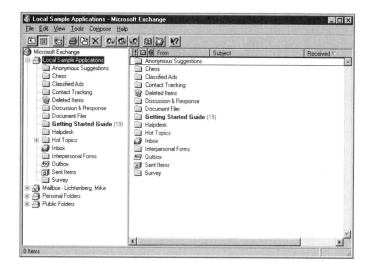

The following sections provide three examples that illustrate the document-management and integration capabilities of Exchange Server. The first example is a library of product literature which is set up in a public folder application; the public folder organizes Microsoft Office documents stored within it by accessing characteristics of those documents. The second example shows how you can use Exchange Server to set up an automated system for requesting and receiving information from a Microsoft SQL Server database. The last example shows how to streamline the collection of information from users through the use of custom forms created with the Exchange Forms Designer. Each of these examples shows you how to create the described solutions.

Product Literature

One particularly useful function of a document library is the storage and organization of documents in a single easy-to-use and easy-to-access location. Exchange Server public folders are particularly well-suited to the tasks of storing and organizing data. Documents of any type can be placed in public folders. Then anyone who has access to the folders can access those documents. Replication allows even users at remote sites to access items placed in public folders. Once items are in a public folder, you can create views to organize the items meaningfully, making it easy to find and retrieve information.

This example shows how to create an Exchange Server public folder application that accomplishes storage and organization of documents pertaining to Company X's product line. Currently, Company X has documentation on its products scattered throughout the organization; some documents reside on users' local computers and some reside in various network directories. Company X wants a single point of storage for all of its product literature. Within this single point of storage, Company X wants the documentation organized by product. So, all documents pertaining to Product X should be grouped together, all documents for Product Y should be grouped together, and so on. By using integration between Microsoft Word for Windows 95 (Word 7.0) and the Exchange Client, this example shows you how to store and organize all of Company X's product documentation in a single product literature public folder. For this example, it is assumed that all documentation is created in Word 7.0.

Setting Up the Public Folder Application The product literature public folder application has two main components: a Microsoft Word 7.0 document template and an Exchange Server public folder. The Word document template contains a custom property which is linked to a field in the document. Figure 30.5 shows the Word template used to create documents for the product literature folder. A public folder view references this custom property in order to organize the contents of the folder into product groups.

FIG. 30.5

Shown here is the Microsoft Word 7.0 document template used in the product literature folder application. The field labeled "Product Name:" is linked to a custom property of the document template. The custom property allows Microsoft Exchange public folder views to reference the contents of the field.

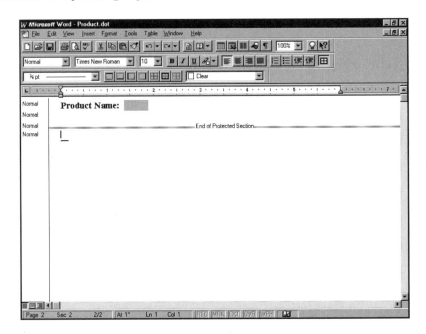

To create a Microsoft Word 7.0 document template with linked custom properties, do the following:

1. In Microsoft Word 7.0, create a new document template by choosing File, New from the menu, selecting the Template option, and clicking the OK button.

2. On the first line of the new document template, type **Product Name:**. Leave the cursor just to the right of the text.

3. Choose Insert, Form Field from the menu to display the Form Field dialog box. Select Text in the Type group box and click the OK button to insert a field at the cursor location. Users of the template will enter in this form field the name of the product their document pertains to.

4. Insert one or two blank lines and then Choose Insert, Break from the menu. The Break dialog box appears. Select the Next Page option and click the OK button to insert a section break at the cursor location.

5. Protect the section you just created by choosing Tools, Protect Document from the menu. In the Protect Document dialog box, select the Forms option and click the Sections button. From the Section Protection dialog box, select the Section 1 check box only, and then click OK to close each dialog box.

6. You now have a field you can link to a custom property. From the menu, choose File, Properties to display the Properties dialog box and select the Custom tab. Figure 30.6 shows the Custom tab.

Part

VI

Ch

30

FIG. 30.6

You use the Custom tab of the Properties dialog box to create linked custom properties.

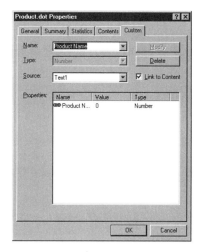

7. Type **Product Name** in the Name drop-down list and select the Link To Content check box. Click the Add button to create a linked custom property and then click the OK button to close the dialog box.

8. Save the new template as PRODUCT.DOT.

To prevent accidental changes to the template, make the new document template read-only by selecting Read-Only Recommended on the Save tab of the Microsoft Word Options dialog box.

Now that you have a Microsoft Word 7.0 template to be used for creating all the product literature for your organization, the next step is to create the Exchange Server public folder in which to store the product literature. Name the folder "Product Literature." Do not grant other persons access to the folder just yet.

▶ **See** "Creating Public Folders," **p. 1008**

After you have created the Product Literature folder, you are ready to set up the folder view. The folder view includes the linked custom property in the Word template. By including the linked custom property in the view, it is possible to group and sort documents stored in the folder by the value of the custom property. To set up a folder view using the linked custom property, follow these steps:

1. Create a simple Word document using the new template. The document does not need to contain anything except the name of a product in the protected form field; you will use it simply to set up and test the folder view.

2. Open the Windows Explorer and the Exchange Client, and then drag and drop the document you just created into the Product Documentation folder.

3. Go to the Exchange Client and choose File, Properties from the menu to open the Folder Properties dialog box. Select the Views tab.

4. Make sure the Folder Views option is selected and click the New button to open the New View dialog box. Name the view "by Product" and then click the Columns button to open the Columns dialog box.

5. Type **Product Name** in the Available Columns list box, as shown in Figure 30.7, and then click the Add button to move this column into the Show the Following list box.

FIG. 30.7

A linked custom property from a Word document is added to a folder view in the Columns dialog box.

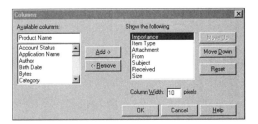

6. When prompted to specify the datatype of the new column, choose Text and click the OK button. This adds the linked custom property in the Word document to the list of columns that will display in the folder. The Show the Following list box also contains the default view columns.

7. If Product Name is not at the top of the Show The Following list, highlight it and then click the Move Up button to move it to the top of the list. Click the OK button to accept the columns you have selected.

8. In the New Views dialog box, click the Group By button to open the Group By dialog box.

9. Select Product Name from the drop-down list to group the items in the folder by the value of the Product Name column. Accept the default grouping and sorting orders by clicking the OK button to close the dialog box. Figure 30.8 shows the completed New View dialog box for the Product Literature application.

10. Click the OK button on the New View dialog box to create the view.

The setup of the Product Literature public folder is now complete. The only things left for you to do are to use the new Word template to create some sample documents, thoroughly test the folder view, and grant permissions to the group of users that will use the application.

▶ **See** "Using Public Folders," **p. 1007**

FIG. 30.8

The completed New View dialog box for the Product Literature folder application is shown here.

Using the Application   The Product Literature folder application is now complete. The Product Literature public folder functions just like any other public folder that you have set up on your Exchange Server, with the exception that the presentation of the items in the folder is slightly different. The most important thing for the application's users to remember is that when creating product literature documents to be organized in the folder, they should always use the PRODUCT.DOT template, instead of NORMAL.DOT or any other Word template.

> **TIP** From time-to-time, you may want to add additional properties to the template. To ensure that all users of the template are using the most recent version, store the template in a shared directory that is accessible to all users.

Follow these steps to use the Product Literature public folder application:

1. Using Microsoft Word 7.0, create one or more documents using the new PRODUCT.DOT template. Remember to fill in the Product Name form field with the name of the product that is being documented.

2. Open the Windows Explorer and locate the documents that you have just created.

3. Open the Exchange Client application and go to the Product Literature public folder.

4. Drag and drop the new documents from Windows Explorer into the Product Literature public folder. The application organizes the documents into a hierarchy based on the value that has been entered in the Product Name form field in each of the documents. The completed folder, containing several documents, is illustrated in Figure 30.9.

Extending the Example   Obviously, this example is a very basic folder application. There are many ways you can extend the application to take advantage of the many capabilities of Exchange Server public folders. By adding additional custom properties to the Word template, such as Product Version and Document Type (for example, Overview, Detailed Specification, or Marketing Information), you can enhance the types of folder views you can create. Also, other applications, including Microsoft Excel for Windows 95 (Excel 7.0) and Microsoft PowerPoint for Windows 95 (PowerPoint 7.0), provide linked custom properties. So, by creat-

Part

VI

Ch

30

ing document templates with linked custom properties in other applications, you can increase the number and type of documents that can be stored in the public folder.

FIG. 30.9

The completed Product Literature public folder application automatically organizes documents into a hierarchy based on the Product Name.

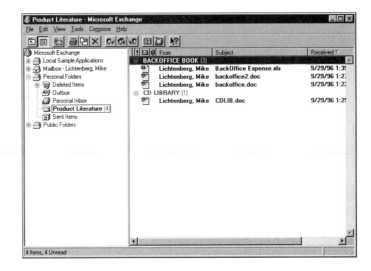

While integration with linked custom properties in Office for Windows 95 documents is a powerful feature, you can use public folders to create many other types of applications. You can create custom forms with the Exchange Forms Designer and associate them with public folders to create robust applications. Forms also can be created to provide unique ways to exchange, organize, and view the information stored in public folders. (See "Creating a Custom Form" later in this chapter for more information about creating custom forms.)

The capability to replicate and easily access public folders makes them excellent candidates for applications which distribute information to persons throughout your organization. Some other examples of public folder applications include the following:

- Bulletin boards
- Discussion forums
- Information-tracking systems

As mentioned earlier, you should examine the sample applications which ship with the Exchange Client for additional information about the types of public folder applications that you can create.

Technical Information

As explained earlier in this chapter, documents in a document library include not just reports, proposals, technical journals, and such, but nearly any type of data. In modern businesses, documents can consist of data stored in remote locations (such as databases) which can be accessed and viewed by users. Using this frame of reference, you can consider the results of a query to a Microsoft SQL Server or Microsoft Access database to be a document. Exchange

Server can be integrated with the BackOffice family of products to allow users in your organization to request and receive data from remote sources. In addition, you can configure Exchange Server to interface with remote data sources in such a way as to make the data stored in the database easily available to a large number of persons. For example, you can populate Exchange Server public folders with data from a remote location.

The following examples show you how the services provided by Window NT Server, Exchange Server, and SQL Server can be integrated. You see how information stored in a SQL Server database can be made available to users of Exchange Server. For the following examples, assume that Company X has stored all the information pertaining to its clients in a Microsoft SQL Server database. Company X wants to make this client information available to its employees by allowing the employees to send and receive database queries via e-mail. In addition, Company X wants to extract information about new clients from the database and post it to a public folder, where a larger number of users have access to the information.

To illustrate the techniques you can use to provide for Company X's needs, the following examples use the pubs database included with Microsoft SQL Server.

Integrating Exchange Server and SQL Server   To accomplish the integration between Exchange Server and SQL Server, you set up several components of each, including the SQL Mail service, a public folder, a database trigger, and a SQL Server scheduled task. SQL Mail is the service that allows you to communicate with the SQL Server database via e-mail messages. You use the public folder as a repository for new client information and set up the database trigger to populate it automatically with data from the SQL Server. In addition, you set up a scheduled task on the SQL Server to reply to incoming database queries.

Microsoft SQL Server includes a set of system and extended stored procedures that you use to manipulate messages received and sent by the SQL Mail service. Table 30.1 lists the available mail-related stored procedures.

Table 30.1   SQLMail System and Extended Stored Procedures

Procedure	Description
xp_deletemail	Deletes a message from the Inbox
xp_findnextmessage	Returns the message following a specified message
sp_processmail	Executes the contents of incoming messages as database queries and returns the query results to the message sender in an attached file
xp_readmail	Reads a message in the Inbox
xp_sendmail	Sends a message to one or more recipients
xp_startmail	Starts an Exchange Client session
xp_stopmail	Stops an Exchange Client session

Part

VI

Ch

30

The first step in mail-enabling the database is to configure the SQL Mail client of SQL Server to work with Exchange Server. To set up SQL Mail, follow these steps:

1. Verify that the Windows NT user account that you are using for the Microsoft SQL Server service is a domain account and has the following characteristics:
   - Is a member of the local Administrators group
   - Has the Password Never Expires attribute set
   - Is able to log on as a service, act a part of the operating system, replace a process level token, and increase quotas

2. At the Microsoft Exchange Server, set up a mailbox for the Windows NT user account that you are using for the MS SQL Server service.

3. Log on to the SQL Server computer, using the Window NT user account for the Microsoft SQL Server service.

> **CAUTION**
>
> You must log on to the SQL Server computer using the Microsoft SQL Server account. If you complete the process of setting up SQL Mail while logged on with a different Windows NT account, you will not be able to start the SQL Mail service.

4. Install the Microsoft Exchange Client.

5. Set up an Exchange Client profile for the Microsoft SQL Server service account. Verify that you can send and receive mail.

6. Start the Mail and Fax application from the Control Panel. Choose the Show Profiles button to display the Exchange Client profile you just created. Make a note of the profile name.

7. From the SQL Server, set up the SQL Mail service to use the Exchange Client profile. When you are done, verify that SQL Mail is working properly.

▶ **See** "Managing User Accounts," **p. 191**
▶ **See** "Setting Up Recipients," **p. 941**
▶ **See** "Using the Exchange Client," **p. 972**
▶ **See** "Using SQL Mail and Alerts to Monitor SQL Server," **p. 1674**

Now that you have configured the SQL Mail service, you are ready to set up the SQL Server to process the incoming queries. To process messages arriving in the SQL Mail Inbox, use the sp_processmail system-stored procedure. This stored procedure allows you to specify exactly how incoming messages are processed. You can specify a required subject line for incoming queries, the permissions under which to execute the query, and the file type and format for the query results. For this example, assume that all queries pertain to the pubs database and that only messages with a subject line of "query" should be processed. To accomplish this, execute the stored procedure as shown in Listing 30.1.

Listing 30.1   *PROCMAIL.SQL*—Command Used to Process Mail in the SQL Mail Inbox

```
exec sp_processmail @subject = 'query', @dbuse = 'pubs'
```

The stored procedure processes all messages currently in the Inbox that match the specified criteria. The results of each query are returned to the query sender in a file attached to an e-mail message.

To automate the processing of incoming mail, schedule a task on the SQL Server to execute this stored procedure (see Figure 30.10).

Part

VI

Ch

30

FIG. 30.10

The Edit Task dialog box is used to schedule a mail system stored procedure for periodic execution. You can schedule tasks to be run on-demand, to be run one time, or to be run as recurring tasks.

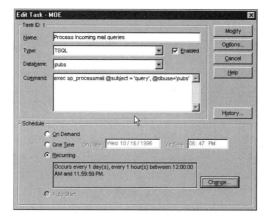

The integration of Exchange Server and SQL Server for the purpose of querying the database is now complete. You are now ready to consider the second of Company X's requirements. Each time a new client is added to the SQL Server database, Company X wants information about the new client to be posted automatically to an Exchange Server public folder.

The first thing you need to do is to create the public folder. Name the public folder "New Clients" and grant permissions to view the items in this folder to everyone in the organization. Grant the user account used by the SQL Server the permission to author items in the public folder. You also may want to enable message aging for the folder so that messages are deleted after a certain amount of time has passed.

▶ **See** "Using Public Folders," **p. 1007**

▶ **See** "Automating Maintenance with the SQL Executive," **p. 1223**

Every Exchange Server public folder has an SMTP address. Exchange Server creates the SMTP address for a public folder by using the name of the folder (with any spaces stripped out) and the domain address. For example, the SMTP address of a folder named New Clients that exists in the domain **gasullivan.com** is **NewClients@gasullivan.com**. Follow these steps to configure the SQL Server to use the SMTP address of the folder when posting messages to the public folder:

1. Using the profile that you set up for the Microsoft SQL Server service, start the Exchange Client. Then locate the New Clients public folder.

2. Choose File, Properties from the menu to open the Properties dialog box.

3. Click the Summary tab and then the Personal Address Book button to add the SMTP address of the public folder to the personal address book for SQL Mail. Figure 30.11 shows the properties of a public folder that has been added to the personal address book.

FIG. 30.11

This figure shows the Properties dialog box of a personal address entry for an Exchange Server public folder.

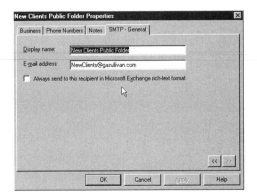

Now you are ready to configure the SQL Server to populate the public folder automatically when new records are added to the database. To post items to a public folder, use the `xp_sendmail` extended stored procedure to send an e-mail message to the folder. This stored procedure allows you to specify all of the details about the message being sent, including recipients, message subject, message body, and message attachments. You can accomplish the necessary automation by creating a database trigger that selects information from the newly inserted row and then calls `xp_sendmail` to post a message containing the selected information. Listing 30.2 shows an example trigger that has been set up on the authors table of the pubs database. Every time a record is inserted into the table, `xp_sendmail` executes and sends a message to the NewClients public folder.

Listing 30.2   _SENDMAIL_TRIGGER.SQL_—Insert Trigger Which Sends a Mail Message

```
CREATE TRIGGER ins_authors ON authors      FOR INSERT
AS
BEGIN
        DECLARE @NEWCLIENT VARCHAR(40)

        SELECT @NEWCLIENT = au_lname
```

```
        FROM inserted

        EXEC master.dbo.xp_sendmail
                'NewClients@gasullivan.com',
                @subject='New Client',
                @message=@NEWCLIENT
    END
```

▶ **See** "Creating Databases and Database Objects," **p. 1183**

Accessing SQL Server Data   The integration of Exchange Server and SQL Server that is necessary to facilitate user queries and public folder postings is now complete. To request information from the SQL server, simply send an e-mail message from an Exchange Client to the SQL Server. The message should have a subject of "query" and contain only a Structured Query Language (SQL) statement in the message body. The SQL Mail client of the database processes the message as a database query and sends a reply back to you with an attached file containing the query results. Figure 30.12 shows a message that has been formatted to query the SQL Server, and Figure 30.13 illustrates the query results that are returned automatically by the SQL Server.

FIG. 30.12

As illustrated here, a query that is sent to a SQL Mail mailbox contains only a valid SQL statement. Unless configured otherwise, the SQL Mail mailbox assumes that incoming messages contain only valid SQL statements.

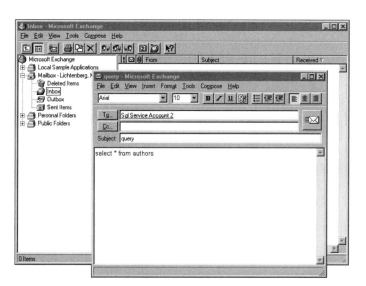

To view information about new company clients, simply access the New Clients public folder and view the postings you find there; the SQL Server automatically posts information to the folder as new records are added to the database. From a user's standpoint, all the integration with the SQL Server database is entirely transparent. Instead of learning a new tool or application to access the SQL Server, Company X's employees can use the familiar Exchange Client interface to request and view information in the database.

FIG. 30.13
The SQL Mail service of Microsoft SQL Server returns query results in an attached file like the one shown here.

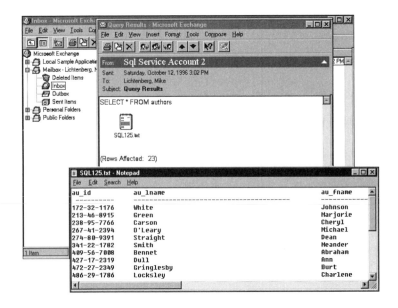

Extending the Example   This example has illustrated ways in which you can integrate Exchange Server with SQL Server and Windows NT Server to provide business solutions. You can use the discussed techniques to extend further the integration of Exchange Server and SQL Server. Some ways in which you can extend the integration include the following:

- Sending mail to the SQL administrator when server processes begin, complete, or result in errors.

- Logging error messages to public folders which are accessible only to system administrators.

- Setting up additional triggers to notify users when events occur. For example, send a notification to marketing personnel when a client is deleted from the database.

In addition, you can use custom forms, which the next section examines in detail, to simplify the process of using Exchange Server to request and receive data from SQL Server databases. More advanced solutions are available through the use of Microsoft Visual Basic and MAPI, which also are discussed later in the chapter.

Company Forms

You can enhance Microsoft Exchange Server's capability to function as a document library by creating custom forms. Custom forms are electronic messaging forms which can replace standard paper documents, such as timesheets and expense reports, in your organization. Forms can include edit fields, check boxes, option buttons, list boxes, tabbed fields, and various other types of fields. You can use forms to send information between users and to post information in folders. By using custom forms to collect and present information, you can enhance the visual presentation of the data.

The following example shows you how to create a custom form and add it to a forms library to be used to eliminate paper documents and improve the efficiency of Company X. Like many organizations, Company X has a number of forms that must be filled out and turned in periodically by employees. These forms include expense reports, vacation requests, timesheets, performance reviews, and personal-information surveys. All of these are maintained by administrative personnel, who must deliver the forms to employees, collect the forms, forward the forms to the appropriate persons, and eventually file the forms for safe-keeping.

Company X wants a way to automate the processes of completing, distributing, and filing the forms, in turn freeing the administrative personnel for more important tasks. You can accomplish this by creating custom forms for each of the paper documents that are to be replaced and then locating the forms in a forms library which is accessible to all employees. This example shows how to create and install the first custom form, a vacation request form, for Company X's library.

Creating a Custom Form   Custom forms for Exchange Server are built using the Exchange Forms Designer. The Forms Designer, which is included with the Exchange Client software, is used to design, build, and install custom forms and form applications. You do not need programming experience to create forms using the Forms Designer, although some experience is helpful. The Forms Designer does resemble Microsoft Visual Basic in that you visually build the message forms and set properties on fields, forms, and windows through the use of simple dialog boxes. In fact, the Forms Designer creates Visual Basic projects for your forms. So, you can use Visual Basic to enhance further the capabilities of your forms. To install the Exchange Forms Designer, follow these steps:

1. As the Exchange Server administrator, copy the EDFSETUP directory from the Exchange Client Setup CD-ROM to the Exchange Server computer from which you will run the Forms Designer Setup program.

TIP To make it easier for Exchange Client users to set up their computers, you should copy the Forms Designer Setup directory to the same computer where the Microsoft Exchange Client Setup Program has been created.

2. To install the Forms Designer on a computer running the Exchange Client, connect to the network server on which the Forms Designer Setup program is located.

3. Run the Setup program in the Forms Designer setup directory.

After you have installed the Exchange Forms Designer, you are ready to create the Vacation Request form. This form contains only two fields that a person requesting a vacation needs to complete—a start date and an end date for the requested vacation. The recipient of the form is pre-filled, so that when the form is sent, it is delivered automatically to the person who evaluates the request. Also, the person requesting a vacation receives a copy of the form message, to ensure that he or she has an electronic copy of the request. The persons requesting and evaluating the request can be any Microsoft Exchange users who have permission to use the form. Once the form has been sent, it can be replied to or forwarded just like any other e-mail message.

T I P   Although the following example creates a new form from scratch, an easy way to create forms is to find another form which nearly suits your needs and modify it. See the sample applications which are included with the Exchange Client for some example forms. Also, Exchange Forms Designer includes several forms templates which you can use to speed the development of new forms.

Here are the steps to follow when creating the custom Vacation Request form:

1. Start the Exchange Forms Designer. A dialog box appears and gives you three choices: create a new form using a form template, create a new form using the Form Template Wizard, or open an existing form project.

N O T E   Forms created using the Exchange Forms Designer are stored in form project files, which have an .EPF extension. ▇

2. Since you are creating a new form, select the Form Template Wizard option and click the Next button. Complete each step of the Template Wizard to create the blank form shown in Figure 30.14 by supplying the following answers to the Wizard prompts:

   - When asked whether the information will be sent to another user, or posted to a public folder, specify that the information on the form will be sent to another user.

   - When asked whether the form will be used to send information or send a response, specify send information.

   - When asked whether the form will have one or two windows, specify one window.

   - When asked to specify a form name and description, enter **Vacation Request** as the form name and any description you prefer.

FIG. 30.14

The Form Template Wizard jump-starts the development process by creating a blank form with many standard properties already set. You can modify the standard property settings to suit your needs.

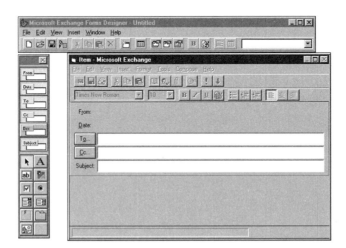

3. Place two entry fields in the lower portion of the custom form below the Subject entry field, by selecting Entry Field from the Forms Designer Toolbox and clicking in the desired location on the form. Arrange the entry fields one above the other. These fields will hold the start and end dates of the requested vacation.

4. Select the top entry field you just added. Choose <u>V</u>iew, Field <u>P</u>roperties from the menu to display the Field Properties dialog box for this field (see Figure 30.15).

FIG. 30.15
Use the Field Properties dialog box to set up the characteristics of fields on custom forms.

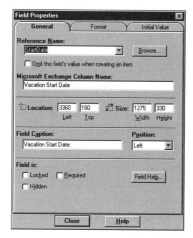

5. On the General tab of the dialog box, enter **StartDate** for the Reference <u>N</u>ame and **Vacation Start Date:** for the Field C<u>a</u>ption.

6. Go to the Format tab of the dialog box. Select Date from the Type drop-down list and m/d/yy from the Format drop-down list. Click the Close button to close the dialog box.

7. Set the field properties for the bottom entry field on the form by repeating steps 4 through 6, entering **EndDate** for the Reference <u>N</u>ame and **Vacation End Date:** for the Field Caption.

8. In the top portion of the custom form, select the entry field with a caption of "To." This is one of the entry fields that was automatically added to the form by the Template Wizard. Choose <u>V</u>iew, Field <u>P</u>roperties from the menu to open the Field Properties dialog box.

9. Select the Initial Value tab of the dialog box. Add the name of the person who approves vacation requests as the initial value. To do this, you can click the T<u>o</u> button to select a name from the Address Book. Then, select the Include the Current User of the Form check box. This ensures that the sender of the form will automatically receive a copy of the vacation request. Click the Close button to close the dialog box.

10. Choose <u>V</u>iew, <u>W</u>indow Properties from the menu to display the Window Properties dialog box. Enter **VacationRequest** for the Window Name and **Request Vacation** for the Window Caption. Remove MAPI_From and MAPI_SentDate from the tab order and add the new entry fields StartDate and EndDate. Arrange the items in the following tab order: MAPI_To, MAPI_Cc, MAPI_Subject, StartDate, and EndDate. The completed dialog box is shown in Figure 30.16. Click the Close button to close the dialog box.

11. Choose <u>V</u>iew, <u>F</u>orm Properties from the menu to display the Form Properties dialog box. Enter **Vacation Request** for the Form Display Name. Click the Close button to close the dialog box.

FIG. 30.16

Use the Window
Properties dialog
box to set the general
characteristics of a form
window, such as the title
bar and tab order.

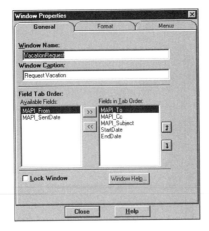

12. Choose File, Save to save the form project. Figure 30.17 shows the completed form.

T I P To maintain different versions of the same form, use File, Save As to save the form to a different form project.

FIG. 30.17

The Vacation Request
custom form is
complete and ready
to be installed into
a forms library.

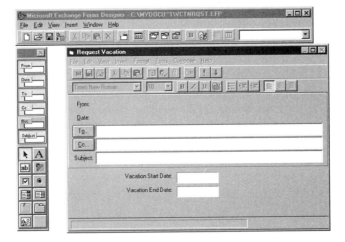

13. Install the new form by choosing File, Install from the menu. This causes a number of actions to take place: the Visual Basic files for this form are created and stored in a directory immediately below the directory in which the forms library was stored; the *.CFG file for this form is created; and the *.EXE file for this form is created. Finally, a Set Library To dialog box appears. For now, install the form into a Folder Form Library such as one of your personal folders or other folder to which only you and perhaps a few other users have access.

N O T E The `*.CFG` and `*.EXE` files which are created during the form installation are used to install the form into additional forms libraries, such as the Organization Library. ■

Now that you have created the Vacation Request form and installed it into a folder, you need to test the form. Installing a form into a folder library adds the form to the Compose menu for that folder. So, by choosing the menu item associated with the new form, you can open the Vacation Request form, fill it out, and send it to a recipient. Do this many times, testing each of the form's features. Once you are satisfied that the form is correct, you are ready to make the Vacation Request form available to your entire organization by installing the form into the Organization Forms form library.

N O T E Forms are stored in one of three types of forms libraries, depending on how they are to be used. The *Organization Forms form library* is used for forms that you want to make available to everyone in your organization. A *folder forms library* is typically for storing forms used with a public folder. You also can use a *personal forms library* to store forms for your personal use. ■

Install the form into the Organization Forms form library by doing the following:

1. Choose Tools, Options from the Exchange Client menus to open the Options dialog box.
2. Select the Exchange Server tab, and then click the Manage Forms button to open the Forms Manager.
3. To make the Organization Forms form library the destination for the new form, click the Set Button above the right-hand list box and select the Organization Forms form library from the Set Library To dialog box when it displays.

N O T E You need to have owner permissions on the destination library to install a form into the Organization Library or public folder form libraries. If the Install button is inactive after you have selected your destination library, you do not have the necessary permissions to install forms into the library. ■

TROUBLESHOOTING

There is no Organization Forms form library. The Organization Forms form library is not created automatically when the Exchange Server is installed. You need to create it before installing forms.

▶ **See** "Using Public Folders," **p. 1007**

4. From the Forms Manager, click the Install button. This opens the standard Open dialog box, as shown in Figure 30.18.
5. Select the `*.CFG` file for the Vacation Request form, and click the Open button. The Form Properties dialog box appears; this dialog box displays information about the Vacation Request form. It allows you to edit several of the form's properties, including its display name, category, and contact.

Part

VI

Ch

30

FIG. 30.18

The Forms Manager allows you to insert, delete, copy, and view the properties of forms.

6. After reviewing the information presented in the Form Properties dialog box, choose OK to install the form.

Using the Custom Form   The Vacation Request form is now complete and ready for use. Users now can easily access the form from within the Exchange Client software. The new form functions very much like a standard e-mail form, except that instead of typing a message, the users need only to fill out the start and end dates for their vacations and then send the form to the recipients. You can send, reply to, forward, and print a form message just like any other message. Follow these steps to use the Vacation Request custom form:

1. From the Exchange Client, select Compose, New Form to display the New Form dialog box (see Figure 30.19). This dialog box displays all the forms which have been installed in the Organization Forms form library.

FIG. 30.19

The Organization Forms form library contains the forms that are used by all users of the Exchange Server installation.

2. Select the Vacation Request form from the list and click the OK button. This opens the form (see Figure 30.20).

N O T E   The first time you execute a form from an Exchange Client computer, the form is downloaded and installed on the local computer before being executed. Subsequent executions of the form use the local copy of the form. However, if the form in the forms library changes, the next time you execute the form, the new copy of the form is downloaded and installed on your local computer. ▪

FIG. 30.20
Shown here is a a
vacation request form
that has been filled out
and is ready to be sent.

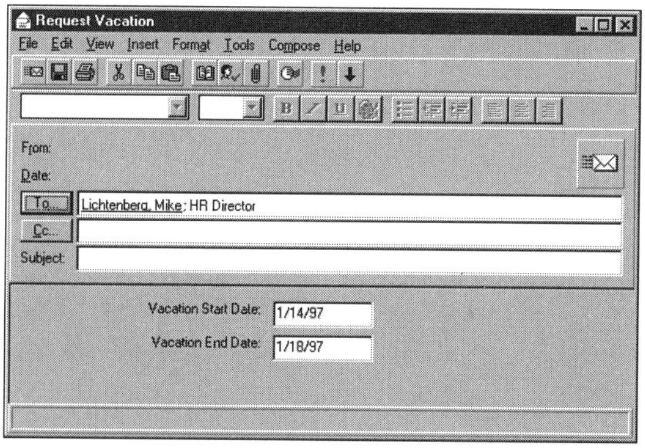

CAUTION

The Exchange Client computer must have enough free disk space to store the form. If the form cannot be downloaded and stored locally, the Exchange Client will not be able to use the form.

3. Fill out the Start Date and End Date information on the form.

4. Choose File, Send to send the form to the recipients.

Be aware that when you send a message using a custom form, the form itself does not travel; only the data entered on the form is actually sent to the recipient. So, if the message recipient does not have access to the forms library used to fill out the form, or at least a replicated copy of that forms library, he or she cannot view the information sent using the form.

Extending the Example   To complete the Company Forms library for Company X, you must convert each paper form that is routinely circulated to employees to an electronic custom form and install it in the Organization Forms form library. Then, to extend further the use of these custom forms, you can provide storage locations for the completed forms by creating public folders that are available only to administrative personnel. By setting up folder views, you can create a filing system for completed forms.

Obviously, the vacation request form that was created in the preceding example is an extremely basic form. You can add many other features to forms using the Forms Designer and customize responses to certain form events. For example, you can specify that when a user chooses to reply to a message sent with the form, a specific custom form window opens instead of the standard response form. You can create custom help messages for each form. The Exchange Forms Designer allows you to customize the look and feel of the form windows, menus, and fields in a variety of ways. You can add frames, tabbed fields, and picture boxes to a form to create complex dialogs for collecting and distributing information. Figure 30.21 shows a complex form which exhibits many of these features.

N O T E   See the *Microsoft Exchange Application Designer's Guide* for more information about extending custom forms. ▪

FIG. 30.21

You can use the Exchange Forms Designer to create complex forms for collecting and presenting information.

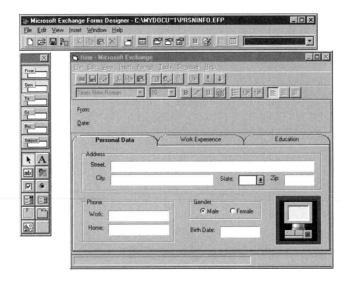

You can combine custom forms with public folders to create robust workgroup solutions. Forms can be designed to post information to public folders and to structure the information stored in public folders. For examples of the types of applications that you can create by combining custom forms with public folders, examine the Discussion & Response, Helpdesk, Survey, and Contact Tracking sample applications.

Because the Exchange Forms Designer creates Microsoft Visual Basic projects from custom forms, persons with programming experience can customize forms in many other ways. By using Visual Basic for Microsoft Exchange Server 4.0, which is included with the Exchange Forms Designer, or by using Microsoft Visual Basic 4.0, you can extend forms to perform many different functions. The following are some examples of form extensions that you can add:

- Performing calculations
- Enhancing validation of user input
- Formatting queries to request data from external databases
- Adding OLE controls
- Manipulating Microsoft Schedule+ objects

In addition, Exchange Server supports all MAPI-compliant forms, meaning that you can use Microsoft Visual C++ and other third-party tools to create forms for use with Exchange Server.

CAUTION

If you use Visual Basic to modify a project that was created by the Exchange Forms Designer, you cannot continue to maintain the form with the Forms Designer. The Forms Designer does not recognize changes made using Visual Basic, and regenerating the form with the Forms Designer overwrites any of the changes you made using Visual Basic.

N O T E For more information about creating and extending custom forms using the Forms Designer, see the *Microsoft Exchange Server Application Designer's Guide*. ■

Using Document Routing to Streamline Workflow

Microsoft Exchange Server provides robust document-routing functionality. By taking advantage of the available routing services, you can dramatically improve the flow of documents through your organization.

Traditionally, paper documents are routed through an organization by means of a manual process. Usually this process involves handwritten or typed routing slips, interoffice mail, and the inboxes and outboxes located on individuals' desktops. Such routing processes are fraught with the potential for delays and loss of information. Interoffice mail sometimes takes a day or two to deliver documents across an organization. Routing slips can be misplaced or misused, and documents can become buried on an individual's desk, causing other recipients on the routing list not to receive the information at all. Worse yet, documents can be inadvertently discarded. Revisions and annotations to routed documents pose another problem with this routing process. Once a routed document has been returned to the original sender, that person is faced with the unenviable task of compiling and deciphering any notes that have been attached to the document and then integrating the suggestions into the document.

Other challenges in the traditional process of routing documents include obtaining confirmation that a document has been received and determining where in the routing process a particular document is. These simple tasks can be time-consuming and frustrating chores, involving lengthy bouts of phone-tag and the passing of messages from person to person.

Exchange Server provides a number of ways for you to automate and simplify all of these tasks. One very simple form of document routing is the Return Receipt options that you can set on Inboxes or individual messages. These options provide a notification when a message is delivered or read. Another way that you can provide document routing is by creating custom forms that forward messages, reply to messages, move messages to public folders, or automatically send notifications. Two other forms of document routing that Exchange Server provides are electronic routing slips, which are integrated into the Microsoft Office suite of applications, and message rules, which are set individually at each Exchange Client installation.

On the following pages, routing slips and rules are examined in more detail. Electronic routing slips allow you to automatically circulate documents to a list of recipients. In addition, when routing a document, you can specify that Exchange Server track revisions and annotations to the document, and when the routing is completed, automatically return the modified document to the original sender. Message rules provide you the capability to set up your Exchange Client to automatically copy, move, forward, and reply to messages. All of these routing capabilities can provide your organization with the capability to streamline its document-routing process and thereby improve workflow. Among the improvements that you can realize are efficient tracking of routed documents, reliable delivery of routed documents, and improved response time to routed documents.

Automatic Form Routing

There are several ways in which Exchange Server facilitates automatic document routing. Electronic routing slips provide powerful message routing capabilities that are integrated directly into Microsoft Office applications such as Word, Excel, and PowerPoint. Rules, which are set up at the Exchange Client, allow you to route messages as they arrive at the Exchange Client mail delivery location.

Routing Slips Electronic routing slips have been a feature of Microsoft Mail Server and Microsoft Office for some time. However, they have also been a poorly understood and rarely used feature of these applications. Routing slips provide you the capability of automatically sending an Office document directly from the application in which you created the document to a list of recipients. The options that can be set for routing slips allow you to do the following:

- Route documents to recipients one at a time or all at once
- Track revisions and annotations to documents
- Track the progress of documents through the routing list
- Return a routed document to the original sender when everyone on the routing list has reviewed it

To fill out a routing slip from within an Office application, follow these steps:

1. Select File, Add Routing Slip from the menu. The Routing Slip dialog box appears (see Figure 30.22).

FIG. 30.22

The Routing Slip dialog box in Microsoft Word 7.0 is used to set up the routing order and recipients for a document. All of the Microsoft Office applications use this dialog box to set up routing slips.

N O T E If you have already created a routing slip for the document on which you are working, the menu selection will be File, Edit Routing Slip instead of File, Add Routing Slip. ▪

 It is a good idea to establish a connection to Exchange Server before filling out a routing slip. You can establish a connection simply by starting the Exchange Client. If you have not done this, a Choose Profile dialog box appears, requiring you to select a profile and establish a connection anyway.

CAUTION

Document routing may not work across electronic mail gateways. You must have mail systems compatible with either MAPI or Vendor Independent Messaging (VIM). Exchange Server is compatible with MAPI. Even if the mail systems are compatible with the specifications listed previously, it is possible that the mail systems may not be able to resolve the addresses on the routing list.

2. Click the Address button on the Routing Slip dialog box to choose the desired members of the routing list. The Exchange Client address book is displayed.

3. Select the recipients of the document, and click the OK button when you are finished.

N O T E   If a person in the address book has already been sent a routed copy of the current document, that person's name has an asterisk next to it and cannot be selected. ▓

 If you select a group alias as a recipient, all members of the alias are considered a single recipient for routing. If you want to route the document to each member of the group alias one after the other, select each individual member of the alias separately.

4. Notice that the recipients you have selected are now listed in the To box of the Routing Slip dialog box. If you will be routing the document to the recipients one after the other and want the recipient to receive the document in a certain order, use the Move arrows to arrange the recipients in the order in which you want the document to be routed.

5. Fill out the Subject and Message text to accompany the routed document. If you have given your document a title, by default this title displays as the subject of the message.

6. In the Route To Recipients group box, you have the option to route the document to all recipients at once or to each recipient one at a time. To route the document to everyone at once, select the All at Once option. To route the document to one recipient at a time, select the One After Another option.

7. To specify that the document be returned to you after it has been routed to each of the recipients, select the Return When Done check box.

8. If you want to follow the progress of the document through the routing list, select the Track Status check box. Selecting this option causes a message to be sent to you each time the document is forwarded to the next recipient in the list.

9. To set the types of modifications that can be made to a document during the routing process, choose Annotations, Revisions, or Forms from the Protect For drop-down list. Choosing Revisions allows recipients to change a document and tracks all changes with revision marks. Choosing Annotations allows recipients to insert annotations, but not change the contents of the document. Choosing Forms allows recipients to enter information into form fields only.

You should password-protect all documents that are sent through a routing list. The settings for password-protected documents can only be modified by someone who knows the password. However, documents which are not password-protected can be unprotected by anyone, allowing them to change the document settings and make untracked revisions.

10. To add the completed routing slip to the document, click the Add Slip button. If you want to route the document immediately, click the Route button. The Clear button clears all recipients and selected options on the routing slip. To cancel the routing slip without saving changes to the routing slip or routing the document, click the Cancel button. If you choose to add the routing slip to the document, you can later send the document to the recipients by choosing File, Send from the menu. Alternatively, when the document is closed, you are notified that the document has a routing slip and asked if you would like to send the document to the first recipient.

Using Rules to Route Messages   At each Exchange Client installation, you can set up rules for routing messages. *Rules* process a set of conditions that you define and, if the conditions are met, take whatever actions you define. Among the actions you can specify for a rule are several which pertain to message routing. You can create rules so that when a message arrives, it can be replied to, forwarded to another recipient, copied to another location (such as a public folder), or moved to a new location.

One simple example of a way to use rules for message routing is the processing of Internet mailing lists. By subscribing an Exchange Client to several mailing lists and setting up a series of rules for forwarding incoming messages, you can automatically populate public folders with the contents of the mailing lists.

To use the Exchange Client AutoAssistants to set up rules for routing messages, do the following:

1. In the Exchange Client, choose Tools, Inbox Assistant, or Tools, Out of Office Assistant from the menu.

2. Click the Add Rule button to open the Edit Rule dialog box.

3. In the group box titled When a Message Arrives that Meets the Following Conditions, specify the conditions that a message must meet in order for the rule actions to execute. Rule conditions can include messages that are received from specific senders, messages sent to specific recipients, messages received directly or carbon copied, and messages which contain specific words or phrases in the subject line or message body. In addition, there are many other advanced conditions you can set. More than one condition can be specified for a single rule.

▶ **See** "Using the Exchange Client," **p. 972**

4. In the Perform These Actions group box, select the actions you want to take for messages meeting the specified conditions. You can specify more than one action for a single rule. The routing actions are highlighted in Figure 30.23. The actions you can specify to route messages include the following:

- **Move messages to a specified folder.** Select the Mo_v_e To check box and then click the _F_older button immediately to the right of the check box to specify the folder into which you want to move messages.

- **Copy messages to a specific folder.** Select the Cop_y_ To check box and then click the Fold_e_r button immediately to the right of the check box to specify the folder into which to copy messages.

- **Forward messages.** Select the For_w_ard check box and then click the _T_o button to specify the recipients to which messages should be forwarded.

- **Send an automated reply to message senders.** Select the Reply With check box and then click the Te_m_plate button to specify the text of the response message.

FIG. 34.23

The Perform These Actions box of the Edit Rule dialog box includes several actions that can be used to automatically route messages. One or more routing actions can be specified for each rule.

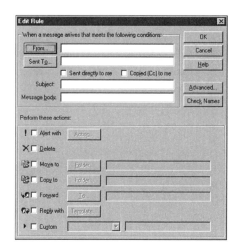

Part

VI

Ch

30

 T I P By default, newly created rules are active. To deactivate a rule, clear the Status check box that displays next to the rule in the Inbox Assistant dialog box.

N O T E All rules are processed on the Microsoft Exchange Server computer. However, if a rule requires access to the computer on which the client software resides (for example, to retrieve an address from a personal address book), the rule's actions cannot be executed until the client logs on. This is also true for rules that require validation of the client's permissions, such as rules that copy or move messages into public folders. Actions such as these also cannot be executed until the client logs on to the server. ▨

The Flow of Routed Documents

Microsoft Exchange Server uses the store-and-forward concept to provide its many services. _Store-and-forward_ means that all server functions are accomplished by passing e-mail messages back and forth between users, servers, and sites. This is different from other workgroup systems such as Lotus Notes, which use active connections to carry out server functions. The store-and-forward architecture of Exchange Server provides a fault-tolerant, reliable system. In addition, this is an ideal architecture for messaging systems, which must support intermittent client connections to a server.

A simple example of the store-and-forward concept in Exchange Server is sending an e-mail message from one person to another. A message is sent by Person A to Person B's mailbox, where it is then *stored*. Person B can then take a number of actions to affect the message, including opening, moving, copying, forwarding, replying, and so on. These actions typify the *forward* action of the store-and-forward concept. Similarly, many internal functions of Exchange Server, including such services as replication and directory synchronization, are achieved using store-and-forward messaging. Messages are sent from a server or server agent, stored, and then acted upon or acknowledged by one or more other servers and agents. In sending information from location to location, acknowledging message receipt, and processing received messages, Exchange Server personifies a "virtual network" based on the store-and-forward concept.

Similarly, the flow of documents and notifications from person to person within an organization also illustrates the concept of a store-and-forward or "virtual network." The topology of any network operating system includes the concepts of servers and network nodes. Packets of information are sent from node to node, as controlled by the server. At each node, rules may be applied which specify how to handle certain types of information packets, notifications may be sent to acknowledge receipt of information packets, packets may be modified, and packets may be stored or sent to another node. Any enterprise that relies on the passing of information, then, can be thought of as a "virtual network."

Information packets in the virtual network—in the form of business documents—flow from node to node, or person to person. Each virtual network node, or person, may have rules to follow for handling specific types of information packets. For example, a manager might always forward a certain type of management memo to each of the people working for him or her. Each node, or person, may send notifications when information packets are received; for example, Person A might leave Person B a voice-mail message advising Person B that an important proposal has been received. In addition, each person, or network node, can modify information packets (make annotations to a weekly report), store information packets (file a document), or route an information packet to the next node (send a routed publication to the next person). As you can see, most modern business enterprises characterize the virtual network.

Routing By exploiting the document-routing capabilities incorporated into Exchange Server and the Microsoft Office applications, you can create an electronic virtual network. Exchange Server functions are the backbone of this virtual network, carrying routed messages and documents from person to person.

Figure 30.24 shows the store-and-forward flow of a document with an attached routing slip that is routed from Person A to Persons B, C, and D, in that order. In this case, the routing slip specified that the document be returned to the original sender when everyone had finished reviewing the document; this return message is the final forwarding of the document.

FIG. 30.24

This diagram shows the store-and-forward routing of a document from Person A to Persons B, C, and D, and then back to Person A.

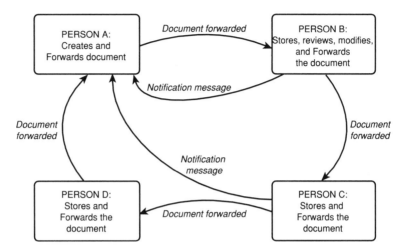

At each store point in the flow of a routed document, you can make a local copy of the document, revise and annotate the document, or simply review the document. Once each person on the routing list finishes with the document, he or she forwards it to the next person on the routing list.

Through integration with Office applications such as Word and Excel, Exchange Server facilitates this routing process. To route a document that has a routing slip attached, follow these steps:

1. In the Exchange Client, open the message containing the routed document. The routed message will look similar to the message shown in Figure 30.25. At the top of the message there may be a message from the original sender of the document. Following this, there is verbiage explaining that the attached document has a routing slip and that you should continue the routing after you have finished reviewing the document. To open and review the routed document, double-click the attached object.

CAUTION

In order to review and forward the routed document, you must have access to the appropriate application to open the document.

2. Review the document and make revisions or annotations.

3. When you have completed reviewing the document, choose File, Send from the menu to open the Send dialog box.

 You can change the order of the remaining persons on the routing list, or add additional members to the routing list by selecting File, Edit Routing Slip from the menu and editing the information on the Routing Slip dialog box.

FIG. 30.25

Routed documents are
attached to messages
similar to the one shown
here.

4. The Send dialog box, as shown in Figure 30.26, gives you the option of either routing
   the document to the next person on the routing list, or sending a copy of the document
   without using the routing slip. Select Route Document and click the OK button to send
   the document to the next person on the routing slip.

FIG. 30.26

The Send dialog box
gives you the routing
options for the current
document.

If you have set up rules to facilitate message routing, documents are evaluated as they are
received at the Exchange Client; if they meet the criteria specified in the rule, then the routing
actions specified by the rule are taken. These actions could include forwarding, moving, and
copying the document. Figure 30.27 shows the flow of a document that was sent to Person A to
Person B and, meeting the criteria of rules set on Person B's Inbox, was automatically forwarded to Person C.

Notifications   Notifications of information delivery and a capability to track information are
critical in any network. This is true even of store-and-forward networks. It is important that you
be able to track the progress of routed documents through a network and to receive verifications that messages have been delivered. Exchange Server provides mechanisms for both
tracking routed messages and sending verifications that messages were delivered.

FIG. 30.27

This diagram shows the Inbox rule evaluation and automatic routing of a document sent from Person A to Person B.

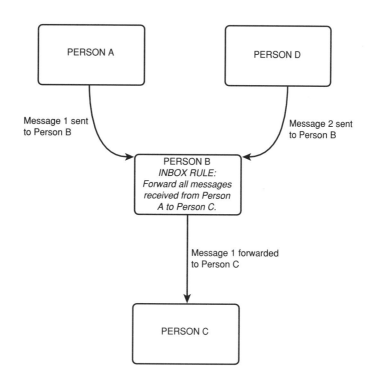

The three most common ways that you can use Exchange Server to provide message delivery notifications are the following:

- Return receipts
- Inbox rules
- Routing slip status messages

Return receipts provide simple notifications to you when a message that you have sent is either delivered or read. To request return receipts for your messages, do the following:

1. Choose Tools, Options from the Exchange Client menu to open the Options dialog box.
2. Go to the Send tab (see Figure 30.28).
3. Click The Item Has Been Read check box to request a return receipt when messages that you send are opened by the message recipient.
4. Click The Item Has Been Delivered check box to request a return receipt when messages that you send are delivered to the message recipient.

FIG. 30.28

The Send tab of the Options dialog box is used to set up your Exchange Client to request return receipts. On this tab, you can also specify the sensitivity and importance of your messages.

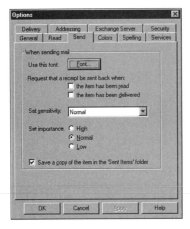

CAUTION

If you are composing a message when these options are set, they are not applied to the current message but are to all messages sent after the one you are currently composing. To request a receipt for a message you are composing, choose File, Properties from the menu and go to the General tab. Select Delivery Receipt or Read Receipt to request the type of receipt you desire.

After setting the return receipt options, you automatically receive a return receipt notification when your messages are delivered or opened. The notification states the action that occurred and the time that the action occurred.

Setting up Inbox rules to notify senders of messages that you have received their messages is identical to the setup of rules for routing messages. When setting up the rule, select the Reply With rule action and put some verbiage in the reply template that notifies senders that their message has been received. (See the section "Automatic Form Routing" earlier in this chapter for more information about using the Inbox Assistant to set up rules for routing messages.)

The most powerful notifications that are available through Exchange Server are those associated with routing slips. Perhaps the most frustrating thing about routing a document to a number of people is keeping track of the document. Too often, the document becomes lost during the routing process, and it becomes a time-consuming chore to find out where the document is located. The notifications available with routing slips remedy this problem. When you set up a routing slip for a document, you have the option to request status reports on the progress of the document. By selecting the Track Status option as the original sender of the document, you receive a status report each time the document is sent to another recipient on the routing list. The notification process at each step of the routing process is illustrated in Figure 30.29.

The routing status report that you receive shows who sent the document and who the recipient was (see Figure 30.30).

FIG. 30.29
This diagram shows how routing status reports are sent to the original sender of a document each time the document is forwarded from one recipient to the next.

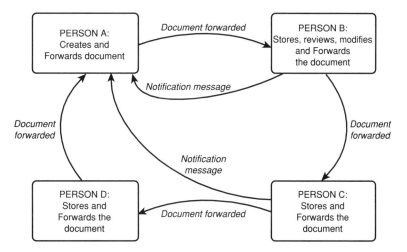

FIG. 30.30
Routing status messages such as this keep you informed about where your documents are located in the routing process.

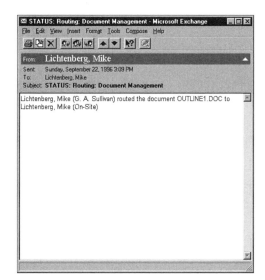

From Here...

You have now learned how to build a document library with Microsoft Exchange Server by taking advantage of the capabilities provided by public folder applications and custom forms, and by integrating various Microsoft Office and BackOffice applications. Along the way, you have learned how to build public folder applications and how to use the Exchange Forms Designer to create and install custom forms. You also have seen how Exchange Server can be integrated with SQL Server. In addition, you have learned how to improve your workflow by taking advantage of the document routing capabilities integrated into Exchange Server and the Office applications.

The following chapters deal with topics related to those covered in this chapter:

- For information on using the Exchange Client, see Chapter 28, "Using Exchange Client Applications."
- For information on creating public folders, see Chapter 29, "Distributing Information with Exchange Server."
- For information on the features of SQL Server, see Chapter 33, "An Inside Look at SQL Server."

CHAPTER 31

Exchange Server Advanced Topics

by Don Benage

In this chapter, you learn how to install and use the advanced security features that complement the security already provided by Windows NT. Although the security built into Windows NT Server helps prevent unauthorized use of the computer equipment in your organization and control access to shared resources, additional measures are needed when messages are sent across the country or around the world. Even in a local environment, if the nature of your information is highly sensitive, these advanced features of Exchange Server play an important part in keeping your information confidential. ■

How to install advanced security for Exchange Server

Find out how to install the Key Manager service and set up advanced security administrators. Learn how to enable a mailbox for advanced security.

How to use Exchange Server's Advanced Security features

Learn how Exchange Server uses public-key technology and sophisticated encryption to digitally "sign" and "seal" your electronic messages.

How to connect Exchange Server to Microsoft Mail (PC) systems

Learn how to configure the Microsoft Mail (PC) Connector so that you can exchange mail with existing users and Post Offices. Learn how to use the Microsoft Exchange Migration Wizard to automatically move mailboxes and messages from an existing Microsoft Mail Post Office to an Exchange Server.

How to connect Exchange Server to the Internet

Discover how to configure the Internet Mail Service so that your Exchange Server system can communicate with the Internet community.

Understanding Server Security

Through the use of public-key protocols, you can attach a digital signature to your message verifying that it could only have been sent by you. You also can employ sophisticated encryption algorithms to encode a message so that it cannot be intercepted and read. Furthermore, you can even apply techniques that detect any tampering or substitution of bogus information. Additional information on public-key systems and other security-related issues is provided in Chapter 46, "Implementing Real-World Security."

New in this release is support for using encryption and digital signatures with Exchange users outside your own organization. By exchanging public-key information with another user (described later in this chapter), you can store their public-key information in your Personal Address Book making it easy to use advanced security features when communicating with that user. This alleviates the limitation of only being able to use these features within your own organization. Both users must be using Exchange Server with advanced security features enabled. You can use these features with Outlook or the Exchange Client.

You learned how to set up a site connector in Chapter 29, "Distributing Information with Exchange Server." In this chapter, you learn how to install and use two additional connectors so that you can send and receive messages with Microsoft Mail (PC) users and the vast community attached to the Internet. You also learn how to migrate mailboxes from a Microsoft Mail system in a manner somewhat similar to the automated extraction of Windows NT account information and subsequent creation of mailboxes that you learned in Chapter 27, "Implementing Exchange Server." The Internet Mail Service (formerly called the Internet Mail Connector) has been improved in this release and is much easier to configure using a new wizard which is described near the end of this chapter.

Using Exchange Server Advanced Security

With the increased use of electronic messaging, and especially with the explosion of the Internet, there is a growing concern for privacy and security. Imagine for a moment that the only type of letter you could send through the traditional mail system was a postcard. This would certainly limit the kind of information you would transmit through the mail and greatly affect its usefulness. Although the situation with electronic messaging isn't quite that bad, perhaps, in some ways this is an apt analogy.

Due to the public nature of much of the infrastructure that makes up the Internet, and the mechanisms employed to transmit network packets, it is very possible for people who are not the intended recipient of a message to gain access to its contents. This is also true on most corporate and organizational networks, unless stringent precautions and considerable expense have been employed to prevent such an eventuality. The growing availability of network-protocol analyzers, at ever-decreasing costs, has put the necessary tools within reach of average citizens. In addition, the informal community of computer "hackers" continues to develop and use ingenious, or at least shrewd, methods to gain unauthorized access to information.

It is worthwhile, therefore, to expend time and energy to learn how to safeguard your information. An important point to bear in mind when learning about these techniques, however, is the old adage that a chain is only as strong as its weakest link. The literature on computer security and crime is filled with stories of organizations that went to great lengths to secure their systems and then threw the operations manual in the (unguarded) dumpster at the back of the building. The hacker community has even coined the phrase "dumpster diving" to describe looking for information that will lead to access to systems. This is just one example of a weak link that might be overlooked and lead to disaster. The lesson: No system will help secure your information if your password is written on a Post-it note stuck to the bottom of your desk drawer.

▶ **See** "Data Security," **p. 1613**

Installing Exchange Server's Advanced Security

Public-key systems, like the one used by Exchange Server, depend on the use of *keys* to "lock" and "unlock" encrypted information. A key in the context of computer-based encryption systems is nothing more than a string of characters. The strength of the encryption and its capability to withstand attempts to break it are directly proportional to the quality and length of the key that is chosen. A long, highly random key provides very good protection. Because long strings of random (or pseudo-random) characters are difficult for humans to remember and inconvenient to enter on a keyboard, most commercial encryption software provides a key-management component that aids the process of generating, storing, and managing the keys being used. Exchange Server provides such a component called the *Key Management server*.

Part
VI
Ch
31

To use the security features of Exchange Server, you must first install the Key Management server (KM server) software. You should use one, and only one, server for this purpose. Users needing advanced security features communicate with the KM server through e-mail and can therefore leverage the features of this component even if it is located in a different site through a connection that does not support Remote Procedure Calls (RPCs). However, you do need an RPC-capable link to the KM server to install and administer advanced security because the Exchange Administrator is the tool you use to do so, and it requires RPC support.

There are two passwords that an administrator will have occasion to use in connection with the KM server. The first is a password that allows you to start the KM service on the Exchange Server computer where it is located. This password is generated during the setup process, cannot be changed, and either can be stored on a floppy disk for easy entry during startup or can be written down and typed in when you start KM server.

CAUTION

Although it is generally a bad idea to write down a password, this one is required to start the KM server. If you lose this password, you must reinstall the KM server software. Therefore, you should record this password on paper and/or a floppy disk and store it in a secure location such as a safe. You need the password (or disk) whenever you start the KM server, so it must be accessible for this operation (which may be required only a few times per year for maintenance, troubleshooting, and so on). Possession of this password does not imply an unauthorized user can easily read encrypted messages, but it may provide assistance to a sophisticated attacker.

The other password is used by an advanced security administrator and must be entered each time an advanced security task is performed. You can assign the role of advanced security administrator to more than one person, and each will have his or her own password. The initial password created by the Setup program is *password*. Procedures to assign additional advanced security administrators and change their passwords follow.

To install advanced security and create your KM server, follow these steps:

1. Log on to the computer that will act as your KM server with an account. The account you use should be a member of the local Administrators group for the computer. The account also must have administrative permissions for the Configuration object on the Exchange Server. Insert the Exchange Server CD into the CD-ROM drive.

2. The Key Manager software is located in the EXCHKM subdirectory. This can be found in the subdirectory for your CPU architecture (I386, ALPHA, or MIPS) under the Setup subdirectory. Find the appropriate directory for your computer and launch the Setup program.

3. After the Welcome screen, the Key Management Server Setup dialog box appears. You can change the installation directory by using the Change Folder button. You also are prompted for a name and organization to register your software. Then click the Typical button, the only option available, to install the KM server with all options. You are prompted to select the service account to use for this service. In general, you can use the same service account that you are using for the rest of your Exchange Server services. After copying files to your computer's disk drive, the Setup program eventually prompts you with another Key Management Server Setup dialog box (see Figure 31.1).

FIG. 31.1
This dialog box indicates the Country Code for the country in which you reside and whether you want Exchange Server Setup to create a KM Server startup floppy disk.

4. This dialog asks for your Country Code and whether you want a floppy disk created that will store the password used to start the KM server. This is a recommended option, but not required. If you create the floppy disk, a KMSPWD.INI file is saved containing the clear text (non-encrypted) password. If you do not create a floppy disk, the password displays on-screen for you to record. Whether you use a floppy disk, a written record, or both (recommended) to maintain this password, it must be kept secure. Click OK. Insert a floppy disk or record the password, and click OK again.

CAUTION

You will not be able to start the KM server without this password! If you lose this password, you will need to reinstall the KM server software.

5. After a short period of time, you see a dialog box indicating that the KM server software has been successfully installed. Click OK.

You should now start the KM server for the first time and change the default administrator's password. To start the KM server, follow these steps:

1. Open the Control Panel on the KM server computer. Double-click the Services icon. In the Services dialog box, scroll down the list until you find the Microsoft Exchange Key Manager service.

2. If you didn't select the appropriate service account during setup, or you need to change the service account for some reason, continue with this step. Otherwise, skip to step 5. Click the Startup button. The Service dialog box appears.

3. In the Log On As box at the bottom of the dialog box, select the This Account option button and then enter the Exchange service account name, or use the ellipsis button to browse for the account.

4. Enter and confirm the password for the Exchange service account (not the startup password) in the appropriate boxes. Click OK to return to the Services dialog box (see Figure 31.2).

Part VI

Ch 31

FIG. 31.2

Use this dialog box to set startup options for the KM server and to start the service. If you have not created a startup floppy disk, you must type the password generated during setup into the Startup Parameters box before clicking Start.

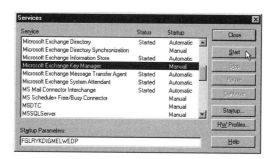

5. Either insert the startup floppy disk into drive A:, or type the startup password into the Startup Parameters box. Make sure that the Microsoft Exchange Key Manager service is still highlighted, and click the Start button. The service starts.

It is important to change the default password for advanced security administrators without delay. You should change the password and assign at least one additional advanced security administrator at this time (in case of an emergency situation or accident). To change the password and add another advanced security administrator, follow this procedure:

1. Start the Exchange Administrator.

2. In the container area (the left pane) of the display, find the site containing the KM server. Click the plus sign to the left of the site name to expand the display if it is not already open. Click the plus sign to the left of the Configuration object to expand its display.

3. Highlight the Configuration object. In the contents area, double-click the Encryption object. The dialog box for the Encryption object appears.

4. The General tab only allows you to change the display name of the object, which you can do if you want. The Permissions tab is used just as other permissions tabs you have already learned about. You can add permissions for one or more accounts if the inherited permissions aren't sufficient. The most important permissions are those granted on the Security tab. Click the Security tab (see Figure 31.3).

FIG. 31.3

This tab of the Encryption object's dialog box is used to select the encryption algorithm (the method used to encode information) for North American sites and all others. Use the button at the bottom of the dialog box to set up advanced security administrators.

5. The Security tab allows you to select the method used for encrypting information. In North America, you can select CAST-64, or the Data Encryption Standard (DES). Outside of North America you can use only CAST-40 because of restrictions that prohibit the export of "strong" encryption technology from the United States. The Key Management server location information cannot be changed.

N O T E   Strong encryption is a relative term used in the field of cryptography to describe the use of algorithms and key lengths that make decryption theoretically impossible. Many encryption algorithms allow you to select a key of varying length to use as a part of the encryption process. In general, the longer the key that is selected, the more difficult the task of decrypting the message. This is not a formal definition, but is accurate enough to be suitable for this discussion. For more information on encryption and the entire field of cryptography, see Applied Cryptography, Second Edition, by Bruce Schneier. ▦

6. Click the Key Management Server Administrators button. The Key Management Server Password dialog box appears (see Figure 31.4).

FIG. 31.4

Enter your personal
security administration
password in this dialog
box.

7. Enter your own password for advanced security administration. If you have not already changed it, the default is *password*. Click the check box if you want the Exchange Administrator to Remember This Password for up to 5 Minutes while you complete additional security administration tasks. If you do not check this box, you are prompted for your password before each task can complete.

N O T E If you finish performing advanced security tasks before five minutes have elapsed, most advanced security dialog boxes have a Forget Password button that causes the Exchange Administrator program to require the password again for any additional tasks. This is recommended to help avoid a situation in which you leave your workstation, perhaps in an emergency, while logged in with advanced security permissions. ■

8. Click OK to continue. The Key Management Server Administrators dialog box appears (see Figure 31.5).

FIG. 31.5

This dialog box allows
you to add or remove
advanced security
administrators or
change their pass-
words.

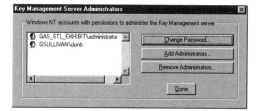

9. Click Change Password. A dialog box labeled Change the Password for the Key Management Server appears. Enter your existing password and a new password, and then verify your new password by entering it again. The password must be at least six characters in length and is case-sensitive. Click OK to return to the Key Management Server Administrators dialog box.

10. Click OK to return to the Encryption Properties dialog box and then click OK once more to close the dialog box.

Adding Advanced Security Administrators

You should grant permissions for one or more additional accounts to perform advanced security tasks such as enabling and revoking the use of advanced security, to act as a backup in the event of some catastrophic accident. If the only person who has this privilege is unable to perform these tasks, the organization is in serious jeopardy of eventual loss of information. While the currently active keys will continue to function, no one will be able to grant new mailboxes this capability, making the system less effective. Eventually, you will need to reinstall the Key Manager, which could lead to information loss.

Part
VI

Ch
31

To create an additional advanced security administrator, follow this procedure:

1. Start the Exchange Administrator.

2. In the container area (the left pane) of the display, find the site containing the KM server. Click the plus sign to the left of the site name to expand the display if it is not already open. Click the plus sign to the left of the Configuration object to expand its display.

3. Highlight the Configuration object. In the contents area, double-click the Encryption object. The dialog box for the Encryption object appears.

4. Click the Security tab.

5. Click the Key Management Server Administrators button. The Key Management Server Password dialog box appears.

6. Enter your own password for advanced security administration. Click the check box if you want the Exchange Administrator to remember the password for up to five minutes while you complete additional security administration tasks. Click OK to continue. The Key Management Server Administrators dialog box appears.

7. Click Add Administrators, and the Add Users dialog box appears.

8. Select the account that should have the capability to enable or revoke advanced security privileges for mailboxes from the Add Users dialog box. Click OK.

N O T E For the account selected to perform advanced security functions, the following additional permissions must already exist or be added. The account must be able to access a computer that can run the Exchange Administrator program. If this is a Windows NT Server, the Log On Locally right must be assigned to the account using the User Manager if the account is not a member of a local group with that privilege. The account does *not* need to be a Windows NT administrator, server operator, or accounts operator. The account also must be given the View Only Admin role (at a minimum) for the site object using the Exchange Administrator. Also, the account must be granted the Admin role for the Encryption object. If the account in question has inherited permissions already, these need not be added. ▓

9. You cannot change the advanced security password for an account without logging on using the account whose password you want to change. Regardless of which account is selected in the list, if you click the Change Password button, you will be changing the password for the currently logged on account. Therefore, the new advanced security administrator should be advised to change his or her password from its default (password) as quickly as possible because you can't do it for them. Click Done to return to the Encryption Properties dialog box; then click OK.

Enabling Advanced Security for Mailboxes

Now you are ready to enable a mailbox for using advanced security and to send a test message to try the new capabilities. A good first mailbox to enable is your own. If you want to enable mailboxes on other sites, you must install the Key Management software on that site. You should not set up another Key Manager service. Allow time for the directory information for the site with the new Key Manager to propagate to other sites. At that time, the Certification Authority (CA) object appears in the contents area of the Configuration object for the site. If this object is not visible, do *not* install the KM server software in this additional site. Investigate why the directory information has not yet replicated (perhaps not enough time has elapsed, or perhaps there is a problem) and wait until the CA object appears.

N O T E For directory information to propagate to other sites, a messaging connector of some type, such as a site connector or X.400 connector, must be established between the two sites. In addition, a directory-replication connector must be created and configured. ▪

▶ **See** "Setting Up a Site Connector," **p. 998**
▶ **See** "Setting Up Bridgehead Replication Servers," **p. 1003**

After you have performed these steps, you then enable mailboxes on home servers in remote sites to use advanced security, in the same manner as for mailboxes in the same site as the KM server. However, because the Exchange Administrator program must connect to the KM server to generate temporary security keys to enable a mailbox, this task must be performed on the site with the KM server. Therefore, a procedure must be developed describing the human interactions that occur for this process. In general, the administrator who generates the advanced security token (see the following described procedure) should provide this token directly to the mailbox owner and should require some reliable proof of identity before doing so.

N O T E You cannot enable advanced security for a distribution list or custom recipient. A mailbox is the only recipient type for which a Security tab is available on the dialog box. However, you can generate security tokens (see the following procedure) in groups to streamline the process of enabling advanced security for a large group. This process is described in the *Exchange Server Administrator's Guide* provided with Exchange Server. You should still distribute the tokens very carefully and individually using a secure channel or method. Exactly how to accomplish this is beyond the scope of this book, but if you want the encryption you are setting up to be worth anything, you should go to some trouble to be sure that this information is kept truly secret. ▪

To enable a mailbox for advanced security, follow these steps:

1. Start the Exchange Administrator.
2. Highlight the recipients container containing the mailbox in which you are interested. In the contents area, double-click the mailbox object. Click the Security tab (see Figure 31.6). You are prompted to enter your KM Server password (your *remembered* password that you created, not an auto-generated token or key).
3. The Current Status for this mailbox should be listed as Undefined. Click Enable Advanced Security. You are prompted to enter your password again unless you selected the Remember This Password for up to 5 Minutes option. After a brief pause for the generation of a new temporary security token, a Microsoft Exchange Administrator dialog box appears (see Figure 31.7).

FIG. 31.6

The Security tab of a mailbox's dialog box is used to enable advanced security features.

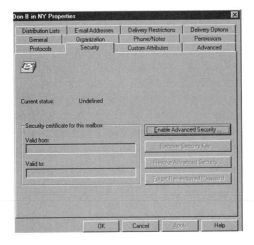

FIG. 31.7

This dialog box displays the new token generated for this mailbox. This token should be supplied to the mailbox owner through some secure means after receiving proof of identity.

4. Record the token and store it in a secure location. Click OK. The mailbox owner now completes the process using this token in the Exchange Client, as described in the next procedure.

To activate advanced security using a temporary security token, follow this procedure:

1. Start the Exchange Client. Make sure that you have logged on with the Windows NT account that has permissions to use the mailbox you want to activate. This is only an issue for administrators because normal users have only one account and one mailbox.

2. Choose Tools, Options. The Options dialog box appears. Click the Security tab.

3. Click Set Up Advanced Security, and the Setup Advanced Security dialog box appears (see Figure 31.8).

4. Enter the token provided by the advanced security administrator. Complete the name for your security file. It should retain an EPF extension. If you want, you can change the location of this file. You can use advanced security on any computer that contains a copy of your security file. It contains encrypted information that allows you to use advanced security features.

FIG. 31.8

The Security tab of the Options dialog box for a mailbox is used to set up advanced security using the temporary token generated by an administrator. You enter your token into the Setup Advanced Security dialog box shown in this figure.

5. At the bottom of the dialog box, enter and confirm a password that you will need every time you want to digitally sign your messages, seal them using encryption, or read messages sent to you using advanced security features. The password must be at least six characters and is case-sensitive. If you forget this password, sometimes referred to as your *remembered password*, an advanced security administrator can reissue your security key so that you can perform this process again.

6. Click OK to complete the process and close the dialog box. This sends your security request to the KM server. When your credentials have been authenticated, you receive a message from the System Attendant on the KM server indicating that your mailbox has successfully been security enabled.

Using Advanced Security Features When Sending E-Mail

Now that you know how to install and enable the advanced security features of Exchange Server, the only thing left to learn is how to use them. The ease of use you will discover when you exercise these capabilities belies the powerful technology being employed to protect your privacy. You may wonder whether your information is, in fact, actually protected. Only the test of time will provide the final answer to that question, but the Entrust Security Technology that Microsoft has licensed from Northern Telecom Limited, employs methods that have stood up to intense scrutiny and attack in the cryptographic community. Unless your security needs to withstand the best efforts of government agencies, it will probably be more than adequate.

To send a message using the advanced security features of Exchange Server, follow these steps:

1. Start Outlook or the Exchange Client. Both of these e-mail clients support the advanced security features of Exchange Server in the same way. They use the same menu choices and toolbar buttons.

2. Compose your message in the usual manner.

3. To encrypt the message, thereby "sealing" it electronically so that no one else can read it, click the Seal Message with Encryption toolbar button (see Figure 31.9). There is no change to the message display, but the message will be encrypted before being sent to the recipients list, and if it is somehow captured on its electronic journey, it will be almost impossible to read.

Part

VI

Ch

31

FIG. 31.9

Use the two toolbar buttons at the far right of the toolbar to activate Exchange Server's advanced security features.

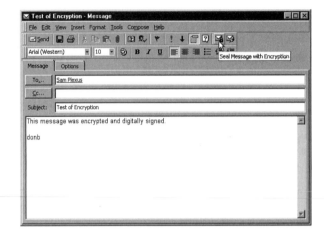

4. To add a digital signature to your message, thereby "signing" it electronically, click the Digitally Sign Message toolbar button. The message does not change its appearance on your screen. You learn how to verify that a message has been digitally signed, and who signed it, in the next procedure.

   You also can choose File, Properties, and use the Security tab on the Properties dialog box for a message to select the option buttons to sign and seal your message without using the toolbar buttons.

5. Click the Send toolbar button to send the message. You are prompted to enter your password to send or read secure items. If some of the recipients have not been enabled to use advanced security, you cannot send them an encrypted message. If this happens, a dialog box similar to the one shown in Figure 31.10 appears. You can either remove the offending name from the list, or send the message in an unencrypted format. In addition, you can use digital signatures with such recipients, but they cannot verify that signature.

FIG. 31.10

This Microsoft Exchange Security dialog box informs you if one or more of the recipients on the To line of a message are unable to receive encrypted messages.

To read a message using the advanced security features of Exchange Server, follow these steps:

1. Start the Exchange Client.

2. Messages with advanced security attributes (encryption or digital signatures) are opened in the same manner as ordinary messages. For example, you can simply double-click the message. When you open a message that has advanced security attributes, you are prompted to enter your advanced security password. After entering the password, you can read the message normally.

N O T E Messages that have been encrypted, with or without digital signatures, appear in your Inbox with a padlock on top of the envelope icon in the Item Type column. Messages that have just been digitally signed appear with an icon depicting the tip of a fountain pen over an envelope in the Item Type column. ■

3. To check the security properties of the message and verify the digital signature (if any) on the message, choose File, Properties.

4. You are prompted to enter your password again, unless you selected the Don't Prompt for Password Again Until Next Microsoft Exchange Logon option the first time you were prompted to enter it. On the Security tab of the Properties dialog box for the message, you can see which security features were used by reviewing which options are checked. If it was digitally signed, you can verify the digital signature.

5. You also can use the Read Digital Signature toolbar button to verify a digital signature (see Figure 31.11). It may be worth noting that after a message is open on your desktop, you can modify the message without the change's being reflected in this dialog box. If security is important to you, you should store your messages in a personal folder file with password protection and encryption on a disk drive that is physically secure. You also should not use the convenient option button that remembers your password and automatically enters it on subsequent Microsoft Exchange logons.

FIG. 31.11

The Verify Digital Signature dialog box shows you the identity of the person who signed the message and verifies that the contents of the document were not altered between the time it was sent and the time you received the message.

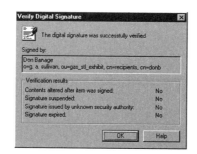

New to this release of Exchange Server is the capability to exchange public keys with an Exchange Server user at another organization. This allows you to exchange encrypted messages and to verify your digital signatures. Support for this feature is built in to both Outlook and the Exchange Client. It is very easy for the recipient of such a message to add the key information directly to their personal address book.

N O T E Your *private* key will not be compromised by sending copies of your public key to another user. In fact, the whole notion of public-key cryptography is based on the fact that knowing a person's public key does not help to discover their private key. This automated process is designed to make it easy to send and manage keys which are long strings of characters that are not easy to copy accurately and distribute without errors. You need not worry about keeping your public key secure. ■

To send another e-mail user a copy of your public security key, follow these steps:

1. Open Outlook or the Exchange Client.
2. Select Tools, Options from the menu.
3. Select the Security tab.
4. Click Send Security Keys. The Security Key Exchange Message displays (see Figure 31.12).

FIG. 31.12

This dialog allows you to send your public key, e-mail address, and other information to an Exchange Server user outside your organization. After they have sent their key to you, the two of you can use encryption and digital signatures.

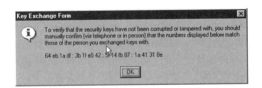

5. Click the Verify Key Integrity button (shown in Figure 31.13). This displays the Key Exchange Form dialog box. Compare these alphanumeric characters with those received by the other party (after the message is delivered) to be sure your key transfer was successful. The recipient needs to send you their security key to complete the process.
6. The *recipient* of a key-exchange message can open the message just like any other. They see a slightly different version of the Security Key Exchange Message (see Figure 31.13). They can easily add this information, including your public key, to their personal address book. Click the Verify Key Integrity button to verify the exchange was successful.

FIG. 31.13

The recipient's version of the Security Key Exchange Message is slightly different than the sender's version, reflecting its different function. Click Add to Personal Address Book to store this information.

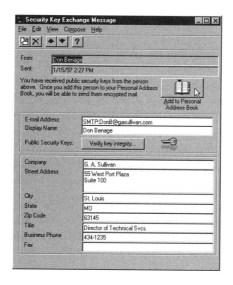

You should now be able to employ the advanced security features of Exchange Server to keep your private information private. It is important to have at least a rudimentary training session for users of advanced security to stress the importance of protecting their private password and selecting a good password in the first place. Using this technology, you should be safe from all but the most dedicated attacks from major governments or the United States' National Security Agency, and perhaps even from those (but don't count on it). When you have implemented these features of Exchange Server, and your people are using it properly, you have taken a big step toward safeguarding your information.

In the remainder of this chapter, you learn about two additional connectors—the Microsoft Mail (PC) Connector and the Internet Mail Service. These gateways allow your Exchange Server system to communicate with other mail systems. The first creates a connection between Exchange Server and a Microsoft Mail for PC Networks version 3.x mail system. You also can configure a connector to Microsoft Mail for AppleTalk Networks, but that is not covered in this book (see Chapter 10, "Using the Microsoft Mail for AppleTalk Connector," in the *Exchange Server Administrator's Guide*). The second connector you learn about is the Internet Mail Service. This gateway is used to exchange messages with the Internet community.

Configuring the Microsoft Mail (PC) Connector

Setting up a connection to MS Mail for PC networks is a process that involves a number of steps. These steps should be taken in the order described. There are several elements involved in this connector, and they depend on each other. It is important, therefore, that you complete one part of the process before moving on to the next.

When installing the Microsoft Mail (PC) Connector, you create a special post office that is compatible with MS Mail. This is called the Microsoft Mail Connector post office, or the *shadow post office*, and it serves as a temporary repository for messages being sent to or received from MS Mail. A Windows NT service called the Microsoft Mail Connector Interchange handles the transfer of messages between Exchange Server and the shadow post office. It also converts the messages to MS Mail format. Another service, the Microsoft Mail Connector (PC) message transfer agent (MTA) transfers messages between the shadow post office and the MS Mail post office.

If you are familiar with MS Mail you know about its original MTA, the MS-DOS-based program EXTERNAL, and its more recent replacement, the Multitasking MTA. The Connector (PC) MTA performs many of the same functions as these utilities. For example, it can deliver mail to MS Mail post offices over a LAN link without the use of the Multitasking MTA or EXTERNAL. However, if you want to connect to a remote post office over an asynchronous dial-up connection or X.25 connection, you must employ one of the older MTAs at the remote site.

The steps for configuring the MS Mail Connector that appear in the following five sections are for a simple connection between Exchange Server and MS Mail. If you have a large MS Mail system, with many post offices and gateways, you must take additional steps to enable message routing to post offices beyond the directly connected post office. You also may want to make new Exchange Server connectors available to the community of MS Mail users. This can be enabled by installing an access component so that the MS Mail post office can use the new connector in much the same way you would configure access to an older MS-DOS-based gateway. Exchange Server users also can take advantage of existing MS-DOS-based gateway products you already have installed. The procedures for these advanced configurations are beyond the scope of this book and are not covered. Refer to Chapter 9, "Connecting to Microsoft Mail for PC Networks," in the *Exchange Server Administrator's Guide* for additional information.

The following steps are necessary to set up the MS Mail (PC) Connector. Each one is covered in detail in the following sections.

1. Configure the MS Mail Connector Interchange.
2. Configure a LAN Connection to MS Mail.
3. Configure the Connector MTA.
4. Configure the MS Mail post office.
5. Test the MS Mail (PC) Connector.

Configuring the MS Mail Connector Interchange

The first step is to configure the Interchange, the component that transfers messages from Exchange Server to the shadow post office and converts them to MS Mail format. To configure the MS Mail Connector Interchange, follow these steps:

1. Start the Exchange Administrator.
2. In the container area (the left pane) of the display, find the site that will contain the MS Mail Connector. Click the plus sign to the left of the site name to expand the display if it

is not already open. Click the plus sign to the left of the Configuration object to expand its display.

3. Highlight the Connections object. In the contents area, double-click the MS Mail Connector object. The dialog box for the MS Mail Connector appears. Click the Interchange tab (see Figure 31.14).

FIG. 31.14

You can use the dialog box for the MS Mail Connector to configure a gateway between Exchange Server and MS Mail for PC Networks. This figure depicts the Interchange tab, the first step in configuring the gateway.

4. You must select an administrator's mailbox to receive status messages. You cannot leave this blank. Click Change and select a recipient from the Address Book. If you have not already established an administrator's mailbox for Exchange Server, consider creating one immediately following this procedure. You can change this selection later if you want.

 A person acting as an Exchange Server administrator will typically still want his or her own private mailbox. If you are in this position, you can create a profile for the Exchange Client that opens an administrator's mailbox for which you have permissions, in addition to your own mailbox. In this way, it is convenient to check both mailboxes and to send messages on behalf of "the administrator." Using this technique, you avoid having to close one mailbox and open another several times per day.

5. Select the primary language you will be using. If the user community makes use of embedded OLE objects, you should leave the Maximize MS Mail 3.x Compatibility check box selected. This increases the size of messages with OLE objects sent through the connector, but users of both systems will be able to view and save these objects. If you clear this check box, MS Mail users will not be able to see embedded objects sent from Microsoft Exchange clients. If you want to enable message tracking, a useful troubleshooting tool, click the check box.

6. Click the General tab. You cannot change the computer name on this tab. It is listed here for viewing only. You can use this tab to set a message size limit for messages that will pass through the MS Mail (PC) Connector.

> **CAUTION**
> Changing the name of the computer is done using the Network icon in the Control Panel and should be
> approached carefully as it can sometimes disrupt services.

You have now configured the Interchange and set limits for message size. You are ready to
continue with the next procedure, configuring a LAN connection to MS Mail.

▶ **See** "Creating an Administrator's Mailbox," **p. 942**

Configuring a LAN Connection to MS Mail

The next procedure shows you how to connect to an existing MS Mail post office over the
LAN. When you have connected, the network and post office names are extracted for you. You
provide only the network path, in the form of a Universal Naming Convention (UNC) name.
This is the same path to which your MS Mail clients have usually (by convention) mapped the
drive letter M: to connect to the post office.

To configure the LAN connection to the MS Mail post office, follow this procedure:

1. Be sure that you have finished the preceding procedure, "Configuring the MS Mail
   Connector Interchange," before continuing. You should have the dialog box for the MS
   Mail Connector object (from the Connections container in the site object) open in the
   Exchange Administrator program. Click the Connections tab.

2. You should see your Exchange Server site's MS Mail address (in Network/Post office
   format) in the Connections list. Click the Create button, and the Create Connection
   dialog box appears (see Figure 31.15).

FIG. 31.15
The Create Connection
dialog box is used to
define a connection,
in this case a LAN
connection, to the MS
Mail post office.

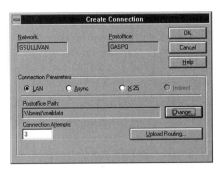

3. Click Change. Enter the network path in the Postoffice Path text box using a UNC name
   (*server**sharename*).

4. If you are connecting to a post office on a non-trusted Windows NT domain or a Novell
   NetWare network, or your Exchange service account is not a valid user on the post office
   server, enter an account and password that is a valid user. Click OK to return to the
   Create Connection dialog box.

5. The Network name and Postoffice name will be filled in automatically. Click OK.

6. An Apply Changes Now dialog box appears giving you a chance to confirm your changes. If you do not want to see this dialog box in the future, clear the check box labeled Confirm Before Connection Changes Are Applied on the Connections tab. The Connections tab should now show the connection between the Exchange Server site and the MS Mail post office in the list box.

You have defined the network connection needed to attach to the MS Mail post office. Now you are ready for the next procedure, configuring the connector MTA.

Configuring the Connector MTA

You can configure multiple MTAs to service this connector. Each MTA is capable of servicing one or more MS Mail post offices, and each is configured to use a particular type of connection. All MTAs are capable of using LAN connectivity. You also can configure an MTA to use Asynchronous connectivity, or to use an X.25 connection. For efficiency and manageability, it is recommended that each MTA be configured to service only one particular type of connection even though an X.25 MTA, for example, also can handle LAN connectivity.

To configure a connector MTA, follow this procedure:

1. Be sure that you have finished the preceding procedure, "Configuring a LAN Connection to MS Mail," before continuing. You should have the dialog box for the MS Mail Connector object (from the Connections container in the site object) open in the Exchange Administrator program. Click the Connector MTAs tab. Click the New button. A New MS Mail Connector (PC) MTA Service dialog box appears (see Figure 31.16).

FIG. 31.16
Use this dialog box to define the properties of a Windows NT service that will act as an MTA for one or more MS Mail post offices. It will transfer mail to and from the MS Mail Connector post office (the shadow post office).

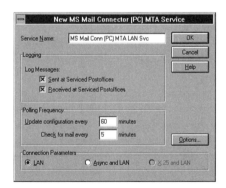

2. Enter a name for the service. The name can be up to 30 characters and can include spaces and some special characters (which should probably be avoided). A descriptive name is better than a creative name.

Part
VI

Ch
31

T I P If the name for the new service you are creating begins with "MS Mail," it will appear in the services list adjacent to the MS Mail Connector Interchange. Because these work in tandem to provide message transfer between the two systems (Exchange Server and MS Mail), they are almost always started and stopped together. Having them appear together in the list can help you remember to use them as a pair.

3. Set your logging preferences using the check boxes. You can turn logging on later if you have problems, or you may want to log messages for an initial shakedown period. You should not need to change the polling frequency although you can if you want. Do not click the Options button. Click OK to finish this task before setting options.

4. Highlight the newly defined MTA service and click the Configure button. Then click Options. The MS Mail Connector (PC) MTA Options dialog box appears (see Figure 31.17).

FIG. 31.17

This dialog box allows you to set message size limits, storage limits, and options for the MTA service.

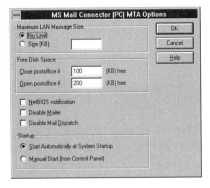

5. Enter any message size and storage limits you want to enforce. You also can select check boxes to Disable Mailer and Disable Mail Dispatch functions of the MTA if you want. This prevents the MTA from delivering and distributing messages to LAN-connected post offices and users. In general, these should not be checked. The mailer capability is similar to the mailer functionality of the External program. Select your Startup options and click OK to return to the dialog box named Configure the MS Mail Connector (PC) MTA Service. Then click OK again to return to the Connector MTAs tab of the MS Mail Connector (PC) Properties dialog box.

6. You now identify those post offices that will be serviced by this MTA. Click the List button. The Serviced LAN Postoffices dialog box appears (see Figure 31.18).

7. Select any post office that you want this MTA to service in the Available LAN Postoffices list box. Click Add to move them to the Serviced LAN Postoffices list box.

8. When you have added all the post offices appropriate for this MTA, click OK.

9. Click the Local Postoffice tab to get the information you need for the next step. Record the Network name and the Postoffice name. The serial number used as a sign-on ID and the password are needed only when configuring an external MS Mail post office that has

been specified as a direct route type connecting with an asynchronous or X.25 connection. Click OK to finish.

FIG. 31.18

This dialog box is used to select the post offices that will be serviced by the MTA you are configuring.

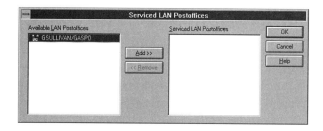

10. To use the connector, you must start the services you have defined. This can be done with either the Control Panel on the local computer or the Server Manager, locally or from a LAN or RAS-connected computer. Open the Services dialog box and start the MS Mail Connector Interchange service and the connector MTA service you just defined.

You have configured the connector MTA. Now you are ready for the next procedure, configuring the MS Mail post office.

Part

VI

Ch

31

Configuring the MS Mail Post Office

Next, you use the MS Mail 3.*x* ADMIN program to define the MS Mail Connector post office as an External post office for your existing MS Mail system. You can perform this task on any system capable of connecting to the post office and running the MS-DOS-based ADMIN program. To configure the MS Mail post office, follow these steps:

1. Start the MS Mail 3.*x* ADMIN program. This typically involves connecting drive letter M: to the shared directory containing the post office and launching ADMIN.EXE.

2. Select External-Admin from the main menu, and then select Create. Enter the information you recorded from the Local Postoffice tab in step 7 of the preceding procedure. For a LAN connection, select Direct for the route type and MS-DOS Drive for direct connection via (see Figure 31.19).

FIG. 31.19

The MS Mail 3.*x* ADMIN program being used to configure an MS Mail External post office address for the Exchange Server's MS Mail Connector post office (the shadow post office).

```
                              ADMIN.EXE
External-Admin
  Create   Modify  Delete  Export  List  Report  Setup
  Create?   Yes   No


     Enter network name:      GASULLIVAN
     Enter postoffice name:   EXTERNAL2
     Select route type:       Direct  Indirect
     Direct connection via:   MS-DOS Drive  Modem  X.25
```

3. Select Yes to confirm the creation of the External post office address.

You also should define at least one address for an Exchange Server recipient in the MS Mail Postoffice Address List. Use the same network and post office name along with the alias name for the recipient in the Exchange Server system. This will be used to test the connection from an MS Mail client in the next procedure.

Testing the MS Mail (PC) Connector

The connector is now defined, and the services have been started. You are almost ready to test the connection. In the last step of the preceding procedure, you defined an address for an Exchange Server mailbox in the MS Mail Postoffice Address List. You now need to create a custom recipient in Exchange Server for at least one user in the MS Mail system so that an Exchange Server client can address a message to an MS Mail user. As you have already learned, the custom recipient can be defined by an administrator on the server, or added to a Personal Address Book by a user.

If you have convenient client workstations to use for the test, use them. If not, you can define two profiles for the Exchange Client to attach to each system and test the connection from a single desktop. Configuring profiles for the Exchange Client to use Exchange Server services has already been discussed. This procedure outlines the process for defining a profile to attach to an MS Mail post office.

▶ **See** "Setting Up Custom Recipients," **p. 950**

▶ **See** "Creating a User Profile," **p. 959**

To create a profile for the Exchange Client to use MS Mail, follow these steps:

1. Open the Control Panel. Double-click the Mail and Fax icon. Click the Show Profiles button in the resulting dialog box.

2. Click Add. The Microsoft Exchange Setup Wizard starts.

3. Click the option button to Manually Configure Information Services and click Next.

4. Enter a name for your profile. If you use multiple profiles, you may want to indicate that this is an MS Mail profile in the name to help distinguish them. Click the Next button. A blank properties dialog box appears.

5. Click the Add button. Select Microsoft Mail from the Available Information Services list box and click OK. The Microsoft Mail dialog box appears (see Figure 31.20).

TROUBLESHOOTING

When the Add button is clicked, MS Mail does not appear in the Available Information Services list box. The Microsoft Exchange Client Setup program does not install this service by default. If you do not see the MS Mail service in the list, you must cancel the profile definition and run the Exchange Client Setup program. Select the Add/Remove button, and make sure that the MS Mail service is included in the Information Services that are installed.

FIG. 31.20

Use the Microsoft Mail dialog box to configure the Exchange Client to use an MS Mail post office.

6. Enter the path to your post office. If you are using a Windows NT or Windows 95 client, you can enter a UNC name of the form *server**sharename*. This is the same name you used in step 4 of the procedure for configuring a LAN connection to MS Mail earlier. Click the Logon tab.

7. Enter the mailbox name and password you will use with this profile. You can set other options if you want, but they are not typically necessary for this simple test procedure. Click OK.

8. Click Add. Select Personal Folders and enter a path and file name, or select a location in the Create/Open Personal Folders File dialog box. Click OK to return to the Properties dialog box for this profile. Click the Delivery tab.

9. Enter or verify the post office and mailbox names, and enter your password. Click OK.

10. There is a short pause while the Exchange Client attempts to connect to the mailbox you entered. When it connects, select your personal folder file in the Deliver New Mail to the Following Location drop-down list. Click OK. Click Next and then click Finish to complete the Wizard.

You have set up all the connector components and identified existing client workstations, or set up new ones, which can connect to each of the two messaging systems (MS Mail and Exchange Server). To test the MS Mail (PC) Connector, follow these steps:

1. Start the Exchange Client using a profile that uses Exchange Server. Compose a message and address it to the custom recipient you defined for the MS Mail mailbox (see Figure 31.21). Click the Send toolbar button, the first button at the far left of the toolbar depicting a moving envelope. Exit from the Exchange Client.

2. Restart the Exchange Client using the profile you just created for an MS Mail mailbox. If you have set the option to select the profile when you start the Exchange Client, an excellent option for administrators, you see a Choose Profile dialog box like the one shown in Figure 31.22.

Part
VI

Ch

31

FIG. 31.21

The Exchange Client, connected to Exchange Server, with a message addressed to an MS Mail recipient. This message will be routed to MS Mail through the MS Mail (PC) Connector.

FIG. 31.22

You can select a profile as you start the Exchange Client by choosing Tools, Options from the menu inside the Exchange Client and using the General tab. A profile defined for an MS Mail mailbox is being selected in this figure.

3. Within a short period of time, the new message should appear. You can choose Tools, Deliver Now if you want. Double-click the message to open it.

4. Click the Reply toolbar button and enter a reply. If you want, you can confirm who your return message is addressed to by double-clicking the name in the To list. A Properties dialog box similar to the one in Figure 31.23 appears.

5. Click OK to close the Properties dialog box. Click the Send toolbar button to send your message. Exit the Exchange Client.

6. Finally, restart the Exchange Client with the Exchange Server profile and confirm that you received the reply. Open the reply and double-click the name in the From list. You should see the properties page for the custom recipient you created earlier (see Figure 31.24).

You have now successfully created, configured, and tested the Microsoft Mail (PC) Connector. In the next section, you learn how to configure the Internet Mail Service.

FIG. 31.23

This figure depicts the Exchange Client, attached to an MS Mail mailbox, receiving and replying to a message from an Exchange Server recipient. This verifies that the MS Mail Connector is transferring mail from Exchange Server to MS Mail.

FIG. 31.24

A message from an MS Mail user with the properties page displaying the custom recipient definition for the sender.

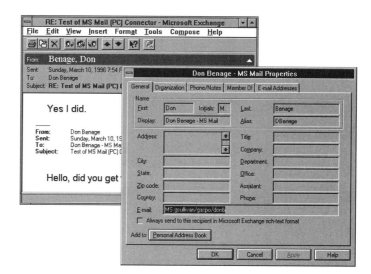

Configuring the Internet Mail Service

The Internet Mail Service (IMS) is a gateway capable of connecting Exchange Server sites to the Internet or any system that supports Simple Mail Transfer Protocol (SMTP). For successful operation, it depends on the use of Transmission Control Protocol/Internet Protocol (TCP/IP), which must be installed and configured before you configure the IMS. For most organizations, you also need information about the Internet service provider (ISP) you are using. In particular, you need the IP address of the SMTP host that will service the IMS. If you are not familiar with your organization's TCP/IP configuration and the Internet service provider you are using, seek assistance from an administrator who is familiar with this subject matter before you continue.

N O T E The Internet Mail Service was called the Internet Mail Connector (IMC) in Exchange Server 4.0. You may still find references to something called IMC in documentation, Registry keys, and Performance Monitor counters. You can assume that these refer to the newly renamed Internet Mail Service. ▨

Like the MS Mail (PC) Connector you just learned about, IMS requires a number of steps for proper installation. To ensure success, you should perform the steps in the order they are given. A complete discussion of the IMS and all its options is beyond the scope of this book. This section presents a basic configuration scenario suitable for small- to medium-sized organizations. If you require advanced configuration information, consult Chapter 11, "Using the Internet Mail Service," in the *Exchange Server Administrator's Guide*.

The following steps are necessary to set up the Internet Mail Service. Each one is covered in detail in the following sections.

1. Gather information about the IP addressing used for your network. Find out if you use a Domain Name Service (DNS) to resolve IP addresses to their host names. Obtain the IP address(es) of any DNS servers. If you are not using DNS, find out who creates and controls the location and distribution of HOSTS files. Find out the domain name and host name for the computer on which you will create the IMS.

2. Gather information about SMTP addressing and hosts. What is the SMTP address for your site? What are the IP addresses of any SMTP hosts that will service the IMS?

3. If it has not already been done, install and configure TCP/IP on the Windows NT server that you will use for the IMS and any additional servers on which it may be required.

4. Add the IMS computer to the DNS, or to the HOSTS file(s) if a DNS is not being used.

5. Configure the IMS using its dialog box in the Exchange Administrator.

6. Start the IMS service and test its operation.
   ▶ **See** "Why Use TCP/IP?," **p. 251**
   ▶ **See** "Name Resolution in the TCP/IP Environment," **p. 280**

Update the DNS or HOSTS Files

When you have collected the necessary information regarding addressing, protocols, and hosts, you are ready to begin. If you are installing and using TCP/IP for the first time, see Chapter 9, "Using TCP/IP with Windows NT Server," for procedures to install and configure TCP/IP. You will also find Chapter 10, "Name Resolution with TCP/IP," very helpful in understanding the role of DNS for resolving domain names and IP addresses. Make sure that you have successfully configured your computers and that the method you have selected for IP address/name resolution is functioning. You should be able to use the TCP/IP diagnostic utility PING to bounce a packet off the SMTP host at your ISP and/or your IMS Server in addition to your DNS server(s) if you are using DNS. You should be able to PING by IP address or host name.

If you use one or more DNS servers, you need to add the computer you will use for the IMS to the DNS servers. There are a variety of implementations for DNS. Windows NT Server provides DNS capabilities starting with version 4.0. All DNS implementations are similar but can contain slight variations. Consult a local expert or the administrator's guide for the DNS in use at your site to verify the exact syntax and options available. The following steps serve as a guide. Instructions for configuring the Windows NT Server DNS are included, as well as generic instructions that should work for most DNS servers. If your DNS is operated by your ISP, discuss with them the appropriate information to update their DNS.

To add the new IMS server to a Windows NT Server DNS, follow these steps:

1. Launch the Windows NT DNS Manager utility.
2. Open the server list and find the domain name to which you want to add records. Highlight the domain name (e.g., company.com).
3. Select DNS, New Record from the menu. The New Resource Record dialog box displays (see Figure 31.25).

Part
VI

Ch
31

FIG. 31.25
You use the New Resource Record dialog box to add records to the DNS.

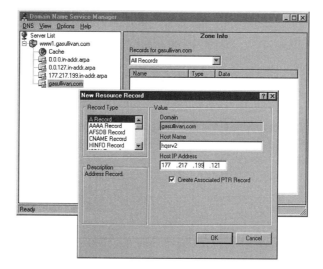

4. Select A Record (an Address record) in the Record Type list. This will contain the IP address and Fully Qualified Domain Name of the IMS computer.
5. Enter the name of the IMS server in the Host Name text box.
6. Enter the IMS server's IP address in the Host IP Address text box.
7. Click the OK button.
8. Again, select DNS, New Record from the menu. The New Resource Record dialog box displays.

9. Select MX Record in the Record Type list box. The MX (mail exchanger) record will specify a computer that will process or forward mail for the domain name specified.

10. Leave the (optional) Host Name blank.

11. Enter the name of the IMS server in the Mail Exchange Server DNS Name text box.

12. Enter a preference number (for example, 10).

13. Click the OK button.

To add the server you will use for IMS to your DNS, follow these steps (if you do not use DNS, see the later procedure for adding the IMS computer to your HOSTS files):

1. Add an A (address) record that contains the IP address and Fully Qualified Domain Name of the IMS computer. For example, using a host name of infosrv2, a domain name of gasullivan.com, and a (sample) IP address of 111.11.11.11, the A record for a typical DNS looks something like this:

```
infosrv2.gasullivan.com    IN A 111.11.11.11
111.11.11.IN_Addr    IN PTR infosrv2.gasullivan.com
```

2. Add an MX (mail exchanger) record to specify each computer that will process mail for the site. This entry contains the SMTP address for your site, as well as the IMS computer. If the SMTP address for the site is external2.gasullivan.com, the entry for a typical DNS should look something like this:

```
external2.gasullivan.com. IN MX 10 infosrv2.gasullivan.com.
```

If your entire organization uses the same IMS computer, the MX record should look like this:

```
gasullivan.com. IN MX 10 infosrv2.gasullivan.com.
```

3. Add an entry with the host and domain name and the IP address of the IMS computer.

To add the server you will use for the IMS to your HOSTS files, follow these steps (this is not necessary if you use DNS servers):

1. A sample HOSTS file is included in the \WINNT\SYSTEM32\DRIVERS\ETC directory. You can update this file directly. It should be left in this location to function properly. It can be edited with Notepad or any text editor capable of editing standard text files.

2. Add an entry with the host and domain name and the IP address of the IMS computer. For example, using a host name of infosrv2, a domain name of gasullivan.com, and a (sample) IP address of 111.11.11.11 the entry would look like this:

```
111.11.11.11    infosrv2.gasullivan.com
```

You should now be able to PING the computer you will use as your IMS server by IP address or host name.

Configuring the Internet Mail Service

The source files for the Internet Mail Service are installed by default when you are using the Enterprise Edition of Exchange Server, but it is not set up on any of your servers. In this section, you learn how to install IMS on a server and configure it so that it is ready to use. A wizard has been added in Exchange Server 5.0 to assist with this process. Although the exact dialog boxes that you see may vary slightly from the following figures (if you make different choices to reflect the needs of your environment), this example provides you with a good example of how this process works.

To add IMS to a server, follow these steps:

1. Start the Exchange Administrator.

2. In the container area (the left pane) of the display, find the site that will contain the IMS. Click the plus sign to the left of the site name to expand the display if it is not already open. Click the plus sign to the left of the Configuration object to expand its display.

3. Highlight the Connections object.

4. Select File, New Other, Internet Mail Service from the menu. This launches the Internet Mail Wizard (see Figure 31.26).

FIG. 31.26

The Internet Mail Wizard provides a checklist of tasks, gathers information about your install-ation, and then installs IMS.

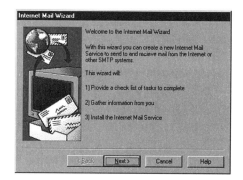

5. Click Next. A checklist of items that need to be done before you continue with the Wizard is presented (see Figure 31.27).

FIG. 31.27

This dialog box has a convenient checklist of items that must precede the installation of IMS.

6. Click <u>N</u>ext. Enter the name of the server on which you want to install IMS. If you intend to use the Remote Access Service (RAS) to send Internet mail through a dial-up connection, click the check box labeled Allow Internet Mail Through a <u>D</u>ial-Up Connection.

7. Click <u>N</u>ext. On the resulting dialog box, indicate which Internet mail addresses will be serviced by this IMS. The typical choice is <u>A</u>ll Addresses.

8. Click <u>N</u>ext. The next dialog box specifies the site address used to generate Internet mail addresses for your users. Enter your site address (e.g., **@company.com**).

9. Click <u>N</u>ext. Specify the administrator's mailbox that will receive Non-Delivery Reports (NDRs). The default creates and/or uses a mailbox named Administrator.

10. Click <u>N</u>ext. You are prompted to enter the password for the service account (see Figure 31.28). Enter the password.

FIG. 31.28

Use this dialog box to confirm the password for the service account that establishes the account context under which the IMS will run.

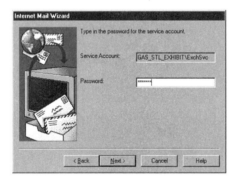

11. Click <u>N</u>ext. The Wizard should be done gathering information and ready to install your IMS. Click <u>F</u>inish. A series of dialog boxes inform you of the progress as IMS is installed and the service is started. A final dialog box indicates that the installation process has succeeded.

There may be additional configuration required for your Internet Mail Service. The next section describes how to make additional changes to the default IMS configuration. These changes can be made immediately, or at any later time as necessary.

To configure the IMS, follow these steps:

1. Start the Exchange Administrator.

2. In the container area (the left pane) of the display, find the site that will contain the IMS. Click the plus sign to the left of the site name to expand the display if it is not already open. Click the plus sign to the left of the Configuration object to expand its display.

3. Highlight the Connections object. In the contents area, double-click the Internet Mail Service object. The dialog box for the Internet Mail Service displays. Click the Internet Mail tab if it is not already displayed (see Figure 31.29).

FIG. 31.29

The Internet Mail tab of the dialog box for the IMS is used to select an administrator's mailbox for non-delivery report (NDR) notifications and to set message content options.

4. Click Change and select a recipient to use for the administrator's mailbox. This mailbox will receive NDR notifications. Click OK to return to the Internet Mail tab.

5. Next, look at the Message Content Information box at the bottom of the dialog box. Select the method IMS should use to format the contents, or *message bodies*, of messages containing special formatting, such as bold, italic, colors, fonts, attachments, or embedded OLE objects. These messages require 8-bit character data, often referred to as a *binary file*, rather than the 7-bit character data used by ASCII text files. Such files do not generally travel through the Internet undamaged. Some of the components making up the Internet were not designed to process 8-bit data.

N O T E The IMS supports both MIME and UUEncode. Multipurpose Internet Mail Extensions (MIME) is the current standard for sending rich message types on the Internet. UUEncode (and UUDecode) are utilities designed originally for UNIX systems to prepare messages for transmission by converting them entirely to 7-bit data. The IMS and Exchange Server can automatically convert outgoing messages to either format and decode either format for incoming messages. You should probably use MIME as your default encoding scheme unless your organization exchanges messages primarily with other systems using UUEncode/UUDecode. Whatever option you select, it can be changed on a per-message basis by choosing File, Send Options from the menu after composing a message. ▪

6. Click the Connections tab (see Figure 31.30). In the Message Delivery box, you can specify whether outbound messages should be routed using DNS for resolution, or if all messages should be routed to the same host. If you are using an Internet service provider and all outbound SMTP addresses will be routed through a single host at your provider, select the option labeled Forward All Messages to Host and enter the IP address of the SMTP host in the text box.

FIG. 31.30

The Connections tab defines the connections between the IMS and other SMTP hosts.

7. Click the Address Space tab (see Figure 31.31). Create address space entries for all e-mail addresses to be routed through this connector. For example, if all SMTP messages will be routed through this connector, click the New Internet button and define an address containing a single asterisk (*), the multi-character wild card in address space names. This causes all messages addressed to SMTP recipients to be routed through this connector.

FIG. 31.31

Use the Address Space tab to enter template addresses that indicate which outgoing messages are to be sent using this service.

8. Click OK to return to the Address Space tab. Then click OK again to save your selections and configure the IMS.

Testing the Internet Mail Service

Now you are ready to test the IMS. You need the SMTP address of at least one recipient with Internet mail capabilities. This should not be a problem. With the explosion of interest in the Internet, many people now have their Internet addresses on their business cards. You must create a custom recipient in the directory using the Exchange Administrator or create an entry in your Personal Address Book.

Start the Exchange Client. Compose a message addressed to the new custom recipient and click the Send button. Now all you have to do is wait. You should either receive a reply or an NDR notification. If you receive an NDR, use the information provided to help diagnose what is not working properly. Look for the easy things first. Are you sure that the address was entered correctly? You also can enable the extensive logging and message tracking capabilities of Exchange Server to make sure that the appropriate routing is occurring within your organization. You also might consider using a link monitor to make sure that the connection between your site and your Internet service provider is remaining active.

▶ **See** "Setting Up Custom Recipients," **p. 950**

▶ **See** "Monitoring Your Site," **p. 1027**

Part
VI

Ch
31

From Here...

In this chapter, you learned how to install, configure, and use Exchange Server's advanced security. You learned how to use the sophisticated security features of Exchange Server to safeguard sensitive information and ensure the integrity of your messages. You also learned how to connect your Exchange Server system to Microsoft Mail (PC) systems and the Internet.

See the following chapters for related information:

■ For information on Exchange Server client software, see Chapter 28, "Using Exchange Client Applications."

■ For more on creating public folders, replicating public folders, and managing directory information, see Chapter 29, "Distributing Information with Exchange Server."

■ To learn about the database component of Microsoft BackOffice, SQL Server, see Chapter 33, "An Inside Look at SQL Server."

■ For an in-depth discussion on the host connectivity component of Microsoft BackOffice, SNA Server, see Chapter 39, "SNA Server Preparation and Installation."

■ For information on the systems management component of Microsoft BackOffice, Systems Management Server (SMS), see Chapter 42, "Preparing for SMS."

SQL Server

CHAPTER 32

An Inside Look at Relational Databases

by Greg Sullivan

SQL Server is fundamentally different from most database products that are familiar to PC users, such as Microsoft Access. SQL Server is an industrial strength RDBMS which you can use to manage information for organizations both small and large. In order to use it effectively, you must have an understanding of RDBMS principles. In addition to being able to use SQL Server more effectively, you can avoid making mistakes and wasting time if you prepare for SQL Server use with some background material.

If you are already familiar with RDBMS technology, and understand how these database products are implemented in PC-based networks, you may want to skim this chapter or even skip it entirely. If this subject matter is new to you, the time you invest in learning the material presented in this chapter will provide rich dividends as you implement SQL Server in the next chapter. ■

Definition of a relational database management system

Learn the fundamental characteristics of a relational database management system (RDBMS) and how SQL Server satisfies these characteristics.

The role of the database administrator

See what the roles and responsibilities of a database administrator are with respect to relational database management.

The database design process

Learn how to design databases properly so that they can be efficiently implemented using SQL Server.

How database design impacts SQL Server

Discover how the effectiveness of your database design impacts your success with SQL Server.

What Is a Relational Database Management System?

A relational database management system (RDBMS) is a software product that structures data in accordance with the relational data model and permits data manipulation based on relational algebra. Users are protected from the low-level technical details associated with manipulating the data because the physical aspects of data management are handled by the RDBMS. See "The Relational Data Model" later in this chapter for more information on data modeling.

The framework of the RDBMS is a collection of tables, consisting of rows and columns, views, indexes, and other objects with related data. SQL provides all the data-definition and update capabilities needed in any database language. With SQL statements, you can create new tables and views, add new data, modify existing data, and perform other functions. Figure 32.1 shows examples of views on relational database tables.

FIG. 32.1

A relational database is a collection of tables.

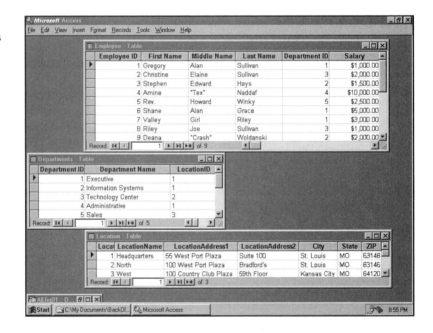

The first, and most important, function of an RDBMS is to provide a means for storing, retrieving, and updating data. Database management systems, in general, were originally conceived to provide an organized way to structure data. By structuring data, the job of managing interaction with the data was simplified.

The basic premise of RDBMS products is to separate data-management functions from application functions. This concept works well when combined with the client-server process model or the I-net process model. The job of data management is isolated to the RDBMS, which is a service provider, or server in the client-server sense, which also applies in the I-net process model. The RDBMS is implemented on a Windows NT platform as a server-based *service*. Applications request data-management services from the RDBMS and process the response. Data-management services include, at a minimum, the capability to define and manipulate data.

Data Definition and Manipulation

With any database management system, you desire the capability to perform the following tasks:

- Define the structure of a database
- Manipulate the database

To define and manipulate a database, it is necessary to have a means for communicating instructions to the database management system. This facility is typically provided via a programming language. Two types of language are necessary to support these activities:

- Data Definition Language (DDL)
- Data Manipulation Language (DML)

In the case of RDBMS products, the DDL and the DML are both provided by the same language—Structured Query Language (SQL). SQL uses relations, and the rules of relational algebra, to transform input into the desired output.

What Is SQL?   SQL is the industry-standard language by which applications communicate with RDBMSes and is the de facto standard on all computing platforms, from mainframes to PCs.

SQL has a long history dating back to the late 1970s. Although many commercial versions of SQL were available during the 1980s, the first SQL standard was not developed until 1986. ANSI and the International Standards Organization (ISO) combined to create this first standard. It was enhanced in 1989 and took on the name SQL-89. Since that time, ISO released a new standard in 1992 known as SQL-92, or SQL2. Currently under development is SQL3, which is significantly more comprehensive than SQL2. SQL also has been formally adopted as an international standard by the International Electrotechnical Commission (IEC) and as a Federal Information Processing Standard (FIPS) for the United States federal government.

SQL is a language of relationships, and these relationships transform user inputs into desired outputs. As an RDBMS communication language, SQL is viewed as a high-level language because queries are English-like in form. SQL queries also are described as non-procedural in form because the user determines what information is necessary to be retrieved, not how to retrieve it. The RDBMS controls manipulation of the database and determines the best data-retrieval method. SQL queries gather sets of data, unlike languages with the capability to return only one record at a time.

▶ **See** "isql and ISQL/w," **p. 1152**

Part

VII

Ch

32

A database language standard provides portability of database definitions and database application programs among conforming environments. Where there is interchange of database information between systems, using a database language standard is appropriate. To support the relational data model, the structures and operations implemented by the RDBMS are defined. Additional components that support data definition, data access, security, programming language interface, and data administration are also defined. SQL is the standard for database applications requiring flexibility in data structures and access paths to the database.

SQL supports data definition by allowing you to communicate the structure of a relational database to the RDBMS. Data definition provides the capability to define the following:

- Table names
- Column names
- Datatypes
- User privileges
- Valid or allowable data values

SQL also provides facilities for data manipulation, including the following:

- Querying the database for data retrieval
- Adding data to the database
- Updating data in the database
- Removing data from the database

With an RDBMS, it is possible to create new tables from existing tables. These new tables can be created through the use of *unions*, *intersections*, or *joins*. A union of two tables creates a third table containing all rows that are either in the first table, the second, or both. An intersection produces a table with rows from the first table that are identical to rows in a second table. To produce a join table, rows in the two tables that have identical values in corresponding columns are used to populate the new table (see Figure 32.2).

▶ **See** "Creating Databases and Database Objects," **p. 1183**

FIG. 32.2
Tables can be joined by linking identical values from columns with corresponding information. This figure shows connections between columns that contain linking values.

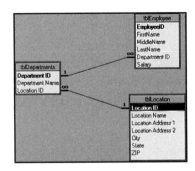

SQL Server provides these basic functions through a language called Transact-SQL. This language is an extension of SQL. As such, it contains all the features of SQL along with several enhancements in support of specific SQL Server features.

Extensions to SQL   Transact-SQL is the language at the heart of Microsoft SQL Server. Transact-SQL provides a control-of-flow language enhancement, designed to extend the power of ANSI-standard SQL. Transact-SQL supports the requirements of mission-critical applications and reduces the need for a more complex programming language to accomplish a desired task. The enhancements provide a powerful programming language to boost system performance, provide stringent data integrity, and efficiently perform complex data manipulation.

ACID

Users interact with the RDBMS by making requests for database management services. Each request equates to a unit of work for the RDBMS. These units of work are referred to as *transactions*. Each transaction typically requires multiple operations on the database to complete it in its entirety.

A single unit of work, or transaction, can be handled easily by any commercial RDBMS. Complexities arise in situations where there are multiple, concurrent users of the same database. In this situation, it is possible for users to simultaneously request operations on the same elements of data. An important property of the RDBMS is to ensure the successful completion of each transaction while providing protection of the data.

This property is often referred to as *ACID*. In 1983, Andreas Reuter used this term to describe the following:

Part
VII

Ch
32

- Atomicity
- Consistency
- Isolation
- Durability

RDBMS products must possess all these characteristics.

Atomicity   When users submit transactions to the RDBMS, they are interested in knowing whether all the operations associated with the transaction completed successfully. If any one operation failed, then the user would prefer to be notified of the failure and have the database returned to its state prior to any of the transaction operations being performed. This all-or-nothing property is referred to as *atomicity*.

To provide this capability, RDBMS products record each operation associated with a transaction in a log file. At the beginning of a transaction, a marker is placed in the log file indicating that a transaction is beginning. Thereafter, each operation is recorded in the log file until all operations are complete. As soon as the last operation is complete, the RDBMS marks the transaction as complete, or *committed*. If a problem occurs, the transaction log is used to *roll back* the transaction.

Consistency   If a failure occurs at any time during the execution of transaction operations, the transaction cannot complete successfully. In this situation, the RDBMS must *undo* the operations it has completed up to the point of failure in the transaction. Ensuring that the database is never left in a corrupt state, even in the event of a transaction failure, is known as *consistency*.

Transaction logging and recovery provide the means for fulfilling this requirement of an RDBMS. If all operations of a transaction are not completed, the RDBMS goes back through the log file, up to the beginning-of-transaction marker, and undoes each operation. This action is known as *rollback and recovery*.

Isolation   The most typical use of an RDBMS today involves multiple, simultaneous users. These users are concurrently attached to the RDBMS and requesting services at the same time. Occasionally, multiple users request at the same time operations on the same element of data. The characteristic of RDBMS products that protects users from operating on the same data at the same time is referred to as *isolation*.

The way an RDBMS addresses the problem is by *locking* the element of data for which the operation is being requested. The data element is locked prior to the operation's being performed and subsequently unlocked after the operation is completed.

The *lock* is typically a logical construct that prevents other users from performing some operation on the element of data for the duration of the lock. In this manner, locked users are protected from operating on data which is incomplete because it may be in the middle of being operated upon.

Deep inside every RDBMS is a set of processes that manages concurrency through the implementation of a locking scheme. The job of the RDBMS is to avoid situations that may arise due to concurrent use of the same data.

One such example is the case of *deadlocks*. This situation arises when one user is awaiting a lock to clear on an element of data while another user is awaiting a lock to clear on an element of data that is locked by the first user. These two users would wait forever for each other's lock to clear. The RDBMS concurrency management function detects this situation, allows one user to proceed, and returns an error to the other user. Other such situations also are handled by the RDBMS to allow users to successfully complete each of their desired operations.

Although this may seem like a simple idea, it is fraught with complexities. Many of the complexities lie in the physical aspects of protecting data stored in the database. Other complications arise because transactions typically involve operations on multiple elements of data at the same time.

Isolation is the property of RDBMS products that ensures that each transaction is performed as if the requesting user were the only user of the RDBMS. Furthermore, each transaction must be performed without interfering with any other transactions being completed at the same time.

Durability   The *durability* property of an RDBMS ensures that the effects of a transaction are permanent. If the RDBMS fails for any reason, including a system crash, the database should include the impact of all completed transactions after restart. Incomplete transactions should not be reflected in any way.

Security

Every organization has an interest in protecting the data stored in its databases. Some data contains confidential information and should not be viewable by certain individuals or groups of individuals. Other data may not be as confidential but is critical information that must be safe from change or damage.

SQL Server provides a means to protect data in these situations. Protection is offered at various levels of the relational data model. In SQL Server, it is possible to secure each identifiable element of data, including tables, rows, columns, and individual fields.

Four types of privileges can be granted:

- Read
- Add
- Update
- Delete

For each element of data, you may assign any or all of these privileges to any given user. In doing so, you establish a security matrix. The rows represent users, the columns represent data elements, and the cells indicate the permitted operations.

The administrator responsible for security should create and manage the security matrix. This is most often the database administrator. See "What Does a DBA Do?" later in the chapter for a thorough discussion of the DBA's responsibilities.

▶ **See** "Using SQL Server Security," **p. 1227**

Part
VII

Ch
32

Distribution Services

Many organizations must physically distribute data across several locations or interact with data from external sources. Usually, you might think of an RDBMS as managing the data within the databases it controls. Given the need to distribute data, however, this notion is obsolete. See the section "Data Distribution" later in the chapter for more information.

One of the more important features expected from modern-day RDBMS products is the capability to manage distributed data. It may be necessary to spread the data across physically separate servers for capacity or performance reasons. It also may be necessary to distribute copies of data to get it closer to the users who need it. Many complications arise when databases are distributed to different physical servers, each with their own RDBMS, in potentially very different locations.

Consequently, it is desirable for an RDBMS to be able to synchronize with one or more instances of a similar RDBMS on another server on the network. In this sense, *synchronization* refers to copying an element of data to the required additional server(s) whenever that element changes. If an RDBMS provides this service, it is said to be able to *replicate* data.

Replication is an important feature of an RDBMS. It also is desirable for a given RDBMS product to be able to replicate to and from competing RDBMS products. In this way, your RDBMS can exist in a heterogeneous computing environment and share data with other database management systems.

▶ **See** "An Introduction to Data Replication," **p. 1244**

N O T E   The capability to distribute data through replication in a manner transparent to users is an important characteristic of modern RDBMS products. It is nice to be able to distribute data across multiple database servers, each running a separate RDBMS. However, it may not be useful if users are required to know the location of every element of data they want to view or modify. Transparency implies that the data is available to users as if it all existed on the same database server. In other words, it should be "transparent" to the user that data is located in multiple physical locations. ▪

Administration Utilities

Many activities are associated with the operation and management of an RDBMS. Database administrators perform these activities, as well as determine and set appropriate configuration parameters for the RDBMS.

To facilitate the convenient administration of an RDBMS, it is customary for RDBMS products to be delivered with a set of administration tools. These tools exist in the form of applications that interact with the RDBMS. The activities supported by these administration tools include the following:

- Configuring the RDBMS
- Setting up users
- Granting user privileges
- Monitoring and performance tuning
- Troubleshooting problems

Much of the administration can be performed from client PCs. This enables administrators to manage the operation of their database management system using a desktop computer. In addition to the administration tools provided by the RDBMS vendor, the open architecture of RDBMS products allows the development of third-party administration tools.

▶ **See** "Surveying the Available Tools," **p. 1146**

What Does a DBA Do?

The database administrator (DBA) is responsible for managing the organization's data, including the hardware, software, tools, and human resources associated with managing data. The DBA typically reports to top-level information systems management and has the authority to make decisions about the application of resources, human and capital, to the business of managing the organization's data. The DBA's domain of responsibility for data management normally encompasses the entire organization.

In small organizations, the DBA role may be only a portion of an individual's overall responsibilities. In such cases, the DBA also may be the network administrator, among other duties. It is most important that someone be assigned responsibility for carrying out DBA functions. In larger organizations, a dedicated person or a team of people performs the role of DBA. For purposes of this discussion, the term DBA applies equally to both situations. Regardless of the size of the organization, all the responsibilities of the DBA must be carried out by someone or some group of people.

N O T E Someone in the organization must perform the role of the DBA. Many organizations overlook the significance of database administration and, therefore, assume that it can be performed by off-site staff or via external support. This attitude eventually leads to serious problems as the organization relies more heavily on the RDBMS to support production systems. ▨

Part

VII

Ch

32

DBA roles and responsibilities divide into two major categories:

- Administrative
- Technical

Administrative functions focus on those aspects of database administration external to the physical act of managing the database, whereas technical functions center on the hardware, software, and data.

Administrative Functions

The DBA is responsible for preparing the database environment, as well as managing its operation. Preparing for a database environment includes dealing with the organization's personnel and technical vendors.

Standards and Procedures Database management and usage should be performed in accordance with a set of standards and procedures. It is the DBA's responsibility to develop these policies. In this manner, all database administrators and users should follow a consistent set of guidelines and operate under a similar set of expectations. Some examples of standards and procedures that the DBA should develop are the following:

- Security policies
- Backup and archival procedures
- Disaster recovery procedures

RDBMS, Tool, and Vendor Selection   The DBA should be responsible for selecting which RDBMS products will be used in the organization. In addition to selecting the RDBMS, the DBA selects associated tools, such as administration and design packages. It also may be the DBA's responsibility to select product vendors and carry out negotiations for the acquisition of these products.

Security   The DBA is responsible for the security of the database. This is one of the most important DBA responsibilities. Management typically views the DBA as the "protector of the data." As such, the DBA selects the database security model, assigns user privileges with respect to the database, and monitors database access among the many activities associated with securing a database.

▶ **See** "Choosing a Security Model," **p. 1164**

Capacity Management   As more applications use the RDBMS and more users manipulate the database, some aspect of RDBMS operation will be overtaxed. It may be that the database has grown beyond the size of available storage capacity. It may be that the number of users has increased to the point where the RDBMS can no longer respond to each user in a reasonable amount of time.

In either case, it becomes apparent that some aspect of the RDBMS has exceeded its capacity. In the first example, the storage device restricts the growth of the database. In the second example, the RDBMS server memory or processor utilization has exceeded reasonable limits of operation.

▶ **See** "Planning Disk Space Usage," **p. 1159**

The DBA has the responsibility of repairing these situations when they occur. More important, the DBA must make sure that these situations never arise by anticipating future needs and configuring servers accordingly.

Backup and Recovery   After an organization becomes dependent on the RDBMS, users expect it to work all the time. Unfortunately, the RDBMS, or the hardware upon which it operates, will eventually fail. When this occurs, it is necessary to return to normal operation as quickly as possible.

To accommodate this situation, the DBA must make a copy of the database at regular intervals. This activity is known as *backing up* the database. The frequency of backups should be dictated by the nature of the data (e.g., historical, mission-critical, private) or the frequency of change of the data (hourly, daily, weekly, etc.). At the time of failure, the DBA can simply restore the database to its state at the time of the last backup.

▶ **See** "Backing Up and Restoring Data," **p. 1234**

Copies of the database should be stored in off-site locations, as well as at the same physical location as the RDBMS. This allows the DBA to restore normal operations even in the event of a disaster in which the entire computing environment is damaged. This responsibility of the DBA is referred to as *disaster recovery*.

Technical Functions

In addition to preparing the database environment, the DBA must manage its operation. These types of activities tend to be hands-on.

Development, Test, and Production Environments Applications usually exist in various states throughout their life cycles. After an application is designed, it is placed into development. During its creation, the application is in the hands of a developer, or a team of developers, who builds the application. Similar to how contractors construct a building, application developers first assemble the foundation, create the structure, and, finally, complete each module. While an application is under construction, developers need access to the RDBMS for testing purposes. The RDBMS designated for application development is known as the *development database server*.

After the application has been assembled and all its individual components have been tested, it is advisable to test the entire application. This testing should be performed in a computing environment similar to the environment in which the application will eventually be put into operation. The RDBMS designated for application testing is known as the *test database server*.

Finally, if the application has passed all tests, it can be placed into production use. It then will be installed onto the production computing environment for operation. The RDBMS designated for live application operation is known as the *production database server*.

> **N O T E** It is necessary to establish separate computing environments for application development, application testing, and application operation. ■

Part

VII

Ch

32

The RDBMS on each database server operates on its own physical data. While it is logically possible to have a single database server (and its own RDBMS) perform each of these roles, it is not recommended to do so. Instead, the development database server, the test database server, and the production database server should all be separate servers physically, each with their own RDBMS.

Many organizations overlook the significance of setting up separate database servers for each of these situations. Application users will be annoyed if application testers take down the RDBMS to test the outcome of a different server configuration. Application testers may also become annoyed with developer experimentation on the RDBMS. These three different groups of people will frequently interfere with one another if they use the same database server; therefore, it is advisable to establish three physically distinct computers for these tasks.

▶ **See** "A Sample Network Architecture," **p. 1137**

Support Application developers and users require assistance from time to time when using SQL Server. An important role of the DBA is to provide support and guidance to developers and users as their needs dictate. At a minimum, the DBA should be responsible for suggesting resources for developers and users to consult for answers to their questions.

Performance Measurement and Tuning   After an application is placed into production, users frequently encounter unacceptable levels of performance. This usually occurs the first time the application is tested and eventually occurs as characteristics of the database change, such as its size. When the performance of the database diminishes, the DBA is called upon to adjust the operational characteristics of the RDBMS to improve performance. This activity is known as *performance tuning*.

As applications are being tested for the first time, developers require the support of the DBA to "get the most" out of the RDBMS. This is a normal part of the process for developing client-server or I-net applications using RDBMS products. The DBA is normally involved in this process.

After applications are placed into production, it is common for developers to move on to other projects or, in some cases, to other jobs. In such cases, the original developers are no longer available to adjust performance characteristics of an application. Because most applications encounter a performance problem sooner or later, the DBA must get involved. In these situations, the DBA inspects the behavior of the application and adjusts the RDBMS to, hopefully, improve performance. At a minimum, the DBA should make recommendations for application improvements that developers can later address.

▶ **See** "Tuning SQL Server," **p. 1236**

Database Design   The topic of whether a DBA should perform database design is frequently debated. The ideal DBA should be capable of doing database design. It is essential that the DBA be qualified in this area to effectively administer the RDBMS.

Nevertheless, many organizations assign DBA responsibilities to individuals with no database design experience. In these situations, conflicts often arise between application developers and the DBA as to how the RDBMS should be configured. Moreover, the DBA can potentially lose control of his/her primary responsibility—the data.

Ideally, your DBA will not only be qualified in database design, but also be the chief database designer in your organization.

Process Model Architecture   Just as the DBA should be qualified for database design, the DBA must also be qualified in the area of application architecture. To do so, the DBA must be an expert on the client-server process model and the I-net process model, and fully understand relational database concepts. See "Technical Underpinnings" later in this chapter for a complete discussion of these topics.

▶ **See** "Selecting Protocols for Client-Server Computing," **p. 1165**

When client-server or I-net applications are developed, some of the processes execute on the RDBMS. In some situations, the DBA is responsible for the development of these server-based processes. At a minimum, the DBA should be responsible for the design decisions that dictate which processes execute on the RDBMS server and which should execute on the client workstation.

Ultimately, the DBA is responsible for performance of the RDBMS server. If the server is overburdened with application processes, then it will have insufficient processing power to manage the database. Again, it is the DBA's responsibility to understand, manage, and possibly develop the server processes.

Designing Databases

Through the continued advancement of database technology and the competition of the open market, more sophisticated uses of data and information become possible and desirable. Without modeling the organization's use of its data and keeping your model current, significant losses are possible. This is due to the continued constraints of currently installed database technologies, when new technology may allow a wider and more profitable use of the data. In addition, if you wait until after system upgrades are implemented to construct and update data models, it becomes extremely costly and difficult to implement database structure changes. For these reasons, database design—and data modeling—should be a key focus when you plan strategies to meet organizational objectives.

Your success with SQL Server will be driven by the effectiveness of your database designs. Now that you have learned what to expect from an RDBMS and the specific features and tools of SQL Server, it is time to explore database design. Database design, and in particular relational database design, is a widely published topic covered in many excellent books and periodicals.

It is beyond the scope of this book to provide a comprehensive coverage of relational database design. However, it is useful to understand relational database design issues as they apply to SQL Server before jumping into the product itself. If you are a relational database expert, this can serve as a review. If you are new to relational databases, it serves as an introduction. You are encouraged to pursue these important topics apart from this book.

Part
VII

Ch
32

Technical Underpinnings

The most successful database designers understand the principles of underlying technologies. Database designers must fully comprehend these principles:

- The client-server process model
- The I-net process model
- Relational database management systems
- Relational database design
- Distributed systems architecture

Current and aspiring database designers also should be well-versed in object-oriented technology. The popular RDBMS vendors, including Microsoft, tend to move their products more toward object-oriented database management with each new release. Although you will rarely hear a major RDBMS vendor refer to its product as an Object Oriented Database Management System (OODBMS), you will notice that the RDBMS products include more and more object oriented features with each new release.

The Relational Data Model   Relational database concepts are based on a branch of mathematics known as relational algebra. It is not necessary to be an expert in relational algebra to be successful with relational database design and implementation. However, those who are adept at mathematics tend to traverse the learning curves associated with applying relational database concepts more quickly than those who are not.

The idea of a relational database first originated in IBM research laboratories in the late 1960s. A researcher, E.F. Codd, set about to address database issues of the day by applying mathematics to the problem. The result of his efforts spawned the popular idea of a relational data model for solving data-management problems.

 T I P   Your knowledge of the principles of the relational data model will influence your success with SQL Server.

In its purest form, the relational data model is simply a foundation for logical modeling. It is commonly misunderstood that at the root of relational database issues is a logical model of the data. Confusion about the relational data model centers on the physical aspects of relational database implementation. These physical implementation issues, such as performance, have little to do with the underlying foundation defined by the relational data model.

Codd's work manifests itself in the form of a relational data model. Relational databases consist of tables with rows and columns. These tables represent *sets* of information. By applying set theory, Codd devised a means for defining which operations can be performed on these sets of data. In turn, this manifestation is what we know as SQL today.

N O T E   Do not confuse Codd's relational data model with your logical data models. Your logical data models are simply an implementation of the theoretical foundation put in place by his work. ▪

SQL Server is an implementation of the relational data model. Microsoft continues to apply the formal aspects of relational theory to the physical implementation of its relational database product. For this reason, it is useful to understand the underlying principles of the relational data model when applying SQL Server to solve your data-management problems.

Client-Server Process Model   Contemporary RDBMS products rely heavily on the client-server process model. It is common for the two to be confused. Many people fail to understand that RDBMS and client-server are two distinct aspects of technology today. RDBMS just happens to be one of the most successful examples of products based on the client-server process model.

In Chapter 1, "An Inside Look at BackOffice," you learned that the fundamental concept of the client-server process model and the I-net process model is to distribute process execution across the computing enterprise. The processes associated with data management are handled by the RDBMS. Popular RDBMS products, such as SQL Server, are delivered as server-based applications.

In turn, the applications you build or purchase that rely on RDBMS also are based on the client-server process model or the I-net process model. This concept manifests itself as process architecture. SQL Server, as do other popular RDBMS products, provides a means for creating processes that can execute on the RDBMS server. The most common type of process that executes on the RDBMS is known as a *stored procedure*.

N O T E A stored procedure is simply a process that executes on the RDBMS. In this manner, it is possible to take advantage of the client-server process model by distributing some of the processing to the server application, which in this case is the RDBMS. ▨

Triggers, or *triggered procedures*, are another example of a type of process supported by SQL Server and other RDBMS products. Triggers, similar to stored procedures, are processes that execute on the RDBMS server application. The difference between triggers and stored procedures is that the execution of a triggered procedure is tied to an event. A triggered procedure executes when a defined event occurs, such as when a data value changes or a table update takes place.

Stored procedures and triggers provide means for placing processes on the RDBMS server application. Your applications also will contain processes that execute on client PCs. These processes interact with the RDBMS for data-management services. As such, your applications rely on the client-server process model and RDBMS services regardless of whether your application is based on the client-server process model or the I-net process model.

Architectural Issues

Successful database designers give ample consideration not only to how the database is structured, but also to how the data is processed and moved. These issues external to the database itself are often referred to as *architectural issues.*

When architects design buildings, they are concerned with, among other things, the functions of the building and the amount of traffic it will bear. They contemplate how many rooms to build, how the rooms should be arranged with respect to one another, how traffic will flow from room to room, and the size of the rooms in comparison to the overall size of the structure.

Database designers have to make similar architectural decisions. In the case of database design, this amounts to determining the following:

- Where, when, and how the data should be processed
- Where, when, and how the data should be distributed
- For what purpose the data exists

Process Model   During database design, it is important to understand the client-server process model, whether you are basing your application on the client-server process model or the I-net process model. You have already seen how this process model manifests itself in SQL Server.

Part
VII

Ch
32

From the perspective of the database designer, process modeling amounts to determining where the data will be processed. On an information network, processes may exist on server computers, such as the computer running SQL Server, and on the client PCs. Some of the important issues that deserve consideration when determining the process model for your application include the following:

■ **Performance.** Typically, server computers possess much more processing capacity than desktop PCs. Because SQL Server is scalable across multiple processors, it is common for the server computers for SQL Server to contain multiple processors. This additional processing power provides some incentive for placing processes on the server computer. On the other side of the coin, you must take into account the number of client PCs that may request the execution of a stored procedure or trigger at the same time. Too many simultaneous requests to execute a server process may overburden the server.

▶ **See** "Tuning SQL Server," **p. 1236**

■ **Network Bandwidth.** Application processes communicate with each other across the network by passing messages back and forth. Client processes generate requests by sending a message to a server process. The server process receives the message, processes the request, and responds with a result. These messages back and forth generate traffic on the network. Consideration must be given to the amount of network traffic created by the interaction defined within your process model. In particular, it is important to understand the amount of network traffic you will generate during peak operating periods. This task is a bit difficult because most networks perform functions other than sending your application's messages back and forth. Your network administrator can assist you in understanding the network implications of your process model.

▶ **See** "Significance of Bandwidth," **p. 72**

■ **Data Integrity.** Isolating data-management rules to processes on the RDBMS is an effective way to preserve the integrity of your data. Those processes that contain the rules by which your organization manages or interprets data are best located in the RDBMS as stored procedures or triggers. This ensures that the rules will be applied consistently because they exist in one place only. Of course, you also should give consideration to the performance implications of placing too many rules on the server.

■ **Maintainability.** A good reason to isolate some processes to the server is that it makes it easier to maintain the application in the future. When you place processes on the RDBMS, as opposed to designing them into each of the client processes, there is only one place to go to make changes. This makes sense so long as each client expects the same behavior of the process. Care must be taken when isolating processes to the server not to penalize client processes by reducing flexibility. Nevertheless, isolating processes to the server can reduce the cost of maintenance.

Even after the most careful consideration of these issues, it is difficult to completely understand exactly how the application will behave once it is constructed and placed into production.

Some techniques are available for predicting performance of a given process model while it still exists on paper. Most of these techniques are somewhat theoretical, however, and difficult to apply.

It is common for application development teams to make their best guess on the process model during design phases. These guesses are based on their experience in similar situations and their understanding of the fundamentals of the underlying technologies. No matter how good a guess is, however, there is always a need to adjust the process model during testing—and sometimes even after the application is placed into production. You should allow for these adjustments to the process model in your work plan during the performance-tuning phase.

 TIP

The process model almost always changes during the performance-tuning phase of application development. You should expect this and, therefore, accommodate it in the development schedule. Developers frequently overlook this when creating work plans for building client-server or I-net applications even though it can sometimes take as long as, or longer than, the software development phase.

Data Distribution   Where should the data be located? Unfortunately, the answer to this question is not as simple as it may seem. In today's world of departmentalized organizations, data exists in many locations and in many forms. Moreover, the same data may exist in multiple locations at the same time. Processed data is frequently sent on to other locations for management reporting purposes.

Few applications today have the luxury of existing in their own world with no need to distribute data. Therefore, it is imperative when designing a database to take into account where, when, and how the data will be distributed. Some of the issues to consider when contemplating data distribution are as follows:

Part
VII
Ch
32

- **Capacity.** Some databases grow so large that they outstrip the storage capacity of the server computer. In other situations, the server computer can accommodate the size of the database but does not perform adequately with so much data to manage. In either case, it is useful to split up the data and physically distribute it across multiple server computers, each operating their own RDBMS. Although this is possible to implement transparently to the users of the data, it is more difficult to administer. Take this into account when contemplating separating data for capacity reasons.

- **Delivery.** Clearly, data should be stored in locations that facilitate its convenient delivery at the time of request. The definition of convenient delivery may be different depending on your perspective. A user prefers to have the data located nearby so that it can be retrieved as quickly as possible, whereas an administrator generally prefers to have the data located in a secure location within the physical domain of the administrator's control. Due to delivery performance requirements, sometimes users in different physical locations all need the same data located at their sites.

Storing the data in a central location is more convenient for the administrator, but it creates a situation in which some users have to wait longer for the data to arrive than others. This is especially true in wide area networks, with users spread across multiple geographic locations. In these cases, it makes sense to place copies of the data at enough locations to accommodate convenient delivery. Therefore, when designing your database, you must decide how many places it must exist to get it where it needs to go as fast as it needs to get there.

■ **Redundancy.** Delivery requirements frequently lead to the need to create copies of the data in other physical locations. How is it possible to have redundant data while preserving the integrity and consistency of the data? The answer to this question lies in a concept known as *replication*. SQL Server, as well as other popular RDBMS products, possesses the capability to "replicate" data in other locations. SQL Server has a built-in replication service that can be applied to any, or all of your data. When you design your database, you must determine how the replication service will manage the distribution of your data in such a manner so as to preserve the integrity and consistency of the data.

Just as with process modeling, it is difficult to accurately predict how the data-distribution plan will affect the behavior of an application. Allow for time during the testing phases to make adjustments to when, where, and how the data is distributed.

T I P   As your application undergoes changes over time, you must contemplate architectural changes, as well. It is a mistake to make significant adjustments to an application without also considering how the data-distribution plan will affect its behavior. Sometimes it is appropriate to change the manner in which data is distributed in response to the changing needs of the users.

▶ **See** "Sample Replication Scenarios," **p. 1246**

Online Transaction Processing and Online Analytical Processing   Presumably, you are storing data in a database for a reason. It makes sense to store and manage the data differently depending on the purpose of the data and the reason for its existence. Today, databases are commonly broken down into two types:

■ Online Transaction Processing (OLTP) databases

■ Online Analytical Processing (OLAP) databases

These two types of databases support distinctly different purposes and, therefore, are designed differently.

OLTP databases are designed and built to support the operations of an organization. Sometimes these types of systems are referred to as *production systems*. The distinguishing feature of a production system is its transactional nature. These databases receive a constant flow of new or updated data with occasional, large bursts of new data or changes to existing data.

OLAP databases, on the other hand, are designed to support decision-making processes. The common term for an OLAP database today is *data warehouse*. A data warehouse is built to accommodate user reporting and ad-hoc queries. The applications that use data warehouses to support decision making and data analysis are frequently referred to as *decision support systems* (DSS).

▶ **See** "Data Warehousing Fundamentals," **p. 1270**

N O T E   One of the most important principles of database design is the separation of OLAP databases from OLTP databases. ▪

Many designers overlook the significance of these two types of databases when designing their applications. OLTP databases should be designed to accommodate the quickest possible input of data into the database. OLAP databases should be designed to accommodate the quickest possible output of data from the database. Remember, OLTP is designed to support production systems (data input), whereas OLAP is designed to support reporting and ad-hoc query activities (data output).

These two types of databases have many differences, which should be accounted for in design. These topics are thoroughly covered in numerous books and a variety of periodicals. For the sake of clarity, however, it may help you now to understand one of the most significant differences.

Decision makers frequently analyze historical data as a part of their thought processes. Retrieving data about the past is necessary to support this task. Therefore, it is often prudent for an organization to retain a fair amount of historical data. It may even make sense to store this data in summarized form, as well as in its original detail, to facilitate faster reporting of summary information.

Historical data and summary data tend to clutter production system databases. The larger a database grows, the less quickly it can accept new data. Those involved with the organization's operations expect their transactions to be accepted quickly and painlessly. As the production database grows, these times tend to increase.

Consequently, it is not wise to burden a production database (OLTP) with all this historical and summary data. It also is not advisable to burden the production database with all the requests for information from the decision makers. The queries against the database also can affect performance for the operations staff.

A better location for historical and summary data is in a separate database (OLAP). This database can be designed and built for the sole purpose of facilitating convenient data retrieval. Decision makers can query this data warehouse without concern for the impact of their query on the production systems. Moreover, the data can be stored in a form more conducive to human analysis.

This example demonstrates one of the important differences between OLTP and OLAP databases. Again, there are many other important reasons for separating production data from reporting data. You are encouraged to pursue this topic further to ensure the best chance for success with your SQL Server database.

Part
VII

Ch
32

Detailed Design Issues

After architects lay out the design for a building, designers arrive to address issues such as appearance and functionality. Such is the case for database designers, as well. After the architectural decisions have been put into place, it is necessary to move into the details:

- Which design tools will be used?
- To what extent will normalization be enforced?
- How will data integrity be preserved?
- How will the data be modeled?
- Which indexing techniques will be applied?

Design Tools   Much as a writer uses a word processor to create a document for recording ideas, a database designer uses a database design tool. Database design tools are sometimes referred to as *computer-aided software engineering* (*CASE*) *tools*. CASE tools exist for activities other than database design, as well.

Database designers use CASE tools to record their ideas and produce design documentation. In relational database design, this implies that the design tool is capable of generating a diagram of the data entities and their corresponding relationships. This is known as an *entity-relationship* (*E-R*) *diagram*. Most popular database design tools support the creation of E-R diagrams, among other design documents.

In addition to design documentation, some CASE tools prepare the source code to create or update the physical database. This source code is created in the DDL for the database of your choice. This function is also known as *schema generation*.

Other CASE tools go far beyond design documentation and schema generation by producing application source code. Given an appropriate amount of information, the tools may be able to create header file definitions for database classes to be used in the application source code. They also may go so far as to generate source code for stored procedures and triggers, based on the rules the tool interprets from the relationships you have defined in your data model.

After the data model is designed in a CASE tool and the schema is generated, you can create your database in SQL Server. As time goes on, you may choose to alter the database layout in SQL Server. If you only change it in SQL Server, the database will become out of sync with the data model in your CASE tool. It is important you always keep your data model in sync with your SQL Server database as this will ensure a stable, well-documented database that will withstand future adjustments and enhancements.

Most CASE tools do not support incremental changes to the data model. If your CASE tool does not automatically re-synchronize the data model with the physical database, you must do so yourself. Regrettably, the task of updating the data model in the CASE tool while keeping it in sync with the database is "manual." To do this job yourself, you must change the data model in the CASE tool, generate the new database definition, export the data, create a new database based on the new definition, and reload the data from the previous database.

Some sophisticated CASE tools automate portions of this task. Other CASE tools promise to provide this type of functionality as they become more tightly coupled with RDBMS products in the future.

Database design tools come in many sizes and flavors. Regardless of your level of expertise, if you are designing a database for SQL Server, you should be using a database design tool for the job. At the very least, it serves as a documentation aid in support of your design efforts.

Normalization   Data in relational databases must be organized in a manner which allows the data to be conveniently accessed by users and easily manipulated by applications. There exists a set of rules for organizing relational databases in order that there is no duplication of data and no loss of information. The process for organizing relational data in this manner is known as *normalization*.

Relational database designers must be knowledgeable about normalization. Even though it is beyond the scope of this book to completely define normalization, it is important to explain the significance of normalization as it relates to your SQL Server implementation.

Normalizing a relational database is a step-by-step process, with each step building on the last. One measure of the effectiveness of a logical data model is the level (i.e., how many steps) to which it is normalized. At the base level of the relational data model is first normal form (1NF). You can also deploy second normal form (2NF) and third normal form (3NF) database designs in SQL Server.

For the most part, the minimum level of acceptance for an OLTP database is 3NF. Denormalizing a 3NF data model for the sake of performance usually leads to difficulty somewhere down the road. You are encouraged to maintain, at least, 3NF with your physical data models. Having said that, you should recognize that this is not always possible in real-world projects. In some cases, logical data models are taken to 3NF, but a denormalized form is implemented.

OLAP databases, however, tend to be somewhat denormalized. In support of user reporting and ad-hoc queries, it is acceptable to intentionally model the database to include repeating groups, for example. Less than 3NF is acceptable in this case because the database is almost never updated by users (it is populated by production databases), and the data is frequently retrieved in groups.

Integrity   Normalized relational databases, by definition, model organizational processes by breaking them down into logical components suitable for processing by SQL Server. A concept at the application level may be modeled in the database design as several components, or entities. It is important that the relationships these entities have with one another are preserved as the data is processed.

For a moment, imagine that you have in your hand an order for several items from one of your customers. In front of you exists a single piece of paper, which you refer to as an order. SQL Server, on the other hand, likely (assuming that 3NF is achieved) captures the order as two or more entities. At a minimum, there exists an order header file that contains attributes such as customer name, ship to address, order date, and order number; and an order detail file that contains information such as item ordered, quantity ordered, item price, and extended price.

While you mentally process this as one object (the order), SQL Server processes this as two objects (the order header file and the order detail file). One aspect of integrity is the preservation of this important concept. If you "tear up" the order, it is entirely eliminated. If you ask SQL Server to delete the order, you must be careful to instruct it to remove both the order header information and the order detail information. Furthermore, you must ensure that either both sets of information are completely removed or nothing is removed.

Accounting for this type of situation is critical to the success of your SQL Server databases. You must familiarize yourself with the various types of integrity and at what level you will enforce their compliance. This is absolutely necessary in order to ensure accurate and consistent data.

Logical Data Model   The first step in database design is to map the application requirements to the database. The database designer, or data modeler, analyzes the requirements and constructs a conceptual model for fulfilling those requirements. In this case, the model is comprised of relational database components. These components go by many names depending on which school of thought you follow. Regardless of the naming scheme used, the same basic concepts apply.

N O T E   Application requirements are not the only possible source of originating information for the data modeler. It is common in today's world for a data modeler to begin from a conceptual object model. Several methodologies exist for mapping object models to relational data models. In fact, there are methodologies that support mapping from relational data models to object models. Design tools are available today that aid in the development of an object model and a data model at the same time, regardless of the direction your methodology takes you. ■

You must follow the principles of relational database technology in designing databases for SQL Server. The process of "mapping" requirements to the database results in the identification of the logical database entities. For each entity, you must define its attributes and how it relates to the other entities. As the entity relationships are defined, the keys are identified. See the section "The Relational Data Model" earlier in the chapter for more information.

N O T E   You are encouraged to study the principles of relational database design if you are not intimately familiar with this topic. ■

As mentioned previously, the pictorial representation of how entities relate to each other is known as an entity-relationship (E-R) diagram. The end result of any logical data modeling exercise is the creation of the E-R diagram. All popular relational data modeling tools support the creation and maintenance of E-R diagrams. Other diagrams that support the logical data model also are available from these tools.

Creating a logical data model is a necessary step in every database design project. It is with the logical data model that the database designers, application architects, and application designers perform mental exercises to validate system behavior. Even after the logical data model is transformed into a physical database, the logical model must remain in sync with the physical aspects of the database to support future decision making.

Physical Data Model   After the logical data model is prepared, analyzed, and approved, it is time to create the physical database. Often the model of the physical database differs from the logical model. Why might the physical database be different from the logical model? The answer lies in the fact that humans analyze the model differently than the RDBMS processes the data.

Logical data models are designed to accommodate the thought processes of a database designer. The representation of the physical database, also known as the *physical data model*, is designed to accommodate the best possible scenario for processing the data by the RDBMS.

Physical data models are concerned with exactly how the data is stored on the storage media. Database designers and database administrators may implement a physical database differently than depicted by the logical data model. This is necessary in most instances due to performance implications. It also may be necessary to accommodate environmental aspects such as the configuration of your network, servers, or client PCs.

After applications are tested and implemented, it is normal for the physical database to undergo changes to improve performance or repair a deficiency in the operational characteristics of the application. This process is known as *performance tuning*.

Part
VII

Ch
32

N O T E   Performance-tuning exercises frequently result in changes to the physical database. This should be expected as a part of optimizing application performance after testing begins. ▨

Again, it is imperative you keep your logical model in sync with your physical database. A common mistake made during this work step is to let the logical data model get out of sync with the physical database. If you allow this to happen, you lose the ability to analyze the database on its logical characteristics. Because this is the best basis from which humans can contemplate such issues, you run the risk of ending up with an inadequate data model. In the real world, damage at this level is irreparable because time is rarely allowed to start over again.

Indexing   One of the most important decisions regarding the physical implementation of the database is how the indexes will be built. Selecting which way to build an index is a function of how you believe it will be used. SQL Server offers the following two ways to build indexes:

- ▨ Clustered
- ▨ Non-clustered

As the name implies, clustered indexing creates indexes such that the indexed order of the rows is the same as the physical order of the rows. Additionally, the lowest level of a clustered index contains the actual data. Because clustered indexes have such a direct relationship to the physical data, they provide the fastest form of data retrieval.

Also, because clustered indexing infers something about the physical arrangement of the data, there can only be one clustered index per table. If a clustered index is desired, the question becomes for which columns should the clustered index be applied. In most cases, the clustered index is generated for the columns that uniquely identify each row—that is, the *primary key*. This certainly makes sense in situations where most searches are performed on the primary key, or when the primary key is used exclusively in WHERE clauses.

However, in some situations it makes sense to apply the only clustered index for a table to columns other than those representing the primary key. These situations include the following:

- Searching columns sequentially, or by a range of values, is best supported by a clustered index.
- Applying a clustered index to a column that is frequently sorted improves ORDER BY or GROUP BY performance.
- Static columns and join columns benefit from clustered indexes.

N O T E   When selecting the indexing method, it is important to know how the table will be queried in most situations. It also is important to know how SQL Server will optimize index usage. For the former, you need know only the application and how the users will use it. For the latter, the best way to gain this knowledge is through training and experience. ◼

Non-clustered indexes typically outperform clustered indexes in situations where key values are being added or updated. On the other hand, non-clustered indexes usually cannot match the retrieval speed of a clustered index. This is because non-clustered indexes are physically one level removed from the data. In particular, the following issues are relevant to considering non-clustered indexes:

- It is possible to have multiple non-clustered indexes per table. However, insert and update operations take longer as indexes are added. This is not a problem in situations where the database is queried far more than updated, such as in OLAP databases.
- Because non-clustered indexes tend to be larger than clustered indexes, the additional storage space required should be weighed against the extra cost of that capacity.
- Non-clustered indexes are of less value in cases where many duplicate index values exist.

These indexing issues, among others, are important aspects of the physical design of your database. Database designers and database administrators will find their time is well spent exploring these issues. Tools like DBCC and the SHOWPLAN option for query analysis are instrumental in helping you develop and refine your database designs. The benefit of experience is valuable in these situations.

▶ **See** "Detailed Design Issues," **p. 1128**

Enterprise Data Model

Another important topic that deserves discussion before leaving the topic of database design is *enterprise data modeling.* An enterprise data model is a database design that supports most, if not all, of an organization's production systems. It also may include one or more data warehouse components in support of the user reporting and query requirements.

The concept of building a single, large database for the entire organization is not new. However, only recently could RDBMS products such as SQL Server deal with the complexities and size of enterprise databases. Because there are many advantages to modeling the enterprise on the whole and because SQL Server can accommodate this approach, many organizations are now at various stages of enterprise data model development or implementation.

Enterprise data models are typically built by a single individual or team of database designers. It should not be a surprise that better data models are developed when the job stays in one group, as opposed to being spread across the organization and into the application development teams.

 T I P Enterprise data models do not eliminate the need for, nor the benefit of, departmental databases. In fact, a well-designed enterprise data model includes rules and processes for synchronizing with departmental databases.

Part

VII

Ch

32

Most enterprise data models are built in increments. This design approach is used primarily because it is difficult to design the entire data model all at once. Rarely is there enough time to finish the entire design before the first application goes into production. Consequently, the enterprise data model tends to grow as each new application is brought into existence. The bigger the enterprise data model gets, the easier it is to build new applications. Each new application has the benefit of the existing data model and associated processes, including stored procedures and other aspects of the database.

Overall, the stability of applications is improved due to the consistency within their foundation—the enterprise data model. For this reason, the up-front investment in enterprise data modeling pays off over time.

From Here...

In this chapter, you were introduced to the underlying technologies upon which SQL Server is based. It is important to understand the technical foundation of SQL Server to be successful in its use. Specifically, you learned the characteristics of an RDBMS, the roles and responsibilities of a DBA, how to design databases, and how database design influences your success with SQL Server.

Refer to the following chapters for more detailed information on SQL Server and related topics:

- For an overview of the Microsoft Distributed Transaction Coordinator and its use in distributed transaction management, see Chapter 30, "An Inside Look at Distributed Transaction Coordinator (DTC) and Microsoft Transaction Server (MTS)."

- For an introduction to Microsoft SQL Server, see Chapter 33, "An Inside Look at SQL Server."

- To learn how to install and configure SQL Server and create databases, see Chapter 34, "Building Your SQL Server."

- For an understanding of the details associated with administering SQL Server, see Chapter 35, "Maintaining SQL Server."

- To learn about SQL Server's data replication features, see Chapter 36, "SQL Server Data Replication."

- To learn how to use SQL Server to build a data warehouse, see Chapter 37, "Data Warehousing with SQL Server."

CHAPTER 33

An Inside Look at SQL Server

by Don Benage

Microsoft SQL Server is the database component of the BackOffice family. It is a relational database management system (RDBMS) designed to allow organizations to effectively manage information and build powerful database applications for deployment in multiuser networked environments. ■

Overview of SQL Server

Gain an understanding of the relational database management system offered as a part of Microsoft BackOffice—SQL Server.

Brief history of SQL Server

Learn how the product began as the first relational database on the PC platform.

Features and tools of SQL Server

Explore the significant features of SQL Server and become acquainted with the tools included with this BackOffice component.

Characteristics of Microsoft SQL Server

Microsoft SQL Server is based on client-server architecture, which divides processing into two components: a front-end, or client component, and a back-end, or server component. SQL Server itself constitutes the back-end database server, with which many different front-end client applications communicate, typically over a local area network (LAN). Its built-in data replication, powerful management tools, and open system architecture provide a platform for delivering cost-effective information solutions for organizations of all sizes. SQL Server provides a complete and integrated system of database management software to meet the challenges facing today's organizations when they deploy large-scale distributed information systems.

Microsoft SQL Server has the following characteristics:

- **Relational database management system (RDBMS).** SQL Server structures data according to the relational data model, and operations proceed according to the rules of relational algebra, originally put forth by E.F. Codd in 1970.

- **SQL-based.** Administrators, users, and application programs use the Structured Query Language (SQL) to interact with SQL Server.

- **Scalable.** You can add additional processors to a SQL Server computer (provided the computer you selected supports multiple processors) to achieve performance gains and greater throughput without any significant reconfiguration of SQL Server itself.

- **High performance.** Microsoft SQL Server has consistently performed well in benchmark testing conducted by the computer industry trade press and various testing laboratories. It is among the top performers available.

A Brief History of Microsoft SQL Server

In 1988, Microsoft, working with industry partners Ashton-Tate and Sybase, introduced its first version of SQL Server, designed to run on the OS/2 operating system. The product was written by Sybase, and marketed by Microsoft and Ashton-Tate. Subsequent to its initial release, Microsoft gradually adopted an increasing responsibility for fixing bugs and implementing SQL Server on OS/2. In 1992, the Microsoft SQL Server team decided to port the SQL Server 4.2 code base to Windows NT. This change required a major rewrite to SQL Server, but provided a powerful, multiprocessing RDBMS for the Windows NT environment.

The first version of SQL Server for Windows NT shipped within 30 days of the release of Windows NT 3.1 in July of 1993. The product was quite successful and showed that direct competition with larger, UNIX-based platforms was not only possible, but also likely. Because of this success, and the competitive posture it engendered, it became obvious that different priorities existed for Sybase and Microsoft. They eventually ended their cooperative development agreement in April of 1994, and Microsoft gained complete control of Microsoft SQL Server development. Microsoft subsequently has added the following features:

- Support for RISC platforms
- A MAPI interface for developing message-enabled database applications
- Data-migration tools
- Integration with OLE object technology and the Microsoft Visual Basic programming system
- Language enhancements that include declarative referential integrity (DRI) and powerful server-based cursor support

A Sample Network Architecture

SQL Server can be implemented in a wide variety of ways. To familiarize you with the way in which SQL Server is set up in a typical network, this section presents some sample scenarios showing representative networking architectures. This should help you plan for an effective implementation at your site and better understand some of the options you have when adding SQL Server to your network. The scenarios illustrated include the following:

- A small, stand-alone SQL Server added to a traditional file-sharing network environment
- A SQL Server integrated with an intranet server, providing database access through World Wide Web (WWW) browser connections to corporate network users
- A wide area network (WAN) with SQL Servers at each geographic location, using replication to consolidate information from each branch at the corporate headquarters location
- A scenario involving two SQL Servers, one used for Online Transaction Processing (OLTP) and one used in an Online Analytical Processing (OLAP) role as a data warehouse in a Decision Support System (DSS)
- A SQL Server that is accessed through queries sent via electronic mail from users attached via the Internet or dial-up Remote Access Service (RAS) connections

Part
VII

Ch
33

Simple SQL Server Scenario

Probably the most common way to deploy a SQL Server, and the simplest, is to add a stand-alone SQL Server to an existing network. This could be a network based on Windows NT Server, using Microsoft networking protocols, or it could be a network using file servers from another vendor such as Novell or Banyan. The SQL Server is installed on a separate computer running Windows NT Server, or on an existing Windows NT Server machine provided there is sufficient processing power available to handle the additional load (see Figure 33.1).

Microsoft SQL Server is specifically designed to be accessible over networking protocols from other vendors (besides Microsoft's own). In particular, existing Novell NetWare client computers using IPX/SPX, and Banyan Vines clients using TCP/IP can access a Microsoft SQL Server without adding additional networking protocols to the client. The SQL Server can be configured to support your existing networking protocol during installation, or at a later time by running Setup. All that is added to the client is appropriate database software; the basic networking software on the client can remain unchanged. This greatly simplifies the installation process and reduces the likelihood of configuration problems. Of course, if you are already using Microsoft networking, you can easily add database support to your client computers without reconfiguring the network software.

FIG. 33.1

A stand-alone SQL Server can be easily deployed in a traditional file-sharing network.

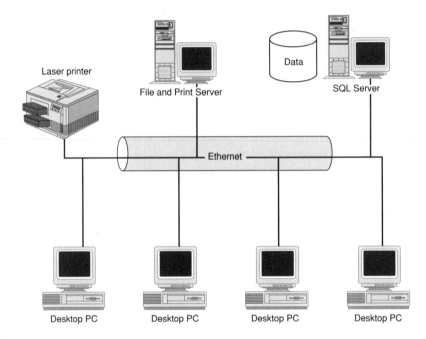

SQL Server with Web Server Integration

In recent years, use of the Internet has exploded. The World Wide Web (or simply, the Web) has become a popular place to exchange information, conduct research, or even engage in business-related activities such as product promotion. More people than ever before are looking at the world through their Web browser. Therefore, it should be no surprise that the need has arisen to integrate SQL Server data with Web servers.

With this arrangement, the client computer does not (usually) communicate directly with the SQL Server at all, but rather establishes a connection to the Web server through the use of a Web browser. No special database software needs to be added to the client computer since it is communicating only with the Web server, using the Hypertext Transport Protocol (HTTP). The Web server, on behalf of the client(s), accesses the SQL Server and presents the data to the client.

N O T E Even though the client computer does not directly access the SQL Server, you should still carefully review the License Agreement for SQL Server and evaluate whether client licenses are required in your situation. In general, accessing a SQL Server through some sort of "gateway" or "concentrator" process on another machine does not alleviate the need for client licenses. A special license may be available specifically designed to support Web server integration scenarios. Check with your software vendor or Microsoft representative for details. ■

You can integrate a SQL Server database with a Web server in a number of different ways. A stored procedure or SQL script can be run at regular intervals, under the control of the SQL Executive, that extracts data from a database, which is then used to update a relatively static Web page. In this scenario, the data from the database is preprocessed and formatted in Hypertext Markup Language (HTML) before the client computer(s) makes a connection. Although this method provides fast access, the information is usually somewhat out of date.

Another option is to have SQL Server process dynamic queries based on user requests. For example, when the user clicks an "update" button, a query is sent to SQL Server; the results are formatted in HTML and then presented to the user's Web browser for display on the client computer.

A third option is to incorporate ActiveX Controls, or other dynamic elements such as a Java applet or Netscape add-in, that are designed to access data from SQL Server or another ODBC data source (see Figure 33.2).

FIG. 33.2
This figure depicts a SQL Server which provides data for a Web server.

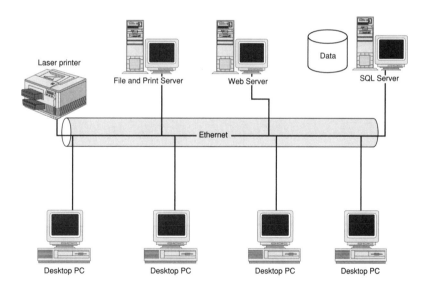

Part
VII

Ch
33

There are other ways to integrate SQL Server with the Web, and, in fact, the methods outlined above are not mutually exclusive. These elements, and others, can be used together on the same Web page, providing the appropriate level of data access required by the user.

Branch Office Data Consolidation Using Replication

Chapter 36, "SQL Server Data Replication," covers replication in detail, but a sample scenario is presented here to give you an idea of the way SQL Server can be integrated into corporate networks. Figure 33.3 depicts a corporation with two branch offices and a headquarters location. At each branch office, line-of-business information (e.g., orders for products or services, customer service requests, or employee evaluation results) are entered into the local SQL Server database. This information is then automatically copied, or replicated, to the corporate headquarters location where it is consolidated.

FIG. 33.3

A typical corporate "rollup" replication architecture with two branch offices and a headquarters location is shown in this figure.

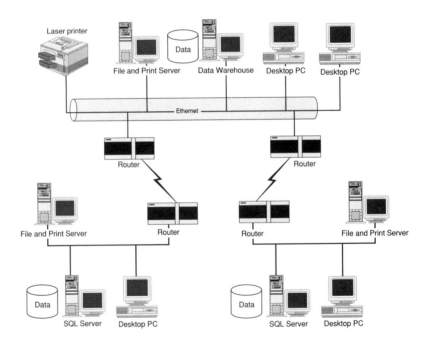

It is also possible to have consolidated data from all regions replicated back out to the branch offices from the headquarters site. In other words, the flow of replicated information need not be just one way. Microsoft SQL Server supports the notion of a single server being both a source of replicated information (a "publisher") and a destination (a "subscriber"). The consolidated information may be replicated throughout the day, or only during off-peak times, depending on the nature of the data and the need for up-to-the-minute updates. In this way, each branch office has the very latest information available to support its activities and operations.

Data Warehousing Scenario

Another rapidly growing area for database products is the *data warehouse*. In addition to using database technology to support OLTP, Information Systems (IS) professionals have learned that a separate source of data, dubbed the data warehouse, is best suited to support the needs of managers and other professionals engaged in data analysis. While these two functions were initially supported using a single database, this architecture did not work well for a variety of reasons.

▶ **See** "Data Warehousing with SQL Server," **p. 1269**

The following scenario shows a network with two SQL Servers (see Figure 33.4). The first supports transaction processing. It has many users, typically clerical workers or telemarketing personnel, entering orders or some other type of recurrent transaction information (e.g., product service requests). The transactions are generally small, and the response time must be rapid since the transaction usually must be processed immediately, potentially with a customer waiting on the phone for confirmation.

FIG. 33.4

Information captured by an OLTP server can be replicated to the data warehouse to support more detailed analysis.

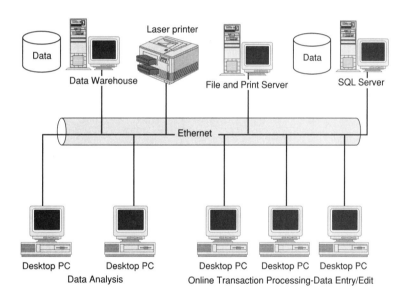

Information from this server is replicated to a second SQL Server where the information is manipulated to leave it in a form more suitable for trend analysis and other decision support activities. The data warehouse typically stores data for a longer period (to support historical analysis), but may not require the same level of detail. Various aggregates (sums, averages, counts) may be pre-calculated and stored in the database to speed analytical queries that frequently use such figures. In addition, the number of users accessing the data warehouse is typically smaller than the transaction-processing server; but the queries processed tend to be complex and require more computational power and time to resolve.

SQL Server with E-Mail Integration

While the most common method for accessing a SQL Server involves a direct connection over a LAN (whether directly by a client computer, or by a Web server on behalf of a client) it also is possible to configure SQL Server to respond to e-mailed requests from computers that access the network using dial-up software or that reach your organization's LAN via the Internet. In such a scenario, the client computer need not have any database software installed at all, just support for the e-mail product being used (see Figure 33.5).

FIG. 33.5
Remote client computers, such as laptops being used by traveling members of your organization, can access SQL Server data through e-mail requests.

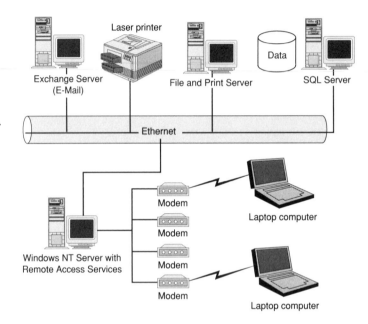

This type of setup is appropriate only when response time can be measured in minutes or hours rather than seconds. It also does not allow the user to be sure the request has been accepted and processed before disconnecting, and may therefore occasionally lead to wasted time and the need for resubmitting a request. In certain situations, however, it can be a useful adjunct to other more conventional approaches.

Surveying Features in Microsoft SQL Server

This section introduces you to some of the features available in Microsoft SQL Server 6.5, which is included in BackOffice 2.5. SQL Server 6.5 was first included in BackOffice 2.0. The next two chapters cover in detail the procedures to follow when using these tools to create and manage databases with SQL Server. They are presented in this section to provide you with an overview of the features and tools the product provides.

Enterprise-Wide Administration

SQL Server 6.5 provides enterprise-wide system administration through an integrated management framework of objects, services, and components. From a single desktop computer, the DBA can manage many SQL Servers by connecting to them over the network and issuing commands. The tool most often selected for this task is the SQL Enterprise Manager, a graphical administration tool that provides easy management of a multiple-server environment, including the following:

- Scheduling
- Administrator alerts
- Built-in replication management interface

SQL Enterprise Manager also makes it easier for the database administrator (DBA) to manage the following:

- Logins
- Access privileges
- User groups
- Devices and databases
- Script development
- Database and transaction log backups
- Database components (tables, views, stored procedures, triggers, indexes, rules, defaults, and user-defined datatypes)

SQL Enterprise Manager also contains a new component called SQL Executive, which replaces the SQL Monitor from version 4.2. SQL Executive enables replication and provides scheduling of SQL Server events, DBCC operations, and other administrative maintenance tasks. Tasks may consist of a T-SQL script, an operating system command to be entered at a command prompt, or one of three special-purpose tasks used to support data replication. You can schedule tasks to occur only once or at regular intervals.

The enhanced SQL Enterprise Manager in version 6.5 includes a Database Maintenance Plan wizard. This wizard guides you through the process of creating a plan for routine maintenance and scheduling automated tasks controlled by the SQL Executive. The Database Maintenance Plan wizard is discussed in more detail later in this chapter (see "The Database Maintenance Plan Wizard").

In addition to the Enterprise Manager, you can automate repetitive tasks by the following:

- Creating SQL scripts specifying maintenance operations. For example, you can run the Database Consistency Checker (DBCC) on all the tables in a database to ensure their basic integrity.

Part
VII

Ch
33

■ Creating Microsoft Visual Basic for Applications (VBA) macros (using Microsoft Excel, for example) that interact with SQL Server through the Distributed Management Object (DMO), SQL Server's OLE interface. This is a feature first implemented in version 6.0 and enhanced in version 6.5. An example of an appropriate use of this capability is creating a graph showing the size of each table in a database.

Some new tools have been added to SQL Server 6.5, including the following:

■ **SQL Web Page Wizard.** This wizard guides you through the process of publishing HTML pages on the World Wide Web that use a SQL Server database.

■ **SQLTrace.** This graphical utility allows you to record and monitor database activity for benchmarking and troubleshooting.

■ **Microsoft Query.** This easy-to-use query tool has been available in the past as part of the Microsoft Excel product, but also can be used as a stand-alone query tool.

Data Integrity

In a client-server database environment, the server enforces integrity rules automatically and provides a reliable foundation for client-server computing. SQL Server uses several mechanisms to enforce data integrity. Starting with version 6.0, SQL Server provided declarative referential integrity (DRI), allowing the DBA to define data-integrity restrictions for a table and relationships between tables and to provide assurances that related key values are consistent. This is done to enforce referential and business-rule integrity, ensuring that cross-references among tables are valid and that changes to the database are consistent with business rules. To provide entity integrity, SQL Server includes unique indexes, ensuring that the values in key columns are unique because each record is a unique row and no two rows have the same values in key columns. SQL Server also uses defaults and rules to enforce domain integrity, ensuring that the values in certain columns are legal.

Distributed Transaction Coordinator

An important new feature added to SQL Server 6.5 is the Microsoft Distributed Transaction Coordinator (MS DTC). The MS DTC combines the component object model (COM) with transaction technology and the two-phase commit protocol. Using this new functionality, software developers can create powerful new applications that create *transaction objects* and enlist the help of *resource managers* (a SQL Server for example) to complete the work of the transaction. The status of transactions can be monitored using new features that have been added to the SQL Enterprise Manager (see Figure 33.6).

FIG. 33.6
Use the SQL Enterprise Manager to monitor the status of transactions using the MS DTC.

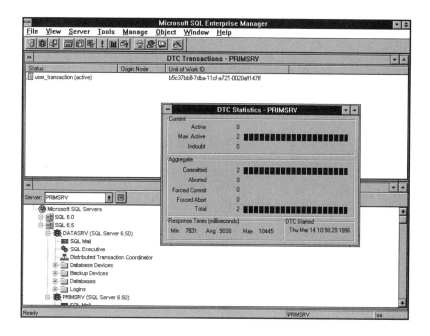

Replication

Microsoft SQL Server 6.0 included data replication as a standard feature of the RDBMS. Through data replication, the user is able to automatically disseminate copies of transactional data across the enterprise from a single source server to one or more destination servers at remote locations. Continuous store-and-forward updates allow for a high availability of synchronized, distributed data. Direct configuration and administration is accomplished through the SQL Enterprise Manager application. The replication stored procedures provide the capability of manual configuration.

In version 6.5, the replication features have gained an important new capability. It is now possible to replicate to ODBC subscribers, including Microsoft Access and ORACLE. In addition, you now can replicate text and image datatypes, something that was not possible with SQL Server 6.0.

Performance Features

Microsoft SQL Server 6.5 provides powerful new features, as well as expansion of existing system tools and procedures. SQL Server 6.5 extends the standard conventions set forth by the

Part
VII

Ch
33

American National Standards Institute (ANSI) by including scrollable, server-based cursors to support forward, backward, absolute, and relative-position cursors. SQL Server 6.5 also includes these features:

- Enhanced database consistency checker (DBCC)
- Advanced configuration options
- Parallel data scans (asynchronous read ahead) on sequential page operations
- Added keywords and reserved words
- Query optimizations
- Enhanced RAISERROR statement
- Session settings
- New system procedures

Language Features

SQL Server 6.5 includes enhanced Transact-SQL features. For example, ANSI-standard compliant CASE expressions have been added, as well as a double-quote delimited identifier feature, which allows the server to bypass language within double quotes. Also included is a new Data Definition Language (DDL), which uses Transact-SQL statements to define databases and database objects and to manage their properties. An enhanced Data Manipulation Language (DML) uses Transact-SQL statements to manipulate database objects, and a Data Control Language (DCL) allows Transact-SQL statements to permit access to database objects.

New for version 6.5, SQL Server has been enhanced to meet the American National Standards Institute (ANSI) SQL-92 standards. SQL Server 6.5 is certified as compliant with the Federal Information Processing Standard (FIPS) 127-2 created by the National Institute of Standards and Technology (NIST). Specific enhancements to Transact-SQL include the following:

- The CREATE SCHEMA statement
- ANSI-standard joins in the SELECT statement
- The GRANT WITH GRANT OPTION and REVOKE GRANT OPTION FOR statements
- ANSI-standard NULL and DEFAULT support
- The DUMP TABLE and LOAD TABLE statements, which allow a single table to be backed up and restored

Surveying the Available Tools

Now that you have been briefly introduced to SQL Server and learned a little about the technology upon which it is based, it is time to learn about some of the actual tools and utilities used to configure and manage SQL Server. This section introduces you to the SQL Enterprise Manager, the main tool used by DBAs to work with SQL Server. It also reviews the other special-purpose tools that complement the SQL Enterprise Manager.

The SQL Enterprise Manager

This tool is an updated combination of the older SQL Administrator and SQL Object Manager tools offered in version 4.2. The SQL Enterprise Manager, as shown in Figure 33.7, is a feature-rich management tool that allows DBAs to manage SQL Servers anywhere on the enterprise network from a single computer running Windows NT or Windows 95.

FIG. 33.7
Here, the SQL Enterprise Manager is connected to the SQL Server named DATASRV.

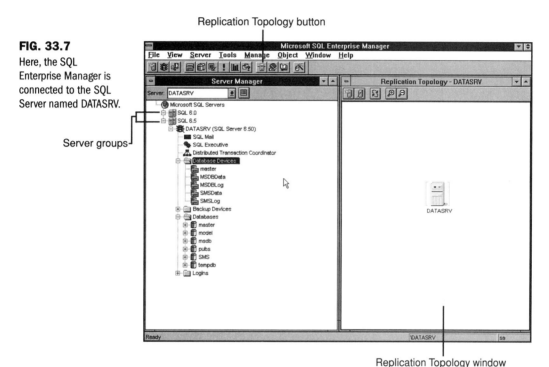

The SQL Enterprise Manager allows each DBA to create *server groups* to organize the SQL Servers for which he or she has administrative responsibility. Another administrator running the SQL Enterprise Manager on a different computer has the freedom to create a different set of server groups reflecting a different view of the network appropriate to a different set of responsibilities.

You now can perform many different tasks using the SQL Enterprise Manager. Most of the things you learn to do in this chapter and the two that follow are done using the SQL Enterprise Manager. The following is a short list of the operations you can perform with this tool:

- List the devices defined on a SQL Server
- List the databases defined on a SQL Server
- List the tables, indexes, stored procedures, and other objects defined for a database

■ View the structure of a table

■ List the definition of a stored procedure or trigger

■ Display the replication topology showing the relationship between publishing and subscribing servers

■ Display the tasks, schedule, and status of the SQL Executive

■ Initiate a transfer of data and associated objects from one SQL Server to another using a capability very similar to the stand-alone SQL Transfer Manager tool

This list is by no means comprehensive, but offers a glimpse at the depth and breadth of the SQL Enterprise Manager's capabilities. You can see that it has been designed to configure and control nearly every aspect of SQL Server operation. The SQL Enterprise Manager is used to demonstrate most operations in the remaining SQL Server chapters.

The Database Maintenance Plan Wizard

For the newcomer to database administration, one of the nicest features added to SQL Server 6.5 is the Database Maintenance Plan Wizard (see Figure 33.8). This helpful tool asks you questions about the nature of your database with a series of dialog boxes, making helpful suggestions along the way (see Figure 33.9). Then, based on the responses you provide, it creates a task for the SQL Executive to execute either daily or weekly. It even can send an e-mail notification summarizing its actions to the person of your choice (see Figure 33.10). Of course, you may change the scheduling of this task manually later.

FIG. 33.8

The Introduction dialog box describes the Database Maintenance Plan Wizard and allows you to select the database with which you want to work.

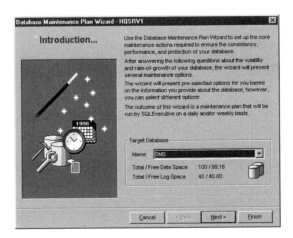

The tasks created by this Wizard use a utility program called SQLMAINT.EXE. This utility provides an easy way to request routine maintenance tasks from a command prompt. You can find it in the MSSQL/BINN directory if you loaded SQL Server in the default location. You can view the available options for this utility by typing **SQLMAINT /?** at the command prompt. When coupled with the Maintenance Plan Wizard, this utility provides a painless way to keep your database in proper working order that is easy to use for the neophyte.

FIG. 33.9

A series of dialog boxes, one of which is pictured here, appears in order to gather information about the characteristics of your particular database.

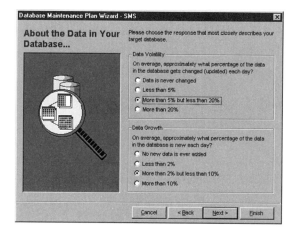

FIG. 33.10

You can specify how often these mainte-nance operations execute and select an operator to be notified by e-mail.

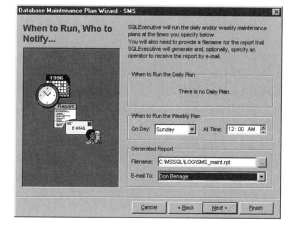

SQL Security Manager

SQL Server supports three different security models, which are described in more detail later. Two of the models offer the capability to use Windows NT user accounts for access to SQL Server. If you have selected one of these two models, the SQL Security Manager will help you manage user accounts. Figure 33.11 depicts a typical Security Manager display showing the Windows NT accounts that have been granted User privilege on this SQL Server.

▶ **See** "Using SQL Server Security," **p. 1127** (Ch. 34)

▶ **See** "Choosing a Security Model," **p. 1164** (Ch. 35)

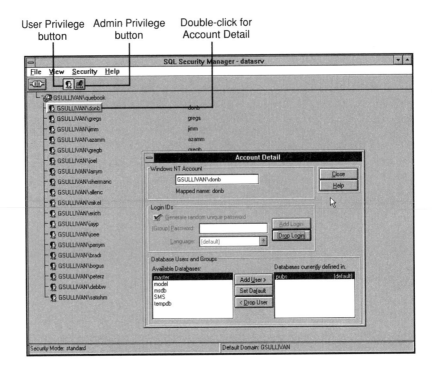

FIG. 33.11

The SQL Security Manager is displaying Windows NT accounts that have been granted User privilege. The Account Detail dialog box displays when you double-click the user's account name.

SQL Transfer Manager

SQL Transfer Manager is an administrative tool from SQL Server 4.2 and 6.0 that has been replaced by a transfer-management interface in the SQL Enterprise Manager. You still can use SQL Transfer Manager, however, and it provides a graphical interface to control the transfer of data and associated objects into and out of SQL Server. This utility is an easy-to-understand and convenient alternative to the older bulk copy program known as bcp (see the "bcp" section later in this chapter). You can use the SQL Transfer Manager to move information between SQL Servers running on dissimilar platforms, the primary reason for continuing to use it. For example, you can transfer information from a SQL Server running on a computer with a MIPS processor to a computer using an Alpha AXP processor or an Intel processor.

The transfer-management interface in the SQL Enterprise Manager provides much of the same functionality as SQL Transfer Manager, but you can use it only when the destination server is running SQL Server version 6.5. You open it by choosing Tools, Database/Object Transfer from the menu after selecting the source database. If you have a mixed server environment, the SQL Transfer Manager may still be useful. If the source server for your transfer is running SQL Server version 6.0, the OBJECT60.SQL script must be run on the source server for the SQL Transfer Manager to function properly.

SQL Administrator

The SQL Administrator is an administrative tool from SQL Server 4.2 that has been replaced by the SQL Enterprise Manager. The SQL Administrator can still be used, however, but you must first run the SQL script (ADMIN60.SQL) that is provided with SQL Server to set up support for this older utility. Most administrators prefer the more powerful and comprehensive SQL Enterprise Manager, and will only continue to run the SQL Administrator during a short transitional period if at all. Figure 33.12 depicts a typical SQL Administrator session showing the device and database management windows.

FIG. 33.12

The SQL Administrator is an older tool from SQL Server version 4.2 that can still be useful in mixed server environments.

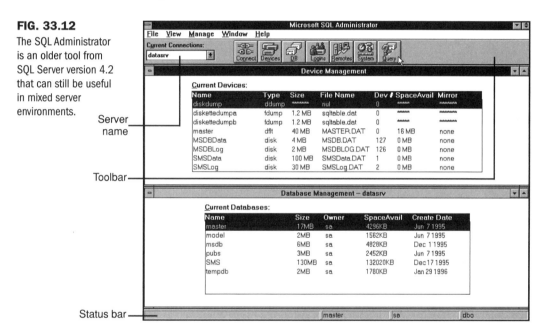

Object Manager

The Object Manager is another SQL Server 4.2 tool that has been replaced by the SQL Enterprise Manager. You run a corresponding script (OBJECT60.SQL) in order to use this tool on SQL Server 6.0. Software developers sometimes prefer this tool if they need a tool that allows them to view the structure and definition of a database, its tables, and associated objects. The Object Manager provides that capability without including the administrative functions for which a developer has no use. Figure 33.13 shows a typical Object Manager display. The Manage Tables window is open to show the definition for the "authors" table.

Part
VII

Ch
33

FIG. 33.13

The Object Manager is a SQL Server 4.2 tool that is still useful, especially for software developers.

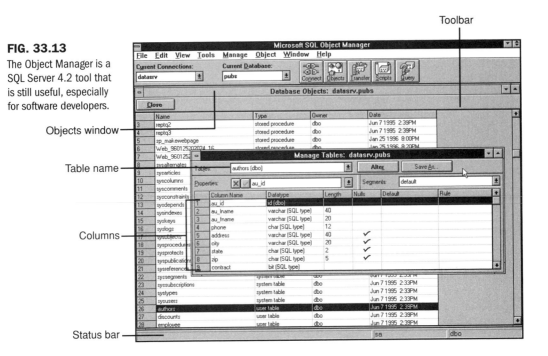

isql and ISQL/w

Traditionally, all management of a database management system was done from a command-line prompt by entering individual commands or executing a prepared script of commands created to perform a specific task. The first versions of SQL Server included a command-line utility called *isql* (for *interactive* SQL). That utility is still available. An updated version of this old standby features multiple windows in a graphical, Windows-based utility called ISQL/w (see Figure 33.14). This tool still allows you to enter individual commands or run scripts, but it also offers some useful capabilities for tracking the behavior of queries in addition to the advantages of a multiwindow environment.

Some DBAs prefer to use a command-line interface and scripts of SQL commands to perform maintenance tasks on their servers. Others prefer the SQL Enterprise Manager with its graphical user interface (GUI), dialog boxes, toolbar buttons, and visual, graphical feedback. It is fair to say that if a repetitive maintenance task needs to be performed on many servers, it can be faster and more reliable to create a script of commands, test them, and then execute them on the target servers. For an operation on a small number of servers, the speed and ease of directly specifying an operation using SQL Enterprise Manager is often a better choice. Of course, a balanced approach using all the available tools is likely the ideal approach.

▶ **See** "Using SQL Scripts and Stored Procedures for Maintenance Tasks," **p. 1219**

FIG. 33.14

ISQL/w is a Windows-based utility for entering command lines or executing SQL scripts.

New Query button

Query tab

Results tab

Execute Query button

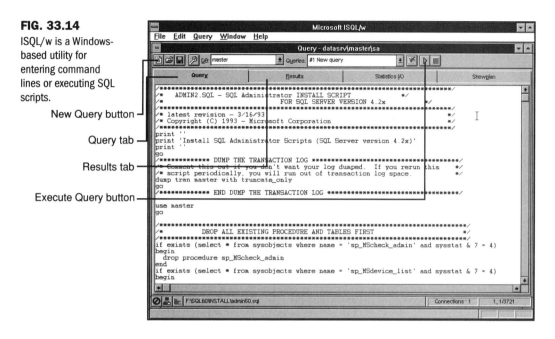

bcp

The bulk copy program (bcp) is the command-line utility traditionally used to get large amounts of data into and out of SQL Server (see Figure 33.15). It is most often used to import data from an operating system "flat file" or other non-SQL Server data source into a SQL Server database.

FIG. 33.15

A bcp command being entered from a Windows NT command prompt. The command shown is using the /? flag to display the full syntax of the command.

▶ **See** "Importing and Exporting Data," **p. 1213**

DBCC

The Database Consistency Checker (DBCC) is a command that plays several special roles in the administration of SQL Server databases. Its primary function is to perform a check on the internal consistency of databases or individual tables. It compares the information in SQL Server's internal system tables with the actual physical database to see whether the information contained in the two locations matches. If the physical database does not match the internal description of its size and location, you can use DBCC to attempt repairs. The DBCC command also is used to set *trace flags*, an advanced feature of SQL Server that is useful in some troubleshooting scenarios. A typical use of the DBCC command is shown in Figure 33.16.

FIG. 33.16

A DBCC command being entered in an ISQL/w window. A DBCC SHOW_STATISTICS command has just executed, and the results are displayed on the Results tab of the Query window.

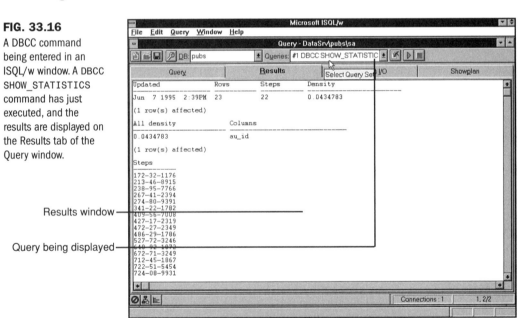

System Procedures

In addition to the commands available in the SQL language, there is a collection of predefined *system procedures*. System procedures also are called *system stored procedures* because they are, in fact, a collection of useful stored procedures created by Microsoft and provided with the product. You can use these procedures to perform many administrative tasks for SQL Server, such as defining users, creating login IDs, setting configuration parameters, and creating devices. Almost everything that you can do with system procedures you also can do using the SQL Enterprise Manager; however, the system procedures provide the ability to make administrative changes in an unattended batch mode. These commands have names beginning with sp_. For example, the system procedure to add a login ID is sp_addlogin. For more information, see "Stored Procedures-System Stored Procedures" in the *Transact-SQL Reference Manual*.

▶ **See** "Stored Procedures," **p. 1194**

From Here...

This chapter introduced you to Microsoft SQL Server, version 6.5. You learned about the product's current features, what new features were added to this version, and future plans for upcoming releases. You also learned about the tools included with SQL Server that allow you to administer the product.

Refer to the following chapters for information related to the issues discussed in this chapter:

- To learn how to install and configure SQL Server and create databases, see Chapter 34, "Building Your SQL Server."
- For an understanding of the details associated with administering SQL Server, see Chapter 35, "Maintaining SQL Server."
- To learn about SQL Server's data-replication features, see Chapter 36, "SQL Server Data Replication."
- To learn how to use SQL Server to build a data warehouse, see Chapter 37, "Data Warehousing with SQL Server."
- For an overview of the Microsoft Distributed Transaction Coordinator and its use in distributed transaction management, see Chapter 38, "An Inside Look at Distributed Transaction Coordinator (DTC) and Microsoft Transaction Server (MTS)."

Part
VII

Ch
33

CHAPTER 34

Building Your SQL Server

by Don Benage and Sherman Cassidy

In the preceding two chapters, you learned about relational database management systems (RDBMS), the role of the database administrator (DBA), designing databases, SQL Server, and the tools provided to manage SQL Server. This background information forms an important foundation as you install SQL Server, create databases, and begin to use SQL Server as a component for building client-server applications.

You are now ready to make specific plans for your server. The first two sections in this chapter provide some guidance on selecting hardware appropriate for use as a server and how SQL Server allocates and uses disk storage. Then you learn about the installation options you must decide upon for your installation to be a success. This discussion is followed by procedures for installing SQL Server and using the SQL Enterprise Manager to create login IDs and usernames. Finally, you learn how to define devices, databases, and various database objects.

If you are not an experienced database designer, spend some time designing your first database, following the guidelines from Chapter 32, before you actually create it on the server. Even database designers with years of experience don't foresee all eventualities, and changes will undoubtedly need to be made on occasion. The design process is an important part of database administration, and it should be approached with a professional attitude. ■

How to plan for installation

Get prepared to install SQL Server. Learn what hardware is required and plan how you will use the space on your disk drives.

How to install SQL Server

Follow step-by-step procedures to install SQL Server on your server hardware. Learn about the various installation options available for character sets, sort orders, and security models.

How to use SQL Enterprise Manager

Find out how the SQL Enterprise Manager can help you customize your installation. Learn how to create server groups and register your server for administration with SQL Enterprise Manager.

How to set up user access and create databases

Learn how to create login IDs and usernames, and how access to database objects is managed. Find out how to allocate storage by creating database devices and how to create databases.

Sizing Your Server

The required capacity of a particular SQL Server depends on several factors. The volume of data is the most obvious element involved in determining the optimal size for a SQL Server database. How much data is required by your applications? Less obvious factors also play a large role in determining how to implement your server. Some factors are presented in the following list and then described in more detail in the following sections:

- The nature of the application
- The users of the database
- The physical access method to the database
- Expansion of the scope of the project
- Unforeseen circumstances

Evaluating the Nature of Applications

The nature of the application and the use of the data are essential factors in determining the size of the database. A database used for storing names and addresses of a political candidate for use in fund-raising is different from a database used in a real-time, process-control environment in a factory. The name-and-address database may be used only two or three times during a two-year period, but contains a large volume of static data; whereas the process-control database could be in use 24 hours a day and contain a small volume of dynamic data.

The Users of the Database

The makeup of the user population that uses the data is also an important factor. For example, if the database will be used only by a group of highly trained database analysts for sophisticated analysis, the design and structure of the database will be substantially different than a database used by a community of data-entry clerks. In many ways this is a reflection of the differences between an On-Line Transaction Processing (OLTP) database and an On-Line Analytical Processing (OLAP) database. The distinctions go beyond these differences, however.

The average level of understanding among members of the user community—their backgrounds and the training that they have received—affects how much effort is required by the database designer to simplify data access. For example, creating views that contain the specific information needed by a particular group greatly simplifies the process of accessing that information. Entire tables of denormalized data are sometimes introduced to simplify and speed access for a particular group of users. In order to implement a successful design, you must consider the nature of the user community.

Physical Access to the Database

The method used to access the data also can have an impact on the design of the database. In particular, a growing number of organizations are providing access to some databases through the Internet, or a corporate intranet. A SQL Server may reside on a machine with a Web server and all access to the data may be through the use of a Web browser. Clearly, this is something that needs to be considered when determining the size of the server. If most users are accessing the data through a separate Web server, the direct impact on the SQL Server will be reduced.

▶ **See** "The Interactive, Dynamic Web Site," **p. 728**

Alternatively, there are a wide range of other applications and utilities that directly access SQL Server databases. They may be applications that directly add and update information to the database, or analytical tools that only read information and calculate totals or other aggregates. Online data entry personnel expect rapid access and fast updates. Analytical users may formulate complex queries that require extensive server resources (memory and processing power) to resolve. The type of user, and the type of access (direct or indirect), can have a profound effect on performance.

Allowing for Expansion and Unforeseen Circumstances

Experienced project managers will tell you that few Information Systems (IS) projects have been implemented without the design changing somewhat during the development cycle. Some changes involve the data model and/or the space requirements for the SQL Server. The following are some changes you may encounter:

- A table being added or deleted
- A column being added to or deleted from a table
- A column size (or even a column datatype) changing
- The need for another index
- A revision to the estimated volume of data
- A change in the scope of the project

Planning Disk Space Usage

A number of techniques can be employed by the DBA to optimize performance and improve fault tolerance. Using Redundant Array of Inexpensive Disks (RAID) technology can improve performance and help protect against drive failures. The Windows NT operating system also provides options for mirroring and striping, methods to protect against data loss and improve access speed. The methods available within SQL Server to control disk space usage include the use of *devices* and *segments*.

▶ **See** "Software RAID," **p. xxx** (Ch. 6)

Part
VII

Ch
34

Devices

Devices are operating system files that SQL Server uses to store databases, transaction logs, and their backups. They allow the DBA to control which hard disks are used to store database files, determine how much space should be used, and preallocate space so that it is not used by another application. When you create a database, you must identify devices for the database and the transaction log. Devices are created on disk drivet, except when they are used to store backups, in which case they also can be created on a tape drive or floppy disk.

Devices used for databases and transaction logs are generally referred to as *database devices*. Database devices store the data, indexes, and transaction logs. Devices used to store backups are referred to as *dump devices*.

Database Devices   Again, database devices store data and indexes. When you create a device, you are asked to supply a logical name and a physical name. The logical name is the name by which the device will be identified within SQL Server. The physical name is the operating system file specification where the device will be stored.

Every time activity occurs in the database, an entry is made in the transaction log. By using a transaction log, SQL Server ensures that either an entire transaction is applied to the database, or none of it is applied. The database is never left in an undefined intermediate state due to a partial transaction being applied and then terminated due to some system failure.

You should store databases and their transaction logs on separate devices. This increases performance and provides for easier administration. Also, if the log device is on a separate drive than the data device, you lessen the risk of losing data. If the data device fails, you can restore the database from the most recent backup (via the LOAD command) and update it with the current transaction log to bring it back to its state at the time that the device failed. If the log device fails, you can immediately DUMP the database to create a fresh backup and reestablish the transaction log.

Dump Devices   You use dump devices to store backups of databases and transaction logs. The importance of dump devices cannot be overstated. It is critical that the DBA define and execute regularly scheduled backups of all databases for which he or she is responsible. If the dump device is created on a tape drive, the physical name must be the Windows NT name for the tape drive.

Two default floppy disk dump devices are created at installation: DISKETTEDUMPA and DISKETTEDUMPB. These provide backward compatibility to earlier versions of SQL Server. With databases becoming larger and larger and tape drives becoming more prominent, backing up databases on floppy disks is rarely done.

Segments

Segments provide the DBA with a way to control disk space usage, which augments the control provided by devices. Whereas devices are required to create databases, segments are optional. A segment also provides the DBA additional flexibility by using segments—tables and indexes can reside on more than one database device. This extra control, if utilized properly, can improve performance. However, using segments introduces another level of complexity and administration, and thus an opportunity for error. Much the same performance gain can be achieved by using RAID drive arrays or Windows NT operating system methods (striping and mirroring) to control disk space usage. These methods are transparent to SQL Server administration tasks and therefore do not add any complexity.

A segment can best be thought of as a piece of a database device on which tables and/or indexes can be explicitly placed by the database administrator. Because the segments are named, and are independently specified, the DBA can indicate that a table should be located on one or more specific segments. Segments must be built on devices and must be used specifically by one database. This allows you to place a database on more than one database device (up to a maximum of 32 segments). The ALTER DATABASE command allows you to expand a database from one device to a segment on another device. The segment on the subsequent device can then be identified when creating tables and/or indexes. If an index already exists, it must be dropped and re-created on the new segment for the entire index to be placed on the new segment.

Even though it is possible to identify multiple segments (for the same database) on one device, it is not recommended because objects placed on the segments would then compete for space. This would negate the performance gain sought by the use of segments.

Some uses for segments include separating a table from its index by placing segments on two separate devices and putting a frequently accessed table on more than one device to spread the work around.

Databases

Before estimating space requirements for your database, it is important to understand certain terminology.

SQL Server uses the following three units of data storage:

- ■ Page (2K, or 2,048 bytes)
- ■ Extent (8 pages)
- ■ Allocation unit (32 Extents)

The smallest amount of space that can be allocated to a database is one allocation unit (256 contiguous 2K pages, or 0.5M). However, when you create devices and databases with the Enterprise Manager (explained later in this chapter), you need to specify the number of megabytes. You cannot enter fractional numbers.

Even though the smallest fragment of space must be at least one allocation unit, SQL Server uses the paging technique to store data. It puts as many data rows from a table (or index rows from an index) onto a page as it can. If an additional row is too large to fit on the remainder of the page, it must be stored on another page.

Each page requires 32 bytes of overhead, which means that only 2,016 bytes are available in each page. Also, one page out of every allocation unit is reserved for use by SQL Server. That page contains information about how data is stored on the other 255 pages. Some overhead is required for various elements to be stored; this overhead varies depending on the type of elements.

Given certain assumptions, you can get a good start on estimating the space required for a SQL Server database by following these steps:

Part
VII

Ch
34

1. Establish the data model. The data model is the end product of an analysis of the application's data requirements. This includes defining the tables to be used, columns in each table, relationships among the tables, and any indexes that should be built.

2. Determine the size (in bytes) of a row in each table.

3. Multiply each row size by the estimated number of rows for that table.

4. Determine the size (in bytes) of a row in each index.

5. Multiply each size by the estimated number of rows for that index.

6. Sum the products.

This gives you a starting point on which to base further calculations and against which to measure future changes. There are formulae in Appendix B of the *SQL Server Administrator's Companion* that you can use to CALCULATE exactly the number of data rows and index rows that can be stored on a page. For these formulae, you need to know the number and datatypes of the columns in the table, as well as the estimated number of records. Because the data model can change many times, especially in the early stages of development, you may need to update these calculations frequently.

Installing SQL Server

In this section, you learn how to install SQL Server. The section guides you through the setup process and explains the dialog boxes and options. If you are installing a server that you intend to put into a production role on your network, you should read through this section completely before actually installing the server because it is important that you get everything right the first time. If you are setting up a test server, you may want to follow along immediately. If you are already familiar with the options you must choose among when setting up your server, you may want to skip ahead to the section "Running the SQL Server Setup Program" later in this chapter.

The machine that you select for your server should be listed on the Hardware Compatibility List (HCL) for Windows NT Server, which is available in the Windows NT Server box and also updated regularly on CompuServe and Microsoft's World Wide Web server on the Internet. You should already have installed Windows NT Server. As a rule of thumb, the server should not be a Primary Domain Controller (PDC) or Backup Domain Controller (BDC), especially on an active network with many users. These types of servers already have a significant load placed on them validating logons. There are exceptions of course. In small networks with only 10 or 20 users, and perhaps only one server, you can install SQL Server on the PDC as long as it is sufficiently powerful and has enough RAM. See "Sizing Your Server" earlier in the chapter, for more details.

Before you launch the setup program, review the next four sections for background information on the choices you make during setup. Some of these selections cannot be changed after setup is complete without a significant effort.

> **CAUTION**
>
> The choices you make for sort order and character set are very important for one simple reason—if you choose incorrectly, you must reinstall SQL Server or rebuild the *master* database to change them. If you have already created databases and entered data, you must rebuild the master database, re-create all other databases, and then reload and rebuild them to reflect the new settings.

Sort Order

The sort order you select determines the way SQL Server sorts information and builds indexes and also determines the information selected in response to a query. Different sort orders can, therefore, have a profound impact on the operation and results that you get when using SQL Server.

There is no right or wrong sort order. For different applications and environments, each of the possible selections can be a sensible choice. Ideally, you should select a sort order that reflects the needs of the specific applications and the expectations of users running the system. For example, most users do not expect upper- and lowercase to have an impact on the results returned by a query. Therefore, a case-insensitive sort order is usually appropriate. There are applications, however, that must distinguish between upper- and lowercase characters when used in ID fields, for example. In these situations, you may need to use a case-sensitive order and develop application program logic to insulate users from this distinction, while still providing the expected results from queries.

If you are installing a single SQL Server to be used in an isolated environment, you only need to make a selection that provides appropriate results for your applications. If you are adding a SQL Server to an existing computing environment that already contains other database servers, it is important that you consult with the DBAs for those systems. If there is any chance that you may need to exchange data, you should make every effort to use the same sort order and character set to avoid data-conversion problems when transferring data.

N O T E The default sort order changed from version 4.2 to version 6.0. The version 4.2 default was binary sort order, which is generally the fastest. This order does not generate results that match the order you would find in a typical dictionary (dictionary order), which can lead to some confusion. The default for version 6.0 is dictionary order, case-insensitive, which is the most intuitive order for users. ▦

Part

VII

Ch

34

Character Set

The decision you make for character set is similar in some respects to the sort order decision. Again, there is no "right" choice for all situations, and the selection you make is most important if your SQL Server will be exchanging data with other SQL Servers. Also, the default changed from version 4.2 to version 6.0.

All character sets use the same characters for the first 128 characters. The differences appear in the second 128 characters, which are used primarily for foreign language support. Many of these characters include diacritical marks. If you are using SQL Server only in English-speaking environments, or if you have only one SQL Server to set up, the character set you select is probably unimportant.

The same character set must be used on both clients and servers for data to display properly. Windows NT clients include an International application icon in the Control Panel that allows you to set the character set for that computer.

Some applications, especially older MS-DOS applications, use extended characters for graphics. These applications are generally written expecting Code Page 437 to be used as the character set. Change the character set used on a computer running Windows NT Workstation and then run the application to see if it displays characters properly. If not, you need to use Code Page 437 to support the application.

> **CAUTION**
>
> If you must exchange data with other SQL Servers, it is critical that you use the same character set. Data entered with another character set displays incorrectly, which confuses users and might lead to serious errors.

N O T E   The default character set changed from version 4.2 to version 6.0. The version 4.2 default was Code Page 850. The default for version 6.0 is ISO 8859-1, which is used as a default by Sybase SQL Servers running on UNIX and VMS. The new default reflects the growing need for Microsoft SQL Servers to interoperate with other database servers in enterprise computing environments.

Choosing a Security Model

Microsoft SQL Server supports three different security models. The following sections outline the characteristics of these three models. The decision you make now is not irreversible. If you decide later to change the security model you are using, you can do so with the SQL Enterprise Manager. The appropriate model to select depends on the type of network you are running and the policies in place for managing resources.

Standard   The standard security model implements an entirely separate user account database specifically for SQL Server. This is the default security model. You create SQL Server login IDs using the SQL Enterprise Manager or system stored procedures. These accounts then can be assigned as users of particular databases and granted specific permissions within those databases.

Integrated   The integrated security model uses the accounts and groups defined in a Windows NT domain for SQL Server as well. Users and groups are created using the User Manager for Domains tool provided with Windows NT Server. Then they can be assigned the capability to use SQL Server with the SQL Security Manager and given specific database access and permissions with the SQL Enterprise Manager or system procedures.

Mixed   Use the SQL Security Manager to assign Windows NT accounts and groups to a SQL Server login ID. You can give each user a separate login ID, or assign a collection of users or group to a single login ID. Additionally, you can create and manage standard model login IDs with no relationship to a Windows NT account.

Selecting Protocols for Client-Server Computing

As you have already learned, SQL Server is a product designed to operate in a client-server environment. In this setting, there must be a mechanism for clients and servers to communicate to pass information and instructions to each other. This is often referred to as an *interprocess communication* (*IPC*) mechanism. SQL Server supports several different *network libraries*, special purpose collections of commands and utilities that enable this client-server communication.

The network libraries are referred to collectively as *Net-Libraries*. When implemented, they take the form of dynamic link libraries (DLLs), which are installed on the computers that use them. For example, SSMSRPCN.DLL is the name of the DLL that contains the Microsoft Multi-Protocol RPC Net-Library. DLLs are a widely used mechanism for implementing capabilities for both operating systems and applications. They are an ideal mechanism for implementing Net-Libraries.

N O T E   It is possible, and even common, to configure a SQL Server to support more than one Net-Library. Servers generally have plenty of processing power to handle multiple network libraries and transport protocols. This makes sense because it allows a single server the capability to support clients with different requirements. Most clients, however, are configured to use one transport protocol and a single Net-Library to conserve the use of client resources. ▨

▶ **See** "Understanding Network Protocols," **p. 110**

The connections between a server and various clients can be characterized as either a *trusted* connection or a *nontrusted* connection. Some network protocols support authenticated connections between clients and servers. In other words, mechanisms are built into the networking protocols to ensure that a client connection is *authentic*—the client is who he claims to be. Other network protocols do not have authentication mechanisms and must rely on higher level protocols to provide authentication services. For example, clients using the Multiprotocol RPC and Named Pipes Net-Libraries can establish trusted connections. A Novell NetWare client using the Sockets Net-Library would establish a nontrusted connection.

The issue of trusted and nontrusted connections is related to the security model you select. Nontrusted connections must use SQL Server's login validation since the connection itself is nontrusted. Therefore, clients using nontrusted connections must use standard security or the standard mode of mixed security. If you want to use integrated security, or the integrated mode of mixed security, you must use a network protocol that supports trusted connections.

Each of the supported Net-Libraries has its own characteristics that make it an appropriate selection for particular environments. Some client configurations limit the possible Net-Library selections you can make. The characteristics of the various Net-Libraries, and suggestions for when they are appropriate, are outlined in the following sections.

Named Pipes   The Named Pipes Net-Library has been available since the very first version of SQL Server was offered by Microsoft. It is still available and is the default IPC protocol installed by the SQL Server setup program. Named pipes support is available for all Windows platforms and MS-DOS. A pair of test utilities, MAKEPIPE and READPIPE, are available to test the function of a named pipes connection. Named pipes can be used over all Microsoft transport stacks including NetBEUI, NWLink IPX/SPX, and TCP/IP. However, you cannot install and use named pipes over native Novell transports. The use of named pipes creates a trusted connection that can be used with any security model.

TCP/IP Sockets   Support for sockets clients extends the reach of SQL Server support to a wide range of TCP/IP transport protocols available from various vendors. The popularity and use of TCP/IP stacks have grown dramatically over the past few years. A Windows-based sockets interface standard allows software companies to create utilities and applications that exist at the upper layers of the OSI seven-layer model. These applications can use the sockets interface to request network transport services. Microsoft has implemented its upper-layer SQL Server client support to operate in this environment. TCP/IP sockets clients create nontrusted connections to SQL Servers. Support is available for all Windows platforms, but not for MS-DOS.

NWLink IPX/SPX   To support SQL Server on networks with clients using native Novell IPX/SPX stacks, Microsoft added the NWLink IPX/SPX Net-Library. This Net-Library uses an SPX interface to request transport services from IPX stacks in a manner analogous to the use of a sockets interface for TCP/IP. IPX/SPX Net-Library clients create nontrusted connections to SQL Server. Support is available for all Windows platforms and MS-DOS.

Banyan VINES   This Net-Library supports SQL Server use in environments using Banyan VINES as a network operating system (NOS). Use of this Net-Library creates a nontrusted connection to SQL Server. Support is available for all Windows platforms and MS-DOS.

Multiprotocol RPC   The Multiprotocol RPC Net-Library is the newest IPC protocol and is also the one that Microsoft recommends for most situations. RPC stands for Remote Procedure Call, and this general purpose IPC mechanism is used widely in Windows NT environments. RPCs are used, for example, to allow Windows NT administrative utilities such as Server Manager to connect to remote Windows NT servers.

This Net-Library is a little different from the others. It actually runs on "top" of named pipes, IPX/SPX, or TCP/IP sockets—hence the name Multiprotocol. Use of the Multiprotocol RPC Net-Library allows the creation of trusted connections over TCP/IP and IPX/SPX (as well as named pipes). This Net-Library is available for all Windows platforms, but not for MS-DOS.

An important new feature available only with this Net-Library is the capability to encrypt information before it is transmitted over the network and then decrypt it at the other end of the connection. Although this introduces additional processing overhead and therefore slows down response time somewhat, this is a critical need if you have stringent security requirements. In today's network environment, you should generally assume that a perpetrator can capture all network traffic for analysis and reconstruction unless you have gone to extraordinary lengths to physically secure your premises.

Running the SQL Server Setup Program

Before installing SQL Server, you should create a service account to be used by the SQL Executive. The SQL Executive is a companion service that works with SQL Server to execute scheduled tasks and support advanced services such as replication. You can run the SQL Executive using a LocalSystem account; however, such an account has access privileges only on the local computer. A SQL Executive service running in this manner has no access rights on other computers and therefore cannot participate in replication or tasks involving additional computers.

It is a good idea to set up a domain account for use by the SQL Executive service. If you are using a master domain model, the account should usually be a member of the master domain. The account must be a member of the Administrators local group on the proposed server and should have Log on As a Service rights. It also is a good idea to set the Never Expire option for the account.

If the computer you use as your server has a CD-ROM drive, you can install your server directly from the CD. If it does not, you can copy the contents of the CD onto a shared network directory using a computer that does have a CD-ROM drive, or simply share the CD.

▶ **See** "Using Service Accounts," **p. 114**

To install SQL Server, follow these steps:

1. Insert the SQL Server CD into the CD-ROM drive on the server, or connect to the shared location of the installation files. Change to the directory that matches the type of computer you have—Intel, MIPs, or Alpha AXP. Run SETUP.EXE.

2. Select the option to install SQL Server and Utilities. Follow the instructions provided, and complete the dialog boxes by selecting options for sort order, character set, and security model as discussed earlier. Online help is available as you go through the process either by clicking Help buttons on dialog boxes or by pressing the F1 function key.

3. The setup process should generally take less than 30 minutes.

Using the SQL Enterprise Manager to Build Your Server

In the next few sections, you have your first opportunity to use the SQL Enterprise Manager. You were introduced to this important tool in the last chapter. Now you learn how to start the SQL Enterprise Manager, create a server group, and register your newly installed SQL Server.

Part

VII

Ch

34

Then you are given a quick tour of the main features and capabilities of the SQL Enterprise Manager.

For these operations you should use an account with system administrator (SA) privileges. You can use the SA account itself, but it is better to create a group called SQLAdmins (or something similar) and assign SA privileges to the group. Then you can control who is an administrator by assigning or revoking membership in the group. For more information, see "What Is a Group?" later in the chapter.

Starting the SQL Enterprise Manager

You can run the SQL Enterprise Manager directly on the SQL Server machine, or remotely by using a computer running Windows NT Workstation (or Windows NT Server) on which you have installed the SQL Server administrative tools. To start the SQL Enterprise Manager, follow these steps:

1. Open the Program Manager. Find the SQL Server program group.

2. Double-click the SQL Enterprise Manager icon.

3. The first time you run SQL Enterprise Manager, the Register Server dialog box appears. You need to create at least one server group and register your server as a member of a server group. See the next section, "Creating Server Groups and Registering Servers," for details on how to complete this process.

TROUBLESHOOTING

An Unable to Connect to Server message appears when trying to register my server.
Make sure that the computer you are using is running at least one network protocol in common with the SQL Server. If you are using TCP/IP, try to PING the SQL Server to check basic connectivity.

Creating Server Groups and Registering Servers

Server groups are a convenient way to organize SQL Servers for administrative purposes. These groups have no significance for data replication, transaction management, or other purpose. No server hierarchy exists as with SMS. These groups merely make it convenient to organize the display of the SQL Enterprise Manager. The server groups created by one DBA can be completely different from those created on another computer by another DBA.

To create a server group and register your server, follow these steps:

1. Start the SQL Enterprise Manager.

2. Choose Server, Register Server from menu, or click the Register Server button on the toolbar. The Register Server dialog box appears, as shown in Figure 34.1.

3. Enter the name of the SQL Server you want to register in the Server box. Alternatively, you can click the List Servers button. When the Select Server dialog box appears, select the server you want to register (see Figure 34.2).

FIG. 34.1

Enter a server's name and an administrator's ID and password in the Register Server dialog box so that the SQL Enterprise Manager can be used to manage the server.

FIG. 34.2

Use the Select Server dialog box to choose a server from the list of available servers. If your server does not appear in the list, enter its name manually.

4. In the Login Information box, select the type of connection you want to establish when you use SQL Enterprise Manager to connect to this server. If the server uses the standard security model, select Use Standard Security. This establishes a nontrusted connection to SQL Server and relies on SQL Server security to verify privileges. You also should select this option if you want to use the standard mode of mixed security. If you are using the integrated or mixed security model and want to use a trusted connection to SQL Server, click Use Trusted Connection. See the section "Choosing a Security Model" earlier in the chapter for more details.

5. If you chose standard security, enter the login ID and password. If you are using a trusted connection, your Windows NT user account validates your access and you need not enter an ID and password here.

6. There is a check box at the bottom of the Register Server dialog box for Display Server Status in Server Manager. If this box is selected (the default), SQL Enterprise Manager displays the status of SQL Server using a stoplight icon in the Server Manager window. This indicates whether SQL Server is started, stopped, or paused and provides a convenient way to view the status of your SQL Servers at a glance.

7. It is now time to select a server group. You may use the default group that is already created (SQL 6.5), or you can create your own group(s) to reflect any organizational plan you want. If you don't want to create a new server group, skip ahead to step 9. To create a server group, click the Servers button. The Manage Server Groups dialog box appears, as shown in Figure 34.3.

Part

VII

Ch

34

FIG. 34.3

Use the Manage Server Groups dialog box to create server groups. Administrators can use these groups to organize the collection of servers for which they have administrative responsibilities.

8. Enter the name of the new server group you want to create in the Name text box. You can create a hierarchy of groups, much like a subdirectory hierarchy on a hard disk. Select either the Top Level Group or Sub Group Of option button. If you chose Sub Group Of, you must select a parent group that will contain this server group in the server group hierarchy displayed. You need not select a parent group if you are creating a top level group. Click Add, and your new server group displays in the hierarchy. Then click Close to return to the Register Server dialog box.

9. Click the Register button. Your SQL Server is now registered as a member of the server group you selected and can be managed from this computer using SQL Enterprise Manager. Repeat steps 3 through 8 for each server you want to manage. When you are finished registering servers, click Close to close the Register Server dialog box.

TROUBLESHOOTING

When changing a server registration, I cannot see the Register button. If you are changing a server registration, the Register button becomes the Modify button. Clicking Modify changes your original server registration.

A Quick Tour of the SQL Enterprise Manager

Now that you know how to start SQL Enterprise Manager and have registered your server, it is time to take a tour of the features and capabilities of this most important management tool. For this section, you should be sitting at a computer with the SQL Enterprise Manager up and running (see Figure 34.4). If you have not already done so, start the SQL Enterprise Manager.

When you use SQL Enterprise Manager, you can use either the menus or toolbar buttons. *ToolTips* are available for the toolbar buttons. If you position the mouse cursor over a toolbar button and pause momentarily, a small box appears near the mouse cursor identifying the toolbar button's function.

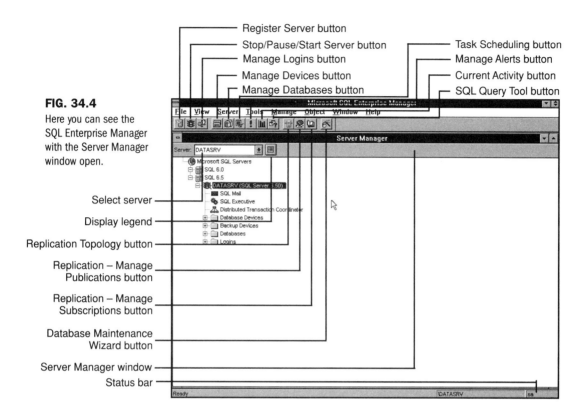

FIG. 34.4

Here you can see the SQL Enterprise Manager with the Server Manager window open.

Register Server button
Stop/Pause/Start Server button
Manage Logins button
Manage Devices button
Manage Databases button
Task Scheduling button
Manage Alerts button
Current Activity button
SQL Query Tool button

Select server
Display legend
Replication Topology button
Replication – Manage Publications button
Replication – Manage Subscriptions button
Database Maintenance Wizard button
Server Manager window
Status bar

Two main windows can open in SQL Enterprise Manager: the Server Manager window and the Replication Topology window. The Server Manager window displays by default whenever SQL Enterprise Manager starts. You open the Replication Topology window by clicking the Replication Topology toolbar button, or by choosing Server, Replication Configuration from the menu. As you execute various tasks, a variety of dialog boxes appear.

By making selections and entering information in the various dialog boxes, you can perform many of the same actions that used to require entering commands in Transact-SQL or using system stored procedures. Of course, you still can use commands to complete these tasks. Using the isql or ISQL/w utility, you can enter individual commands or run scripts containing sequences of commands that have been saved in a file. You may even prefer this option if you must perform an operation repeatedly on many different servers.

A drop-down list box at the top of the Server Manager window allows you to select the server on which you want to focus. Alternatively, you can simply double-click a server to connect to the server and display information about the various objects defined on the server. To the right of the Server drop-down list box is a button that displays a legend describing the various icons and symbols used in the Server Manager window (see Figure 34.5).

Part
VII

Ch
34

FIG. 34.5

The Server Legend window provides a convenient reference for all the icons and symbols used in the SQL Enterprise Manager's various displays.

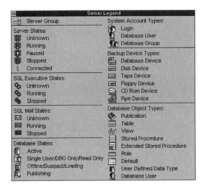

In addition to making selections from menus or using toolbar buttons, you also can use the right mouse button to display context-sensitive menus for many objects in the Server Manager window and the Replication Topology window. By positioning the mouse pointer over an object and clicking the right mouse button, you can initiate many tasks such as creating or deleting an object or editing its structure. The SQL Enterprise Manager is used extensively throughout the rest of the SQL Server chapters to illustrate how to perform various management functions.

▶ **See** "isql and ISQL/w," **p. 1152**

▶ **See** "Using SQL Scripts and Stored Procedures for Maintenance Tasks," **p. 1219**

Creating Login IDs and Usernames

In this section, you learn how to create login IDs for SQL Server users and how to assign them to particular databases that they need to use. This section also provides an overview of SQL Server security and defines some terms that apply to this area of SQL Server administration. Although the concepts are not difficult, the ways in which users are given accounts, log on to SQL Server, and are granted permissions to various objects are handled a little bit differently in SQL Server than in Windows NT Server. Some terminology is a little different, as well. After the differences have been explained, they should no longer be confusing, and you should be able to effectively manage user access to SQL Server.

The way in which users gain access to SQL Server depends on the security model you select when installing SQL Server. If you select integrated security, the domain accounts already defined for use by Windows NT Server are used for SQL Server access, as well. A trusted connection is made between the client workstation and the server. The SQL Security Manager allows you to manage accounts using integrated security. Standard security implies a completely separate set of user accounts, and the connections between client workstations and the server are nontrusted connections. Mixed security allows you to use either integrated or standard security. See "Choosing a Security Model," earlier in the chapter, for more information on this topic.

Understanding Users, Usernames, and Login IDs

Newcomers to SQL Server are frequently confused by the differences between login IDs and usernames. This situation is worsened by the frequent practice of using the term *user* to refer to a SQL Server *username*. You are about to learn the difference between a login ID and a username. After you understand what is meant by a username, you should be able to tell from the context whether the term *user* is meant to refer to an actual person or a SQL Server defined username. This should eliminate the confusion.

The procedures for creating each of these entities are given as they are defined, but you may want to read this entire section before actually creating new login IDs or usernames.

 T I P   SQL Server uses the term *login* rather than Windows NT's *logon*. Do not let this slight difference confuse you. SQL Server uses the term login for historical reasons. The meaning is the same.

What Is a Login ID?   Anyone who wants to access information in a SQL Server database must have a *login ID* (often shortened to *login*). When a user (an actual person) connects to SQL Server using an application program or administrative utility, a login process occurs. If it is a nontrusted connection, SQL Server prompts the user to enter a login ID and corresponding password. If it is a trusted connection, the login ID is implicit using the account that was mapped to the user's Windows NT account with the SQL Security Manager, or the default login ID if no mapping was created. If a default login ID has not been established, the server denies the user access. In other words, even in situations in which the user is not prompted to enter an ID and password, a specific login ID is being used, and a security context for the user is established or denied.

A valid login ID and password allow a user to connect to a server, but do not provide access to any of the databases defined on that server. To use one or more databases, the login ID must be associated with a username, and the username must be assigned permissions for specific databases and database objects.

Often, the username is identical to the login ID. This is another potential source of confusion, so it is important to be accurate. Even if the two match, a login ID of Sam, for example, is a different entity from the username Sam.

To create a new login ID, follow this procedure:

1. Start SQL Enterprise Manager.
2. In the Server Manager window, open a server group by clicking the plus sign (+) to the left of the group name. Select the server you want to manage.
3. Click the Manage Logins toolbar button, or choose <u>M</u>anage, <u>L</u>ogins from the menu. The Manage Logins dialog box appears (see Figure 34.6).

Part

VII

Ch

34

FIG. 34.6

Use the Manage Logins dialog box to create login names, assign passwords, and grant database access.

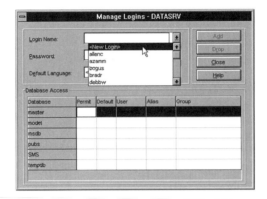

4. Click the drop-down button to the right of the text box and select New Login from the list. The text box clears, and you can enter a new login ID name.

5. Enter a password for the login ID. Users who connect to SQL Server with the default login ID need to know this password.

6. Select a default language for this login ID in the Default Language drop-down list.

7. In the Database Access box, you can make multiple selections as appropriate. You need not make any assignments now if you just want to create the login ID. You can make all other selections later.

   Select the Permit box for each database you want the default login ID to be permitted to use. Click the Default box for the one database that will become the current database when this login ID is used. The username this login ID will use within a database is listed in the User column. The default username is the same as the login ID. You can change this if you want by typing another name in the box. Alternatively, you can select the Alias box for a database and select a username that has already been defined to be used as an alias for this login ID. A login ID may be assigned only one username (or alias) per database. Finally, you can select one group in the Group box per database. This group is in addition to the public group that contains all users.

N O T E It is a good idea to give all login IDs a default database other than master. This discourages users from creating objects in the master database, which is generally a bad practice. ▨

8. Click Add. The confirm password dialog box appears. Carefully reenter the password to confirm it and click OK.

9. Repeat steps 4 through 8 if you want to add another login ID. Click Close to close the Manage Logins dialog box.

What Is a Username?   A username is used to assign a login ID access rights to a database and objects within the database. A particular login ID can be assigned to only one username for a given database, but more than one login ID can be assigned to the same username. For example, if the login ID Sam is assigned to the username Sam for the PUBS database, the Sam login ID cannot also be assigned to the Fred username in PUBS. Another login ID, Sue for example, could be assigned to the Sam username in PUBS. The username Sam would then be an *alias* for the login ID Sue in the PUBS database.

To create a new username for a database, follow this procedure:

1. Start SQL Enterprise Manager.

2. In the Server Manager window, open a server group by clicking the plus sign (+) to the left of the group name.

3. Select the server you want to manage and open the Databases folder. The databases on the server are listed. Select the database for which you want to create a username.

4. Choose Manage, Users from the menu. The Manage Users dialog box appears, as shown in Figure 34.7.

FIG. 34.7
Use the Manage Users dialog box to assign SQL Server usernames to login IDs for access to a database.

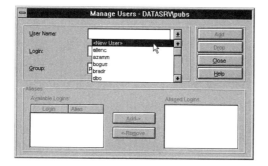

5. Enter a new username in the User Name drop-down list box. If a name already appears in the text box, click the drop-down button at the far right of the box and select New User from the list. A username can be up to 30 characters. The first character must be a letter, or either of the symbols # or _. The rest of the characters can be letters, numbers, or most symbols. If you leave the name blank, a name that matches the login ID (see next step) is created for use in the database.

6. Select a login ID from the Login drop-down list.

7. If you want, you can add this username to one group in addition to the public group, which automatically contains all usernames.

8. Click Add. The Add button becomes a Modify button, indicating that the new username has been added to the database.

9. If this username is to be used as an alias for more than one login ID, you may select login IDs in the Available Logins box and click Add. This adds these logins to the Aliased Logins box. When any aliased login ID uses this database, it uses the username just created as an alias. Click Modify.

10. Click Close.

Part

VII

Ch

34

What Is an Alias?   Whenever two or more login IDs share a username, that username is called an *alias*. You can use any username as an alias. An alias can be an appropriate way to provide several users with the same access rights. Aliases are commonly used to allow more than one user (each with a login ID but sharing a single username) to act as a database owner (DBO). If you intend to alias a number of users to a single username, it is best to create a username that indicates a type of person or a role (like Engineer or Sales), rather than a proper name (like Sam), to avoid confusion.

To assign a username as an alias for more than one login ID, follow this procedure:

1. Start SQL Enterprise Manager.
2. In the Server Manager window, open a server group by clicking the plus sign (+) to the left of the group name.
3. Select the server you want to manage and open the Databases folder. The databases on the server are listed. Select the database for which you want to create an alias.
4. Choose Manage, Users from the menu. The Manage Users dialog box appears (see Figure 34.8).

FIG. 34.8

You also can use the Manage Users dialog box to assign a username as an alias for more than one login ID to use within a particular database.

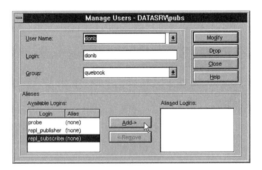

5. Select a username from the User Name drop-down list.
6. The primary login ID associated with this username appears in the Login drop-down list box.
7. Select login IDs in the Available Logins box and click Add. This adds these login IDs to the Aliased Logins box. When any aliased login ID uses this database, it will use the username just created as an alias. Click Modify.
8. Click Close.

What Is a Group?   A group is a collection of usernames created to simplify the assignment of access rights. When a username is created in a database, it is automatically added to the built-in group *public* and cannot be deleted. You also can create other groups. Each username may be added to one additional group besides public. You can remove a username from that additional group and add it to a different group if you later want to change the username's membership.

If you have a database with many usernames defined, it is a good practice to use groups to manage permissions. In such a database, it may be easier to create the groups first and then add usernames to the appropriate group as they are created.

To add a group to a database, follow these steps:

1. Start SQL Enterprise Manager.

2. In the Server Manager window, open a server group by clicking the plus sign (+) to the left of the group name.

3. Select the server you want to manage and open the Databases folder. The databases on the server are listed. Select the database for which you want to create a group.

4. Choose Manage, Groups from the menu. The Manage Groups dialog box appears (see Figure 34.9).

FIG. 34.9
Use the Manage Groups dialog box to create a group of users for the purpose of granting database access.

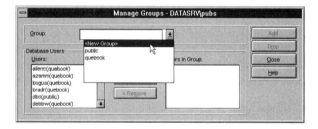

5. Enter a new group name in the Group drop-down list box. If a name already appears in the text box, click the drop-down button at the far right of the box and select New Group from the list. A group name can be up to 30 characters. The first character must be a letter or either of the symbols # or _. The rest of the characters can be letters, numbers, or most symbols.

6. If you want, you can add usernames to membership in the group. Select usernames from the Users list box in the Database Users box. Click the Add button in the center of the dialog box to add them to the group. They then appear in the Users in Group list box.

7. When you are done adding users, click Add in the upper-right corner of the dialog box.

Understanding Special Users and Login IDs

You must understand some special login IDs, usernames, and roles to effectively administer security for SQL Server.

System Administrator (SA)   When you install SQL Server, it creates the *sa* login ID automatically. This login ID allows full access to all databases, database objects, and commands. A number of operations can be initiated only by the *system administrator* (SA). Anyone who knows the password for the sa login ID can act as SA for the server. In addition, with integrated security, you can use the SQL Security Manager to map one or more Windows NT accounts to the sa login ID. When these users attach to SQL Server using a trusted connection, they act in the role of SA.

N O T E   The person acting in the role of system administrator frequently uses the sa login ID.
A lowercase sa refers to the login ID. An uppercase SA is an abbreviation for the role of
system administrator. ▪

SAs are not subject to any security checks after they connect. They can perform any operation
and manage all objects in all databases. An SA can temporarily take on the role of another
username by using the following command:

```
SETUSER ['ID']
```

The SA is the owner of the master database and is treated as the DBO of any databases he
uses.

Default Login ID   When a user connects to SQL Server using a trusted connection, an implicit login process occurs. If the SA has used the SQL Security Manager to map the user's
Windows NT account to a SQL Server login ID, that login is used. If no mapping has been
created, SQL Server uses the default login ID (if it has been created). You can create a default
login ID during SQL Server installation or by using the SQL Enterprise Manager.

To create a default login ID with SQL Enterprise Manager, follow these steps:

1. Start SQL Enterprise Manager.
2. In the Server Manager window, open a server group by clicking the plus sign (+) to the
   left of the group name. Select the server you want to manage.
3. Choose Server, Configurations from menu. The Server Configuration/Options tabbed
   dialog box appears, as shown in Figure 34.10. Click the Security Options tab.

FIG. 34.10

Use the Security
Options tab of the
Server Configuration
dialog box to select
the security model
used by this server and
configure other security-
related settings.

4. Your current settings display. If the Default Login text box is empty, enter a login ID to use as the default. Click OK to close the dialog box and save your new setting. This does not create the login ID, however; it only sets the default. So, if this login ID already exists, you are finished. On the other hand, if you need to create a new login ID to match the default entry you just made, continue with step 5.

5. Click the Manage Logins toolbar button, or choose Manage, Logins from the menu. The Manage Logins dialog box appears (see Figure 34.11).

FIG. 34.11

You can use the Manage Logins dialog box to assign database access to the default login ID.

6. Enter the same name you used in step 4 into the Login Name drop-down list box. If a name is already listed in the text box, click the drop-down button to the right of the text box and select New Login from the list.

7. Enter a password for the login ID. Users who connect to SQL Server with the default login ID need to know this password.

8. Select a default language for this login ID from the Default Language drop-down list.

9. In the Database Access box, you can make multiple selections as appropriate. Select the Permit box for each database you want the default login ID to be able to use. Click the Default box for the one database that you want to be the current database when this login ID is used. The username this login ID will use within a database is listed in the User column. The default username is the same as the login ID. You can change this if you want by typing another name in the box. Alternatively, you can select the Alias box for a database and select a username that has already been defined to be used as an alias for this login ID. You can assign a login ID only one username (or alias) per database. Finally, you can select one group in the Group box per database. This group is in addition to the public group, which contains all users.

10. Click Add. The Confirm Password dialog box appears. Carefully reenter the password to confirm it and click OK.

11. Click Close to close the Manage Logins dialog box.

Part

VII

Ch

34

Visitor Login IDs   If you have a number of users that need only occasional access to SQL Server, you may want to create a visitor login ID that these casual users can share. This is done as a convenience for the SA. Rather than create individual login IDs for all these users, you create a single login ID (named *visitor*, for example) and provide the login ID and password to users who fit the description of a visitor. Typically such a login ID has very limited access to databases and database objects. This is usually done by the use of guest usernames, discussed later in the chapter (see "The Guest Username").

The Database Owner (DBO)   The creator of a database is the database owner (DBO). On a newly installed SQL Server, the sa login ID is the DBO of the master database. The SA can grant the capability to create databases to specific login IDs. If a user connects to SQL Server with one of these login IDs and creates a database, the user has the special username "DBO" in that database. In other databases, the user is known by whatever username has been assigned to that user's login ID.

Only one login ID can be assigned DBO status in a database. You can transfer DBO status to a different login ID (using sp_changedbowner) and alias multiple login IDs to DBO. The DBO has all privileges in a database and can act as an administrator of that database, granting other users permission to access the database, creating objects, and assigning permissions to objects.

Database Object Owners   A DBO can grant permission for users to create objects in the database. When a user then creates an object, that user becomes the *object owner*. The object owner must grant permission for other users to access or modify the object, including the DBO or SA. However, the DBO or SA can impersonate any other user in the database, including the database object owner, and thereby grant permissions. No special login ID or username is associated with an object owner.

The Public Group   All usernames added to a database are automatically added to a special group named *public*. You cannot drop usernames from this group, or drop the group itself. Access permissions assigned to the public group create a minimum set of permissions shared by all usernames in a database. You can add usernames to one group in addition to *public*.

The Guest Username   By creating a username of *guest* in a database, you create a username context for any login ID that has not been explicitly assigned a username or alias for that database. Therefore, any user who can connect to SQL Server (with their own login ID, a visitor login ID, or the default login ID) can use the database with the access permissions assigned to *guest*, even if the login ID they use has not been assigned a username or alias. When the guest username is created, it automatically inherits the access permissions granted to the public group. An SA or the DBO can change these permissions.

Creating Devices

As stated earlier in the chapter, a device is the foundation upon which databases, transaction logs, and backups reside. The method to create devices used for databases or transaction logs is different from the method for creating devices for backups of the databases and transaction logs. The following sections explain both methods.

Backup (Dump) Devices

Backup devices are very important. They allow recovery should a hard drive crash. It cannot be stressed enough that every DBA should design and implement a disaster recovery plan. Part of this plan is a regularly scheduled backup (with the DUMP DATABASE command) to a dump device. Before you can do this, however, you need to create the appropriate device(s) to which to back up the databases and transaction logs. You can create dump devices on disk drives, tape drives, and floppy disk drives. Two default floppy disk backup devices are created.

NOTE The terms *dump* and *backup* are synonymous in the context of SQL Server discussions. Starting with version 6.5, there is a growing use of backup rather than dump. Beginners occasionally confuse dump and *drop*—a serious error! To drop an object is to discard or delete it, something you certainly don't want to do if you intend to back it up. ■

To create a backup device, perform the following steps:

1. Start SQL Enterprise Manager.
2. In the Server Manager window, open a server group by clicking the plus sign (+) to the left of the group name.
3. Select the server you want to manage. Click the plus sign next to the server name to open the list of objects and services on the server.
4. Select Backup Devices in the list and click the right mouse button.
5. Select New Backup Device from the resulting pop-up menu. The New Backup Device dialog box appears (see Figure 34.12).

FIG. 34.12
Use the New Backup Device dialog box to create a backup device (also known as a dump device) to be used as the target of a backup procedure.

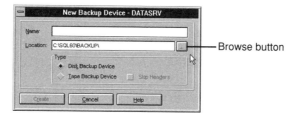

Browse button

Part
VII

Ch
34

6. Enter the backup device Name. This is the logical name of the device.
7. Enter the physical name for the dump device in the Location box. The name should be of the form *drive:\path\filename* for a local disk drive, or *\\servername\sharename\path\filename* for a shared network drive. A tape drive should have a name of the form *\\.\TAPEx* where *x* is replaced with an integer starting with 0 for the first tape drive, 1 for the second, and so on.
8. Select the type of backup device you want to create using the option buttons.
9. Click Create.

Database Devices

Database devices are an integral part of SQL Server. Database devices are where all data and transaction logs are stored. As with dump devices, when you create a database device, you must supply both a logical and a physical name. The logical name is what SQL Server uses to identify a device. A physical name is the actual file name (including path) that identifies the device to the operating system.

When you create a device for a database, you also should create a log device on a separate drive. This allows you to recover the database in case the drive containing the database crashes. (Remember, you must have in place and execute a regularly scheduled DUMP for this plan to work.) Also, creating the transaction log on a device separate from the one that contains the database improves performance and allows you to back up the transaction log without backing up the database.

To create a database device, perform the following steps:

1. Start SQL Enterprise Manager.
2. In the Server Manager window, open a server group by clicking the plus sign (+) to the left of the group name.
3. Select the server you want to manage. Click the plus sign next to the server name to open the list of objects and services on the server.
4. Select Database Devices in the list and click the right mouse button.
5. Select New Database Device from the resulting pop-up menu. The New Database Device dialog box appears, as shown in Figure 34.13.
6. Enter the database device Name. This is the logical name of the device.

FIG. 34.13
Use the New Database Device dialog box to define the name, size, and location of a new database device.

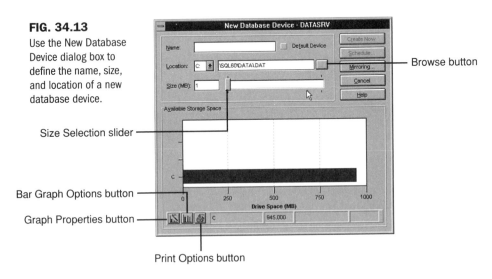

7. Select the drive on which to put the device. (SQL Server allows you to place devices on local disks only—that is, placed on the computer on which SQL Server is installed, even though it can be managed from a workstation.)

8. If you want to change the default path, overwrite the name in the Location drop-down list's text box, or click the ellipsis (...) button to browse the directory structure of the server. Enter the size in megabytes. The minimum size for a database device is 1M. The relative size of the proposed device (compared to available space) displays in a bar chart that changes dynamically as you enter the number.

9. Select the Default Device check box if you want to add this database device to the pool of default devices used to store newly created databases when a device is not specified.

10. Click OK. SQL Server adds the database device.

Creating Databases and Database Objects

Databases consist of objects. These objects store not only the data, but also supporting objects that make it possible for SQL Server to maintain data integrity and referential integrity, enforce business rules, and provide a mechanism to make the application-development process easier for all concerned. The primary objects contained in a database are tables. You can create other objects, such as indexes, defaults, and rules, at the same time you create a table, or add them later. Some of these objects can be created using the SQL Enterprise Manager or with Transact-SQL statements. See "CREATE DATABASE Statement" in the *TRANSACT-SQL Reference Manual*. Views, triggers, and stored procedures must be created using Transact-SQL statements.

To create a database using the SQL Enterprise Manager, follow these steps:

1. Start SQL Enterprise Manager.

2. In the Server Manager window, open a server group by clicking the plus sign (+) to the left of the group name.

3. Select the server you want to manage. Click the Manage Databases toolbar button; the Manage Databases dialog box appears (see Figure 34.14).

FIG. 34.14
The Manage Databases dialog box provides a graphical representation of the databases defined on a server.

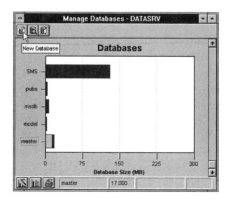

4. Click the New Database button. The New Database dialog box appears, as shown in
    Figure 34.15.

FIG. 34.15

Use the New Database
dialog box to define a
new database.

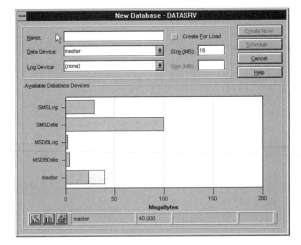

5. A graph appears representing the various devices defined on this server, the size of each
    device, and the amount of available space. A default device to contain the new database is
    automatically entered in the Data Device drop-down list box.

6. Enter a name for the new database in the Name text box.

7. If you want, you can change the default data device by using the Data Device drop-down
    list. You also can select <new> from the list if you want to define a new device. Use the
    same procedure you have already learned for creating a new device to create a device
    during database creation. Refer to the section "Creating Devices" earlier in this chapter.

8. Enter a size for the data device in the Size (MB) text box. By default, this is filled in with
    the largest amount of space available on the selected device. As you enter numerals, the
    graphic display is updated to reflect the size of the proposed database.

9. Select a device to contain the transaction log for this database from the Log Device drop-
    down list. Again, you can select <new> from the list if you want to define a new device.
    Enter a size for the log device in the Size (MB) text box.

    Always store the transaction log for a database on a separate device from the database
    itself. This improves performance and allows you to make backups of the log. As a rule
    of thumb, the size of the log should be 10 to 25 percent of the database size.

10. If you want to load a backup into this database before it is used, click Create For Load.

11. Click OK to create the database.

After you have created the database, you can begin creating the database objects. You now can
implement the planning that you've done for the database and its objects. Before you begin,
however, review your data model for potential problems. This means that your plan must be

documented, not just worked out in your head. Any database requiring the power of SQL Server should be documented and reviewed by at least one other person. It is always easier to do this before the database objects are created than after.

Just a few of the issues you should resolve before proceeding with creating database objects follow:

- Have all tables been identified and defined?
- Have all columns been identified for each table?
- Has the datatype and/or length of each column been established?
- Have you determined whether each column can contain a null value?
- Has a set of valid values been determined for each column?
- Has a default value been considered for each column?
- Have any key fields been identified for all tables?
- Have all possible indexes been defined to optimize performance?
- Have all the business rules been identified?
- Have you determined how application developers will present the data to the eventual users?
- Have you determined how data integrity will be enforced?
- Have you determined how referential integrity will be enforced?

If you answered no to any of the preceding questions, you are not ready to create database objects. It cannot be stressed enough that proper planning is essential in creating and maintaining a SQL Server database along with a client-server application. Don't fool yourself by believing that you can plan as you go. It just won't work.

You can create several supporting objects during the creation of a table object by using the Advanced Features button. However, the following sections demonstrate how you can create these objects independently of one another to introduce you to the various facilities of the SQL Enterprise Manager. This should be useful later when you are maintaining the database structure.

Part
VII

Ch
34

Tables

The Table object is used to store the data in the database. It is the basis to which all other objects are related. Tables are conceptually comprised of rows and columns, much like spreadsheets. When tables are created, each column must be identified as a certain datatype. This tells SQL Server how to store the data in the table as well as how much space to use to store the data. Table 34.1 presents a list of the datatypes available and the number of bytes required for each.

Table 34.1   Datatypes

Datatypes	Bytes Required
binary(n)	n
varbinary(n)	0–255
char(n)	n
varchar(n)	0–255
datetime	8
smalldatetime	4
decimal(p,s)	1–17 (depending on the precision)
numeric(p,s)	1–17 (depending on the precision)
float(n)	8
real	4
int	4
smallint	2
tinyint	1
money	8
smallmoney	4
bit	1 (up to 8 bit columns can be stored in one byte)
timestamp	Same as binary(8)
user-defined	Variable datatypes
text	Stored as series of linked 2K pages
image	Stored as series of linked 2K pages

A number of questions should come to mind when designing tables:

- What data do I need in the tables?
- How will these tables be related to one another?
- What type of data will be stored?
- Are there any columns whose data items are optional?
- Are there any columns whose data items must fall within a certain range of values?
- Are there any columns whose data items must be restricted to values based on a value stored in another column or table?
- Are there any columns whose value will be the same in a large percentage of the rows?

The answers to these questions may necessitate the need to create one or more of the following supporting objects:

- Indexes
- Defaults
- Rules
- Views
- Triggers
- Stored procedures

Tables fall into one of two categories: *permanent* or *temporary*. Permanent tables exist until they are explicitly dropped. Temporary tables subdivide into two types: *local* and *global*. Local temporary tables exist until the current session is terminated. Global temporary tables exist until all sessions using the table have been terminated. To create temporary tables, you must use the CREATE TABLE command or the SELECT INTO command. See "CREATE TABLE Statement" in the *TRANSACT-SQL Reference Manual*.

To create a permanent table, you must know the columns required for the table, as well as the datatypes for all the columns. It also is a good idea to know which columns may contain a null value. To create a permanent table, perform the following steps:

1. Start SQL Enterprise Manager.
2. In the Server Manager window, open a server group by clicking the plus sign (+) to the left of the group name.
3. Select the server you want to manage. Click the plus sign next to the server name to open the list of objects and services on the server.
4. Click the plus sign next to the Databases folder to open the list of databases on this server. Highlight the database on which you want to create the table.
5. Choose <u>M</u>anage, <u>T</u>ables from the resulting pop-up menu. The Manage Tables dialog box appears, as shown in Figure 34.16.

FIG. 34.16

The Manage Tables dialog box is used to create a table by defining the columns, their datatypes, their size, and any constraints that apply to the columns.

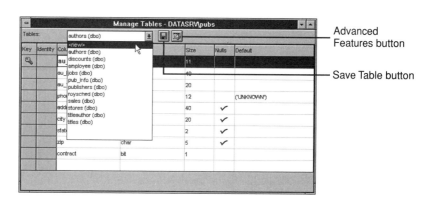

Advanced Features button

Save Table button

Part

VII

Ch

34

6. You can now begin entering the column names for the table. For each column identified for the table, you can enter the following pieces of information:

   - Column name
   - Datatype
   - Size (if applicable)
   - Nulls
   - Default

7. You may notice two additional columns in the dialog box labeled Key and Identity. These are read-only. You learn to create indexes and identity columns in the next section, and defaults in another section later on.

8. After you have entered the column names and their datatypes, click the Save Table toolbar button. The Specify Table Name dialog box appears so that you can specify the table name (see Figure 34.17).

FIG. 34.17

Use this dialog box to enter a name for the new table.

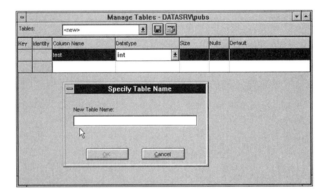

9. Enter the table name and click OK.

Indexes

Indexes are used to increase response time during the execution of queries. Much like the index of a book, an index provides a way to find a piece of information quickly without having to look at each record sequentially to determine whether it meets the search criteria. SQL Server furnishes two types of indexes: *clustered* and *nonclustered*.

Building a clustered index physically orders the rows of the table being indexed based on the key specified for the index. In other words, the table is stored in clustered index order. Therefore, each table can have one, and only one, clustered index. A non-clustered index leaves the existing table as is, and creates a separate index based on the index key.

You can identify an index as a unique index, which means that the column(s) identified in the index must be unique in the table (that is, no two rows in the table can contain the same value). An example would be a Social Security number (SSN) on a personnel table. Because no two people should possess the same SSN, a unique index is appropriate. If an attempt was made to add a record whose SSN already existed in the table, an error would result. Column(s) identified in a unique index cannot allow a NULL value.

> **N O T E** This is actually the subject of debate among database aficionados. The uniqueness of Social Security numbers is *not* guaranteed. Depending on the size of the population and range of years tracked by your database, this may be a poor choice for a unique index. In practice, it works most of the time, but it does highlight the care you must take when selecting unique indexes. ■

Other columns do not accommodate a unique index, such as a state column. If a personnel department must produce reports based on the employee's state, it makes sense to create an index on the field. However, because the state field cannot be unique for every row on the table, a unique index cannot be built on the state column.

After you have created the table, you can enter any necessary indexes. As stated earlier, an index is primarily for reducing response time during the execution of queries. However, indexes also can provide a way to enforce data integrity. For example, you can create a unique index on the Social Security number of a personnel file, thereby prohibiting the addition of records with duplicate Social Security numbers.

To create an index, perform the following tasks:

1. Start SQL Enterprise Manager.
2. In the Server Manager window, open a server group by clicking the plus sign (+) to the left of the group name.
3. Select the server you want to manage. Click the plus sign next to the server name to open the list of objects and services on the server.
4. Click the plus sign next to the Databases folder to open the list of databases on this server. Highlight the database on which you want to create the index.
5. Choose Manage, Indexes from the menu. The Manage Indexes dialog box appears, as shown in Figure 34.18.

FIG. 34.18
Use the Manage Indexes dialog box to define and modify indexes for tables in the database.

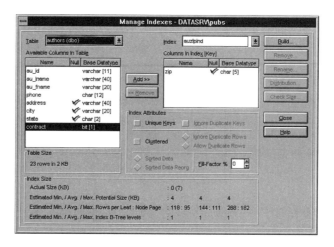

Part
VII

Ch
34

6. This dialog box allows you to create and maintain all indexes in a database. First, you must select the table on which you want to create an index from the Table drop-down list in the upper-left corner of the dialog box. When a table is selected, its columns display in the Available Columns In Table list box directly below the Table drop-down list box. The list box also displays whether each column may contain a null value and the datatype of the column.

7. If any indexes currently exist for the selected table, they appear in the drop-down list to the right of the one for the tables. To create a new index, you must enter the name of the index in the drop-down list box. You now can highlight individual columns and make them part of the index you are creating by clicking Add. As you do this, the column disappears from the Available Columns In Table list box and appears in the Columns In Index (Key) list box. To remove a column from the index, highlight it and click Remove.

8. If you want the index to be for a unique key, click the Unique Keys check box in the Index Attributes area. If the Unique Keys check box is checked, you also can indicate whether to ignore duplicate keys by clicking the Ignore Duplicate Keys check box.

9. You also can specify whether the index should be clustered. If so, you also can indicate whether SQL Server should allow duplicate rows. This option can be specified only when a non-unique clustered index exists.

10. The Sorted Data option is valid only when creating a clustered index on an existing table. If you select Sorted Data, SQL Server does not perform the sort step of the index build (because you indicated that the data already is sorted in index order). If the data exists in a different order from what the index specifies, the command will be rejected and the new (incorrect) index will not be built.

11. If you are an experienced DBA who wants to exercise more control over how much of each page should be left available for subsequent rows in the table, you can make an entry in the Fill Factor box. This is relevant only at the time of index creation on an existing table and only useful when you can accurately predict how the data in the table will change in the future.

12. Click the Build button. SQL Server creates the new index.

Defaults

If a certain column will contain the same value in a large percentage of the rows in a certain table, you can create a *default*. If a record is inserted into the table and a value is not supplied for the column in question, it is set automatically to the value specified in the default.

Defaults allow you to avoid providing a value if the value of the column will be the same in most rows. The easiest way to define a default is to enter it when you create a table using the method mentioned previously. The rightmost column in the Manage Tables dialog box is used to provide a default for the column in the table. If you want to define a default that can be used by many columns in various tables in the database, you must define the default a different way.

To define a default to be used throughout the database, perform the following tasks:

1. Start SQL Enterprise Manager.

2. In the Server Manager window, open a server group by clicking the plus sign (+) to the left of the group name.

3. Select the server you want to manage. Click the plus sign next to the server name to open the list of objects and services on the server.

4. Click the plus sign next to the Databases folder to open the list of databases on this server. Highlight the database on which you want to create the default.

5. Choose Manage, Defaults from menu. The Manage Defaults dialog box appears with three tabs: Defaults, Column Bindings, and Datatype Bindings, as shown in Figure 34.19.

FIG. 34.19

Use the Column Bindings tab on the Manage Defaults dialog box to bind a default value to one or more columns in one or more tables.

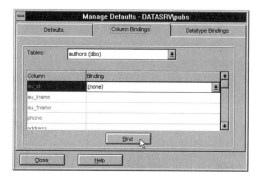

6. Make sure that the Defaults tab has been selected and enter the name of the default in the Defaults drop-down list box.

7. Enter the description of the default in the Description text box. If you enter a string for the description, it must be enclosed in quotation marks.

8. Enter a value for the default.

9. Click Add. Even though you have added the default, you still need to associate it with columns in tables in the database. To apply the default to specific columns, you must now "bind" the default to the columns.

10. Select the Column Bindings tab on the Manage Defaults dialog box (refer to Figure 34.19).

11. Select the table that contains the column to which you want to associate the default. Select the column in the table.

12. Click Bind.

Part
VII

Ch
34

Rules

This object allows a DBA to specify the set of values that are legal for insertion into specific columns or user-defined datatypes. For example, with a state column in a personnel table, there are 51 legitimate values in the United States (one for each state and one for the District of Columbia). You can create a rule that specifies that the value inserted (or updated) into this column must be one of those 51 values. Otherwise, the insert (or update) results in an error.

You can specify the following criteria in a rule:

- Specific values (the 51 legal state codes for example, AK, NY, and so on).
- A range of values (a number between 1 and 51).
- Formatting (such as a field that requires that the first two characters be letters and the next three characters be numbers).

Using rules can result in more reliable data in the database because some validation can be done at the server level. Rules are created in much the same way as defaults. The only difference is that you select Rules from the Manage menu. In addition, the description must contain the condition(s) for the rule instead of a single value for a default. After you create a rule, you must bind it to a column(s) in the database in the same manner you learned to bind defaults to columns in a database. Refer to the "Defaults" section earlier in the chapter.

Views

After the relational database is constructed, logical presentations of data cannot always be accomplished by referring to one table alone. The process of taking the data as stored in tables and making it available in a logical presentation can be made easier by using a *view*. A view is simply a method of presenting data in a table format different from the underlying table(s) used for storage.

A view is sometimes called a *virtual table*, meaning that the data in a view (in most cases) can be manipulated and displayed as though it were in a table. The data itself is not stored in the view, but in the underlying tables on which the view is based. A view is stored in the database as instructions for creating the presentation of the data from the actual tables.

The following benefits make views a valuable tool in SQL Server:

- You can construct views so as to show only specific rows and/or columns, thus making it easier for the DBA to limit what users can see in the database.
- Views can reference one or more tables, joining separate tables on columns that correspond to each other.
- In most cases, views can be treated as though they were tables with updates applying to the underlying tables.

To define a view, use the CREATE VIEW statement in conjunction with the SELECT statement from the Transact-SQL language. If you are not experienced with using Transact-SQL, you should review "Retrieving Data with Queries" in the *Database Developer's Companion*. You also should practice executing queries with the ISQL/W utility provided with SQL Server.

To create a view in SQL Server, perform the following tasks:

1. Start SQL Enterprise Manager.

2. In the Server Manager window, open a server group by clicking the plus sign (+) to the left of the group name.

3. Select the server you want to manage. Click the plus sign next to the server name to open the list of objects and services on the server.

4. Click the plus sign next to the Databases folder to open the list of databases on this server. Highlight the database on which you want to create the view.

5. Choose Manage, View. The Manage Views dialog box appears (see Figure 34.20).

FIG. 34.20

Use the Manage Views dialog box to enter the definition for a new view or modify an existing view.

Execute button

6. <New> appears in the Views drop down list and CREATE VIEW <*view name*> AS in the lower portion of the dialog box. To finish creating the view, replace <*view name*> with the name of the view you want to create, and enter a SELECT statement that specifies the tables and columns to include in the view below.

7. Click the Execute button (a green triangle pointing to the right). The view is created. You may now treat the newly created view as if it were a table in the database for most operations.

Triggers

Triggers are a particular type of stored procedure executed automatically when changes are made to the data in a table. They can be built for inserting new rows into a table, updating existing rows in a table, or deleting existing rows in a table. They are used primarily for enforcing referential integrity and data integrity. Triggers are based on one table only, but can affect changes on other tables if necessary. For example, suppose that a customer goes out of business and needs to be deleted from a table in a database. All of that customer's ship-to locations also should be deleted from another table in the database. This is called a *cascading delete*, and you can accomplish it by using a trigger. You also can use a trigger to prevent the deletion if that customer has an outstanding unpaid balance.

Part
VII

Ch
34

Stored Procedures

There is often a need for software applications to execute the same functions from various places in the application. Instead of creating the Transact-SQL statements to execute these functions at every location where it is needed, you can use stored procedures. A stored procedure is a series of Transact-SQL statements grouped together and compiled the first time they are run. Subsequent executions usually are faster than a standard Transact-SQL batch (even if the batch contains the exact same statements) because they have been compiled and do not need to be recompiled and interpreted each time.

Stored procedures can accept up to 255 parameters. This allows standard calculations or processes based on one or more variables to be coded into a stored procedure. Procedures also can call other stored procedures, which allows some code reuse within SQL Server itself. Version 6.0 of SQL Server contains an enhancement to the EXEC statement that allows you to execute a dynamically built SQL statement. This allows you to program an iterative process in which a SQL statement can execute a variable number of times, depending on the process and the items for which the process was called.

There also is the opportunity to provide limited access to information from tables a user does not have permission to view. Permission to execute a stored procedure can be granted to the user, and the stored procedure may return specific data from tables to which the user does not normally have access.

Stored procedures also can provide a way to enforce business rules. For example, a mail order house could have a table built for sales records and have a stored procedure be responsible for entering new rows into the table. The stored procedure could check the outstanding unpaid balance for the customer, and if it happens to be over a defined threshold, reject the attempt to add a record to the table and inform the user that the customer's unpaid balance must be reduced before further sales to that customer are allowed.

Stored procedures allow you to do just about anything you can imagine with a SQL Server database. With very few exceptions, you can combine Transact-SQL statements to provide the required functionality. A thorough understanding of Transact-SQL is recommended to take full advantage of stored procedures.

You create stored procedures in much the same way as views, except that stored procedures are not limited to the SELECT statement. To create a stored procedure in SQL Server, perform the following tasks:

1. Start SQL Enterprise Manager.
2. In the Server Manager window, open a server group by clicking the plus sign (+) to the left of the group name.
3. Select the server you want to manage. Click the plus sign next to the server name to open the list of objects and services on the server.
4. Click the plus sign next to the Databases folder to open the list of databases on this server. Highlight the database on which you want to create the stored procedure.

5. Choose <u>M</u>anage, Stored <u>P</u>rocedures from the menu. The Manage Stored Procedures dialog box appears (see Figure 34.21).

FIG. 34.21

Use the Manage Stored Procedures dialog box to enter the definition for a new stored procedure or modify an existing stored procedure.

6. <New> appears in the Procedures drop-down list box and CREATE PROCEDURE *<procedure name>* AS in the lower portion of the dialog box. To finish creating the stored procedure, replace *<procedure name>* with the name of the stored procedure you want to create and enter the Transact-SQL statements that comprise the stored procedure in the window below.

7. Click the Execute button (a green triangle pointing to the right). The stored procedure is then created.

From Here...

In this chapter, you learned how to prepare for and then execute SQL Server installation. You learned how to select an appropriate sort order, character set, security model, and network protocol. The chapter introduced the SQL Enterprise Manager and explored the procedures for creating login IDs and usernames to provide access to SQL Server and database objects. You learned how to create database and dump devices and, finally, how to create databases and database objects.

The following chapters cover topics related to those discussed in this chapter:

- For an understanding of the details associated with administering SQL Server, see Chapter 35, "Maintaining SQL Server."

- To learn about SQL Server's data replication features, see Chapter 36, "SQL Server Data Replication."

- To learn how to use SQL Server to build a data warehouse, see Chapter 37, "Data Warehousing with SQL Server."

- For information on the host connectivity component of BackOffice, SNA Server, see Chapter 39, "SNA Server Preparation and Installation."

- For information on the systems management component of BackOffice, Systems Management Server (SMS), see Chapter 42, "Preparing for SMS."

Part
VII

Ch
34

CHAPTER 35

Maintaining SQL Server

by Don Benage

In the last chapter, you learned the basics of setting up SQL Server, creating databases, and creating database objects. By combining these skills with the information about database design, you are well on your way to being successful with SQL Server. In this chapter, you learn about keeping SQL Server running properly. You learn techniques for monitoring the health of SQL Server and some proactive steps you can take to ensure that no problems arise. Procedures for importing and exporting data also are discussed. ■

How to use SQL Enterprise Manager for database administration

Extend your knowledge of SQL Enterprise Manager with new techniques to perform database administration and maintenance tasks.

How to import and export data

Learn how to automatically transfer database objects from one SQL Server to another. Find out how to use the SQL Enterprise Manager to generate Transact-SQL (T-SQL) scripts that re-create database objects on other servers.

How to use SQL scripts, stored procedures, and the SQL Executive for maintenance tasks

Find out how to build script files containing T-SQL commands that you can use to perform maintenance tasks. Learn how to create stored procedures that can be run manually, or scheduled and executed by the SQL Executive.

How to use SQL Server security

Learn how to use the SQL Security Manager to manage Windows NT accounts that need SQL Server access and how to grant database access and object permissions to SQL Server usernames.

Database Administration with the SQL Enterprise Manager

To avoid problems, follow the guidelines already provided in this book for sizing the computer you select to build your SQL Server and adhere to sound database design principles. It is only natural, however, for conditions to change as you put databases into production use. Over time, some design decisions made initially are no longer valid. You may need to add tables and relationships to reflect new requirements. New triggers also may be needed to enforce changing business rules.

As information is added, the data itself may develop characteristics that suggest changes. Perhaps after months in production it becomes evident that "hot spots" have developed in the database—some areas are very active, whereas other areas are used rarely. By performing some tuning, you may be able to balance the distribution of data and improve performance.

You've already been introduced to SQL Enterprise Manager. Now it's time to learn some additional functions provided by this powerful tool that can help keep your server healthy.

Creating Groups of Servers

In general, each SQL Server administrator creates his own server groups and can organize the servers he manages in any manner that is convenient and sensible. It is possible, however, to share the server groups created by one user with other administrators. In version 6.0 (and later), you can manually copy the SERVERS.BIN file, which is usually located in the \SQL60\BINN directory, to another database administrator's (DBA's) computer after creating a desirable set of server groups and registering appropriate servers.

Version 6.5 replaces the SERVERS.BIN file with registry entries. The SQL Enterprise Manager is a 32-bit application and cannot, therefore, be run on 16-bit Windows operating systems. Both Windows NT and Windows 95 computers can run the SQL Enterprise Administrator, and both of these operating systems use a hierarchical database called the *Registry* to contain configuration information, largely replacing the use of configuration files such as WIN.INI and SYSTEM.INI. If you upgrade an existing SQL Server 6.0 installation, the information in SERVERS.BIN migrates into the Registry the first time you run SQL Enterprise Manager.

N O T E Many INI files have been retained on 32-bit Windows platforms for compatibility with older applications. They are used much less than in the past, however, and their use should eventually cease. ■

Although the SERVER.BIN file is no longer used, it is still possible to share a particular configuration for SQL Enterprise Manager. To set up a shared configuration, follow these steps:

1. Select a computer on which to store the shared configuration information. This should be a computer that is always running and available, such as a server. You can use a server to store the information even if you use Windows NT Workstation and Windows 95 desktop computers to run SQL Enterprise Manager.

2. On the computer you have selected, start SQL Enterprise Manager, create the server groups you desire, and register your SQL Servers.

3. Exit the SQL Enterprise Manager. This saves the group and server registration information in the Registry on the local computer. You then can connect to this computer from other administrative workstations and use the shared configuration. At each computer that you want to share this configuration, complete the remaining steps.

4. Start SQL Enterprise Manager.

5. From the menu, choose Tools, Preferences/Configure. The Configure SQL Enterprise Manager dialog box appears (see Figure 35.1).

FIG. 35.1

Use the Configure SQL Enterprise Manager dialog box to select the computer whose shared configuration you want to use and make other global settings affecting the operation of SQL Enterprise Manager.

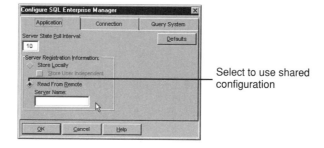

Select to use shared configuration

6. Select the Application tab.

7. In the Read From Remote text box, enter the name of the server containing the configuration information. Use the form *servername*. Click OK.

▶ **See** "Creating Server Groups and Registering Servers," **p. 1168**

Checking Space Utilization

Because SQL Server allows you to preallocate space for databases by creating database devices, it is less likely than other applications to suddenly run out of space due to actions by another user or application. It is still important, however, to take an active approach toward space management on SQL Servers. A number of techniques can be helpful in this area. Some you execute manually on an ad hoc basis, whereas you can set up others to automatically help monitor the use of storage space on servers. This section outlines both approaches.

A number of questions arise when you want to characterize a server's storage. Following is a short list of questions that might be of interest:

■ What devices have been defined on a server?

■ What database(s) and/or log(s) have been placed on a device?

■ How much, if any, available space is left on a device?

■ On which device(s) has a database been placed?

■ How much, if any, available space is left in a database?

Part

VII

Ch

35

You can find the answers to these questions by using isql or ISQL/w and running system stored procedures (for example, sp_helpdb and sp_helpdevice). You also can use the SQL Enterprise Manager to view the status of devices and databases on a server. The information displays in bar graph format. New in version 6.5 is the capability to set options to control the format of the graphs and output them to a printer.

To view a graph depicting the devices that have been defined on a server, follow these steps:

1. Start SQL Enterprise Manager.

2. In the Server Manager window, open a server group by clicking the plus sign (+) to the left of the group name. Select the server you want to manage.

3. Click the Manage Devices toolbar button, or choose Manage, Devices from the menu. The Manage Database Devices dialog box appears, as shown in Figure 35.2.

FIG. 35.2

The Manage Database Devices dialog box provides a graphical display of the currently configured database devices. Toolbar buttons are available to create, edit, or delete devices.

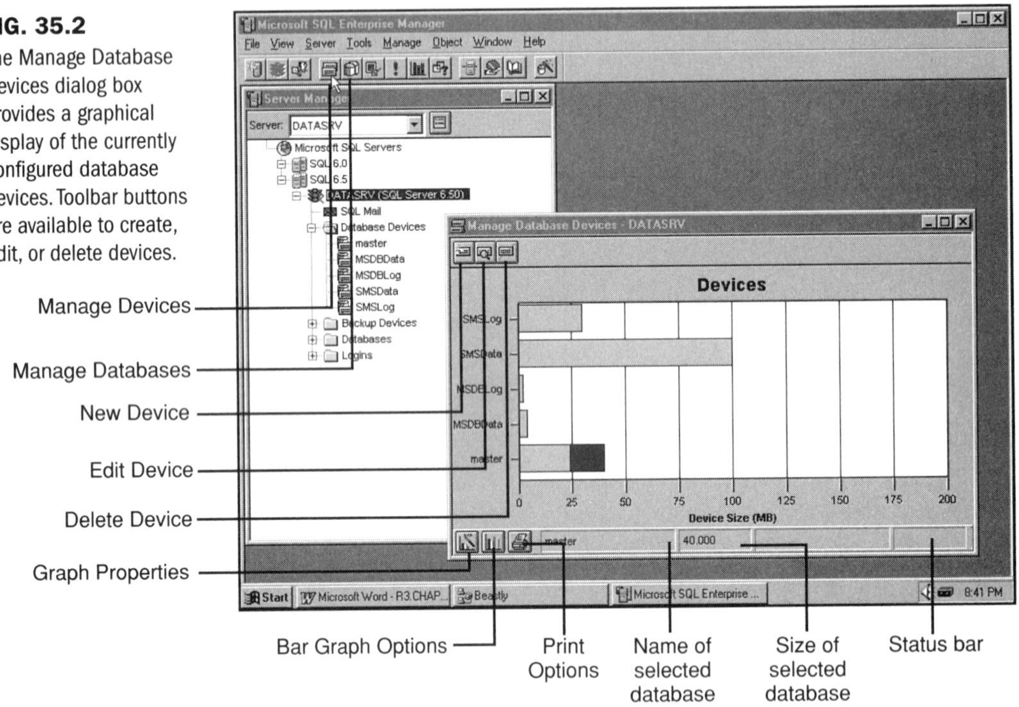

Manage Devices
Manage Databases
New Device
Edit Device
Delete Device
Graph Properties

Bar Graph Options — Print Options — Name of selected database — Size of selected database — Status bar

4. All the devices defined on this server are displayed in a bar graph. Two different colors show the space used and the space available.

NOTE When viewing a device graph in SQL Enterprise Manager, bear in mind that "space used" implies that one or more databases have been placed on this device and are "using" the space. The databases may be nearly empty, but they still use the space. The space has been preallocated to the databases shown and is no longer available. If you want to gauge how much actual data is on a server, you must view the space used in the Manage Databases dialog box. ■

5. If you want to view the databases on a device, click the Edit Device toolbar button. The Edit Database Device dialog box appears, as shown in Figure 35.3.

FIG. 35.3

The Edit Database Device dialog box provides a display of the databases stored on a device. You can use it to expand the size of a database device, an operation that can be scheduled for off-peak hours. You also can use it to set up mirroring for a device.

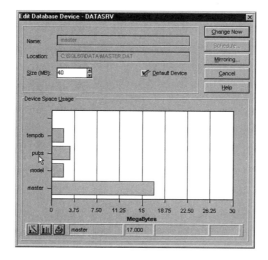

6. The total size of the device is listed in the Size (MB) box. By clicking a database name at the left of the graph, you can list the name, size of the database, and free space in the status bar at the bottom of the graph. If you position your mouse over one of the bars, the status bar changes to reflect information about that device.

To view a graph depicting the databases defined on a server, follow these steps:

1. Start SQL Enterprise Manager.

2. In the Server Manager window, open a server group by clicking the plus sign (+) to the left of the group name. Select the server you want to manage.

3. Click the Manage Databases toolbar button, or choose Manage, Databases from the menu. The Manage Databases dialog box appears (see Figure 35.4).

Part
VII

Ch
35

FIG. 35.4

The Manage Databases dialog box provides a display showing the currently defined databases on a server. Toolbar buttons are available to create, edit, or delete databases.

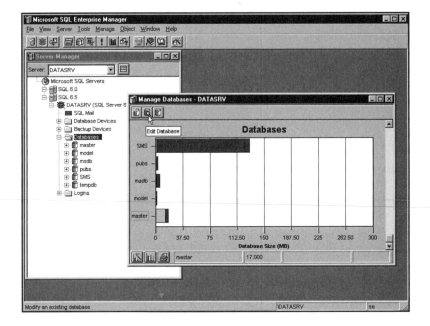

4. All the databases defined on this server are displayed in a bar graph. Two different colors show the space used and the space available.

5. If you want to view database information, configuration options, and permissions for a particular database, click the name of the database to the left of the graph (or click anywhere on the bar itself) and then click the Edit Database toolbar button. The Edit Database dialog box appears (see Figure 35.5).

6. Click the Database tab if it is not already selected. The creation date, database owner, size of the database and log, data space available, and log space available are all displayed. By clicking the Options tab, you can view and set options for this database. By clicking the Permissions tab, you can view and grant permissions for the database. See the sections "Setting Database Options" and "Understanding Object Ownership and Permissions" later in this chapter for more information.

You can expand devices, but you cannot shrink them. To expand a device, you again have the option of using a command (DISK RESIZE) or SQL Enterprise Manager. To expand a device with SQL Enterprise Manager, follow these steps:

1. Start SQL Enterprise Manager.

2. In the Server Manager window, open a server group by clicking the plus sign (+) to the left of the group name. Select the server you want to manage.

3. Click the Manage Devices toolbar button, or choose Manage, Devices from the menu. The Manage Database Devices dialog box appears.

FIG. 35.5

The Edit Database dialog box is a three-tabbed dialog box used to change the size of a database, set database options, and grant permissions.

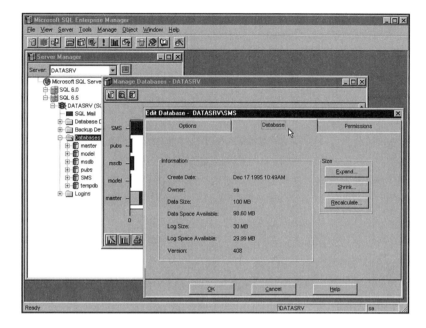

4. All the devices defined on this server are displayed in a bar graph. Two different colors show the space used and the space available.

5. If you want to view the databases on a device, click the Edit Device toolbar button. The Edit Database Device dialog box appears.

6. The total size of the device is listed in the Size (MB) box. You can enter a larger number to expand the size of this device. You cannot shrink a device using this technique.

N O T E To achieve the effect of shrinking a device, you must back up all data on the device, drop the device, delete the physical file that contained the device, create a smaller device with the same name, and reload databases. ■

If you decide, after looking at the databases on your server, that one of the databases needs to be larger or smaller, you can use the SQL Enterprise Manager to expand or shrink a database. To expand a database, use this procedure:

1. Start SQL Enterprise Manager.

2. In the Server Manager window, open a server group by clicking the plus sign (+) to the left of the group name. Select the server you want to manage.

3. Click the Manage Databases toolbar button, or choose Manage, Databases from the menu. The Manage Databases dialog box appears.

4. All the databases defined on this server are displayed in a bar graph. Two different colors show the space used and the space available.

Part
VII

Ch
35

5. Select the database you want to resize by clicking the name of the database to the left of the graph (or click anywhere on the bar itself). Then click the Edit Database toolbar button. The Edit Database Device dialog box appears.

6. Click the Database tab if it is not already selected. The creation date, database owner, size of the database and log, data space available, and log space available are all displayed. Click Expand. The Expand Database dialog box appears (see Figure 35.6).

FIG. 35.6

Use the Expand Database dialog box to increase the size of a database. You can optionally schedule the expansion for a later time when the server is less busy.

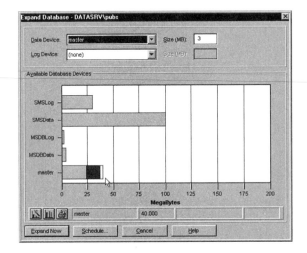

7. A graph appears depicting the devices defined on this server. The graph uses two colors to indicate used and free space. In the Data Device drop-down list, select the device on which you want to expand this database. In the Size (MB) text box, enter the amount of additional space to allocate to this database. As you enter numerals in the text box, the graph is dynamically updated with a third color indicating the relative amount of new space to be added. You also can use the same technique to select a device and amount for expansion of the transaction log.

8. You now have the option to execute the expansion now or schedule it for later. If you want to execute the expansion operation immediately, click Expand Now. The expansion begins, and you are finished with this task.

Because database expansion can take some time and may impact throughput on an active database in the middle of a busy period, you may want to schedule expansion of production databases for off-peak time periods. If you want to create a task to initiate the expansion operation at a later time, click the Schedule button. The Schedule Database Expansion dialog box appears, as shown in Figure 35.7.

FIG. 35.7

The Schedule Database Expansion dialog box allows you to schedule when database expansion should occur.

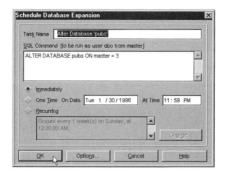

9. This dialog box represents a task that has automatically been created to complete the expansion operation. The task name and SQL Command (ALTER DATABASE) have already been entered. Typically, you would schedule the task to run one time at an appropriate date and time. Click OK to schedule the task.

To shrink a database, use this procedure:

1. Start SQL Enterprise Manager.

2. In the Server Manager window, open a server group by clicking the plus sign (+) to the left of the group name. Select the server you want to manage.

3. Click the Manage Databases toolbar button or choose Manage, Databases from the menu. The Manage Databases dialog box appears.

4. All the databases defined on this server are displayed in a bar graph. Two different colors show the space used and the space available.

5. Select the database you want to resize by clicking the name of the database to the left of the graph (or click anywhere on the bar itself). Then click the Edit Database toolbar button. The Edit Database Device dialog box appears.

6. Click the Database tab if it is not already selected. The creation date, database owner, size of the database and log, data space available, and log space available are all displayed. Click Shrink. A warning, shown in Figure 35.8, informs you that the database must be put into single-user mode before the shrink operation can proceed.

FIG. 35.8

This warning from SQL Enterprise Manager informs you that the database must be set to single-user mode.

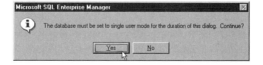

7. Clearly this is an operation that cannot be performed during active use of the database. If it is an appropriate time to proceed, click Yes to continue. The Shrink Database dialog box appears (see Figure 35.9). SQL Enterprise Manager automatically sets the single-user option and clears it when the operation is complete or has been canceled.

FIG. 35.9

The Shrink Database dialog box allows you to reduce the size of a database.

8. The minimum size to which you can reduce this database displays at the top of the dialog box. Enter the size you want in the Database Size (MB) text box, or use the up and down arrows to select a size. Click OK to initiate the shrink operation.

 After shrinking a database, you should dump the master database. See "Backing Up and Restoring Data" later in this chapter for more information.

Managing Transaction Logs

Almost every activity that occurs on a SQL Server is recorded in a transaction log *before* it occurs so that, in case of emergency, it can be *rolled back*. There are exceptions—actions that are not logged—but they are special cases that are discussed later in the chapter. Each database has its own *syslogs* system table, also referred to as its *transaction log*. You can place the transaction log on the same database device as the data or on another database device.

 It is usually a good idea to place the transaction log on a different device from the data. This may result in better performance, especially if the device is on a different physical drive with a different controller. It also allows you to save transaction log dumps so that you can completely restore the condition of your database in the event of a media failure.

Under normal circumstances, you cannot turn off transaction logging. However, if you are adding a large amount of information to a database, you may want to limit the amount of logging that occurs. For example, you can limit logging when using the fast mode of the bulk copy program, bcp. This improves the speed of the bulk copy operation, and the original data you are copying into the database serves temporarily as a backup copy. After the operation is complete, however, you must resynchronize the data and the log by dumping the database.

Transactions are bracketed by BEGIN TRANSACTION and COMMIT TRANSACTION statements. Conceptually, when a transaction has been *committed* it has been written to disk and is *durable*. SQL Server maintains its effects even if there is a catastrophic failure. The following paragraphs outline the means by which this is implemented.

As processing occurs, the log grows. Obviously, there must be some mechanism by which the size of the log is reduced or it would soon fill the device. This mechanism is known as *truncating* the log, and you can configure SQL Server to perform this task automatically, or you can initiate it manually, usually after dumping the log. The Truncate Log on Checkpoint database option controls whether automatic log truncation occurs. See the next section, "Setting Database Options," for the procedure to change this and other database options.

When a COMMIT TRANSACTION statement is issued, all logging for the transaction is immediately written to disk. It is possible that some of the actual data pages may not be immediately written to disk, but remain in the data cache in memory. These are *dirty pages*. If additional cache memory is required, SQL Server always writes dirty pages to disk before reallocating cache to another operation.

Try to avoid allowing dirty pages to exist in memory for long periods of time, even when SQL Server doesn't need the data cache for another operation. At a *checkpoint*, SQL Server flushes all data cache buffers, physically writing the information to disk. You can initiate checkpoints manually by issuing the CHECKPOINT statement. SQL Server also initiates implicit checkpoints.

If the Truncate Log on Checkpoint option is set, SQL Server attempts to truncate the transaction log at the completion of implicit checkpoints. At that point, the transaction has been logged and written to disk, and the data itself has been written to disk (there are no dirty pages in cache). SQL Server truncates the transaction log up to the page containing the oldest transaction that has not been committed, rolled back, or replicated. This process occurs approximately every 60 seconds. The transaction log also will be truncated after the log has been backed up with a DUMP TRANSACTION statement. Truncating the log without backing it up is usually appropriate only in development or test environments. See the next section, "Setting Database Options," for more information.

It is important to manage the relationship between the size of the transaction log and the amount of logging that occurs so that the transaction log never becomes full. A full transaction log generates an 1105 error and processing stops. You can use the Performance Monitor to monitor the size of the transaction log for a database. By setting an alert based on this counter, it is possible to automate the process of dumping and truncating the log. This is a more appropriate method for managing transaction log size in production environments than using the Truncate Log on Checkpoint option.

Two other situations occur that can cause the log to fill up, even if you have an appropriately sized log and are initiating log truncation at regular intervals. Because only committed transactions can be truncated, a *stranded* transaction caused by an application error can prevent truncation and cause the log to grow abnormally large. If the user process that caused the problem cannot be completed, it can be forcibly stopped, and the transaction rolled back. Also, some transactions cause extensive logging because of their nature. Deleting a table or updating every row in a table are good examples. These transactions should be broken down into multiple transactions that each accomplish part of the work with log truncation occurring after each stage. Table deletions can usually be replaced with the TRUNCATE TABLE command, which logs only space-deallocation operations. For more information, see "Stopping Processes" in Chapter 24 of the *Administrator's Companion*. This manual is part of the SQL Server documentation set and is included in SQL Server Books On-line for SQL Server 6.5. An icon to launch the online books is included by default in the Microsoft SQL Server 6.5 program group.

Setting Database Options

To set database options, such as the Truncate Log on Checkpoint option, follow these steps:

1. Start SQL Enterprise Manager.
2. In the Server Manager window, open a server group by clicking the plus sign (+) to the left of the group name. Select the server you want to manage.
3. Open the Databases folder by clicking the plus sign (+) to the left of the folder. Select the database you want to manage.
4. Position the mouse cursor over the name of the database and click the right mouse button. A context-sensitive menu appears, as shown in Figure 35.10.

FIG. 35.10

The SQL Enterprise Manager makes extensive use of context-sensitive pop-up menus, which are accessed with a right-click (click the right mouse button).

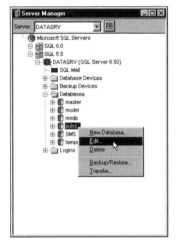

5. Select Edit from the menu. The Edit Database dialog box appears (see Figure 35.11).
6. Set or clear the desired options by clicking the check boxes.
7. Click OK.

Setting and Responding to Alerts

The DBA's job is demanding. Managing and maintaining active production databases requires the administrator to monitor many potential problem areas and take corrective action before problems occur. If a problem does surface, the administrator must identify and correct it quickly.

FIG. 35.11

Use the Options tab of the Edit Database dialog box to set database options. For example, with this tab, you can set the database to operate in single-user mode for maintenance operations.

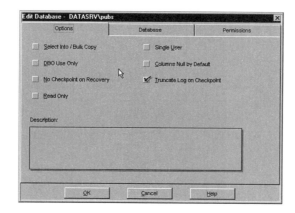

SQL Server provides a powerful alert-processing mechanism that can be a tremendous aid to DBAs. A range of error conditions, from severe to relatively benign, can be monitored. A group of *operators* can be defined, usually composed of administrators and database owners. A schedule can be created that specifies which operators should be notified when certain types of alerts occur and what days and times they are "on call." When an alert condition is detected, an e-mail message is sent to the appropriate operator. With optional third-party software and services, an e-mail message can activate a pager.

To define operators, follow these steps:

1. Start SQL Enterprise Manager.

2. In the Server Manager window, open a server group by clicking the plus sign (+) to the left of the group name. Select the server you want to manage.

3. Click the Manage Alerts toolbar button, or choose Server, Alerts from the menu. The Manage Alerts dialog box appears. Select the Operators tab if it is not already active (see Figure 35.12).

4. Click the New Operator toolbar button to define a new operator, or click the Edit Operator toolbar button to edit an existing operator. Defining a new operator is demonstrated here, but editing an existing operator is essentially the same. The New Operator dialog box appears (see Figure 35.13).

Part
VII

Ch
35

FIG. 35.12

The Operators tab of the Manage Alerts dialog box displays a list of operators who have been defined. They can subsequently be assigned responsibility for one or more alerts.

Manage Alerts

New Alert

Edit Alert

Delete Alert

New Operator

Edit Operator

Delete Operator

Refresh Display

Task Engine Options

Manage Messages

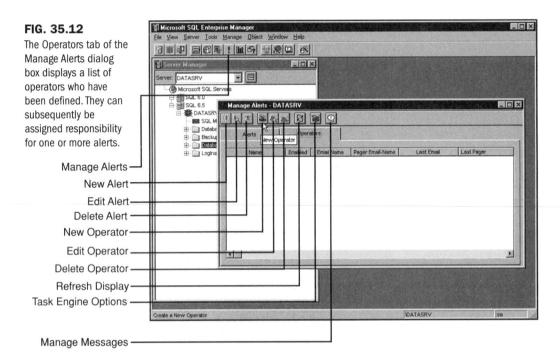

FIG. 35.13

Use the New Operator dialog box to define administrative operators who are responsible for various alerts triggered by error conditions.

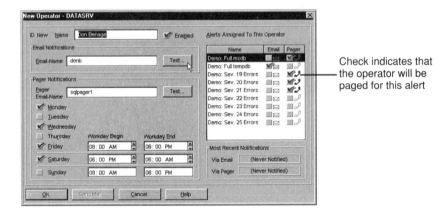

Check indicates that the operator will be paged for this alert

5. Enter a name for the new operator. If you want this operator activated immediately, be sure the Enabled option is selected. You can enable and disable operators to reflect availability based on vacations, special projects, and so on.

6. Enter an e-mail name for the new operator. To receive e-mail alert notifications, you must set up SQL Mail.

7. In the Alerts Assigned to this Operator box, click the e-mail or pager option buttons to select which alerts are the responsibility of this operator and the method of notification. E-mail is sent immediately. If you are using third-party paging support, identify the schedule for this operator to receive pages.

8. Click OK.

   ▶ **See** "Using SQL Mail and Alerts to Monitor SQL Server," **p. 1674**

To view and define alerts, follow these steps:

1. Start SQL Enterprise Manager.

2. In the Server Manager window, open a server group by clicking the plus sign (+) to the left of the group name. Select the server you want to manage.

3. Click the Manage Alerts toolbar button, or choose Server, Alerts from the menu. The Manage Alerts dialog box appears. Select the Alerts tab if it is not already active, as shown in Figure 35.14.

FIG. 35.14

The Alerts tab of the Manage Alerts dialog box lists the defined alerts, the conditions that trigger the alerts, and information about the last time each alert was raised.

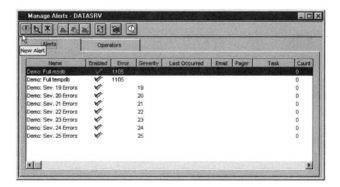

4. Click the New Alert toolbar button to define a new alert, or click the Edit Alert toolbar button to edit an existing alert. Defining a new alert is demonstrated here, but editing an existing alert is essentially the same. The New Alert dialog box appears (see Figure 35.15).

Part
VII

Ch
35

FIG. 35.15

The New Alert dialog box allows you to define a new alert by specifying the conditions that will trigger the alert, defining a response, and assigning an operator.

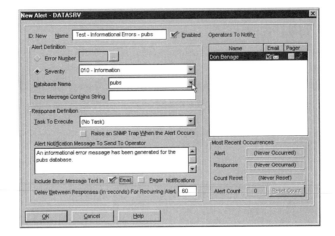

5. Enter a name for the new alert. Be sure the <u>E</u>nabled button is selected to activate the new alert.

6. In the Alert Definition box, select either a specific Error Nu<u>m</u>ber or <u>S</u>everity level that you want to monitor. You can narrow the scope of the alert further by selecting a particular database and/or entering a character string that the error message must contain to fire the alert.

7. In the Response Definition box, indicate what should happen when the alert is fired. You can execute a predefined task and/or send an alert notification message to specific operators. You can include the error message text in the notification message if you want. In SQL Server 6.5, you can raise a Simple Network Management Protocol (SNMP) trap when the alert occurs so that an SNMP console application can recognize the alert, as well.

8. Select the operators to notify for this alert.

9. Notice that you can open this dialog box later by using the Edit Alert button to view the contents of the Most Recent Occurrence box.

10. Click OK.

You can set alert engine options that affect the way all alert operations are handled. These options include a *fail-safe* operator who is notified if all other pager notifications for an alert fail. You also can designate another server to which any unhandled events can be forwarded. SQL Server errors of a specified severity generate events that are sent to the event log of the specified server.

To view and define alert engine options, follow these steps:

1. Start SQL Enterprise Manager.

2. In the Server Manager window, open a server group by clicking the plus sign (+) to the left of the group name. Select the server you want to manage.

3. Click the Manage Alerts toolbar button, or choose Server, Alerts from the menu. The Manage Alerts dialog box appears. Select the Alerts tab if it is not already active.

4. Click the Engine Options toolbar button. The Alert Engine Options dialog box appears, as shown in Figure 35.16.

FIG. 35.16

Use the Fail-Safe tab of the Alert Engine Options dialog box to establish an operator to contact if all other operators are unavailable.

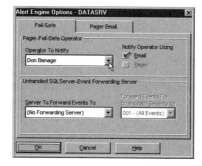

5. If you want to use fail-safe options, enter the name of the operator who will receive fail-safe notifications and/or the name of the server to forward unhandled events.

6. Click the Pager Email tab, as shown in Figure 35.17.

FIG. 35.17

The Pager Email tab of the Alert Engine Options dialog box allows you to enter the proper e-mail account for use by SQL Mail.

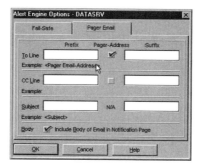

7. You can use this dialog box to format the To Line, CC Line (CC for *carbon copy*), and Subject Line of e-mail notifications sent for pager alerts. You can combine prefixes and suffixes with operator e-mail names to create special addresses for pager e-mail.

8. Click OK.

Importing and Exporting Data

SQL Server provides a number of ways to get information into and out of databases. The command-line bulk copy utility, bcp, has been available since the first release of SQL Server. It allows an operating system file containing structured data to be imported into a SQL Server database table. You also can use bcp to export information from tables to files. For more information on bcp, see "Using the Bulk Copy Program," in Chapter 11 of the *Administrator's Companion*.

Part
VII

Ch
35

The SQL Transfer Manager is a newer, graphical utility. It transfers information, both data and objects, from one SQL Server to another. With the release of SQL Server 6.5, the SQL Transfer Manager is no longer a part of the product. Instead, the SQL Enterprise Manager has a transfer-management interface that offers essentially the same capabilities and performs in much the same way. The interface is organized a little differently and should be easier for most people to use. You can also use SQL Enterprise Manager to generate a Transact SQL (T-SQL) script that can re-create a database object on another server. This section describes the use of SQL Transfer Manager and SQL Enterprise Manager for the transfer of data and objects.

Using the Transfer-Management Interface in SQL Enterprise Manager

The transfer-management interface is implemented as a series of dialog boxes that allows you to select a destination server and specify the options you want for the transfer of data and objects. There are many options for this new interface. The Advanced Options box on the Transfer Objects dialog box described later in this section offers two buttons that aren't described: Choose Objects and Scripting Options. This section provides a basic overview of the interface. Online help is available and provides detailed information on all options.

To use SQL Enterprise Manager to transfer information from one SQL Server to another, follow these steps:

1. Start SQL Enterprise Manager.

2. In the Server Manager window, open a server group by clicking the plus sign (+) to the left of the group name. Select the server you want to use as the source of the information that will be transferred.

3. Open the Databases folder by clicking the plus sign (+) to the left of the folder. Select the database you want to manage.

4. Select Object, Transfer from the menu. The Transfer Objects dialog box appears (see Figure 35.18).

FIG. 35.18
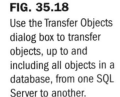
Use the Transfer Objects dialog box to transfer objects, up to and including all objects in a database, from one SQL Server to another.

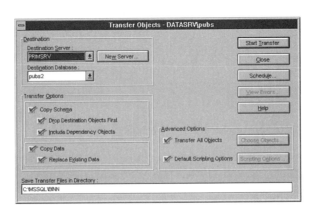

5. In the Destination box, select a Destination Server and a Destination Database using the drop-down lists. If the server you want to use as a destination server does not appear in the list, you can register a new server by clicking the New Server button.

TROUBLESHOOTING

The transfer-management interface does not let me select a version 6.0 server as a destination.
You are not doing anything wrong. The transfer-management interface allows only version 6.5 servers as destinations. The source server can be versions 4.x or 6.x.

6. If you want to transfer all objects in a database and start the transfer immediately, simply click Start Transfer. You see a series of progress indicators and then a message box informing you the transfer is complete. Your transfer is done, and you can click Close to exit the transfer-management interface and skip the remaining steps.

7. To schedule the transfer for a later time, perhaps when the load on the server is at a minimum and users are not connected to the databases involved in the transfer, click Schedule. The Schedule Transfer dialog box appears (see Figure 35.19).

FIG. 35.19
Use the Schedule Transfer dialog box to create a task that initiates the transfer you have specified at a later time.

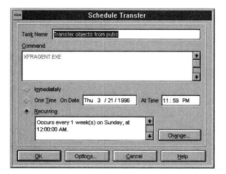

8. Enter the date and time you want the transfer to occur. You can specify a recurring schedule if you want this transfer to occur at regular intervals. Click OK to register the task and return to the Transfer Objects dialog box. Click Close to exit the transfer-management interface.

▶ **See** "Creating Server Groups and Registering Servers," **p. 1168**

Using SQL Transfer Manager

Although the SQL Transfer Manager is no longer included in version 6.5, it is still a useful tool for those organizations that have older versions of SQL Server in operation. This section outlines the procedures for its use.

Part
VII

Ch
35

To use SQL Transfer Manager, follow these steps:

1. Start SQL Transfer Manager. The SQL Transfer Manager Connect dialog box appears. Enter the names of the source and destination servers. Enter the appropriate login IDs and passwords.

2. Click Connect. The SQL Transfer Manager dialog box appears, as shown in Figure 35.20.

FIG. 35.20

Use the SQL Transfer Manager dialog box to specify the source and destination databases and the objects to transfer.

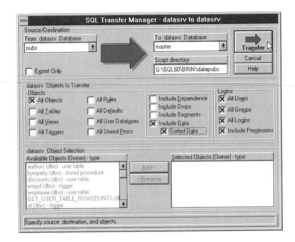

3. Using the From Database drop-down list, select the database from which to transfer data or objects. Select the To Database in the same manner.

4. Specify the objects to be transferred. The default selection is All Objects, which transfers the entire database.

5. You can use SQL Transfer Manager to copy the data, or simply to create an identical, but empty, database structure. If you want to include the data, select the Include Data check box.

6. If you want to transfer security information (which is appropriate if the same users will need to access the information on the new server), select the appropriate check boxes in the Logins area of the dialog box. You should select all the boxes if you want identical permissions for all users and groups currently defined.

7. The Export Only check box determines whether the actual transfer occurs. If this box is checked, scripts are created (and saved in the location specified in the Script directory text box) that can later be run to create all specified objects. If the Export Only check box is cleared, the scripts are still created, and all objects and data are transferred.

8. Click Transfer. If you want to interrupt the transfer process after it has started, press Ctrl+C.

Using SQL Enterprise Manager to Generate SQL Scripts

To use SQL Enterprise Manager to generate a script for re-creating a particular object, follow these steps:

1. Start SQL Enterprise Manager.

2. In the Server Manager window, open a server group by clicking the plus sign (+) to the left of the group name. Select the server you want to manage.

3. Open the Databases folder by clicking the plus sign (+) to the left of the folder. Select the database you want to manage.

4. Open the database containing the object of interest. Open the Objects folder and then the folder containing the type of objects (tables, stored procedures, rules, and so on) you need.

5. Position the mouse cursor over the object and click the right mouse button. A context-sensitive menu appears, as shown in Figure 35.21.

FIG. 35.21
You use the context-sensitive menu for a table object to initiate the generation of SQL scripts.

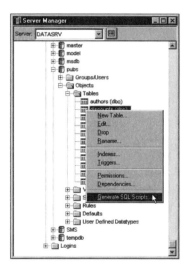

6. Select Generate SQL Scripts from the menu. The Generate SQL Scripts dialog box appears (see Figure 35.22).

Part
VII

Ch
35

FIG. 35.22

The Generate SQL Scripts dialog box allows you to specify the scripts you want to create. You can specify the objects for which scripts should be generated and the type of scripts.

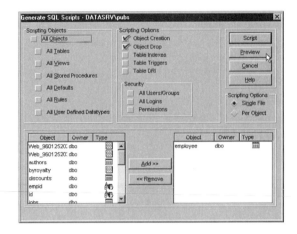

7. Use the <u>A</u>dd and R<u>e</u>move buttons to identify additional objects for which you want to generate scripts. The object you selected earlier in step 5 should already appear in the list on the right side of the dialog box.

8. Select scripting options and identify the security statements you want to add (if any).

9. Click <u>P</u>review to view the SQL statements that will be generated based on your current selections. The Object Scripting Preview dialog box appears (see Figure 35.23). Alternatively, you can click the Scri<u>p</u>t button from the main dialog box to generate the script without a preview.

FIG. 35.23

The Object Scripting Preview dialog box provides you with the opportunity to view generated scripts prior to saving them to disk.

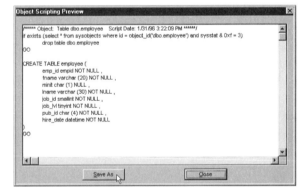

10. If you are not satisfied with the current results, click <u>C</u>lose and return to step 7.

11. When you are satisfied with the SQL statements that will be generated, click the <u>S</u>ave As button. A standard Save As dialog box appears so that you can name the file and save it in the location you choose.

Using SQL Scripts and Stored Procedures for Maintenance Tasks

In addition to the commands available in the SQL language, it is possible to create a program or *script* containing one or more SQL commands. You can save these scripts in an operating system file on a hard disk or floppy disk. You then can retrieve and execute them using a command-line utility such as isql or ISQL/w.

A script file can be created using any editor, such as Notepad or WordPad (included with most versions of Windows), or entered directly into ISQL/w where it can be executed immediately or saved for later. Files that you have created and saved can be loaded in ISQL/w and executed, or provided as a parameter to the isql command directly from the operating system prompt.

It also is possible to save a script in SQL Server as a stored procedure. This causes SQL Server to compile the SQL statements in the script and store them in the database. Because SQL Server has already compiled the statements, execution time is generally faster. In addition, this procedure now can be called by application programs or initiated from clients using command-line utilities if they have permission to run the procedure. So turning a script into a stored procedure allows you to control access with SQL Server security, makes it potentially available to all clients, and can improve execution speed.

▶ **See** "Stored Procedures," **p. 1194**

An enhancement to the EXEC statement first introduced in version 6.0 allows you to provide a variable argument to EXEC. This mechanism gives you the capability to write general purpose scripts to which you can give the name of a database, table, or other object as an argument. In addition, it is possible to query a system table for the names of all objects of a certain type (for example, tables in a database) and execute a script sequentially on each of them. This creates exciting opportunities for using short, elegant scripts to perform routine maintenance chores on SQL Server. Some examples of maintenance scripts that are applicable to specific situations are provided in the *Administrator's Companion*. See "Creating Supplemental Stored Procedures" in Chapter 24 of the *Administrator's Companion* for additional examples.

To use ISQL/w for script creation and execution, follow these steps:

1. Start ISQL/w. The Connect Server dialog box appears (see Figure 35.24).

FIG. 35.24
Use the Connect Server dialog box to specify the name of the server you want to connect to and the type of connection you want to use.

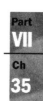

Part VII

Ch

35

2. Enter the name of the server to which you want to connect. Select the type of connection you want to use and, if you are using an untrusted connection (Standard Security), enter your SQL Server login ID and password. If you are using a trusted connection, leave this blank. Click Connect, and a Query window appears, as shown in Figure 35.25.

FIG. 35.25

This figure depicts a query window being displayed in ISQL/w.

New Query

Load SQL Script

Save Query/Result

Query Options

Remove Current Query Set

Execute Query

Cancel Executing Query

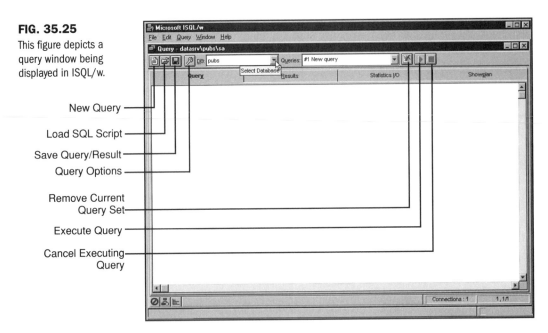

3. Select the database you want to manage from the DB drop-down list. You now can click your mouse cursor anywhere in the query window to get an insertion point and begin entering and editing a query. Alternatively, you may want to use a full-featured editor to create a text file with an extension of SQL. You then can load and execute it here. To load a previously prepared T-SQL script, click the Load SQL Script button. An Open File dialog box appears, as shown in Figure 35.26.

FIG. 35.26

Use the Open File dialog in ISQL/w to browse for and open an existing script file containing T-SQL statements for subsequent modification or execution.

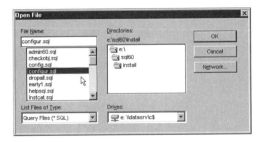

4. Your script is now visible in the Query tab of the Query window (see Figure 35.27).

FIG. 35.27

A query has been opened and is about to be executed in this figure.

5. Before executing the query, there are two optional buttons you can select to provide additional information about the query execution process. The two options are the Display Statistics I/O button and the No Execute button, both of which are located in the lower-left corner of the query window. Click the Display Statistics I/O button to activate the use of the Statistics I/O tab. Click the Execute Query button to run your query. If the No Execute button has been selected, the query will be parsed, and an execution plan will be determined, but the query will not actually be executed. The Results tab appears automatically (see Figure 35.28). Use the Results tab to view the results of executing the query, or see the execution plan if No Execute is selected.

6. To view the statistics on input and output operations for the query, click the Statistics I/O tab. A bar graph summarizing input and output operations required to resolve the query appears, as shown in Figure 35.29.

7. To view a graphical Showplan output, click the Showplan tab. A chart appears, indicating index usage and table scans needed to resolve the query (see Figure 35.30).

Part
VII

Ch
35

FIG. 35.28

The Results tab of a Query window in ISQL/w displays the outcome when a query is executed.

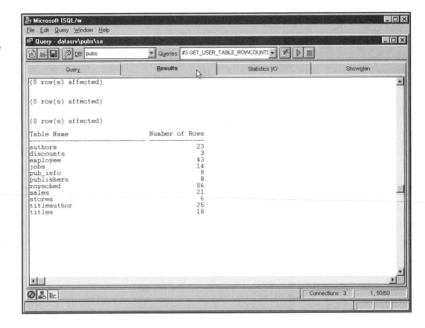

FIG. 35.29

When a query executes (and you have clicked the Statistics I/O toolbar button) the Statistics I/O tab displays a bar graph summarizing the input/output operations required to resolve the query.

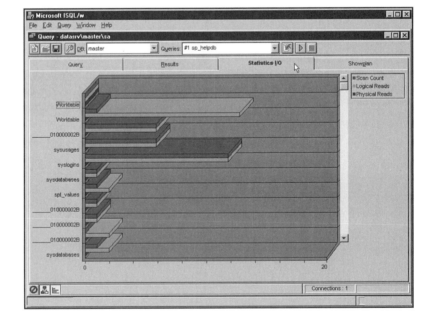

FIG. 35.30

The Showplan tab provides a graphical representation of the plan used to resolve the query. The indexes used, and any table scans that were required, are represented on the display.

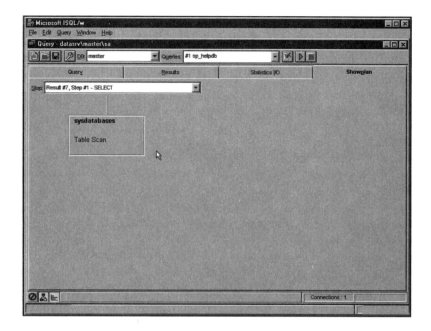

8. Click the Remove Query toolbar button if you no longer need a query. Click the New Query toolbar button to open a new query window and continue. You can use the Queries drop-down list to select a query from among active queries.

Automating Maintenance with the SQL Executive

You have already learned how to use alerts to automate a response to particular conditions that may arise during SQL Server operation. In this section, you learn how to use the SQL Executive to execute routine tasks that you have defined. A task may consist of Transact SQL statements or an operating system command line with parameters. The replication components of SQL Server also use the SQL Executive to launch special tasks associated with the replication process.

You can enter single T-SQL statements directly in the Command box of a New Task dialog box. T-SQL scripts can either be compiled as stored procedures and called with a T-SQL command, or saved as an operating system file and executed as a command-line process using isql.

An example of a task ideally suited to this type of automation is the creation of backups for your data and transaction logs. A typical schedule might involve backing up, or *dumping*, the database (data and log) once a week and dumping just the transaction log each night when processing activity is at a minimum.

Part
VII

Ch

35

To create a task for routine maintenance, follow these steps:

1. Start SQL Enterprise Manager.

2. In the Server Manager window, open a server group by clicking the plus sign (+) to the left of the group name. Select the server you want to manage.

3. Click the Task Scheduling toolbar button, or choose Server, Tasks from the menu. The Task Scheduling dialog box appears, as shown in Figure 35.31.

FIG. 35.31

The Task Scheduling dialog box lists the currently defined tasks including those not currently enabled.

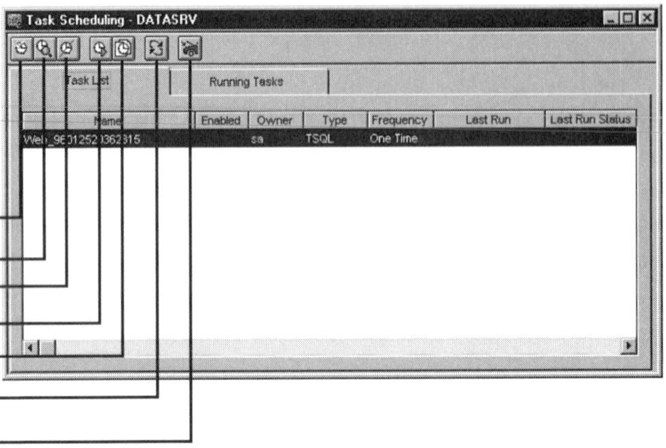

New Task

Edit Task

Delete Task

Run Task

Task History

Refresh

Task Engine Options

4. Click the New Task toolbar button, and the New Task dialog box appears, as shown in Figure 35.32.

FIG. 35.32

You define new tasks by using the New Task dialog box.

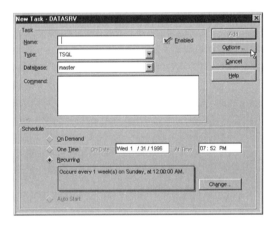

5. Enter a name for the task in the Name text box. Select the type of task this will be: T-SQL or CmdExec. It is possible to create your own tasks using the special types for replication (Distribution, LogReader, and Sync), but it is not usually necessary.

   ▶ **See** "An Introduction to Data Replication," **p. 1244**

6. Make sure that the Enabled check box is selected if you want this task activated immediately, even if you aren't scheduling it to execute until later. From the Database drop-down list, select the database this task will be executed on.

7. Enter the command that will actually perform the task in the Command box. You can specify additional options for the command by clicking Options. A Task Options dialog box appears (see Figure 35.33).

FIG. 35.33
Use the T-SQL Task Options dialog box to set error recovery and notification options for this task.

8. If you want someone notified about the success or failure of this task, select an operator for SQL Server to e-mail. You also can write success or failure notification to the Windows NT Application Event log. You also can indicate a retry delay and number of retry attempts to perform in the event of failure. Click OK to return to the New Task dialog box.

9. Select the appropriate option button in the Schedule box. On Demand tasks are used by alerts and executed manually using the Run Task toolbar button from the Task Scheduling dialog box. Auto Start tasks are used by replication processes and are launched automatically every time the SQL Executive starts.

   One Time tasks run at the date and time specified and then are disabled but not deleted. Recurring tasks launch at regular intervals that you specify. Click Change if you need to modify the schedule for a recurring task, and the Task Schedule dialog box appears (see Figure 35.34).

Part
VII

Ch
35

FIG. 35.34

Use the Task Schedule dialog box to specify the scheduled times at which this task should run.

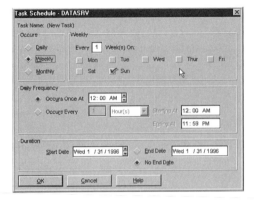

10. Make appropriate selections to indicate the recurring interval when this task should launch. Click OK to return to the New Task dialog box.

11. Click Add to add the task.

You may want to view already defined tasks, check the status of currently running tasks, or review the history of a task.

To monitor the status of tasks, follow these steps:

1. Start SQL Enterprise Manager.

2. In the Server Manager window, open a server group by clicking the plus sign (+) to the left of the group name. Select the server you want to manage.

3. Click the Task Scheduling toolbar button, or choose Server, Tasks from the menu. The Task Scheduling dialog box appears.

4. Some task status information displays directly in the Task List tab of the Task Scheduling dialog box. You can see the frequency of the task, when it last ran, and the status (success or failure) of the last run. For additional status information on a particular task, highlight the task and click the Task History toolbar button. The Task History dialog box appears, as shown in Figure 35.35.

FIG. 35.35

The Task History dialog box displays the history for a particular task including when it executed, the status of its execution, and the disposition of any operator e-mails.

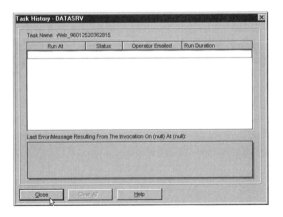

5. You can see a list of times when the task has run, the status (success or failure) of the task, whether an operator was e-mailed, and the amount of time it took for the task to execute. The Last Error/Message displays any messages that were generated when the task last executed.

6. Click Clear All if you want to clear the history for this task. Click Close to return to the Task Scheduling dialog box.

7. To see which tasks are actively running on the server, select the Running Tasks tab. The Running Tasks dialog box appears, as shown in Figure 35.36.

FIG. 35.36
If you have any actively running tasks, they display in the Running Tasks tab of the Task Scheduling dialog box.

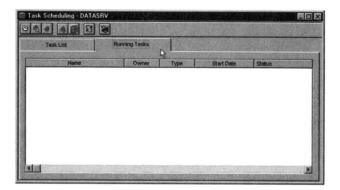

8. The name, owner, type, start date, and status of running tasks display.

Using SQL Server Security

You have already been introduced to SQL Server Security concepts. In Chapter 34, "Building Your SQL Server," you learned about the different security models supported by SQL Server and how this selection impacts logging on to SQL Server. In this section, you learn a few important security-related techniques, after a brief recap of information already presented.

SQL Server can support users gaining access over two types of connections: trusted and nontrusted. Using Integrated security, SQL Server validates users based on their Windows NT user ID and establishes a trusted connection. With Standard security, SQL Server does not rely on any external security authority and uses a nontrusted connection to accept a login ID and password that are created and managed by SQL Server. Mixed security allows the use of either type of connection.

You can create native SQL Server login IDs with T-SQL statements or by using SQL Enterprise Manager. These can be used to log on using Standard security, or they can be associated with a Windows NT user ID with Integrated or Mixed security. The SQL Security Manager is the tool that accomplishes this mapping of Windows NT accounts to SQL login IDs. If you are using only Standard security, the SQL Security Manager plays no useful role for your server.

Part
VII

Ch
35

However you connect to SQL Server, the login ID you are using (explicitly, or through an implicit mapping) is associated with a username when you use a database. The username may match the login ID, or it may be completely different. Some administrators, especially with Integrated security, prefer to have users' IDs match with usernames to keep things simple. In other cases, a collection of IDs may all be mapped to the same username (which would then be an alias) to provide equivalent privileges to those users.

Having connected to SQL Server and initiated use of a particular database, the access privileges you accrue depends on the rights *granted* to you by the system administrator (SA) or database owner. The SA can grant the capability to create databases to other users. The creator of a database automatically becomes the database owner (DBO). Only the DBO can grant privileges to create, use, and modify objects in a database. The SA, however, can impersonate any user in a database.

The next section introduces you to the SQL Security Manager and describes how to map Windows NT user accounts to SQL login IDs. Next, you learn how to use SQL Enterprise Manager to grant privileges to create databases and then, within a database, grant privileges to create and use objects. Remember that anyone can use SQL Enterprise Manager. A user's login ID and username in a database determines exactly what operations a user can or cannot perform.

▶ **See** "Choosing a Security Model," **p. 1164**

Using the SQL Security Manager

SQL Security Manager is useful for SQL Servers running Integrated or Mixed security. You can use this tool to map Windows NT groups (and the users in those groups) to SQL login IDs. You also can add users to SQL Server databases or determine the access privileges a user has been assigned on a particular SQL Server.

The SQL Security Manager maps an entire Windows NT group to SQL login IDs in one operation. You cannot specify an individual Windows NT account to be mapped. These groups can be granted user privileges or SA privileges. A suggested strategy to simplify the process and make it manageable as users' needs change over time is as follows:

- Create Windows NT local groups (not global groups) that correspond to the desired categories of SQL Server users.

  For example, create a group called SQLAdmins, or something similar, and add any users who will be responsible for administration of SQL Server.

- Also create one or more groups of users that will receive only user privileges. For easier management of permissions, it is a good idea to create multiple groups that correspond to different access needs in SQL Server.

  For example, if you need to allow a group of users specific privileges for an inventory application, you might create a group called InvUsers. Perhaps some of the users are managers and require different permissions. You then should create an additional group called InvMgrs, for example, to facilitate this process.

The first time you use SQL Security Manager, you either need to log on using the built-in sa login ID, or be logged on to Windows NT with an account that is a member of the Windows NT Administrators local group. By default, this group includes the global group Domain Admins if you are using Windows NT domain security. Also by default, this group receives SA privileges during SQL Server setup. If you are using integrated security, and your Windows NT account meets the criteria outlined earlier, you do not need to enter a login ID or password.

If you are not a Windows NT administrator but are a member of a newly created SQLAdmins group that will be assigned SA privileges (following the suggestion made earlier), you should connect the first time using the built-in sa login ID. Then use the following procedure to grant SA privileges to the SQLAdmins group. The next time you connect, you do not need to enter a login ID and password, as your Windows NT account status (as a member of the SQLAdmins group) maps you to SA privileges.

To use the SQL Security Manager to map a Windows NT group to SQL Server login IDs and grant them user privilege, follow these steps:

1. Start the SQL Security Manager. The Connect Server dialog box appears (see Figure 35.37).

FIG. 35.37
Use the Connect Server dialog box to specify the name of the server you want to connect to and the type of connection you want to use.

2. Enter the name of the server you want to manage, or select the name from the Server drop-down list. If needed, enter a Login ID and Password. Click Connect. The SQL Security Manager window appears, as shown in Figure 35.38.

FIG. 35.38
The SQL Security Manager window is depicted in this figure. A single Windows NT group (quebook) from the GSULLIVAN domain has been granted user privileges on this server.

Establish a connection to a SQL server

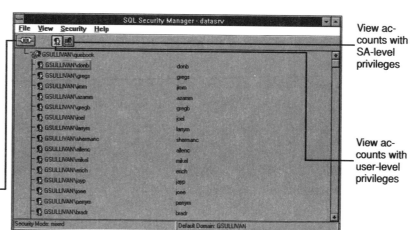

View accounts with SA-level privileges

View accounts with user-level privileges

3. To assign a Windows NT group user privilege in SQL Server, click the User Privilege toolbar button. From the menu, choose Security, Grant New. The Grant User Privilege dialog box appears (see Figure 35.39).

FIG. 35.39

The Grant User Privilege dialog box allows you to assign user privileges on the SQL Server to which you are connected for selected Windows NT groups.

4. Select the option button for either Local Groups or Groups on Default Domain. If you are following the suggested guidelines, the Windows NT groups you defined should be local groups defined in the domain, not local groups defined in the account database of the computer running SQL Server. Therefore, you should select Groups on Default Domain.

TROUBLESHOOTING

My newly defined groups appear when I select Local Groups. You have created the new groups improperly. Start User Manager for Domains and re-create the local groups in the proper Windows NT domain. Do not use the User Manager tool. Make sure that you run User Manager for Domains.

5. If you want each user in the group to have her own SQL Server login ID, make sure that the Add Login IDs for Group Members check box is selected. If you don't, these users will all be assigned the default login ID when they use SQL Server. Be sure to define the default login ID if you clear this check box.

6. You can add these users to a database and make that database their default database. This is usually a good idea. If you don't explicitly make an assignment, the master database will be a user's default database. It is usually not appropriate for users to create new databases in the master database.

7. Click Grant.

   ▶ **See** "Default Login ID," **p. 1178**

To use the SQL Security Manager to map a Windows NT group to SQL Server login IDs and grant them SA privilege, follow these steps:

1. Start the SQL Security Manager. The Connect Server dialog appears.

2. Enter the name of the server you want to manage, or select the name from the Server drop-down list. If needed, enter a Login ID and Password.

3. Click Connect. The SQL Security Manager window appears.

4. To assign a Windows NT group SA privilege in SQL Server, click the SA Privilege toolbar button.

5. From the menu, choose Security, Grant New. The Grant System Administrator Privilege dialog box appears (see Figure 35.40).

FIG. 35.40

The Grant System Administrator Privilege dialog box allows you to assign SA privileges on the SQL Server to which you are connected for selected Windows NT groups.

6. Select the option button for either Local Groups or Groups on Default Domain. If you are following the suggested guidelines, you should select Groups on Default Domain and choose the group called SQLAdmins (or the other name you chose for the system administrator's group).

7. The Add Login IDs for group members and the Add Users to Database check boxes are dimmed because all users in this group will be mapped to the sa login ID. They are assigned *master* as their default database.

8. Click Grant.

To see what privileges a group has been granted, follow this procedure:

1. Start the SQL Security Manager.

2. Click the User Privilege toolbar button.

3. Press the Ctrl key and double-click the group name. The Account Detail dialog box appears (see Figure 35.41).

4. The name of the Windows NT group and the mapped SQL Server group are displayed. View or modify information as necessary.

N O T E In general, it is a good idea to let SQL Server generate random unique passwords for the login IDs created for users in a group. The passwords are not necessary when using integrated security. Because your Windows NT account and password establish a trusted connection, you need not enter a login ID and password when prompted. However, if you do not place a password on the account, the account may be compromised under Mixed security, should you ever change to a Standard security model. ▇

Part
VII

Ch
35

5. Click Close.

FIG. 35.41

The Account Detail dialog box provides the opportunity to add a Windows NT group to a database.

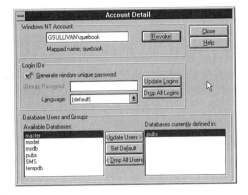

Understanding Object Ownership and Permissions

An SA can use SQL Enterprise Manager to allow users to create databases. Alternatively, the SA can create databases and then assign the ownership of a database to a different (single) user. Only one user can be the DBO; however, other users can be aliased to the DBO and thereby act as database owners.

An SA or DBO can use SQL Enterprise Manager to assign permissions for a user or group. Permissions can be assigned to access and use various database objects or to use particular T-SQL statements. Statement permissions are set for an entire database—they are not object-specific. For example, if a user is granted permission to use the CREATE RULE statement, that user can create rules for columns in any table in the database.

To grant permissions for database objects using SQL Enterprise Manager, follow these steps:

1. Start SQL Enterprise Manager.

2. Select the server you want to manage. Open its database folder and select the database whose permissions you want to view or modify.

3. Choose Object, Permissions from the menu. The Object Permissions dialog box appears, as shown in Figure 35.42. Select the By Object tab.

FIG. 35.42

The By Object tab of the Object Permissions dialog box allows you to select an object in a database and assign permissions for one or more users and groups in the database.

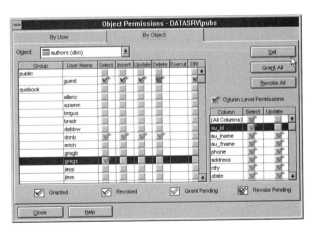

4. Select an object from the Object drop-down list. The current set of permissions for this object displays. New selections you make are marked *pending* until you click Set at the end of this procedure.

5. You can choose Grant All to grant all permissions to all users. Revoke All revokes all permissions. Sometimes it is helpful to use these buttons to start with and then selectively add or remove specific permissions by clicking individual check boxes to fine-tune your selection.

6. If you want to set column-level permissions, select a table or view in the Object drop-down list. Then select a user or group name from the list of names and click the Column Level Permissions check box. Click the appropriate check boxes indicating which columns may be selected or updated by the selected user or group.

7. Click Set to grant the selected permissions.

To grant permissions to use particular T-SQL commands, follow this procedure:

1. Start SQL Enterprise Manager.

2. Select the server you want to manage. Open its database folder and double-click the database whose statement permissions you want to view or modify. The Edit Database dialog box appears (see Figure 35.43). Select the Permissions tab.

FIG. 35.43

The Permissions tab of the Edit Database dialog box allows you to grant permissions for the creation of database objects to particular users.

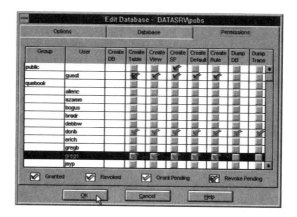

3. The current set of permissions are indicated by check marks. As you grant new permissions, they are indicated as *pending* until you click OK to update your new selections. Make changes by clicking the check boxes.

4. Click OK to update your permission changes.

N O T E The capability to grant the Create DB permission is given only to an SA and may be applied only to users of the master database. Therefore, there is no check box for this permission when viewing user databases or the sample PUBS database. ▩

Part
VII

Ch
35

Using Dial-Up Access to SQL Server

The Remote Access Service (RAS) included with Windows NT Server provides users who are not directly attached to a LAN, or connected via a WAN link, to gain access to resources on the network using a variety of methods. These methods include dial-up telephone access, the use of ISDN connections, or the use of an X.25 packet switched network. See Chapter 12, "Implementing Remote Access Service (RAS)," for more information on RAS.

RAS works very well with most SQL Server applications. Because SQL Server was designed using the client-server process model, the processing workload divides between clients and servers. A client typically passes a request for information to SQL Server, which processes and resolves the request and returns only the appropriate answer set over the connection. If the connection is a relatively slow link, this distinction is important.

All administrative tools, with the exception of the SQL Transfer Manager, work well over a RAS connection. Obviously, it is not a good idea to initiate a large transfer operation over a slow connection.

The *Administrator's Companion* describes how to set up remote servers and remote users. Do not confuse this terminology with the similar concepts used for RAS. In SQL Server terminology, a "remote" server is defined so that a user on the "local" server can execute stored procedures on the "remote" server. The remote server is usually on the same LAN or WAN as the local server.

SQL Server does not support the concept of a domain, like Windows NT Server does. In other words, you cannot have a group of SQL Servers automatically share the same login IDs. As you have already learned, you define SQL Server usernames and groups only within a particular database, not across an entire server, and certainly not across multiple servers. With integrated security, it is possible to use SQL Security Manager to map the same domain groups to each SQL Server on a LAN, thereby creating the same login IDs on all servers, but they do not stay synchronized automatically. There is no default process that automatically keeps the login IDs for all SQL Servers the same.

In practice, this is not a problem. The nature of database server usage, and the appropriate use of groups to assign permissions, makes the task of managing access to databases a relatively straightforward task. This discussion has been provided to eliminate any potential confusion from arising due to the similar terminology used by different BackOffice components.

Backing Up and Restoring Data

The SQL Enterprise Manager includes an easy-to-use interface to facilitate backing up and restoring data. You also can use T-SQL commands (DUMP and LOAD) to achieve the same purpose. For a large site with many active databases, it is a good idea to create an automated backup regimen using T-SQL tasks that the SQL Executive launches for performing routine backups. In addition, third-party tape backup products that are compatible with Microsoft SQL Server are available with many advanced features.

This section outlines rudimentary backup procedures that you can use on an *ad hoc* basis to provide a backup of essential data. Before you put a system into production, you should spend time to thoroughly familiarize yourself with backup and restore operations. Procedures for creating a backup (dump) device have already been described.

▶ **See** "Backup (Dump) Devices," **p. 1181**

To back up a database to a disk dump device, follow these steps:

1. Start SQL Enterprise Manager.

2. In the Server Manager window, open a server group by clicking the plus sign (+) to the left of the group name. Select the server you want to manage.

3. Open the Databases folder by clicking the plus sign (+) to the left of the folder. Select the database you want to back up.

4. Choose Tools, Database Backup/Restore from the menu. The Database Backup/Restore dialog box appears (see Figure 35.44).

FIG. 35.44

This dialog box allows you to specify the source database and the destination dump device for a backup operation. You also can designate additional options, including scheduling the backup for a later time.

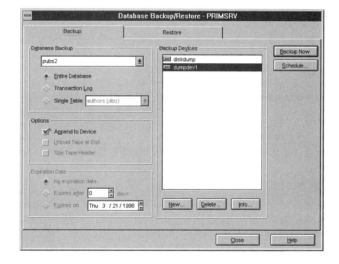

5. If you want, you can select a different database to back up instead of the one you originally highlighted. Use the drop-down list in the Database Backup box.

6. Select the information you want to back up—the entire database, the transaction log, or a single table.

7. Select the backup (dump) device that will be the destination of the backup. You can define a new dump device by clicking New.

8. Click Backup Now to begin the backup operation. A progress indicator provides feedback on the process. When it is finished, a Backup Completed! message appears.

Part
VII

Ch
35

Tuning SQL Server

A natural concern for any DBA is improving performance of SQL Server to achieve optimum levels. Entire books have been written on the subject of database performance tuning. In fact, the topic of SQL Server performance may best be described as *query optimization* since the desired result is faster query performance.

A holistic approach to performance is the most effective. Such an approach encompasses not only hardware and software configuration, but also proper database design, appropriate indexing strategies, and balancing the desire for maximum consistency and concurrency through appropriate locking strategies. It is beyond the scope of this book to provide all the intimate details required to wring out every last transaction per second (tps) possible. Nonetheless, this section provides some general guidelines on performance improvement and specific steps for configuring SQL Server that should be of benefit in nearly all situations.

General Guidelines

It should go without saying that no matter how carefully you configure your server, if you implement poorly designed databases, performance suffers. All too often, performance is considered only after the database is implemented and performance is unacceptable, when it should be part of the design process from the beginning. Some rules of thumb to consider when designing and implementing your database follow:

- Start with a sound logical model.
- Identify those query operations which are most time-critical, and factor this information into your database design.
- Do not take the normalization process too far. This requires some judgment, but in general, a highly normalized database requires more joins and more input/output operations to resolve a query.
- Consider your locking strategies carefully. SQL Server offers a variety of locking levels which can have a big impact on multiuser access (concurrency). You want to maximize access (with as few locks on the smallest amount of data possible) while maintaining consistency (ensuring that the data is accurately updated and each user is provided the latest valid data available).
- Keep transactions as short as possible.
- When creating a group of stored procedures, or even *ad hoc* queries, that update multiple tables, try to update the tables in the same order in all procedures and queries. This reduces the chance of deadlocks and hence improves performance.
- Use the fill factor parameter on tables that are frequently receiving inserts to allocate some room to grow. At regular intervals, rebuild these tables to maintain the fill factor desired. This can be done with the DBCC DBREINDEX command in most cases.

In addition to the database design guidelines provided above, there are some basic statements about hardware selection and configuration:

- When selecting a server, strongly consider a machine that supports multiple processors, even if you plan to start with just one. Support for multiprocessor machines is a powerful capability of Windows NT Server, and it is very easy to make the necessary configuration changes to use an additional processor. To move from a single processor to two or more, rerun the Windows NT Server setup program after adding the additional processor(s), and it will change the single processor kernel to the multiprocessor kernel.

- Set the "SMP concurrency" parameter in SQL Server to zero (0), and SQL Server will use one less than the total number of processors (with two or more). If you have a dedicated server, you can consider setting this parameter to –1 instructing SQL Server to use all processors.

> **CAUTION**
>
> Setting SMP concurrency to –1 causes the performance of a local session on the console to be extremely sluggish. You should make this change only on a dedicated server that is always administered remotely (no one ever logs in directly on the console of the server).

- You should try to use multiple SCSI (Small Computer Systems Interface) disk drives in a RAID (Redundant Array of Inexpensive Disks) drive array. This is almost always better than using a single large disk drive. Use a hardware-based RAID configuration if possible (i.e., one that is implemented directly by the manufacturer using special drive controller hardware). If you can't use a hardware-based RAID drive array, use the capability of Windows NT Server to create a RAID array.

Configuring RAM

For most organizations, the amount of RAM added to a server is an important concern. Large amounts of memory are not likely to be truly inexpensive in the foreseeable future. And even in situations where plenty of memory is available, you must still configure the server properly to achieve appropriate benefits. The capability to effectively use the memory in a given server is therefore important. A few areas bear special attention and are discussed in the following section.

SQL Server Memory   The setup program (in versions 6.0 and 6.5) assigns memory to SQL Server based on the amount of total memory installed in the computer. If your server has less than 32M of RAM, SQL Server is assigned 8M. If your server has 32M or more, SQL Server is assigned 16M.

In some situations, this straightforward approach needs to be improved upon. For example, if you are setting up a very large server to handle gigabytes (G) of data, you will want to configure your server with 128M of RAM (or more) and assign much more than 16M to SQL Server. In addition, servers participating in replication scenarios typically need more memory in general and more assigned to SQL Server.

Part
VII

Ch
35

As you increase the amount of memory in your server, you still need to reserve some for the operating system itself. In other words, you must not configure SQL Server to use *all* of the computer's memory. In addition, if you have other processes running on the same server (e.g., SMS), you should take that into account, as well. For a server running only SQL Server, Table 35.1 suggests a good place to start when configuring your server memory.

Table 35.1   SQL Server Memory Configuration

Total System Memory	SQL Server Memory
32	16
64	40
128	100
256	216
512	464

To assign more memory to SQL Server, follow this procedure:

1. Start SQL Enterprise Manager.

2. Open the appropriate server group and select a server to manage.

3. Choose <u>S</u>erver, <u>C</u>onfigurations from the menu. The Server Configuration/Options dialog box appears, as shown in Figure 35.45. Select the Configuration tab.

FIG. 35.45

Use the Configuration tab of the Server Configuration/Options dialog box to change the value of various SQL Server configuration parameters. Alternatively, you can use the `sp_configure` system procedure to change these values.

4. The amount of memory assigned to SQL Server appears in the Running column. This amount indicates the number of 2K blocks of memory assigned, so 16M appears as the number 8192. Enter the new amount for the memory option in the Current column.

T I P One kilobyte (1K) equals 1024 (2^8) bytes or characters.

---

5. Click OK.

6. This change does not take effect until SQL Server is stopped and restarted. You can use the Stop/Pause/Start button on the SQL Enterprise Manager toolbar (the stoplight button) or the SQL Service Manager utility program. If there are active users, you should wait until a later time when the server is not being used. Alternatively, you can pause the server, notify users to sign off, wait an appropriate time period, and then stop and restart the server. See the next section, "Using the Performance Monitor," for information on monitoring SQL Server's resource utilization during operation.

The manner in which SQL Server allocates memory is relatively complex, as one might expect. An overview of the way SQL Server uses memory follows:

■ SQL Server uses a certain amount (approximately 2M) of static overhead to contain the program itself.

■ Configurable options have an impact on memory usage. Significant options are user connections, open databases, open objects, locks, and devices. The DBCC MEMUSAGE statement provides a per-resource value for these items, which can then be multiplied by the setting for that option. Be sure when performing the calculation to use the same scale (bytes or megabytes) for all figures.

■ You can estimate the total cache size (data + procedure cache) by subtracting both the static overhead and the memory used by configurable options from the total SQL Server memory setting. The remaining memory is the approximate total cache size.

Procedure Cache   SQL Server allocates some of its memory to cache frequently used procedures. There are a number of approaches for estimating an appropriate size for the procedure cache, but all of them yield only a "best guess" to use as a starting point. Validate your settings with regular testing if maximum performance is critical to your organization.

One approach to estimating procedure cache size is the following:

1. Analyze the stored procedures defined on your server and identify those frequently used throughout a normal work day.

2. Estimate the average size of the query plan for these procedures. The smallest plan size is one page (2K). You can use the DBCC MEMUSAGE command to determine the query plan size for a procedure.

3. You want at least one copy of all frequently used procedures to fit in the cache to avoid swapping. Therefore, multiply the number of frequently used procedures by the average size of these procedures to calculate a minimum procedure cache size. For example, ten frequently used procedures with an average size of ten pages yields a size of 100 2K pages, or approximately 2M. Add an additional 10 to 20 percent for additional procedures that are used less often.

Part

VII

Ch

35

Remember that this is a rough approximation. You must perform testing if you want to be sure that your settings are appropriate.

The procedure cache option is set using the same steps outlined previously for changing the memory option (see the preceding section, "SQL Server Memory"). The setting does not represent a number of pages, however, but rather a percent of the total cache space allocated to the procedure cache. The rest is allocated to the data cache.

Anytime you are testing something, it is a good idea to change one item at a time and then measure possible effects. This is made somewhat more difficult when changing options on SQL Server because a change to a single setting can affect more than one item. If you want to increase the size of the procedure cache while maintaining the same data cache size, you must increase both the memory and the procedure cache settings.

User Connections   SQL Server allocates approximately 37K for each defined user connection. This space is allocated even if some connections are unused. Although there is always a tendency to allocate a few extra connections to handle unusual situations, it is important to limit the number of user connections as much as possible.

Increasing user connections decreases the total cache size (and hence the size of both the data and procedure cache) unless you increase the memory option. To maintain the same total cache size while increasing user connections, you would need to increase the memory option by approximately 19 (2K) pages for each user connection.

Using Performance Monitor

You can use the Windows NT Performance Monitor to monitor the performance of SQL Server (see Figure 35.46). When SQL Server is installed on a Windows NT Server, new objects and counters are added to the Performance Monitor configuration. In addition, an icon that launches Performance Monitor with some standard objects and counters selected is added to the SQL Server program group.

You can create your own predefined set of counters to monitor and save it in a file so that you can easily use this configuration again. You can even define an icon to automatically launch Performance Monitor and load this predefined configuration. If you are doing benchmark testing, you may want to explore the Performance Monitor in detail. You also can log measurements made with Performance Monitor in addition to displaying them in a real-time graph. The Windows NT Resource Kit includes a manual entirely devoted to this powerful tool.

Remember that as soon as you measure something, you have changed it somewhat. To minimize the overhead associated with performance-monitoring activities, you should connect to the SQL Server under investigation from a Windows NT workstation that contains the SQL Server administration tools and run Performance Monitor from there. In addition, you should turn on only the disk-performance counters while you are actively benchmarking your server. Remember to turn them back off when you are finished.

In addition to the predefined settings provided with SQL Server, some important counters are outlined in the following sections.

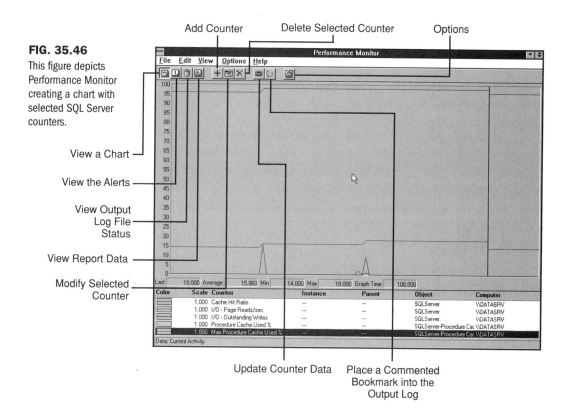

FIG. 35.46
This figure depicts Performance Monitor creating a chart with selected SQL Server counters.

Add Counter
Delete Selected Counter
Options

View a Chart
View the Alerts
View Output Log File Status
View Report Data
Modify Selected Counter

Update Counter Data
Place a Commented Bookmark into the Output Log

RAM   Memory management is one of the most important performance-improvement areas you can explore. Ideally, you want to maximize the use of cache and minimize the amount of physical I/O required. The primary counter to monitor for cache utilization is the Cache Hit Ratio. This counter measures the percentage of time that requests are resolved using information (pages) in the data cache avoiding the need to physically read information from disk. This counter monitors the use of the data cache, not the procedure cache. You want this counter to be high.

New in SQL Server 6.5 is the Procedure Cache object. Some objects that might warrant particular scrutiny are the Max Procedure Cache Used % and the Procedure Cache Used %. By watching the Procedure Cache Used % over time, you can tell if you have allocated too much space to the procedure cache. The Max Procedure Cache Used % tells you what was needed at peak usage. If this represents a single spike during a short period of unusual activity, you may want to try a smaller procedure cache percentage setting.

DiskPerf   To measure physical disk activity, you must first activate the counters associated with the Physical Disk object. The counters are off by default because they slow down disk access. The Windows NT Server System Guide lists the overhead as 1.5 percent on a 386-class computer. You must be a Windows NT administrator (not a SQL Server SA) for the computer you want to monitor. At a command prompt, type the command **diskperf** to see if these counters are on or off and view a help screen for additional details about the command.

Part
VII

Ch
35

After turning on these counters, you can view a number of key counters related to SQL Server. Of particular interest are I/O – Page Reads/sec and I/O – Outstanding Writes. The first of these counters represents the number of physical page reads per second. Ideally, you want this number to stay low and the Cache Hit Ratio to be high. Many factors affect this counter, including the size of the data cache, the use of indexes, the formulation of queries, and the overall design of your databases. No amount of tuning can make up for a poor design.

The I/O – Outstanding Writes counter can indicate whether your disk subsystems are up to the job of running SQL Server with the load that you are placing it under. If this counter remains high over a long period of time, it indicates that the I/O subsystem on this computer is not able to keep up with the demands being made. A faster subsystem, such as a high-performance disk array, might have a significant impact on performance.

From Here...

In this chapter, you learned how to prepare for and then execute SQL Server installation. You learned how to select an appropriate sort order, character set, security model, and network protocol. The SQL Enterprise Manager was introduced, and the procedures for creating login IDs and usernames to provide access to SQL Server and database objects were explored. You learned how to create database and dump devices and, finally, how to create databases and database objects.

For more information on the topics discussed in this chapter, refer to the following chapters:

- To learn about SQL Server's data replication features, see Chapter 36, "SQL Server Data Replication."

- To learn how to use SQL Server to build a data warehouse, see Chapter 37, "Data Warehousing with SQL Server."

- For an overview of the Microsoft Distributed Transaction Coordinator and its use in distributed transaction management, see Chapter 38, "An Inside Look at Distributed Transaction Coordinator (DTC) and Microsoft Transaction Server (MTS)."

- For information on the host connectivity component of BackOffice, SNA Server, see Chapter 39, "SNA Server Preparation and Installation."

- For information on the systems management component of BackOffice, Systems Management Server (SMS), see Chapter 42, "Preparing for SMS."

CHAPTER 36

SQL Server Data Replication

by Don Benage

At this point, you have been introduced to enough administrative techniques to handle common situations that arise when using SQL Server. This chapter explores an advanced topic—*data replication*. This technique is not required for every SQL Server installation, but it can be a powerful addition to the basics that you have learned already. The introduction provided here should get you well on the way to exploiting this capability in your SQL Server implementations. ∎

Learn about how data replication is used

Several scenarios that involve data replication are explored to help you understand why data replication is so important, and how it can be put to good use. This provides the necessary background for you to decide whether you need to use replication and how to construct your network to exploit this feature.

How to set up replication using SQL Enterprise Manager

Explore the possibilities offered by replicating data. Use SQL Enterprise Manager to create a distribution database and then "publish" data on a publication server. Create a subscription server and complete the replication process.

How to view data replication in action

Learn how to use SQL Enterprise Manager to monitor the tasks involved in replication and to view tables for evidence of data replication.

Learn about the Replication architecture

Discover the different roles servers can play in the replication architecture—publication, distribution, and subscription servers. Review the capabilities of each and learn how to create and configure them.

An Introduction to Data Replication

Many situations occur in the daily operation of an organization that involve the need to have the same information in more than one location. This situation naturally occurs in large organizations with many geographic locations, but it also is common in smaller organizations with branch offices. A growing use of data replication, as a component of building a *data warehouse*, is appropriate even at a single location. For instance, you can replicate data from an online transaction-processing system to a data warehouse on another server for analysis.

Data Replication and Its Purpose

Put simply, data replication is a process that automatically copies information from one database to one or more additional databases. In the context of high-end database products like Microsoft SQL Server, data replication implies that this data transfer occurs successfully while maintaining a high degree of consistency and reliability. In other words, the information transferred is generally available within seconds or minutes of a change being made, rather than hours, and the transfer is accomplished accurately.

Traditional methods, such as sending a weekly tape with new information, for example, can accomplish moving information slowly, but the servers involved are never (or rarely) synchronized with one another. Other available techniques, such as the two-phase commit (2PC) protocol, can replicate information to one or more servers and *guarantee* that the information at all locations is identical by preserving the ACID nature of transactions involving multiple servers. However, 2PC requires that all servers, and the communications links between them, be available or the transaction cannot occur. Due to the realities of network management and computer reliability, it is relatively common for one of the components to be unavailable. With 2PC, a transaction involving multiple servers comes to a halt if a single component fails.

N O T E You may recall from Chapter 32, "An Inside Look at Relational Databases," that the term *ACID* is an acronym representing four potential properties of a transaction: atomicity, consistency, isolation, and durability.

▶ **See** "ACID," **p. 1113**

N O T E When the Microsoft Distributed Transaction Coordinator is explored in Chapter 38, "An Inside Look at Distributed Transaction Coordinator (DTC) and Microsoft Transaction Server (MTS)," you learn about an important new tool that can improve the management of 2PC processing, thereby making it more practical than in the past.

Replication strikes a balance between availability and consistency. Replication is useful in situations where information must be kept loosely synchronized. It does not guarantee that at every instant in time all copies of a particular data element will be identical. This is not a serious limitation. Many situations require the level of availability and consistency provided by SQL Server's replication.

Many sales organizations, for example, publish new pricing on a weekly or monthly basis. The distribution of this information often involves physically delivering a printed copy, a process that is subject to routine interruptions and failures. An automated mechanism that can provide all sales offices and distributors with pricing information that is current to within 30 minutes (or less) would be a welcome change.

N O T E   The actual time required for replication events to take place can vary dramatically. It depends on the amount of information, the speed of the communications link, and the additional workload being handled by the servers involved. With small amounts of information on a high-speed LAN, replication can occur in less than a minute. However, the real-world situations in which replication is most useful often involve performance constraints, such as high-traffic networks and exchanges across large-scale WANs. Establishing a set of reasonable expectations is an important part of the planning process. ▨

Replication Terminology

Before exploring replication in more detail, it is useful to learn some basic terminology. Microsoft has adopted a metaphor to help describe and define replication using SQL Server. A server that replicates information is said to *publish* it and is known as a *publisher* or *publication server*. Servers that receive the information are *subscription servers* or *subscribers*.

Another role in the process is that of moving the information. This may be done by the publication server, or an entirely separate computer. The server that performs this process is called the *distribution server* or *distributor*. Therefore, the publisher and distributor may refer to the same machine.

Replicated information is described with a number of special terms. A *publication* is a group of tables published as a unit. A publication is made up of one or more *articles*. Each article represents information from a single table. An article may contain an entire table or a *partition*. A horizontal partition contains only selected rows; a vertical partition contains only selected columns. Partitioning is also known as *filtering*. Publications and articles are replicated from a *publication database* to one or more *subscription databases* located on subscribers.

Overview of the Replication Process

When setting up replication, it is helpful to have at least a rudimentary understanding of the processes involved and the manner by which information moves through the various stages of replication. After you have a basic understanding of the process, you will be ready to work through a sample replication scenario, an excellent way to learn this material.

This section presents a simplified view of replication to help you get started without becoming overwhelmed in details. The replication functionality in Microsoft SQL Server has many options and provides features to meet many real-world challenges. After working through a simple example, you can start expanding the complexity of your implementations.

You already know the three distinct roles played by servers in a replication event: publisher, distributor, and subscriber. As mentioned earlier, the distribution server can be the same computer as the publisher, or it can be a separate computer. Furthermore, a server may act as both a publisher and a subscriber. It is possible, for example, for a server to replicate information to itself, although it is difficult to imagine a use for this setup other than as a demonstration. A more likely situation is for a publisher of one publication to act as a subscriber of a different publication from another publication server.

Under ordinary circumstances, you want the publication database and subscription database(s) to be *synchronized* before having the publisher replicate its first new transactions to subscribers. This job can be handled automatically by a special synchronization process (a Sync task). In the case of large databases and slow communications links, you may want to perform manual synchronization using one or more high-speed tape dump devices, for example, to back up the publisher and restore to the subscriber. This is a more involved process but is often more practical than attempting the transfer of many megabytes or gigabytes of information over a slow link.

When a publication is created, the LogReader task on the distribution server reads the transaction log of the publication server and copies transactions that have been earmarked for replication. They are copied to the *distribution database* on the distribution server. The Distribution task on the distribution server is now responsible for moving the information to the appropriate subscription databases on all subscribers.

Sample Replication Scenarios

SQL Server data replication can be used in different environments and for different reasons. In order to familiarize you with the way in which replication is typically set up, this section presents some sample scenarios showing representative architectures. This should help you plan for an effective implementation at your site. These scenarios (or very similar ones) were first introduced in Chapter 33, "An Inside Look at SQL Server." This section discusses the scenarios in more detail and explores the role that replication plays in supporting these setups. The scenarios illustrated include the following:

- A scenario involving two SQL Servers, one used for Online Transaction Processing (OLTP) and one used in an Online Analytical Processing (OLAP) role as a data warehouse in a Decision Support System (DSS).

- A replication scenario in which a SQL Server supporting traditional transaction processing replicates selected information to a SQL Server integrated with a Web server.

- A wide area network (WAN) with SQL Servers at each geographic location, using replication to consolidate information from each branch at the corporate headquarters location.

Replication to a Data Warehouse

The next chapter, "Data Warehousing with SQL Server," explores data warehousing in more detail, but it is discussed briefly here because of the role played by replication. Data warehousing has become an area of intense interest and activity in the last several years. In addition to using database technology to support OLTP, Information Systems (IS) professionals have learned that a separate source of data, dubbed the *data warehouse*, is best suited to support the needs of managers and other professionals engaged in data analysis. While these two functions were initially supported using a single database, this architecture did not work well for a variety of reasons.

Because the data warehouse is typically populated with information originally created or captured by an OLTP database, the idea of using replication to move selected information to the data warehouse naturally suggests itself. At regular intervals selected by the database administrator (DBA), information that has been entered into the organization's databases can be copied to a separate SQL Server.

In a large organization, there may be a number of SQL Servers operating at a department level, and each of them may replicate information to the data warehouse. In this situation, the data warehouse is a subscriber to a number of publishing servers. This type of use is very similar to the corporate roll-up example covered in the third scenario in this section (see "Replication to a Headquarters Location").

Figure 36.1 shows a network with two SQL Servers. The first supports transaction processing. It has many users, typically clerical workers or telemarketing personnel, entering orders or some other type of recurrent transaction information (such as product service requests). The transactions are generally small, and the response time must be rapid since the transaction must usually be processed immediately.

FIG. 36.1

Replication allows you to populate a data warehouse with information from an OLTP system.

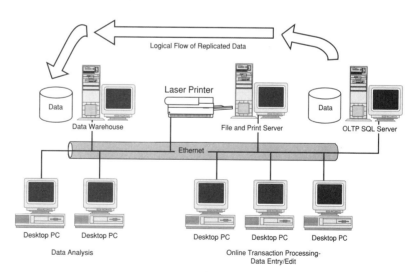

Information from this server is replicated to a second SQL Server where the information is manipulated to leave it in a form more suitable for trend analysis and other decision-support activities. The data warehouse typically stores data for a longer period (to support historical analysis), but may not require the same level of detail. Various aggregates (sums, averages, counts) may be precalculated and stored in the database to speed analytical queries which frequently use such figures. In addition, the number of users accessing the data warehouse is typically much smaller, but the queries that are processed tend to be much more complex and require more computational power and time to resolve.

Because of the different nature of the data on the two servers, replication will only accomplish the first part of the task, creating two (or more) roughly identical sets of data. In this situation, the data from the OLTP system will be replicated in the same form in which it is stored on the OLTP system, but after it is received on the subscribing server (the data warehouse server) it will usually be "massaged" in a variety of ways. This is done, for example, to make it easy to express analytical queries ("how did sales in the third quarter of this year compare with last year's third quarter") and to resolve them quickly. The synchronization task, which plays an important role in many SQL Server scenarios, is less critical in this environment.

Replication to Support Web Server Integration

In addition to data warehousing, another similar phenomenon is growing substantially. Integrating SQL Server with a Web server has some of the same goals as a data warehouse—make it easier for a particular group of users to make use of database information. There are differences, however.

The typical application of Web server/database integration is designed to present the data through an extremely easy-to-use interface. The user community being served is generally much less sophisticated than the analyst using a data warehouse and does not require the capability to form complex queries (or want the responsibility of formulating them).

When using a Web server front end, the client computer does not (usually) communicate directly with the SQL Server at all, but rather establishes a connection to the Web server through the use of a Web browser (see Figure 36.2). One advantage is that database software does not need to be added to the client computer. This can be a significant advantage if you want to present information to an extremely large group of users (such as all Internet users!) or to users that are completely outside the boundaries of your organization.

FIG. 36.2

Adding a SQL Server to provide database information to a Web server creates a powerful combination that can solve a number of different needs.

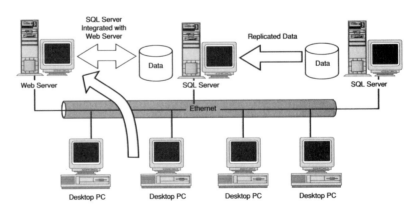

N O T E Even though the client computer does not directly access the SQL Server, you still should carefully review the License Agreement for SQL Server and evaluate whether client licenses are required in your situation. In general, accessing a SQL Server through some sort of "gateway" or "concentrator" process on another machine does not alleviate the need for client licenses. A special license may be available specifically designed to support Web server integration scenarios. Check with your software vendor or Microsoft representative for details. ■

The primary reason for using replication in this situation is, again, to avoid burdening the OLTP server with the task of responding to requests for information made, in this case, by the Web server. Because of the need to keep OLTP systems running at top speed, replication is a good fit. Even the job of distributing the data can move from the OLTP server so that the impact of replicating the data is minimal. Once the information arrives at the subscribing server, there is less concern about responsiveness. The subscribing server may even be the Web server depending on load, response-time requirements, and the power of the hardware being used.

It is worth pointing out that Web servers are frequently being used, in ever increasing numbers, to provide information to customers. In such situations, it still makes sense to use replication to "share the load" among two or more SQL Servers, but responsiveness of the Web server may still be of primary concern. In this case, replication helps by allowing the power of multiple machines to be applied to manage the same information in two distinct environments.

Replication to a Headquarters Location

Figure 36.3 depicts one of the classic uses of replication—a corporation with branch offices and a headquarters location. Information is entered into a SQL Server database at each branch (e.g., orders for products or services, customer service requests, or employee evaluation results). The SQL Server then automatically copies, or replicates, this information to the corporate headquarters location where it is consolidated for reporting purposes. It may even be manipulated further and replicated again into a corporate data warehouse.

Consolidated results may be replicated back to the branch locations from the headquarters site. Microsoft SQL Server supports the notion of a single server's being both a source of replicated information (a "publisher") and a destination (a "subscriber"). The consolidated information may be replicated throughout the day, or only during off-peak times, depending on the nature of the data and the need for up-to-the-minute updates. In this way, each branch office can have the very latest information available to support their activities and operations.

FIG. 36.3

This figure depicts a typical corporate "roll-up" replication architecture with two branch offices and a headquarters location.

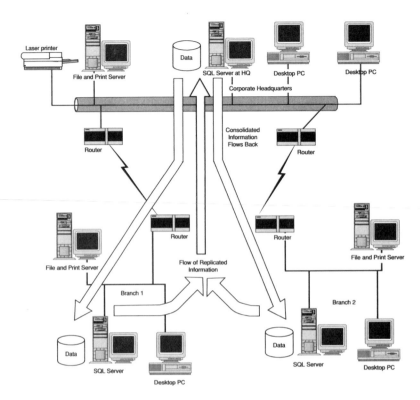

The Role of the SQL Executive

You were briefly introduced to the SQL Executive and the process of creating and scheduling tasks in earlier chapters. The SQL Executive is a Windows NT service responsible for executing scheduled tasks. A user (usually an SA) can create the tasks, or SQL Server can generate them automatically to support replication or some other operation.

The SQL Executive plays an active role in replication. It might even be called the *engine* of the replication process. You use three special-purpose tasks to implement replication—the Sync, LogReader, and Distribution tasks. As you complete the dialog boxes used to tell SQL Server about your replication needs, the SQL Executive creates and runs these tasks automatically. You can later use SQL Enterprise Manager to monitor what tasks are spawned and check their success or failure.

A Complete Example—Start to Finish

An example is helpful to illustrate the manner in which SQL Server implements data replication. Although this example may not coincide with the needs of your organization, it is generic enough that the concepts involved apply to virtually every use of replication. After you understand how this situation is set up, you will be well on your way to using replication successfully. Subsequent sections describe in detail how to actually perform the operations described here.

This example involves only two servers: DATASRV and PRIMSRV. DATASRV is the publisher and the distributor. PRIMSRV is a subscriber to publications on DATASRV. A publication is created from the information found in the sample database included with SQL Server—pubs—to make it easier for you to follow the example with your own servers. PRIMSRV uses a database named pubs2 as the subscription database. The *titles* table from the pubs database on DATASRV is replicated to the pubs2 database on PRIMSRV.

N O T E   It is only a coincidence that the sample database provided with SQL Server happens to be based on an example involving publishers. The pubs database has been provided as a sample for several years and was used well before replication brought about servers in the role of *publisher*. Hopefully, this won't make the replication scenario more difficult to follow. Clearly the subject matter of the information in the database has no impact on the replication process. ■

Both servers are members of the domain named INTERNAL. PRIMSRV is the Primary Domain Controller (PDC) for the INTERNAL domain, and DATASRV has been configured with the *server* role (that is, it is not a domain controller). The master domain model is being used for the servers on this network. A one-way trust relationship has been established between the INTERNAL resource domain and the GSULLIVAN master domain. INTERNAL trusts GSULLIVAN. Both SQL Servers (and both SQL Executives) are running in the security context of the same master domain service account (GSULLIVAN\sqlsvc).

Setting Up Replication with the SQL Enterprise Manager

It is possible to set up replication by using commands entered from a command prompt or saved in a script or stored procedure. Until you have worked through a number of examples using SQL Enterprise Manager, you should avoid using manually generated commands. As you become an advanced replication administrator, the capability to use custom procedures is a powerful complement to the easy-to-use graphical interface.

Figures 36.4 through 36.22, which depict the replication process, are from a computer running Windows 95. The SQL Enterprise Manager and the two SQL Servers are all version 6.5. Some of the dialog boxes have been enhanced from version 6.0, but most are very similar. The concepts are identical. If you are using version 6.0, you should still be able to follow the procedures provided here with only minor differences. The biggest single change made to replication from version 6.0 to 6.5 is the capability to replicate to ODBC subscribers. In particular, the use of Microsoft Access and ORACLE subscribers is supported.

Setting up replication is a process involving many steps. There are some natural stopping points along the way, or you may proceed rapidly through the entire process. In an actual production environment, there might be a delay while waiting for synchronization to occur. It is common to schedule automatic synchronization for off-peak hours, or to accomplish synchronization manually.

Publication and Distribution Servers

The first step in configuring replication is to install publishing on the publication server. At the same time, you establish a distribution database on the distribution server. In the example presented here, the publisher is also the distributor—the server named DATASRV. To install publishing and create the distribution database, follow these steps:

1. Start SQL Enterprise Manager. If you haven't already done so, register both servers that you will use for replication. Establish an active connection to both servers by clicking the plus sign next to the server name. (Although this is not strictly necessary, it is a convenient way to be sure that you have no connectivity problems before beginning.)

2. Highlight the server you want to use as the publisher (DATASRV, in the example). From the menu, choose Server, Replication Configuration, Install Publishing. The Install Replication Publishing dialog box appears (see Figure 36.4).

FIG. 36.4

Use the Install Replication Publishing dialog box to initiate the creation of the distribution database that will be used in the replication process.

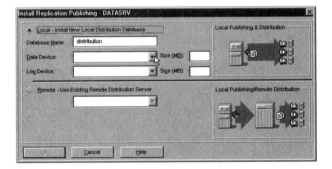

3. In this dialog box, you can specify a local or remote distribution server. Select Local if you want to use the publication server as the distribution server as well. To use another server, select Remote and enter the name of the server you want to use as the distribution server. The example calls for a local distribution server.

4. The name of the distribution database defaults to "distribution." You can enter another name if you want.

5. Next, you must create the database devices for the data and transaction log. From the Data Device drop-down list, select New. The New Database Device dialog box appears, as shown in Figure 36.5.

6. Enter a name for the new device that will contain the distribution database. In general, you should not use this device as a default device. Select a drive location for the device in the Location drop-down list. A path and file name for the device is offered as a default which you can override if you want.

7. Next, you either can type a size for the device directly in the Size drop-down list box, or move the slider control to the right of the drop-down list with your mouse. A corresponding size is entered in the Size box, and the graphical display of available drive space is updated to reflect the size of the potential new device. When you are satisfied with your

selections, click Create Now. If everything works properly, you should receive confirmation that the device has been created.

FIG. 36.5

Use the New Database Device dialog box to create a device on which to store the distribution database.

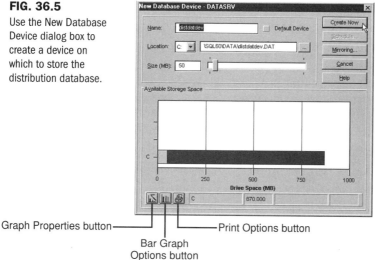

Graph Properties button ————

Print Options button

Bar Graph Options button

8. Repeat steps 5 through 7 for the log device. The log device does not need to be as large as the data device.

 TIP A good rule of thumb for the log device size is from ten to 30 percent of the data device size.

After creating both devices, you return to the Install Replication Publishing dialog box with all the options for a local distribution database completed (see Figure 36.6).

FIG. 36.6

This figure depicts the Install Replication Publishing dialog box with the newly created data and log devices. At this point, you are ready to create the distribution database.

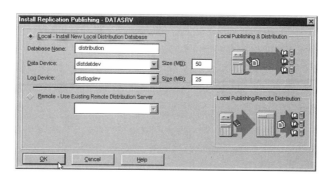

9. Click OK. After a short interval for processing, an information window appears, confirming that Replication Publishing (the distribution database) has installed successfully. You also are asked if you want to continue by adding publishing databases and subscribers at this time (see Figure 36.7).

FIG. 36.7

This dialog box provides
confirmation that the
distribution database
has been successfully
created.

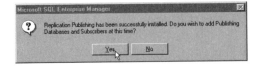

10. Click Yes, and the Replication Publishing dialog box appears, as shown in Figure 36.8.

FIG. 36.8

The Replication
Publishing dialog
box is used to enable
publishing to a specified
list of servers. You also
can control which data-
bases can be used for
creating publications.

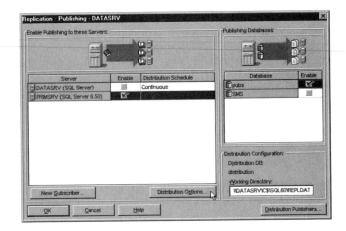

11. In this dialog box, you tell SQL Server which servers should be allowed to subscribe to
    this publication server. This is one method of limiting the availability of publications to
    selected subscribers. You also can open this dialog box later (by choosing Server,
    Replication Configuration, Publishing from the menu) and disable a subscriber for this
    publisher with a single mouse click.

12. For the purposes of the example, DATASRV enables publishing to PRIMSRV and
    establishes pubs as a publishing database. Click OK.

13. This is a natural stopping point. If you want, click the Replication Topology toolbar
    button and view the results of your efforts (see Figure 36.9).

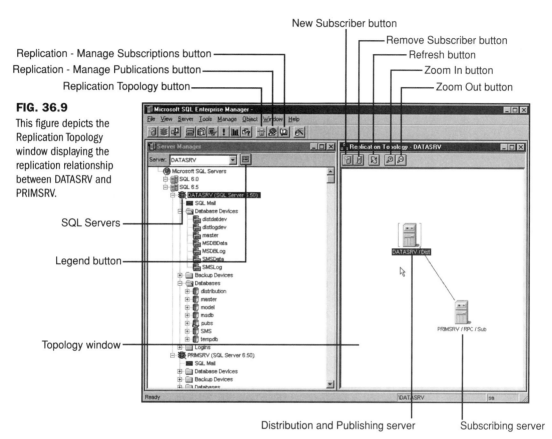

New Subscriber button

Remove Subscriber button

Refresh button

Zoom In button

Zoom Out button

Replication - Manage Subscriptions button

Replication - Manage Publications button

Replication Topology button

FIG. 36.9

This figure depicts the Replication Topology window displaying the replication relationship between DATASRV and PRIMSRV.

SQL Servers

Legend button

Topology window

Distribution and Publishing server

Subscribing server

Articles and Publications

To create a publication on your publication server, follow these steps:

1. Start SQL Enterprise Manager. Click the Replication Topology toolbar button, or choose Server, Replication Configuration, Topology from the menu. The Replication Topology window appears (see Figure 36.10).

FIG. 36.10

The Replication Topology window provides a graphical representation of the relationship between publishing and subscribing servers.

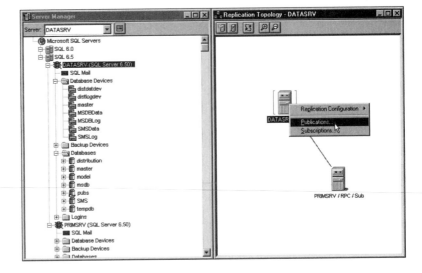

2. Using the right mouse button, click the publication server. A context-sensitive menu appears.

3. Select Publications, and the Manage Publications dialog box appears, as shown in Figure 36.11.

FIG. 36.11

The Manage Publications dialog box displays a list of any currently defined publications. Use this dialog box to initiate the creation, modification, or deletion of publications.

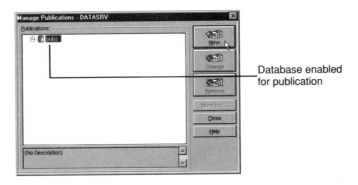

Database enabled for publication

4. Any databases that you enabled for publication appear in the Publications window. At this point if you click the plus sign to open the database, no publications appear because none have been defined. Click New, and the Edit Publications dialog box appears (see Figure 36.12).

5. Enter a Publication Title and Description for the publication. Leave the (default) Transaction Based option button selected.

FIG. 36.12

The Edit Publications dialog box is a multitab dialog box used to specify the data included in a publication and other parameters affecting the replication process.

6. On the Articles tab, find the table(s) you want to publish in the Database Tables box. Highlight it and click Add. For the example, select and add only the Titles table. If you want to refine further instructions for an article (such as defining a partition), highlight the article and click Edit. The Manage Article dialog box then appears, as shown in Figure 36.13.

FIG. 36.13

Use the Manage Article dialog box to specify a table to be replicated. Alternatively, you can indicate a horizontal or vertical partition (rows or columns) to be replicated.

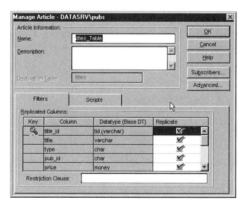

7. In this dialog box, you can change the name of an article and enter a description. Using the Filters tab, you can define a vertical partition by selecting particular columns, or a horizontal partition by entering a Restriction Clause. The Scripts tab allows you to control the action SQL Server takes when an INSERT, UPDATE, or DELETE occurs on a table marked for replication. You also can customize the initial table synchronization schema script.

For the example, you should not make any changes. If you return to this dialog box later, after processing for this publication has occurred, the blank portions of the dialog box will be replaced by the default results. Click OK to return to the Edit Publications dialog box. Click the Synchronization tab (see Figure 36.14).

FIG. 36.14

The Synchronization tab of the Edit Publications dialog box allows you to select the method used for synchronization. You can select a date and time that the synchronization process will occur if you don't want to initiate the process now.

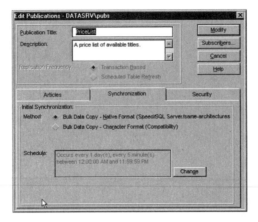

8. This tab controls the method and schedule for automatic synchronization. Click Change to view the schedule for the synchronization event and the Task Schedule dialog box appears (see Figure 36.15).

FIG. 36.15

This is the Task Schedule dialog box for the Initial Synchronization event that precedes replication of transactions.

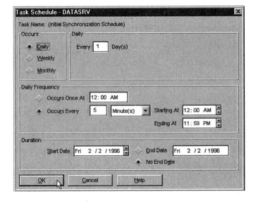

9. Theoretically, it is necessary to perform synchronization only once. Thereafter, transactions are distributed to subscribers as they occur. In practice, it may be appropriate to apply a synchronization event at some regular interval (for example, weekly or monthly) to be certain that subscriber data is identical to the publisher. Remember, replication is based on a loose consistency model, and data is not guaranteed to be identical.

For the purposes of the example, change the schedule to reflect a task that occurs one time approximately one hour in the future. This gives you time to set up the subscriber before synchronization occurs. You can manually run the task before the scheduled time if the subscriber is ready and you don't want to wait. After a task completes, it is disabled but not deleted, so you can always use it again if needed. Click OK to return to the Edit Publication dialog box and then select the Security tab (see Figure 36.16).

FIG. 36.16

The Security tab of the Edit Publication dialog box allows you to limit the servers that are able to view and subscribe to this publication.

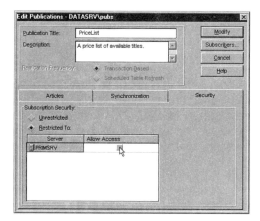

10. You can restrict the visibility of this publication to only certain subscribers. For the example, either leave the Unrestricted option checked, or click the Restricted To option and click the check box to Allow Access for the subscription server (PRIMSRV).

11. Click Add. (Note that if you edit an existing publication, this button becomes the Modify button.) The publication is created, and tasks are launched for the synchronization event.

Subscribing Servers

So far, you have created a publication server (DATASRV), *enabled* publication to PRIMSRV, and created a publication. You are now ready to set up a subscription server. Before doing so, a short explanation about certain commands is appropriate to help you avoid confusion.

Using SQL Enterprise Manager, you can select commands from a menu, use a toolbar button, or use the right mouse button to activate a context-sensitive pop-up menu. All available methods for a particular command yield the same results. Those new to replication are sometimes confused by the similarity of some commands. This is amplified by the fact that there are two or three ways to specify the same command.

Two main dialog boxes have publishing as their subject matter: the Replication Publishing dialog box and the Manage Publications dialog box. You use the first for configuring which servers are enabled to subscribe to a publisher and specifying the publication databases. The second you use to actually create publications. Likewise, there is a Replication Subscribing dialog box and a Manage Subscriptions dialog box. These two dialog boxes are used similarly to their publishing counterparts: one to configure subscribing and one to create actual subscriptions.

To subscribe to a publication, follow these steps:

1. Start SQL Enterprise Manager if it is not already running.

2. Open the Replication Topology window. Right-click the subscription server (PRIMSRV in the example) and select Replication Configuration, Subscribing from the menu. The Replication Subscribing dialog box appears, as shown in Figure 36.17.

FIG. 36.17

The Replication Subscribing dialog box allows you to restrict the publishing servers that can be used by this server as a subscriber.

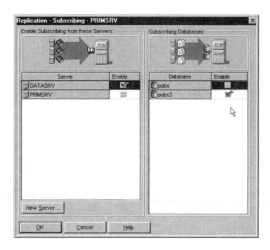

3. Use this dialog box to specify the publishing servers this subscriber can use and which databases can be used as the destination for replicated data. For this example, you should not need to make any changes. Click OK.

4. Right-click the subscription server again and select Subscriptions from the pop-up menu. The Manage Subscriptions dialog box appears, as shown in Figure 36.18.

FIG. 36.18

The Manage Subscrip-tions dialog box lists the current subscriptions and is used to initiate subscribing to available publications.

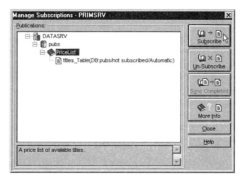

5. The publication servers that this subscriber has enabled appear in the Publications window. By opening the server and then the publication databases on the server, you can see the publications and articles available to this subscriber. You can get additional information about a publication by selecting it and clicking More Info. For this example, select PriceList and click More Info. The Publication Info dialog box appears (see Figure 36.19).

6. Confirm that this is the publication to which you want to subscribe, and then click Close to return to the Manage Subscriptions dialog box. With PriceList still selected, click Subscribe. The Subscription Options dialog box appears (see Figure 36.20).

FIG. 36.19

The Publication Info dialog box describes the contents of a publication and its synchronization schedule.

FIG. 36.20

The Subscription Options dialog box allows you to specify the destination database for the replication and to select the type of synchronization you want to apply.

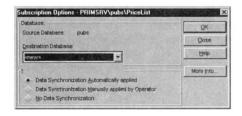

7. Select the option Data Synchronization Automatically Applied. For this example, the destination database (and the transaction log and devices for each) must be created. Select New from the Destination Database drop-down list, and the New Database dialog box appears.

8. Enter a name for the subscription database (**pubs2** in the example).

9. Next, you need to create the database devices for the data and transaction log. In the Data Device drop-down list, select New. The New Database Device dialog box appears (see Figure 36.21).

10. Enter a name for the new device that will contain the subscription database. This device should not be used as a default device. Select a drive location for the device from the Location drop-down list. A path and file name for the device is offered as a default that you can override if you want.

11. Next, you can either type a size for the device directly in the Size drop-down list box, or you can move the slider control to the right of the drop-down list box with your mouse. A corresponding size is entered in the Size box, and the graphical display of available drive space will be updated to reflect the size of the potential new device. When you are satisfied with your selections, click Create Now. If everything works properly, you should receive confirmation that the device has been created in an information window.

FIG. 36.21

The New Database Device dialog box provides the opportunity to define a new device for the database and/or the transaction log.

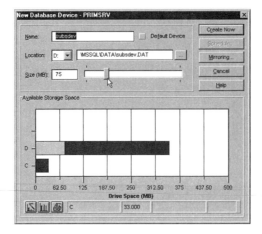

12. Repeat steps 9 to 11 for the log device. The log device does not need to be as large as the data device.

T I P   A good rule of thumb for the log device size is from ten to 30 percent of the data device size.

13. You should now be back to the New Database dialog box with the data and log devices created and specified. Click Create New to create the subscription database.

14. You return to the Subscription Options dialog box with the newly created database entered in the Destination Database list box. Click OK.

15. You then return to the Manage Subscriptions dialog box (see Figure 36.22). The display should now indicate that you are subscribed, but not synchronized. Click Close.

FIG. 36.22

This figure depicts the Manage Subscriptions dialog showing a publication with a subscribed but not synchronized status.

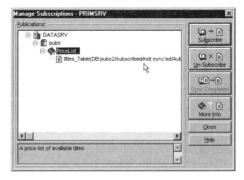

Congratulations! You have a completely configured replication. With no further action on your part, the synchronization event you scheduled will take place at the specified time. Any changes you make to the pubs database on the publication server (DATASRV) will be automatically replicated to the subscriber (PRIMSRV).

Monitoring the Status of Replication Events

Now that you've configured replication, you'd probably like to see replication in action—see some changes to the publication database appear in the subscription database as well. In this section, you learn techniques for monitoring the status of replication events. You follow the progress of the replication example to see its effects.

There are a number of ways to see the effects of replication. You can view the tasks that are created and running to perform replication actions. You also can see that the new subscription database has been created and that the replicated table has automatically been created by the synchronization process. You can enable e-mail or event log notification of the success or failure of tasks, such as the distribution task, to leave evidence that the process is working. And, of course, you can make a change in the publishing table and then view the subscriber to see if the change has been replicated.

To view the tasks used for replication, follow these steps:

1. Start SQL Enterprise Manager.

2. You want to review the tasks that have been launched on the distributor. Select the distribution server (DATASRV) in the Server Manager windows and click the Task Scheduling toolbar button. The Task Scheduling dialog box appears, as shown in Figure 36.23.

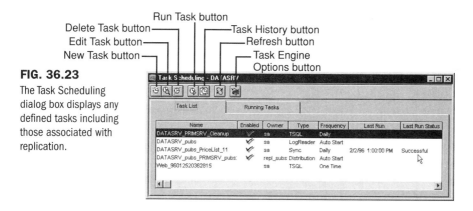

FIG. 36.23

The Task Scheduling dialog box displays any defined tasks including those associated with replication.

3. Depending on the schedule you established for the synchronization event earlier, your Sync task may not have run yet. If you want, you can highlight the Sync task and click the Run Task toolbar button to run the task immediately.

4. Click the Running Tasks tab (see Figure 36.24). The LogReader and Distribution tasks should be Active. Close the Task Scheduling dialog box when you are finished viewing.

To check the subscription database for evidence that the synchronization process has completed, follow these steps:

1. Start SQL Enterprise Manager.

FIG. 36.24

This figure shows the Running Tasks tab of the Task Scheduling dialog box displaying active replication tasks.

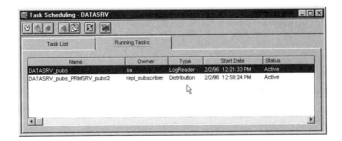

2. In the Server Manager window, select the subscription server and open its Databases folder. Find the destination database you specified when you created the subscription and open its folder (pubs2 in the example).

3. Open the Objects folder and then the Tables folder. If the Sync task has completed, you should see the table it created (titles in the example).

4. Right-click the table and select Edit from the pop-up menu. The Manage Tables dialog box displays the structure of the table created during the synchronization process (see Figure 36.25). It should contain the columns you specified (all columns in the example—no partitioning was specified).

FIG. 36.25

You can use the Manage Tables dialog box to view the structure of an existing table.

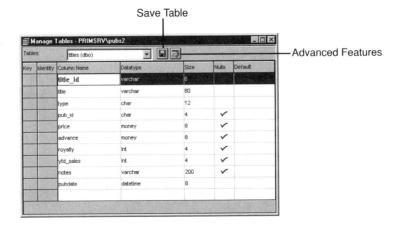

Monitoring tasks and viewing the newly created tables in the subscription database provide circumstantial evidence that replication is working, but there is no substitute for actually changing the data on the publisher and seeing the change reflected in a subscriber. To see replication in action, follow this procedure:

1. Start SQL Enterprise Manager.

2. Highlight the publication server (DATASRV) and click the SQL Query Tool button on the toolbar (this button was called the Query Analyzer in version 6.0).

3. Highlight the subscriber (PRIMSRV) and click the SQL Query Tool button again.

4. Click anywhere in the first query window (the one for DATASRV) to make it the active window; then choose <u>W</u>indow, Tile <u>H</u>orizontally from the menu. Your display should look something like Figure 36.26.

SQL Query Tool

FIG. 36.26

SQL Enterprise Manager is shown in this figure with a query window open for both publisher and subscriber, a convenient arrangement for testing replication.

New Query

Load SQL Script

Save Query/Result

Query Options

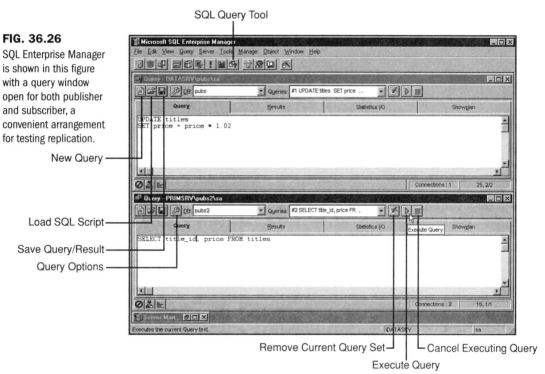

Remove Current Query Set — └ Cancel Executing Query

Execute Query

5. In the top (publisher) window, select the name of the publication database from the <u>D</u>B drop-down list.

6. In the subscriber window, select the name of the destination database (the subscription database).

   In the example, the pubs database should be selected on DATASRV, and pubs2 should be selected on PRIMSRV.

7. Because replication can happen very quickly, you should view the destination table before replication to verify its contents. In the example, the new titles table in the pubs2 database should still have the original values that were installed with SQL Server unless you have used pubs.

8. To verify the current contents, enter the following query in the Query tab of PRIMSRV's window: **SELECT title_id, price FROM titles**. Click the Execute Query button and view the results in the <u>R</u>esults tab of the dialog box.

9. In the Query tab of the publisher's window, enter a Transact-SQL (T-SQL) statement to modify some of the data in the publication. For this example, the titles table is modified

to reflect a two-percent price increase on all titles. This can be done with the following T-SQL statement which you should enter into the query window: **UPDATE titles SET price = price * 1.02**.

10. Click the Execute Query button. In the Results tab, you should see that all rows have been updated.

11. Click the Execute Query button in the subscriber's window again. You may already see the replication reflected by changed prices. If not, wait a few minutes and try again. You should see the updated prices in the Results tab (see Figure 36.27).

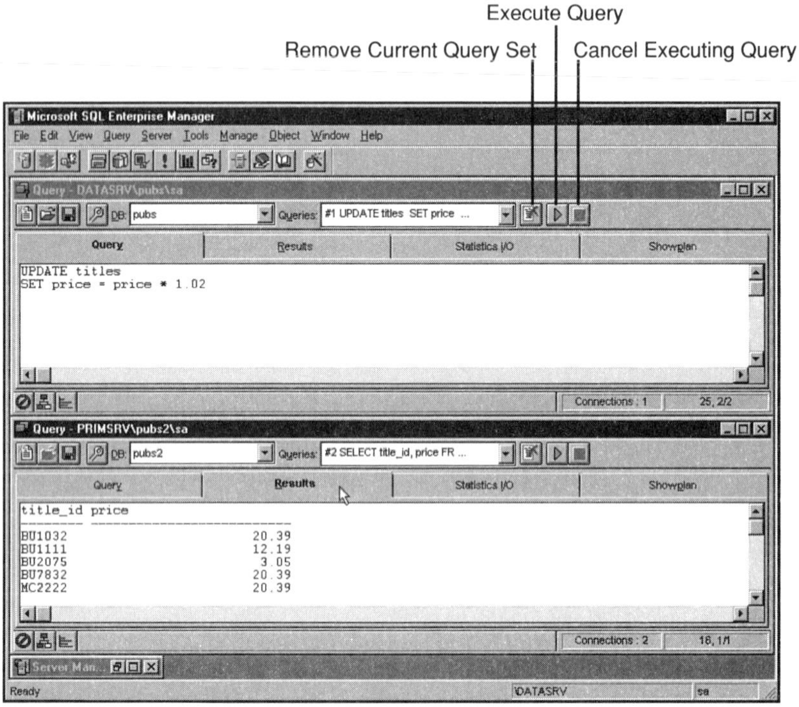

FIG. 36.27

The Results tab allows you to display the results of a query that has executed. In this case, it shows the replicated information.

From Here...

In this chapter, you learned some advanced features of Microsoft SQL Server. You were introduced to the procedures for setting up data replication and how to see the process of replication take place. You also learned about distributed transactions and a new tool included in SQL Server version 6.5, the Distributed Transaction Coordinator. The chapter also described the various tools for monitoring the status of distributed transactions and resolving problem transactions.

For information on related topics, see the following chapters:

- For a review of the procedures for administering SQL Server, see Chapter 35, "Maintaining SQL Server."

- To learn about using SQL Server to establish a data warehouse, see Chapter 37, "Data Warehousing with SQL Server."

- To learn about using multiple SQL Servers to process distributed transactions, see Chapter 38, "An Inside Look at Distributed Transaction Coordinator (DTC) and Microsoft Transaction Server (MTS)."

Data Warehousing with SQL Server

by Kevin Runnels

Most companies have geared their information systems around On-Line Transaction Processing (OLTP) systems. They have found that they end up being data rich and information poor. They can get reports of extremely detailed information regarding specific transactions, yet can't derive the strategic information they need to make informed business decisions. They see lots of trees, but miss the forest. They want to be able to "slice and dice" the data based on specific criteria. They want important trends to "jump out at them" from reports. They want to be able to drill down from summary data to look at underlying detail. They want to know the data they are looking at is correct and complete. They want quick access times for queries, and they don't want to learn SQL. They want a data warehouse. ■

Data warehouse teamwork

Discover the necessary steps to ensure success in planning your data warehouse project by soliciting user involvement and managing expectations.

Data warehouse process flows

Explore the process of extracting data and transforming it into business information for decision support.

OLTP versus data warehousing

Learn to discern the marked differences between traditional transaction processing and the specialized structure of the data warehouse.

Dimensional modeling

Expand the way you look at your business data and explore new approaches in schema design such as the star schema.

Analysis and decision support

Uncover different analysis options and presentation techniques for your published warehouse data.

Future directions

Look into the future of data warehousing with performance-enhancing structures and a discussion of Microsoft's Active Data Warehouse Framework.

Data Warehousing Fundamentals

The capability to construct a data warehouse, as it is known today, hasn't existed until relatively recently, whereas OLTP systems have been around for decades. The power of modern desktop servers, with multiple CPUs and multiprocessor-aware operating systems such as Microsoft Windows NT Server, now offer raw processing speeds and mass storage options that previously existed only in the mainframe shop. The software available for these machines is also vastly superior to that which was previously available, providing more complex data structures, faster indexing and querying, and much improved user interfaces.

Technology provides the means to capture, store, and analyze ever larger amounts of data. Businesses have found benefits in applying these new tools to manipulate the transaction-based data collected by their companies to provide information to support decision making and measures of company performance in ways that were not previously possible. An entire industry has sprung up to support the use of computers in decision making and help managers derive meaning from the megabytes of data collected within their companies. The application of this technology has resulted in the concept of data warehousing.

Data Warehouse Defined

Data warehousing is actually an aggregate of many concepts. The core concept is that data collected by a company, usually by some type of On-Line Transaction Processing System (OLTP), is validated and reorganized into categories or subjects that represent something meaningful to the end users of the data. The reorganized data is published to end users in an integrated, static format that they can use as the source of an enterprise-wide Decision Support System (DSS). Managers and analysts can use the reorganized data as a basis for such diverse activities as tracking trends in supplier costs/quality, identifying customer profiles, analyzing the effects and utilization of special marketing promotions, and so forth. The methods and techniques employed to get the data from the raw state to the meaningful state, as well as the tools used to examine and present this data, are what make up data warehousing.

N O T E The concept of "publishing" information in the data warehouse is very important. Publishing infers that the data is of high quality, meaning it has been examined for accuracy, completeness, and consistency, and that it represents something modeled at a single point in time. It is important that the person responsible for managing the data warehouse take responsibility for the quality of data and make users aware of any issues that may compromise the validity of the information they are presented. ▪

The Data Warehouse Process Model

There are essentially four major components to the Data Warehouse Process Model, as shown in Figure 37.1. The data warehouse typically pulls in data from several data sources, usually production OLTP systems, but can include data purchased from syndicated data sources. This data is then cleansed (reconciling differences in formats, transaction dates, currencies, translating codes, etc.). Once it has been processed to a uniform, intermediate format, the data is then loaded into the data warehouse where it is reorganized into a format that allows for quick access of summarized information while still supporting queries down to the detailed level.

FIG. 37.1
The four stages of Extracting, Cleansing, Loading, and Accessing information in the data warehouse are general categories. In most data warehouses, these general categories describe several processes.

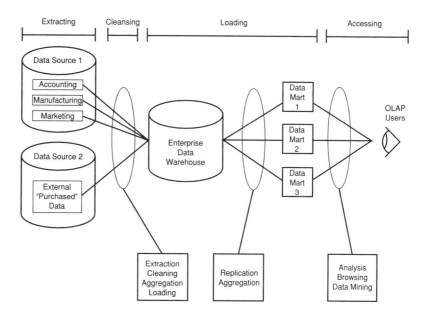

The overall design will reflect end users' understanding of their business around "dimensions" such as time, product, supplier, and so on. Once the data is published in the data warehouse, users access it using specially developed On-Line Analytical Processing (OLAP) software.

Developing the Foundation of the Data Warehouse

The technical construction of the data warehouse will be built upon the foundation of the requirements you will discover from interviewing the end users of the system. This will be a time-consuming process, but the time you spend designing the data warehouse will be paid back many times over when you actually implement your design. Be prepared to spend more time interviewing users and developing requirements than is spent on the technical side of implementing the warehouse.

Determine who in your organization will be using the data warehouse. Keep in mind that the user base will increase after the warehouse is successfully deployed; so take into consideration not only those people or departments that have an immediate need for the warehouse, but also those that you can forsee having a future need. Cultivate a relationship with the people you interview that makes them aware that they are part of a team in successfully designing and building the data warehouse. Make sure that everyone involved understands that the project is going to involve them from the beginning and some people may be involved in maintaining the warehouse indefinitely. Make the initiative of building and maintaining the warehouse a group initiative.

You must also organize the interviews in terms of the number of people you interview at one time, the makeup of those groups, and how to keep the interviews on track in providing information that you need to build effective and complete requirements.

Determining Who to Interview

When interviewing users, it is important to manage several aspects of the interviewing process. You should be aware of what different roles people play in the organization and try to interview a good cross-section of the people who know what information would be useful to have in the data warehouse, as well as people who understand how the information is gathered and can determine the quality of the information. You want to talk to the people who will help you determine what information the data warehouse must contain, as well as those people who can help you determine how to obtain that information and make sure that it represents what the end user believes that it represents.

You are going to interview top executives and managers to determine organizational goals and corporate priorities. Include key management personnel and obtain strong support by involving them in the definition of the data warehouse. Managers are key to defining what information is needed on a macro scale.

You also need to seek the input of administrative and clerical personnel. They often are the ones who have the clearest understanding of what sources of information are available within the company and are usually the best judges as to the quality of the data.

Don't neglect interviewing the Information Systems professionals that maintain the existing OLTP systems. Make sure that they are aware that the data warehouse is a supplement to, and not a replacement for, the systems that they administer. Discuss issues such as how specific fields are used, what certain codes mean, how different systems in the company relate to each other, where and how information is collected and shared, and so forth. These people will also be instrumental in designing new systems to capture information that will ultimately end up in the warehouse.

Conducting the Interviews

Try to keep the number of people that you are interviewing at any one point in time to a relatively small number. Many people are inhibited in voicing their opinions and expectations in a group setting, but are not so demure in public e-mail discussions. Also, some people are so vocal and opinionated that they can dominate the group and only the limited number of issues that they are interested in are discussed. If you interview small groups and find that different people have direct conflicts in expectations or requirements, reschedule a larger meeting with those specific individuals to work out a compromise.

 T I P Maintain a public folder discussion group in Microsoft Exchange regarding ongoing issues and directions being taken in the design and maintenance of the warehouse. Don't allow the "but I was told..." type of statements to damage the project. Keep everything out in the open as much as possible.

Try to see that people prepare for the meeting and prime them with some simple questions to get them started thinking about the issues, questions such as "What are the measures of success within your group or department?" and "What kind of information would make the biggest impact to the success of your department?"

Deriving Your Requirements from the Interviews

The discovery of requirements is not a simple process. Different managers are going to want very different kinds of information. Information needs will change over time, and the discovery of one piece of information may naturally lead to a need for more and different information. A data warehouse can be a political hot potato and you need to be careful that you include in the requirements phase everyone who will be a user, or could become a potential user, of the information the data warehouse will contain.

Part VII

Ch

37

Unfortunately, it is a fact of life that some needs cannot be predicted and will make themselves known later. That is why it must be made clear that the data warehouse project will live day by day and is not built and then forgotten. Do not assume that you can interview users, get requirements, and then go off for six months or a year and bring back something useful. Reorganizations, acquisitions, personnel changes, new product introductions, new marketing programs, changes in production systems, as well as any number of other issues, are going to affect how the warehouse is built and maintained.

Once you feel that you understand what information is needed in the data warehouse, prepare a document that describes what information is to be stored and what reports will be produced in the initial deployment of the data warehouse. Let the users examine the reports and make their additions and modifications to include things they will want to be able to obtain from the warehouse. If information is requested that you simply cannot provide from in-house systems, point this out to the users who requested the information. Let them know that the information is unavailable, but challenge them to come up with a solution. If the information is important enough, they will locate an outside source from which the information can be purchased, or they will suggest a new in-house system to begin capturing the information they require. The point is to let the user take responsibility in developing or discovering new data sources. Your job will be large enough in coordinating these data sources into a coherent data warehouse strategy.

OLTP Systems versus Dimensional Data Warehousing

Since order taking and accounting systems are usually the first systems that a company computerizes, a technique of storing transactions that support those systems was developed and has been widely adopted for most data storage needs. Since data warehousing involves accessing and analyzing information in a much different manner than traditional transaction processing systems, a different technique is used to store the information in the database. This has resulted in the multidimensional data warehouse.

OLTP/RDMS Schemas

The traditional OLTP system is concerned with the storage and manipulation of data at the basic level of the individual transaction. The major goal of OLTP systems is to store and manipulate, as quickly and efficiently as possible, large amounts of data.

The most popular form of database in use today is the Relational Database Management System (RDMS). It has allowed marked increases in the speed at which data can be stored and accessed due to the concept of entity relationships (ERs). The data to be stored is normalized into individual tables to eliminate redundancy and the tables are "joined" by specified keys. Examining the data in a single table in an RDMS system will usually not tell you very much about the information contained in the database. The data contained in each row within the table will usually not be related to the other rows in the table. Each row of data must be joined to another row, or rows, from another table until you have joined together enough data to build up a complete transaction. These joins represent how the data is logically linked together to allow meaning to be derived by relating data from one table to another based upon logical keys. Individual data items are stored only once in this model, with pointers (joins) linking together the related data among tables. As a result of this technique, additions, changes, and deletions can be made very quickly because the database has to access the data in only one place. Figure 37.2 illustrates a simple entity relationship (ER) diagram.

FIG. 37.2
A typical Entity
Relationship diagram.

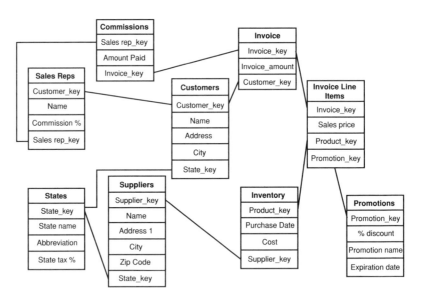

While the ER technique has many advantages, in practice the diagrams can become extremely large and complex, with many tables and many joins between those tables. Any two tables can have many paths between them, making navigation difficult. Also, when databases with many records are involved, joining across multiple tables can have very poor results in terms of execution speed.

Data Warehousing Schemas

Data warehouses are frequently implemented on an RDMS platform, but the schema looks dramatically different. The requirements you discovered during your user interviews are frequently couched in terms that describe how the user perceives individual operational transactions, such as "accounting information," "customer information," or "product inventory information." This is a by-product of the widespread use and familiarity of users to OLTP systems. Your challenge is to sift through these categories to identify the fundamental dimensions of the underlying data.

Part
VII
Ch
37

An example might be a case in which a CEO tells you that his company sells books. The books are either hardbacks or paperbacks. Now, there are many authors of these books. The books the company sells fall into certain subject areas, such as biographies and fiction. The company sells the books in stores all across the country, and it measures its performance over time. From this information you identify a central fact table and the resulting dimension tables. This schema is commonly referred to as a star schema and is shown in Figure 37.3.

FIG. 37.3

The star schema is the most common schema structure used in data warehousing.

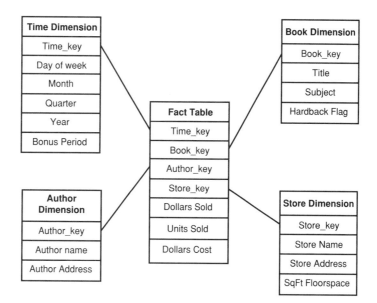

Dimensional Modeling

Data warehouses are inherently multidimensional. Multidimensionality essentially means that you model your business by determining what is to be measured (facts), what level of detail the facts will be measured (grain), how many different ways you want to examine the facts (dimensions), and what levels to summarize the fact grain (aggregates). You also store information that explains or describes what is stored in the data warehouse (metadata).

Facts

The fact table is the central hub of your data warehouse and is where the important numeric measurements are stored. Fact tables typically include many attributes, the majority of which should be keys to the dimensions or numeric facts. The most useful facts are numeric and additive. Additive means that they can be added up over any dimension, or any combination of dimensions. Adding, or aggregating, the data from the fact tables is the most common type of query the users of a data warehouse execute. A typical fully additive fact would be the price paid for a product. This price can be added across dimensions such as time, geographic location, product type, etc.

Sometimes numeric facts are semi-additive. This means that they make sense when added up against some dimensions, but not all dimensions. For example, a measure of square footage adds up to the total square footage of your facility when measured by the department dimension. However, the square footage measurement doesn't make sense if applied against the time dimension. There are also numeric attributes that are not additive at all, such as percentages. Of course, you can have text attributes as facts, but since they can't be added over the dimensions, they are of little value.

Grain

The grain of the data warehouse is the level of detail of the information that is stored in the fact table. Common grains are based on a time series, such as daily, weekly, monthly; however, you can use the individual transaction as the ultimate low level of granularity. The more detail you store, the lower the level of the grain. Granularity is a significant design decision, as you need to determine the trade-off between speed and drill-down capabilities. Your low-grained warehouse may have excellent drill-down capabilities, allowing decision support personnel to get down to individual transactions, but suffer from sluggish performance. Highly grained warehouses may offer faster performance but are shallower in terms of what detailed information can be retrieved and reported.

N O T E In data warehousing terminology, a "high" level of granularity means that there is less detail. A "low" level of granularity means that there is more detail. This usage may be different than what you've normally used when discussing the general idea of "granularity." ▪

Dimensions

The dimension tables store the descriptions of the different dimensions you identified by interviewing the users of the warehouse. It is easier to think of the dimension tables as being the criteria that will be used in queries or as the column headings you will want to see in your reports. For instance, you may want to look at book sales based on author, store, or over some period of time. Each of those three criteria represents a dimension.

The warehouse should always have a time dimension, as time is a critical element of any business and the historical nature of the data in the warehouse always has time as a dimension. Other dimension tables contain many fields, such as Title, Category, Address, and so forth.

The dimension fields are usually text based, though numeric information that is a valuation of something that is relatively constant also can be a dimension. Some measures of dimensions that are relatively common across industries include geographic areas, company structure (departments, zones, etc.), and financial-modeling scenarios such as budgeted expenses versus actual expenses.

Aggregates

Data warehouses that have a low level of granularity often employ aggregates to provide significant performance improvements over accessing large numbers of base-level facts. Since the best facts are numeric and additive, they can be easily summarized. These summarized records serve as the basis for a new fact table. When a new aggregate fact table is created, an accompanying aggregate dimension table must also be created.

For instance, using the example of the publishing company, you may decide that a frequent measure made of the business is the sale of books by subject areas by store. The new subject aggregate fact table is shown with a subject key that joins it to the newly created subject dimension. This fact table contains summarized facts on the new subject dimension. The new dimension table contains the subject key and hardback flag, but drops the Title attribute from the original Book dimension. The Book attribute pertained only to an individual book, and this dimension pertains to individual subjects. Figure 37.4 illustrates the additional aggregate fact and aggregate dimension tables.

FIG. 37.4

Aggregation tables.

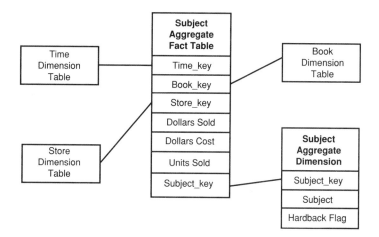

Metadata

The standard definition of *metadata* is "data about data." Metadata provides a blueprint to users that exposes which raw bits and bytes are actually Social Security numbers, credit card balances, and so forth. It also includes information regarding the common algorithms that was used in summarizing or processing raw data before it was integrated into the warehouse, the structure and formatting of the data as it is to be published, actual (or estimated) volumes of data by major dimensions, and so forth. By providing incorrect metadata, the information in a warehouse becomes so much scrambled noise and loses any capability for providing useful information.

 It is a good idea to keep metadata stored as a time series. For instance, if a field from source data is remapped to a different representation in the warehouse in a couple of years, the users should be aware of when and why this reclassification occurred.

Data Extraction

The first thing you should expect when you look at extracting data is problems with the existing systems. It is amazing the number of problems that have existed for years that are suddenly uncovered. You find that users use only part of the information they receive on a report and simply have no understanding, or have a misunderstanding, of other information in the same report. "That number is never right, we just ignore it," could portend more serious problems. The warehouse is a read-only repository, so you must ensure that the data is correct before it makes it into the warehouse. If erroneous data is published by the warehouse, it won't make any difference that the problem resided in a feed from a data source, the credibility of everything in the warehouse becomes suspect.

 Sometimes you can't wait for an existing system to be "fixed" so that it provides good information. In this instance, move ahead without the data. Make sure that the users who wanted the suspect information included in the warehouse understand why it was excluded. Let the users drive the fixes to the OLTP system.

You may also find that you need to store data that is not kept in any OLTP system. Many times users make adjustments to data that has been produced by the OLTP and those adjustments exist only in a file on someone's PC. You should insist that these types of situations be avoided and have systems developed that capture those adjustments as a new data source for your warehouse or that the adjustments the user has made on the PC are fed back to the original OLTP and are reflected in the OLTP's data before it is extracted and fed to the data warehouse.

Data Cleaning

Cleaning up data that feeds the warehouse is one of the more difficult and time-consuming tasks you will face. You must identify inaccuracies, anomalies, redundancies, and so on, before you damage the integrity of the data in the warehouse and your reputation. No matter how responsive the data access, no matter how pretty the user interface, no matter how powerful the data-analysis tools, nothing causes users to abandon the warehouse project more quickly than to find that it contains inaccurate information.

Data redundancy is a problem wherein the same piece of information comes to the warehouse from two different data sources. Multiple records can exist because of a business name change, an acquisition, a typographical error, and various other reasons.

Different reporting units must be converted to a standard. Different departments might report the same information based on different units—for example, one reports on "days," whereas another uses "hours."

 T I P It makes sense to assign specific individuals to specific data sources to ensure that someone familiar with the underlying data is responsible for certifying the quality of the information allowed into the data warehouse. Don't appoint a single individual to be responsible for the entire data-cleaning effort and expect them to understand the detail involved in translating and transforming disparate data sources.

Translations on specific facts need to be performed on data from different data sources because they contain facts that are the same but are represented differently. For example, one system may report Male and Female as "M" and "F," whereas another codes them as "1" and "0." These data elements must be translated to the form that is standard within the warehouse.

You also must check for referential integrity, where you account for any parent/child relationships that should exist between different data elements. If a data stream contains a header that says four credit card detail records exist but those detail records cannot be found in the rest of the data, then the entire transaction that relates to the credit card entries should be dropped.

You also want to apply user-defined business rules against the data to determine if it should be loaded. *Business rules* express policies that define what constitutes data that you want to include in your warehouse and how that information is represented. For instance, you may specify relationships between data elements for excluding information where the `customer name = "Martha's Cookie Co."` and `Territory = "Region5"` because that same customer's data is fed to you from a different data source as "Eifert's Bakery, Inc.".

You may also have a business rule that generates additional information that is derived from the information provided by the data source. For example, you may create additional cost entries expressed as a percentage of the sales made by Eifert's Bakery, Inc. because you have a contractual agreement to pay the original founders a percentage of sales for three years after you purchased the company. If that information is not being captured by any other data source, you can create it on-the-fly by using this specialized business rule.

Architectures

The architecture on which you choose to implement your data warehouse can take several different forms, depending on your company's budget, support staff, number of users, network topology, and business needs. Three distinct architectures include the centralized, federated/functional, and tiered.

The *centralized* platform is the simplest structure and provides efficiencies in administration and support. It can be overwhelmed, however, if your OLTP runs on the same platform or in instances of heavy user demand. Performance issues are the overriding concern when deploying on a centralized platform. The centralized structure also represents a single point of failure in the case of a catastrophe. By storing all of the information in the data warehouse on one server, you run the risk of losing access to anything in the warehouse if that server is unavailable.

The second type of structure, referred to as a *federated* or *functional* structure, houses data based on the function it serves. This model might have one server that houses financial information, a second server that houses manufacturing information, and so forth. These functional servers also are called *data marts*. Federated structures distribute the information contained in the data warehouse so that if a problem is encountered accessing a server, only the type of information that was stored on that server will be unavailable. This may allow some users to continue productively using the warehouse in times of temporary equipment failure because the information they require may not reside on the equipment that is experiencing the problem.

The third physical structure, the *tiered* structure, is based on the level of data summarization in your warehouse. The tiers of the structure are organized so that highly summarized data is on one server, more detailed summaries are on a second server, and so on. The information is not stored on different machines by specialized function, as in the federated structure, but by the level of granularity or aggregation of the information contained in the data warehouse. The tiered structure allows you to use a different hardware server based on the anticipated amount of traffic that it will service. If most of the traffic in the data warehouse is at the transaction level, you could supply a more powerful server to store that information. If the highly summarized data is being used infrequently by a relatively small number of users, you could house that data on a smaller PC.

Data Marts

Data marts are essentially subject-specific data warehouses. Modeling a single subject, such as a line of business, provides advantages in design, querying, and maintaining, and is quicker, easier, and cheaper to implement. A small data warehouse is not necessarily considered a data mart. Size is not the determining factor as much as the single subject format. However, the single subject format does result in smaller, more manageable databases than an Enterprise-wide data warehouse. Enterprise-wide data warehouses are not easy to design, implement, or maintain. Companies have spent millions of dollars constructing mammoth data warehouses that ended up being abandoned because of costs, time constraints, or poor implementation.

Data marts are thought of as being *independent* or *dependent* in nature. An independent data mart has its own data sources, does its own validation and data scrubbing, and generally follows the data warehouse process model for its single-subject area. It can sometimes act as a data source to a larger enterprise data warehouse.

Dependent data marts are clients of the enterprise data warehouse. The single-subject data they contain was first collected and processed by the enterprise data warehouse, which then extracted or replicated the information to the data mart. The dependent data warehouse is essentially a subject-specific node of the distributed enterprise data warehouse.

A recent trend has been for companies to begin building data marts that are structured so that they can eventually be integrated in to a distributed enterprise data warehouse. The simplicity of the data mart allows for relatively quick "proof of concept" demonstrations as to the value of the data warehousing concept, and with proper design, the enterprise data warehouse can evolve specifically and purposefully towards a larger enterprise design. This incremental building block approach requires close cooperation between the individual subjects being modeled in the data marts, such as departments or lines of business.

Part
VII

Ch
37

On-Line Analytical Processing (OLAP)

On-Line Analytical Processing is a term that has varied in meaning since data warehouses were first formulated. There are essentially three different types of OLAP tools:

- The Executive Information System (EIS)
- The report generators and query tools
- The data-mining tools

The Executive Information System

At the highest and most general level is the Executive Information System (EIS). Executives, loosely defined, are senior managers who do not have the time or inclination to do any data analysis. The analysis function is typically done for them and presented in an executive briefing. The EIS is the published output of the data warehouse, summarized, categorized, and presented in a concise, easy-to-use format.

This output may look like a Microsoft PowerPoint slide presentation with hot buttons available for additional information that emphasizes other components of the presentation. Some EIS systems may include "links" to the Internet for news or information that is not contained in the data warehouse. However, by providing the link from the EIS, you have essentially extended the warehouse to include information which you have no control over and has not been subjected to the "data scrubbing" process. As EIS systems become more and more "slick" and Web-like, you should take care always to identify to the user what is "external" information and provided on an "as is" basis. Microsoft's future adoption of the Web browser interface to Windows NT will encourage even more of this sort of presentation.

Reporting and Querying Tools

Reporting and querying make up the largest portion of the OLAP market and are usually what people mean when they use the generic term "OLAP." OLAP provides a means for users to interactively query the information contained in the warehouse, browse for unexpected or unusual information, and then follow up by performing additional queries and "drilling down" into lower levels of detail if something interesting is discovered.

Common presentation formats include summarizing based on subtotaled information by category and on cross tabulations, where the data is summarized by different categories in a grid. Cross tabulations can be extremely insightful, especially when they can be "pivoted" similar to the PivotTables found in Microsoft Excel. Some OLAP tools also offer advanced modeling capabilities that derive results and create aggregations and consolidations. Trend analysis, forecasting, optimizations, correlations, and other statistical analysis features also are found in this group of tools.

ROLLUP and *CUBE*

As was discussed earlier in the chapter (see the section "Aggregates"), data warehouse users frequently need access to summarized data. It is always the correct approach to anticipate these needs and design aggregate fact and dimension tables. However, because of the nature of ad hoc queries, you can't always know with certainty which data will need to be summarized. This is where the performance of the data warehouse can be severely affected.

Microsoft SQL Server 6.5's native SQL scripting language, called Transact-SQL, can aggregate values using the SUM, AVG, COUNT, and other operators as found in standard SQL. New to version 6.5 are two new operators in CUBE and ROLLUP that can aggregate results to a deeper level.

Both ROLLUP and CUBE are used with the "GROUP BY" clause of standard SQL. An example of the standard GROUP BY SQL and resultset are shown as follows:

```
SELECT ProductTypeID, ProductID, SUM(QtyOnHand)
FROM MyTable
GROUP BY ProductTypeID, ProductID
```

ProductTypeID	ProductID	SUM
Type_1	Product_A	10.00
Type_1	Product_B	5.00
Type_2	Product_A	25.00
Type_2	Product_B	3.00
Type_2	Product_C	100.00
Type_3	Product_A	34.00

Using the ROLLUP operator, you can create convenient subtotal aggregates to feed your OLAP system:

```
SELECT ProductTypeID, ProductID, SUM(QtyOnHand)
FROM MyTable
GROUP BY ProductTypeID, ProductID
WITH ROLLUP
```

ProductTypeID	ProductID	SUM
Type_1	Product_A	10.00
Type_1	Product_B	5.00
Type_1	NULL	15.00
Type_2	Product_A	25.00
Type_2	Product_B	3.00
Type_2	Product_C	100.00
Type_2	NULL	128.00
Type_3	Product_A	34.00
Type_3	NULL	34.00

The NULL values in the resultset indicate that the SUM column contains the sum of all of the SUM values above it for the column in which the NULL value appears. This expresses a common subtotal, or hierarchical view of information commonly seen in reporting and OLAP systems.

By using the CUBE operator, you can "super-aggregate" the resultset even further. In addition to the hierarchical subtotals, the resultset contains cross-tabulated values. Remembering that NULL values are inserted in the columns where the row contains the sum for all values of that column, the same query using the CUBE operator looks like this:

```
SELECT ProductTypeID, ProductID, SUM(QtyOnHand)
FROM MyTable
GROUP BY ProductTypeID, ProductID
WITH CUBE
```

ProductTypeID	ProductID	SUM
Type_1	Product_A	10.00
Type_1	Product_B	5.00
Type_1	NULL	15.00
Type_2	Product_A	25.00
Type_2	Product_B	3.00
Type_2	Product_C	100.00
Type_2	NULL	128.00
Type_3	Product_A	34.00
Type_3	NULL	34.00
NULL	NULL	177.00
NULL	Product_A	69.00
NULL	Product_B	8.00
NULL	Product_C	100.00

As you can see, the first three NULL values represent the hierarchical "subtotal" values you get when using ROLLUP. However, the line with a NULL for ProductTypeID and ProductID represents the "grand total" of the summarized subtotals. The NULL values in the ProductTypeID column show the summarized values for each corresponding ProductID.

T I P Although the CUBE and ROLLUP operators provide an easy way to produce summarized and cross-tabulated results from your data warehouse, they do not substitute for the correct application of Aggregate tables. CUBE and ROLLUP result in the creation of two worktables and the additional I/O can slow system performance. Aggregate table access is faster by several orders of magnitude, and if you anticipate the need for specific aggregations, then plan ahead for them by using Aggregate tables.

WOLAP

The Internet, and especially the World Wide Web, is becoming ubiquitous in today's computing environment. OLAP vendors have responded to this by enabling their products to work with Web browsers and have coined the term *WOLAP*, which stands for *Web-Enabled On-Line Analytical Processing*. Corporate developers are adapting the Web paradigm to corporate intranets, so WOLAP products also are now being used internally, without ever reaching the Internet. Most WOLAP products provide access to the warehouse by one or more of the following three methods:

- Pre-creating static HTML pages
- Creating HTML pages on-the-fly
- Client-side ActiveX or Java components

Pre-creating static HTML pages is usually acceptable for only the most basic of OLAP needs. Executive Information Systems can be created using this approach, as analysis is not done at that level. Screens are generated between data loads of the warehouse, usually every 24 hours, that will represent the new information for the next day. The EIS will allow hypertext linking between the screens to allow the executive to peruse a standard presentation package.

OLAP analysis, at a basic level, also can be done with HTML layouts. The user can rotate two dimensions by picking the variables to be modeled through a drop-down combo box and clicking a "generate" button to see the results. Drill-down capabilities also can be provided by hypertext links. This information is generated interactively as the user requests it.

ActiveX controls and Java applets provide the most powerful access method. These software components run on the client computer and minimize communication between the client and the server by handling the presentation and manipulation of data on the client side.

Microsoft has announced a SQL report-writing product, code named "Gutenberg." This report writer is a WOLAP product which allows publishing, viewing, and retrieving of Excel pivot tables and works through Excel or Internet Explorer. SQL Server centrally stores the templates and data needed to produce the report.

In the future, it is likely that Internet-enabled OLAP tools will utilize component-based functionality communicating with the server via direct TCP/IP. This will enable the software to bypass the Web HTTP interface and communicate directly with OLAP server using an Object Request Broker, such as the native Windows NT Server 4.0 Distributed Component Object Model (DCOM). This will provide even more functionality than the common browser interface and will allow corporate developers to design for a single architecture that will work transparently across the corporate network or the Internet.

Data Mining

Data mining is the newest and least understood form of OLAP. The term is often incorrectly used to describe reporting and querying tools. Data-mining tools search for and discover unrecognized patterns within data stored in the warehouse using sophisticated mathematical, statistical, and artificial intelligence (AI) techniques. The analyst doesn't really drive the analysis, so much as he is led through the analysis by the data-mining software.

The information produced by data-mining tools can be categorized as being Classes/Clusters, Associations/Sequences, or Forecasts.

Classes and *Clusters* are the most common type of data-mining information generated. Classes can be graphically represented using Venn diagrams where the overlapping portions of the circles represent the "mined" information. For instance, you can query the data warehouse to determine what percentage of a company's customers are college graduates, who purchase action/adventure novels and drink "Zipee Blend" coffee in the coffee shop. Clusters are a similar type of information generated by data-mining tools, except this type of information is discovered by the the software's anaysis of the data, without predefining the query. The data mining software discovers the overlapping relationships on its own by using sophisticated pattern-matching algorithms.

Associations are a classification where one event is associated with another. An example is an analysis that states that 70 percent of all shaving cream purchases are followed by the purchase of aftershave. *Sequences* are similar to this, except that the association of one event with the other is not immediately followed by, but statistically happens within some period of time, after the first event. An example of this is that 70 percent of new car owners buy floor mats within two weeks of the car purchase, or that 30 percent of new parents increase their pre-tax 401K contributions within one year after the birth of a child.

Forecasting involves estimating what will happen in the future based upon what has happened in the past. Forecasting is an inherently risky business, as dropping one variable out of the forecast could have a substantial effect on the outcome. As different factors interrelate, misjudgment of just a proportion of a variable can have a sweeping impact on the result of the forecast. Data-mining software is used to sift through all data at the disposal of the software to determine associations and variables, as well as their proportions, that will serve as inputs to the forecast. The software finds relationships that only the most astute, professional forecaster with many years of experience would find.

N O T E   Data-mining software is necessarily computation intensive. The client workstation used for data mining purposes should have a higher speed processor, higher resolution graphics for complex graphical representations of information, and more local storage space for intermediate work files, than the average OLAP workstation. ▨

This sophisticated form of analysis is done by large companies who have the time and deep pockets necessary to purchase, implement, and understand the results of the data-mining software. Aerospace firms, large retailing chains, and financial institutions have been the early adopters of this technology.

To temper all this good news somewhat, it is important not to oversell the data-mining concept. Data mining is effective only with well-designed data warehouses that correctly model the appropriate facts and dimensions of the enterprise and contain accurate, verified, consistent information. Data-mining packages are also relatively expensive. You are much better served in spending the money to model, build, and maintain the data warehouse and derive the benefits from that process rather than to try to purchase shrink-wrapped expertise and answers.

Performance Issues

Data warehouses can, or rather *will*, become quite large. At the present time, the majority of data warehouses are at or below the 100 gigabyte threshold. There are data warehouses in operation, however, that are over a terabyte in size. These numbers should scare you. The performance of the data warehouse is of primary consideration in its design. Queries that relax one or more dimensions can end up retrieving thousands, if not millions, of fact records. Some of the design decisions that can be made in preparation for the growth of the warehouse include Random Access Memory (RAM) issues, indexing, parallel processing, and distributed architectures.

RAM

Not surprisingly, the amount of RAM in your server makes a large performance difference. According to Microsoft, SQL Server requires a minimum of 16M of RAM, 32M if you use replication features. Realistically, you shouldn't have less than 64M of RAM for even the smaller data marts. With the price of memory becoming less and less expensive, consider putting 128M on the server.

Indexing

Appropriate indexing is the most powerful tool in delivering reasonable performance in your data warehouse. OLTP systems are slowed substantially by having many indexes on a single table because of all of the delete and add operations they must support. Since the warehouse is a read-only database, many indexes give you the benefit of fast access times without the concern of slow updates. Avoid a table scan at all costs.

As data warehouses support a large number of ad hoc queries, it will be difficult in the beginning to determine which indexes you need to build. After users have begun running queries against the warehouse, they will report which types of analyses are taking too long. From their input, do a detailed query analysis to determine the proper type of index to implement.

TIP In instances where you create a compound index, remember that your SQL `Where` clause must include the first column specified in the index. `Create index myindex on mytable (firstkey, secondkey, thirdkey)` will only be used when your SQL query contains `firstkey` as a component of the `Where` clause (i.e., `Select mycolumn from mytable where firstkey = myvalue`). The SQL query `Select mycolumn from mytable where secondkey = myvalue` would not use the index and would result in a table scan.

Clustered indexes are also frequently useful in data warehousing applications as they are especially useful for OLAP queries such as finding a range of values, columns frequently referenced in "order by" clauses, and when a column is not part of a primary key.

Multiprocessing

When using Windows NT Server and Microsoft SQL Server for the data warehouses, you can take advantage of multiple processors. Microsoft SQL Server can take advantage of this by using different processors for simultaneously making a join between tables, providing raw CPU cycles to an intensive data-mining statistical calculation, and sorting data to an intermediate table. Since multiprocessor support is a feature of the NT Server operating system and Microsoft SQL Server, you can implement this step fairly easily. In the past, information systems professionals had to take additional steps through software to use extra processors. While throwing more hardware at the problem will help, it is not the only or the best step you can take to increase performance. Most performance issues in data warehouses are related to input/output (I/O) operations.

Partitioning

Partitioning data improves retrieval performance by physically segmenting the data based upon a logical design. Stable data, such as that found in a data warehouse, can be partitioned with good results. Partitioning is usually thought of as being "vertical" or "horizontal." *Vertical partitioning* is a technique by which a table is split, by attribute, into two or more columns. This is usually done to move infrequently accessed attributes into a separate column and reduce the size of the primary table. This frequently results in a star schema derivative referred to as a snowflake schema. *Horizontal partitioning* splits a table based on rows, where related rows are moved into separate tables based on some criteria. This criteria could be functional department, product type, and so forth. This results in the data mart construct described earlier in the "Data Marts" section.

If you can correctly anticipate the most frequently accessed data, grouped logically in the vertical or horizontal partitions, you can vastly improve the performance of standard queries. The downside is that ad hoc queries that are not anticipated do not see the performance improvement and actually run more slowly.

Microsoft SQL Server allows customers to partition their database and applications among different SQL Servers running on different nodes of the network. If a user that is connected to a server on one node needs to access partitioned data that resides physically on another node, the request can be made through Transact SQL or a remote procedure call to the server on the other node. SQL Server and OLE transactions manage the data-integrity issues between the servers.

When data is distributed onto different machines, there needs to be a way to share information between those nodes. Data replication in Microsoft SQL Server takes care of this for you. Replication propagates changes to a SQL server running at one location to one running at another location. This is useful when individual data marts have been constructed so that they share common reference data, such as codes for specific products or validating information. The SQL Enterprise Manager component of SQL Server implements a "publish" and "subscribe" metaphor. By cascading this replication, you can distribute large amounts of information between machines. Replication also is done in transaction units, so everyone sees a consistent view of the database from a single point in time. Publication can be immediate, periodic, or on demand.

Network Architecture

Just as it doesn't matter what the top speed of your Ferrari is when the freeway is jammed, so it is with SQL Server when you have a slow network connection. You can have 128M of RAM, quad processors, intelligent indexing, and efficient data partitioning strategies, and it is all for naught if you're on a 4M token ring network. This area becomes especially significant if you're distributing your data warehouse over multiple servers on a LAN or WAN.

Microsoft's Data Warehousing Strategy

Microsoft is increasing the visibility of Microsoft SQL Server in the data warehousing market by combining new technologies, as well as allying themselves with industry leading data warehouse tool vendors. The Microsoft Alliance for Data Warehousing was formed in late 1996 between Microsoft and eight other companies to design, test, and evaluate a technology Microsoft calls the "Microsoft Active Data Framework." The Active Data Framework consists of an extensible set of COM-based interfaces to simplify integration and management of data warehouse solutions. It will provide a common architecture and interface for different products involved in data cleaning, data extraction, OLAP tools, and so on. Specific areas that will be addressed are data acquisition and transformation services, a metadata model, data distribution and replication, and administration.

Microsoft's Alliance for Data Warehousing

The founding members of the alliance are leading tool manufacturers whose products represent various phases of the data warehousing process model. All of the following vendors offer additional product information and some provide free evaluation copies of their software from their Web sites:

- **Business Objects SA (www.BusinessObjects.com)** is an OLAP vendor whose product, Business Objects, provides data analysis and graphical representation of OLAP results. It is also the publisher of BusinessQuery, a Microsoft Excel add-on that provides querying capabilities.

- **Execusoft Systems, Inc. (www.Execsys.com)** offers Symbiator, which provides near real-time replication from a wide range of different data sources such as IBM's DB2 and Microsoft SQL Server.

- **Informatica Corporation (www.Informatica.com)** has PowerSuite, which is a comprehensive set of tools that address all the phases of the data warehousing process model.

- **NCR Corporation (www.NCR.com)** is well known for its TeraData database, in wide use as a platform for large data warehouses, and also markets various multiprocessor servers.

- **Pilot Software (www.pilotsw.com)** produces various data-mining and OLAP tools that are integrated with Microsoft SQL Server and Microsoft Excel.

- **Platinum Technology, Inc. (www.platinum.com)** has several products geared toward data warehousing and Microsoft SQL Server, notably the InfoPump, which allows access to data from various mainframe sources.

- **Praxis International (www.Praxisint.com)** offers the data-replication program OmniReplicator, which moves heterogenous enterprise data into data warehouses.

- **SAP AG (www.SAP.com)** produces various client/server software and has over 200 applications running SAP R/3 with Microsoft SQL Server.

Microsoft Active Data Warehouse Framework

Microsoft's Active Data Warehouse Framework (ADWF) is made up of four components. These components mirror the data warehouse process flow and include data-transformation services, data-movement interfaces, and a metadata repository.

Data Transformation Services   The goal of Data Transformation Services is to help get data into and out of Microsoft SQL Server. The services will be administered through the existing Enterprise Manager tool.treat and will treat each transformation as a "package." These packages can consist of multiple steps and will take inputs from multiple data sources and send data to multiple data storehouses in a single transformation. Standard transformations will include date transforms, field mappings (both one-to-one and many-to-one), enumerated code lookups, among other things. Typically the transformations will be done on the server using Microsoft's VBScript or JavaScript. If the transformations are too complex or are running too slowly, you can produce your own transformation service as an ActiveX component and exploit the exposed Data Transformation Services API.

Data Movement Interfaces   Microsoft is working closely with industry leaders to integrate SQL Server as a data mart from larger systems such as NCR's TeraData system. Announced data sources currently include Oracle, DB/2, VSAM, and IMS. The data movement out of SQL Server also will support different interfaces. Microsoft is currently talking about exporting data directly into Microsoft Excel pivot tables for use in cross-tab analysis and exporting to HTML for Web publishing.

Metadata Repository The Metadata Repository is the result of a collaborative effort between Microsoft and Texas Instruments. This repository has been specifically designed for the specialized needs of data warehousing. The repository will hold metadata, data-lineage information, and transformation packages. It also will support an open COM interface for integration with other packages.

Microsoft and OLAP Microsoft has not released a dedicated OLAP product. They have purchased, however, the OLAP technology developed by Panorama Software Systems and have announced that this technology will be integrated into a future version of Microsoft SQL Server.

From Here...

In this chapter, you learned about what critical steps should be taken in planning a data warehouse and involving the user community. The data warehouse process flow was outlined, and the different stages of moving data from OLTP systems to the data warehouse were explained. A discussion of star schemas, multidimensional modeling, and architectures addressed the commonly used structure and storage options used in data warehouse systems. Future directions with Microsoft's plans for SQL Server and the data warehousing market were outlined.

For additional information on the topics discussed in this chapter, please reference the following chapters:

- For an understanding of the details associated with administering SQL Server, see Chapter 35, "Maintaining SQL Server."
- To learn about SQL Server's data replication features, see Chapter 36, "SQL Server Data Replication."

An Inside Look at Distributed Transaction Coordinator (DTC) and Microsoft Transaction Server (MTS)

by Don Benage

This chapter explores the subject of distributed transaction processing. Microsoft is creating a growing number of tools and technologies to help manage applications that execute on multiple computers. This distributes the processing load and provides a collection of other benefits, as well. Not every user of SQL Server requires distributed transaction services. However, this is a rapidly growing area of computing technology, and many businesses and organizations can benefit from these tools, even if they are not yet aware of the benefits.

Some of these techniques have existed in the past, but have been available only on large, expensive platforms costing hundreds of thousands, or even millions of dollars. Part of the attraction of these tools is that they are now available on low-cost, commodity-priced computing platforms. This puts the technology within the reach of much smaller organizations.

Definition of the Microsoft Distributed Transaction Coordinator (DTC)

Learn about the nature of distributed transaction processing and explore some existing methods for implementing this functionality. Find out about a new addition to SQL Server version 6.5 that will help you implement transactions that access and update databases on more than one server.

How to use the Microsoft Distributed Transaction Coordinator (DTC)

Learn how to monitor distributed transactions and how to use new tools to resolve problem transactions that may occur due to such causes as hardware failures or disruptions in network communications.

Installation of Transaction Server

Learn how to install the Microsoft Transaction Server, and set up the sample applications that are provided with the product to help you learn how this powerful new tool functions.

This chapter provides an overview of two key components Microsoft offers for distributed transaction processing: Distributed Transaction Coordinator (DTC) and Transaction Server. The DTC was introduced with SQL Server 6.5. It greatly simplifies the process of developing and deploying distributed applications. Transaction Server 1.0 was released in January of 1997 and builds on the functionality offered by DTC. It provides a COM-based programming model and forms the basis of an entirely new computing architecture that you can use to build state-of-the-art distributed systems. ■

Why Are Distributed Transactions Important?

Before spending time learning about products that help implement distributed transactions, it is worth asking why they are so important. Why are Microsoft, ORACLE, and others working feverishly to deliver technology for this capability? Is this really necessary? What are the benefits and the risks? Part of the answer lies in the fact that this is not new technology. It is being implemented in new ways on new platforms, but the underlying technology is at the heart of many large systems that have been in place for years. The revolutionary aspect of the recent developments in this area is the dramatically reduced cost for these tools and the ability to implement them on commodity-priced equipment instead of expensive proprietary hardware.

The use of PCs as computing platforms began with the invention of the microprocessor. They were first built and used by hobbyists as an interesting novelty occasionally pressed into service in some customized control function (e.g., control lighting) or to play games. With the invention of VisiCalc in the early 1980s, the use of small, inexpensive computers to perform business functions was launched. Over the next decade the primary use for PCs was *personal productivity*, a term describing the use of a PC to help an individual perform their own work. Even the term PC, *personal computer*, implied the individual nature of the applications that were being implemented on these machines.

However, a growing number of application developers began using these inexpensive platforms for real line-of-business applications—systems that were used to actually run the business as opposed to analyzing results or making office workers more productive. Although this use of PCs was initially disparaged by some IS professionals (especially mainframe-centric individuals who didn't really know much about the smaller machines), they have proven to be a useful tool in building these important systems. This is no longer a novelty; it has become a full-fledged industry. And it is distinct from *workgroup* applications (although those are also important), which are really just an extension of personal productivity tools into group productivity tools.

The focus of this discussion is core applications like billing, payroll, and inventory management. It also includes applications specific to particular industries, such as banking, finance, manufacturing, and retailing. To deliver applications that are useful in medium-to-large organizations involved in this type of work, you must provide much more computing power than is available on a single desktop computer. It is essential to be able to deliver applications managing gigabytes of data that are simultaneously accessed by hundreds of people.

As already discussed, these systems have been built in the past using large minicomputers and mainframes. What hasn't been available is a computing architecture built with desktop PCs and servers that have the following characteristics:

- Economical to acquire, deploy, and maintain.
- Very high reliability (used to run the business!).
- Capability to recover from catastrophic failure quickly with little or no loss of information.
- Capable of handling (very) large amounts of data.
- Capable of supporting dozens of users with simultaneous access.
- Provide strong security features (with auditing) so that you can control who has access.
- High availability of data (can't "lock" important information for exclusive use by one process or user for long periods of time).
- Able to develop and deploy new applications quickly to reflect changes in business and industry.
- Able to maintain existing applications.
- Support the capability to leverage existing application components through reuse where appropriate.
- The tools used to build applications are reasonably straightforward to learn and use so that developers can be quickly and economically trained.
- The tools and programmatic interfaces used are "open" and based on industry standards (or at least, they should not be poorly documented, proprietary tools created by a small company which is about to go out of business!).
- Possible to effectively implement applications for small, medium, and large systems, and the price of the system should grow gradually as the size of the system grows with no large increases at certain points in the growth path.
- The entire architecture is capable of continuing to evolve to meet challenges that no one has yet foreseen.

Part
VII

Ch
38

After looking at this list it should be obvious that creating such an architecture is no easy task. On the other hand, such an architecture can provide organizations with a real advantage in this era of global competition and rapid change. Systems that meet these criteria offer tremendous benefits to the organization lucky enough to possess them. History has shown that truly great strategic information systems can yield a competitive advantage in the marketplace, whereas poor systems can cripple even the best people and organizations, frustrating their efforts and making them ineffective.

Taking a collection of small computers, some networking equipment, some software, and a group of trained and talented people and producing a system that can meet these requirements is still a mix of science and art. The two tools discussed in this chapter are very powerful components that can make the job much *easier*, but it is by no means easy. Still, the capabilities provided by these components can be valuable additions to your information systems that help you meet the lofty goals outlined above.

The Distributed Transaction Coordinator (DTC)

So far, you have learned about using single SQL Servers and using replication to keep information on two or more servers loosely consistent with each other. In the discussion about replication, the 2PC protocol was mentioned as a potential tool for implementing transactions involving more than one SQL Server—distributed transactions. The 2PC protocol has some strengths and some weaknesses. Although it solves many problems associated with distributed transactions, it can be difficult to implement and manage.

▶ **See** "SQL Server Data Replication," **p. 1243**

A complete discussion of 2PC is beyond the scope of this book. However, a brief overview will help you to understand the rudiments of this technology and the powerful new components that Microsoft has added to make the use of distributed transactions more practical. This discussion of 2PC is a deliberate simplification designed to help managers and SAs understand the role and importance of 2PC in distributed transaction processing. Developers wanting to use this technology are urged to seek additional resources, such as the *Guide to Microsoft Distributed Transaction Coordinator* which is provided with the product.

Sample Transaction Scenario

Assume that you are running an application on a desktop computer that needs to update databases on two SQL Servers as part of a single transaction (see Figure 38.1). Naturally, you would like them both updated, or you would like the transaction to fail and both servers to be left unchanged. You could then try the transaction again later; but most important, the data on each server would remain in a consistent state, and the data regarding the proposed transaction also would remain consistent. The transaction either happens or it doesn't—all or nothing.

FIG. 38.1
In this diagram, a client is attempting to work with two SQL Servers as individual entities. The transactional capability of SQL Server alone is not sufficient in this scenario.

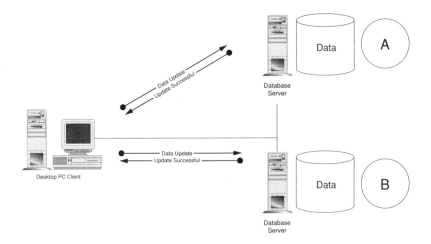

Trying to implement this behavior is harder than it might appear at first. For this technology to be useful, it must continue to work when one or more computers fail *at the worst possible moment*. Anyone who has used computers for even a short period of time knows that they can and do fail. SQL Servers have the capability to log transactions in a write-ahead log and either commit them or roll them back. Furthermore, this capability is robust enough to handle system failures and power outages. However, this facility alone is not enough to implement distributed transactions.

Suppose that your application has sent update instructions to both databases and is ready to commit the transaction. It could send a commit instruction to the first server (call it A), wait for a confirmation, and then send a commit to B. But what if B, or the communications link between the client and B fails after A has committed and before B gets the message? The rule has been broken. You did not achieve an all-or-nothing transaction. You could try sending the commit instruction to both at the same time, but this is really no better.

Two additional elements are needed. You must ask your servers to achieve a *prepared* state in which they can durably commit or roll back. In other words, if the computer fails in the prepared state, it can be restored to the prepared state, still ready to commit or roll back. Additionally, you need a *commit coordinator* to help this process take place. Of course, the application itself could take on this role, but managing the states of multiple SQL Servers in a durable manner is a lot to expect from a typical application program.

With these additional elements, the following process can occur (see Figure 38.2). When an application is ready to commit its updated information, it notifies the coordinator. The coordinator instructs the SQL Servers to prepare to commit. They each attempt to adopt the prepared state. If one (or both) fails, the coordinator records in a log that the transaction has failed and advises both servers to roll back the transaction. A failed server would check with the coordinator when it was running again and find out that the transaction should be rolled back. The coordinator also can recover from a failure and remember the status of the pending transaction.

Part
VII

Ch
38

FIG. 38.2

A distributed transaction using 2PC protocols is depicted in this figure. The transaction coordinator is shown as a separate machine for clarity, but could actually be implemented on one of the Database Servers.

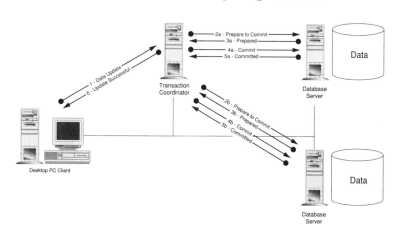

If both servers report that they have successfully prepared, the coordinator records that the transaction should commit and advises both servers to commit the transaction. If a server or communications link fails at this point, all three components (the two SQL Servers and the coordinator) are able to restart and achieve the prepared state again. The coordinator's log "reminds" them all to commit the transaction. If the commit takes place (as it usually does), the application has successfully completed a distributed transaction.

A full analysis of all the possible failures that could occur, at all the worst times, requires a good deal of thought. For this discussion, suffice it to say that the 2PC mechanisms described provide a reliable and automatic problem resolution in most failure situations. A few conditions still require human intervention, however. One such case is an extended outage of a server or communications link that leaves elements in the databases locked. If the locked element is a table of all available rooms at a hotel, the front desk personnel will undoubtedly expect the situation to be resolved quickly.

Role of the DTC in Transaction Processing

SQL Server has included support for the 2PC protocol in the past. Application programmers using the C/C++ programming languages could access 2PC functionality by using the DB-Library interface provided by Microsoft for developing SQL Server applications. Procedures were provided on servers that allowed them to take on the role of commit coordinator.

The Microsoft Distributed Transaction Coordinator (DTC) adds important new components to help implement distributed transactions and make the management of 2PC a practical undertaking. Each server has a full DTC service that will coordinate transactions with other servers. Using the DTC, a server can take on the role of commit coordinator for certain transactions. In addition, the DTC can help resolve problem (or in-doubt) transactions by communicating with other DTC services running on other servers involved in a transaction.

A client-side interface to DTC is available for Windows NT and Windows 95 computers. This interface allows developers to create applications using distributed transactions and leverage the facilities provided by the full DTC service running on SQL Servers. The client components of DTC do not include a full DTC service, even on Windows NT clients. Also, the DTC client is available only for 32-bit versions of Windows (Windows 95 and Windows NT).

T I P It is possible for a stored procedure running on an SQL Server to launch a distributed transaction on behalf of a 16-bit client. Therefore, older Windows clients can still benefit from DTC functionality.

In addition, a set of management utilities has been added to SQL Enterprise Manager. The utilities include graphical tools that allow you to dynamically monitor the state of transactions on SQL Servers running the DTC service. You can open multiple windows to monitor transactions occurring on multiple servers from a single workstation. The DTC extensions to SQL Enterprise Manager also allow an administrator to manually resolve problem transactions arising from equipment or application failure.

N O T E Although SQL Enterprise Manager can be run on Windows 95, the DTC utilities are available only when using SQL Enterprise Manager on a Windows NT computer. ■

For application developers, DTC offers new tools to support distributed transactions. A new statement in T-SQL, BEGIN DISTRIBUTED TRANSACTION, allows the creation of stored procedures that use DTC to coordinate transaction execution on multiple servers. This dramatically simplifies the development of stored procedures involving remote servers. In addition, an API for C/C++ programmers that conforms to the OLE Component Object Model has been provided for DTC. Using this interface, an application developer can create transaction objects and enlist the services of transaction resource managers and transaction coordinators to process those objects.

At this point, Microsoft SQL Server is the only available resource manager, but an OLE Transaction interface definition has been published, and other resource managers will be created by Microsoft and other software companies. Some level of interoperability is offered with several existing transaction-processing monitors, including Encina, Top End, and TUXEDO, and particularly with Microsoft's new Transaction Server (formerly code-named Viper).

Part
VII

Ch
38

Managing DTC with SQL Enterprise Manager

The DTC server components are installed automatically when you set up SQL Server 6.5, or upgrade SQL Server 6.0 to version 6.5. You can start the DTC service just like any other service using the Control Panel on the local computer, or using the Services dialog box in the Server Manager utility provided with Windows NT Server. You also can start the service using the SQL Service Manager or SQL Enterprise Manager.

The rest of this section focuses on the DTC capabilities added to SQL Enterprise Manager. This administrative tool has been enhanced with functionality to completely monitor and manage DTC capabilities. To start the DTC service with SQL Enterprise Manager, follow these steps:

1. Start SQL Enterprise Manager.

2. In the Server Manager window, open a server group and select the server you want to manage.

3. If the SQL Server service is not yet running on the server, click the Services button—the one that looks like a stoplight—on the toolbar. The SQL Server Manager dialog box appears.

4. Click the green Start/Continue portion of the stoplight control. When SQL Server starts, click the Done button.

5. Now click the plus sign to the left of the server name. The services and objects on the server are listed.

6. Right-click the DTC icon. It is typically listed just below the SQL Executive icon and labeled Distributed Transaction Coordinator. Select Start from the pop-up menu. After a brief pause, the icon turns green to indicate the service has started.

The DTC Configuration dialog box allows you to control the behavior of the DTC service. You can configure parameters that affect viewing transactions in the Transactions window, the tracing information sent to the Trace window, and the location and size of the DTC log file. To configure the DTC service, follow this procedure:

1. Start SQL Enterprise Manager.

2. In the Server Manager window, open a server group and select the server you want to manage. If SQL Server and the DTC service are not running, start the services.

3. Right-click the DTC icon. Select Configure from the pop-up menu. The DTC Configuration dialog box appears, as shown in Figure 38.3.

FIG. 38.3

Use this dialog box to configure the displays that monitor the distributed transaction coordinator service and its behavior.

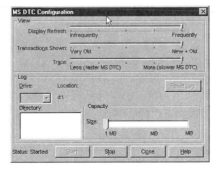

4. Using the Display Refresh slider bar, you can configure DTC to update the display at intervals from 1 to 20 seconds with a default value of five seconds. Updating the display more frequently adds administrative overhead to transaction processing and can cause reduced performance.

5. The older a transaction, the more likely it will have difficulty completing. The Transactions Shown slider controls how old a transaction must be before being displayed in the Transactions window. You can set values from one second to five minutes.

6. The Trace slider controls how much trace information is sent to the Trace window. You can specify no tracing, increasing levels of error, warning and informational traces, or all trace information.

7. You can change view settings while the DTC service is running. To change log settings, you must stop the DTC service. You can then change the location and size of the log.

To view the status of active transactions, follow these steps:

1. Start SQL Enterprise Manager.

2. In the Server Manager window, open a server group and select the server you want to manage. If SQL Server and the DTC service are not running, start the services.

3. Right-click the DTC icon. Select Transaction from the pop-up menu. A DTC Transactions window for the selected server appears (see Figure 38.4).

FIG. 38.4

This figure depicts a DTC Transactions window for the server HQSRV1. There are three active transactions and one preparing to commit.

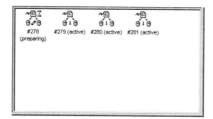

4. You can select another server and open a transactions window for it, as well. It is possible to monitor the transactions on a number of servers simultaneously using tiled or cascaded windows.

5. In the transactions window, you can monitor transaction states and manually resolve in-doubt transactions (see Figure 38.5).

FIG. 38.5

You can manually resolve in-doubt transactions by right-clicking the transaction in the transactions window and selecting the appropriate action.

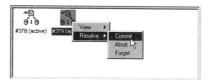

CAUTION

You should not manually force transactions until you thoroughly understand the interaction of all members of a DTC system. Please review the *Guide to Microsoft Distributed Transaction Coordinator* carefully before using this utility to resolve transactions.

To view the traces being sent (at the level you configured DTC to provide), follow these steps:

1. Start SQL Enterprise Manager.

2. In the Server Manager window, open a server group and select the server you want to manage. If SQL Server and the DTC service are not running, start the services.

3. Right-click the DTC icon. Select Trace from the pop-up menu. A DTC Traces window for the selected server appears.

4. You can select another server and open a traces window for it, as well. It is possible to monitor traces from a number of servers simultaneously using tiled or cascaded windows.

A DTC service maintains statistical information about its performance. To view the statistics that have accumulated for a DTC service, follow these steps:

1. Start SQL Enterprise Manager.
2. In the Server Manager window, open a server group and select the server you want to manage. If SQL Server and the DTC service are not running, start the services.
3. Right-click the DTC icon. Select Statistics from the pop-up menu. A DTC Statistics window for the selected server appears, as shown in Figure 38.6.

 T I P   The statistics for a DTC service are cleared and restarted whenever the DTC service is stopped and restarted.

FIG. 38.6
This figure depicts a DTC Statistics window for the server HQSRV2.

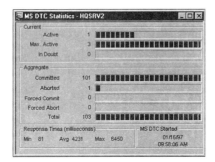

Microsoft Transaction Server (MTS)

Microsoft Transaction Server 1.0 (MTS) was released in January of 1997, and it builds on the functionality offered by DTC. It provides a COM-based programming model with a relatively simple Application Programming Interface (API) that makes it easy for developers to create powerful, distributed applications. Applications are created largely as though they were designed for a single user to execute on a desktop computer. With minor additions, these applications can be invoked in a Transaction Server environment. Transaction Server provides all the needed additional capabilities to make the application multiuser and leverages DTC to provide distributed transaction processing. Transaction Server therefore forms the basis for a powerful three-tiered distributed computing architecture.

A simple example of the way an MTS environment might be set up is provided in Figure 38.7. Desktop PC clients may be either so-called "fat" Win32 systems (running either Windows 95 or Windows NT) or "thin" clients running a Web browser. MTS servers manage *packages* of components. These components may be developed in-house or purchased from third-party software vendors. They are then pulled together in one or more packages that you can deploy as a unit sharing resources (e.g. memory) and security settings. MTS also manages a shared pool of ODBC data connections to a variety of data providers which can be traditional database servers or files on a mainframe.

FIG. 38.7
This figure depicts a sample MTS environment showing various elements of a three-tiered architecture.

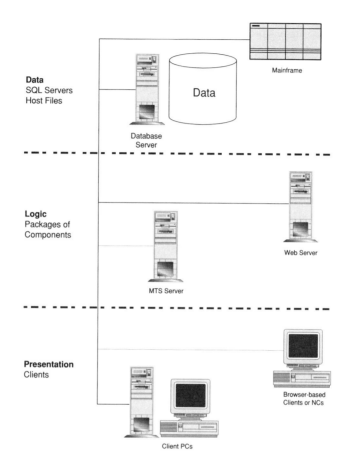

Although the example above describes three tiers, there is nothing inherent in the design of MTS that limits it to this structure. It is possible to break a computing system into more than three logical tiers, and MTS is designed in a manner which makes it straightforward to implement a variety of system architectures including multitiered designs. The three-tiered model is natural in some respects and is starting to be widely used, but need not be the only deployment alternative with MTS.

N O T E   The operating systems and applications that are installed on PCs have gotten much larger as they have grown in sophistication. With the advent of the HTTP-based Web browser, application developers started exploring the capability of using this relatively "thin" tool as the basis for server-based applications. The traditional application architecture with its executable files and Dynamic Link Libraries (DLLs) has been characterized as "fat" because of the amount of information (programs, configuration files, and data) that must be stored on the client.

It is worth noting, however, that browsers (from Netscape, Microsoft, and others) continue to get "fatter" as more features are added. In addition, browser-based applications have not yet reached the level of performance and sophistication offered by the more traditional Win32 client. It remains to be seen how fat the thin client will need to become to match the functionality offered by Win32 clients. ■

The next few sections provide an introduction to Transaction Server. You learn how to install the product, go through a quick tour of MTS in action, and review the product's features.

Installing Transaction Server

There are two ways that MTS can be installed—as a *production server* or as a *development server*. If you plan to experiment with MTS and use the development tools to create distributed applications, you will want to install the Software Developer's Kit (SDK) in addition to MTS. If you are implementing a solution that has already been developed, you will probably prefer to install only MTS. The procedures for installing MTS and its options are provided below.

To install MTS, follow these steps:

1. Launch the Setup program. If you are installing the evaluation copy of MTS from the Microsoft Web site, you launch a self-extracting compressed file called MTXEVAL.EXE.

2. You are reminded that you should close other programs that are running. If you are installing the evaluation copy, a license agreement is presented which you must agree to in order to continue with the installation. Click I Agree to continue.

3. A Name and Organization dialog box opens so that you can register your copy of the software. Enter your name and organization and then click OK.

4. The Product ID number is presented. This number is required in order to get product support. You can write it down now, or access it later by choosing Help, About from the menu in Transaction Server Explorer (the administration tool described later in this chapter). Click OK.

5. You are now given the opportunity to change the default directory where MTS will be installed. Either click Change Folder to change the directory or accept the default. Click OK.

6. A dialog box appears which allows you to select the type of installation you want to make (see Figure 38.8). These instructions describe the development installation, but the typical installation without development tools is very similar. Click the large button labeled Microsoft Transaction Server Development.

FIG. 38.8
This dialog box allows you to select a development installation of MTS with the SDK and samples, or a production installation including only the MTS product itself.

7. The resulting dialog box—shown in Figure 38.9—allows you to select the individual optional components you want to install. Make your selections and click <u>C</u>ontinue.

FIG. 38.9

Use this dialog box to select the individual components you want to install.

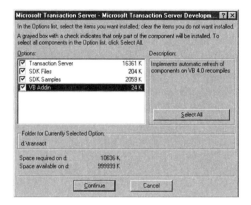

8. A dialog box appears which asks if you want to set the System Server Process identity. This is nothing more than the service account that the Transaction Server service will run under. You can set the service account now, or set it later using the Transaction Server Explorer, or the Services Control Panel applet. If you haven't already created a service account you want to use, simply change this setting later. Click <u>N</u>o to continue.

9. The next dialog box that appears asks you whether to run the DTC. You can either decide now to start the DTC service automatically on this server, or start and stop it as needed using the Transaction Server Explorer, or other service starting utilities (e.g., Control Panel, Services). Click <u>Y</u>es or <u>N</u>o to continue.

10. The setup program begins copying files to your hard disk. When it is finished, it prompts you to restart Windows NT to complete the installation. Be sure you have closed all other applications and saved your work. Then click the <u>R</u>estart button. You have successfully installed MTS.

Features of Transaction Server

Transaction Server is used to deploy mid-tier logic implemented in the form of ActiveX components. These objects receive requests from clients, apply some sort of logic (e.g., business rules) to the requests, and then call on appropriate resource managers to resolve the requests. The ActiveX components can be written with a variety of languages, including those listed in Table 38.2 in the section "Packages of Components" later in this chapter. Once these components are written, they are combined to form *packages*. The packages are then deployed, usually on Windows NT servers, to act as intermediaries for clients wishing to access shared resources.

Because of MTS's capability to manage the linkage between many clients accessing many resource managers (e.g., databases) while applying application logic, the application architecture you can create using these building blocks has some very desirable characteristics:

■ **Scalable.** Applications can be implemented using one server or scaled to many multi-processor servers handling hundreds of users.

■ **Distributed.** Applications which span multiple machines are coded in a manner almost identical to an application designed to run on a single computer.

■ **Multiuser.** MTS automatically provides thread management, assists with shared memory management, and offers other capabilities that make it easier to take existing single-user components and run them safely in a multiuser environment.

■ **Reliable.** Through the use of transactional technologies like DTC and OLE TX, the MTS environment ensures that discrete units of work are always either done completely, or not done at all. Atomicity is always maintained. The data accessed through MTS resource managers remains in a consistent state, even with many users accessing diverse resources on multiple machines. In addition, using the latest SQL Server products you can achieve a high degree of concurrency and processing throughput.

COM and DCOM

Much of the distributed nature of the MTS product comes as a direct result of the use of the Component Object Model (COM) and Distributed Component Object Model (DCOM) as the basis for MTS component building. A full discussion of these specifications is beyond the scope of this book—see *Special Edition Using ActiveX* from Que. But a brief introduction is included here as an aid to understanding the underlying mechanisms that make MTS work.

The basic COM specification uses a message-based architecture to allow one process to communicate with another. Each COM component is implemented as a *server*. The word *server* is obviously used in a different sense here than a file server of some sort. The component, or server, does create its own context and serves an interface, or multiple interfaces, to the outside world. Calling processes may use these interfaces to access the services offered by this component. There are two types of servers—in-process or local server. Both of these types of components execute on the same machine as the caller. In-process servers are usually implemented as DLLs, and therefore they run in the same process as the caller (see Figure 38.10).

FIG. 38.10
This figure depicts a simple call from one process to an in-process server.

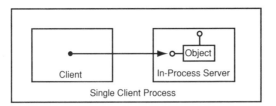

Local server components run in a separate process on the same computer as shown in Figure 38.11. Through the use of a *proxy* and a *stub*, the calls from one to the other are easily handled. The proxy looks like the actual component being called to the calling process. The proxy communicates with the stub through an Inter-Process Communication (IPC) mechanism. The stub then communicates with the component, appearing to be the original calling process. The caller and component have been separated, but remain on the same machine.

FIG. 38.11

In this figure a call is made from one process to a local server process running on the same machine.

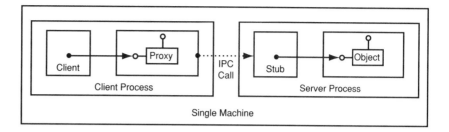

The DCOM specification adds a third type of server—remote server. In this instance, the IPC mechanism used for local server calls has been replaced with a Remote Process Communication (RPC) mechanism. The original caller and component implementations are retained, as is the use of the proxy and stub; only the communications mechanism has changed (see Figure 38.12). The substitution of remote servers for local servers is nearly transparent to the developer, making the process of partitioning an application into components much more straightforward. The application logic can be located where you want to put it, and the "plumbing" between components is managed by MTS.

Part

VII

Ch

38

FIG. 38.12

The DCOM remote server implementation is shown in this figure.

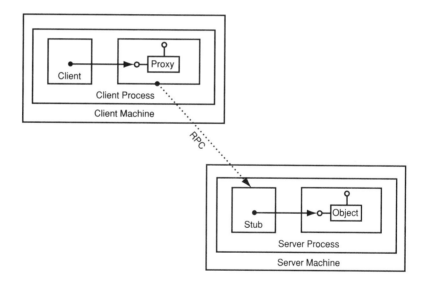

Packages of Components

After you have either purchased off-the-shelf components, written your own, or both, you can create collections of components called *packages*. You can manage a package of components as a unit. The components in the package can share security settings and can access other shared resources through the use of MTS's Shared Property Manager (SPM). They also can share a pool of ODBC connections to database resources. Allocating memory and processing on a one-to-one basis with clients becomes inefficient when handling large numbers of clients. A shared pool is more efficient and scales better as the number of clients grows.

When access to distributed database resources is required, the services of Microsoft's DTC (described in the first part of this chapter) are used to efficiently provide a message-based architecture capable of maintaining the atomic nature of transactions across machine boundaries. Communications with database *resource dispensers* are handled using a variety of protocols. Currently, OLE Transactions (OLE TX) is used. Other protocols will be added in the future, according to Microsoft's public announcements (see Table 38.1).

Table 38.1   Database Access Protocol Support for MTS

Protocol	When
OLE TX	Now
Transaction Internet Protocol (TIP)	Q1 '97
XA	Q2 '97
SNA LU 6.2	Q3 '97

The MTS development environment provides a very flexible programming environment. As already noted, the focus of most developers is on creating components designed for single-user environments without regard for distributed applications issues. They can work in a variety of languages, including those listed in Table 38.2.

Table 38.2   Languages Supported for MTS Development

Language	Manufacturer
Delphi	Borland
Visual Basic	Microsoft
Visual C++	Microsoft
Visual J++	Microsoft
PowerBuilder	PowerSoft
Café	Symantec

After components are created, they are packaged to facilitate setting security and deploying on a particular machine. Packages can be effectively managed using the Transaction Server Explorer. You can even split a package for deployment across server boundaries by partitioning the package for multiple-machine installation. The use of the Transaction Server Explorer is described in the next section, "Using MTS."

Using MTS

The tool used to package components, and then deploy the packages, is the Transaction Server Explorer. This administrative console for MTS is a graphical utility that allows you to manipulate and control the components which build a multitiered MTS architecture. In addition to these component-based activities, you also can use the Transaction Server Explorer to start and stop the DTC, change the service account settings, or perform other administrative tasks.

To use the Transaction Server Explorer to manage MTS, follow these steps:

1. Launch the Transaction Server Explorer by using the Start menu or double-clicking the appropriate icon. The basic Explorer interface displays (see Figure 38.13).

FIG. 38.13

The Transaction Server Explorer is shown in this figure with My Computer selected in the left pane, and the contents of My Computer displayed in the right pane.

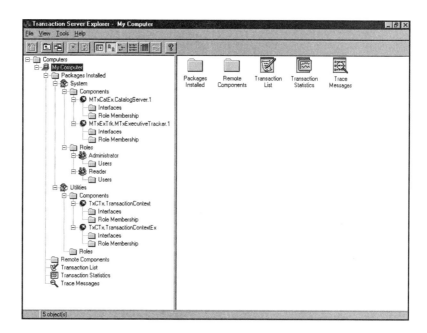

The Transaction Server Explorer uses a two-pane display. The left pane is presented in hierarchical fashion, showing the computers that are being managed. If you select an object in the left pane, its contents are shown in the right pane.

Right-clicking an object generally opens a context-sensitive menu with choices pertinent to the object selected.

2. Click the plus sign (+) to the left of an object to open the hierarchical display of its contents in the left pane.

3. To add other computers to the display (after MTS has been installed on the machine), click the Computers folder and select File, New from the menu. Enter the name of the computer you want to manage. Click OK.

4. To create a new package, click the Packages Installed folder in the left pane and select File, New from the menu. The Package Wizard starts (see Figure 38.14).

FIG. 38.14

You use the Package Wizard to install pre-built packages and to create empty packages which can then be filled with components.

5. Click the large button labeled Create an Empty Package.

6. In the next dialog box, enter a name for the new package and click Next.

7. Select the account context that this package will be run under. It can execute with the same status as the currently logged on user, or it can be run using a different account, such as a service account, for its security status. Select an account and click Finish. The new package is created.

8. To add a component to a package, highlight the package in the left pane and select File, New from the menu. The opening dialog for the Component Wizard, which is very similar to the Package Wizard, will be displayed. You can Import component(s) that have already been added to your system registry by being installed on this computer. For this example, however, click Install new component(s).

9. The Install Components dialog will be displayed. Click the Add files button. The Select Files to Install dialog appears (see Figure 38.15).

FIG. 38.15

ActiveX components created with a variety of languages can be integrated into a single package for deployment on this computer, or to be exported to other machines.

10. Select the component you want to install and click the Open button. Then click Finish to complete the wizard. The component will be added to your package, and will appear in the right pane of the display when the package is selected in the left pane.

11. To set properties for a package, click the Packages Installed folder in the left pane; then right-click the package in the right pane. Select Properties from the pop-up menu (see Figure 38.16).

FIG. 38.16

Most objects in the Transaction Server Explorer provide pop-up menus when right-clicked.

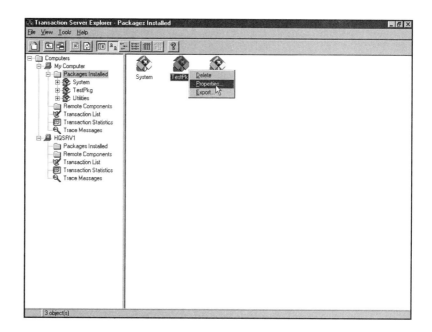

12. A four-tabbed dialog box of package properties displays (see Figure 38.17). On the General tab you can enter a description of the package, or view the package's unique Package ID. Click the Security tab.

13. The Security tab allows you to select the authorization level to be used for this package (see Figure 38.18). Use the drop-down list labeled Authentication Level for Calls, and click the check box labeled Enable authorization checking to use this feature. Click the Advanced tab.

14. The Advanced tab is used to set Server Process Shutdown options. Select either Leave Running When Idle, or specify a number of minutes of idle time before you shut down com-ponents in this package. Click the Identity tab.

15. The Identity tab is used to select the account ID that will be used when executing com-ponents in this package. Choose Interactive User or select This User, and choose a user account from the Set Package Identity dialog box. Click OK.

16. To monitor transactions as they occur after you have deployed your packages, click the Transaction List or Transaction Statistics icons in the left panel of the display. The active

transactions display (see Figure 38.19), or transaction statistics for all activity since the DTC was started are provided (see Figure 38.20).

FIG. 38.17

This is the General tab of a package's Properties dialog box showing the Package ID and a description of the package.

FIG. 38.18

The Security tab allows you to set more stringent authorization requirements for components in this package.

Microsoft plans to continue the evolution of MTS into the future, where it will become a key component of multimachine architectures. Microsoft has publicly announced plans to add data-dependent message routing (useful in partitioning large applications) and durable queues which would maintain the queue of messages even in the event of catastrophic failure. These and other features will likely be delivered by, or derived from, the Microsoft Message Queue (MSMQ) Server, a product which was code-named Falcon. It will be interesting to see how these technologies are combined to extend and improve the powerful features already included in the first release of MTS.

FIG. 38.19

By clicking the Transaction List icon in the left pane, you display any active transactions in the right pane.

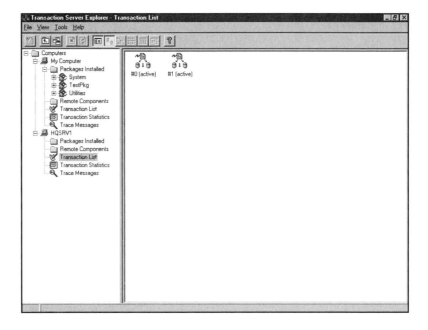

FIG. 38.20

Transaction Statistics reflect the activity on this server since the DTC service was started, or since the settings were last cleared.

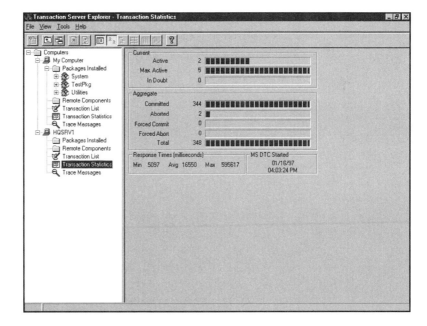

From Here...

In this chapter, you learned some advanced features of Microsoft SQL Server. You were introduced to the procedures for setting up data replication and how to see the process of replication take place. You also learned about distributed transactions and a new tool included in SQL Server version 6.5, the Distributed Transaction Coordinator. The various tools for monitoring the status of distributed transactions and resolving problem transactions were described.

See the following chapters for related information:

- For a review of the procedures for administering SQL Server, see Chapter 35, "Maintaining SQL Server."

- To find out how to replicate data from one SQL Server to another, see Chapter 36, "SQL Server Data Replication."

- To learn about using SQL Server to establish a data warehouse, see Chapter 37, "Data Warehousing with SQL Server."

- For information on the host connectivity component of BackOffice, SNA Server, see Chapter 39, "SNA Server Preparation and Installation."

- For information on the systems management component of BackOffice, Systems Management Server (SMS), see Chapter 42, "Preparing for SMS."

SNA Server

SNA Server Preparation and Installation

by Daniel Garcia and Jim Marshbank

Microsoft's Systems Network Architecture (SNA) Server is a key component of the Microsoft BackOffice suite of server-based applications. It provides a way of accessing existing IBM mainframe-resident and AS/400-resident data from your desktop PC. Although the major focus of this chapter is on the SNA Server installation process, it is important that you understand some of the broad concepts behind IBM's SNA and Microsoft's SNA Server and the various network models in which they function. Therefore, before launching into a detailed discussion of the actions required to install SNA Server, a significant portion of this chapter overviews IBM's SNA and Microsoft's SNA Server to include a brief survey of some of SNA Server's more important features. ■

Learn the basic concepts behind SNA Server

Enhance your understanding of SNA Server by learning what SNA really is, seeing some different SNA models, and becoming familiar with key SNA Server features.

How to prepare for your SNA Server installation

Acquaint yourself with the recommended installation preparation actions, planning decisions that need to be made early on, and helpful forms to document planned installation and configuration parameters.

How to install SNA Server with the SNA Server Setup program

Obtain the details on selecting SNA Server components to install, choose a license mode, choose an SNA Server role, client-server protocols, and network subdomain name.

How to perform some common SNA Server administrator tasks after installing SNA Server

Find out how the SNA Server Setup program can be used to accomplish postinstallation actions. Step-by-step procedures are provided for some common SNA Server administrator tasks.

Understanding SNA Server

With the growing popularity of client-server computing in local area network (LAN) and wide area network (WAN) environments, businesses are demanding robust PC-based client-server solutions that provide accessibility to and control of corporate data across the enterprise. Although a large percentage of these businesses could benefit by moving from a traditional legacy (mainframe) system to a LAN-based PC environment, industry analysts agree that many of them will continue to run mission-critical applications on mainframe systems, not LAN-based PCs. This, coupled with the generally accepted position that traditional mainframe-style computer environments will continue to play a key role in major business enterprises for the foreseeable future, indicates that a significant number of businesses will establish and maintain computing environments that consist of multiple systems of various types in use simultaneously. Even if they eventually decide to migrate away from a mainframe environment to a pure LAN-based PC client-server environment, that migration will probably be a long, arduous process during which data and applications residing on diverse types of platforms will need to be accessible across a variety of environments.

The challenge, therefore, is to build transitional strategies that leverage existing computing environments without jeopardizing reliable, fast, and secure access to corporate data via the desktop PC. These strategies must identify cost-effective solutions that make legacy data and applications accessible to heterogeneous collections of PCs and networks. At the same time, the capabilities of host systems or PCs cannot be sacrificed during the migration to a pure LAN-based PC client-server environment. Any candidate solution must convincingly deal with a few critical management concerns if businesses are to implement new technologies in ways meaningful to their business operation. One concern is how to maintain control of sensitive information and manage access to that information in a secure and highly centralized manner while distributing client-server applications as close as possible to the end users. The other management concern is how to ensure that LAN administrators have total management control of all the PC desktops across the entire enterprise environment.

Some of the most prevalent enterprise computing environments today involve IBM mainframe-stored corporate data available only through IBM's Systems Network Architecture (SNA) network. Therefore, candidate solutions need to be cleanly integrated and closely coupled with these SNA networks to provide rapid, secure, and reliable data accessibility in a way that also convincingly satisfies the management-control concerns of the enterprise. The Microsoft SNA Server, designed and developed for compatibility with IBM's proprietary SNA network, is just such a solution.

What Is SNA?

IBM's SNA, originally defined in the 1970s, is a set of communications protocols and message-format specifications that provide for the integration of IBM hardware and software into a networked environment called an SNA network. While this architecture is indeed proprietary, the specifications embodied within it are well documented and available for third-party vendors to use in developing SNA-compatible hardware and software products, which can then be integrated into SNA networks. As a matter of fact, the popularity of SNA environments and their wide use around the world have created a *de facto* standard recognized throughout the industry.

Hierarchical SNA Model　The traditional SNA specification represents a hierarchical model (a vertical architecture) in which each device communicates with a more intelligent device above and a less intelligent device below. The IBM mainframe is at the top of the hierarchy. It is referred to as a *Physical Unit Type 5* (PU 5) in standard SNA terminology. There can be only one PU 5 in an SNA domain, and it handles the actual computing. The typical applications that run on the PU 5 are Time Sharing Option (TSO), NetView (IBM's network management package), databases, the SNA network software called VTAM (Virtual Telecommunications Access Method), and other user-developed applications.

Below the PU 5 in the hierarchy is the PU 4, an IBM front-end processor that is directly connected to the PU 5 via a high-speed connection. The PU 4 is a highly intelligent device that handles the communications between the PU 5 and the users, devices, and applications throughout the network. The IBM cluster controller, PU 2, is the next device down in the hierarchy, as reflected in Figure 39.1.

FIG. 39.1

A simple diagram of the hierarchical SNA model.

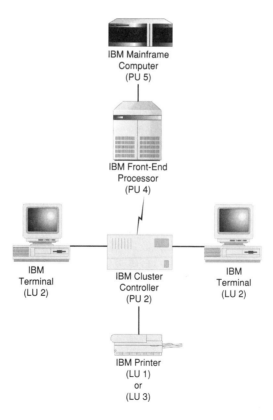

IBM Mainframe
Computer
(PU 5)

IBM Front-End
Processor
(PU 4)

IBM
Terminal
(LU 2)

IBM Cluster
Controller
(PU 2)

IBM
Terminal
(LU 2)

IBM Printer
(LU 1)
or
(LU 3)

Part

VIII

Ch

39

The PU 2 communicates with the PU 4 via telephone line, token ring connection, local cable, or other physical connections. It directly controls the unintelligent devices at the bottom of the hierarchy on the SNA network. These unintelligent peripheral hardware devices consist of equipment such as CRT terminals, tape drives, and printers. The SNA network software knows these actual hardware devices only as logical addresses, and, therefore, they are generically referred to as *logical units*, or LUs. LUs are of different types, and each unique type communicates with the PU 2 via a uniquely defined set of protocols in the SNA. Two of the more common LU types are CRT terminals (LU 2) and IBM 3287 printers (LU 1 and LU 3). Any user-defined device, which is by default nonstandard, is an LU 0.

Peer-Oriented SNA Model   While IBM's SNA was originally developed for its hierarchical S/370 mainframe-oriented hierarchical network, it has evolved to accommodate the IBM AS/400 intelligent peer-oriented networks, as well. In the peer-oriented SNA model, a horizontal model in which computers communicate directly with each other, each computer depends mostly on its own intelligence and does not rely heavily on help from a higher level device. Communication can be initiated anywhere, not just from a top-down host. The peer-oriented model is the general direction in which all computer networks are evolving, and IBM's stated direction for the future evolution of its SNA networks is to employ Advanced Peer-to-Peer Networking (APPN).

The peer-oriented SNA model of an APPN network is not completely horizontal, however (see Figure 39.2). The larger computers in the IBM SNA-APPN network are usually AS/400s, which handle all network routing functions and normal computing functions, as well. These network peers, referred to as PU 2.1 devices, may offer various levels of service and network intelligence.

The smaller computers, which are associated with the PU 2.1s, are typically PCs that provide terminal and printer emulation. These PCs appear as LU device type 6.2 and are therefore called LU 6.2 devices. These devices, as well as programs in an SNA-APPN network, appear as LU 6.2 entities that communicate via LU 6.2 sessions by using Advanced Program-to-Program Communication (APPC) protocols. Two separate and totally independent programs running in an SNA-APPN network, each one appearing as an LU 6.2 session, also can communicate directly by using APPC.

FIG. 39.2

A simple diagram of the Advanced Peer-to-Peer Networking (APPN) SNA model.

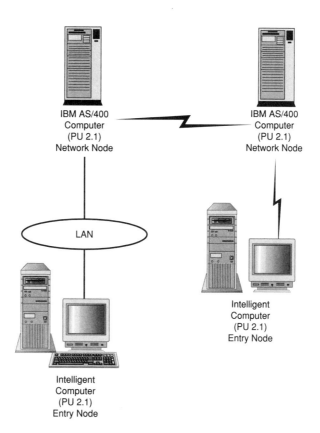

IBM AS/400
Computer
(PU 2.1)
Network Node

IBM AS/400
Computer
(PU 2.1)
Network Node

LAN

Intelligent
Computer
(PU 2.1)
Entry Node

Intelligent
Computer
(PU 2.1)
Entry Node

Part
VIII

Ch
39

What Is SNA Server?

SNA Server provides a sophisticated, user-friendly business solution for accessing existing IBM mainframe-resident and AS/400-resident data from your desktop PC. It is essentially a high-speed internetworking gateway between the PC and IBM SNA network, connecting LAN-based PCs with IBM host systems running SNA protocols. As a server process running under the Microsoft Windows NT Server operating system, it is composed of both hardware and software components and is capable of concurrently running communications protocols from both the Windows NT network environment and the IBM SNA network environment. Additionally, the SNA Server provides extensions to other networking protocols such as TCP/IP and IPX. The SNA Server thus provides a high-speed window between the SNA network and the Windows NT network environments through which bidirectional communications can occur.

SNA Server emulates IBM S/370 and S/390 mainframe terminals, IBM AS/400 terminals, and IBM 3287 printers through its high-speed, bidirectional communications capability. It actually functions as a server node to the IBM SNA network and provides LAN-based PCs with direct access to data and applications residing on IBM mainframes and IBM AS/400 hosts. Because the PC can emulate an IBM terminal, applications running on the IBM host can display application screen faces and data directly on the PC. These data screens can then be manipulated and application processes communicated back to the IBM host system.

One obvious additional benefit of having this data available at the PC is the capability to use standard desktop productivity software with the IBM host data. You can easily use word processors, spreadsheets, and presentation packages to manipulate and utilize the data in routine office productivity functions such as the following:

- Drafting letters
- Generating reports
- Calculating statistical summaries
- Developing professional presentations

Additionally, the printer-emulation software allows you to gain access to and capture IBM print data at your network printer. You can even transfer files between the IBM host system and your LAN-based PC by using SNA Server.

SNA Server in the Hierarchical SNA Model   As an internetworking gateway, SNA Server concurrently runs two separate and different networking protocols. This capability allows the SNA Server to essentially belong to two separate networks at the same time, as shown in Figure 39.3. The SNA Server fits into the SNA network by emulating the IBM PU 2 (cluster controller) and multiple LUs of type 1, 2, or 3. Thus, the SNA network sees the SNA Server as a PU 2 with associated LUs. Client software applications within the Windows NT network that emulate LU 0 through LU 3 devices can then communicate with the PU 5 (IBM host) through the PU 4 (IBM front-end processor).

FIG. 39.3

A view of how the Microsoft SNA Server fits into the hierarchical SNA network model. Note that the SNA server is included in both the Windows NT and IBM SNA environments.

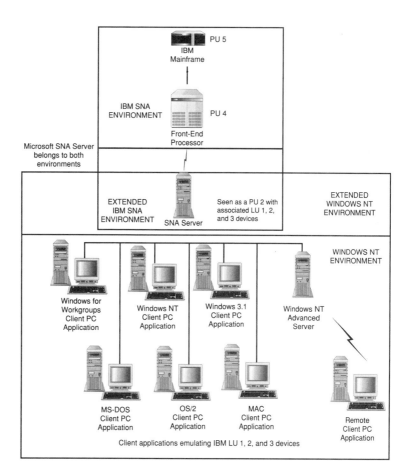

SNA Server in the Peer-Oriented SNA-APPN Network

As in the hierarchical SNA model, the SNA Server belongs to both the SNA network and the Windows NT network simultaneously. In the case of the peer-oriented SNA network model, the SNA Server fits into the SNA-APPN network by emulating the IBM PU 2.1 network node with its associated LU 6.2 sessions (see Figure 39.4). It appears to the SNA-APPN network as a PU 2.1 peer device and also as an APPN Low Entry Network (LEN) node. It allows software applications in the Windows NT network that emulate LU 6.2 devices to communicate with PU 2.1 devices or LU 6.2 applications within the SNA network.

Part
VIII

Ch
39

FIG. 39.4

A view of how the Microsoft SNA Server fits into the peer-oriented SNA APPN network model. Note that the SNA server is included in both the Windows NT and IBM SNA environments.

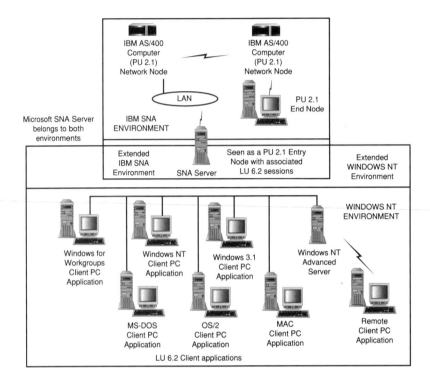

Surveying Features in Microsoft SNA Server

Numerous features have been designed into the SNA Server to make it one of the most powerful, reliable, and user-friendly internetworking products available today. Many of these features also greatly simplify the LAN administrator's difficult job of managing and controlling the enterprise network. Some of the more significant features are presented in the following list and then described in the rest of the chapter:

- Enhanced, but still familiar, graphical user interface
- Tight integration with Windows NT Server
- Centralized monitoring and control
- Enterprise configuration flexibility
- Highly secure, reliable, and efficient
- Numerous host service options
- Numerous host connectivity options
- Comprehensive client-server support
- Robust administrative and diagnostic tools
- LU pooling
- Support for Remote Access Service (RAS)

Graphical User Interface (GUI)   SNA Server was designed to have the same look and feel as Windows NT 4.0, thus potentially reducing your training and support costs. State-of-the-art GUI functionality, icon-based visual feedback, easy-to-understand dialog boxes with drag-and-drop features, and dynamic-data updating help to make SNA Server intuitive to use and administer. Intelligent integration and design of dialog boxes has also minimized the number of windows necessary for installation and simplified setup and configuration tasks.

The SNA Server Manager program eases the burden of SNA Server network administration by employing standard Windows NT Explorer functionality to configure and manage all SNA Server components. Unique icons allow you to readily identify connection types and LU types, as well as specific servers, connections, users, and LU pools. SNA Server Manager also allows remote configuration and management of SNA servers.

Tight Integration with Windows NT Server   The installation of SNA Server on top of the Windows NT Server operating system provides a tight integration with the Windows NT Server graphical tool set. This not only simplifies management of the host/PC interconnection for LAN administrators but also ensures the viability of other SNA Server features such as security and centralized monitoring and control. Windows NT Server tools such as the User Manager, Server Manager, Performance Monitor, Event Viewer, and Control Panel applets actually appear as seamless extensions of the SNA Server, as follows:

- **User Manager.** This tool allows you to create and manage all user and group accounts on the domain. SNA Server shares the accounts established by User Manager and, therefore, any account created on the Windows NT Server or the SNA Server is automatically registered for use on the other server, as well. This single-account database design allows you to specify which users and groups defined in the Windows NT Server domain will also be users and groups on the SNA Server.

- **Server Manager.** A logical grouping of servers is called a *domain*. Server Manager allows you to manage various accounts on one or more domains. You can switch between domains, view all the servers on the selected domain, attach to servers on the domain, and manage servers on the domain. You also can alter the properties for each of the servers on the domain.

- **Performance Monitor.** This tool is used to measure the performance of any server, including installed SNA servers, accessible over the network. Things such as connections, LUs, and adapter throughput and transmission volume can be measured on SNA servers. Monitored results are dynamically updated and can be viewed as charts, tables, and logs. In some cases, client response times can be monitored, but the client emulator needs to support the NetView Response Time Monitor (RTM) for this to be possible.

- **Event Viewer.** You can use this tool to record and view predefined events that occur on the Windows NT server or SNA server. Event Viewer is very flexible and can easily be tailored to suit a variety of conditions and monitoring needs. For example, you can set the type and severity of events you want to be recorded, and you can put limits on the size of the log file. You can even provide disposition instructions that will automatically be carried out when the log file becomes full so that remaining events can still be recorded.

■ **Control Panel.** This is a collection of tools for Windows NT Server and SNA Server. It allows you to start and stop services; install, configure, or remove network cards; install, configure, start, and stop system drivers; and monitor who is connected to your computer, as well as identify the shared resources in use.

▶ **See** "Surveying the Administrative Tools of Windows NT Server," **p. 186**

Centralized Monitoring and Control   The SNA Server's seamless integration with the Windows NT Server allows you to manage all the SNA servers from a single computer. The SNA Server Manager program, which you can run from any Windows NT platform, provides all the tools the SNA or LAN administrator needs to manage the daily operation of network interactions. From the IBM mainframe side, the NetView program, resident on the IBM host computer, provides the capability for the host operators to communicate with the SNA server. The following list briefly describes some of the more important functions that can be performed through centralized management of the SNA Server environment:

■ **Troubleshooting.** The SNA Server either directly or indirectly provides a wide array of helpful troubleshooting tools such as the SNA Trace tool, support for the RTM, support for the NetView utilities NVAlert and NVRunCmd, Windows NT Performance Monitor, and Windows NT Event Viewer.

■ **User and LU management.** The SNA Server Manager program allows monitoring and management of users, groups, and sessions for users assigned SNA Server access. It also allows you to create LUs for specific connections and group them into pools and then to assign specific users or groups to the various LU pools as a way of controlling access to SNA Server resources.

■ **Configuration management.** The SNA Server Manager program allows you to manipulate multiple configuration files between and among primary and backup SNA servers. This facilitates hot backup in the event the primary server is lost. Additionally, because every SNA server in the domain knows what the other servers are doing, new sessions can be distributed to less busy servers automatically to better balance the workload on each SNA server.

■ **Link services management.** SNA Server Manager program allows you to install, configure, and remove link services, and it also displays the mapping between the Windows NT device driver names and the SNA connections.

■ **Connection management.** SNA Server Manager allows you to monitor the status of SNA servers and connections as being active, inactive, pending, or stopping. It also allows you to create, remove, start, and stop connections; and it facilitates connection activation by providing options for manually starting the connection, having the connection start automatically upon SNA Server startup, or starting the connection on demand as clients have a need for it.

■ **Remote administration.** The SNA Server Manager program can be used across routers, bridges, and Remote Access Service (RAS) links to allow central management of distributed SNA servers. However, because the SNA Server can be connected to only one remote domain at a time, you can perform administration operations on only one remote domain at a time.

Enterprise Configuration Flexibility   SNA Server can be physically located in two distinct enterprise configurations: centrally at the main corporate office or data center or in a distributed fashion where SNA servers are located at branch offices. In the centralized configuration, one or more SNA servers are located in a single place, usually a controlled access data center, to maximize reliability (hot backups and load balancing are simplified) and security. Also with the centralized configuration, a single routable protocol (such as TCP/IP or IPX) can be used on all WAN links to connect clients on the WAN to SNA servers at the central site.

In the branch configuration, SNA servers can be at each branch office, possibly even utilizing existing Windows NT Server platforms that are already performing control functions for printing, database management, e-mail distribution, and fax operations. This configuration usually reduces heavy traffic on the WAN and improves management responsiveness to user needs and configuration changes since LUs, connections, security, and users can be managed locally at the branch office. Because remote administration of the local branch SNA Server also can be performed from another site (the data center or home office, for example) using RAS or NetView, there is not necessarily a need to have trained troubleshooting personnel at the branch office.

Highly Secure, Reliable, and Efficient   Controlled logon to the Windows NT Server domain provides enhanced security, meeting the U.S. government's C2 level. Administrators can exercise tight local and remote access control from the LAN, the IBM host, or both through the use of a single-user-account database in the Windows NT Server domain. Additionally, administrators can implement SNA Server's host security features—single sign-on, password synchronization, and data encryption. For more information, see the "Implementing Security" section later in this chapter.

Reliability is achieved through the *hot backup* capability, a unique benefit of the SNA Server's LU pooling feature. Hot backup is the term applied to the capability of immediately switching to the backup SNA Server when the primary SNA Server fails or becomes unavailable. This switching occurs without session interruption and without losing any session functionality or data. If you want to maximize the hot backup potential of your SNA Server, you should assign LUs from more than one SNA Server in each LU pool. Thus, if an SNA Server stops working, pool users can still get LU access through another SNA Server. In fact, the pool users will probably not even be aware that a server has malfunctioned. See the "LU Pooling" section later in this chapter for more information.

Efficiency is achieved through load balancing, another direct benefit of SNA Server's advanced LU pooling feature. In multiple SNA Server configurations, load balancing is the capability of each SNA Server to automatically route new LU sessions to the least-busy SNA Server. This dynamic routing of traffic across multiple servers minimizes response time and improves user productivity. You can prevent automatic load balancing by specifying which SNA Server should run a particular transaction program (TP). You accomplish this by using unique TP names or by associating each TP with a unique local LU alias. If you do not require specific control over SNA Server choices, however, you can certainly gain efficiency by allowing the SNA servers to distribute new workloads automatically based on existing TP availability.

Part
VIII
Ch
39

Numerous Host Service Options   SNA Server provides several features that expand SNA connectivity. The addition of these features gives administrators the flexibility needed in today's mixed networking environments:

- Host Print service for LU 1, LU 3, Intelligent Printer Data Stream (IPDS), and SCS transparent mainframe printing, and SCS line printing and 3812 pass-through emulation AS/400 printing.

- Shared Folders service for allowing non-SNA clients to access AS/400 files using Windows NT Server file sharing.

- TN3270 service for TN3270 and TN3270E emulation, and TN3287 printing.

- TN5250 service for TN5250 emulation.

- APPC File Transfer Protocol (AFTP) and FTP-AFTP gateway service for file transfer between hosts and clients.

- ODBC/DRDA driver for Windows, Windows 95, Windows NT Workstation clients, and Windows NT Server for client access to DB2 mainframe and DB2/400 databases.

- 3270 and 5250 emulation applets for Windows, Windows 95, and Windows NT clients (one user license per server).

- Demo host facility for offline development, training, and product demonstrations.

Numerous Host Connectivity Options   SNA Server connects to the SNA network through a data link that is a combination of both hardware and software. The hardware is composed of a circuit board (communications adapter) that is installed in the SNA Server platform and provides a physical connection to the SNA network. These physical connections can be made using one of the following seven possible connection types:

- 802.2 connection type for Ethernet, token ring, or FDDI network configurations using the 802.2 communications protocol.

- Synchronous Data Link Control (SDLC) using leased telephone lines dedicated to the connection at all times, or switched telephone lines connected as needed.

- X.25 for public or private packet-switching networks using the X.25 Qualified Logical Link Control (QLLC) protocol.

- Distributed Function Terminal (DFT) using local coaxial cable or twisted pair for the direct physical connection to an IBM cluster controller.

- Channel, which provides a direct channel attachment to an IBM mainframe.

- Twinax, which provides a direct twinaxial connection to an IBM AS/400.

- Distributed Link Service, based on Microsoft's SNA Open Gateway Architecture (SOGA).

The software part of the data link is embedded in an SNA Server component called *Link Services*. It provides communications between the SNA Server and the hardware communications adapters. Although a single link can support only a single adapter, each link can support multiple sessions.

Comprehensive Client-Server Support   SNA Server supports all the SNA application programming interfaces (APIs), LU protocols, PU protocols, and data-link protocols. SNA APIs also support both synchronous and asynchronous calls. Synchronous calls support the native SNA communications schemes, but asynchronous calls can be more efficient in client-server environments. This is because asynchronous calls improve client-server I/O handling through the pipelining of I/O operations and independent processing of I/O requests while the application is performing other tasks.

The APIs supported by SNA Server include the following:

- APPC and EHNAPPC for developing 5250 emulators, as well as applications that communicate peer-to-peer with other APPC applications using the LU 6.2 protocol.
- CPI-C for developing applications that communicate peer-to-peer with other applications using the LU 6.2 protocol.
- CSV for developing applications that include tracing of API calls, communication with NetView, and EBCDIC-to-ASCII conversion.
- LUA for developing applications that need direct access to the LU 0, LU 1, LU 2, and LU 3 data streams.
- APPC Sync-point for developing distributed transaction-processing applications.

N O T E   The EHLLAPI for developing applications that interface with existing 3270 or 5250 applications is available from independent software vendors, but is not supplied by Microsoft. It is not currently included in the SNA Server applets. ▨

The LU protocols supported by SNA Server include:

- LU 0
- LU 1
- LU 2
- LU 3
- LU 6.2
- TN3270
- TN3270E
- TN3287
- TN5250

The PU protocols supported by SNA Server include:

- PU 2.0
- PU 2.1
- APPN LEN Node
- Downstream PUs (DSPUs)

Part

VIII

Ch

39

The data-link protocols supported by SNA Server include:

- 802.2/LLC
- SDLC
- X.25/QLLC
- DFT
- Twinax
- Channel
- Distributed Link Service

SNA Server also provides native support for many client-server protocols, including the following:

- TCP/IP
- Microsoft Networking (Named Pipes)
- Remote Access Service (RAS)
- IPX/SPX
- Banyan VINES IP
- AppleTalk

SNA Server's flexibility in the area of client-server support allows you to mix clients using these protocols together, in any fashion, on the same SNA Server. For example, you can mix NetWare clients running the IPX protocol with TCP/IP clients on the same SNA Server.

The number of client systems supported by SNA Server is large, so connecting to practically any client desktop system with SNA Server is relatively easy. The client systems currently supported by SNA Server are the following:

- Windows 3.x
- Windows for Workgroups
- Windows NT version 3.1
- Windows NT Workstation version 3.5 or later
- Windows 95
- MS-DOS
- Macintosh
- UNIX
- OS/2

Robust Administrative and Diagnostic Tools   As mentioned earlier, the tight integration of SNA Server with the Windows NT Server provides a number of graphical tools that you can use not only to manage the network but also to perform diagnostic appraisals of the network functions and components. The diagnostic tools allow you to monitor and trace events and collect event information leading up to a specific problem occurrence. Thus, with effective event monitoring, you can tell the exact state of the system at the time of the difficulty.

The SNA Server Manager program can dynamically provide data on the server status (inactive, pending, active, stopping), connection status (inactive, pending, active, stopping), and the LU status (active or inactive, associated user, computer name). The SNA Server Trace program, which can be executed without stopping the SNA Server, collects information on the activity between and within the SNA Server components. This information can be extremely valuable in diagnosing configuration problems and improving performance.

The RTM, an IBM NetView function that measures response time between a host and a 3270 session, is another valuable diagnostic tool, but for you to use it your 3270 emulator must be capable of supporting it. SNA Server Manager allows you to tailor the RTM by specifying such things as when the collected data should be sent and what triggers will cause the RTM to register responses from the host computer.

IBM's NetView is a network management system that runs on the IBM host. It is helpful to the network administrator because it receives alerts from the Windows NT system, or NT-based applications, and forwards these alerts to the host computer and the network administrator. It is also helpful in diagnosing problems and improving performance on the network. The NetView service that provides this functionality is called NVAlert. A companion service of NetView, NVRunCMD, runs as a background process on the SNA Server and is a command-line interface to the Windows NT Server. It is extremely useful in responding to NVAlert messages for diagnostic querying or for providing simple fixes to problems. For example, if a NetView operator receives an alert indicating an application could not find a particular file, the NetView operator could intervene by executing a command (via NVRunCMD) on the Windows NT Server to copy the file to an area where it could be found by the application needing it.

LU Pooling   LU pools are groupings of 3270, LUA, or downstream LUs organized by the administrator in such a way as to maximize access to the LUs in the pool. A pool user, LUA application, or downstream system can get LU access as long as only one of the pooled LUs is available and functioning. One or more LUs in the pool can cease to function without affecting pool access by other users, applications, or downstream systems, just as long as a single pool LU continues to work. The primary benefits of LU pooling are hot backup, load balancing, session efficiency, and administrative efficiency. For a brief discussion of hot backup and load balancing, see the section "Highly Secure, Reliable, and Efficient" earlier in this chapter.

Session efficiency applies to cases where intermittent users need to use a limited number of resources. These intermittent users could be pooled together to represent a smaller number of users and find their access needs sufficiently met. For example, if nine 3270 users need infrequent access to a particular resource, they may find that access is sufficiently provided by a pool of only four 3270 LUs.

Administrative efficiency is achieved through the administrator's use of the SNA Server Manager program to assign LU pools to users or groups of users. This eliminates the need to assign LUs to users individually. Additionally, with SNA Server's drag-and-drop functionality, creating pools and assigning users or groups to them is extremely fast and easy.

Part
VIII

Ch
39

Remote Access Service (RAS) Support   RAS allows network clients in remote locations to participate in the full functionality and features of the network. RAS servers can be configured on any Windows NT-based platform (including SNA Server) as long as SNA clients have access to SNA gateway resources from remote workstations. Connectivity for RAS can be achieved through the use of asynchronous dial-up modems, X.25 adapters, or ISDN connections. All SNA Server functions, application-to-application communications, administration, and emulation are possible with an RAS connection. Additionally, because RAS supports Windows NT logon and domain security disciplines, callback, and data encryption, secure network access by remote clients is ensured.

SNA Server version 2.1 put a new twist on this RAS feature. It is called the *SNA RAS*. It is similar in most respects to the RAS feature just described, but it has additional significant benefits in that it can use the SNA network itself as the physical connection between the RAS server and the SNA Server. Administrators can create virtual LAN connections between Windows NT systems across an existing SNA network by essentially integrating SNA Server's LU 6.2 transport with the standard RAS architecture. Because SNA RAS uses SNA remote transports such as synchronous X.25 and SDLC, there is no longer a need for corporate customers with large SNA-WAN backbones to have to create LAN-to-LAN networks or install dial-up modems in each remote branch office. Thus, network administrators who need to manage remote offices connected to corporate mainframes or AS/400s through existing SDLC lines can now do so easily.

Preparing for SNA Server

Before you install any network server, it is always wise to do some detailed preliminary planning. But preliminary planning becomes an absolute necessity when you are preparing for an SNA Server network environment. SNA Server environments are extremely varied in how they are put together and what they do. For example, SNA servers may access IBM mainframes, AS/400s, remote peer systems, or a combination of all three. Their communication lines and adapters also vary from slow speed to high speed and are capable of supporting a range of traffic loads from light to very heavy. Because SNA Server environments are so varied, the configuration parameters for any particular environment also must be varied. Fortunately, SNA Server was designed to supply many standard default values. Invariably, however, unique parameters for one thing or another seem to always be required to make your system work. It is, therefore, imperative that parameters be defined in advance, system constraints identified before installation, and configuration options intelligently selected to best fit the needs of the enterprise.

Selecting a Management Model

One of the first decisions you must make when planning the installation of SNA Server environments is how to organize the SNA Server domains. Two management models for organizing domain distributions are possible, with each one possessing certain advantages and disadvantages. You must have an understanding of the business enterprise requirements, the existing environment, applicable resource constraints, and enterprise growth projections to select a management model that is right for your particular enterprise, both today and in the future.

Branch Configuration of SNA Server Domains   In the branch model, SNA servers in the enterprise are geographically separated and spread out across multiple LANs, with each network domain containing one or more servers and the clients supported by those servers. An enterprise consisting of a corporate or home office and one or more branch offices is depicted in Figure 39.5. In this typical example, a different SNA server is physically located at each branch office and is part of the LAN supporting that branch office. The branch SNA server also is connected to the IBM front-end processor (PU 4) or AS/400 located at the home office or data center. This connection is a Synchronous Data Link Control (SDLC) connection using leased telephone lines (dedicated to the connection at all times) or switched telephone lines (connected only when needed).

FIG. 39.5

The view of a typical branch SNA Server configuration with geographically separated SNA servers supporting independent LANs.

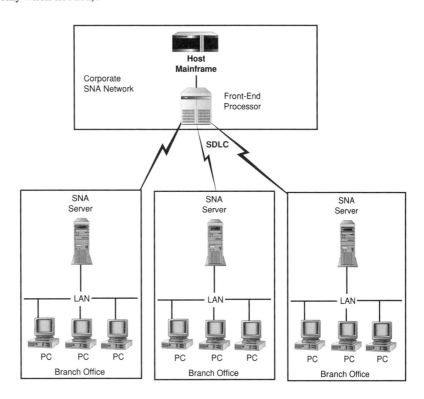

Part
VIII

Ch
39

Because each SNA server has its own communications link with the home office PU 4 or AS/400, transmission contention such as what would occur over a common WAN backbone is avoided. You also can install the SNA Server on an existing branch office server platform already being used for printing, e-mail, fax, and local database support. This would reduce traffic on the WAN between the branch office and the home office and increase responsiveness to branch users through local management control of connections, LUs, and security. Additionally, because branch office domains are typically smaller, server platforms could be smaller and SNA Server components would probably be easier to configure and manage. Because SNA

Server's graphical tools and remote administration features would be available via Remote Access Service (RAS) or NetView, there probably would not be a requirement for having trained SNA support personnel on site at the branch office to administer or troubleshoot the local SNA network. Another important consideration is that the distributed SNA Server configuration could easily take advantage of existing distributed networks and decrease the number and type of physical changes required to implement a new SNA Server network.

Centralized Configuration of SNA Server Domains   The alternative to the branch configuration of SNA servers is the centralized approach. With the centralized configuration, SNA servers are all in one place (a data center, for example) and on the same WAN with all the clients, regardless of location. These servers and clients all use the same networking protocol (TCP/IP, for example) to connect and communicate throughout the network. Using the example of the typical branch office enterprise environment once again, all the SNA servers would be located at the home office or central data center, as portrayed in Figure 39.6. Each branch office has its own LAN domain that is also a part of the enterprise WAN. Access to the SNA server(s) supporting the branch LAN is obtained via a combination of SDLC connections and WAN bridges or routers. Each SNA server in the data center is connected to the IBM front-end processor (PU 4) or AS/400 via a token ring LAN or directly attached to the host mainframe channel.

FIG. 39.6

The view of a typical centralized SNA Server configuration with SNA servers located in the same facility.

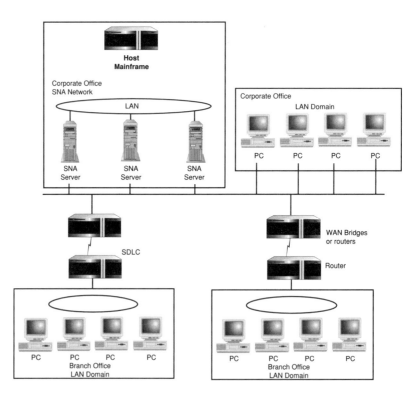

This centralized approach provides several benefits:

- Having the SNA servers located in one place maximizes reliability and security, facilitates the arrangement of hot backups and load balancing, simplifies server management, and reduces the potential need for SNA Server expertise at remote sites.
- The same WAN environment can be used for other purposes, as well, such as SQL Server, e-mail, and printer- and file-sharing support.
- Configuration is simplified because only one communications protocol is used throughout the WAN.

Filling Out the Planning Forms

Planning forms serve a useful function in identifying and organizing all the information required during SNA Server installation and configuration. Work with the system administrator of the remote host, peer, and/or downstream system to obtain the required information for the various forms. The following forms are included in the *Microsoft SNA Server Version 2.1 Administration Guide* and are reprinted in Appendix A of this book:

- Server Resources Planning Form
- Server Information Form
- Initial Connection Settings Form
- 802.2 Settings Form
- SDLC Settings Form
- X.25 Settings Form
- Channel Settings Form
- 3270 LUs Form (for Individual LUs)
- 3270 LUs Form (for Ranges of LUs)
- 3270 LU Pools Form
- Users and Groups Form
- Local APPC LUs Form
- Remote APPC LUs Form
- Mode Properties for LU-LU Pairs Form
- CPI-C Properties Form
- 3270 RTM Settings Form

Part
VIII

Ch
39

Defining Connectivity Options

As discussed earlier, communications between the SNA Server and the SNA network can occur over various types of connections, which are determined by the type of physical wire or cable across which the data is passed, the communications adapter installed in the SNA Server platform, and the communications protocol used to control the communications process.

Two of these connection types use special coaxial or other cables and adapters to connect directly to the IBM mainframe or AS/400 host. These are referred to as the *Channel* connection, which provides direct channel attachment to the mainframe, and the *Twinax* connection, which provides a twinaxial connection to an AS/400. Several other connection types are possible, with each type having an associated link service.

Link services allow the SNA Server to communicate with host, peer, or downstream computers over specific data links composed of communications adapters, physical wires or cables, and protocols. The following sections examine each of these connection types and their associated link services in more detail.

Data Link Control (DLC) 802.2 Link Service   This link service facilitates communications between the SNA Server and host, peer, or downstream computers over token ring, Ethernet, and FDDI LANs using the standard 802.2 communications protocol. For example, if your environment has client devices communicating with each other over a token ring or Ethernet network, and these client devices need to communicate with IBM mainframes, AS/400s, or other downstream SNA devices, the SNA Server should be configured with the DLC 802.2 link service (see Figure 39.7).

FIG. 39.7

The view of a typical environment suitable for the use of the DLC 802.2 link service.

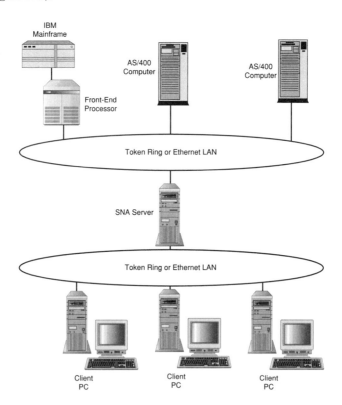

SDLC Link Service   The SDLC link service controls communications between the SNA Server and the host, peer, or downstream computers over telephone lines that are either *switched* or *leased* (see Figure 39.8). Switched lines are basically dial-up lines that are activated when you dial the telephone number of the computer to which you want to connect. Leased lines, on the other hand, are dedicated lines that are constantly active between the SNA Server and the host, peer, or downstream computer. Leased lines are essentially point-to-point type circuits that physically connect two geographically separated computers to each other.

FIG. 39.8

The view of a typical environment suitable for the use of the SDLC link service.

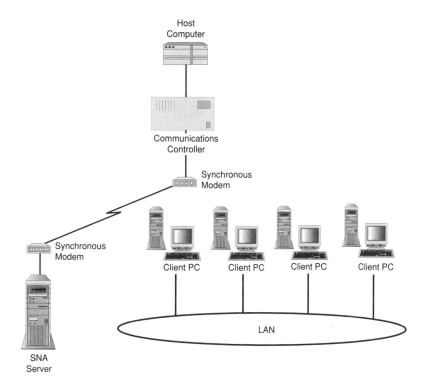

Another characteristic of the SDLC link service is the requirement for a full-duplex or half-duplex synchronous modem at each end of the telephone line. Data to be transmitted must pass from the computer, through the synchronous modem, and to the communications line for transmission to the distant end. Then, at the other end, the data being received must pass from the communications line, through another synchronous modem, and then into the receiving computer. The advantage of using a full-duplex modem is that the modem can accommodate two-way communications simultaneously. In other words, the modem can send and receive data at the same time. The half-duplex modem also can send and receive data, but not simultaneously. It must complete one operation (for example, sending data) before it can begin the other (receiving incoming data).

X.25 Link Service   This link service supports the communications between the SNA Server and the host, peer, or downstream computers through the use of *packet-switching networks*, as reflected in Figure 39.9. These packet-switching networks are classified as either *public* or *private*, depending on the accessibility of the network to the general public. Public packet-switched networks transmit data over public telephone circuits; whereas private packet-switched networks transmit data over private circuits installed and maintained for the exclusive use of the network owner.

FIG. 39.9
The view of a typical environment suitable for the use of the X.25 link service.

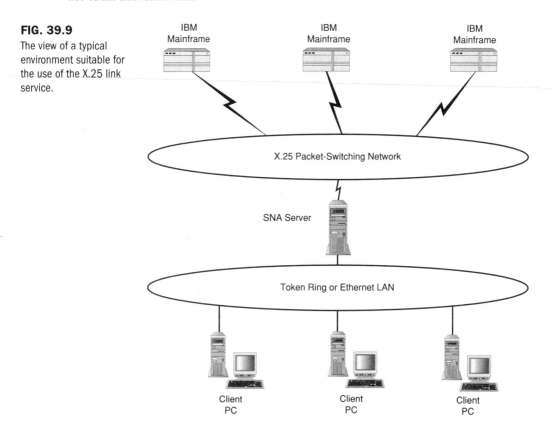

Public networks can reduce a corporation's line costs by using the existing communications lines of a communications service provider (AT&T, for example), but there are several reasons why a corporation may still need to pay the high installation and maintenance fees to have their own private network. For example, the corporation may have sufficiently high traffic loads to make a private network more cost effective, or they may need a packet-switched network in an area where public packet-switched services are not available. The increased security afforded through centralized management and control of the private network may also be sufficient justification for the high cost of owning and operating the private network. In many cases, however, the most cost effective solution is to utilize a mix of private and public packet-switching networks to handle nationwide communications needs.

N O T E The X.25 link service must use the X.25 Qualified Logical Link Control (QLLC) protocol when communicating in an SNA network environment. ■

Distributed Function Terminal (DFT) Link Service   The DFT link service controls the communications between the SNA Server and the host systems over coaxial cable or twisted-pair wire. The cable (or wire) directly connects the SNA Server to the IBM cluster controller, as shown in Figure 39.10. It is also possible to connect SNA Servers to peer systems via the mainframe host using this link service. Multiple sessions are supported by the DFT link service.

FIG. 39.10
The view of a typical environment suitable for the use of the DFT link service.

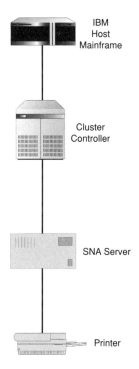

IBM
Host
Mainframe

Cluster
Controller

SNA Server

Printer

Part
VIII

Ch
39

Distributed Link Service   The Distributed Link Service, based on Microsoft's SNA Open Gateway Architecture (SOGA), implements the use of a LAN protocol (TCP/IP, IPX/SPX, or Banyan VINES IP) for communications between SNA Server computers at branch sites with SNA Server computers at a centralized site, as shown in Figure 39.11. LAN protocols are still used for communications between client computers and branch site SNA Server computers, and the SNA protocol is still used for communications between the host and centralized site SNA Server computers.

FIG. 39.11

The view of a typical environment suitable for the use of the Distributed Link service. Note that SNA servers are located at each site. This configuration combines the branch and centralized models discussed in the "Selecting a Management Model" section earlier in this chapter.

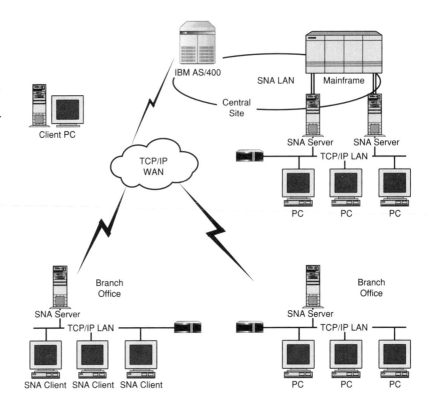

Understanding Client-to-SNA Server Protocols

SNA network client devices usually exist on a separate LAN connected to the SNA Server platform via an 802.2, SDLC, or X.25 connection. The network software and protocols for the client devices are dependent upon the network operating system controlling the client devices, as well as the physical adapter, contained within each client device, which allows that client device to communicate with the client LAN. You can configure SNA Server to support the following types of network software and protocols:

- Microsoft Networking (Named Pipes)
- Novell NetWare (IPX/SPX)
- Banyan VINES IP
- TCP/IP
- AppleTalk (for Macintosh networks)

Client platforms can be controlled by any one of several different operating systems as long as the proper networking software and protocols are used. In Figure 39.12, notice that for each operating system identified, at least one of the required combinations of networking software and/or protocols must be installed in the client device in order for the SNA Server to communicate with that client.

FIG. 39.12

Relationship of various client operating systems to required networking software and protocols.

For SNA Server Clients Running	One or More Required Network Software Protocols
Windows NT version 3.1 Windows NT Advanced Server version 3.1 Windows NT Server version 3.5 Windows NT Workstation version 3.5	Microsoft Networking (the network software included in Windows NT) NWLink of equivalent IPX/SPX services Microsoft TCP/IP or equivalent Win32 Windows Sockets version 1.1 interface Banyan Enterprise Client version 5.52 for Windows NT
Windows NT version 3.x Windows for Workgroups	The network software included in Windows for Workgroups LAN Manager version 2.x Novell Netware (IPX/SPX) version 3.10 or later, or any ODI driver Microsoft TCP/IP or equivalent Win32 Windows Sockets version 1.1 interface
MS-DOS operating system version 3.2 or later	LAN Manager version 2.x Novell Netware (IPX/SPX) version 3.10 or later Banyan VINES version 5.52
OS/2 operating system version 1.21 or later	No additional required
Macintosh Computer with System 6.0.2 or later and Finder version 6.0 or later	Macintosh platform with AppleTalk access Emulator software

Implementing Security

SNA Server security is provided and enforced through three different design factors, which when implemented properly provide a stable, highly controllable security environment meeting the government's stringent C2 security-level standard. These design factors are as follows:

- The SNA Server architecture itself
- The use of the Windows NT-based server operating systems
- The client logon process
- Single sign-on
- Password synchronization
- Data encryption

Part
VIII

Ch
39

Security Through the SNA Server Architecture　　The SNA Server architecture has been designed to make it impossible to bypass SNA Server security features. Regardless of which SNA Server components are communicating, and regardless of which transport components are being used for that communication, everything must pass through a single SNA Server component—the DMOD Service Layer. The DMOD enforces SNA security features by applying defined security constraints and conditions to all communications that pass through it.

Security Through Windows NT-Based Server Operating Systems　　Because SNA Server must operate under the control of a Windows NT Server operating system, the Windows NT security features provide the bulk of the security for SNA Server. This security involves controlling access at two different levels:

- Access to mainframe and/or AS/400 resources
- Access to the tools and files used to create or change accounts and LUs

Access to Mainframe and/or AS/400 Resources　　Remember that SNA Server uses the same user accounts database as the Windows NT-based servers, so you can specify which Windows NT domain users and groups will also be SNA Server users and groups. They have to be created only once for use by both Windows NT and SNA Server.

Mainframe access, however, is defined through use of the 3270 LU. So for users and/or groups to gain access to mainframes through 3270 emulation, they must be associated with 3270 LUs. You accomplish this by assigning specific 3270 LUs or LU pools (defined for mainframe access) to them. In this way, you can control access to the mainframe by controlling which 3270 LUs or LU pools are assigned to which users or groups of users.

Access to the Tools and Files Used to Create and Change Accounts and LUs In a way similar to that for the mainframe, access to the AS/400 is defined and controlled by the LU. But unlike the 3270 LU used by the mainframe, the design of LU 6.2 (the specific type of LU used with the AS/400) is not nearly as restrictive. As long as a user has an account in the Windows NT domain and has specific information about the 6.2-type LUs configured in SNA Server, that user can gain access to the AS/400 that those LUs communicate with. To prevent this, you must exercise tight control over accounts and LU information available to the users. Because this information is contained in the SNA Server configuration file, it is essential to control access to this file through the use of file-access restrictions and security permissions.

The capability to assign security permissions on a file-by-file basis is available in Windows NT, but only if the file to be protected is stored on an NT file system (NTFS) partition on the internal hard disk. If the file is stored on a file allocation table (FAT) or high-performance file system (HPFS) partition instead, file-level security features cannot be implemented. Therefore, always install SNA Server software on an NTFS partition. This is especially critical for SNA servers used in the primary and backup roles because they contain the main configuration files for all the other SNA servers in the domain.

Security Through the Client Logon Process The logon process is the first level of security for the SNA Server because the user is identified to the Windows NT domain and to the SNA servers through this process. If the user cannot be identified by the Windows NT server during logon, it does not give the user access to any domain resources, SNA Server resources included.

SNA Server handles the logon process differently depending on the networking software being used by the client system. If Microsoft Networking (used for Windows for Workgroups, Windows 95, Windows NT-based systems, and Windows or DOS systems running LAN Manager) is being used, a valid logon causes the user to be logged on across the network automatically through encryption and secure protocols. Thus a single correct logon gains a user access to both the Windows NT domain and all the SNA servers in the domain. Non-Microsoft Networking (such as Novell NetWare, TCP/IP, and Banyan VINES) requires two logons—one for access to the Windows NT domain and one for access to the SNA servers in the domain. The same password for both logons can be used, but no information is sent from the SNA Server to the client system until both logons have been completed successfully.

Single Sign-On One security problem that all administrators and users face is the use of multiple user names and passwords. This creates a potential security problem, since many users are forced to write their user names and passwords on paper, often in plain view for everyone to see. SNA Server solves this problem by implementing a single sign-on feature for APPC host connections. Thus, users need to remember only one user name and password for all APPC host and LAN/WAN connections. Once users log on to the Windows NT domain and start an APPC host application, SNA Server automatically logs the user into the APPC host application.

Password Synchronization   Users who access several network resources and host computers face the challenge of managing multiple passwords. This is especially true when users are required to change their password on a regular basis. SNA Server—along with third-party host software when needed—allows users to keep one password for all host and LAN/WAN connections. When users change their password as required for either the Windows NT domain or host, the password is automatically synchronized to the new password on all other systems.

Data Encryption   In an SNA environment, the username and password are sent from client to host as clear text, thus creating a potential security problem. SNA Server solves this problem with data encryption. Data encryption of communications between the SNA Server and client is implemented on a per-user basis.

Implementing Auditing

Auditing is a feature provided through the Windows NT Server operating system. The system performs auditing when specific events are recorded in an event log as they occur. When you set up the auditing feature, you can specify which events to audit. When the specified event occurs, such as a member of the Administrator Group changing the configuration file, for example, the system automatically records information concerning that event.

Auditing is also an important method of collecting security-related information. When auditing is used, however, system resources must be used for tracking and recording audited events. This means you pay a small price in performance overhead for each event audited. Additionally, if you audit numerous events, the size of the event log can quickly get very large. Therefore, you should carefully select which events to audit so that useless event log entries are avoided and system performance is not unnecessarily affected.

Choosing a Server Role

When planning for the SNA Server environment, one of the planning decisions you must make is how many SNA servers should be present in the network and what each of their roles should be. SNA server can be installed to function in any one of three different roles: primary server, backup server, or member server.

When the SNA Server is installed as a primary server, it contains the main configuration file for the entire domain. This configuration file contains information about the SNA Server resources available in the domain, such as link services, LUs, domain users, and so on. There can be only one primary SNA server in a domain, and typically it is the first one installed.

N O T E   As used in this section, the term "domain" actually refers to a subdomain under the Windows NT domain. Numerous SNA Server subdomains can exist under a single Windows NT domain, but each subdomain can have only one primary SNA Server (and up to 14 backup SNA servers). Thus, a Windows NT domain can support several primary SNA servers as long as each primary SNA Server is in a separate subdomain under the Windows NT domain. ■

You can install up to 14 backup SNA servers on the domain. Any of these backup servers can automatically take over as the primary server if the primary server ever fails or if domain connection to the primary server is ever lost. The primary SNA server ensures that a current read-only copy of the domain's main configuration file is replicated and stored on the backup SNA server(s) each time the configuration is changed and saved on the primary server. Then if the primary SNA server is ever lost, the backup SNA servers have all the necessary files and information about the domain to immediately take over the primary SNA server functions. Because the configuration file is a read-only copy of the main configuration file, it cannot be changed or saved while the backup server is functioning as the primary server. You can actively manage the current configuration, however, without altering the configuration file.

If the SNA server is not a primary or backup server, it has to be a member server. Member SNA servers do not contain configuration files, but they do perform normal SNA Server functions by applying configuration-file information as necessary through communications with the primary SNA server.

Installing SNA Server with the SNA Server Setup Program

Because the SNA Server Setup program requires the capability to access the Windows NT Registry, you must be logged on to the Windows NT Server as an administrator when you start the SNA Server Setup program. When you start the SNA Server Setup program, you see several dialog boxes concerning the license agreement, name and organization information, and SNA Server product identification number. If you have installed other Microsoft BackOffice products, you have undoubtedly seen similar dialog boxes for entering identification information. The buttons at the bottom of the dialog box allow you to continue with the Setup program after entering the information, go back to edit the information you have just entered, obtain help on the Setup program, and exit from the Setup program.

After completing the dialog boxes mentioned above, the Microsoft SNA Server Setup dialog box appears with the installation path. The default installation path displayed is C:\SNA. You can accept this default path or change the installation path to one of your own choosing. Be sure to type in the full installation path if you choose your own, and be careful to use an empty directory so that SNA Server Setup does not inadvertently overwrite files needed by other programs on your system.

Selecting SNA Server Components

A different Microsoft SNA Server Setup dialog box appears, starting the installation process. Clicking the only large button starts the installation process. You also can exit setup at this time. Clicking the large button brings up the Microsoft SNA Server Select Components dialog box, as shown in Figure 39.13. All components are listed to the left and a brief description of each component appears to the right when a component is selected. Double-clicking any component listed selects or deselects it, as denoted with the appearance or absence of a check mark next to the component. Specific Link Services are selected by checking the Link Services component and clicking the Change Option button. This brings up the Microsoft SNA Server Link Services dialog box, where you select or deselect specific link services.

FIG. 39.13

The Microsoft SNA Server Select-Components dialog box shows the components available for installation. Any components can be added or removed after the initial setup by running the setup program again.

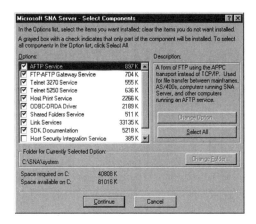

Entering Server Domain Account Information

The Setup program next prompts for a Windows NT domain, Windows NT user account, and password. The current Windows NT domain you are logged on is listed by default. The domain must be one in which you have administrative privileges, since SNA Server will run its services under this account. You can enter an existing account or have the Setup program create a new account by entering new information in the Server Domain Account Information dialog box. If a new account is created, it will then have the same privileges as the account currently logged on.

Choosing a License Mode

The Choose License Mode dialog box appears next. You must choose one of two client licensing modes—Per Server or Per Seat. In most cases, you will select the client licensing mode that is currently in place. The Per Server option gives you the opportunity to add or remove client licenses.

Selecting the Server Role

When the licensing mode setup actions have been completed, Setup directs you to designate a role for this SNA Server by displaying the Choose Server Role dialog box. For a description of the different SNA Server roles, see the section "Choosing a Server Role" earlier in this chapter.

The Primary Server option is automatically selected as the default. If this is the role you want the SNA Server to have, simply click the Continue button. Otherwise, click one of the other desired options. Because the SNA Server can be designated for only a single role, clicking one of the options clears the highlighting from any other option.

> **CAUTION**
>
> When an SNA server is going to function as a primary server, the SNA Server software needs to be installed on an NTFS hard disk partition so that file-level security permissions can be used to control access to critical configuration files. If necessary, exit SNA Server Setup, establish an NTFS partition on the SNA Server installation platform, and then rerun SNA Server Setup to install the SNA Server software on the NTFS partition.

Selecting Client-Server Protocols

The Setup program next checks for installed client-server protocols. If it detects more than one client-server protocol, the Select Client/Server Protocols dialog box appears (see Figure 39.14).

FIG. 39.14

The Select Client/Server Protocols dialog box shows all client-server protocols that have been automatically detected by the SNA Server Setup program.

The detected protocols become available for selection. Other protocols may be listed but may be grayed out and unavailable for selection if they were not detected on your system. You can deselect the protocol(s) you do not want SNA Server to use by clicking the marked check box.

Selecting a Network Subdomain Name

The last piece of information SNA Server needs is the network subdomain name. Starting with SNA Server version 2.11, several SNA Server subdomains can exist in a Windows NT domain. This facilitates the existence of several SNA primary servers in one Windows NT domain. Each SNA Server subdomain can contain one primary server and 14 backup servers. At least one of the SNA Server subdomains can have the same name as the Windows NT domain. After entering a subdomain name in the Network Subdomain Name dialog box and clicking Continue, the Setup program begins to install components to the hard disk.

Completing Installation of SNA Server

The SNA Server Setup program displays the Microsoft SNA Server Setup dialog box when the SNA Server software files have been successfully installed. At this point, there is still a significant number of SNA Server configuration tasks that need to be accomplished by running the SNA Server Manager program. These tasks are explained in detailed in Chapter 40, "Building SNA Server."

The following items are contained in the Microsoft SNA Server (Common) menu, which is accessible from the Programs menu of the Start menu:

- 3270 Applet
- 32bit ODBC Administrator
- 5250 Applet
- Host Account Manager
- Host Security Setup
- Manager
- Release Notes
- SDK Documentation
- Setup
- SNA Formats Guide
- Trace
- Trace Viewer

Part

VIII

Ch

39

Using the SNA Server Setup Program After Initial Installation

When you run Setup from the Microsoft SNA Server (Common) menu, one of the first things it does is check for the presence of installed SNA Server files and configuration data. If it detects your completed installation and finds the configuration file, it asks whether you want to stop SNA Server services and then displays the Microsoft SNA Server Setup dialog box. From this dialog box, you can perform the following tasks:

- **Add/Remove.** Adds or removes SNA Server components.
- **Reinstall.** Repeats the last installation of SNA Server and restores missing files and settings.
- **Remove All.** Removes SNA Server.

Changing SNA Server Properties

Follow these steps to redefine the SNA subdomain name, network transports (client-server protocols), and SNA Server role:

1. In the Windows NT Server Start Menu, choose Programs, Microsoft SNA Server (Common), and then Manager.

2. Select the SNA Server computer from the SNA Server directory tree located in the left pane of Microsoft SNA Server Manager.

3. Either right-click the SNA Server and select Properties, or choose View, Properties.

4. When the SNA Server Properties dialog box appears, click the Server Configuration tab and then click Change.

5. When the Server Configuration dialog box appears, change the SNA subdomain name, network transports (client-server protocols), and SNA Server role as needed, and click Save.

From Here...

This chapter briefly introduced the basic concepts of IBM's SNA and how the Microsoft SNA Server fits into a typical SNA network environment. Required SNA Server installation actions were covered in detail, including some of the recommended preinstallation planning activities and postinstallation uses of SNA Server Setup.

The following chapters provide related information:

■ For information on using the Windows NT Server administrative tools as the SNA Server administrator, see Chapter 7, "Administering Windows NT Server."

■ For information on building the SNA Server and establishing the connections between the SNA Server and the host mainframe or AS/400 system, and configuring the logical units and downstream connections so that clients can access network resources, see Chapter 40, "Building SNA Server."

■ For information on managing the SNA Server on a daily basis as the SNA Server administrator, see Chapter 41, "The Role of the SNA Server Administrator."

Building SNA Server

by Daniel Garcia and Jim Marshbank

After the initial installation of SNA Server has been successfully completed, you must use the SNA Server Manager program to build SNA Server. This initial build process requires you to configure the server and the SNA Server-to-host connections. Then you must implement the SNA Server (make it operational) by configuring the logical units (LUs).

This chapter examines the concepts and procedures for configuring SNA Server, configuring the SNA Server-to-host connections, and configuring the logical units (LUs). Additionally, this chapter examines the procedures for configuring SNA Server's alternative host connectivity features, including the Host Print Service, TN3270 Service, TN5250 Service, and Shared Folders Service.

When you have completed the procedures in this chapter for your particular installation, your SNA server should be capable of supporting client communications with the host system. ■

How to configure your SNA Server

Learn what is needed to configure the properties of an SNA Server.

How to add and configure link services

Learn what the link service properties are and how to add and configure link services.

How to complete the detailed configuration of SDLC, 802.2, X.25, and Channel connections

See additional configuration tabs for each of these connections and gain an understanding of what the different configuration parameters actually do.

How to create and configure logical units (LUs)

Learn what the different LU types actually do. Then follow a series of detailed, step-by-step procedures to create and configure your 3270, APPC, LUA, and downstream LUs individually or several at one time.

How to configure the Host Print Service

Learn how to provide 3270 and 5250 printer emulation to allow clients to print to a network printer from mainframe and AS/400 applications.

Configuring Your SNA Server

Start SNA Server Manager by opening the Start Menu and choosing Programs, Microsoft SNA Server (Common), and Manager. This causes the SNA Server Manager display to appear as shown in Figure 40.1. The SNA Server Manager window has the look and feel of Windows NT Explorer. The window is double-paned—the left pane displays the domain hierarchy of SNA Servers and services, while the right pane displays the contents of an item selected on the left pane.

FIG. 40.1

The SNA Server Manager is used to configure and manage SNA servers.

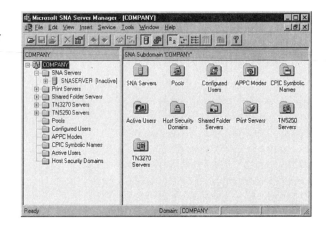

Perform the following steps to configure your SNA server:

1. In the left pane, select the server to be configured from the SNA Servers folder.

2. From the View menu, choose Properties; or right-click the SNA Server selected and click Properties. The Server Properties dialog box appears (see Figure 40.2).

FIG. 40.2

The first step in building an SNA server is configuring it. The SNA Server Properties dialog box is used to define the basic parameters for the SNA server.

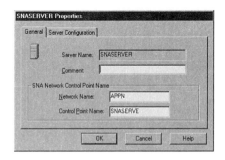

3. In the Comment box, enter any comment you want to assign to the server. Comments can be up to 25 characters long. You may want to enter a comment, for example, that describes the role of the server (primary, backup, and so on), or you can leave this box blank. Entries in this box are optional.

4. In the SNA Network Control Point Name area, enter the Network Name and Control Point Name if required. Generally, if the SNA Server will be accepting incoming calls that use Format 3 Exchange Identifiers (XIDs) (the default type of incoming call identifiers), or if it is to be used for 6.2-type LUs, you should specify both the Network Name and the Control Point Name. These two names work together to identify this local server node to the other network resources. For this reason, if either of the names is supplied, the other name also should be supplied. The SNA host system administrator should advise you as to whether these two names are required, and if so, what the names should be.

When used, each name can contain up to eight alphanumeric characters (including the special characters @, #, and $). Lowercase letters are automatically converted to uppercase.

5. Click OK.

N O T E When you are connecting to a host system and you are using a Network Name, the Network Name must match the NETID parameter in the VTAM Start command for the local VTAM system, and the Control Point Name must match the CPNAME parameter in the PU definition for the host.

When you are connecting to an AS/400 system, the Network Name must match the RMTNETID parameter in the AS/400 APPC controller description. If this value is *SAME, then use the Local Network ID parameter in the AS/400 Network Attributes display (use the DSPNETA command). The Control Point Name must match the RMTCPNAME parameter in the AS/400 APPC controller description. ▪

Adding Link Services

A *link service* defines the protocol used between the SNA Server software and the installed communications adapter and enables communication with that adapter's device driver.

Perform the following steps to add a link service to your SNA server:

1. In the left pane, select the server to add link services to from the SNA Servers folder.

2. From the Insert menu, select Link Service; or right-click the server, select Insert and click Link Service. The Insert Link Service dialog box appears (see Figure 40.3).

FIG. 40.3

Most of the link services listed in the Insert Link Service dialog box reflect the manufacturer of the communications adapter and link service type.

3. Select the desired link service and click <u>A</u>dd. The Properties dialog box for that link service appears.

N O T E Several link services can only be installed using the setup program from the earlier version of SNA Server. To add these link services, open SNA Server Manager, and choose External Link Services from the <u>T</u>ools menu. The Setup program from the earlier version of SNA Server appears. The same options as described in "Configuring Link Services" later in this chapter are available in this setup as well. ▨

Depending on the link service being added, additional tabs may appear to solicit your input of required configuration constraints. For example, if you select the Barr Systems SDLC link service (for the Barr T1-SYNC adapter card), an additional tab appears for card configuration settings.

If you add the DLC 802.2 link service, SNA Server checks for the presence of DLC software. If none is detected, a message box appears informing you that you must install DLC software before continuing.

Configuring Link Services

You have to properly configure the link services before adding an SNA Server-to-host connection. The following sections discuss how to configure link services.

DLC 802.2 Link Service   Follow these steps to configure the DLC 802.2 link service:

1. Add the DLC 802.2 Link Service. The DLC 802.2 Link Service Properties dialog box appears, as shown in Figure 40.4.

FIG. 40.4

Icons represent token rings or Ethernet local area networks in use with DLC 802.2 connections.

If you have already added this link service, select the Link Services folder under the appropriate SNA server on the left pane of SNA Server Manager. Select the link service to configure; then choose <u>V</u>iew, <u>P</u>roperties, or right-click the selected link service and click <u>P</u>roperties. The DLC 802.2 Link Service Properties dialog box will then appear.

2. In the Title box of the DLC 802.2 Link Service Properties dialog box, either accept the default title or enter a new title name for this link service. Title names can be up to 40 characters long.

3. In the Adapter box, click the drop-down list box to display the list of communications adapter cards. Then select the communications adapter card you are using.

4. In the Local Service Access Point (SAP) box, enter the local SAP number, which is used for access to certain services on an 802.2 connection within an SNA network. This number, which is usually four for an SNA Server, must be evenly divisible by four and be in the range from 4 to 252.

5. Click OK. SNA Server Manager copies the required files and displays the Insert Link Service dialog box. You can add more new link services now if you choose.

6. Click Finish to create adapter bindings and return to SNA Server Manager.

N O T E If your SNA environment includes an SNA server on an Ethernet LAN and communications between SNA Server and remote hosts, peers, or downstream systems is accomplished via routers, you may have to make adjustments to the Windows NT Registry. The FrameType Registry entry indicates the type of frames the 802.2 link service needs to send over the Ethernet LAN. You need to ensure that the frame type used by SNA Server matches the frame type used by the routers. Check with the local network support staff to determine what type of frames the routers pass.

The FrameType can only be set on an SNA Server and is in the following Registry section:

`HKEY_LOCAL_MACHINE\SYSTEM\CurrentControlSet\Services\DLCLinkServiceName\`
`Parameters\ExtraParameters`

SDLC Link Service   Follow these steps to configure the SDLC link service:

1. Add the SDLC Link Service. The SDLC Link Service Properties dialog box appears, as shown in Figure 40.5.

FIG. 40.5
The SDLC icon is displayed for SDLC connections.

If you have already added this link service, then select the Link Services folder under the appropriate SNA server on the left pane of SNA Server Manager. Select the link service to configure; then choose View, Properties, or right-click the link service selected and click Properties. The SDLC Link Service Properties dialog box will then appear.

2. The Mode Settings tab is shown by default. In the Service Title box, either accept the default title or enter a new service title name for this link service. Service Title names can be up to 40 characters long.

3. The Line Type area contains three options. Choose one by clicking the radio button adjacent to the option. The options include the following:

   - **Leased.** Choose this option if you will be using a dedicated telecommunications line.

   - **Switched: Modem-Stored Number.** Choose this option if your modem is capable of storing a phone number and is configured to dial the number when the Data Terminal Ready status is detected. See "Using Server-Stored Numbers" later in this chapter.

   - **Switched: Manual Dial.** Choose this option if you will be manually dialing the phone number when prompted by the SNA Server.

4. Click the Constant RTS (Request To Send) check box if you want the SDLC adapter to be in constant readiness to send data. In this mode, the adapter keeps a high priority on maintaining its own RTS state and signals the remote end to set a high priority on maintaining its CTS (Clear To Send) state, as well.

   In contrast, if Constant RTS is turned off (by clicking the marked Constant RTS check box to clear the mark), the SDLC adapter must establish its RTS state and then wait for the remote end to establish its CTS state before the adapter can send data. Therefore, transmission delays are minimized when RTS is on. For higher throughput, turn on RTS whenever you can.

CAUTION

Constant RTS must be turned on if the link service is configured for use by a full-duplex connection, and it must be turned off if the link service is configured for use by a multidrop connection.

---

5. Click the Card Configuration tab. Depending on the specific SDLC link service, several settings appear asking you to enter information applicable to your communications adapter—Adapter Type, Interrupt, IRQ Level, DMA, DMA Channel, DMA Level, Base Address, I/O Address, Data Rate, Maximum BTU Size, Internal Clocking, Device Name. Consult your specific adapter's documentation for information about your card's configuration settings.

N O T E   The IBM SDLC and IBM MCPA adapters lack coprocessors. Therefore, they cannot handle full-duplex transmission at high transmission speeds. If you are using one of these adapters and want to use a transmission speed greater than 9600 baud, you must use the SNA Server Manager program to set the half-duplex mode for the adapter. ▪

6. If the Dialer Settings tab is available in the SDLC Link Service Properties dialog box, select it and configure the following setting as indicated:

- **COM Port.** Select the number of the COM port. For example, for COM2, select 2.

- **Baud Rate.** Select the desired transmission rate. The default is 9600.

- **Incoming String.** Type the command string to be sent to the modem when an incoming call is detected. If your modem accepts the standard AT command set, the default command string (AT&F&C1&S1&D3&Q1Q1S0=1) will be appropriate in most cases. See "Modem Command Strings" later in this chapter.

- **Outgoing String.** Type the command string to be sent to the modem when an outgoing call is detected. If your modem accepts the standard AT command set, the default command string (AT&F&C1&S1&D3&Q1Q1S0=0DT) will be appropriate in most cases. See "Modem Command Strings" later in this chapter.

7. Click OK. SNA Server Manager copies the required files and displays the Insert Link Service dialog box. You can add more new link services now if you choose.

8. Click Finish to create adapter bindings and return to SNA Server Manager.

X.25 Link Service   To configure the X.25 link service, follow these steps:

1. Add the X.25 Link Service. The X.25 Link Service Properties dialog box appears, as shown in Figure 40.6.

FIG. 40.6

The IBM X.25 Link Service Properties dialog box for a computer using an IBM SDLC communications adapter on dedicated communications lines.

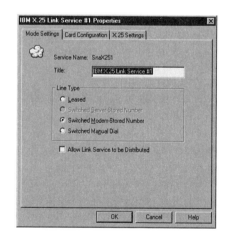

If you have already added this link service, then select the Link Services folder under the appropriate SNA server on the left pane of SNA Server Manager. Select the link service to configure; then choose View, Properties, or right-click the link service selected and click Properties. The X.25 Link Service Properties dialog box will then appear.

2. The Mode Settings tab is shown by default. In the Title box, either accept the default title or enter a new service title name for this link service. Service Title names can be up to 40 characters long.

3. The Line Type area contains four options. Choose one of these options by clicking the radio button adjacent to the option. The options are as follows:

- **Leased.** Select this option if you are using dedicated lines.

- **Switched Server-Stored Number.** Select this option if the adapter card to which your synchronous modem is attached has a serial port built into it.

- **Switched Modem-Stored Number.** Select this option if your modem can store a phone number. Make sure that you configure your modem to dial the stored number when it senses a Data Terminal Ready (DTR) status.

- **Switched Manual Dial.** Select this option if you will be dialing the number manually when prompted by the SNA Server.

4. Click the Card Configuration tab. Depending on the specific SDLC link service, several settings appear asking you to enter information applicable to your communications adapter—Adapter Type, Interrupt, DMA, DMA Channel, Base Address, I/O Address, Device Name. Consult your specific adapter's documentation for information about your card's configuration settings.

5. If the Dialer Settings tab is available in the X.25 Link Service Properties dialog box, select it and configure the following settings as indicated:

- **COM Port.** Select the number of the COM port. For example, for COM2, select 2.

- **Baud Rate.** Select the desired transmission rate. The default is 9600.

- **Incoming String.** Type the command string to be sent to the modem when an incoming call is detected. If your modem accepts the standard AT command set, the default command string (AT&F&C1&S1&D3&Q1Q1S0=1) will be appropriate in most cases. See "Modem Command Strings" later in this chapter.

- **Outgoing String.** Type the command string to be sent to the modem when an outgoing call is detected. If your modem accepts the standard AT command set, the default command string (AT&F&C1&S1&D3&Q1Q1S0=0DT) will be appropriate in most cases. See "Modem Command Strings" later in this chapter.

6. Click the X.25 Settings tab to configure X.25 communications.

7. In the Local NUA Address box, enter the local X.25 address. The address must be 15 decimal digits in length with no embedded spaces. The last 3 digits are used to route information between stations having the same 12-digit address. No defaults are available for this box.

8. The Default L3 Window Size parameter applies only to switched virtual circuit (SVC) connections and specifies the maximum number of packets that can be transmitted before an acknowledgment from the receiver is required. In the Default L3 Window Size box, accept the default value of 2; or click the drop-down list box to display the full list of possible values and then click the desired value to be used as the default L3 window size.

9. The Default L3 Packet Size setting defines the maximum length of the data each packet can contain when transmitted over SVC connections. In the Default L3 Packet Size box, accept the 128 standard default setting; or click the drop-down list box to expand the list

box and display all the allowable values, and then click the desired value to be used as the default L3 packet size.

10. The L2 Window Size parameter specifies the number of frames that can be sent to the network by the SNA Server before an acknowledgment from the receiver is required. In the L2 Window Size box, accept the standard default of 7; or click the drop-down list box to expand the list box and display all the allowable settings, and then click the desired setting to be used as the default L2 window size.

11. The T1 Timeout parameter defines the length of time a local station (system) should wait for a receiving station to respond to a transmission before it tries the transmission again. This parameter is specified in tenths of a second, with the allowable range being from 1 to 100, and the default value being 30. In the T1 Timeout box, either accept the default or enter another number in the allowable range, being careful to use a number greater than the normal frame relay time needed between the local and remote systems.

12. The N2 Retry Limit box specifies the maximum number of times a particular transmission should be attempted. The allowable range is from 1 to 100, with the default being 10. Either accept the default or enter another valid number.

13. The Accept Reverse Charge check box indicates whether the SNA Server should accept incoming calls that are flagged to have the long distance charges reversed or charged to the receiving SNA Server. Reverse charge calls are indicated by the data contained in the call packet. Click the empty check box to select it if you want the incoming reverse charge calls to be accepted by the SNA Server.

14. The Startup Restart check box indicates whether a restart should be performed each time the link is activated. The default setting is for the restart to be performed each time. Click the marked check box to turn off the option so that a restart will not be performed each time the link is activated.

15. The Incoming Filter check box indicates whether calls to X.25 addresses other than the local one are filtered out. The default setting is for the calls to be filtered out. Click the marked check box to turn off the option so that calls to X.25 addresses other than the local one will not be filtered out.

16. The Select Standby check box indicates whether a standby line can be used. A standby line is essentially a backup line included on some modems that can handle the transmission in the event the primary modem line fails. The default setting has this option turned off. Click the empty check box to turn on the option for the standby (backup) line to be selected to handle the transmission.

17. Channel range specifications for your X.25 link must agree with the configuration used by your X.25 carrier. Therefore, you must specify a channel range for at least one of the channel types using the X.25 link service in accordance with the following guidelines. The only default available is for the Two-Way SVC channel. That default is 0001-0004:

- Channel numbers may range from 1 to 4096.

- When entering channel numbers, you must use the format A–B where A represents the beginning channel number, and B represents the ending channel number.

Part
VIII

Ch
40

- Although there is no requirement for the number of channels used by switched or permanent virtual circuit types, the total number of channels among all types must be from 1 to 16.

- Channel number ranges must be unique and cannot overlap.

- At least one SVC incoming or SVC two-way channel must have a range specified if incoming calls are to be received.

- A PVC channel range must be specified if a PVC connection uses the link service.

- When configuring more than one channel type, assign channel numbers to the selected channel types in ascending order, adhering to the following channel type ordering sequence from the lowest channel numbers to the highest channel numbers: PVCs (use lowest channel numbers), incoming SVCs, two-way SVCs, and outgoing SVCs (use highest channel numbers).

18. In the Data Rate box, you can leave the data rate default set to High, or click the Low radio button to set the data rate to a slower speed if your line quality is poor and errors occur at the high rate setting.

19. Because encoding specifies the encoding pattern for the data, it must be set the same for both the sending and receiving computers. In the Encoding box, leave the default set to NRZ (nonreturn to zero), or click the NRZI (nonreturn to zero inverted) radio button to switch to the NRZI encoding scheme.

20. If other options are displayed, select the appropriate option or supply the additional information as required.

21. Click OK. SNA Server Manager copies the required files and displays the Insert Link Service dialog box. You can add more new link services now if you choose.

22. Click Finish to create adapter bindings and return to SNA Server Manager.

DFT Link Service   To configure the DFT link service, perform the following steps:

1. Add the DFT Link Service. The DFT Link Service Properties dialog box appears (see Figure 40.7).

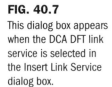

FIG. 40.7

This dialog box appears when the DCA DFT link service is selected in the Insert Link Service dialog box.

If you have already added this link service, then select the Link Services folder under the appropriate SNA server on the left pane of SNA Server Manager. Select the link service to configure; then choose <u>V</u>iew, <u>P</u>roperties, or right-click the link service selected and click <u>P</u>roperties. The DFT Link Service Properties dialog box will then appear.

2. Examine the current title of the link service and leave it as is if it is acceptable. Otherwise, delete the default title and enter a new title for the link service. Title names can be up to 40 characters long.

3. In the DFT Base Addresses Available box, either accept the default address or select a new address for the adapter.

4. If additional DFT adapters need to be configured, add the link service again and select a different DFT Base Address.

5. Click OK. SNA Server Manager copies the required files and displays the Insert Link Service dialog box. You can add more new link services now if you choose.

6. Click <u>F</u>inish to create adapter bindings and return to SNA Server Manager.

Twinax Link Service   To configure the Twinax link service, perform the following steps:

1. Add the Twinax Link Service. The Twinax Link Service Properties dialog box appears (see Figure 40.8).

FIG. 40.8
This dialog box appears when the IBM Twinax link service is selected in the Insert Link Service dialog box.

If you have already added this link service, then select the Link Services folder under the appropriate SNA server on the left pane of SNA Server Manager. Select the link service to configure; then choose <u>V</u>iew, <u>P</u>roperties, or right-click the link service selected and click <u>P</u>roperties. The Twinax Link Service Properties dialog box will then appear.

2. Examine the current title of the link service and leave it as is if it is acceptable. Otherwise, delete the default title and enter a new title for the link service. Title names can be up to 40 characters long.

3. In the <u>I</u>nterrupt box, select the interrupt for the adapter.

4. In the I/O Address box, select the I/O address for the adapter.

5. In the Page Address box, select the computer's memory address space the adapter will use. This setting only appears for IBM twinax adapters.

6. In the Work Station Address box, select the workstation address for the adapter. The workstation address must match the host's workstation address.

7. Click OK. SNA Server Manager copies the required files and displays the Insert Link Service dialog box. You can add more new link services now if you choose.

8. Click Finish to create adapter bindings and return to SNA Server Manager.

Channel Link Service   To configure the Channel link service, perform the following steps:

1. Add the Channel Link Service. The Channel Link Service Properties dialog box appears, as shown in Figure 40.9.

FIG. 40.9

This dialog box appears when the Polaris ESCON link service is selected in the Insert Link Service dialog box.

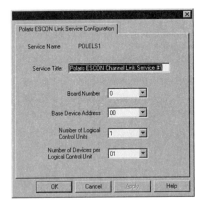

If you have already added this link service, then select the Link Services folder under the appropriate SNA server on the left pane of SNA Server Manager. Select the link service to configure; then choose View, Properties, or right-click the link service selected and click Properties. The Channel Link Service Properties dialog box will then appear.

2. Examine the current title of the link service and leave it as is if it is acceptable. Otherwise, delete the default title and enter a new title for the link service. Title names can be up to 40 characters long.

3. Several settings are present depending on the specific Channel link service. Enter information applicable to your communications adapter. Consult your specific adapter's documentation for information about your card's configuration settings.

4. Click OK. SNA Server Manager copies the required files and displays the Insert Link Service dialog box. You can add more new link services now if you choose.

5. Click Finish to create adapter bindings and return to SNA Server Manager.

Distributed Link Service   Configuring SNA Servers for the Distributed Link Service (DLS) involves configuring SNA servers at a central site and branch sites. Configuring the SNA server at a central site involves adding one or more link services. In order to make these link services distributed or available to a branch site SNA server, select the Allow Link Service to be Distributed check box. This option is located on the default tab of a link service Properties dialog box.

Configuring the SNA server at a branch site involves the following steps:

1. Add the Distributed Link Service. The Distributed Link Service Link Service Properties dialog box appears, as shown in Figure 40.10.

FIG. 40.10

The Distributed Link Service is added and configured on SNA servers located at branch sites.

If you have already added this link service, then select the Link Services folder under the appropriate SNA server on the left pane of SNA Server Manager. Select the link service to configure; then choose <u>V</u>iew, <u>P</u>roperties, or right-click the link service selected and click <u>P</u>roperties. The Distributed Link Service Properties dialog box will then appear.

Part
VIII

Ch
40

2. Examine the current title of the link service and leave it as is if it is acceptable. Otherwise, delete the default title and enter a new title for the link service. Title names can be up to 40 characters long.

3. In the <u>L</u>ink Type box, select a distributed enable link type that exists on an SNA server at the central site.

4. In the <u>R</u>emote Link Services box, enter the name of the link service on the SNA server using the format \\<i>server</i>\<i>service</i>.

5. In the <u>A</u>lternate Link Services box, enter the names of alternate or backup link services on the SNA Server computer using the format \\<i>server</i>\<i>service</i>.

6. Click OK. SNA Server Manager copies the required files and displays the Insert Link Service dialog box. You can add more new link services now if you choose.

7. Click <u>F</u>inish to create adapter bindings and return to SNA Server Manager.

Using Server-Stored Numbers

If you choose Switched Server-Stored Number for a line type when configuring your link service, the following modem setup requirements must be fulfilled in order for a phone number to be accepted from the SNA Server:

- Accept dial commands in ASCII format consisting of eight data bits, no parity bit, and one stop bit.
- Do not dial when the DTR signal is sensed.
- When ready to accept dial commands, set Clear To Send (CTS) and Data Set Ready (DSR) to on.
- After accepting the dial command, set DSR to off.
- Set DSR back to on only when the dialed connection is made.
- Change to the synchronous mode after completing dial-up.
- Change back to the dial-up mode if DTR status is lost and then reacquired.

Modem Command Strings

When the SNA Server creates a dial string to send to the modem, it actually appends the phone number specified through SNA Server Manager to the outgoing command string supplied through the installation and configuration of the SDLC link service by the SNA Server Setup program. For modems that accept the standard AT command set, the outgoing default command string of AT&F&C1&S1&D3&Q1Q1S0=0DT will probably be appropriate. Using this command string as a reference, the effect each element has on the modem is described in the following list:

- **AT** is the standard prefix for modem command strings.
- **&F** instructs the modem to reset itself to its initial factory-installed defaults.
- **&C1** instructs the modem to track the status of the Carrier Detect (CD) line.
- **&S1** instructs the modem to raise the Data Set Ready (DSR) line after it has dialed.
- **&D3** instructs the modem to reset when the Data Transmit Ready (DTR) line is lost.
- **&Q1** instructs the modem to go into command mode and switch to the synchronous mode after dialing.
- **Q1** turns off the modem result codes.
- **S0=0** sets the modem for outgoing calls by turning off the auto-answer mode.
- **DT** instructs the modem to dial the number following it (the one appended by the SNA Server) using tone dialing. If this element were DP, the modem's actions would be the same except that pulse dialing would be used instead of tone dialing.

The incoming default command string (AT&F&C1&S1&D3&Q1Q1S0=1) will also probably work well for modems that accept the standard AT command set. The elements do the same thing as in the outgoing command string just described, except that the S0=1 element instructs the modem to answer the phone after one ring.

Configuring SNA Server-to-Host Connections

A connection is assigned to the SNA Server in SNA Server Manager. This connection makes communications between the SNA Server and the host system possible. But before the connection can be configured, a specific connection type must be selected and assigned to the SNA Server. After that, a two-phase configuration process occurs in which the properties common to essentially all the connection types are configured, and then the properties unique to each connection type are configured. The following sections discuss these procedures in detail, for each connection type, from the perspective of a new installation. For the most part, these procedures also supply sufficient guidance for viewing and/or modifying existing connection configurations.

Assigning New Connections to the SNA Server

To assign a new SNA Server-to-host connection, complete these steps:

1. In the left pane of SNA Server Manager, select the SNA server to add a connection.

2. From the Insert menu, select Connetion, and then select the connection type to add—SDLC, 802.2, X.25, Channel, DFT, TwinAx. The Connection Properties dialog box appears (see Figure 40.11).

FIG. 40.11
The General tab settings reflect the characteristics of the connection.

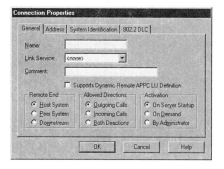

Part
VIII

Ch
40

Configuring Common Connection Properties

In the Connection Properties dialog box, the General tab is used to configure properties common to all the connection types. After you configure the common properties in the General tab, additional properties specific to the connection type you have assigned for your SNA Server-to-host communications are configured by selecting the other tabs present. This section details the steps required to configure the common connection properties. The following sections then detail the procedures for configuring the basic and advanced properties for each connection type.

The following steps detail the procedure for configuring the properties common to all the different connection types:

1. In the Name box, enter a unique name for this connection. The name has a maximum length of eight alphanumeric or special (@, #, and $) characters and cannot be the reserved name SNASERVR.

N O T E The first step is really a continuation of the procedure described earlier for assigning a new connection to the SNA Server. The last step of that procedure concluded with the Connection Properties dialog box (for the connection type assigned) displayed. ▪

2. In the Comment box, enter any comment up to 25 characters. Entries in this box are optional.

3. In the Link Service box, click the drop-down list box and select the desired link service from the list. Remember the link service allows this connection to access your installed communications adapter. If the link service you need is not listed, you must cancel this part of the configuration and go back to add the appropriate link service.

4. In the Remote End area of the Connection Properties dialog box, select the remote system type for this particular connection. If this is a "direct-connect" connection (Channel type, Twinax type, or DFT type), the correct remote end is automatically selected. The available types are as follows:

   - **Host System.** This is usually a mainframe system that controls interactions to the devices connected to it. If this connection will be using dependent Advanced Program-to-Program Communication (APPC), select this type of remote system. Also, select this type of remote system if this connection will be used for 3270 or LUA LUs.

   - **Peer System.** This can be any size computer system that communicates with another computer system on an equal basis, and each computer system shares communications control. Do not select this type of remote system if the connection will be using dependent APPC.

   - **Downstream.** This can be any client system that accesses host connections available on the SNA Server directly instead of using the SNA Server client-server interface.

N O T E Downstream connections cannot be the DFT, Twinax, or Channel connection type but can be of the 802.2, X.25, or SDLC type. ▪

5. In the Allowed Directions area of the Connection Properties dialog box, select the appropriate call directions: Outgoing Calls, Incoming Calls, or Both Directions. The default selection is the Outgoing Calls option. For an SDLC-type downstream connection, Outgoing Calls must be selected. For Channel, Twinax, and DFT connections, the call direction is preselected.

6. The Activation setting applies only to outgoing calls. Therefore, if the Allowed Directions setting (described in step 7) includes outgoing calls, a default option will be highlighted. You can accept the default option or override it by making your own selection. If the connection is configured to accept incoming calls, the connection starts listening for calls whenever the SNA Server starts. The options for the Activation setting are as follows:

   - **On Server Startup.** This is the default option for 802.2 and DFT connections. When this option is selected, the connection starts whenever the SNA Server used by this connection starts. This option results in faster access time for the first user who connects after SNA Server startup and is the best choice when communications line charges are fixed regardless of time used rather than assessed for only the time used. Therefore, this option is best for X.25 permanent virtual circuit connections, SDLC leased-line connections, and 802.2 connections.

- **On Demand.** This is the default option for all connection types except 802.2 and DFT connections. When this option is selected, the connection starts when the user tries to activate an LU session on the connection and it stops when the session is completed. The cost benefits of this option are obvious as line charges are assessed only for the time used. This option would be best suited for SDLC switch-line connections and X.25 switched virtual circuit connections.

- **By Administrator.** When this option is selected, the administrator must control the connection activation on a case-by-case basis.

7. Click the other tabs to configure additional properties for SDLC, 802.2, X.25, and Channel connections; or click OK to accept these initial configuration settings and exit the dialog box. Because DFT and Twinax connections only require the settings in the General tab of the Connection Properties dialog box, their configurations are completed by also clicking OK.

Completing Configuration of SDLC Connections

After the initial connection settings have been made in the Connection Properties dialog box, use the following steps to configure additional SDLC connection properties:

1. Click the Address tab in the Connection Properties dialog box (see Figure 40.12).

FIG. 40.12

Use the Address tab to define the address parameters for an SDLC connection.

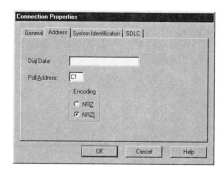

2. In the Dial Data box, enter the telephone number (up to 40 characters) of the modem to be called. If your modem is attached to an SDLC adapter with a built-in COM port, it probably is capable of accepting a phone number from the SNA Server. In this case, enter the phone number that the SNA Server should send to your modem. Be sure to use the format expected by your modem. If your modem accepts only manually dialed numbers, then enter the phone number as it should appear in the pop-up message when the SDLC connection starts.

N O T E The Dial Data box in the Address tab is available only if the SDLC connection is using a switched line. Because leased SDLC lines are essentially point-to-point lines not requiring a phone number to establish the distant-end modem connection, this Dial Data box is not available for SDLC connections using leased lines. ■

3. In the Poll Address box, either accept the C1 default value or enter a two-digit hexadecimal number that uniquely identifies this SNA Server connection to the remote system. If the remote system is an IBM host mainframe, contact the host system administrator for the ADDR parameter in the VTAM PU definition. The poll address and the ADDR parameter must match. If the remote system is a peer system, however, the poll address can be any value except those reserved for special use (00 and FF).

4. In the Encoding box, specify the encoding scheme your modem should use for this connection. Both the local and remote modems should use the same encoding scheme. Also, when multiple SDLC connections using the same link service will be accepting incoming calls, the encoding scheme for all the connections must match. The two possible schemes are Nonreturn to Zero (NRZ) and Nonreturn to Zero Inverted (NRZI). Contact your host system administrator to determine the NRZI setting in the LINE/ GROUP definition in VTAM. Your modem's encoding scheme must match this setting. If VTAM does not specify a setting, use the standard default setting of NRZI.

5. Click the System Identification tab in the Connection Properties dialog box, shown in Figure 40.13.

FIG. 40.13

The System Identification tab allows you to define identification parameters for an SDLC connection.

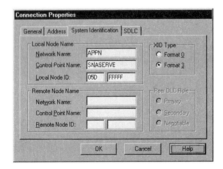

6. In the Local Node Name area, enter the Local Node ID, an eight-digit hexadecimal value that uniquely identifies the local SNA Server to the remote host, peer, or downstream system. After the first three digits (the block number) of the Local Node ID are typed, the cursor positions itself in the second half of the Local Node ID box so that the remaining five digits (the node number) can be entered. Be sure that you use the same Local Node ID for all the connections and link services on this SNA Server. The default Local Node ID value is 05D FFFFF. The block number portion of the Local Node ID cannot be 000 or FFF, and the node number portion cannot be 00000, as these values are reserved.

N O T E   Coordinate the Local Node ID value with the remote system administrator so that
corresponding VTAM parameters in the host system can be set up to match the Local Node
ID. For host systems, the block number should match the IDBLK variable, and the node number should
match the IDNUM variable in the VTAM PU definition.

7. In the Remote Node Name area, enter the Network Name and Control Point Name if
    they are required. The Network Name identifies the remote system's SNA network
    and is required if you will be using Format 3 XIDs. Likewise, the Control Point Name
    identifies the remote system on the SNA network and is required if Format 3 XIDs will
    be used.

    These two names work together to identify this system to the other network resources.
    For this reason, if either of the names is supplied, the other name should also be
    supplied. The SNA host system administrator should advise you as to whether these two
    names are required, and if so, what the names should be.

N O T E   When you are connecting to a host system and you are using a remote Network Name, the
name must match the NETID parameter in the VTAM Start command for the remote VTAM
system. The remote Control Point Name also must match the SSCPNAME parameter in the VTAM Start
command for the remote VTAM system. In such cases, the remote Network Name and remote Control
Point Name should be supplied by the remote system administrator.

    When used, each name can contain up to eight alphanumeric characters (including
    the special characters @, #, and $). Lowercase letters are automatically converted to
    uppercase.

    If this connection will access an AS/400 host, use the network name of the AS/400 in the
    Network Name box and the AS/400 name in the Control Point Name box.

8. Also in the Remote Node Name area, enter the Remote Node ID, an eight-digit hexadeci-
    mal value that uniquely identifies the remote host, peer, or downstream system. The
    remote system administrator should provide the proper value to enter. After the first
    three digits (the block number) of the Remote Node ID are typed, the cursor positions
    itself in the second half of the Remote Node ID box so that the remaining five digits (the
    node number) can be entered. The block number portion of the Remote Node ID cannot
    be 000 or FFF, and the node number portion cannot be 00000, as these values are
    reserved.

9. In the XID Type area, specify the type of identifying information the SNA Server should
    send. Two formats (types) are available: Format 0 and Format 3. When Format 0 XIDs
    are used, only the Node ID is sent. You should use this type only for hosts that do not
    support Format 3 XIDs, which send up to 100 bytes of identification information,
    including the Local Node ID and Control Point Name. If independent APPC LUs are
    going to be used on this connection, Format 3 XIDs must be specified. Format 3 is also
    the default XID type.

10. Click the SDLC tab in the Connection Properties dialog box, shown in Figure 40.14.

FIG. 40.14

You use the SDLC tab to
define SDLC parameters
for an SDLC connection.

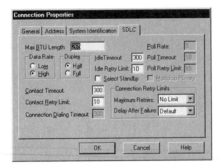

11. In the Max BTU Length box, either accept the default value of 265 or enter a new value
from 265 through 16393 to represent the maximum length of the *basic transmission unit*
(BTU). A BTU, also known as an *I-frame*, is the number of bytes that can be transmitted
in a single data-link control frame. If you are using a mainframe host connection, the
Max BTU length should be equal to or less than the value specified for the MAXDATA
parameter in the VTAM PU definition. If you are using a downstream connection, you
should specify a Max BTU length equal to or less than the maximum supported value of
the downstream system. Contact the host or downstream system administrator for the
values to use.

12. In the Data Rate area, select the setting appropriate for your modem. The Low setting
increases the reliability of transmissions over lines that are noisy and produce errors at
higher rates of speed. The High setting gives faster transmissions and is the default
setting.

TROUBLESHOOTING

There are errors occuring at the High setting. Poor-quality lines may be the problem. Try transmitting
with the Low setting selected to see if the errors disappear.

13. In the Duplex area, select the setting appropriate for your modem. If you did not set the
Constant RTS option for any of your adapters during installation using the SNA Server
Setup program, then only the default setting of half-duplex (Half) is available. Otherwise,
both half-duplex and full-duplex (Full) are available.

N O T E   Because IBM SDLC and MPCA adapters cannot handle full-duplex transmission at high
speeds due to the lack of a coprocessor, you should use the half-duplex setting when you
want to use transmission speeds greater than 9600 baud. ▪

14. In the Contact Timeout box, either accept the default value of 300 or enter a new value
from 5 through 300 to represent the length of time, in tenths of a second, the local

system should wait after an unsuccessful connection attempt before trying to connect to the remote system again. Contact timeout is applicable only for outgoing calls and, therefore, is ignored for incoming calls.

15. In the Contact <u>R</u>etry Limit box, either accept the default value of 10 or enter a new value from 1 to 20 to specify the maximum number of times the local system should attempt to make a given connection. Contact timeout is only applicable for outgoing calls and, therefore, is ignored for incoming calls.

16. In the Connection <u>D</u>ialing Timeout box, either accept the default value of 300 or enter a new value from 10 through 500 to represent the length of time, in seconds, the user or modem will have to actually dial the number of the remote system. This setting is available only when switched SDLC lines are used for outgoing calls. If manual dialing is required, allow sufficient time for the remote system to answer and establish the connection.

17. In the <u>I</u>dle Timeout box, either accept the default value of 300 or enter a new value from 1 through 300 to represent the length of time, in tenths of a second, the local system should wait for a transmission response before trying again. The idle timeout is only applicable for sessions in which the SNA Server is functioning in a secondary link role and, therefore, affects all host mainframe and some peer system sessions.

18. In the Idle <u>R</u>etry Limit box, either accept the default value of 10 or enter a new value from 1 through 255 to represent the number of times the local system should attempt to transmit data to the remote system without getting a response. The idle retry limit is applicable only for sessions in which the SNA Server is functioning in a secondary link role and, therefore, affects all host mainframe and some peer system sessions.

19. For the <u>S</u>elect Standby check box, the default for this setting is off (the check box is empty, or unmarked). If your modem is capable of supporting a standby line and you want to activate that capability, simply click the <u>S</u>elect Standby check box to select it.

20. In the <u>P</u>oll Rate box, either accept the default value of 5 or enter a new value from 1 through 50 to represent the number of polls per second that should occur. Poll rate can be specified only if the remote system is a peer or downstream system. Otherwise, this box is unavailable.

21. In the Poll <u>T</u>imeout box, either accept the default value of 10 or enter a new value from 1 through 300 to represent the length of time, in tenths of a second, the local system should wait for a poll response before polling the remote system again. Poll timeout is applicable only for sessions in which the SNA Server is functioning in the primary link role and, therefore, affects all downstream and some peer system sessions.

22. In the Poll Retry <u>L</u>imit box, either accept the default value of 10 or enter a new value from 1 through 255 to represent the number of times the local system should poll the remote system without getting a poll response. The poll retry limit is applicable only for sessions in which the SNA Server is functioning in the primary link role and, therefore, affects all downstream and some peer system sessions.

23. Click the <u>M</u>ultidrop Primary check box to select it if you are using a leased line for the SDLC connection to a downstream system and the SNA Server will be functioning as a

primary node communicating with multiple secondary nodes at the same time (using the same transmission mechanisms). Deselect the check box when the SNA Server is not functioning in a multidrop capacity.

24. If you want to change the connection activation limit defaults (also called *retry timers*), change the settings in the Connection Retry Limits area. The two activation limits available for modification are described in the following list:

   - **Maximum Retries.** This is the number of times the SNA Server should attempt to establish the connection with the host. When the specified number of unsuccessful attempts has been made, the SNA Server quits trying and makes the appropriate entries in the event log. Any number of attempts can be specified, from 1 through No Limit, with No Limit being the default.

   - **Delay After Failure.** This is the number of seconds the SNA Server should wait after each failed attempt before it tries once again to establish the connection. The permissible range for this timer limit is from 5 seconds to 255 seconds, with 10 seconds being the default.

25. Click OK to accept the settings and exit the SDLC Connection Properties dialog box, or click Cancel to exit the dialog box without accepting the settings.

Completing Configuration of 802.2 Connections

After the initial connection settings have been made in the Connection Properties dialog box, use the following steps to configure additional 802.2 connection properties.

1. Click the Address tab in the Connection Properties dialog box (see Figure 40.15).

FIG. 40.15
Use the Address tab to define the address parameters for a DLC 802.2 connection.

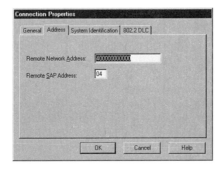

2. In the Remote Network Address box, enter the 12-digit hexadecimal network address of the remote host, peer, or downstream system. This network address should be provided by the SNA host system administrator or network administrator. The standard default Remote Network Address is 400000000000.

3. In the Remote SAP Address box, enter the remote system access point (SAP) address, or as recommended in most cases, accept the default of 04. SAP addresses must be two-digit hexadecimal numbers, evenly divisible by four, in the hexadecimal range between

04 and EC. Coordinate with the remote system administrator to determine the proper Remote SAP Address value.

4. Click the System Identification tab in the Connection Properties dialog box, shown in Figure 40.16.

FIG. 40.16

Use the System Identification tab to define identification parameters for a DLC 802.2 connection.

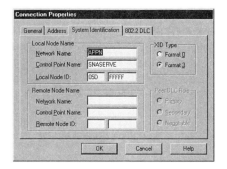

5. In the Local Node Name area, enter the Local Node ID, an eight-digit hexadecimal value that uniquely identifies the local SNA Server to the remote host, peer, or downstream system. After the first three digits (the block number) of the Local Node ID are typed, the cursor positions itself in the second half of the Local Node ID box so that the remaining five digits (the node number) can be entered. Be sure that you use the same Local Node ID for all the connections and link services on this SNA Server. The default Local Node ID value is 05D FFFFF. The block number portion of the Local Node ID cannot be 000 or FFF, and the node number portion cannot be 00000, as these values are reserved.

N O T E Coordinate the Local Node ID value with the remote system administrator so that corresponding VTAM parameters in the host system can be set up to match the Local Node ID. ▨

6. In the Remote Node Name area, enter the Network Name and Control Point Name, if required. The Network Name identifies the remote system's SNA network and is required if you will be using Format 3 XIDs. Likewise, the Control Point Name identifies the remote system on the SNA network and is required if Format 3 XIDs will be used. These two names work together to identify this system to the other network resources. For this reason, if either of the names is supplied, the other name should also be supplied. The SNA host system administrator should advise you as to whether these two names are required, and if so, what the names should be.

When used, each name can contain up to eight alphanumeric characters (including the special characters @, #, and $). Lowercase letters are automatically converted to uppercase.

If this connection will access an AS/400 host, use the Network Name of the AS/400 in the Network Name box and the AS/400 name in the Control Point Name box.

Part

VIII

Ch

40

N O T E When you are connecting to a host system, and you are using a remote Network Name, the name must match the NETID parameter in the VTAM Start command for the remote VTAM system. Also, the remote Control Point Name must match the SSCPNAME parameter in the VTAM Start command for the remote VTAM system. In such cases, the remote Network Name and remote Control Point Name should be supplied by the remote system administrator. ▪

7. Also in the Remote Node Name area, enter the Remote Node ID, an eight-digit hexadecimal value that uniquely identifies the remote host, peer, or downstream system. The remote system administrator should provide the proper value to enter. After the first three digits (the block number) of the Remote Node ID are typed, the cursor positions itself in the second half of the Remote Node ID box so that the remaining five digits (the node number) can be entered. The block number portion of the Remote Node ID cannot be 000 or FFF, and the node number portion cannot be 00000, as these values are reserved.

8. In the XID Type area, specify the type of identifying information the SNA Server should send. Two formats (types) are available: Format 0 and Format 3. When Format 0 XIDs are used, only the Node ID is sent. This type should be used only for hosts that do not support Format 3 XIDs, which send up to 100 bytes of identification information, including the Local Node ID and Control Point Name. If independent APPC LUs are going to be used on this connection, Format 3 XIDs must be specified. Format 3 is also the default XID type.

9. Click the 802.2 DLC tab in the Connection Properties dialog box, shown in Figure 40.17.

FIG. 40.17

The DLC 802.2 tab is used to define DLC 802.2 parameters for a DLC 802.2 connection.

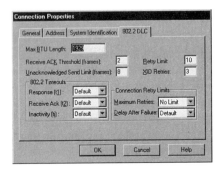

10. In the Max BTU Length box, enter the maximum length of the basic transmission unit (BTU), using values in the range from 265 to 16393. A BTU, also known as an I-frame, is the number of bytes that can be transmitted in a single data-link control frame (see Figure 40.18).

11. In the Receive ACK Threshold (frames) box, either accept the default value of 2 or enter a new value from 1 through 127 to represent the maximum number of frames the local system can receive before it is required to send a response to the remote system.

12. In the Unacknowledged Send Limit (frames) box, either accept the default value of 8 or enter a new value from 1 through 127 to represent the maximum number of frames the local system can send before it receives a response from the remote system.

FIG. 40.18

These are the suggested Max BTU lengths to use under the stated conditions.

Criteria	Default Value	Suggested Max BTU Length
For host connections		< or = MAXDATA parameter in VTAM PU definition
For downstream connections		< or = maximum value supported by the downstream system
For token ring adapter transmitting at 4 Mbps	1929	< or = 4195
For token ring adapter transmitting at 16 Mbps	1929	16393
For Ethernet adapter	1493	< or = 1493

13. In the Response (t1) box for 802.2 Timeouts, enter the amount of time the local system should wait before attempting to retransmit to a nonresponding remote system. This setting has two default values. One is for a remote system on a local ring (default is expressed in milliseconds), and the other is for a remote system on a remote ring (default is expressed in seconds). These default values are 400 milliseconds and 2 seconds, respectively. If you choose to enter a specific timeout value rather than accepting the default values, the timer always waits the specified amount of time regardless of whether the remote system is on a local or a remote ring. Therefore, it is usually best to use the default values if they are sufficient.

14. In the Receive ACK (t2) box for 802.2 Timeouts, enter the maximum amount of time the local system should wait before acknowledging receipt of a transmission. This setting should be less than the value used for the Response Timeout (t1) setting. Acknowledgments are sent automatically at the expiration of this timer unless some other condition has already prompted an acknowledgment. This setting has two default values. If the remote system is on a local ring, the default value is 80 milliseconds; and if the remote system is on a remote ring, the default value is 800 milliseconds. If you choose to enter a specific timeout value rather than accept these default values, the timer always waits the specified amount of time regardless of whether the remote system is on a local or a remote ring. Therefore, it is usually best to use the default values if they are sufficient.

15. In the Inactivity (ti) box for 802.2 Timeouts, enter the maximum amount of time the local system should wait before shutting down an inactive link. This setting has two default values, depending on whether the remote system is on a local or remote ring. These default values are 5 seconds and 25 seconds, respectively. If you choose to enter a specific timeout value rather than accept these default values, the timer always waits the specified amount of time regardless of whether the remote system is on a local or remote ring. Therefore, it is usually best to use the default values if they are sufficient.

16. In the Retry Limit box, enter the number of times, from 0 to 255, the SNA Server should retransmit a frame without receiving a response from the remote host, peer, or

downstream system. The default value is 10. If 0 is used for the retry limit, the SNA Server will use its internal default retry limit.

17. In the XID Retries box, either accept the default value of 3 or enter a new value from 0 through 30 to represent the number of times the local system should retransmit an identifying message when the remote system is not responding.

18. If you want to change the connection activation limit defaults (also called *retry timers*), change the settings in the Connection Retry Limits area. The two activation limits available for modification are described as follows:

   - **Maximum Retries.** This is the number of times the SNA Server should attempt to establish the connection with the host. When the specified number of unsuccessful attempts has been made, the SNA Server quits trying and makes the appropriate entries in the event log. Any number of attempts can be specified, from 1 through No Limit, with No Limit being the default.

   - **Delay After Failure.** This is the number of seconds the SNA Server should wait after each failed attempt before it tries once again to establish the connection. The permissible range for this timer limit is from five seconds to 255 seconds, with ten seconds being the default.

19. Click OK to accept the settings and exit the 802.2 Connection Properties dialog box, or click Cancel to exit the dialog box without accepting the settings.

Completing Configuration of X.25 Connections

After the initial connection settings have been made in the Connection Properties dialog box, use the following steps to configure additional X.25 connection properties:

1. Click the Address tab in the Connection Properties dialog box, shown in Figure 40.19.

FIG. 40.19

The Address tab lets you define address parameters for an X.25 connection.

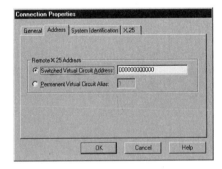

2. In the Remote X.25 Address area, enter the 12-digit or 15-digit hexadecimal Switched Virtual Circuit Address of the remote host, peer, or downstream system. If you use a 15-digit address, the last three digits are used for routing between host, peer, and downstream systems having the same 12-digit address. This network address should be provided by the SNA host system administrator or network administrator. If the host is a

system using VTAM, this address value also must match the DIALNO parameter in the VTAM PORT definition.

3. Click the System Identification tab in the Connection Properties dialog box, shown in Figure 40.20.

FIG. 40.20

You use the System Identification tab to define identification parameters for an X.25 connection.

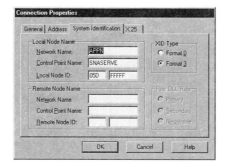

4. In the Local Node Name area, enter the Local Node ID, an eight-digit hexadecimal value that uniquely identifies the local SNA Server to the remote host, peer, or downstream system. After the first three digits (the block number) of the Local Node ID are typed, the cursor positions itself in the second half of the Local Node ID box so that the remaining five digits (the node number) can be entered. Be sure that you use the same Local Node ID for all the connections and link services on this SNA Server. The default Local Node ID value of 05D FFFFF can be used if the connection is using a permanent virtual circuit (PVC) because the destination address will be preset. The block number portion of the Local Node ID cannot be 000 or FFF, and the node number portion cannot be 00000, as these values are reserved.

N O T E Coordinate the Local Node ID value with the remote system administrator so that corresponding VTAM parameters in the host system (if used) can be set up to match the Local Node ID. Ensure the block number matches the IDBLK parameter, and the node number matches the IDNUM parameter value in the VTAM PU definition.

5. In the Remote Node Name area, enter the Network Name and Control Point Name if they are required. The Network Name identifies the remote system's SNA network and is required if you will be using Format 3 XIDs. Likewise, the Control Point Name identifies the remote system on the SNA network and is required if Format 3 XIDs will be used. These two names work together to identify this system to the other network resources. For this reason, if either of the names is supplied, the other name should also be supplied. The SNA host system administrator should advise you as to whether these two names are required, and if so, what the names should be.

When used, each name can contain up to eight alphanumeric characters (including the special characters @, #, and $). Lowercase letters are automatically converted to uppercase.

Part

VIII

Ch

40

If this connection will access an AS/400 host, use the network name of the AS/400 in the Network Name box and the AS/400 name in the Control Point Name box.

NOTE When you are connecting to a host system, and you are using a remote Network Name, the name must match the NETID parameter in the VTAM Start command for the remote VTAM system. Also, the remote Control Point Name must match the SSCPNAME parameter in the VTAM Start command for the remote VTAM system. In such cases, the remote Network Name and the remote Control Point Name should be supplied by the remote system administrator. ■

6. Also in the Remote Node Name area, enter the Remote Node ID, an eight-digit hexadecimal value that uniquely identifies the remote host, peer, or downstream system. The remote system administrator should provide the proper value to enter. After the first three digits (the block number) of the Remote Node ID are typed, the cursor positions itself in the second half of the Remote Node ID box so that the remaining five digits (the node number) can be entered. The block number portion of the Remote Node ID cannot be 000 or FFF, and the node number portion cannot be 00000, as these values are reserved.

7. In the XID Type area, specify the type of identifying information the SNA Server should send. Two formats (types) are available: Format 0 and Format 3. When Format 0 XIDs are used, only the Node ID is sent. This type should be used only for hosts that do not support Format 3 XIDs that send up to 100 bytes of identification information, including the Local Node ID and Control Point Name. If independent APPC LUs are going to be used on this connection, Format 3 XIDs must be specified. Format 3 is also the default XID type.

8. Click the X.25 tab in the Connection Properties dialog box, shown in Figure 40.21.

FIG. 40.21
Use the X.25 tab to define X.25 parameters for an X.25 connection.

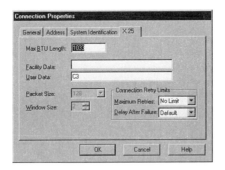

9. In the Max BTU Length box, either accept the default value of 256 (host connections) or 1033 (peer connections), or enter a new value from 265 through 16393 to represent the maximum length of the basic transmission unit (BTU). A BTU, also known as an I-frame, is the number of bytes that can be transmitted in a single data-link control frame. If you are using a mainframe host connection, the Max BTU length should be equal to or less than the value specified for the MAXDATA parameter in the VTAM PU definition. If you are using a downstream connection, you should specify a Max BTU length equal to or

less than the maximum supported value of the downstream system. Contact the host or downstream system administrator for the values to use.

10. In the Facility Data box, enter up to 126 hexadecimal characters to request non-default X.25 network functions for a particular SVC connection. If required, this facility data information string can be obtained from your network and/or remote system administrator. The Facility Data box is available only for connections using SVCs.

11. In the User Data box, either accept the default value of C3 (specifies the QLLC protocol) or enter an even number of hexadecimal characters (32 maximum) to supply required user data to the network. One of the primary pieces of user information supplied in this way is the communications protocol used by the X.25 network. Required user data strings can be obtained from your network administrator. The User Data box is available only for connections using SVCs.

12. In the Packet Size box, either accept the default value of 128, or enter a new value from the following permissible set of values: 64, 128, 256, 512, or 1024. This value represents the maximum number of bytes, not including header information, that can be transmitted in a single frame. Coordinate with your network administrator to determine this value. Packet size is applicable only to connections using PVCs.

13. In the Window Size box, either accept the default value of 2 or enter a new value from 1 through 7 to represent the maximum number of frames the local system can send without receiving a response from the remote system. Coordinate with the remote system administrator to determine this value. Window size is applicable only to connections using PVCs.

14. If you want to change the connection activation limit defaults (also called retry timers), change the settings in the Connection Retry Limits area. The two activation limits available for modification are described in the following list:

   - **Maximum Retries.** This is the number of times the SNA Server should attempt to establish the connection with the host. When the specified number of unsuccessful attempts has been made, the SNA Server quits trying and makes the appropriate entries in the event log. Any number of attempts can be specified, from 1 through No Limit, with No Limit being the default.

   - **Delay After Failure.** This is the number of seconds the SNA Server should wait after each failed attempt before it tries once again to establish the connection. The permissible range for this timer limit is from 5 seconds through 255 seconds, with 10 seconds being the default.

15. Click OK to accept the settings and exit the X.25 Connection Properties dialog box, or click Cancel to exit the dialog box without accepting the settings.

Completing Configuration of Channel Connections

After the initial connection settings have been made in the Connection Properties dialog box, use the following steps to configure additional Channel Attached connection properties:

1. Click the Address tab in the Connection Properties dialog box, shown in Figure 40.22.

Part
VIII

Ch
40

FIG. 40.22

You use the Address
tab to define address
parameters for a
Channel connection.

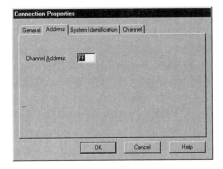

2. In the Channel <u>A</u>ddress box, either accept the FF default value or enter a two-digit
   hexadecimal number from 00 through FF that uniquely identifies this channel.

3. Click the System Identification tab in the Connection Properties dialog box (see
   Figure 40.23).

FIG. 40.23

Use the System
Identification tab to
define identification
parameters for a
Channel connection.

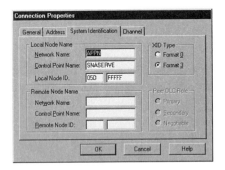

4. In the Local Node Name area, enter the <u>L</u>ocal Node ID, an eight-digit hexadecimal value
   that uniquely identifies the local SNA Server to the host system. After the first three
   digits (the block number) of the <u>L</u>ocal Node ID are typed, the cursor positions itself in
   the second half of the <u>L</u>ocal Node ID box so that the remaining five digits (the node
   number) can be entered. Be sure that you use the same <u>L</u>ocal Node ID for all the
   connections and link services on this SNA Server. The default <u>L</u>ocal Node ID value is
   05D FFFFF. The block number portion of the <u>L</u>ocal Node ID cannot be 000 or FFF, and
   the node number portion cannot be 00000, as these values are reserved.

N O T E   Coordinate the <u>L</u>ocal Node ID value with the host system administrator so that corresponding VTAM parameters in the host system can be set up to match the <u>L</u>ocal Node ID. For
host systems, the block number should match the IDBLK variable, and the node number should match
the IDNUM variable in the VTAM PU definition. ■

5. In the Remote Node Name area, enter the Net<u>w</u>ork Name and Control <u>P</u>oint Name if
   they are required. The Net<u>w</u>ork Name identifies the remote system's SNA network and
   is required if you will be using Format 3 XIDs. Likewise, the Control <u>P</u>oint Name

identifies the remote system on the SNA network and is required if Format 3 XIDs will be used. These two names work together to identify this system to the other network resources. For this reason, if either of the names is supplied, the other name should also be supplied. The SNA host system administrator should advise you as to whether these two names are required, and if so, what the names should be.

When used, each name can contain up to eight alphanumeric characters (including the special characters @, #, and $). Lowercase letters are automatically converted to uppercase.

N O T E   When you are connecting to a host system, and you are using a remote Network Name, the name must match the NETID parameter in the VTAM Start command for the remote VTAM system. Also, the remote Control Point Name must match the SSCPNAME parameter in the VTAM Start command for the remote VTAM system. In such cases, the remote Network Name and the remote Control Point Name should be supplied by the remote system administrator. ■

6. Also in the Remote Node Name area, enter the Remote Node ID, an eight-digit hexadecimal value that uniquely identifies the remote host, peer, or downstream system. The remote system administrator should provide the proper value to enter. After the first three digits (the block number) of the Remote Node ID are typed, the cursor positions itself in the second half of the Remote Node ID box so that the remaining five digits (the node number) can be entered. The block number portion of the Remote Node ID cannot be 000 or FFF, and the node number portion cannot be 00000, as these values are reserved.

7. In the XID Type area, specify the type of identifying information the SNA Server should send. Two formats (types) are available: Format 0 and Format 3. When Format 0 XIDs are used, only the Node ID is sent. This type should be used only for hosts that do not support Format 3 XIDs that send up to 100 bytes of identification information, including the Local Node ID and Control Point Name. If independent APPC LUs are going to be used on this connection, Format 3 XIDs must be specified. Format 3 is also the default XID type.

8. Click the Channel tab in the Connection Properties dialog box, shown in Figure 40.24.

Part
VIII
Ch
40

FIG. 40.24

The Channel tab allows you to define Channel parameters for a Channel connection.

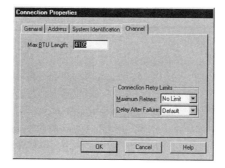

9. In the Max BTU Length box, either accept the default value of 4105 or enter a new value from 265 through 16393 to represent the maximum length of the basic transmission unit (BTU). A BTU, also known as an I-frame, is the number of bytes that can be transmitted in a single data-link control frame. If you are using a mainframe host connection, the Max BTU length should be equal to or less than the value specified for the MAXDATA parameter in the VTAM PU definition. Contact the host system administrator for the values to use.

10. If you want to change the connection activation limit defaults (also called retry timers), change the settings in the Connection Retry Limits area. The two activation limits available for modification are described in the following list:

- **Maximum Retries.** This is the number of times the SNA Server should attempt to establish the connection with the host. When the specified number of unsuccessful attempts has been made, the SNA Server quits trying and makes the appropriate entries in the event log. Any number of attempts can be specified, from 1 through No Limit, with No Limit being the default.

- **Delay After Failure.** This is the number of seconds the SNA Server should wait after each failed attempt before it tries once again to establish the connection. The permissible range for this timer limit is from 5 seconds to 255 seconds, with 10 seconds being the default.

11. Click OK to accept the settings and exit the Channel Connection Properties dialog box, or click Cancel to exit the dialog box without accepting the settings.

Configuring the LUs

Two types of LUs can be created and configured using the SNA Server Manager program. The following list presents the LU types and their primary use qualifications:

- **3270 LU.** Provides access to IBM mainframe environments. 3270 LUs include Display LU, Printer LU, Application LU (LUA), and Downstream LU. A Display LU provides access to mainframe terminal sessions. A Printer LU provides access to mainframe printer sessions. An Application LU (LUA) provides access to a connection by LUA applications.

    LUA applications, which allow communications between a PC and an IBM host, use LU 0, LU 1, LU 2, or LU 3 protocols. A Downstream LU allows an SNA Server to support communications between an IBM host and clients that do not use the SNA Server client-server interface (Macintosh systems, IBM Communications Manager/2 systems, and so on).

- **Advanced Program-to-Program Communications (APPC) LU.** Provides access to AS/400 environments using 5250 emulation. Allows transaction programs (TPs) on peer systems to communicate with each other over the SNA network. APPC LUs use LU 6.2 protocols.

The following sections contain step-by-step procedures for creating and configuring each of these LU types.

Creating and Configuring 3270 LUs

You can create and configure 3270 LUs individually or in groups called *ranges*. When created as a range of LUs, all the LUs in the range have the same properties. You can go back, however, and modify these properties on an individual basis for each LU. The following sections first present the procedures for creating and configuring individual 3270 LUs and then give similar procedures for creating and configuring a range of 3270 LUs.

Individual 3270 LUs   To create and configure 3270 LUs individually, follow these steps:

1. In the left pane of SNA Server Manager, select the SNA server to be configured from the SNA Servers folder. Next, double-click the Connections folder and select the connection from either the left or right pane.

2. From the Insert menu, choose 3270 and then click any LU type (Display LU, Printer LU, Application LU (LUA), or Downstream LU); or right-click the selected connection, choose Insert, 3270, and click one of the LU types. The 3270 LU Properties dialog box appears (see Figure 40.25).

FIG. 40.25

You use the 3270 LU Properties dialog box to define the LU number and name along with a few other parameters.

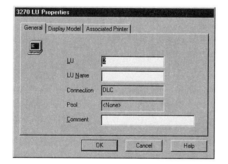

Part
VIII

Ch
40

The General tab is displayed by default. The 3270 LU Properties dialog box for a Display LU has additional tabs for more settings to configure.

3. In the LU box, enter a number for this LU. Although valid numbers range from 1 through 254, SNA conventions dictate that LU numbers always start with 2, not 1. Therefore, the permissible values are really 2 through 254. This number must correspond to the VTAM SysGen parameter, LOCADDR, in the VTAM generator on the host computer. Coordinate with the SNA host administrator for the number to use and enter that number here. If the number you entered has already been assigned to an LU, a message box appears telling you to enter a different number because duplicate LU numbers are not permitted.

N O T E   LUs for DFT connections do not require an LU number but instead use a Port Number (the DFT adapter number with permissible values from 1 through 4) and an LT number (the Logical Terminal number configured at the 3174 for this coaxial cable with permissible values from 1 through 5). ▨

N O T E   The LU number identifies this LU to the IBM host. It does not need to match the Downstream LU number, which identifies the LU to the downstream system. ▨

4. In the LU Name box, enter a unique name for this LU. This name can contain a maximum of eight characters (alphanumeric and the special characters @, #, and $).

5. Several boxes require no entry:

   • No action is required in the Connection box. It simply displays the connection for the LU you are creating and configuring.

   • No action is required in the Pool box. It simply displays the pool for the LU. None is listed when creating new LUs.

   • The Comment box is optional. If you do decide to enter a comment, you can enter up to 25 characters of freeform text.

6. If configuring a Printer, Application, or Downstream LU, then click OK to exit the dialog box and accept the settings; or click Cancel to exit the dialog box without accepting the settings.

   If configuring a Display LU, then click the Display Model tab.

7. In the Display Model tab, either accept Model 2 as the default or click the radio button next to the desired display model. The model determines the number of lines and the number of characters per line to be displayed. Some emulators are capable of emulating only certain display models, so you should refer to your emulator documentation to determine the display model constraints of your specific emulator.

8. The Model Can Be Overridden check box is, by default, selected so that the display model can be overridden by using the 3270 terminal emulation program. If you do not want to be able to override the display model, deselect the check box.

9. Click the Associated Printer tab.

   No action is required in the Display LU box. It simply displays the LU name for the LU. None is listed when creating new LUs.

10. In the Associated Printer LU box, select a printer LU to associate with this Display LU. None are listed by default and when no printer LUs exist.

11. Click OK to exit the dialog box and accept the settings, or click Cancel to exit the dialog box without accepting the settings.

Range of 3270 LUs   Perform these steps to create and configure a range of consecutively numbered 3270 LUs:

N O T E It is not possible to create and configure a range of LUA LUs for DFT connections. You must configure them one at a time. ■

1. In the left pane of SNA Server Manager, select the SNA Server to be configured from the SNA Servers folder. Then double-click the Connections folder and select the connection from either the left or right pane.

2. From the Insert menu, select 3270 and then click Range of LUs. This starts the LU Creation Wizard, as shown in Figure 40.26.

FIG. 40.26
The LU Creation Wizard lets you create several LUs at a time.

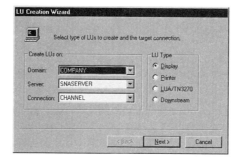

3. In the Create LUs On area, the information in the Domain, Server, and Connection boxes reflects the connection selected in step 1. You can change these settings if you need to create LUs for a different domain, server, or connection.

4. In the LU Type area, click the radio button next to the appropriate choice: Display, Printer, LUA/TN3270, or Downstream.

5. Click Next. A new dialog box appears, as shown in Figure 40.27.

Part
VIII

Ch
40

FIG. 40.27
The same basic information for creating an LU is still needed for creating a range of LUs.

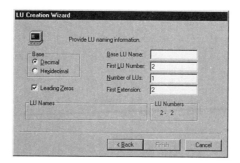

6. In the Base area, click the desired radio button to specify the numbering system to be used for the extension numbers. The default is Decimal. This selection does not affect LU numbers.

7. The Leading Zeros check box is selected by default so that the option is active. Deselect the check box to turn off the option. Leading zeros ensure that LU names display in the proper sequence.

8. In the Base LU Name box, enter a unique name for the LU range. The LUs in the range will have names composed of this Base LU Name and an extension number, and each name can contain a maximum of eight characters (alphanumeric and special characters @, #, and $). Therefore, the permissible length of the Base LU Name really depends on the number of digits (1, 2, or 3) you will be using for the extension number. For example, if you plan to use two-digit extension numbers (to cover up to 99 individual LUs), the Base LU Name must be limited to six characters. Keep this in mind when entering the Base LU Name.

9. In the First LU Number box, enter a number for the first LU. Although valid numbers range from 1 through 254, SNA conventions dictate that LU numbers always start with 2, not 1. Therefore, the permissible values are really 2 through 254. This number must correspond to the VTAM SysGen parameter, LOCADDR, in the VTAM generator on the host computer. Coordinate with the SNA host administrator for the number to use. If the number you entered has already been assigned to an LU, a message box appears telling you to enter a different number because duplicate LU numbers are not permitted.

10. In the Number of LUs box, enter the number of LUs you want in the range. The SNA Server numbers them sequentially from the first number specified.

N O T E   Even though the host administrator may instruct you to use LU numbers that are not consecutive, you can still create a range of sequential LU numbers and then modify the individual LU numbers after they have been created.

11. The First Extension box displays the default first extension, which is the First LU Number entry in the upper portion of the Add LU Range dialog box. Either accept this default or enter a new first extension number. If the Base LU Name is six characters, the First Extension number cannot be greater than two digits (01–99), so as not to violate the maximum length permitted for the LU name. The permissible decimal range of values is 0 through 999, and the permissible hexadecimal range of values is 0 through FFF.

12. No action is required in the LU Numbers area (which simply displays the range of LU numbers you just created), or in the LU Names area (which simply displays the range of LU names you just created). So click Finish to exit the wizard and accept the settings, or click Cancel to exit the dialog box without accepting the settings.

Creating and Configuring APPC LUs

Advanced Program-to-Program Communications (APPC) uses LU 6.2 to provide communications capability between *transaction programs* (TPs) on peer systems. TPs either initiate communications (in which case they are called *invoking TPs*), or they respond to communications (in which case, they are called *invokable TPs*). APPC needs at least one LU for each direction of communications and, therefore, uses one local LU and one or more remote LUs to establish communications between TPs. Unlike the other LUs discussed in this chapter, the local APPC LU is assigned to a server, not a connection.

Local APPC LUs   To assign and configure a local APPC LU, follow these steps:

1. In the left pane of SNA Server Manager, select the SNA server to be configured from the SNA Servers folder.

2. From the Insert menu, choose APPC and then click Local LU; or right-click the selected SNA server, choose Insert, APPC, and click Local LU. The Local APPC LU Properties dialog box appears (see Figure 40.28). The General tab displays by default.

FIG. 40.28

Use the Local APPC LU Properties dialog box to define the Local APPC LU.

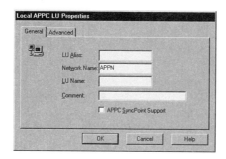

3. In the LU Alias box, enter a unique name for this LU that identifies it to the local TPs. This name can contain a maximum of eight characters (alphanumeric and the special characters @, #, and $). Even though this alias needs to be unique on the server, the alias can be the same as the LU name.

4. In the Network Name box, enter the network name identifying the SNA network. This name can contain a maximum of eight characters (alphanumeric and the special characters @, #, and $). For independent LUs, this network name is required. For dependent LUs, the network name is optional. Even though the network name may be optional, you are wise to assign one anyway because it provides an easy way to identify the network when reviewing monitoring and diagnostic tools such as the Windows NT Event Viewer.

   The SNA host or peer system administrator should advise you as to what the name should be because it needs to match the NETID parameter in the VTAM Start command for host systems operating under VTAM. The default network name is the network name for the SNA Server; or if no SNA Server network name has been specified, the default is APPN.

> **N O T E** If this server will be used to communicate with numerous hosts over several different connections, the network name should be the same as the subarea of the host with which this LU will communicate. ▨

5. In the LU Name box, enter a unique name identifying this LU. This name can contain a maximum of eight characters (alphanumeric and the special characters @, #, and $). For independent LUs, this name is required because it identifies this LU to the other network components. For dependent LUs, the name is optional. Even though the name may be optional, you are wise to assign one anyway because it provides an easy way to identify the LU when reviewing monitoring and diagnostic tools, such as the Windows NT Event Viewer. This LU name can match the LU alias for this LU.

Part
VIII

Ch
40

6. In the Comment box, enter a comment up to 25 characters long. Comments are optional, so if you desire, you can leave this box blank.

7. The APPC SyncPoint Support check box is not selected by default, so the option is inactive. To turn on the option, simply select the check box. APPC Syncpoint support is used by specialized transaction programs (TPs).

8. Click the Advanced tab to configure additional settings for the Local APPC LU, as shown in Figure 40.29.

FIG. 40.29

The Advanced tab for the Local APPC LU Properties dialog box allows you to define additional characteristics for the Local APPC LU.

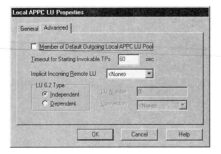

9. When an invoking TP requests an LU session from the SNA Server, the SNA Server first tries to satisfy the request with the Default Local APPC LU specifically assigned to the user or group controlling the invoking TP. If this is not possible, SNA Server then tries to satisfy the request by using an available LU in the Default Outgoing Local APPC LUs pool. You can make a local LU a member of this pool by selecting the Member of Default Outgoing Local APPC LU Pool check box. If you do not want this local LU to be a member of the pool, deselect the check box.

10. In the Timeout for Starting Invokable TPs box, either accept the default of 60 or enter a new value from 1 through 3600 to represent the maximum number of seconds the SNA Server should wait for the invokable TP to respond to a start request from the invoking TP. Allow sufficient time (usually greater than 60 seconds) in those cases where the invokable TP will be started manually by the operator.

11. SNA Server has the flexibility of accepting incoming requests for LU sessions from many different remote LUs that have not been defined on the SNA Server. To enable this flexibility, click the Implicit Incoming Remote LU drop-down list box to display the list of remote LUs and then select a remote APPC LU that defines the properties for SNA Server to use. Then when an unknown remote LU requests a session with a recognized local LU, SNA Server uses the properties defined in the implicit incoming remote LU to control the session. If you do not want SNA Server to accept session requests from unknown remote LUs, select None from the drop-down list.

12. In the LU 6.2 Type area, select either Independent or Dependent, as appropriate. Independent APPC LUs can communicate directly with a peer system and can support multiple parallel sessions. Dependent APPC LUs require support from the local host system to communicate with a remote peer, and they can support only a single session for each LU.

N O T E   If the local LU will be used to communicate with a remote LU over a Distributed Function
Terminal (DFT) connection, the local LU 6.2 Type must be Dependent. ▨

13. The LU Number box is available only if the LU 6.2 Type is Dependent. In this case, enter
a number in the range 1 through 254 to identify the dependent LU. The number must be
unique on the connection. Coordinate with the host system administrator because this
number must match the LOCADDR parameter in the VTAM LU definition or in the NCP
Gen. If the LU 6.2 Type is Independent, the LU Number box is disabled.

N O T E   The permissible range of numbers is 2 through 254 if the local dependent LU will be
partnered with a remote LU using a DFT connection. ▨

14. The Connection box is available only if the LU 6.2 Type is Dependent. In this case,
choose the connection from the drop-down list. If the LU 6.2 Type is Independent, the
Connection box is disabled.

15. Click OK to exit the dialog box and accept the settings, or click Cancel to exit the dialog
box without accepting the settings.

Remote APPC LUs   To assign and configure a remote APPC LU, follow these steps:

1. In the left pane of SNA Server Manager, select the SNA Server to be configured from the
SNA Servers folder.

2. From the Insert menu, choose APPC and then click Remote LU; or right-click the
selected SNA Server, choose Insert, APPC, and then click Remote LU. The Remote
APPC LU Properties dialog box appears (see Figure 40.30). The General tab displays
by default.

FIG. 40.30

The Remote APPC LU
Properties dialog box
lets you define the
Remote APPC LU.

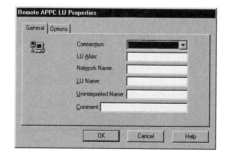

3. In the Connection drop-down list box, select the connection that will be used to access
this remote APPC LU.

4. In the LU Alias box, enter a unique name for this LU that identifies it to the local TPs.
This name can contain a maximum of eight characters (alphanumeric and the special
characters @, #, and $). Even though this alias needs to be unique on both the connec-
tion and the server, the LU Alias can be the same as the LU Name for the LU.

5. In the Network Name box, enter a unique network name identifying the SNA network. This name can contain a maximum of eight characters (alphanumeric and the special characters @, #, and $). The SNA host or peer system administrator should advise you as to what the name should be because it needs to match the NETID parameter in the VTAM Start command for host systems operating under VTAM. The default network name is the network name for the SNA Server; or if no SNA Server network name has been specified, the default is APPN.

6. In the LU Name box, enter a unique name identifying this LU. This name can contain a maximum of eight characters (alphanumeric and the special characters @, #, and $). For a remote LU partnered with an independent local APPC LU, this name is required because it identifies the remote LU to the other SNA network components. For a remote LU partnered with a dependent local APPC LU, the name is optional. Even though the name may be optional, you are wise to assign one anyway because it provides an easy way to identify the remote LU when reviewing monitoring and diagnostic tools such as the Windows NT Event Viewer. This LU Name can match the LU Alias for this LU.

7. The Uninterpreted Name box must contain the remote LU name (as defined on the remote system services control point, or SSCP) if the remote LU will be partnered with a dependent local APPC LU. This name can contain a maximum of eight characters (alphanumeric and the special characters @, #, and $). This Uninterpreted Name can match the LU Alias and LU Name for this LU.

8. In the Comment box, enter a comment up to 25 characters long. Comments are optional, so if you want, you can leave this box blank.

9. Click the Options tab to configure additional settings for the Remote APPC LU, as shown in Figure 40.31.

FIG. 40.31

The Options tab for the Remote APPC LU Properties dialog box is used to define additional characteristics of the Remote APPC LU.

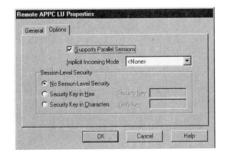

10. The Supports Parallel Sessions check box specifies whether this remote LU will be used to support multiple concurrent (parallel) sessions when paired with an independent local APPC LU. To enable parallel session support, select the check box. If you do not want to enable parallel session support, deselect the check box. If the remote LU is partnered with a dependent local APPC LU, parallel session support is not possible, and the check box must remain unmarked (parallel session support is disabled).

N O T E If a remote LU is to support parallel sessions, you must use it with a mode whose parallel session limit value is greater than one. ▓

11. SNA Server has the flexibility of accepting incoming requests for LU sessions from many different remote LUs whose mode names have not been defined on the SNA Server. You can enable this flexibility by selecting a mode that defines the properties for SNA Server to use from the Implicit Incoming Mode drop-down list. Then when an LU session request is made, but the named mode is not recognized by the SNA Server, the SNA Server uses the properties defined in the implicit incoming mode. If this remote APPC LU has been earlier designated as an implicit incoming remote LU for a local APPC, then a mode must be selected from the Implicit Incoming Mode drop-down list. Otherwise, you may select None from the drop-down list.

12. Configure remote LU session security in the Session-Level Security area. Three options are available:

    - By default, the No Session-Level Security option is enabled, meaning that session-level security has been turned off. You cannot activate session-level security unless the security keys for the APPC session and the remote LU match.

    - Click the Security Key in Hex radio button if you want the security key to be in hexadecimal, and then enter a 16-digit hexadecimal number for the security key.

    - Click the Security Key in Characters radio button if you want the security key to be in characters, and then enter an eight-character string (alphanumeric and special characters @, #, period, and $) for the security key.

13. Click OK to exit the dialog box and accept the settings, or click Cancel to exit the dialog box without accepting the settings.

Creating and Configuring APPC Mode Definitions   An APPC Mode determines the session properties for an LU-LU pair. SNA Server contains several APPC Mode definitions:

- ▓ **#BATCH.** For batch-oriented sessions
- ▓ **#BATCHSC.** For batch-oriented sessions with a minimal level of routing security
- ▓ **BLANK.** For sessions using a default mode name
- ▓ **#INTER.** For interactive sessions
- ▓ **#INTERSC.** For interactive sessions with a minimal level of routing security
- ▓ **QPCSUPP.** For all AS/400 sessions
- ▓ **QSERVER.** ODBC drivers

To create and configure an APPC Mode definition, follow these steps:

1. From the Insert menu, choose APPC and then click Mode Definition; or from the left pane of SNA Server Manager, right-click the APPC Modes folder, choose Insert, APPC, and then click Mode Definition. The APPC Mode Properties dialog box appears (see Figure 40.32). The General tab displays by default.

FIG. 40.32

Use the APPC Mode
Properties dialog box to
create and configure
APPC Modes.

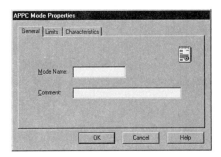

If you want to edit the configuration of an existing APPC Mode definition, click the APPC
Modes folder, right-click the APPC Mode definition displayed in the right pane, and click
Properties. The APPC Mode Properties dialog box will then appear.

2. In the Mode Name box, enter a unique name for this mode. This name can contain a
maximum of eight characters (alphanumeric and the special characters @, #, and $).

3. In the Comment box, enter a comment up to 25 characters long. Comments are optional,
so if you want, you can leave this box blank.

4. Click the Limits tab, as shown in Figure 40.33.

FIG. 40.33

The Limits tab is used
to set APPC session
properties.

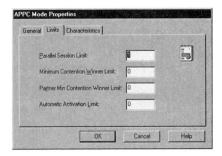

5. In the Parallel Session Limit box, either accept the default value of 1 or enter a new value
from 1 through 1024 to represent the maximum number of sessions allowed with this
mode. If two or more sessions are allowed, they will be conducted in parallel; that is,
multiple concurrent sessions will be conducted between an APPC LU pair in which two
TPs perform multiple operations simultaneously.

N O T E   Because dependent local APPC LUs cannot support parallel sessions, you must specify "1"
if the local APPC LU to be used with this mode has been defined as dependent. ■

6. In the Minimum Contention Winner Limit box, either accept the default of zero or enter
a new value from zero through the Parallel Session Limit defined in step 5. This value
represents the minimum number of sessions in which the local LU must be able to
initiate communications without first obtaining permission from the partnered LU (that
is, be the contention winner).

7. In the Partner Min Contention Winner Limit box, either accept the default of zero or enter a new value from zero through the Parallel Session Limit defined in step 5. This value represents the minimum number of sessions in which the partner LU must be able to initiate communications without first obtaining permission from the local LU (that is, be the contention winner).

N O T E The sum of the values used for the Minimum Contention Winner Limit and the Partner Min Contention Winner Limit cannot be greater than the value used for the Parallel Session Limit. ▨

8. In the Automatic Activation Limit box, enter a value from zero through the Minimum Contention Winner Limit value defined in step 6. This value represents the maximum number of contention winner sessions that can be activated for the local LU whenever the connection for this mode starts.

9. Click the Characteristics tab, as shown in Figure 40.34.

FIG. 40.34

The Characteristics tab is used to set APPC communication properties.

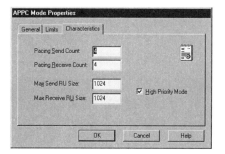

Part
VIII

Ch
40

10. The High Priority Mode check box is selected, by default, so that this mode should be given communications preference over other low-priority modes. If you want this mode to have a lower priority, deselect the check box.

11. In the Pacing Send Count box, either accept the default of 4 or enter a new value from zero through 63 to represent the maximum number of frames the local LU can send before it receives an SNA pacing response from the partner LU. If you enter zero in the box, the local LU can send an unlimited number of frames without receiving a response.

12. In the Pacing Receive Count box, either accept the default of four or enter a new value from zero through 63 to represent the maximum number of frames the local LU can receive before it sends an SNA pacing response to the partner LU. If you enter zero in the box, the local LU can receive an unlimited number of frames without sending a response.

13. In the Max Send RU Size box, either accept the default of 1024 or enter a new value from 256 through 16384 to represent the maximum size for RUs sent by the TP(s) on the local system.

14. In the Max Receive RU Size box, either accept the default of 1024 or enter a new value from 256 through 16384 to represent the maximum size for RUs received by the TP(s) on the remote system.

15. Click OK to exit the dialog box and accept the settings, or click Cancel to exit the dialog box without accepting the settings.

Grouping the LUs into Pools

As mentioned in Chapter 39, "SNA Server Preparation and Installation," LU pools are groupings of 3270 Display, LUA, or Downstream LUs organized by the administrator in such a way as to maximize access to the LUs in the pool. A pool user, LUA application, or downstream system can get LU access as long as only one of the pooled LUs is available and functioning. Several actions are required before an LU pool can become fully operational:

- The LUs for the pool have to be configured.
- The pool needs to be created.
- Configured LUs need to be assigned to the pool.
- The pool needs to be assigned to specific users, LUA applications, or downstream systems.

Because earlier sections of this chapter discussed the steps for configuring the various types of LUs, this section explains how to create and configure new 3270 Display, LUA, and Downstream LU pools using the SNA Server Manager.

LU Pools

Perform the following steps to create and configure your LU pool:

1. From the Insert menu, choose Pool and then click either 3270 Display LU Pool, LUA LU Pool, or Downstream LU Pool; or from the left pane of SNA Server Manager, right-click the Pools folder, choose Insert, Pool, and then click either 3270 Display LU Pool, LUA LU Pool, or Downstream LU Pool. The Pool Properties dialog box appears, as shown in Figure 40.35.

FIG. 40.35

The Pool Properties dialog box allows you to create and configure an LU Pool.

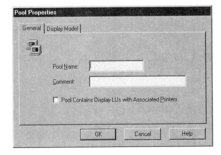

If you want to edit the configuration of an existing Pool, click the Pools folder, right-click the Pool in the right pane, and click Properties. The Pool Properties dialog box will then appear.

2. The General tab displays by default. The Pool Properties dialog box for a 3270 Display LU Pool has additional tabs for more settings to configure.

3. In the Pool Name box, enter a name identifying this LU pool. This name can contain a maximum of eight characters (alphanumeric and the special characters @, #, and $). This name must be unique from any other LU or pool name, except APPC LU names.

4. In the Comment box, enter any comment up to 25 characters. Entries in this box are optional.

5. For a 3270 Display LU Pool, the Pool Contains Display LUs with Associated Printers check box is present and, by default, deselected. If the display LUs are associated with printer LUs, select the check box by clicking it.

6. If configuring an LUA or Downstream LU Pool, then click OK to exit the dialog box and accept the settings; or click Cancel to exit the dialog box without accepting the settings.

   If configuring a 3270 Display LU Pool, then click the Display Model tab.

7. In the Display Model tab, either accept Model 2 as the default or click the radio button next to the desired display model. The model determines the number of lines and the number of characters per line to be displayed. Some emulators are capable of emulating only certain display models, so you should refer to your emulator documentation to determine the display model constraints of your specific emulator.

8. The Model Can Be Overridden check box is deselected by default so that the display model cannot be overridden by using the 3270 terminal emulation program. If you want to be able to override the display model, select the check box by clicking it.

9. Click OK to accept the settings and exit the Pool Properties dialog box, or click Cancel to exit the dialog box without accepting the settings.

Part
VIII

Ch
40

Assigning LUs to Pools

Now that the LU pools have been created and configured, you can assign specific LUs to the pools by following these steps:

1. In the left pane of SNA Server Manager, select the SNA server to be configured from the SNA Servers folder. Next, double-click the Connections folder, and then select the connection to display the LUs in the right pane.

2. Select one or more LUs to assign to a Pool and right-click the selected LUs, and choose Assign To, Pool, and click the Pool name. Alternatively, drag the selected LUs and drop them in the Pool listed below the Pools folder on the left pane.

Follow these steps to remove LUs from an LU pool:

1. In the left pane of SNA Server Manager, select the Pool from the Pools folder.

2. From the right pane, select one or more LUs to remove and choose Delete from the Edit menu; or right-click the LUs selected and click Delete. A confirmation dialog box appears.

3. Click Yes to remove the LUs, or click No to cancel.

Assigning LU Pools to Users and Groups

The LU pool provides access to the LUs contained within it only after the pool has been assigned to a user or group of users. But users must possess accounts on the network before they can be recognized by the SNA Server. After their accounts are properly established on the network, the users can be added to the list used by SNA Server, and they also can be assigned LU pools. The users can then gain access to the host system(s) to which the LUs in the assigned pools connect.

Adding a Network User or Group

Earlier chapters in this book discussed the procedures for establishing user and group accounts on the network. Therefore, this section assumes that you have already established your network user and group accounts. It is now time to add them to the list used by the SNA Server. The steps that follow describe how to do just that:

1. In the left pane of SNA Server Manager, select the Configured Users folder.

2. From the Insert menu, choose User; or right-click the Configured Users folder, choose Insert, and then click User. The Add Users and Groups dialog box appears, as shown in Figure 40.36.

FIG. 40.36
The Add Users and Groups dialog box lists all Windows NT domain users and groups for a given domain.

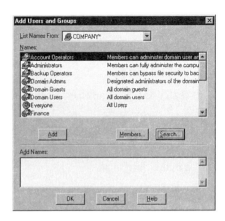

3. In the List Names From box, click the drop-down list box to display a list of available domains. From this list, either select the name of the local SNA Server or select the domain that contains the users and/or groups to be added.

4. From the list of users and groups displayed in the <u>N</u>ames area of the dialog box, select the users and/or groups to be added.

5. Click <u>A</u>dd and then click OK to exit the dialog box and accept the settings, or click Cancel to exit the dialog box without accepting the settings.

Configuring User or Group Properties

Now that the new user(s) and/or group(s) have been added, their user properties need to be reviewed and, if necessary, modified. Perform the following steps to configure these user properties:

1. In the left pane of SNA Server Manager, double-click the Configured Users folder and select the user or group.

2. From the <u>V</u>iew menu, choose <u>P</u>roperties; or right-click the user or group, and then click <u>P</u>roperties. The Properties dialog box for that user or group appears (see Figure 40.37). The User Properties tab displays by default.

FIG. 40.37

The User Properties tab of the User/Group Properties dialog box is used to enable Client-Server Encryption.

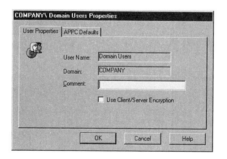

3. In the <u>C</u>omment box, enter any comment up to 25 characters. Entries in this box are optional.

4. The Use Client-Server Encryption check box is deselected by default so that the option is inactive. To turn on the option, simply click the check box to select it. The Use Client-Server Encryption option enables encrypting communications between the client and the SNA Server.

5. Click the APPC Defaults tab to select the local and/or remote APPC LUs to serve as the default when the specified user starts APPC programs (see Figure 40.38).

6. In the Local APPC LU box, either accept the default of None or click the drop-down list box to display a list of local APPC LUs. Select the desired local APPC LU to serve as the default to be used when the user starts APPC programs (TPs, 5250 emulators, APPC applications, and so on).

7. In the Remote APPC LU box, either accept the default of None or click the drop-down list box to display a list of remote APPC LUs. Select the desired remote APPC LU to serve as the default to be used when the user starts APPC programs (TPs, 5250 emulators, APPC applications, and so on).

Part
VIII

Ch
40

FIG. 40.38

The APPC Defaults tab of the User/Group Properties dialog box allows you to select the local and/or remote APPC LUs to serve as the default when the specified user starts APPC programs.

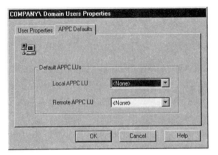

8. Click OK to accept the settings and exit the Properties dialog box, or click Cancel to exit the dialog box without accepting the settings.

Assigning the LUs or LU Pools

Now that you have added and configured the new user(s) and/or group(s), you can assign one or more LUs or LU pools to them. Follow these steps to assign LUs to a user or group:

1. In the left pane of SNA Server Manager, select the SNA server to be configured from the SNA Servers folder. Next, double-click the Connections folder, and select the connection to display the LUs in the right pane.

2. Select one or more LUs to assign to a user or group; then right-click the selected LUs and choose Assign To, User, and click the user or group. Alternatively, drag the selected LUs and drop them in the user or group listed below the Configured Users folder on the left pane.

Follow these steps to assign LU pools to a user or group:

1. In the left pane of SNA Server Manager, double-click the Pools folder, and select the Pool below the folder or from the right pane.

2. Right-click the selected Pool, choose Assign To User, and then click the user or group. Alternatively, drag the selected Pool and drop it in the user or group listed below the Configured Users folder on the left pane.

Configuring the Host Print Service

The Host Print service provides 3270 and 5250 printer emulation for clients, allowing mainframe and AS/400 applications to print to a network printer. The Host Print service supports LU1, LU3, Intelligent Printer Data Stream (IPDS), SCS transparent mainframe printing, SCS line printing, and 3812 pass-through emulation AS/400 printing.

Configuring a 3270 Print Session

To create and configure a 3270 print session, follow these steps:

1. In the left pane of SNA Server Manager, double-click the Print Servers folder, and select the SNA server to configure from the Print Servers folder or the right pane.

2. From the Insert menu, choose Print Server and then click 3270 Session; or right-click the selected SNA Server, choose Insert, Print Server, and then click 3270 Session. The 3270 Print Session Properties dialog box appears (see Figure 40.39). The General tab displays by default.

FIG. 40.39

The 3270 Print Session Properties dialog box lets you define a 3270 printer session.

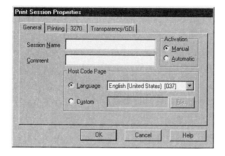

3. In the Session Name box, enter a unique name for this print session. This name can contain a maximum of 32 characters.

4. The Comment box is optional. If you do decide to enter a comment, you can enter up to 25 characters of free-form text.

5. In the Host Code Page area, select either Language or Custom. Select Language and choose a language code in the drop-down list. Select Custom if your language code does not appear in the Language drop-down list, and click File to open a user-specified custom language code file.

6. In the Activation area, select either Manual or Automatic. Manual activates the print server manually, and Automatic activates the print server automatically.

7. Select the Printing tab, as shown in Figure 40.40.

Part

VIII

Ch

40

FIG. 40.40

Use the Printing tab on the 3270 Print Session Properties dialog box to define printing options.

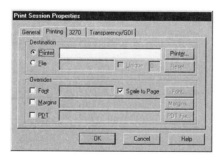

8. In the Destination area, select Printer or File. Printer sends print jobs to a printer. Click the Printer button to open the Print Setup dialog box, and select and configure a printer. File sends print jobs to a file. Click the Unique check box to print each job to a new file. Click Reset to reset the print job sequential numbering scheme.

9. The Overrides area is used to set custom print options. These settings override the same settings defined on the host. Click the check boxes to implement custom settings. Click on Font, Margins, and PDT to display their respective dialog boxes, make your selections, and click OK.

10. Select the 3270 tab, as shown in Figure 40.41.

FIG. 40.41

The 3270 tab on the 3270 Print Session Properties dialog box allows you to define the LU name and the job and page properties.

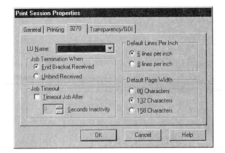

11. In the LU Name box, select a 3270 printer LU for the print session. All available 3270 printer LUs in the SNA Server subdomain are listed. If no 3270 printer LUs are listed, then you must create a 3270 printer LU to further proceed.

12. In the Job Termination When area, select either End Bracket Received or Unbind Received.

13. In the Job Timeout area, click the Timeout Job After check box and enter a number from 1 to 99 in the Seconds Inactivity box to set a time parameter for terminating print jobs.

14. In the Default Lines Per Inch area, select either 6 lines per inch or 8 lines per inch.

15. In the Default Page Width, select either 80 Characters, 132 Characters, or 158 Characters.

16. Select the Transparency/GDI tab, as shown in Figure 40.42.

FIG. 40.42

Use the Transparency/ GDI tab on the 3270 Print Session Properties dialog box to define special parameters to send print jobs.

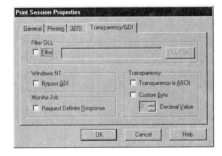

17. Use the Filter DLL to process the printer data stream with a third-party or custom DLL. In the Filter DLL area, click the Filter check box, click DLL File, and open the file.

18. In the Windows NT area, click the Bypass GDI check box to circumvent the Windows printing format system and send the printer data stream directly to the printer.

19. In the Monitor Job area, click the Request Definite Response check box to send a print job completed message to the host.

20. There are two selections in the Transparency area. Click the Transparency is ASCII check box to indicate that transparent data from the host is in ASCII and no translation from EBCDIC to ASCII is required. Click the Custom Byte check box to send the printer data stream in transparent mode. Specify the character designated to start a sequence of transparent data in the Decimal Value list.

21. Click OK to exit the dialog box and accept the settings, or click Cancel to exit the dialog box without accepting the settings.

22. Start the Host Print Service by selecting the SNA server in the Print Servers folder; then choose Start from the Service menu, press the F5 key, or right-click the SNA server and click Start.

Configuring an APPC Print Session

To create and configure an APPC print session, follow these steps:

1. In the left pane of SNA Server Manager, double-click the Print Servers folder and then select the SNA server to configure from the Print Servers folder or the right pane.

2. From the Insert menu, choose Print Server and then click APPC Session; or right-click the selected SNA server, choose Insert, Print Server, and then click APPC Session. The APPC Print Session Properties dialog box appears (see Figure 40.43). The General tab displays by default.

FIG. 40.43
The Print Session Properties dialog box defines an APPC printer session.

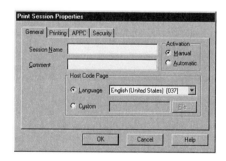

3. In the Session Name box, enter a unique name for this print session. This name can contain a maximum of 32 characters.

4. The Comment box is optional. If you do decide to enter a comment, you can enter up to 25 characters of freeform text.

5. In the Host Code Page area, select either Language or Custom. Select Language and then choose a language code in the drop-down list. Select Custom if your language code does not appear in the Language drop-down list, and click File to open a user-specified custom language code file.

6. In the Activation area, select either Manual or Automatic. Manual activates the print server manually, and Automatic activates the print server automatically.

7. Select the Printing tab, as shown in Figure 40.44.

FIG. 40.44

The Printing tab on the APPC Print Session Properties dialog box defines printing options.

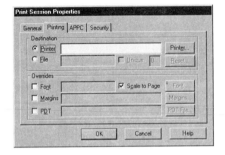

8. In the Destination area, select Printer or File. Printer sends print jobs to a printer. Click the Printer button to open the Print Setup dialog box, and select and configure a printer. File sends print jobs to a file. Click the Unique check box to print each job to a new file. Click Reset to reset the print job sequential numbering scheme.

9. The Overrides area is used to set custom print options. These settings override the same settings defined on the host. Click the check boxes to implement custom settings. Click Font, Margins, and PDT to display their respective dialog boxes, make your selections, and click OK.

10. Select the APPC tab, as shown in Figure 40.45.

FIG. 40.45

The APPC tab on the APPC Print Session Properties dialog box allows you to define APPC properties for the printer session.

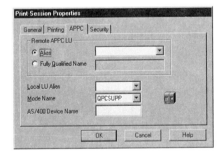

11. In the Remote APPC LU area, accept the default, or either click another Alias from the drop-down list, or select Fully Qualified Name and enter a Remote APPC LU.

12. In the Local LU Alias box, click the local LU alias from the drop-down list.

13. In the Mode Name box, accept the default of QPCSUPP or click the mode from the drop-down list.

14. In the AS/400 Device Name box, enter the the AS/400 printer device name.

15. Click the Security tab, as shown in Figure 40.46.

FIG. 40.46

Use the Security tab on the APPC Print Session Properties dialog box to set a user ID and password for the printer session.

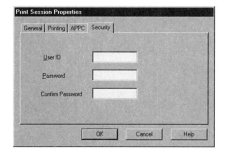

16. In the User ID box, enter a user ID for this printer session.

17. In the Password box, enter a password.

18. In the Confirm Password box, enter the password again.

19. Click OK to exit the dialog box and accept the settings, or click Cancel to exit the dialog box without accepting the settings.

20. Start the Host Print Service by selecting the SNA server in the Print Servers folder; then choose Start from the Service menu, press the F5 key, or right-click the SNA server and click Start.

Configuring the TN3270 Service

The TN3270 service provides TN3270 connectivity to a mainframe and supports TN3270, TN3287, and TN3270E protocols, giving clients terminal emulation and printing capabilities.

Part

VIII

Ch

40

> **CAUTION**
>
> TN3270, TN5250, and Telnet Services all default to "well-known" TCP port number 23. Port conflicts will result from running more than one of these services on the same computer. To avoid port conflicts, either run only one of these services on a particular computer or edit the Services file to use unique port numbers for each service. The Services file is located in the SystemRoot\SYSTEM32\DRIVERS\ETC\ directory. If you run more than one of these services and have not edited the Services file, only the first service will function.

To configure the TN3270 Service, follow these steps:

1. In the left pane of SNA Server Manager, double-click the TN3270 Servers folder and then select the SNA server to configure from the TN3270 Servers folder or the right pane.

2. From the View menu, choose Properties; or right-click the selected SNA Server and choose Properties. The TN3270 Server Properties dialog box appears (see Figure 40.47). The General tab displays by default.

FIG. 40.47

The General tab on the TN3270 SNA Server Properties dialog box is used to enable several session and event logging options.

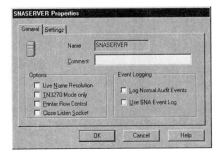

3. Two boxes do not require entries:

- No action is required in the Name box. It simply displays the TN3270 Server you are creating and configuring.

- The Comment box is optional. If you do decide to enter a comment, you can enter up to 25 characters of freeform text.

4. In the Options area, four settings are available as follows:

- Click Use Name Resolution check box only if your SNA Server computer is configured to use a domain name resolver. The domain name resolver allows you to enter the host name of a computer rather than the IP address.

- Click the TN3270 Mode only check box if your TN3270 emulator has problems negotiating with the TN3270 Service, and thus fails to connect. Most TN3270 emulators negotiate function support with the SNA Server, since the TN3270 Service supports TN3270, TN3270E, and TN3287. Selecting this option disables support for TN3270E and TN3287.

- Click the Printer Flow Control check box to have the TN3270 Service send all messages to a TN3270 printer client as response required. This ensures that the TN3270 printer client processes all of the data it receives before it is sent more.

- Click the Close Listen Socket check box to enable the TN3270 Service to stop listening for incoming requests (on this socket) after all of its LUs are in use.

5. In the Event Logging area, click Log Normal Audit Events to log successful client connection and successful client termination. Click Use SNA Event Log to record all TN3270 Service event messages to the event log used by the SNA server.

6. Click the Settings tab, as shown in Figure 40.48.

7. In the Idle Timeout box, either accept the default of 120 minutes or enter a new number. This parameter sets the length of time a session is inactive before the TN3270 Service disconnects the client.

8. In the Init Status Delay box, either accept the default of 2 seconds or enter a new number. This parameter sets the time delay between the TN3270 Service connection to a host session and the TN3270 Service connection to a TN3270 emulator.

FIG. 40.48

The Settings tab on the TN3270 SNA Server Properties dialog box is used to define several connection parameters.

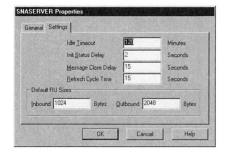

9. In the Message Close Delay box, either accept the default of 15 seconds or enter a new number. This parameter sets the time between sending the message to the TN3270 emulator and closing the connection with the TN3270 emulator. This allows a user to see any error messages displayed before the screen is cleared after a disconnect.

10. In the Refresh Cycle Time box, either accept the default of 15 seconds or enter a new number. This parameter sets the delay time between status updates on the display.

11. In the Default RU Sizes area, either accept the Inbound RU size of 1024 and Outbound RU size of 2048, or enter new numbers (in bytes). The minimum value for inbound or outbound RU size is 256 bytes.

12. Click OK to exit the dialog box and accept the settings, or click Cancel to exit the dialog box without accepting the settings.

Now that the TN3270 Service is configured, you can assign specific LUA LUs to the TN3270 Server by following these steps:

1. In the left pane of SNA Server Manager, select the SNA server from the SNA Servers folder. Next, double-click the Connections folder, and select the connection with LUA LUs that you want to assign to the TN3270 Server.

2. Select the LUA LUs. Right-click the selected LUA LUs, choose Assign To, TN3270 Service on, and then click the SNA server. Alternatively, drag and drop the LUA LUs to the SNA server in the TN3270 Server folder. A new icon for the LUA LU will appear once it is assigned to a TN3270 Server.

Now that LUs are assigned to the TN3270 Server, you can configure the LUA LUs by following these steps:

1. Select the LUA LU to configure, and choose Properties from the View menu; or right-click the selected LUA LU and then click Properties. The LUA LU Properties dialog box appears (see Figure 40.49). The General tab displays by default.

2. The LU box displays the LU number assigned to this LUA LU. You can enter a new LU number, but if the number you entered has already been assigned to an LU, a message box appears telling you to enter a different number because duplicate LU numbers are not permitted.

Part **VIII**

Ch **40**

FIG. 40.49

The LUA LU Properties dialog box enables you to define the LU number and name along with other parameters.

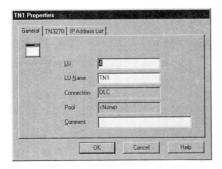

3. The LU Name box displays the LU name assigned to this LUA LU. You can enter a new unique name for this LU. This name can contain a maximum of eight characters (alphanumeric and the special characters @, #, and $).

4. Several boxes do not require entries:

   • No action is required in the Connection box. It simply displays the connection for the LU you are creating and configuring.

   • No action is required in the Pool box. It simply displays the pool for the LU. None is listed when creating new LUs.

   • The Comment box is optional. If you do decide to enter a comment, you can enter up to 25 characters of freeform text.

5. Select the TN3270 tab, as shown in Figure 40.50.

FIG. 40.50

You use the TN3270 tab on the LUA LU Properties dialog box to define display and terminal types.

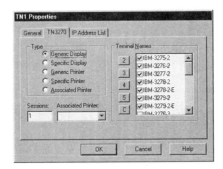

6. In the Type area, the following five settings are available:

   • Select Generic Display to assign the display LU to a client that either requests this LU by name or does not specify a particular LU. This is the default.

   • Select Specific Display to assign the LU to a client that only requests this LU.

   • Select Generic Printer to assign the display LU to a client that either requests this LU by name or does not specify a particular LU. The terminal name will default to IBM-3287-1.

- Select Specific Printer to assign the LU to a client that only requests this LU. The terminal name will default to IBM-3287-1.

- Select Associated Printer to associate a printer LU with a display LU. The terminal name will default to IBM-3287-1.

7. In the Sessions box, enter the the number of TN3270 sessions allowed for the LU.

8. In the Associated LU box, select an Associated LU from the drop-down list if Associated Printer is selected in the Type area.

9. In the Terminal Names area, click the numbered buttons to the left of the list box to select a terminal model. The default is IBM Terminal Model 2. You can select or deselect individual terminal types for the TN3270 Service to accept or reject client requests from TN3270 emulators using those terminal types. Clicking C (Clear) deletes all selections.

10. Select the IP Address List tab, as shown in Figure 40.51.

FIG. 40.51

The IP Address List tab on the LUA LU Properties dialog box is used to add and remove client IP addresses.

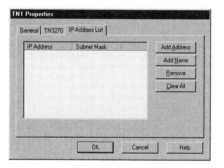

11. Click Add Address to assign an IP Address and Subnet Mask to this LU. If no entries are added, then all users are allowed to connect through the TN3270 Service.

12. Click Add Name to assign a host name to this LU. If no entries are added, then all users are allowed to connect through the TN3270 Service.

13. Click Remove to delete a selected entry in the list.

14. Click Clear All to delete all entries in the list. This allows all users to connect through the TN3270 Service.

15. Click OK to exit the dialog box and accept the settings, or click Cancel to exit the dialog box without accepting the settings.

16. Start the TN3270 Service by selecting the SNA Server in the TN3270 Servers folder; then choose Start from the Service menu, press the F5 key, or right-click the SNA Server and click Start.

Part

VIII

Ch

40

Configuring the TN5250 Service

The TN5250 service provides TN5250 connectivity to an AS/400 and supports TN5250 terminal emulation, giving clients terminal emulation capabilities.

> **CAUTION**
>
> TN3270, TN5250, and Telnet Services all default to "well-known" TCP port number 23. Port conflicts will result from running more than one of these services on the same computer. To avoid port conflicts, either run only one of these services on a particular computer or edit the Services file to use unique port numbers for each service. The Services file is located in the `SystemRoot\SYSTEM32\DRIVERS\ETC\` directory. If you run more than one of these services and have not edited the Services file, only the first service will function.

To configure the TN5250 Service, follow these steps:

1. In the left pane of SNA Server Manager, double-click the TN5250 Servers folder and then select the SNA server to configure from the TN5250 Servers folder or the right pane.

2. From the Insert menu, choose TN5250 AS/400 Definition; or right-click the selected SNA server, choose Insert, and click TN5250 AS/400 Definition. The AS/400 Definition Properties dialog box appears, as shown in Figure 40.52. The General tab displays by default.

FIG. 40.52

You use the General tab on the AS/400 Definition Properties dialog box to define AS/400 parameters.

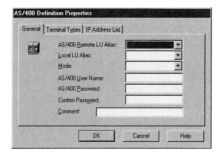

3. In the AS/400 Remote LU Alias box, select a remote LU alias from the drop-down list.

4. In the Local LU Alias box, select a local LU alias from the drop-down list.

5. In the Mode box, select QPCSUPP. This mode is required for a TN5250 connection.

6. In the AS/400 User Name box, enter the AS/400 user name that will be used to establish TN5250 connections. All TN5250 connections will inherit the permissions of this account.

7. In the AS/400 Password box, enter the password for the user name assigned in step 6.

8. In the Confirm Password box, enter the same password as in step 7.

9. The Comment box is optional. If you do decide to enter a comment, you can enter up to 25 characters of freeform text.

10. Click the Terminal Types tab, as shown in Figure 40.53.

FIG. 40.53

The Terminal Types tab on the AS/400 Definition Properties dialog box allows you to define several connection parameters.

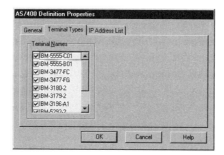

11. In the Terminal Names area, select terminal types for the TN5250 Service to accept client requests from TN5250 emulators using those terminal types. Deselect a terminal type if you want the TN5250 Service to reject client requests from TN5250 emulators using that terminal type. All terminal types are selected by default.

12. Click the IP Address List tab, as shown in Figure 40.54.

FIG. 40.54

Use the IP Address List tab on the AS/400 Definition Properties dialog box to add and remove client IP addresses.

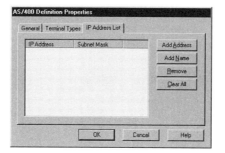

Part

VIII

Ch

40

13. Click Add Address to assign an IP Address and Subnet Mask to this LU. If no entries are added, then all users are allowed to connect through the TN5250 Service.

14. Click Add Name to assign a host name to this LU. If no entries are added, then all users are allowed to connect through the TN5250 Service.

15. Click Remove to delete a selected entry in the list.

16. Click Clear All to delete all entries in the list. This allows all users to connect through the TN5250 Service.

17. Click OK to exit the dialog box and accept the settings, or click Cancel to exit the dialog box without accepting the settings.

18. Start the TN5250 Service by selecting the SNA Server in the TN5250 Servers folder; then choose Start from the Service menu, press the F5 key, or right-click the SNA Server and click Start.

Configuring the Shared Folders Service

The Shared Folders service provides non-SNA clients access to PC files stored in AS/400 shared folders by using Windows NT file sharing. It is possible to configure multiple shared folders on multiple AS/400s for access by clients.

To configure the Shared Folders Service, follow these steps:

1. In the left pane of SNA Server Manager, double-click the Shared Folders Servers folder, and then select the SNA server to configure from the Shared Folders Servers folder or the right pane.

2. From the Insert menu, choose Shared Folders and click AS/400 Definition; or right-click the selected SNA server, choose Insert, Shared Folders, and then click AS/400 Definition. The AS/400 Definition Properties dialog box appears (see Figure 40.55).

FIG. 40.55

The Shared Folders Servers AS/400 Definition Properties dialog box is used to define AS/400 parameters.

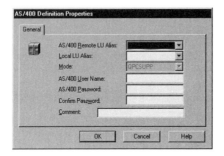

3. In the AS/400 Remote LU Alias box, select a remote LU alias from the drop-down list.

4. In the Local LU Alias box, select a local LU alias from the drop-down list.

5. No action is required in the Mode box. It simply displays the required mode, QPCSUPP, for shared folders.

6. In the AS/400 User Name box, enter the AS/400 username that will be used to establish TN5250 connections. All shared folders connections will inherit the permissions of this account.

7. In the AS/400 Password box, enter the password for the username assigned in step 6.

8. In the Confirm Password box, enter the same password as in step 7.

9. The Comment box is optional. If you do decide to enter a comment, you can enter up to 25 characters of freeform text.

10. Click OK to exit the dialog box and accept the settings, or click Cancel to exit the dialog box without accepting the settings.

Now that AS/400 definition is configured, you can create a folder definition for each shared folder to which you will be connecting. Follow these steps:

1. In the left pane of SNA Server Manager, double-click the Shared Folders Servers folder; select the SNA server to configure; and then select the AS/400 definition below the SNA server or from the right pane.

2. From the Insert menu, choose Shared Folders and click Folder Definition; or right-click the selected SNA Server, choose Insert, Shared Folders, and then click Folder Definition. The Shared Folder Properties dialog box appears, as shown in Figure 40.56.

FIG. 40.56

The Shared Folder Properties dialog box defines shared folder properties for Windows NT.

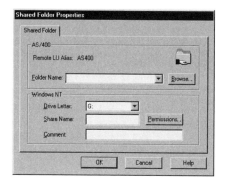

3. In the Folder Name box, enter the name of an AS/400 shared folder, or click Browse and select an AS/400 shared folder from the drop-down list.

4. In the Drive Letter box, select a drive from the drop-down list.

5. In the Share Name box, accept the default share name (same as the folder name), or enter the share name to enable clients to share the folder.

6. Click Permissions to limit access to the shared folder. The Access Through Share Permissions dialog box appears, in which you can add and remove users and groups, and select the type of access. The default is the Everyone group has Full Control.

Part VIII

Ch 40

CAUTION

You must configure shared folders security by using the Permissions button. Do not configure shared folders security in Windows NT Explorer.

7. The Comment box is optional. If you do decide to enter a comment, you can enter up to 25 characters of freeform text.

8. Click OK to exit the dialog box and accept the settings, or click Cancel to exit the dialog box without accepting the settings.

9. Start the Shared Folders Service by selecting the SNA Server in the Shared Folders Servers folder; then choose Start from the Service menu, press the F5 key, or right-click the SNA Server and click Start. The shared folder appears in Windows NT Explorer or the Network Neigborhood on the SNA server.

N O T E   Macintosh clients cannot access the AS/400 shared folders drive because Windows NT
Services for Macintosh only supports NTFS volumes. The AS/400 shared folders appear as
a FAT partition on an NTFS volume. ▓

From Here...

This chapter examined the concepts and detailed the procedures necessary to set up SNA
Server, add and configure link services, configure its connections to the host computer system,
configure LUs, and configure several alternative services. You should now be familiar with the
various parameters used to configure the SDLC, 802.2, X.25, Channel, DFT, Twinax, and DLS
connections and be able to apply these parameters properly. You should know how to configure
3270 LUs and local and remote APPC LUs. You should be knowledgeable about the actions
required to group LUs into pools, and assign LUs and LU pools to users and groups. Lastly, you
should know how to configure the Host Print Service, TN3270 Service, TN5250 Service, and
Shared Folders Service.

The following chapters cover topics related to those in this chapter:

■ For information on using the Windows NT Server administrative tools as the SNA
Server administrator, see Chapter 7, "Administering Windows NT Server."

■ To review basic SNA concepts and SNA Server installation procedures, see Chapter 39,
"SNA Server Preparation and Installation."

■ For information on managing the SNA Server on a daily basis as the SNA Server
administrator, see Chapter 41, "The Role of the SNA Server Administrator."

CHAPTER 41

The Role of the SNA Server Administrator

by Daniel Garcia and Jim Marshbank

The preceding SNA Server chapters explored, in detail, the steps necessary to install and configure the SNA Server. Critical activities such as planning the SNA Server installation, using the SNA Server Setup program, and using the SNA Server Manager program to configure link services, connections, and logical units (LUs) have now brought you to the important task of managing the SNA Server operational environment on a daily basis. The individual usually responsible for this management duty is called the *SNA Server administrator.*

The primary role of the SNA Server administrator in managing the SNA Server operational environment can be categorized into three main functions that are performed on a regular basis. These functions include the following:

How to administer servers, connections, and logical units (LUs)

Learn how to start and stop SNA servers and connections, reset LUs, and manage configuration files. Follow detailed procedures to perform daily SNA Server administrator connection management functions.

How to control access to SNA Server and host resources

Enhance your understanding of Window NT Server and SNA Server security features by walking through step-by-step procedures for granting access and permissions to users and groups. Learn how to monitor security-related events and change SNA Server administrative access ownership.

How to diagnose problems with SNA Server

Familiarize yourself with routine diagnostic tools available to the SNA Server administrator for viewing server and connection status. Learn how to use standard Windows NT Server monitoring tools for tracking response time, performance, and events.

- Managing connectivity to host computer resources
- Managing access to SNA Server and host resources
- Diagnosing problems

This chapter explores each of these functions in detail and, where appropriate, outlines the step-by-step procedures necessary to perform specific tasks associated with them. ■

Managing Connectivity to Host Computer Resources

The productivity of users on the SNA network depends heavily on the daily management of the services, connections, LUs, and resources used to establish and maintain effective and efficient connectivity between the user, SNA Server, and host computer. The SNA Server administrator is the person who keeps this connectivity viable so that network productivity is maximized.

Connectivity management is a daily responsibility, not only from the perspective of monitoring the network for reduced efficiencies and problem identification, but also from the perspective of coping with the numerous enterprise changes that occur as a result of routine business dynamics. The SNA Server administrator uses the SNA Server Manager program to accomplish most of these connectivity management responsibilities.

The following sections focus on the most common administrative procedures you need to effectively administer your SNA Server and its associated connections. Bear in mind, however, to fully use these procedures and manage the connectivity between the SNA Server and the host computer, you must have full administrative privileges for the Windows NT Server on which the SNA Server resides. The following administrative functions are described:

- Starting and stopping servers and connections
- Resetting LUs
- Changing the domain of focus
- Deleting SNA resources
- Working with configuration files
- Changing the primary SNA server

Starting and Stopping Servers and Connections

The SNA Server, and the connections that allow it to communicate with the client PCs and host systems, must be started before they can be of any use.

N O T E You have to configure connections before you can start them. Refer to Chapter 40, "Building SNA Server," for detailed information on configuring connections. ■

You can start and stop all servers and connections manually in SNA Server Manager. SNA Server Manager dynamically displays four connection states for servers and connections—Active, Pending, Stopping, and Inactive.

Stopping a connection frees up that connection (unless it is of the dedicated type) and makes it available for other possible uses. Connections can be stopped individually, or all the connections on a server can be stopped simultaneously by stopping the SNA Server itself. You also may need to stop the SNA Server to activate configuration changes. Although SNA Server Manager dynamically updates the running server when most configuration changes are made, stopping and restarting the server may still be necessary to activate certain changes.

> **CAUTION**
>
> You must ensure that all active users have logged off the remote host or peer system before stopping the SNA Server. Also, ensure that active users on a particular connection have logged off before stopping the connection. Failure to ensure that each user has logged off could result in an unstable or nonfunctional remote host or peer system.

Starting SNA Servers and Connections   Follow these steps to start SNA servers and connections:

1. From SNA Server Manager, select the server or connection that you want to start.

2. In the SNA Server Manager menu, choose Service, Start; or right-click the server or connection and then click Start.

Stopping SNA Servers and Connections   Follow these steps to stop SNA Servers and connections:

1. From SNA Server Manager, select the server or connection that you want to stop.

2. In the SNA Server Manager menu, choose Service, Stop; or right-click the server or connection and click Stop.

3. When the confirmation dialog box appears, click Yes.

Resetting Logical Units (LUs)

You can eliminate minor problems with an LU by resetting it, or in other words, by stopping it and allowing it to restart as needed. If your system has APPC LUs configured on it, you also can deactivate individual LU-LU sessions when necessary. Only LUs in the Active, SSCP, or In Session states can be reset.

Resetting an LU   The procedure for resetting an LU is as follows:

1. From SNA Server Manager left pane, click the connection associated with the Active or In Session LU that you want to stop. This causes all the LUs associated with the highlighted connection to be listed in the right pane of SNA Server Manager.

2. Click the LU you want to reset. Remember that the status of the LU must be Active, SSCP, or In Session.

3. In the SNA Server Manager menu, choose Service, Stop; or right-click the LU and click Stop.

4. When the confirmation prompt appears, click Yes.

Resetting an LU in an LU Pool   To reset an LU in an LU pool, follow these steps:

1. Double-click the Pools folder in SNA Server Manager to list the LU Pools.

2. Click the LU Pool containing the LU you want to reset. This causes all the LUs contained in the highlighted LU Pool to be listed in the right pane of the SNA Server Manager.

3. Click the LU you want to reset. Remember that the status of the LU must be Active, SSCP, or In Session.

4. In the SNA Server Manager menu, choose Service, Stop; or right-click the LU and click Stop.

5. When the confirmation prompt appears, click Yes.

Deactivating an APPC LU-LU Session   To deactivate an APPC LU-LU session, follow these steps:

1. In SNA Server Manager, click the SNA Server containing the local APPC LU associated with the LU-LU session you want to deactivate.

2. Double-click the local APPC LUs folder to list the local APPC LUs.

3. Click the local APPC LU associated with the LU-LU session you want to deactivate. This causes all LU-LU sessions contained in the highlighted local APPC LU to be listed in the right pane of the SNA Server Manager.

4. Click the LU-LU session you want to deactivate.

5. In the SNA Server Manager menu, choose Service, Stop; or right-click the LU-LU session and click Stop.

6. When the confirmation prompt appears, click Yes.

Changing the Domain of Focus

You may be required at some time to work with SNA servers in different domains. You can gain access to these other SNA servers (provided that you have sufficient privileges) by changing the domain of focus. To change to a different domain, follow these steps:

1. In the SNA Server Manager menu, choose File, Open Subdomain to display the Open Subdomain dialog box shown in Figure 41.1.

FIG. 41.1

SNA Server Manager can be used to view and manage all of the SNA Subdomains on your network.

2. In the Subdomain box, enter the name of an SNA Server subdomain or a Windows NT domain.

3. A new SNA Manager window displaying the subdomain appears. To switch to the previous subdomain, select the Window menu and click the subdomain name, which is

listed at the bottom of the <u>W</u>indow menu. To view all subdomains, select the <u>W</u>indow menu and click <u>T</u>ile or <u>C</u>ascade. A blank window appears if no computers running SNA Server are found in the subdomain.

Deleting SNA Resources

It is easy to delete SNA resources (server, connection, LU, LU pool, LU assignments to LU pools or users/groups, users/groups) by simply selecting a resource in SNA Server Manager and pressing the Delete key on your keyboard. The resource will not be deleted until you confirm the deletion request by clicking <u>Y</u>es (or Yes to <u>A</u>ll if more than one item is being deleted simultaneously) in the confirmation message box.

> **CAUTION**
>
> You must ensure that all active users have logged off the remote host or peer system before deleting any SNA Server resources. Also ensure that active users on a particular SNA Server resource have logged off before deleting the resource. Failure to ensure that each user has logged off could result in an unstable or nonfunctional remote host or peer system.

N O T E   SNA Server Manager locks the configuration file when you make a configuration change. The status bar will flash CONFIG LOCK when the configuration file is locked. Any changes made will not be available until the configuration file is saved. Only after you save the configuration file is the lock released and the status bar cleared. If there are any SNA servers in the subdomain, they will be dynamically updated. Also, when a configuration file change has occurred, SNA Server Manager running on other computers in the subdomain is not updated and the status bar will display OUT OF DATE. If an SNA server is in an OUT OF DATE status, you must close and reopen SNA Server Manager. ▨

Working with Configuration Files

You can manipulate configuration files in many ways. Some of the more common administrative operations you can perform on configuration files include the following:

- Saving the current configuration
- Backing up the current configuration
- Restoring a configuration from a backup configuration file
- Copying configuration files between SNA servers

Saving the Current Configuration   To save the current configuration displayed in SNA Server Manager, choose <u>F</u>ile, <u>S</u>ave. The configuration file is saved to the Primary SNA Server and reloaded the next time you start SNA Server. If the configuration file cannot be saved to the Primary SNA Server for any reason, you should back up the configuration file in accordance with procedures described in the next section so that the information is not lost.

N O T E   A back-up of the configuration file should be kept at all times as a safety precaution to
system crashes, file corruption, and so on. If changes to the configuration file are made on
a regular basis, then back up the configuration file on a regular basis as well. ■

Backing Up the Current Configuration   To back up the current configuration, perform these
steps:

1. In the SNA Server Manager menu, choose File, Backup Configuration to display the
   Save As dialog box shown in Figure 41.2.

FIG. 41.2
The Save As dialog
box provides all the
information you need to
select the location and
file name in which to
save the backup
configuration file.

2. Specify the location and file name for the configuration file. The default file name
   extension for a backup configuration file is SNA. This dialog box has the same functionality as the standard Windows Save As dialog box with which you are probably already
   familiar.

3. Click Save. The configuration file is saved in the specified location using the specified file
   name and file name extension.

Restoring a Configuration from a Backup Configuration File   To restore a configuration
from a backup configuration file, follow these steps:

1. In the SNA Server Manager menu, choose File, Restore to display the Open dialog box
   (see Figure 41.3).

FIG. 41.3
The Open dialog
box provides all the
information you need to
select the location and
file name from which to
restore the configuration
file.

2. Specify the location and file name of the configuration file you want to restore. This dialog box has the same functionality as the standard windows Open dialog box with which you are probably already familiar.

3. Click Open, and the configuration file is restored. SNA Server is now ready for operation.

Copying Configuration Files Between Servers When you change and save the configuration file, the primary SNA server is designed to replicate the configuration file to each of the SNA servers designated with "backup" roles. If this replication does not complete normally for any reason, you should use the following procedure for manually copying the configuration file to the backup servers:

1. On the primary SNA server, open a command-prompt window.

2. Access the directory on the primary SNA server hard drive containing the configuration file. On standard installations, this is C:\SNA\SYSTEM\CONFIG.

3. There is a directory on the backup SNA server that is shared so that the primary SNA server can access configuration files on both the primary and backup SNA servers as necessary. This directory is commonly referred to as the *share point directory* and, on standard installations, is located at the network path *servername*\COMCFG where *servername* is the name of the backup SNA server. You can access this share point directory on the backup SNA server using standard network commands.

4. Copy the COM.CFG file from the primary SNA server directory path C:\SNA\SYSTEM\CONFIG to the backup SNA server share point directory *servername*\COMCFG.

5. Answer Yes when the confirmation prompt appears.

Changing the Primary SNA Server

Earlier chapters discussed the SNA Server roles, which consist of the primary, backup, and member roles. The primary SNA server has control over its portion of the Windows NT domain (called a *subdomain*) and is the keeper of the master configuration file for its subdomain. Therefore, only one primary SNA server can be in each subdomain.

The backup SNA server is supplied a read-only copy of the last-saved configuration file so that it can assume primary responsibilities automatically in the event the primary SNA server fails or its connection is lost. When a primary SNA server is unavailable, the backup SNA server is used to stop and start servers, connections, and LUs, but the configuration file cannot be changed or saved. Within a single subdomain, 14 backup SNA servers can coexist, with each one having its own copy of the last-saved configuration file (as supplied by the primary SNA server).

These primary and backup servers communicate with each other in two ways to ensure that configuration information and data pertaining to operational status remain current:

- Backup SNA servers replicate the SNA Server configuration file (COM.CFG) from the primary SNA server each time the configuration is changed and saved by SNA Server Manager.

■ SNA servers send broadcast messages to each other to notify the other SNA servers of major status changes in the server, such as when the SNA Server service is started or stopped.

Thus, any backup server in the subdomain can automatically assume primary SNA server responsibilities in the event the primary can no longer function in its role. This is only a temporary recovery measure, however, to allow user activity to continue, essentially uninterrupted, until the primary server comes back online or until the SNA Server administrator manually changes the roles of the servers in the subdomain. Of course, there could be less traumatic reasons for switching server roles. For example, you need to be able to change SNA Server roles when you acquire a "bigger and better" PC to replace the existing primary SNA server. Another reason for a server role change might be the need to restructure an existing subdomain and use some of its resources to form a second subdomain. Regardless of the reason, there is certainly ample justification for the need to change SNA Server roles from time to time.

Perform the following steps to change the primary SNA server:

1. Use SNA Server Manager to back up the configuration file on the current primary SNA server. See "Backing Up the Current Configuration" earlier in the chapter.

2. Open a command-prompt window in Windows NT Server on the primary SNA server.

3. At the command prompt, type **net stop snabase** and press Enter.

4. Change the role of the current primary SNA server to backup or member.

5. Open a command-prompt window on the server that will become the new primary SNA server.

6. At the command prompt, type **net stop snabase** and press Enter.

7. On the server that will become the new primary SNA server, use SNA Server Manager to assign the primary role to the new SNA Server, as outlined in Chapter 39, "SNA Server Preparation and Installation."

   ▶ **See** "Selecting the Server Role," **p. 1343**

8. In the SNA Server Manager menu on the new primary SNA server, choose File, Restore, and select the backup configuration file saved in step 1 of this procedure.

9. Open a command-prompt window on the server that used to be the primary SNA server.

10. At the command prompt, type **net start snabase** and press Enter.

11. Open a command-prompt window on the new primary SNA SERVER (server that used to be the backup SNA Server).

12. At the command prompt, type **net start snabase** and press Enter.

Managing Access to SNA Server and Host Resources

With the degree of dependence placed on automation and its associated resources in the normal operation of business enterprises today, obvious importance is placed on controlling who can see and use the programs, data, and resources of the enterprise network. In an era when the inability to retrieve and manipulate electronic data equates to a serious loss of productivity, businesses are willing to heavily invest time and capital to prevent the intentional, as well as accidental, destruction of critical data files and software components. Fortunately, SNA Server and the Windows NT Server environment in which it operates possess powerful security features that allow you to manage and control access to the SNA Server and host resources.

Using SNA Server Security Features

SNA security features are embodied within the security mechanisms of the Windows NT Server. When you first install SNA Server, a security foundation equivalent to that already present in the Windows NT Server domain is established automatically. When you configure the security features of SNA Server, you add to this basic security functionality. The configuration parameters you specify for this additional security are actually implemented through the design architecture of the Windows NT Server itself. For example, basic Windows NT Server security concepts such as domains, user accounts, user permissions, and logons are automatically extended into the SNA Server network by virtue of the Windows NT Server operating system under which the SNA Server was installed. The following sections take a closer look at some of the SNA Server security features that actually supplement the basic security provided through the Windows NT Server.

Windows NT File System The NT file system (NTFS) provides a level of file security not possible with the file allocation table (FAT) or high-performance file system (HPFS), which are prevalent on IBM and compatible PCs today. Files stored on FAT and HPFS partitions can be easily accessed and modified by anyone that can log on to the computer. This is not the case with files stored on NTFS partitions. Files (or entire directories) on NTFS partitions can be protected by setting security access permissions on them, which range from no access to full control. This is an important capability when you consider the critical nature of the SNA Server configuration file.

The configuration file, which is created by SNA Server Setup and stored on both primary and backup SNA servers, contains SNA access information such as SNA user and group names and the LUs they are permitted to use. If not properly protected, this file can be accessed by anyone who can log on to the system. Potentially, the file can then be modified to grant unauthorized users full control of system resources, or otherwise tampered with to cause unreliable system performance or make system resources totally inaccessible to even authorized users. By installing SNA Server on an NTFS partition, you can easily protect this critical configuration file from this kind of unauthorized access and tampering.

Part

VIII

Ch

41

CAUTION

Do not use administrative tools to set permissions on the SNA Server configuration file directly. Doing so may block necessary SNA Server access to this file, which is required when working across the network. Instead, use the SNA Server Manager to increase SNA Server security.

If you do install SNA Server on a FAT or HPFS file system, you can still use the Subdomain Properties in the SNA Server Manager program to limit user capability to view and modify the configuration file, but you cannot set access restrictions on the configuration file itself. You can still control Read and Change permissions on the share, which gives the SNA servers access to the configuration file; but, again, you cannot protect the configuration file directly from unauthorized access. All things considered, it is certainly much better (and much safer) to install SNA Server software on NTFS partitions so that you can enjoy the configuration file protection afforded through file-level security controls.

Logon Process   Access control is enhanced by requiring users to successfully log on to the Windows NT Server domain as a first step in gaining access to any resources on the SNA Server network. It is essentially the first level of security for the SNA Server because the user is identified to the Windows NT domain and to the SNA servers through this logon process. If the Windows NT Server cannot identify the user during logon, it does not give the user access to any domain resources, SNA Server resources included.

SNA Server handles the logon process differently, depending on the client operating system and networking software being used. If Microsoft Windows 95 or Microsoft Windows NT is being used, a single valid logon gains a user access to both the Windows NT domain and all the SNA servers in the domain. If another operating system and Microsoft networking is being used, a single valid logon gains a user access to both the Windows NT domain and all the SNA servers in the domain. If another operating system and non-Microsoft networking (such as Novell NetWare, TCP/IP, and Banyan VINES) is being used, two logons are required—one for access to the Windows NT domain and one for access to the SNA servers in the domain. The same password for both logons can be used, if desired, but no information is sent from the SNA Server to the client system until both logons have been completed successfully.

Notice that in all cases, after the logon process for a particular SNA Server is completed successfully, the user is automatically granted access to the other SNA servers in the domain as well. This occurs without additional interaction between the SNA servers and the user. The other domain servers simply repeat the logon verification automatically without involving the user.

Other logon processes may be required by the host mainframe or AS/400 systems to more tightly control the resources on the host system. If the host logon process, by itself, provides sufficient access control over the required resources, it may make sense to ease access controls on the SNA Server and let the host logon process provide the necessary resource control. One way to do this is by allowing open-ended access to LUs instead of restricting access to LUs. You can create open-ended access to LUs through the standard built-in Guest account by following these steps:

1. From SNA Server Manager, double-click the Configured Users folder.
2. In the SNA Server Manager menu, choose Insert, User; or right-click the Configured Users folder, select Insert, and click User. The Add Users and Groups dialog box appears (see Figure 41.4).

FIG. 41.4

The Add Users and Groups dialog box lists all Windows NT domain users and groups for a given domain.

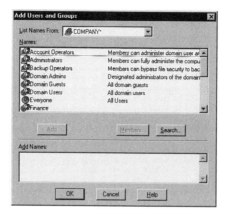

3. In the List Names From drop-down list, select the domain in which the built-in Guest account is located.

4. In the Names list, scroll as necessary to display the Guest account name. Then click the name Guest. The selection remains highlighted.

5. Click Add to place the Guest account name in the Add Names box.

6. Click OK to close the Add Users and Groups dialog box. The new Guest account just added should be displayed within the Configured Users folder.

7. Assign LU(s) and/or LU Pool(s) to the Guest account as outined in Chapter 40, "Building SNA Server."

8. In the SNA Server Manager menu, choose File, Save to save the configuration.

You also can create open-ended access to LUs through the account called Everyone by following the preceding steps to add the account to the list of configured users recognized by SNA Server and assigning LU(s) and/or LU Pool(s) to the Everyone account.

Understanding Permissions

Permissions allow you to limit or totally restrict a user's capability to access and manipulate resources, files, or programs on the SNA Server. More specifically, you can use SNA Server Manager to establish administrative permissions for SNA Server and thus control access to the configuration file (when using NTFS) and the SNA Server Manager program. Because this program is used to modify the SNA Server configuration and to enable resources (servers, connections, services, and so on), you should judiciously apply and carefully manage administrative permissions on a continuing basis. The next few sections detail the procedures for the following tasks:

- Granting administrative access to users and groups
- Changing currently assigned administrative permissions
- Removing administrative access from users and groups

Part
VIII

Ch
41

Granting Administrative Access   To grant administrative access, follow these steps:

1. Select the subdomain icon on the left pane of SNA Server Manager.

2. In the SNA Server Manager menu, choose View, Properties; or right-click the subdomain icon and then click Properties. The SNA Subdomain Properties dialog box appears. Click the Config File Security tab, as shown in Figure 41.5.

FIG. 41.5

Use the Config File Security tab in the Subdomain Properties dialog box to set security on the configuration file for the domain specified.

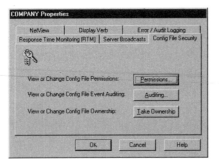

3. Click the Permissions button to display the SNA Subdomain Permissions dialog box (see Figure 41.6). Note that the current domain of focus is listed in the SNA Subdomain box and the Owner box lists the account name designated as the owner of the capability to grant or deny administrative access to the SNA Server. The Name list displays the accounts (both groups and users) that currently have access permissions. The Type of Access box displays the type of access currently assigned to the entry highlighted in the Name list.

N O T E   The procedure for taking ownership is described in the section "Changing SNA Server Administrative Access Ownership" later in this chapter. ▪

FIG. 41.6

The SNA Subdomain Permissions dialog box allows you to grant a specific level of access to groups or individual users for the domain specified.

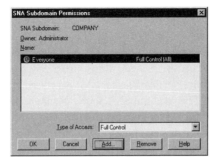

4. Click Add to display the Add Users and Groups dialog box, as shown in Figure 41.7.

5. In the List Names From drop-down list, select the domain to which the users or groups to be added belong. Only trusted domains are listed.

FIG. 41.7

The Add Users and Groups dialog box lists all Windows NT domain users and groups for a given domain.

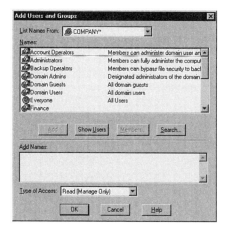

6. From the list of users and groups displayed in the <u>N</u>ames area of the dialog box, select the one to be added.

   If you want to search for a particular user or group, continue with step 7. Otherwise, skip to step 13.

7. Click <u>S</u>earch to display the Find Account dialog box.

8. In the Find <u>U</u>ser or Group box, enter the name of the user or group for which you are searching.

9. Select the search domain by doing one of the following:

   - Click Search A<u>l</u>l to search in all the domains.

   - Click Search <u>O</u>nly In to search in a particular domain. If you select this option, you also must select one of the domains in the list box below the radio buttons. The <u>S</u>earch button does not become available until you do.

T I P If you want to select the Search <u>O</u>nly In option, click the desired domain in the list box below the search option radio buttons instead of clicking the Search <u>O</u>nly In radio button. When you click one of the listed domains, SNA Server Manager automatically highlights the Search <u>O</u>nly In radio button. Thus, you can reduce two required mouse clicks to only one.

Part
VIII

Ch
41

10. Click <u>S</u>earch to start the search. When the search is completed, the results appear in the Search <u>R</u>esults list box, or you are notified that the indicated search item could not be found in the selected domain.

11. Repeat steps 8 through 10 as necessary.

12. Highlight the desired search results in the Search <u>R</u>esults list box, and click <u>A</u>dd to place the selected search results in the A<u>d</u>d Names list box of the Add Users and Groups dialog box. If you want to select more users and/or groups from the <u>N</u>ames list box, continue with step 14. Otherwise, skip to step 17.

T I P To select multiple sequential search result entries, click the first one in the sequence, hold down the Shift key, and click the last one in the sequence. All the search result entries in the range are highlighted.

To assign multiple nonsequential search result entries, hold down the Ctrl key while clicking each search result entry. Each selection remains highlighted.

13. In the Names list, select the user(s) and/or group(s) to receive administrative permissions.

14. Click Add to add the selected user(s) and/or group(s) to the Add Names box.

15. In the Type of Access drop-down list, select the type of access you want the account(s) listed in the Add Names box to have. The possible types of access are as follows:

- **No Access.** Prohibits a user or group from running SNA Server Manager or the snacfg command-line program, or reading and writing the configuration file. This type of access overrides all other permissions that apply to a particular user. If the user belongs to a group that has full control, for example, the user is denied administrative access because No Access overrides the Full Control permissions. Other members of the group retain full control.

- **Full Control.** Permits a user or group to run SNA Server Manager, to run the snacfg command-line program, to read and write the configuration file, and to change the administrative permissions assigned to other accounts. Assign this type of access to SNA Server administrators who will be starting and stopping SNA Server services, permanently changing the SNA Server configuration, managing other SNA Server user and group permissions, and removing SNA Server software from Windows NT Server-controlled PCs.

- **Read (Manage Only).** Permits a user or group to run SNA Server Manager, to run the snacfg command-line program, and to read the configuration file. Users or groups are prohibited from permanently changing the SNA Server configuration because they cannot write to the configuration file. Assign this type of access to SNA Server administrators who will be viewing, starting, and stopping SNA Server services.

- **Read/Write.** Permits a user or group to run SNA Server Manager, to run the snacfg command-line program, and to read and write the configuration file. Assign this type of access to SNA Server administrators who will be starting and stopping SNA Server services and permanently changing the SNA Server configuration.

- **Special.** Permits an SNA Server administrator to tailor a set of administrative permissions for a particular user or group of users. You can selectively assign administrative permissions for managing domains, reading domains, writing domains, viewing permissions, changing permissions, and changing owners.

CAUTION

Creating special cases and permitting exceptions to the norm usually complicate management and control responsibilities and increase the risk of inadvertent or unauthorized access. Creating special permission sets also potentially increases risks. For this reason, limit the use of special types of access and use the standard types of access whenever possible.

16. Click OK to close the Add Users and Groups dialog box and redisplay the SNA Subdomain Permissions dialog box.

17. Click OK to close the SNA Subdomain Permissions dialog box. Click OK to close the SNA Subdomain Properties dialog box and redisplay the SNA Server Manager window.

Changing Currently Assigned Administrative Permissions   To change currently assigned administrative permissions, perform the following steps:

1. Follow steps 1 through 3 as described in the section "Granting Administrative Access" earlier in this chapter.

2. In the Name list, click the user or group for which you want to change the administrative permissions.

3. In the Type of Access drop-down list, select the type of access you want the account(s) listed in the Name box to have. The possible types of access are described as follows:

   - **No Access.** Prohibits a user or group from running SNA Server Manager or the snacfg command-line program, or reading and writing the configuration file. This type of access overrides all other permissions that apply to a particular user. If the user belongs to a group that has full control, for example, the user is denied administrative access because No Access overrides the Full Control permissions. Other members of the group retain full control.

   - **Full Control.** Permits a user or group to run SNA Server Manager, to run the snacfg command-line program, to read and write the configuration file, and to change the administrative permissions assigned to other accounts. Assign this type of access to SNA Server administrators who will be starting and stopping SNA Server services, permanently changing the SNA Server configuration, managing other SNA Server user and group permissions, and removing SNA Server software from Windows NT Server-controlled PCs.

   - **Read (Manage Only).** Permits a user or group to run SNA Server Manager, to run the snacfg command-line program, and to read the configuration file. Users or groups are prohibited from permanently changing the SNA Server configuration because they cannot write to the configuration file. Assign this type of access to SNA Server administrators who will be viewing, starting, and stopping SNA Server services.

   - **Read/Write.** Permits a user or group to run SNA Server Manager, to run the snacfg command-line program, and to read and write the configuration file. Assign this type of access to SNA Server administrators who will be starting and stopping SNA Server services and permanently changing the SNA Server configuration.

Part
VIII

Ch
41

- **Special.** Permits an SNA Server administrator to tailor a set of administrative permissions for a particular user or group of users. You can selectively assign administrative permissions for managing domains, reading domains, writing domains, viewing permissions, changing permissions, and changing owners.

4. Click OK to close the SNA Subdomain Permissions dialog box. Click OK to close the SNA Subdomain Properties dialog box and redisplay the SNA Server Manager window.

Removing Administrative Access   You can deny a user or group administrative access by removing the user/group name from the Name list of the SNA Subdomain Permissions dialog box or by assigning the No Access type of access to the user/group to be denied. Of these two methods, assigning No Access is usually the fastest and surest way of removing administrative access. Because the No Access option overrides all other administrative permissions, you do not have to worry about the user(s) gaining access through another group (with access) to which the user(s) may belong. On the other hand, if you deny access to a user by removing the user account from the Name list in the SNA Subdomain Permissions dialog box, you must make sure that you have considered all the possible groups to which the user belongs. Otherwise, the user may be able to gain access through another group that you failed to consider. See the earlier section "Changing Currently Assigned Administrative Permissions" to remove access by assigning the No Access option to the user or group.

To remove administrative access by removing the user account from the Name list in the SNA Subdomain Permissions dialog box, follow these steps:

1. Follow steps 1 through 3 as described in the section "Granting Administrative Access" earlier in this chapter.

2. In the Name list, click the user or group you want to remove.

3. Click Remove. The highlighted account name is removed from the Name list.

4. Click OK to close the SNA Subdomain Permissions dialog box. Click OK to close the SNA Subdomain Properties dialog box and redisplay the SNA Server Admin window.

Changing SNA Server Administrative Access Ownership

Ownership is a concept implemented through the Windows NT Server operating system and applies to all server types operating in a Windows NT environment. Essentially, the owner of the capability to administer SNA Server (the Administrator account, by default) has greater administrative permissions than anyone else. As a matter of fact, the owner always has (or can always get) full administrative access. This is important to know in cases where administrative permissions may have been inadvertently removed or overly restricted in SNA Server Manager. In such cases, the owner can always go in and grant themselves Full Control and then reinstate removed access or relieve access restrictions as necessary.

Ownership normally includes owning all copies of the configuration file as well, even those on backup SNA servers. Because you must have an account on a server before you can own the configuration file for that server, there could be potential problems in domains where multiple SNA servers exist. Therefore, ownership must be restricted to accounts that exist on every

SNA server in the domain, whether primary or backup servers. This is why the Administrator group account is the default owner—it is a built-in account on every Windows NT-based server.

Ownership of the capability to administer the SNA Server can be seized, however, by any user or group granted Full Control or Special access with Change Owner permissions. In multiple server domains, this user or group has to have an account on every primary and backup SNA Server, or not be able to seize ownership for the server where the account does not exist. The current owner instead retains ownership. Ownership on servers where the accounts do exist, however, pass to the user or group seizing ownership.

If a user takes ownership while being logged on in an account that is a member of the Administrator group, ownership passes to the Administrator group, not the individual user attempting to seize ownership. Indeed, this is the recommended method of ensuring a successful transfer of ownership—through the Administrator group.

To take ownership, follow these steps:

1. Log on to the Windows NT Server using the account you want to acquire ownership status, and then open SNA Server Manager.

2. Select the subdomain icon on the left pane of SNA Server Manager.

3. In the SNA Server Manager menu, choose View, Properties; or right-click the subdomain icon and then click Properties. The SNA Subdomain Properties dialog box appears. Click the Config File Security tab (refer to Figure 41.5).

4. Click Take Ownership to display the Owner dialog box (see Figure 41.8).

FIG. 41.8
Use the Owner dialog box to acquire ownership of the capability to administer SNA Server.

5. Click Take Ownership. This closes the Owner dialog box and redisplays the SNA Subdomain Properties dialog box.

6. Click OK to return to the SNA Server Manager window. If no messages to the contrary appear, ownership was successfully transferred.

Part
VIII

Ch
41

Setting Up Auditing to Monitor Security-Related Events

Auditing is a feature provided through the Windows NT Server operating system. Auditing is performed by the system when specific events are recorded in an event log as they occur. When you set up the auditing feature, you can specify which events to audit. Then when the specified event occurs, such as a member of the Administrator Group changing the configuration file, for example, the system automatically records information concerning that event.

Auditing is also an important method of collecting security-related information. When auditing is used, however, system resources must be used for tracking and recording audited events.

This means you pay a small price in performance overhead for each event audited. Additionally, if numerous events are audited, the size of the event log can quickly get very large. Therefore, you are wise to carefully select which events should be audited so that useless event log entries are avoided and system performance is not unnecessarily affected.

N O T E Installing SNA Server on FAT or HPFS partitions rather than NTFS partitions severely limits your possibilities for auditing. In these cases, the only event that actually results in log entries is the starting of SNA Server Manager. Although this might still be helpful, it is certainly less useful than being able to log numerous types of SNA Server processes. ■

To set up auditing to monitor security-related events, perform the following actions:

1. If auditing has already been turned on in the domain, and File and Object Access has been selected with the Success and Failure options activated, skip to step 8. Otherwise, continue with step 2 to turn auditing on and select the required options.

2. Click the Start button and select Programs, Administrative Tools (Common), and click User Manager for Domains. The User Manager window appears.

3. In the User Manager menu, choose Policies, Audit to display the Audit Policy dialog box shown in Figure 41.9.

FIG. 41.9
Any number of events can be audited; however, system performance will suffer as more events are audited.

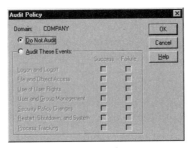

4. If Audit These Events is already turned on, skip to step 6. Otherwise, click the Audit These Events radio button.

5. Click the Success and Failure check boxes across from File and Object Access to select these options. Both these check boxes should be selected, or marked with an X when you finish.

6. Click OK to close the Audit Policy dialog box and redisplay the User Manager window.

7. In the User Manager menu, choose User, Exit to close the User Manager window.
   If SNA Server Manager is already active, skip to step 9. Otherwise, continue with step 8 to start SNA Server Manager.

8. Click the Start button and select Programs, Microsoft SNA Server (Common), and click Manager. The SNA Server Manager window appears.

9. Select the subdomain icon on the left pane of SNA Server Manager.

10. In the SNA Server Manager menu, choose View, Properties; or right-click the subdomain icon and then click Properties. The SNA Subdomain Properties dialog box appears. Click the Config File Security tab (refer to Figure 41.5).

11. Click Auditing to display the SNA Subdomain Auditing dialog box shown in Figure 41.10.

FIG. 41.10

The SNA Subdomain Auditing dialog box displays the Events to Audit as being unavailable until a user or group is added to the Name box.

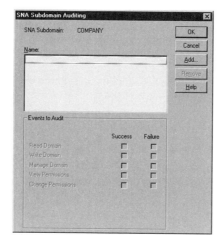

12. Click Add to display the Add Users and Groups dialog box (refer to Figure 41.4).

13. In the List Names From drop-down list, select the domain that the users or groups you want to add belong to. Only trusted domains are listed.

14. Click Show Users to display user and group accounts in the Names list.

    If you want to search for a particular user or group, continue with step 15. Otherwise, skip to step 21.

15. Click Search to display the Find Account dialog box.

16. In the Find User or Group box, enter the name of the user or group for which you are searching.

17. Select the search domain by doing one of the following:

    - Click Search All to search in all the domains.

    - Click Search Only In button to search in a particular domain. If you select this option, you also must select one of the domains listed in the list box below the radio buttons. The Search button does not become available until you do.

18. Click Search to start the search. When the search is completed, the results appear in the Search Results list, or you are notified that the indicated search item could not be found in the selected domain.

19. Repeat steps 16 through 18 as necessary.

20. Highlight the desired search results in the Search Results list, and click Add to place the selected search results in the Add Names list of the Add Users and Groups dialog box. If

you want to select more users and/or groups from the Names list box, continue with step 21. Otherwise, skip to step 23.

21. In the Names list, select the user(s) and/or group(s) whose actions you want to audit.

22. Click Add button to add the selected user(s) and/or group(s) to the Add Names box.

23. Click OK to close the Add Users and Groups dialog box and redisplay the SNA Subdomain Auditing dialog box. The Name list should now display the users and groups for which you can specify actions to be audited.

24. In the Name list, select a user or group.

25. In the Events to Audit area of the SNA Subdomain Auditing dialog box, select the events you want to audit for the user or group selected.

26. Repeat steps 24 and 25 for each of the users and groups listed in the Name list. If no actions are specified for a user or group, that user or group is deleted from the Name list when you perform step 27.

27. Click OK to close the SNA Subdomain Auditing dialog box and redisplay the SNA Subdomain Properties dialog box. Click OK to return to the SNA Server Manager window.

Diagnosing Problems

The tight integration of SNA Server with the Windows NT operating systems has provided a number of tools that you can use not only to manage the network, but also to perform diagnostic appraisals of the network functions and components. SNA Server and Windows NT Server both contain numerous diagnostic tools that are invaluable in determining why SNA Server configuration and/or network problems may be occurring. These diagnostic tools allow you to monitor and trace events and collect event information leading up to a specific problem occurrence. Some of the most commonly used diagnostic tools are the following:

- SNA Server Manager
- Windows NT Server Event Viewer
- Windows NT Server Performance Monitor
- NetView
- 3270 Response Time Monitor (RTM)
- SNA Server Trace

You can use these tools to gather information regarding problem events and system status related to servers, connections, LUs, interfaces, and general system events. The type of detailed troubleshooting information you need to gather dictates which specific tool, or combination of tools, you should use. When these tools are used properly, you should be able to tell the exact state of the system at the time the problem occurred.

The SNA Server administrator is normally responsible for keeping the SNA environment running at peak efficiency. These same tools can be used to do that. By properly monitoring critical events through such tools as the RTM and performance monitor, the SNA Server administrator can fine-tune the SNA Server and its network on a continuing basis.

The following sections explore the available diagnostic tools and describe the detailed procedures you must follow to use them. The major diagnostic tools to be covered are as follows:

- SNA Server Manager for obtaining information about the status of servers, connections, and LUs

- SNA Server Manager for setting up event log parameters

- Windows NT Server Event Viewer for viewing logged information about application events on the SNA network

- Windows NT Server Performance Monitor for obtaining real-time information on system performance

- NetView for obtaining data about personal computer (PC) alerts (errors) via a mainframe host system

- Response Time Monitor (RTM) for obtaining data about the amount of time it takes a host system to respond during 3270 sessions

- SNA Server Trace for obtaining information about internal activities on the SNA network

SNA Server Manager for Status Information

When it is apparent that a particular SNA service is experiencing some type of difficulty, it may be necessary to start, stop, reset, or completely modify the service. Before you take any of these actions, however, you should first gather some status information about the SNA Server itself, the connections it is using, and the assigned LUs. Apply these procedures, described in the following sections, to perform these tasks:

- View the status of an SNA Server

- View the status of a connection

- View the status of a non-Advanced Program-to-Program Communication (APPC) LU

- View the status of an APPC LU-LU pair

- View the active LUs

Viewing the Status of an SNA Server   The procedure for viewing the status of an SNA Server is as follows:

1. Click the Start button and select Programs, Microsoft SNA Server (Common), and click Manager. The SNA Server Manager window appears.

2. From the left pane of SNA Server Manager, double-click the Server folder whose status you want to view. The server's status appears next to the server's icon below the particular folder or on the right pane of the SNA Server Manager (see Figure 41.11).

Part
VIII

Ch
41

FIG. 41.11

The SNA Server Manager dynamically provides server status information.

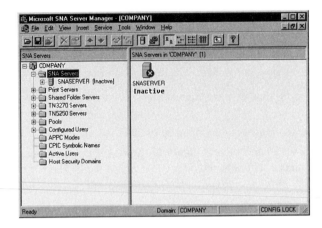

3. The SNA Server Manager reflects one of the following for the current server status:

- **Active.** When this status is reflected, the number of licensed users and sessions also is displayed.

- **Inactive.** This status is reflected when the server is not connected to a host or when the server has been stopped.

- **Pending.** This status appears temporarily whenever the server is in a transitional state, such as when it is going from a stopped state to a started state.

- **Stopping.** This is the status given when the server is stopping.

- **Active [Out of Date].** This status indicates that the server needs to be restarted so that internal parameters can be updated with the latest configuration changes.

- **Error.** This status indicates that SNA Server Manager cannot access the server due to the occurrence of an unexpected condition.

Viewing the Status of a Connection   To view the status of a connection, perform these steps:

1. Click the Start button and select Programs, Microsoft SNA Server (Common), and click Manager. The SNA Server Manager windows appears.

2. From the left pane of SNA Server Manager, double-click the SNA Server folder, and expand the server's hierarchy tree to view its folders.

3. Double-click the Connections folder. Each connection's status appears next to its icon below the particular folder, or on the right pane of the SNA Server Manager (see Figure 41.12).

FIG. 41.12

The SNA Server Manager dynamically provides connection status information.

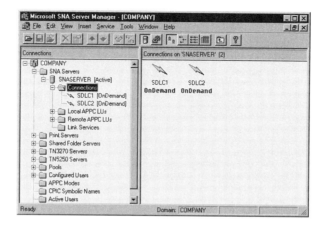

4. The SNA Server Manager reflects one of the following for the current connection status:

- **Active.** When this status is reflected, the number of licensed users and sessions also is displayed.

- **Inactive.** This status is reflected when the connection is not operational or when the connection has been stopped.

- **Pending.** This status appears temporarily whenever the connection is in a transitional state, such as when it is going from a stopped state to a started state.

- **Stopping.** This is the status given when the connection is stopping.

- **On Demand.** This status, which is possible only when connections are configured as On Demand connections, indicates that the connection can be started whenever it is needed.

- **Incoming.** This status, which is possible only when connections are configured as Incoming connections, indicates that the connection is ready to receive incoming calls.

Viewing the Status of a Non-APPC LU   To view the status of a non-APPC LU, follow these steps:

1. Click the Start button and select Programs, Microsoft SNA Server (Common), and click Manager. The SNA Server Manager windows appears.

2. From the left pane of SNA Server Manager, double-click the SNA Server folder, and expand the server's hierarchy tree to view its folders.

3. Double-click the Connections folder.

4. Select the connection for which you want to view the status of its LUs. The LUs status appears on the right pane of the SNA Server Manager, as shown in Figure 41.13.

Part
VIII

Ch
41

FIG. 41.13

The SNA Server Manager dynamically provides LU status information.

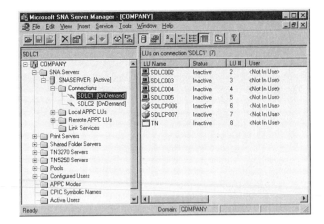

5. The SNA Server Manager reflects one of the following for the current LU status:

- **Inactive.** This status indicates that the LU is not operational and is unavailable for use.

- **In Session.** When this status is reflected, the LU is being used.

- **SSCP.** This status indicates that the LU is in use but has not yet been bound to a specific host application.

- **Available.** This status indicates that the host has recognized the LU as available for use.

- **Pending.** This status indicates that a user is trying to use the LU but cannot access it because the connection is inactive or the host has not recognized the LU as being available.

- **Unavailable.** This status is possible only on Downstream LUs.

Viewing the Status of an APPC LU-LU Pair   Perform the following steps to view the status of an APPC LU-LU pair:

1. Click the Start button and select Programs, Microsoft SNA Server (Common), and click Manager. The SNA Server Manager window appears.

2. From the left pane of SNA Server Manager, double-click the SNA Server folder, and expand the server's hierarchy tree to view its folders.

3. Double-click either the Local APPC LUs folder or Remote APPC LUs folder.

4. Select the local or remote APPC LU for which you want to view the status of its LU-LU pairs. The APPC LU-LU pair status appears on the right pane of the SNA Server Manager, as shown in Figure 41.14. Note that it contains any LUs that have been partnered with the local or remote APPC LU (LU-LU pairs).

FIG. 41.14

The SNA Server Manager dynamically provides LU-LU pair status information.

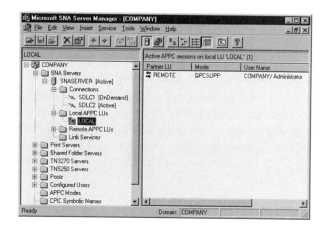

Viewing LUs in Use by an Active User

To view LUs in use by an active user, follow these steps:

1. Click the Start button and select Programs, Microsoft SNA Server (Common), and click Manager. The SNA Server Manager window appears.

2. From the left pane of SNA Server Manager, click the Active Users folder.

3. Active users are displayed on the right pane of the SNA Server Manager (see Figure 41.15). Select the All, 3270, or APPC radio button above the list of active users to view particular LUs being used. All is selected by default.

FIG. 41.15

The SNA Server Manager dynamically provides status information of LUs in use by active users.

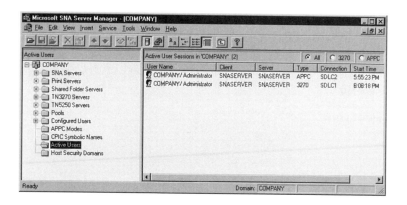

Part

VIII

Ch

41

SNA Server Manager for Event Log Parameters

SNA Server Manager also is used to set several parameters for capturing SNA Server event information. This captured event information is then recorded in one of three logs, depending on the nature of the event. Events related to system activities are recorded in the System Log; application-related events are recorded in the Application Log; and events related to security (such as accessing and/or modifying the SNA Server configuration file) are recorded in the Security Log. You can manipulate the following event log parameters through SNA Server Manager:

■ Specify the server on which the event logs will be stored.

■ Specify the general level of events to be recorded. The three levels available record all activities, general activities only, or significant system activities only. Each of these levels, in turn, generates a corresponding volume of log information. Naturally, the level that captures every possible recordable event accounts for the largest volume of data. Although this is good from a troubleshooting perspective, the size of the log file may become unwieldy.

■ Specify a server (in addition to the local server) to which pop-up error messages should be routed. These pop-up messages relate to activities on the SNA network and do not include SNA Server Admin messages.

SNA Server Manager provides you with a dialog box for setting these parameters. To access the dialog box and configure the parameters, follow these steps:

1. Click the Start button and select Programs, Microsoft SNA Server (Common), and click Manager. The SNA Server Manager window appears.

2. Select the subdomain icon on the left pane of SNA Server Manager.

3. In the SNA Server Manager menu, choose View, Properties; or right-click the subdomain icon and then click Properties. The SNA Subdomain Properties dialog box appears. Click the Error/Audit Logging tab (see Figure 41.16).

FIG. 41.16

The Error/Audit Logging tab on the SNA Subdomain Properties dialog box enables you to specify a level of logging detail, as well as indicate where to send server pop-up messages.

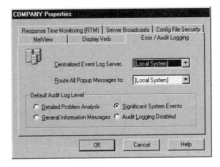

4. In the Centralized Event Log Server box, either accept the default, or click the drop-down list box to select a server from the list. This entry specifies the server on which the event logs should be stored. The local system default entry stores the logs on the server running SNA Server Manager.

5. In the Default Audit Log Level area of the dialog box, click the desired button to specify one of the following logging levels:

• **Detailed Problem Analysis.** This level captures all recordable events.

• **General Information Messages.** This level captures only general activity events.

- **S̲ignificant System Events.** This level captures only major events.
- **Audit Logging Disabled.** This option turns off the logging feature altogether, and no data of any type is captured.

6. In the R̲oute All Server Popup Messages To box, either accept the default entry of Local System, or click the drop-down list box to select a remote server from the list. This entry specifies the server (in addition to the local server) that pop-up error messages should be routed to.

N O T E Pop-up messages always display on the local SNA Server regardless of the server specified in the R̲oute All Server Popup Messages To box. The remote server specified in this box, if any, displays pop-up messages at the same time they display on the local SNA Server. ▪

7. Click OK to accept the settings and exit the SNA Subdomain Properties dialog box, or click Cancel to exit the dialog box without accepting the settings.

Windows NT Server Event Viewer

The event logs discussed in the preceding section can tell you the sequence and types of events that took place up to a selected point in time and, therefore, are very useful to product support technicians who may be working with you to solve a particularly stubborn problem. Before they can be useful, however, you must be able to view them. This is what the Windows NT Server Event Viewer allows you to do. It is designed to provide you with flexible options for controlling the display and viewing of captured event data (specifically SNA Server event data in this case). By selecting appropriate commands from the L̲og, V̲iew, and O̲ptions menus in the Event Viewer, you can tailor the log views from many computers in many different ways. Additionally, because event log data is recorded in log files (with the default extension of .EVT) and stored in SYSTEM32\CONFIG of the WINNT root directory, you can copy and print it like any other text file. This is useful when a remote support technician requests a copy of the log files for your server to assist in troubleshooting a problem.

▶ **See** "Surveying the Administrative Tools of Windows NT Server," **p. 186**

Windows NT Server Performance Monitor

The Performance Monitor is a Windows NT Server graphical tool that allows you to measure the performance of computers on the network and display that performance measurement as a continuously plotted line(s) on a graph. Because the measurements are plotted on a continuous basis, the line graph is an excellent performance-monitoring tool.

▶ **See** "Surveying the Administrative Tools of Windows NT Server," **p. 186**

To monitor performance on your SNA Server, follow these steps:

1. Click the Start button and select P̲rograms, Administrative Tools (Common), and click Performance Monitor. The Performance Monitor window appears.

2. In the Performance Monitor menu, choose E̲dit, A̲dd To Chart to display the Add To Chart dialog box (see Figure 41.17).

FIG. 41.17

The Add To Chart dialog box lets you tailor the view and specify measuring parameters for the Performance Monitor.

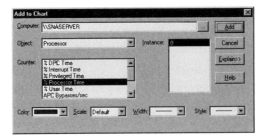

3. In the Computer box, enter the name of the SNA Server computer you want to monitor. If you are currently operating on the SNA server you want to monitor, you do not need to do anything here because the computer on which you are currently operating always appears as the default computer. If you are not operating on the SNA server you want to monitor, click the drop-down list box to select an SNA server from the list, or manually type in the name of the desired SNA server.

4. In the Object box, click the drop-down list box and select one of the following objects from the list, depending on what you want to monitor:

   - SNA Connections
   - SNA Logical Unit Sessions
   - SNA 3270 Response Times

5. In the Counter box, click the drop-down list box and select one of the counters from the list, depending on what you want to monitor. If you do not know what a particular counter measures, highlight the counter and click Explain. A definition for the counter appears at the bottom of the dialog box.

6. Click Add to add the counter's tracking line to the graph. If multiple counters are added to the graph, each counter's tracking line will have a different appearance.

NetView

IBM's NetView is a network management system that runs on the IBM host. It is helpful to the network administrator because it receives alerts from the Windows NT system, or NT-based applications, and forwards these alerts to the host computer and the network administrator. It also is helpful in diagnosing problems and improving performance on the network. The NetView service that provides this functionality is called NVAlert.

A companion service of NetView, NVRunCMD, runs as a background process on the SNA Server and is a command-line interface to the Windows NT Server. It is extremely useful in responding to NVAlert messages for diagnostic querying or for providing simple fixes to problems. For example, if a NetView operator receives an alert indicating an application could not find a particular file, the NetView operator can intervene by executing a command (via NVRunCMD) on the Windows NT Server to copy the file to an area where it can be found by the application needing it.

NetView alerts can be sent through any host connection except a Distributed Function Terminal (DFT) connection. You can specify through which host connection the NetView data should be sent by doing the following:

1. Click the Start button and select Programs, Microsoft SNA Server (Common), and click Manager. The SNA Server Manager window appears.

2. Select the subdomain icon on the left pane of SNA Server Manager.

3. In the SNA Server Manager menu, choose View, Properties; or right-click the subdomain icon and then click Properties. The SNA Subdomain Properties dialog box appears. Click the NetView tab shown in Figure 41.18.

FIG. 41.18

The NetView tab in the SNA Subdomain Properties dialog box is simply used to specify a connection through which the management data should be sent.

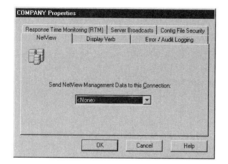

4. In the Send NetView Management Data to this Connection drop-down list, select a non-DFT host connection.

5. Click OK to accept the connection and clear the SNA Subdomain Properties dialog box.

Response Time Monitor (RTM)

The RTM, an IBM NetView function that measures response time between a host and a 3270 session, is another valuable diagnostic tool. But to use it, your 3270 emulator must be capable of supporting it. SNA Server Manager allows you to tailor the RTM by specifying such things as when the collected data should be sent and what triggers will cause the RTM to register responses from the host computer. Perform the following actions to configure RTM settings:

1. Click the Start button and select Programs, Microsoft SNA Server (Common), and click Manager. The SNA Server Manager window appears.

2. Select the subdomain icon on the left pane of SNA Server Manager.

3. In the SNA Server Manager menu, choose View, Properties; or right-click the subdomain icon and then click Properties. The SNA Subdomain Properties dialog box appears. Click the Response Time Monitoring (RTM) tab shown in Figure 41.19.

FIG. 41.19

The Response Time Monitoring (RTM) tab in the SNA Subdomain Properties dialog box allows you to specify when RTM data should be sent, how long the timers should run, and the threshold intervals.

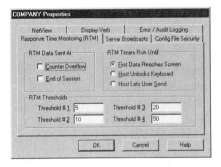

4. In the RTM Data Sent At area of the dialog box, select the appropriate option(s) by clicking the check box to mark it with a ×. If you want to disable one of the options, click the marked check box to unmark it (remove the ×). The options are as follows:

- **Counter Overflow.** Select this option if you want RTM data sent to the host when the number of responses from the host exceeds the size of the available counter.

- **End of Session.** Click this check box if you want RTM data sent to the host at the end of each LU-LU session.

5. RTM timers start running automatically when the local computer starts to send data. The point at which the timers stop, however, depends on the option selected in the RTM Timers Run Until area of the dialog box. This setting determines when the RTM will recognize the host as having responded and therefore stop the timers. Click one of the following options to establish the timer stopping point:

- **First Data Reaches Screen.** Select this option if you want RTM timers to stop when data reaches the local screen.

- **Host Unlocks Keyboard.** Select this option if you want RTM timers to stop when the host unlocks the local keyboard.

- **Host Lets User Send.** Select this option if you want RTM timers to stop when the host lets the local computer send more data.

6. RTM Thresholds settings are defined as intervals (in tenths of a second) at which the RTM will save its count of host responses and restart the count. The permissible range of values is from 1 to 1,000 tenths of a second. The default values of 5, 10, 20, and 50 cause the RTM to save the count of host responses during the intervals from 0.0 to 0.5 seconds, from 0.5 to 1.0 seconds, from 1.0 to 2.0 seconds, and from 2.0 to 5.0 seconds. Either accept these defaults or enter new interval values in the interval number boxes provided.

7. Click OK to accept the settings and close the SNA Subdomain Properties dialog box.

SNA Server Trace

The SNA Server Trace program, which you can execute without stopping the SNA Server, collects information on the activity between and within the SNA Server components. This information can be extremely valuable in diagnosing configuration problems and improving performance. Tracing is possible on client computers running other operating systems, as well (Microsoft Windows, MS-DOS, or OS/2), but it has to be activated with special commands or with lines in an initialization file.

The result of running the SNA Server Trace program is a file, with a file name extension of .TRC, which is stored in the TRACES subdirectory of the SNA Server root directory. You can manipulate these files like any other text file, and support technicians often request these files for troubleshooting purposes when log files alone prove inadequate.

When you begin to gather information for troubleshooting suspected system problems, start with event log data instead of SNA Server trace data. Event log information is much easier to understand and interpret than trace information and is usually adequate in diagnosing the cause of common system ailments. If the logs prove inadequate for discovering root causes for stubborn system problems, however, do not hesitate to start collecting trace data. It will provide much more detail on the SNA Server components possibly involved in the problem. Solicit the assistance of qualified technical support personnel, if necessary, to interpret the trace data.

The remainder of this chapter discusses procedures for running the SNA Server Trace utility for SNA Server and Windows NT-based client systems. For details on how to set up and activate the trace utility for other client computers running Windows, MS-DOS, or OS/2, refer to your *Microsoft SNA Server Administration Guide*.

Determining Software Components and Tracing Types   Before you begin to set up the tracing activity, you must first determine which SNA software component(s) will most likely provide the best diagnostic data for the problem being investigated. The choices you have available for tracing include the following:

- SNA application
- SnaServer, the SNA Server software component that functions as a Physical Unit (PU) 2.1 node and interacts with clients and other nodes on the SNA network
- SnaBase, the SNA Server software component that maintains service name and status lists
- SnaPrint, the SNA Server software component that maintains Host Print service
- SNA Manage Client
- SNA MngAgent
- SNA Server Manager
- Link services added in SNA Server Manager
- Other services, such as Shared Folders, TN3270, and TN5250

After you select the software component(s), you must then decide which type of tracing to perform on the component(s). The tracing types available are described in the following list:

- **Internal.** This type traces activity inside SNA Server software components. This type of tracing is primarily suited to product support technician use because the difficulty of interpreting internal tracing data is beyond the knowledge base of the typical SNA or network administrator.

- **Message.** This type traces messages passed into and out of particular SNA Server software components and includes messages sent to and received from the SNA network.

- **Application Programming Interface (API).** This type traces information passed into and out of an SNA Server DLL communicating with an application. API traces only apply to SNA applications. They do not apply to the other three SNA Server software components mentioned earlier.

Starting the SnaTrace Utility Locally or Remotely Through SNA Server Admin To start the SnaTrace utility locally or remotely through SNA Server Admin, follow these steps:

1. Click the Start button and select Programs, Microsoft SNA Server (Common), and click Manager. The SNA Server Manager window appears.

2. In the SNA Server Manager menu, choose Tools, Trace. The Trace Settings dialog box appears (see Figure 41.20).

FIG. 41.20

The SNA Server Trace program has the ability to gather detailed information on all SNA Server resources.

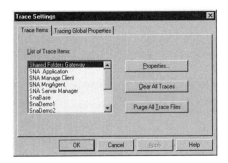

NOTE You also can start the SnaTrace utility remotely by typing **snatrace** *servername* at the command prompt on an SNA server, or you can start it locally on a Windows NT-based client by typing **snatrace** at the command prompt. After entering either command, the Trace Settings dialog box appears. ▪

Enabling or Disabling Trace Options with the SnaTrace Utility After starting the SnaTrace utility and displaying the Trace Settings dialog box as described in the preceding section, follow these steps to configure the trace options:

1. In the List of Trace Items list box, select a service from the list. The list contains the SNA Server software components mentioned in the section "Determining Software Components and Tracing Types" earlier in this chapter, in addition to an entry for each link service added and configured in SNA Server Manager.

2. After a service is selected, click Properties to select the type of tracing from the Trace Properties Sheet dialog box.

3. In the Internal Trace tab of the Trace Properties Sheet dialog box, select options for internal tracing by clicking the appropriate check box(es) to mark the box(es) (with a ×) to enable internal tracing, or click a marked check box (removes the ×) to disable tracing for that internal type. Not enabling internal tracing does not affect other trace options.

4. In the Message Trace tab of the Trace Properties Sheet dialog box, select options for message tracing by clicking the appropriate check box(es) to mark the box(es) (with a ×) to enable message tracing, or click a marked check box (removes the ×) to disable tracing for that message type.

5. In the API Trace tab of the Trace Properties Sheet dialog box, select options for API tracing by clicking the appropriate check box(es) to mark the box(es) (with a ×) to enable API tracing, or click a marked check box (removes the ×) to disable tracing for that API type.

6. Repeat steps 1 through 5 for each service being traced.

7. Click OK.

From Here...

This chapter detailed the routine procedures necessary to administer and manage connectivity and access to SNA Server and host computer resources. It also discussed the various diagnostic tools available to the SNA Server administrator and how these tools should be used.

See the following chapters for related information:

- For information on using the Windows NT Server administrative tools as the SNA Server administrator, see Chapter 7, "Administering Windows NT Server."

- To review basic SNA concepts and SNA Server installation procedures, see Chapter 39, "SNA Server Preparation and Installation."

- To review information on building the SNA Server and establishing the connections between the SNA Server and the host mainframe or AS/400 system, see Chapter 40, "Building SNA Server."

Part
VIII

Ch
41

Systems Management Server (SMS)

CHAPTER 42

Preparing for SMS

by Don Benage and Tim Darby

With the advent of distributed, heterogeneous networking in the enterprise environment, the installation, management, and maintenance of software packages has become a major cost issue for organizations. In addition, network management has become increasingly difficult as the complexity of the enterprise network has increased.

Microsoft Systems Management Server (SMS) is a key component of the Microsoft BackOffice suite of server-based applications. SMS provides system administrators with the capability to do the following:

- Collect and maintain an inventory of computer hardware and software

- Perform distribution, installation, and configuration of software packages

- Manage server-based, networked applications

- Perform network protocol and traffic analysis

- Perform remote diagnosis of network problems and troubleshooting of networked desktop PCs

The Microsoft SMS system provides network administrators with a centrally managed enterprise network solution that allows for the execution of these functions from a single Windows NT-based computer.

Explore the features of Systems Management Server (SMS)

Learn about the features and characteristics of this member of the BackOffice suite.

Learn how servers are organized in a site hierarchy

Discover how SMS sites relate to Windows NT domains. Learn about the different roles that servers can play in an SMS site.

Examine the components of SMS Servers

Find out what this product can provide your organization. Learn about its advanced features that go well beyond basic software distribution and inventory.

Examine the components of SMS Clients

Explore the features of the SMS client applications. Discover how they work synergistically with server components to help you manage your network.

In this chapter, you learn what the term *systems management* means. You also learn the key features of Microsoft SMS and how you can use this product to address systems management requirements for an enterprise-wide network. You explore the components of SMS and learn how you can link SMS components into a hierarchy of servers and client workstations that encompasses the entire enterprise network. In addition, you learn about the various roles servers play in an SMS environment and the work they perform. At the end of this chapter, you will be fully prepared to install SMS and begin using it to make network management easier. ■

Planning for SMS

It is tempting to skip the planning stage and jump right into the setup program. Don't do it. SMS is a sophisticated product with more than a dozen major components. With a little planning, setting up SMS is not a difficult job. But if you skip the planning stage, you will almost certainly need to repeat much of the work a second time after repairing mistakes.

If your schedule permits, set up SMS for the first time in a test environment on a separate network segment not attached to your corporate network. Some of the decisions you make during the setup process can have a profound impact on the network, and SMS has options to automatically install itself on all the computers in your enterprise. By exercising caution until you have spent some time learning about SMS, you can avoid initiating an unwanted operation that impacts most or all of your network.

> **CAUTION**
>
> Be careful with two options in particular. Automatically detecting logon servers and automatically configuring workstation logon scripts are operations that can have an enormous impact on your network. These features can even reach across routers to other geographic locations! The problem is that you may not want particular servers to become logon servers and you may need to control how your client workstations log on to SMS. When you are ready for them, these two capabilities can save you hours of work and are a powerful feature of SMS. By default, these options are turned off.

It is unrealistic to assume that you can install SMS on a large enterprise network and aggressively begin using all its functionality immediately. A measured approach to implementation is generally more successful. First, spend a little time working with SMS in a lab environment to familiarize yourself with its operation and test compatibility with your desktop computers and application suite. Then, set up a central site server and add a single logon server and a few workstations to the site. Set up a few packages for inventory only. After a day or two, set up a package for distribution and installation on a few workstations. Review the log files to see what they report. If all goes well, you can quickly add other servers and workstations to the SMS system.

SMS uses another BackOffice component, SQL Server, as the repository for all the information it collects and manages. Although you don't need to be an expert on SQL Server to use SMS, it is important that you be able to back up and restore the information collected by SMS in case of a computer failure or other catastrophic event.

In addition to SQL Server administration, the full use of SMS delivers features that affect a number of different areas in network administration. It therefore requires expertise in these different areas. It may be appropriate to involve a team of people with a variety of skills to work together with SMS. For example, SMS can automate the installation of software packages. However, you must still be familiar with the process of manually installing software on a single machine to use SMS effectively to automate software installation.

▶ **See** "Backup (Dump) Devices," **p. 1181**

Understanding Systems Management

The management of both large and small networks requires the network administrator to perform certain tasks. Many of these tasks are time consuming and repetitive. They can cause systems to be unavailable while the work is performed, adding to the cost of the operation.

The Desktop Management Task Force (DMTF) is an advisory council formed through the collaboration of computer industry organizations for the purpose of delivering an open standard for the management of networked desktop systems. The goal of these standards is to enable the creation of products to simplify network administration and to control the prohibitive costs of managing a network.

Another standard established for the purpose of managing networks is the Simple Network Management Protocol (SNMP) developed primarily by the UNIX-based community to monitor and troubleshoot routers and bridges. SNMP provides a mechanism for viewing and correcting problems with networked environments, independent of the diverse hardware platforms and networking software implementations.

As networks become more and more distributed and heterogeneous, the need for a uniform, standards-based network management strategy becomes evident. Standards like SNMP and the work of the DMTF have laid the foundations necessary for managing large, complex networks. Until recently, however, available products focused on the networking components themselves and allowed only limited management and control of desktop PCs.

Exploring Systems Management Server

Microsoft SMS is a key component of the Microsoft BackOffice suite that allows system administrators to perform centralized administration of networked desktop PCs.

Support for Industry Standards

SMS supports a variety of industry standards. By supporting these standards, Microsoft has made it possible for other companies like Digital Equipment Corporation (DEC) and Hewlett-Packard (HP) to build upon the basic functionality of SMS and add important additional functionality. Some standards supported and used by SMS include the following:

- Desktop Management Interface (DMI) standard defined by the DMTF.
- Management Information File (MIF) standard defined by the DMTF.
- Simple Network Management Protocol (SNMP) using the Windows NT SNMP Service. SMS also can convert Windows NT events into SNMP traps.
- NetView by IBM using the SNA Server NetView Alert Service.

Integration with BackOffice

The integration of BackOffice applications is evident in the design of SMS. It is implemented as a set of Windows NT Server services, with complementary client applications and administrative utilities. SMS also leverages services built into the base server operating system to perform a multitude of functions. It takes advantage of Windows NT Server services such as the Replicator Service, Remote Access Service, and the Server Service. The SMS Administrator tool complements standard tools like User Manager for Domains, Event Viewer, Server Manager, and File Manager to provide a powerful set of utilities for system management. Figure 42.1 depicts the relationship of SMS to other BackOffice components.

FIG. 42.1

SMS relies on the Microsoft BackOffice components NT Server and SQL Server to do its work.

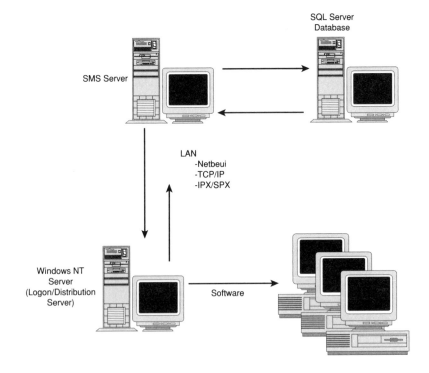

SMS is tightly integrated with other components in the BackOffice suite. It uses SNA Server for sending information over SNA-based communication links to other sites on the enterprise network using site-to-site communications. It also uses the SQL Server relational database to store its system configuration information, inventory information, network topology, and software package distribution information.

By creating custom MIFs on desktop computers, you can include additional information in the SQL Server database specific to your organization. You can include, for example, the location of a computer, the name of the person who normally uses it, and that person's phone number with the inventory information for a particular computer. SMS includes two sample applications for creating MIFs.

Because SMS uses SQL Server as its data repository, it is possible to create applications and custom reports based on SMS information. A large number of applications and development tools have been created to access and manipulate information in SQL Server databases. A full range of tools, from easy to complex, is available. You can add to the information stored in your database and use a broad range of tools to display forms and print reports based on that information.

Management Flexibility

SMS can manage networks of all sizes and shapes. Whether the organization consists of a simple 20-node local area network (LAN) or a large-scale wide area network (WAN), SMS provides the tools to manage the environment effectively. SMS is capable of administering a broad base of platforms including the following:

- Windows NT Server
- Novell NetWare
- LAN Manager
- Windows NT Workstation
- Windows 95
- Windows for Workgroups
- Windows 3.x
- MS-DOS
- IBM OS/2
- Apple Macintosh
- UNIX (through third-party add-ons)

SMS allows administrators to perform all tasks from a central location using a single Windows NT-based machine. You can run the SMS Administrator directly on an SMS server or on computers running Windows NT Workstation. You must set up your central site server and any other primary site servers manually. You also must configure the communications components and special SMS services called *senders* that move information between sites. After these steps are complete, you can automate the rest of the SMS installation.

▶ **See** "Setting Up Your Site," **p. 1474**

Surveying Features in Microsoft SMS

The SMS system provides a comprehensive set of features for managing the networked desktop environment within the enterprise. To allow network administrators to perform effective systems management, SMS offers the following features and functions (see Figure 42.2):

- Hardware and software inventory
- Management of applications that are run from servers
- Software distribution and installation
- Remote control of client workstations and other troubleshooting utilities

FIG. 42.2
This figure depicts the major features of Microsoft SMS.

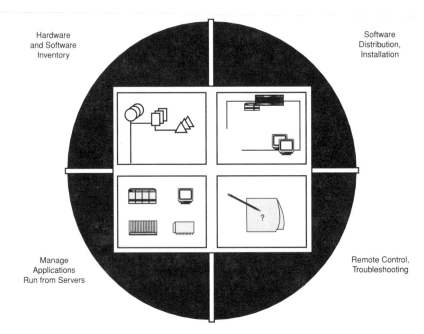

Hardware and Software Inventory

Software Distribution, Installation

Manage Applications Run from Servers

Remote Control, Troubleshooting

Computer Systems Inventory

The SMS database maintains an inventory of all computers on the network—both servers and desktop computers. As part of the inventory collection process, SMS gathers and stores information about the items in the following list. Although this list is representative of SMS' capabilities, SMS also recognizes other components:

- Central Processing Unit (CPU), for example, Pentium, 486, 386, and so on
- Amount of Random-Access Memory (RAM)
- Hard disk drives, their sizes and the amount of storage space used and available
- Video display device

- Mouse or other pointing device
- CD-ROM drives
- Network adapters
- Operating system used by the computer

You can separately control when hardware and software inventory information is collected. The hardware inventory scan is very fast. The exact time varies depending on the specific computer, but it is typically three to eight seconds. Because it is so fast, it is common to let SMS scan hardware daily or even each time the user logs on to the network. Software inventory can take considerably longer because the hard disk drives must be scanned. On a large hard disk, this can take more than 30 seconds. Consider scanning for software only once a month to avoid antagonizing users. The flow of information during inventory collection is depicted in Figure 42.3.

FIG. 42.3

Inventory data flows from workstations to logon servers and then is stored in the SMS SQL Server database.

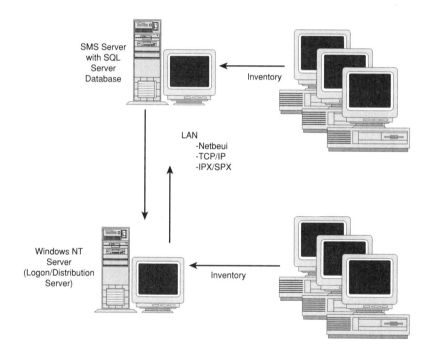

You do not need to explicitly add computers to the SMS database. If you want, SMS automatically detects all logon servers and updates the logon scripts of all users on the network. Then, as users log on, it detects, collects, and stores inventory information about their computers. If you prefer, you can manually add selected servers and update the logon scripts of selected users.

As a user logs on to an SMS-administered network, SMS collects inventory information about the computer and processes it, eventually storing the information in its SQL Server database. The SMS system then allows administrators to view inventory information about the computers on the network using the SMS Administrator. Administrators also can develop and execute custom queries against the SMS database to obtain inventory information.

Software (Package) Distribution to Desktop PCs

As the size of the enterprise network grows, you need to have an effective method of distributing software to network users. The SMS system provides the capability to perform software distribution, installation, and maintenance in a timely and cost-effective manner. The other capabilities that SMS includes, such as inventory, also aid in the implementation of a software distribution and installation strategy.

 T I P Administrators can query the inventory database to determine which computers on the network have the necessary disk space available to install a software package.

SMS gives you the capability to automatically distribute, install, and configure software through the use of *packages*. Packages are made up of information about a software application and how to install it. This information may include custom scripts that perform installation tasks. The distribution and installation of software applications is shown in Figure 42.4.

FIG. 42.4
The software distribution and installation process sends out packages and the source files that go with the packages to logon servers and then to workstations.

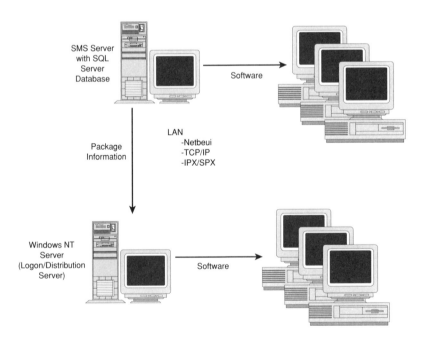

SMS Server with SQL Server Database

Software

Package Information

LAN
-Netbeui
-TCP/IP
-IPX/SPX

Windows NT Server (Logon/Distribution Server)

Software

An SMS package can distribute:

- Commercial software
- Custom software
- Version upgrades of currently installed software
- Virus-detection software
- Data files
- Updated HTML pages for Internet Information Servers
- Batch files used to perform system administration tasks

A client-based utility called the Package Command Manager displays a menu of available commands (typically software setup commands) that can be run on a workstation. This utility supports two methods of software installation: you can force the installation of a package, or allow the user to selectively install one or more applications. Using the first method, the new software is installed automatically on the user's PC the next time the user logs on. The SMS administrator also may specify that a package installation should not be forced if the user is currently connected to the network over a slow link such as a dial-up line. Using the second method, users are given the option of installing the software at their convenience. The second method also allows users to reject software installations they do not want.

> **CAUTION**
>
> Although SMS provides network administrators with a powerful mechanism for distributing and installing applications, it is still important to follow the guidelines for software licensing agreements provided by various software vendors.

Management of Networked Applications

SMS also provides a means of distributing and installing packages on servers (see Figure 42.5). Once installed, they can be run as shared applications from client PCs. SMS also provides the capability to offer these applications to one or more groups of users defined in the Windows NT user account database. As these users log on to the network, icons for the shared applications are added dynamically to their Windows desktops. This capability is called *Program Group Control*.

N O T E   SMS versions prior to 1.2 did not support Program Group Control on Windows 95 PCs. ■

Part
IX

Ch
42

FIG. 42.5

The flow of information for distributing applications to distribution servers for subsequent use by networked workstations.

SMS Server

Windows NT (Distribution Server)

Shared Application Packages

Application Share

WIN/NT Logon Server

Shared Program Groups

Into

Clients (Running Shared Applications)

Networked applications offer users the following advantages:

- A central location for all user application software makes it easier to update or change.

- Availability of applications is based on user groups, not on the PC being used. Therefore, when users move from one computer to another, the applications that they use move with them.

- The capability to use multiple servers as network application servers helps to balance network load.

 TIP The networked application environment presents administrators with added challenges in terms of complying with software licensing agreements. Using Windows NT Server, it is possible to specify the maximum number of users who can connect to a shared directory. You should make sure enough licenses are available for all potential users of a software package.

Network Protocol Analysis

The Network Monitor utility allows the SMS network administrator to monitor the information sent over the network cable for analysis of network traffic and troubleshooting network problems. Figure 42.6 shows a typical display as network information is being *captured* for analysis.

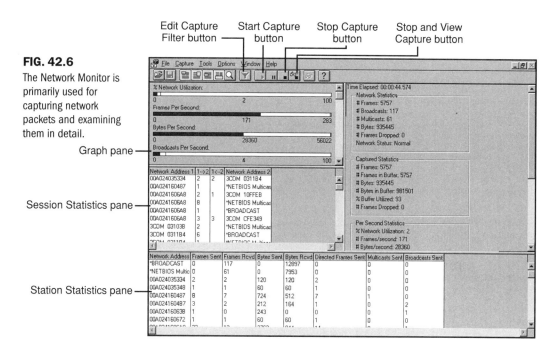

FIG. 42.6
The Network Monitor is primarily used for capturing network packets and examining them in detail.

Network protocol analysis allows the network administrator to "see" the packets of information transmitted on the network cable. This information can be used to develop historical data on network usage and analyze network traffic flow for better use of the network. By studying the information provided by Network Monitor, the network administrator can make informed decisions on how the network could be re-routed to alleviate congestion in certain areas and to better tune the performance of network operations. In addition, problems with a connection or interaction between two specific machines can be investigated in greater detail.

Remote Diagnosis and Troubleshooting

The Help Desk utilities provided with SMS allow the network administrator to connect remotely to client PCs and gain control of the mouse and keyboard for troubleshooting purposes (see Figure 42.7).

The Help Desk utilities also allow the network administrator to perform the following functions:

- Remotely reboot client PCs
- Chat with a remote user by interactively typing messages to each other (useful when you are helping a user without access to a phone)
- Execute a program on a remote client PC
- Transfer a file to and from a remote client PC
- Obtain information about memory usage in a client PC as programs are executing

Part
IX

Ch
42

- List device drivers loaded into memory
- Define alerts for reporting problems and system failures
- Enable the creation of trace logs to provide a detailed log of SMS system activity and errors

FIG. 42.7
The Remote Control utility from the Help Desk tools can be used from an administrative console on Windows NT Workstation or Windows NT Server to operate the mouse and keyboard of another workstation on the network. The remote computer's display is visible inside the window with the striped border.

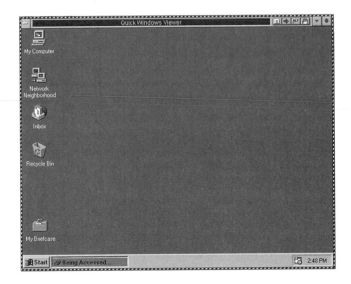

 The Remote Control utility gives you a means for providing quick user training sessions. By taking control of the client PC's mouse and keyboard, you can walk the user through learning to use a new software application. This is practical only for brief tutorials.

New Features in Microsoft SMS 1.2

SMS 1.2 provides a number of performance and ease-of-use enhancements and two big additions: remote control for Windows NT workstations and program group control for Windows 95 workstations. The new support for Simple Network Management Protocol (SNMP) is a welcome addition both for administrators who rely solely on SMS and those who employ management stations from other vendors.

Windows NT Enhancements

Support for Windows NT machines was not up to par with the other Windows platforms in previous versions of SMS. SMS 1.2 corrects these deficiencies by providing Remote Control and an improved Inventory Agent. The Remote Control feature under Windows NT allows you to specify the list of administrators that are to use this feature. The Inventory Agent under Windows NT now installs automatically as an NT service. As such, the inventory agent's security context gives it privileges to access all the resources of the workstation and eliminates the need for a user with sufficient privileges to be logged on to the workstation in order to process the complete inventory.

Windows 95 Enhancements

Program Group Control, which is a necessary component for running shared applications from SMS distribution servers, is now available under Windows 95. The PDF files for both the standard and professional versions of Office 95 are now included.

SNMP

SMS now supports SNMP traps for network management. SMS treats SNMP traps as a new architecture, and you can query the traps and set SMS alerts on them, just as you can with other SMS architectures. This support has two components:

- **Windows NT Events Translator.** This software is an add-on to NT servers and workstations that translates Windows NT Events of your choosing to SNMP traps. These are standard SNMP traps that can be sent to SMS or to any SNMP-based network management station that receives traps. It requires NT 3.51 or later.

- **SNMP Trap Receiver.** Using the Trap Receiver, SMS can receive SNMP traps from Windows NT machines configured to generate traps as well as any network device that is capable of sending an SNMP trap. You can specify the criteria that SMS uses to decide which traps to accept.

Bigger Software Auditing Database

The SMS software auditing database, contained in the file AUDIT.RUL, has been expanded to include definitions for over 5,000 software applications. AUDIT.RUL is a text file that you can use as-is or modify to add your own package definitions.

Improved Network Monitor

Network Monitor supports many more protocols including PPTP, Java, NNTP, GRE, and SMTP and includes the following additional functions:

- **Top User/Consumer.** Gives you an indication of which machine is using the most network bandwidth.

- **Find Network Routers.** Analyzes network traffic and correctly identifies routers and their associated port addresses.

- **Address Resolution.** Identifies the network address of any computer name that you enter using the following address resolution techniques: Domain Name Service (DNS), Local Address Database, NetBIOS, SAP, and SMS Remote Database. You can specify the order in which SMS uses these techniques.

- **Protocol Distribution.** Identifies the different protocols in use on your network and ranks them according to how much bandwidth each is using.

Part

IX

Ch

42

Client Mapping

You now can map client computers to an SMS domain-site combination. This means that you can allow SMS to automatically assign logon scripts in configurations that have multiple sites in one domain. You also can map a client computer to a specific server, which means you can choose the logon server if you have multiple domain controllers.

Improved Reporting

SMS includes Crystal Reports version 4.5 for retrieving information from the SMS database and printing reports. This version of Crystal Reports lets you create SMS reports in HTML format so you can put them up on your corporate web server.

Now that you have been given an overview of SMS and its capabilities, the following sections explore in detail the features and functions of this powerful product.

Understanding Sites and Domains

In Chapter 4, "Enterprise Planning and Implementation," you learned about Windows NT domains and some of the organizational structures that various BackOffice products use. This chapter discusses the *site hierarchy* used by SMS and expands the relationship between sites and domains.

SMS sites do not necessarily correspond directly to Windows NT domains. It may be logical, and convenient, to set up SMS sites to correspond exactly to domains, but it is not required. For example, you may have a single SMS site span multiple Windows NT domains, as illustrated in Figure 42.8.

If you are using a master domain model, it is common to have a master domain server at each geographic location. This may entail having servers from the master domain belonging to many SMS sites, as illustrated in Figure 42.9. Such a configuration makes sense if you need only one domain for security but want to have multiple SMS sites subject to separate systems management control. Domains are created to enforce security. Sites are created to enable systems management. These two functions may or may not correspond.

▶ **See** "Understanding BackOffice Structures for Organizing Servers," **p. 104**

> **CAUTION**
>
> If you want to implement the Use All Detected Servers option, which can be a convenient way to add servers to a site, you cannot have different servers from a single domain belong to multiple sites. This option detects all servers within the domain that contains the site server where the option is set and adds them to the site. If some of the servers belong to different sites, a serious configuration problem will occur.

FIG. 42.8
This figure depicts an SMS site spanning three domains.

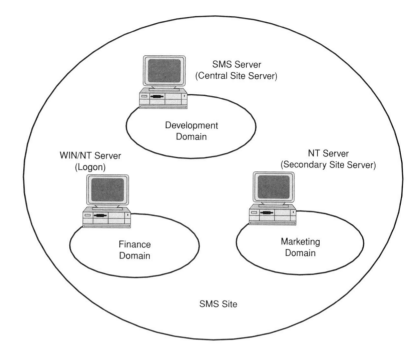

FIG. 42.9
A Windows NT domain can encompass several SMS sites.

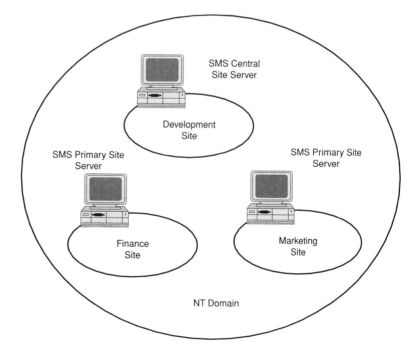

An Overview of the Site Hierarchy

SMS uses two distinct types of sites: *primary sites* and *secondary sites*. A primary site has its own SQL Server database, and a secondary site does not. A secondary site must be linked to a primary site in a *parent/child* relationship. A primary site uses SQL Server to store information about itself and any secondary sites linked to it. A primary site doesn't necessarily have secondary (child) sites; but, secondary sites, if they exist, must be linked to a primary (parent) site.

A primary site also can be linked to other primary sites. In this case, one primary is to be the child of another primary. Every SMS installation has one *central site*. This is the primary site at the top of the hierarchy. All other sites, primary and secondary, are linked to the central site. All information about the entire SMS system is transmitted to the central site. Information in the SMS hierarchy flows upstream and is eventually reported to the central site. An administrator of the central site can manage systems anywhere in the SMS system. An administrator of a primary site farther down in the hierarchy can manage that primary site and any child sites, but does not have the capability to manage the parent site.

The main reason for creating a primary site with its own database is to allow that site, and any child sites, to be managed as a separate entity. If you want to separate administrative duties for a subset of your network, you can create a primary site and possibly one or more secondary sites that encompass the computers you want to manage separately. You then can assign administrative control of that primary site to an individual or group.

A secondary site is necessary when you have a group of computers at a geographic location that does not require a separate administrator, but does need to be managed as a distinct entity. By creating a secondary site that encompasses these computers, administrators of the primary site can manage them, but they can still be treated separately. The installation of a software package, for example, could be scheduled for only the secondary site.

N O T E Each site is designated by a three-character code. The codes are arbitrary and are not case-sensitive, but they must be unique across the entire SMS enterprise. One individual or administrative group should be responsible for assigning site codes to avoid conflicts. If you are setting up a site that needs to be added to an existing SMS system, get a site code from an administrator of that system. ▪

Understanding Different Server Roles

A large enterprise network has many servers performing different tasks. SMS allows you to use multiple servers to perform the work required. This helps avoid single points of failure and allows the SMS system to span large geographic areas with many servers and desktop PCs. It also gives the designer of the SMS system a great deal of flexibility when deciding what resources are required and how to implement different elements of the SMS system.

Server-based components fill a number of different roles. These different components work in harmony to perform systems management tasks. A particular server may be dedicated to performing only SMS tasks, or SMS components may be added to a server already in place and doing other work. You can make the right choices regarding configuration and sizing of servers only by analyzing the work to be done. See "Sizing Your Server" later in this chapter.

SQL Server

As you already learned, SMS stores all its information in a SQL Server database. This may be an existing SQL server, or a new server set up just to support SMS. It may be on the same machine that is used as the primary site server or on a separate machine.

Primary Site Server

Primary site servers must be installed from the distribution media, either floppy disks or CD-ROM. You can think of the primary site server as the hub of activity in an SMS site. Most of the server-based services that perform the work of SMS reside on the site server. A directory structure is set up on the hard disk drive you specify as a work area as SMS processes jobs, to store information in interim form before it is moved to the SQL Server database and to maintain some configuration information about the site.

Secondary Site Server

Secondary site servers are similar to primary site servers but there are differences. No SQL Server database is at a secondary site, so all information is forwarded to the parent primary site rather than stored in a local database. The administration tools are not installed on secondary site servers because there is no local administrative capability. Secondary site servers can be installed automatically from a primary site server without using the distribution media.

Logon Servers

A server that contains logon scripts, processes user logon requests, and is added to the SMS site is called a *logon server*. It is used as a temporary repository for inventory collection. As users log on to the network and their computer is scanned, the resulting inventory information is placed in a subdirectory on the logon server. By modifying users' logon scripts, either manually or automatically, you can control which computers are added to the SMS system. A logon server also can act as a distribution server.

Distribution Servers

A *distribution server* has two primary functions: a temporary repository for package distribution and the location for shared network-based applications. Packages set up to be installed on desktop computers (workstations) first are stored on a distribution server. If the SMS system has been designed properly, the distribution server for a particular workstation is located on the same high-speed network segment. A logon server also can be a distribution server.

Helper Servers for Running Senders or Other Services

The server-based components of SMS are implemented primarily as services. Six primary services process SMS tasks. By default, they are installed on the site server. SMS also includes components designed to move information from one site to another called *senders*. Each sender type is designed to move information over a particular type of link. The three types of senders are as follows:

- LAN senders
- RAS senders
- SNA senders

You do not need to understand the functions performed by these services to use SMS effectively. However, the more you understand about their operation, the better you can be at troubleshooting problems. Perhaps the most important thing to know is that it is possible to move some of the services off the site server to a *helper* server. If the workload placed on your site server is too great, you can reconfigure your site so that some services are relocated to another server with available processing power. Senders are particularly good candidates for location on a separate server. Helper servers also must be logon servers.

Understanding Machine Groups

In some situations, it is useful to select particular computers and group them together for systems management functions. Such a collection is called a *machine group*. For example, in a large corporation, members of the Audit department might be dispersed throughout the organization. The computers used by these individuals would require the use of different applications from those being used by most of the people around them. By placing these computers in a machine group, you can schedule the automatic installation of software for all auditors whatever their physical locations.

Organizing Your Enterprise

Now that you know more about the components of an SMS system, it is important that you spend some time planning. Think about what you want SMS to do for your organization. Here is a short list of the questions you should be able to answer:

- Will you be using SMS to collect and maintain inventory information?
- Will you want to use SMS to distribute and install applications?
- How many applications need to be installed?
- What size are the applications and how often will you need to install or upgrade your applications?
- How many computers do you have?
- How fast is your network?
- What is the current bandwidth utilization on your network?

Geographically

As you plan your SMS system, it is very helpful to have a diagram of your network that shows wide-area links (bridges, routers, brouters, and network hubs) and clearly identifies slower links that could become bottlenecks. Indicate the type of link (LAN, RAS, or SNA) between network segments. It is a good idea to show on the diagram the number of computers and users on each network segment. Also indicate where administrators are located and areas that need to be managed autonomously. If your network has redundant components or areas particularly likely to be cut off from the enterprise network in case of a component failure, indicate it on the diagram. A sample diagram is shown in Figure 42.10.

FIG. 42.10
This figure depicts a sample network diagram showing the geographical relationship of various network components.

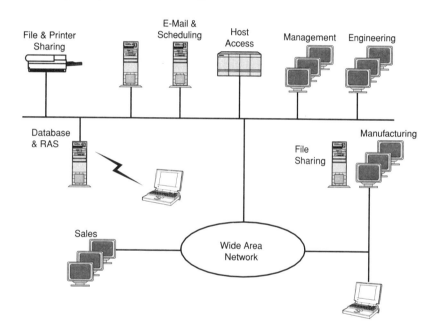

Functionally

To your existing geographic map, overlay functional considerations. Try to map groups of users with similar computing platforms and needs. Don't forget to indicate the smaller, special purpose groups that may have special needs. As you estimate application needs, the frequency of update information, and the size of the information to be distributed, you can better decide where to place distribution servers and senders.

Sizing Your Server

Microsoft provides guidelines on the BackOffice CD for sizing your server(s). In addition, BackOffice components that you purchase separately include guidelines regarding system requirements. Chapter 3, "Planning for BackOffice," contains a detailed discussion about sizing BackOffice servers.

Part
IX

Ch
42

Some useful rules of thumb regarding the resources needed for different server roles are presented in the following list. These should be viewed as guidelines only:

■ SMS does not generally make heavy demands on a SQL Server database. It may be possible to use an existing database server or add other work to a SQL Server established for SMS at a later date. For better performance, the SQL Server should be installed on a different computer than the primary site server.

■ Primary site servers run a number of server-based services. During package distribution, compression minimizes the amount of information to be transmitted. These are processor-intensive tasks. Primary site servers therefore benefit substantially from multiple processors.

■ The work performed by primary site servers also benefits from the addition of RAM. Use the system requirements given by Microsoft as absolute minimums. If your budget can support it, and especially if you intend to use SMS aggressively, additional RAM is an excellent investment.

Now that you've learned about the hierarchy in an SMS system and the different types of servers, it is important to understand the components of SMS that are installed on the servers and clients. These are the server-based services, administrative utilities, and client-based applications that actually perform the work of the SMS system.

Understanding Server Components

Most of the components that make up an SMS system are Windows NT services that run in background mode on a server. This section presents an overview of these services to aid your understanding of SMS processes.

▶ **See** "A Flexible Set of Services," **p. 54**

SMS Services

SMS includes these services:

■ SMS Executive

■ SMS Site Hierarchy Manager

■ SMS Site Configuration Manager

■ Package Command Manager

■ Inventory Agent

■ SMS SNA Receiver (if an SNA Sender is installed)

The SMS Executive itself consists of component parts that can be controlled separately, or as a group. The following components make up the SMS Executive:

■ Inventory Data Loader

■ Inventory Processor

- Despooler
- Scheduler
- Applications Manager
- Maintenance Manager
- SMS Alerter
- Site Reporter
- LAN Sender
- RAS Sender (if installed)
- SNA Sender (if installed)

You can move the first four items to a helper server if you want to off-load some of the processing from the site server. If you install one or more of these services on a helper server, the SMS Executive also is installed, and the services then run as components of the SMS Executive on the helper server.

SMS Service Manager

The SMS Service Manager is the utility that gives you the greatest level of control over the execution state of individual services and components of the SMS Executive (see Figure 42.11). Using the Services applet in the Control Panel, you must start and stop all the SMS Executive components as a group. With the SMS Service Manager, you can start, stop, pause, and continue all SMS services, and control the components of the SMS Executive individually. You also can enable or disable tracing for the individual services.

FIG. 42.11

The SMS Service Manager can be used to control the individual server-based services that make up SMS.

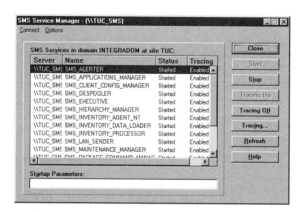

Part
IX

Ch
42

You can use the standard Windows NT tools for controlling services to control SMS services, also. These two tools are the Server Manager, which can control services on the local or remote servers, and the Services applet in the Control Panel, which can control services only on the local computer. Neither of these tools can separately control the individual components of the SMS Executive. Only the SMS Service Manager offers that level of control.

Although the SMS Service Manager lets you turn the services of SMS on or off, another tool, the SMS Administrator, allows you to assign work to the SMS system and to monitor the status of the jobs you create.

SMS Administrator

A common misconception among those new to SMS is that the SMS Administrator program does the work of SMS. The SMS Administrator is not the workhorse of SMS. It is a powerful program that lets you create packages and jobs that then are carried out by the various SMS services. The SMS Administrator also allows you to view much of the information stored in the SQL database used by SMS (see Figure 42.12). But the SMS services act as the "engines" of an SMS system.

Jobs button   Package button   Program Groups button

FIG. 42.12
Use the SMS Adminis-
trator to manage all
facets of the SMS
system.

Sites button

Site

Domain

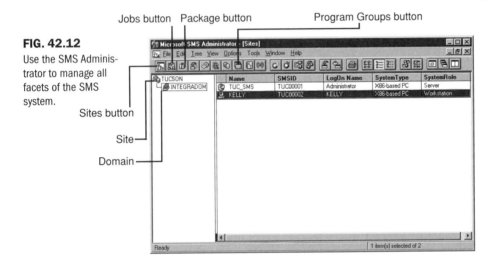

You can think of the SMS Administrator as the "master control panel" for the SMS system. You can use it to set properties of sites and initiate the many tasks that SMS executes for you. The next five sections describe some of the things that you can create or define with the SMS Administrator.

Packages   A *package* is an object that you define using the SMS Administrator. It defines an application or arbitrary group of files to the SMS system. A package optionally can have up to three separate purposes. You can define a package for inventory, for installation on a desktop PC, or for installation and sharing on a network server.

The package includes information about the application's configuration. Depending on the type of package you have created, the package also may include the location of the files that make up the application and information about how to identify the package for inventory purposes.

Microsoft has included some package definition files (PDFs) with SMS. These text files contain settings for each of the three areas of package definition. You can import these PDFs to quickly define packages for popular applications from Microsoft. There also are PDFs for operating systems from Microsoft.

Jobs   *Jobs* consist of instructions for the SMS system to carry out. The system itself creates some jobs to accomplish tasks, and you can define jobs to manipulate packages. You can think of a job as a package combined with a target for installation and a schedule.

You can select the target for package installation in several ways. You can select an individual desktop PC, a single server, or an entire site. You also can use a machine group as the target for a job. You can even create a query that selects a subset of the site and uses the resulting group of computers as the target for your job.

With many applications you run on computers, you get almost instant results. Most of the jobs you create using SMS happen more slowly, over a period of minutes, hours, or even days. Using the SMS Administrator program, you can track the status of your jobs. By checking the status of jobs and by reviewing updated inventory information, you can verify the current condition of your SMS system.

Program Groups   If you have installed and shared network-based applications, you can create program groups using the SMS Administrator and assign them to particular groups of users. You can assign a program group, with icons for the applications that you have shared, to groups of users defined in a Windows NT Server or NetWare user account database. When users in these groups log on to the network, a Program Manager program group is built dynamically. If the user logs off one computer and logs on to another, the shared application icons follow them to the new desktop.

This capability is available only on computers running Windows 3.x, Windows for Workgroups, Windows 95, and Windows NT. To provide the dynamic building of groups on the desktop, you must be running the Program Group Control utility on the client computer. See the section "Understanding the Client Components of SMS" later in this chapter.

Queries   *Queries* are one of the most powerful features of the SMS system. After you set up SMS, it takes a period of time before the inventory information on all the computers you've added to the system has been collected. For various reasons (vacations, illnesses, and so on), it usually takes from one to two weeks before the system has an accurate description of all machines in the system.

After SMS has been operational long enough to have a complete inventory, you can use the query capability of the SMS Administrator to answer many interesting questions. Here are some sample queries that SMS is capable of answering:

Part

IX

Ch

42

- Which computers are currently running Microsoft Word version 6.0?
- How many computers have an Intel 486 processor?
- How many computers have 16M of RAM installed?
- Which computers have more than 30M of available disk space on their hard disk drive and are running Microsoft Excel version 4.0?

It doesn't take much imagination to see how useful this capability can be. Without a system like SMS, these questions are so time-consuming to answer that they usually don't get asked. In a large enterprise network, by the time you get an answer (over a period of days or weeks), it is already out of date and incorrect. SMS gives you up-to-the-minute answers quickly and easily.

Experiment with this capability and use it to your fullest advantage. It is one of the best examples of the leverage you get by installing SMS. After you set up your SMS system, which admittedly takes a significant amount of effort, you are repaid for your work by being able to do things you couldn't do before. With your SMS system in place, it should take less than five minutes to answer any of the preceding sample questions.

Alerts   *Alerts* provide the administrator of an SMS system with a powerful tool for automated management. Alerts are based on queries. You define a query that quantifies an area of interest. For example, if your organization owns licenses for one hundred copies of Microsoft Excel, you can define a query to count the number of machines that have Excel installed. Then, using the SMS Administrator, you can create an alert that notifies you when the hit count is greater than one hundred. The alert can create an entry in a log, execute a command line, or send a message to a particular user or computer.

Like queries, alerts are powerful tools that are often overlooked. It is common to get so focused on installing software and monitoring inventory that alerts are forgotten. Experiment with alerts, and you will discover how valuable they can be. They can help you find problem areas before users are inconvenienced or shut down and help keep your network operational.

Understanding the Client Components of SMS

In addition to server-based components and the objects created by the SMS Administrator program, a number of components that run on client workstations play an integral role in the SMS system. These components vary slightly depending on the type of client you are using. See Appendix B, "Client System Requirements," in the *SMS Getting Started Guide*.

In general, the SMS client components are set up to run automatically. The administrator of an SMS system can use the SMS Administrator to make settings in the Clients dialog box that control which client components load by default on workstations (see Figure 42.13). After these settings are made, the SMS system automatically sets up workstations that are added to the system.

Computers are usually added to the SMS system when a user at a particular computer logs on to the network with a logon script that has been changed to include SMS components. It also is possible to connect manually to the site server and run the client setup utility.

The next five sections describe SMS utilities that run on client workstations and perform client setup, configuration, and communications with SMS servers.

FIG. 42.13

In addition to setting the client components that are loaded by default, you can use the SMS Administrator program to control Package Command Manager polling and the very useful ability to automatically configure workstation logon scripts.

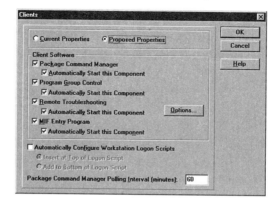

Client Setup and Configuration

A number of logon scripts and programs handle the tasks of adding a workstation to the SMS system, setting up the client computer, and making sure that, on subsequent logons, it is still configured properly and no changes are required. In many SMS systems, these components can be set up and run automatically, without the administrator's needing to initiate their use manually. The components that play a role in setup and configuration are the following:

- **SMSLS.BAT (or SMSLS.CMD for OS/2 computers).** This is the SMS logon script. It initiates client involvement in the SMS system by calling the SETLS program, which sets the logon server for a client and starts the client setup program.

- **SETLS.** This program uses information from the SMSLS.INI file to choose a logon server. After a logon server has been chosen, the client setup and inventory agent programs can be run. The two versions of this program—SETLS16 and SETLS32—support different types of clients.

- **Client Setup.** There are three different versions of client setup. They are CLI_NT.EXE, CLI_DOS.EXE, and CLI_OS2.EXE. These utilities perform myriad services. Client setup sets up new clients, but it also takes care of upgrade, reconfiguration, and removal operations. Seven optional switches can be used to control this command.

- **SMSRUN.** This utility creates program groups on the client and starts components that have been set to start automatically in the Clients dialog box of the site properties. The two versions of SMSRUN—SMSRUN16 and SMSRUN32—support different types of clients.

- **SMSSVR.** This utility is not installed on the client. It is run by a client from a logon server to upgrade or remove SMS components. It works in conjunction with the client setup program to complete these actions.

Part

IX

Ch

42

If this list seems a bit daunting, don't worry. You will not usually need to run these utilities manually. SMS is good at automating client installation. The one exception is the client setup program, which can be run manually from a workstation to include it in an SMS system without modifying any user logon scripts.

Inventory Agent

The Inventory Agent is responsible for scanning the hardware and (optionally) the software on a computer. It reports what it finds to the logon server. This information then is incorporated into the SMS database on the SQL Server being used by SMS. It also can collect files to be included in the database, for example, CONFIG.SYS.

Package Command Manager

The Package Command Manager is the component that initiates installation of software packages on client computers (see Figure 42.14). It can automatically launch installation for mandatory packages, or offer a menu of optional packages for selection by the user. A package can be set up so that it is optional for a period of time and then becomes mandatory.

FIG. 42.14

The Package Command Manager displays pending commands by default, but you can also look at commands that have previously executed or have been archived.

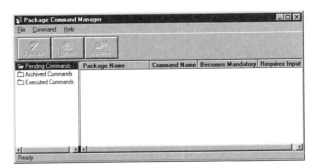

Program Group Control

Program Group Control is available only on computers running Windows 3.x, Windows for Workgroups, Windows 95, or Windows NT. This component uses two programs, APPSTART and APPCTL, to create Start Menu items or Program Manager groups that include icons to launch shared, network-based applications (see Figure 42.15). These groups are built dynamically as the user logs on, based on the groups the user is a member of and the assignments made by the administrator of the SMS system.

When a user launches an application from one of these groups, Program Group Control is responsible for finding an available server from a list of servers that contain the shared application. It then connects to the server and launches the application. When the user exits the application, Program Group Control disconnects the client from the server.

FIG. 42.15
Start Menu items (or Program Manager groups) can be created dynamically by Program Group Control.

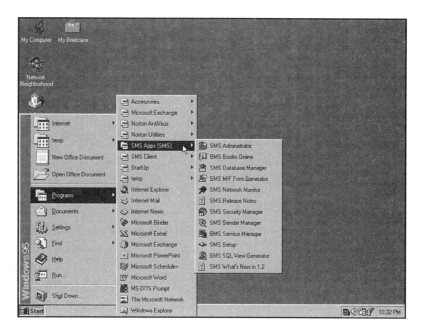

Help Desk Options

There is a configuration utility that you can run on client PCs to allow the user to configure how the remote troubleshooting options can be used (see Figure 42.16). This utility is available only for computers running Windows 3.x, Windows for Workgroups, Windows 95, and Windows NT. You also can configure help desk options from a command line on a computer running MS-DOS.

FIG. 42.16
The Help Desk Options dialog box allows you to select the SMS Help Desk components you want to enable for use on your workstation.

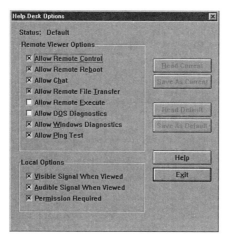

From Here...

In this chapter, you were introduced to the components that make up SMS. You learned about the various Windows NT Server services that comprise the server-based components and about the client components that work together so that a computer inventory can be created and users can automatically install software. You also learned how servers are organized in a site hierarchy and the various roles servers can adopt in an SMS site.

This completes the overview of SMS system components and operations. You should now have a solid understanding of most of SMS's mechanisms and be well prepared to successfully use SMS to manage your network. In the next chapter, you set up your server, create the primary site, and use the SMS Administrator program to set properties for your site. You then learn how to use SMS to inventory the computers on your network.

See the following chapters for related topics:

- For information on setting up your SMS site and collecting inventory information, see Chapter 43, "Implementing SMS."
- For information on automatically distributing and installing software and using the Help Desk features of SMS, see Chapter 44, "The Role of the SMS Administrator."
- For information on establishing policies for improved security and specific guidelines for securing your site, your servers, and client workstations, see Chapter 46, "Implementing Real-World Security."
- For information on developing a proactive approach to avoiding network problems and server outages, see Chapter 48, "Proactive Network Administration."

CHAPTER 43

Implementing SMS

by Don Benage and Tim Darby

So far you have learned why Systems Management Server (SMS) is so important and what it can do for your network. In this chapter, you learn how to set up SMS on your network and use it to make your work more productive. Detailed information is provided to help you set up a primary site server for your central site, install other primary site servers and secondary site servers, and implement the site relationships you have already planned. You learn how to add logon servers and clients to a site. Finally, you learn the basics of defining packages and jobs, a topic explored in more detail in Chapter 44, "The Role of the SMS Administrator."

As noted in Chapter 42, "Preparing for SMS," it is wise to proceed carefully when implementing SMS. The automatic installation features of SMS are powerful and potentially dangerous. The default settings are safe, but with a few clicks of the mouse you can tell SMS to automatically detect logon servers and update logon scripts. Depending on how your network is set up, SMS will find servers and clients, even those across routers in other cities. If this is what you want to happen, and it proceeds according to plan, it saves a tremendous amount of time and effort. If it happens by accident, it can result in a lot of unwanted network traffic on your WAN lines and a lot of work to undo the configuration. Take the time to review Chapter 46 and complete the recommended planning process if you haven't already done so. ■

▬ **How to set up your Systems Management Server (SMS) site**

Learn how to establish basic site properties that control the behavior of SMS at your site. Find out how to establish a relationship with other sites if necessary.

▬ **How to add sites and computers to the SMS site hierarchy**

Discover how to expand SMS sites and how to add both servers and client workstations to an SMS site. Learn how to set up communications between physical locations.

▬ **How to use SMS to inventory computers on your network**

Find out how to automate the collection of inventory information for your network, how to view the information you have collected, and how to use queries.

▬ **How to audit the software on your network**

Explore the auditing capabilities of SMS. Learn how to check workstations for a large list of potential software packages that may be installed and how to view the results.

Setting Up Your Site

In this section, you learn how to set up your first primary site server. This is the server that will be your central site server unless you are adding an SMS site to an existing SMS system. Set up the computer you will be using according to the manufacturer's instructions and install Windows NT Server. After you have completed these tasks, you are ready to install your primary site server.

During the setup process, you need the following key pieces of information:

- A three-character site code
- A login ID and password for SQL Server
- The name of the SQL Server and the database (usually SMS) you will use
- The database device name
- The log device name
- The name of the computer you will use as your site server
- The name of the domain in which the computer resides
- The SMS service account that you have established and its password

> **CAUTION**
>
> If you are adding a site to an existing SMS system, you must be sure that you have a unique three-character site code. This code must be unique across the entire SMS system. Check with the administrator of the existing SMS system to get an unused code.

Be sure that you have these available before you start. Site codes for all sites should be available from the planning process carried out earlier.

The database administrator (DBA) for the SQL Server you will be using can provide the database information in addition to a SQL Server ID and password. This account needs sa (system administrator) or dbo (database owner) privileges for the SMS database. The SMS service account can be created by an administrator of the domain containing the account. If you are using a master domain model, the SMS service account should be a master domain account. The computer name and domain name you can find by logging on to the proposed site server computer and double-clicking the Network icon in the Control Panel.

▶ **See** "Preparing for SMS," **p. 1445**

 If you are using Integrated or Mixed security for SQL Server, you can use your Windows NT domain account as the ID for SQL Server. Be sure to GRANT this ID sa or dbo privileges for the SMS database and log.

▶ **See** "Creating a Service Account," **p. 195**

If the SQL Server that will store your SMS database is running on a different computer from what you will use for your SMS site server, the SMS database, and an appropriately sized log file, should already be created, as well. You can create SQL Server devices, the SMS database, and the log file with the SQL Enterprise Administrator. If the same server will be used for SMS and SQL Server, the SMS Setup program automatically creates the SMS database.

Part

IX

Ch

43

 TIP Use the following information as a general rule for estimating the sizes of your database devices:

- **SMSData device.** The number of clients you will manage multiplied by 20K per client.

- **SMSLog device.** 20 percent of the SMSData device size or 5M, whichever is greater.

- **TempDB.** 20 percent of the SMSData device size or 20M, whichever is greater.

If you haven't already done so, log on to the computer that will be your primary site server. You must log on with an account that has administrator privileges on this computer. Make sure that the account you are using, and the SMS service account, have access privileges to the SMS database on the SQL Server you will be using. If you are using a master domain model, this should be a master domain account.

Insert the CD-ROM containing SMS. The BackOffice CD contains a Setup program for the entire BackOffice product suite and separate directories containing Setup programs for the individual BackOffice components.

You can install SMS as part of a BackOffice installation process that includes multiple components. The following procedure describes how to install the SMS component separately. You need to run the Setup program for SMS, which you can do in several ways.

N O T E Primary site servers, including the central site server, must be either primary domain controllers or backup domain controllers. You cannot use a Windows NT server that has been configured with the role "Server." ▨

▶ **See** "Understanding the Server's Role," **p. 109**

To launch the Setup program, you must know the directory in which it is located. You can select Find, Files or Folders from the Start menu on the taskbar to find the location of the SMS Setup program. The exact location depends on the specific product you are using (SMS itself, BackOffice, CPU type, upgrade, and so on); but for BackOffice 2.5 for Intel processors, it should be located in the \sms1 2\smssetup\x86 directory. Follow these steps:

1. Choose Run from the Start menu.

2. In the Run dialog box, enter **D:\sms12\smssetup\x86\SETUP** (for example) as the command line. If your CD-ROM has a different drive letter than D, substitute the appropriate drive letter.

N O T E You can also open an Explorer window (choose Start, Programs, Windows NT Explorer), navigate to the above drive and folder, and double-click the file SETUP.EXE. ▨

3. Click OK.

You also can open a command prompt window and enter **D:SETUP** as the command line.

After you have started the Setup program for SMS, follow these steps:

1. Read the Welcome Screen.

2. Click Continue. The Registration dialog box appears.

3. Enter your name, organization name, and the product identification number. Click Continue.

4. Verify the information you just entered, and either correct it or click Continue again. The Installation Options dialog box appears (see Figure 43.1).

FIG. 43.1

Use the SMS Installation Options dialog box to select the type of SMS installation you want to perform.

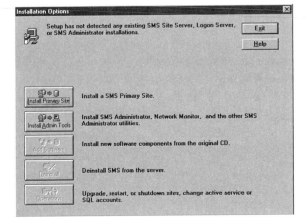

5. Click Install Primary Site. The Licensing dialog box appears.

6. If you agree with the terms of the license agreement, click the check box to signify your agreement. Click OK. The Systems Management Server Setup dialog box appears.

7. This dialog box provides important reminders about the steps you should have already taken prior to starting Setup. Make sure that you have completed these steps and then click Continue.

8. The Installation Directory dialog box appears after the Setup program checks for necessary disk space.

9. Specify the directory where you want to install the SMS system. By default, SMS chooses the root directory of the NTFS partition that has the largest amount of free space available. You should have at least 100 megabytes (M) of available space on the drive you select.

10. Click Continue. The Setup Install Options dialog box appears, as shown in Figure 43.2.

FIG. 43.2

The SMS Setup Install Options dialog box allows you to select the SMS components that you want to install.

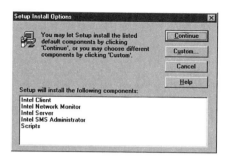

Part

IX

Ch

43

11. The Setup Install Options dialog box lists the default components that Setup is about to install. You can select additional components to install by clicking Custom. If you are unsure, use the default selection. You can run the Setup program again later if you need to add additional components to support other types of computers. When you have selected all the components you want to install, click Continue. The SQL Database Configuration dialog box appears, as shown in Figure 43.3.

FIG. 43.3

The SQL Database Configuration dialog box lets you specify the SQL Server you want to use and enter the login ID and password required to connect to SQL Server. You also must enter the database name, database device, and log device you want to use.

12. Enter the name of the SQL Server, the account that SMS will use to log on, the password, the name of the database, the database device, and the log device. Click Continue. The Primary Site Configuration Information dialog box appears (see Figure 43.4).

CAUTION

The three-character site code you enter in the Primary Site Configuration dialog box must be unique across the entire SMS system. If you are becoming part of an existing SMS system, contact the SMS administrator to obtain a unique site code.

FIG. 43.4

Use the Primary
Site Configuration
Information dialog box
to specify the unique
three-character site
code that will identify
this site. You also must
enter other site-specific
information and specify
the server and domain
that will contain the site
server.

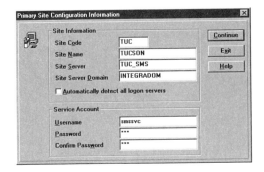

13. Fill in the dialog box. The three-character site code is the unique code discussed earlier. The site name is not as critical as the site code but is used as a label in the Sites window of the SMS Administrator program. You should choose it carefully to make it easy to identify the site. The site server name is simply the name of the computer on which you are currently running the Setup program. Enter the name of the domain that this computer resides in, as well. Then enter the SMS service account information. Click Continue.

CAUTION

You should use the Automatically Detect All Logon Servers option only if you are sure that you understand the ramifications of this selection. In particular, you should not use this option if you want the site server domain to span multiple sites. See "Automatically Adding Servers to Your Site" later in this chapter.

14. If you have not already granted the SMS service account the Log On as a Service right (which can be accomplished with User Manager for Domains), you receive an Account Error message box asking you if this right should be granted. Click Yes to continue.

15. SMS attempts to verify the user account you entered. In addition, if the SQL Server that you specified does not have maximum user connections set to a number larger than 20, SMS displays the SQL Connections dialog box. Enter a number greater than 20 and click Set.

 A good rule of thumb for SQL Connections is to add 20 (or more) to the existing number of connections if you have additional databases. If the SQL Server is used only for SMS, 20 connections should be plenty. You can change this setting later using the SQL Enterprise Administrator if needed.

16. SMS will now complete installation of all components. It will also set up the site database and start all SMS services. The SMS Setup Progress dialog box appears to confirm that the Setup program is still active and display its current progress. When it is complete, the Setup Success dialog box appears.

17. Click OK.

To be certain that everything has been installed properly, you should verify that all SMS services have been started and check the event log for possible errors. You can check the status of SMS services using the SMS Service Manager. Check the event log using the Windows NT Event Viewer. SMS events appear in the applications log.

Setting Basic Site Properties

Many properties affect the behavior and performance of an SMS system. For some SMS systems, you can leave these properties at default settings, but you may want to change a few. This section shows you how to view the current properties safely, without changing anything, and how to make changes when needed.

To change the site properties, you must first start the SMS Administrator program. This utility is the master control panel for the entire SMS system. It allows you to change settings for server-based services and select the client components to install. It also allows you to establish the site hierarchy of your SMS system and to control the flow of information within the system.

To start the SMS Administrator program, follow these steps:

1. Log on to the SMS primary site server or any Windows NT computer on which the SMS tools have been installed.

2. From the Start menu, select Programs, Systems Management Server, SMS Administrator. The Microsoft SMS Administrator Login dialog box appears (see Figure 43.5).

N O T E   SQL Server uses the term *login ID*, whereas all other BackOffice components use the term *logon*. Don't let this slight variation in terminology bother you. The terms are interchangeable and have the same meaning. ■

FIG. 43.5

The SMS Administrator Login dialog box allows you to gain access to the SQL Server database for SMS so you can run the SMS Administrator program.

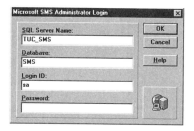

3. Enter the SQL Server Name that contains the SMS database, which is usually the same as the name of the computer running SQL Server.

4. Enter the name of the Database—usually SMS.

5. Enter the Login ID and Password for SQL Server. Click OK.

> **CAUTION**
>
> If you are still using the sa (system administrator) ID with no password, change it soon. Complete your immediate tasks, but don't put this important task off for long. Failing to change the sa password and create new logins for other users with varying levels of access privileges is a common mistake made by beginners, and it leaves your SMS database open to unauthorized access, tampering, and deletion.

6. The SMS Administrator starts and presents you with the Open SMS Window dialog box, shown in Figure 43.6. This dialog box makes it easy to open the windows that you work with when you use the SMS Administrator. Select the windows you want to work with. For now, you need only the Sites window open.

FIG. 43.6

Use the Open SMS Window dialog box to open selected windows when you start the SMS Administrator. You can open these windows later using toolbar buttons if you prefer.

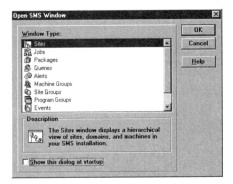

7. You can open these windows with toolbar buttons, as well. You may prefer to clear the Show This Dialog at Startup check box if you don't want to see this dialog box each time you start the SMS Administrator. Click OK.

8. If you see the Sites window, you have successfully started the SMS Administrator (see Figure 43.7).

Now that you know how to start the SMS Administrator program, you can learn a safe procedure for viewing the properties that control your site without any danger of accidentally changing something. Because a few actions in the SMS Administrator program can lead to network-wide changes involving hundreds of computers, SMS has been designed to make it difficult to change settings by accident.

The dialog boxes that allow you to change properties for the SMS system have two option button controls. One indicates that you are viewing the current properties, and the other indicates that you are viewing proposed changes to the properties (look ahead to Figure 43.9 for an example of a dialog box with these option buttons). When the Current Properties button is selected, all the other controls on the dialog box are grayed out, indicating that changes are unavailable. As long as you don't click the Proposed Properties button, you cannot change any site properties. You can safely view all the current selections.

FIG. 43.7

The Sites window in the SMS Administrator displays the site hierarchy.

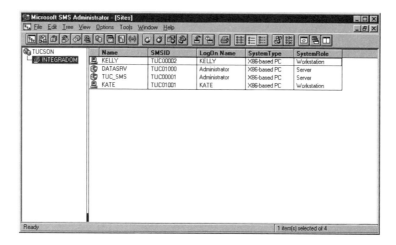

To open the Site Properties dialog box, follow these steps:

1. Start the SMS Administrator program.

2. Open the Sites window.

3. Highlight the primary site name in the left pane of the window by clicking it once.

4. Choose File, Properties. The Site Properties dialog box appears (see Figure 43.8).

FIG. 43.8

The Site Properties dialog box displays the site code, site server name, and various other site properties.

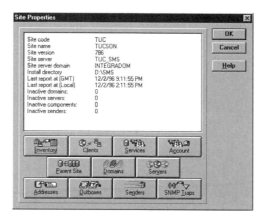

5. You can now view some of the site's properties such as the site code, site server name, and site server domain. You also have buttons that allow you to call up other dialog boxes with additional properties. These dialog boxes are discussed in the next four sections of this chapter.

6. If you just want to view the properties do not click the Proposed Properties option button on any of the additional properties dialog boxes (Services, Inventory, Parent Site, and so on). As long as you leave the Current Properties button selected, you cannot make accidental changes.

7. Click OK to close the dialog boxes when you are done viewing property settings. If you are prompted to confirm an update to the site, choose <u>N</u>o.

Site Services Settings   An SMS system works in cycles. When you give SMS a job to do, it typically takes several minutes to an hour or more for SMS to complete the job. This makes sense, given the nature of the work SMS is designed to perform. At regular intervals, a new cycle begins, and SMS checks to see what work, if any, it should perform.

The Services dialog box controls the speed of the SMS system. It does this by controlling the interval between cycles for seven of the SMS server-based services. These services are responsible for carrying out jobs and coordinating system events in the SMS system. By making the interval between cycles longer or shorter, and exercising good judgment about how many jobs you create, you can control the amount of work that SMS is given in a particular time period. You have the choice of the following four settings for the Response rate:

- <u>V</u>ery Fast
- <u>F</u>ast
- <u>M</u>edium
- <u>S</u>low

The <u>V</u>ery Fast speed is appropriate to use only for testing in a small SMS environment. Setting your site services to <u>V</u>ery Fast can potentially waste processing power by causing the SMS services to frequently poll for work that isn't there and initiate unnecessary monitoring processes.

The following four services poll the SMS database for updates at a regular polling interval:

- Site Hierarchy Manager
- SMS Alerter
- SMS Scheduler
- Applications Manager

In addition, three other services have specific monitoring intervals affected by the Response rate:

- Site Configuration Manager
- Maintenance Manager
- Despooler

Table 43.1 shows the polling interval setting shared by four of the services and the monitoring intervals used by three other services (Maintenance Manager, Site Configuration Manager, and Despooler), based on the setting you select.

Table 43.1   Response Rate Settings (in Minutes)

Setting	Very Fast	Fast	Medium	Slow
Polling Interval	1	5	15	30
Maintenance Manager	12	60	180	360
Site Configuration Manager	24	120	360	720
Despooler	24	120	360	720

To change the Response rate settings for a site, follow this procedure:

1. From the Site Properties dialog box, click Services. The Services dialog box appears, as shown in Figure 43.9.

FIG. 43.9

You change the Response rate setting for SMS Site Services by using the Services dialog box.

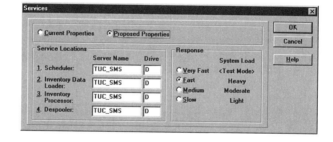

2. Select the Proposed Properties option button.
3. Select the option button that corresponds to the Response rate that you want.
4. Click OK. Then click Yes when prompted to confirm an update to the site.

You also can move some services to other servers using the Services dialog box. If you are using SMS for a lot of package distribution, you may want to move some of the workload off the site server and onto a helper server. You can move the following four services to a helper server:

■ Scheduler
■ Inventory Data Loader
■ Inventory Processor
■ Despooler

To move these services, follow this procedure:

1. From the Site Properties dialog box, click Services. The Services dialog box appears (see Figure 43.10).

FIG. 43.10

To change the Location of SMS Site Services use the Services dialog box.

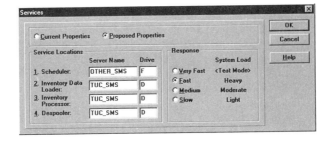

2. Select the Proposed Properties option button.

3. On the line corresponding to the service you want to move, enter the name of the server and the disk drive you want to use in the Server Name and Drive text boxes. Make sure that you have designated a server that is already running and attached to the network. Also make sure that the SMS service account has administrative rights on the server you designate.

4. Click OK. Then click Yes when prompted to confirm an update to the site. SMS automatically finds the server, installs the services on the new computer(s), uninstalls the services from the original server, and synchronizes everything. This may take some time—be patient.

Default Client Component Settings   You can control which of the client components of SMS install on client workstations as they are added to the SMS system. By making selections on the Clients dialog box, you control which, if any, of the components are added to a new client workstation and whether they start automatically.

To set default client setup properties for a site, follow these steps:

1. From the Site Properties dialog box, click Clients. The Clients dialog box appears (see Figure 43.11).

FIG. 43.11

You set default client setup properties for a site by using the Clients dialog box.

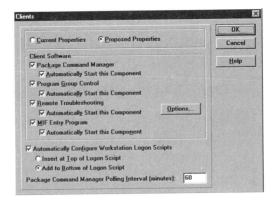

2. Select the Proposed Properties option button.

3. Select the components you want to load by default on all clients added to the site. You also can indicate whether you want them to load automatically when the client workstation starts.

> **CAUTION**
>
> Automatically Configure Workstation Logon Scripts is one of the powerful and potentially dangerous SMS options that you should be careful with. Used properly, it is a tremendously helpful tool. Before you proceed with this option, you should have manually added and tested a representative sample of various workstations, alerted appropriate support personnel and the user community that a change is occurring, and prepared an emergency plan if something goes wrong.

4. If you want SMS to update logon scripts automatically for the entire site, select the corresponding box. You can instruct SMS to add its instructions at the top or the bottom of existing logon scripts. If a particular user doesn't have a logon script, she or he is set up to run SMSLS.BAT, the SMS logon script.

5. You can set options for remote troubleshooting of Windows NT clients by clicking the Options button, which brings up the Remote Troubleshooting Options (see Figure 43.12). You can specify which users or groups are permitted to access Windows NT clients, you can have SMS install special accelerated video drivers on NT clients, and you can specify the default network protocol to be used with NT clients.

FIG. 43.12

The Remote Trouble-shooting Options dialog box allows you to specify parameters that affect the way Windows NT clients are accessed.

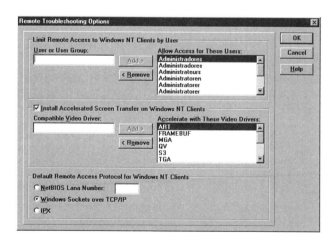

6. Click OK. Then click Yes when prompted to confirm an update to the site.

Inventory Settings   To change the inventory properties for your site, follow this procedure:

1. From the Site Properties dialog box, click Inventory. The Inventory dialog box appears, as shown in Figure 43.13.

FIG. 43.13

Use the Inventory Properties dialog box to set the frequency at which you want inventory information collected for a site.

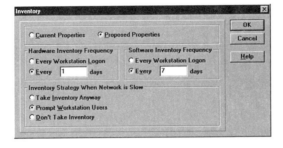

2. Click Proposed Properties.

3. Make selections for the hardware inventory frequency, the software inventory frequency, and the slow network strategy. Hardware inventory happens quickly enough (usually under ten seconds) that it is negligible at most sites with the majority of computers. It is often done at every logon or once a day. Software inventory on the other hand can take quite a bit longer, even several minutes. You also may want to consider how current your information needs to be. A good place to start with these settings is to set hardware frequency to every (1) day and software to every seven days.

4. Inventory can take significantly longer on a slow network link. Your situation should dictate your strategy. If you have a group of users that requires the services SMS offers but are always on the other side of a slow link, you will probably want to take inventory anyway. If the usual scenario for a slow link is a laptop, that has been taken home or on a trip, connecting to the network over a Remote Access Service (RAS) line, then you are likely to already have inventory information for that computer and can wait until it returns to the office for an update.

5. Click OK. Then click Yes when prompted to confirm an update to the site.

SMS Service Account Settings   In accordance with a sound security policy, you should change these settings at regular intervals just as you should regularly change passwords for all accounts.

To change the SMS service account and password properties for a site, follow these steps:

1. From the Site Properties dialog box, click Account. The Account dialog box appears (see Figure 43.14).

FIG. 43.14

The Account dialog box is used to change SMS service account properties.

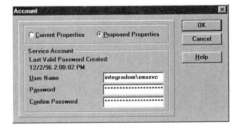

2. Select the Proposed Properties option button.

3. Enter the User Name (ID) that you want to use for the SMS service account. This account with its associated rights is the security context that all SMS services run under. In other words, when an SMS service attempts an action, its capability to perform that action depends on the rights associated with this account. The user name is not case-sensitive—that is, upper- and lowercase letters are treated the same. If you are using a master domain model, this account should be a master domain account. Enter the name with the following format: *domain\name*.

4. Enter the password associated with the account. For security reasons, you do not see the letters of the password as you enter them.

5. Enter the password again to confirm that you entered it accurately. SMS does not check that the password is valid for this account, so if you enter an incorrect ID or password, the services will not be able to start the next time they are shut down and restarted.

6. Click OK. Then click Yes when prompted to confirm an update to the site.

N O T E Changing the Account properties for a site does not create an account. The account must have already been created with User Manager for Domains or by some other method. In addition, changing the account properties does not affect the SQL Server account used.

You also can use the SMS Setup program to change the service account. The SMS Setup program allows you to change both the service account and the SQL Server account. Furthermore, the Setup program checks that the ID and password are valid, which the Account dialog box does not do. However, the Setup program only works on primary site servers. You must use the Account dialog box, as illustrated in the preceding steps, to change the service account for secondary site servers. ◼

CAUTION

It is a good idea to change the account being used at regular intervals, rather than simply change the password. This is due to the nature of SMS and the time that elapses while some actions are carried out. If you simply change the password and the site server is rebooted while the service account change is being done, your server can get caught in a state in which some services will have the correct password and some won't.

Implementing Your Site Relationship

If you have set up a primary site server and want to add it to an existing SMS system, you need to make an entry in the Parent Site Properties dialog box. In this dialog box, you can specify the parent (primary) site that you will attach the current site to as a child site. For this site relationship to function, you must have operational senders and addresses set up for the two sites. It is helpful if you have already done this before implementing the site relationship. See the section "Setting Up Communications Between Physical Locations" later in this chapter.

In the simplified case where you are connecting to another site on the same LAN, you do not need to worry about creating senders because the LAN sender is installed by default. You do still need to create an address, but you can do this directly as part of the site relationship procedure, discussed in the steps immediately following.

To change the parent site properties for a site, follow this procedure:

1. Start the SMS Administrator program.

2. Open the Sites window.

3. Highlight the primary site name in the left pane of the window by clicking it once.

4. Choose File, Properties. The Site Properties dialog box appears.

5. Click Parent Site. The Parent Site dialog box appears, as shown in Figure 43.15.

FIG. 43.15

Use the Parent Site dialog box to create a site relationship with another site. The other site becomes the parent of the current site.

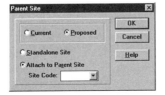

6. Select the Proposed Properties option button.

7. Click Attach to Parent Site and enter the three-character site code of the primary site that is to be the parent of this site, or select it from available sites in the drop-down list. The parent site only shows up in the list if you have already defined an address for the proposed parent site. If the address has already been created, skip to step 11.

8. If you have not defined an address for the parent site, a message box prompts you to create an address. Click Yes. The Address Properties dialog box appears (see Figure 43.16).

FIG. 43.16

The Address Properties dialog box allows you to define the type of connection between two sites.

9. The Destination Site Code should already be filled in with the proposed parent site code. Select the type of connection you will use to communicate between these sites from the Type drop-down list. Your choices are the three sender types—LAN, RAS, and SNA. Then click Details. A Lan Address From *sitecode* To *sitecode* dialog box appears (see Figure 43.17).

FIG. 43.17
Details for the Address Properties dialog box are entered into a dialog box that is specific to the type of connection between the sites. This figure depicts a LAN Address dialog box.

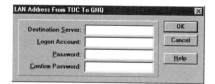

10. Enter the name of the site server for the destination site in the Destination Server box.

11. Enter the Logon Account that the sender will use to access the other site. You can use the SMS service account that you have already defined, or you can define an account for use by senders. If you are using a master domain model, this account should be a master domain account.

12. Enter the Password and then confirm the password. Click OK.

13. Click Yes when prompted to confirm an update to the site.

Adding Computers to the SMS System

After you have finished the installation process for the primary site server and set basic properties for your site, you are ready to connect to other sites. This process begins by telling SMS about other sites that you want to be part of the same SMS system. You establish communications with other sites by setting up connections using a Wide Area Network (WAN), a Systems Network Architecture (SNA) network, or a Remote Access Service (RAS) link. Then you define the SMS components used to move information from one site to another—*senders, outboxes,* and *addresses.*

If you have only one site, you can skip the sections about establishing communications. With a single site, you can still use the default LAN sender, described in the next section; but because this is set up automatically during site installation, no further action is necessary on your part.

You are also ready to add additional computers to your local SMS site, as a task separate from adding other sites. SMS can automatically scan for computers or allow you to manually add only the machines you want. Once again, remember to be careful with the automatic scan. On some networks, this process can "see" as far as 16 router hops!

Setting Up Communications Between Physical Locations

Three key entities are involved in communicating between sites:

- Senders
- Outboxes
- Addresses

A *sender* is a Windows NT service that moves instructions and data from one site to another. It uses one of three means of communication:

- Local Area Network (LAN)
- Windows NT Remote Access Service (RAS)
- Systems Network Architecture (SNA) link

These communications links must be established independently of SMS. For example, if you are going to use an SNA link, you need to install Microsoft SNA Server to create the SNA link. If you want to use RAS as a method of connectivity, you need to install a RAS server at each site. In addition, with both RAS and SNA senders, you have multiple options for the type of link. RAS, for example, supports connections over a standard phone line, X.25 network, or ISDN, and there is a different sender for each of these connections. SMS provides two different SNA senders corresponding to the two types of SNA connections supported. There are different sender types for each of these different links. Configuring a LAN sender is easier, but you should make certain that both sites are running at least one common LAN protocol.

The instructions and data processed by senders are temporarily stored in *outboxes*. After you have installed a sender, you must configure an outbox for the sender to use. An outbox is simply a directory on a server's hard disk that a sender uses to pick up instructions and data that need to be transferred to another site. All senders of a particular type share the same outbox. When you install a site server, an outbox for each type of sender is created on the site server's hard disk. There are six types of outboxes, corresponding to the six different senders.

You also need to create addresses for other sites that your site will communicate with. An address defines the information needed to connect to another site, including the destination site code and the type of sender to use. A site can have multiple addresses defined for a particular destination site. SMS automatically keeps statistics on the speed with which jobs are processed using different addresses. The SMS system reviews the requirements for a specific job, and other current system status information, and chooses the fastest means possible.

A default LAN sender is created automatically when you install a primary site. In addition, an outbox for each type of sender is created on the primary site server. If you need to manage additional sites linked to your primary site via a phone connection or an ISDN line, you need to define additional senders to move data between sites over these links. You may even want to install an additional LAN sender on a server besides the site server to offload work from the site server and improve throughput of site-to-site data.

> **CAUTION**
> The default LAN sender created during site setup is used to help manage the local site in addition to connecting to other sites linked by a network connection. Even if you do not need to connect to other remote sites, do not delete the original LAN sender.

You need three pieces of information to define a sender:

- Sender type
- Name of the server where the sender is installed
- Drive letter for the hard disk drive on which the sender will be installed

To define a new sender, follow these steps:

1. Start the SMS Administrator program.
2. Open the Sites window.
3. Highlight the site name in the left pane of the window by clicking it once.
4. Choose File, Properties. The Site Properties dialog box appears.
5. Select Senders. The Senders dialog box appears.
6. Select the Proposed Properties option button. Click Create. The Sender Properties dialog box appears.
7. Select the type of sender you want to create from the drop-down list.
8. Enter the name of the server on which you want to install the sender.
9. Enter the drive letter for the disk drive on which you want to install the sender.
10. Click OK. When asked to confirm updating the site, click Yes.

By reconfiguring the outbox for a particular type of sender, you can control when those senders are active and the priority level of jobs they will process during specific hours of the day. For example, you may not want LAN senders to process any jobs at all during the busiest part of the business day, to handle only high-priority jobs during the evening, and to process all types of jobs during the night when traffic is lightest. In addition, if you install a sender on a server other than the site server, you may want to move the outbox for that type of sender to the same server.

As an additional example, you may decide to install RAS and a RAS sender on a server other than the site server. You would then probably want to move the RAS outbox to that same computer to reduce network traffic and improve throughput. You also may rename outboxes if you want. You cannot create new outboxes, but you can move or rename the outboxes created originally.

To reconfigure an outbox, follow these steps:

1. Start the SMS Administrator program.
2. Open the Sites window.
3. Highlight the site name in the left pane of the window by clicking it once.
4. Choose File, Properties. The Site Properties dialog box appears.
5. Select Outboxes. The Outboxes dialog box appears (see Figure 43.18).
6. Click the Proposed Properties option button.
7. Select the outbox you want to reconfigure. Click Properties. The Outbox Properties dialog box appears, as shown in Figure 43.19.

FIG. 43.18

Select the Outbox you want to reconfigure using the Outboxes dialog box.

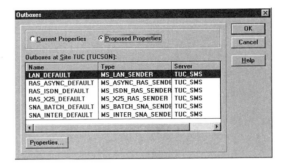

FIG. 43.19

Reconfiguring an Outbox is accomplished using the Outbox Properties dialog box.

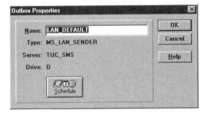

8. Make the changes you want to the name, server, and drive for the outbox. By default, all outboxes are on the site server.

9. If you want to change the schedule for this outbox, click Schedule. The Outbox Schedule dialog box appears (see Figure 43.20).

FIG. 43.20

The Outbox Schedule dialog box allows you to set the hours of operation for a particular outbox and the priority of jobs that will be handled at specific time intervals.

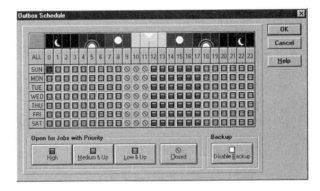

10. Highlight any block of time you want to change by clicking and holding down the mouse button on a particular cell in the grid and dragging to the opposite corner of the block you want to change. This area of the grid changes color to indicate that it has been selected.

11. Click one of the buttons to indicate what type of jobs should be handled, if any, during this block of time. To prevent a particular sender type from being active during a block of time, highlight that block and click Closed.

12. Repeat steps 10 and 11 as often as required. When you are through changing the schedule, click OK.

13. Click OK on the Outbox Properties and Outboxes dialog boxes. When asked to confirm updating the site, click Yes.

To use a sender, SMS also must have at least one address defined to connect to another site. In addition, the other site must have an address to reach your site, because the communications need to be bidirectional. Both of these addresses are created automatically for any secondary sites that are set up. Only the addresses between primary sites need to be created manually.

To define an address for another site, take the following steps:

1. Start the SMS Administrator program.

2. Open the Sites window.

3. Highlight the site name in the left pane of the window by clicking it once.

4. Choose File, Properties. The Site Properties dialog box appears.

5. Select Addresses. The Addresses dialog box appears, as shown in Figure 43.21.

FIG. 43.21

The Addresses dialog box allows you to create, modify, or delete addresses.

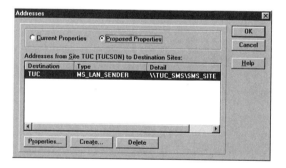

6. Click the Proposed Properties option button.

7. Click Create. The Address Properties dialog box appears (see Figure 43.22).

FIG. 43.22

Use the Address Properties dialog box to create a new address.

8. Enter the site code you want to communicate with in the Destination Site Code box. Using the Type drop-down list, select the type of sender you want to use to move information between these sites. Click Details. A dialog box with the specific properties for the type of sender you selected appears. The example shown in Figure 43.23 is for a LAN sender.

FIG. 43.23
You can set properties
for a LAN sender
address by using the
LAN Address From
sitecode To *sitecode*
dialog box shown here.

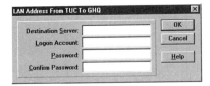

9. Enter the name of the destination server in the Destination Server box.

10. Enter the ID for the account that the sender will use in the Logon Account box.

11. Enter the password for the account and confirm it in the boxes provided.

12. Click OK in the Address Properties and Addresses dialog boxes. When asked to confirm updating the site, click Yes.

Adding Other Sites to the SMS System

You are now ready to add other sites to your SMS system. The communications components between sites should already be established. Specifically, you should have servers set up at your remote sites with Windows NT Server and the necessary sender(s) for the type of communications link present. If you will be connecting to the site with RAS, for example, then you need a RAS sender established on the server at that site. It is a good idea to manually test the reliability of the link between the central site and any other sites. You can connect to the server at a site over a WAN or RAS link and transfer a file of moderate size to see whether the link stands up to a workload.

After the server and its sender have been established at a remote site, it is not necessary to have an on-site administrator. It is possible to build the server for a remote site at your main location, complete some basic testing, and then ship it to the remote site. Removing the need for an on-site administrator at each location is one of the main benefits of a well-run SMS system.

It is occasionally useful to be able to completely shut down a remote server, power it off, and then turn it back on again. If you have set up your server on a computer from the Hardware Compatibility List (HCL) for Windows NT Server, applied all available service releases, and tested the server for a "burn in" period of a few days, you should have very few surprises. You may, however, encounter an intermittent hardware failure or a problem with power surges. For these and a handful of other reasons, you may want to install a device that allows you to power cycle the computer remotely. A number of devices are available that let you turn a computer off and back on using a telephone or LAN connection. If a person isn't available to provide occasional assistance, one of these devices can be very helpful.

Adding Primary Sites   To create other primary sites, follow the same procedure as you did with the original central site server. These servers must be configured by running SETUP from the distribution media (usually CD). There is no automatic installation procedure for primary sites. After these servers have been installed, you should set basic site properties and implement the site relationship using the procedures outlined in the first section of this chapter.

Adding Secondary Sites   A secondary site is a site that does not contain its own SMS database. No one administers it locally; someone at its (primary) parent site handles its administration. A secondary site cannot have any subsites beneath it as child sites.

Secondary sites are created by an administrator of the primary site who will manage the new secondary site. A server must already be prepared to have the secondary site components installed. This server might have Windows NT Server installed and configured at the primary site and then shipped to the secondary site. Alternatively, the server can be prepared at the secondary site by a person with Windows NT experience or a visiting administrator.

The server should be a member of the appropriate domain. If you are using a master domain model, the secondary site server's domain may need a trust relationship established with the domain containing its parent primary site server. Alternatively, it may be a member of the same domain as its parent.

At the primary site, you also must be sure that the sender that will be used to communicate with the new secondary site is operational, as well as any communications services that will be used by the sender (for example, RAS or SNA). If you are using a LAN sender, you need only verify that the LAN or WAN link to the other site is functioning properly and the SMS service account has the appropriate permissions.

If you are using a RAS or SNA sender, make sure that these communications services are operational at the secondary site and that the primary site can successfully connect. Finally, if you are using an SNA sender, you must install an SNA receiver at the secondary site. The secondary site server also must be running SNA Server.

To create a secondary site, you need the following information:

- A three-character site code.
- A name for the new site.
- The name of the computer you will use as the secondary site server.
- The location for the directory that SMS will create on the new site server. This must be a fully qualified path name and must specify an NTFS partition.
- The name of the domain in which the computer resides.
- The type of sender that will be used for the installation.
- The type of computer (architecture) of the secondary site server (the default is INTEL X86).
- The SMS service account that you have established and its password. This is the account that will be used by all services that run at the secondary site.

CAUTION

Make sure that you have a unique three-character site code. This code must be unique across the entire SMS system.

Site codes for all sites should be available from the planning process carried out earlier. The database administrator for the SQL Server that you will be using can provide the database information, in addition to a SQL Server ID and password. This account needs sa or dbo privileges for the SMS database. The SMS service account can be created by any administrator of the domain containing the account. If you are using a master domain model, the SMS service account should be a master domain account. You can find the computer name and domain name by logging on to the proposed site server and double-clicking the Network icon in the Control Panel.

To create a secondary site server, follow these steps:

1. Start the SMS Administrator program.

2. Open the Sites window.

3. Highlight the site name in the left pane of the window by clicking it once.

4. Choose File, New. The New Secondary Site dialog box appears (see Figure 43.24).

FIG. 43.24

Use the New Secondary Site dialog box to initiate the creation of a secondary site and its site server.

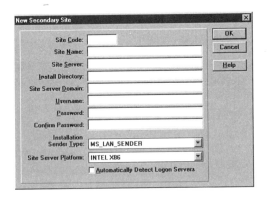

5. Enter the information required in the dialog box.

6. If you are using an account from a trusted domain, you must enter the Username as *domain\username.*

7. If desired, select the check box to Automatically Detect Logon Servers. Click OK.

CAUTION

The Automatically Detect Logon Servers option should be used only if you are sure that you understand the ramifications of this selection. In particular, you should not use this option if you want the site server domain to span multiple sites. See "Automatically Adding Servers to Your Site" later in this chapter.

8. If you chose LAN sender in the Installation Sender Type drop-down list, you are done. If you selected an RAS or SNA sender, you must define addresses for the two sites' senders to use when communicating. You first enter the address the secondary site will use to

contact its parent and then the address that the parent primary site will use to connect with the new secondary site. Click OK.

9. When asked to confirm the creation and installation of a new site, click Yes.

10. If you are using an SNA sender, you should be sure that the SNA receiver is installed and started at the secondary site. You can do this by using the Windows NT Server Manager utility.

Part
IX
Ch
43

After you have completed the preceding process, the secondary site is installed and configured automatically. This process may take several hours depending on the speed of the communications link and the workload the SMS system is already processing. While this process is occurring, an "under construction" icon appears in the Sites window of the SMS Administrator program. If you want to check the status of the site installation, select the secondary site and then choose File, Properties. A Job Properties dialog box appears. During installation, the site goes through four phases, which can be viewed in this Properties dialog box.

You've already learned how to connect to other sites. Now you learn how to add entire domains and individual computers, both servers and clients, to your own site.

Adding Domains

This section describes the steps you take to add an entire domain to your SMS site. It is usually appropriate to add an entire Windows NT domain to a site at one time. A simple configuration for an SMS system is to set up SMS sites that directly correspond to your Windows NT domains. Each site encompasses a single domain. Another common configuration is a single SMS site spanning multiple Windows NT domains. Alternatively, you may have a situation where a single Windows NT domain encompasses more than one SMS site. This can be particularly appropriate when you are using a master domain model. One or more servers from your master domain may be placed at each site. The next section discusses how to set up an SMS system where one domain contains servers located at multiple sites.

If you want, SMS can automatically detect and add all servers in the domain you are adding to the SMS system. Alternatively, you can add the domain and then select specific servers within the domain to be added to the SMS system. This is strictly a matter of personal preference. The Use All Detected Servers option is an easy and powerful way to handle a domain with multiple servers; however, there is a relationship between power and responsibility. If something goes wrong, a manual "one-at-a-time" process is less catastrophic than an automated multiple server process. And there is at least a small chance that something will go wrong. You must weigh the safety versus ease of installation tradeoff and decide what is best in your situation.

CAUTION

You should use the Use All Detected Servers option if you have enabled the Automatically Configure Workstation Logon Scripts option for this site. Logon scripts are not set up automatically for a domain with the Use Specified Servers option set. See the section "Automatically Adding Client Workstations to Your Site" later in this chapter.

To add a domain to the site, take the following steps:

1. Start the SMS Administrator program.
2. Open the Sites window.
3. Highlight the site name in the left pane of the window by clicking it once.
4. Choose File, Properties. The Site Properties dialog box appears.
5. Select Domains. The Domains dialog box appears, as shown in Figure 43.25.

FIG. 43.25

The Domains dialog box lets you add, modify, or remove domains. The domains currently defined in this site are listed.

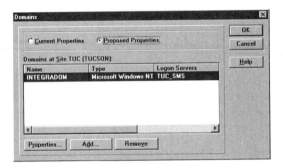

6. Click the Proposed Properties option button.
7. Click Add. The Domain Properties dialog box appears (see Figure 43.26).

FIG. 43.26

Use the Domain Properties dialog box to select the servers from a domain that will be used as logon servers. You can use all servers or select them by name.

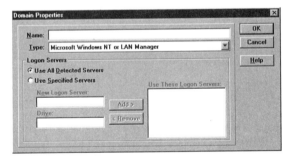

8. Enter the Name of the domain you want to add. If you are adding a Windows NT or LAN Manager domain, the domain must already exist. If you are adding a NetWare domain, you are free to create a unique domain name under which you can group one or more NetWare servers. Select the Type that describes the network operating system being run on the servers in this domain.

9. Click the option button corresponding to your preference for adding logon servers in the domain to the SMS system. Select Use All Detected Servers if you want to add the servers in the domain automatically, or Use Specified Servers to add selected servers manually.

10. Click OK. When asked to confirm updating the site, click Yes.

Managing a Domain Containing Multiple Sites

If you intend to create multiple SMS sites that all contain servers from a single Windows NT domain, you need to add that domain to each site manually. You should not select the option to Use All Detected Servers for such a domain. Use the Domains dialog box to add the domain to each site that contains one or more servers from this domain. Make sure that you select the Use Specified Servers option and manually add each server from this domain to the site. See "Manually Adding Servers to Your Site" later in the chapter.

Adding Servers

At this point, your central site server should be up and running, and you also may have created a site hierarchy by adding other primary and secondary sites to your SMS system. You do not need to create your entire site hierarchy before you begin adding servers to your sites. The only prerequisite is that you have at least one primary site server with its associated database.

You can add servers to a site one at a time or have the SMS system automatically scan for, or enumerate, all the servers in the site server domain. In this section, you learn how to add servers using both methods. The best method to use depends on your particular situation. Guidelines for selecting the best method for your site are given in the section "Adding Domains" earlier in this chapter.

Automatically Adding Servers to Your Site   For the site domain (the domain that contains the site server) there are two methods to tell the SMS system to automatically detect all logon servers. You can set the option during the installation of the site, or you can later change the properties for the site domain using the Domains dialog box. For domains other than the site domain, you must change the Use All Detected Servers setting for the domain in question, using the Domains dialog box.

> **CAUTION**
>
> If you have a domain that spans multiple sites, you'll want the server(s) at each site to be part of that site. Using the option to automatically detect logon servers in this situation will cause all the servers from all your sites to be included in the central site.

When you set up a primary site, the Primary Site Configuration Information dialog box includes the option to Automatically Detect All Logon Servers. During the installation of secondary sites, the New Secondary Site dialog box includes the option to Automatically Detect Logon Servers. Selecting this option when installing either type of site causes the Use All Detected Servers option for the site domain to be set. Conversely, if you do not select this option during installation, the Use All Detected Servers for the site domain is not set. See "Setting Up Your Site" and "Adding Secondary Sites" earlier in this chapter.

You can change the Use All Detected Servers setting for any domain, including the site domain, by accessing the Domains dialog using this procedure:

1. Start the SMS Administrator program.

2. Open the Sites window.

3. Highlight the site name in the left pane of the window by clicking it once.

4. Choose File, Properties. The Site Properties dialog box appears.

5. Select Domains. The Domains dialog box appears.

6. Click the Proposed Properties option button.

7. Select the Domain you want to configure and click the Properties button. The Domain Properties dialog box appears (see Figure 43.27).

FIG. 43.27

The Domain Properties dialog box is shown here with settings for the INTEGRADOM domain. Only two servers, DATASRV and TUC_SMS will be used as logon servers.

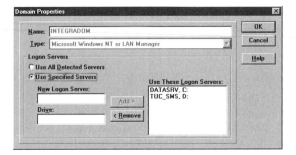

8. Click the Use All Detected Servers option button to turn on this setting (see Figure 43.28).

FIG. 43.28

Setting the Use All Detected Servers property causes all servers in the domain to be used as logon servers.

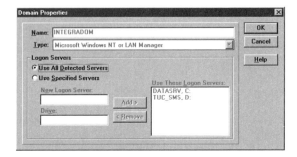

9. Click OK. When asked to confirm updating the site, click Yes.

Manually Adding Servers to Your Site   To manually add logon servers, take the following steps:

1. Start the SMS Administrator program.

2. Open the Sites window.

3. Highlight the site name in the left pane of the window by clicking it once.

4. Choose File, Properties. The Site Properties dialog box appears.

5. Select Domains. The Domains dialog box appears.

6. Click the Proposed Properties option button.

7. Select the Domain you want to configure and click the Properties button. The Domain Properties dialog box appears.

8. Click the Use Specified Servers option button to turn on this setting.

9. Enter the name of the logon server you want to add in the New Logon Server box (see Figure 43.29). If you want, you can specify on which drive (for LAN Manager and Windows NT servers), or on which volume (for NetWare servers) the SMS components should be located. By default, SMS uses the drive or volume with the largest amount of free space.

FIG. 43.29

This figure depicts the process of manually adding Logon Servers using the Domain Properties dialog box.

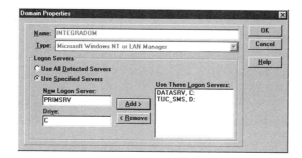

10. Click OK. When asked to confirm updating the site, click Yes.

Adding Client Workstations (PCs)

The addition of client workstations to the SMS system is driven by one of three events:

■ The logon script for a user is manually modified to include SMSLS, the SMS logon script. The user subsequently logs on and the computer being used is added.

■ The Automatically Configure Workstation Logon Scripts option is set for a site. Subsequently, the logon scripts for all users are modified to include the SMSLS logon script for SMS. When users next log on, their computers are added to the SMS system.

■ A user or an SMS administrator logs on to the computer, manually attaches to the SMS_SHR share on the logon server, and executes SMS procedures to add the workstation to the system.

 Be sure that client workstations have their date and time set accurately. If your clients are running LAN Manager software or Windows NT, you can synchronize their time with the site server using the following command:

```
net time \\siteserver /set
```

A similar feature is available to set NetWare clients' time the same as their logon server. Make sure that NetWare servers' times are set the same as the site server.

Automatically Adding Client Workstations to Your Site   If you want to automate the process of adding client workstations to your site, you should use the Automatically Configure Workstation Logon Scripts option for the site. This option only works if two other conditions are met:

- The Use All Detected Servers option must be set.
- For Windows NT or LAN Manager networks, the Replicator service must be operational because it is the mechanism used to update logon scripts on all logon servers in a domain.

Because this option depends on the Use All Detected Servers option, you cannot use it in situations where a single domain spans multiple sites. You cannot use Use All Detected Servers in such a scenario and, therefore, you also cannot use Automatically Configure Workstation Logon Scripts. You can, however, manually set up these domains, and they can still participate in the SMS system.

 TIP SMS 1.2 gives you the capability of using logon scripts in the single domain/multiple site situation by allowing you to map your clients to a domain/site combination.

To set Automatically Configure Workstation Logon Scripts for a site, use the following procedure:

1. Start the SMS Administrator program.
2. Open the Sites window.
3. Highlight the primary site name in the left pane of the window by clicking it once.
4. Choose File, Properties. The Site Properties dialog box appears.
5. Click Clients. The Clients dialog box appears (refer to Figure 43.11).
6. Click the Proposed Properties option button. Then click Automatically Configure Workstation Logon Scripts. You can instruct SMS to add its instructions at the top or the bottom of existing logon scripts. If a particular user doesn't have a logon script, his or her account is set up to run SMSLS.BAT, the SMS logon script.

CAUTION

Automatically Configure Workstation Logon Scripts is one of the powerful and potentially dangerous SMS options that you should be careful with. Used properly, it is tremendously helpful. Before you proceed with this option, you should have manually added and tested a representative sample of various workstations, alerted appropriate support personnel and the user community that a change is occurring, and prepared an emergency plan if something goes wrong.

7. Click OK. Then click Yes when prompted to confirm an update to the site.

For this option to function properly in a Windows NT domain, you must make sure that the Replicator service is operational. The administrator for the site domain may have already configured this service for existing logon scripts. If not, an administrator for the domain needs to set up the Replicator service.

Manually Adding Client Workstations to Your Site   To manually add a single client worksta-

tion to your SMS system, you can do one of two things:

- Change the logon script for the user who uses that workstation.
- Log on at the workstation, connect to the SMS_SHR share on the logon server, and manually run the SMS logon script.

If you plan to manually change logon scripts for selected users instead of using the Automatically Configure Workstation Logon Scripts option for a site, you must manually copy a number of SMS files to the directory containing logon scripts on your logon servers. If you are using the Replicator service, you should copy the files to the SCRIPTS directory in the REPL$ share. If you are not using Replicator, you should copy the files to the NETLOGON share. Copy the following files from the SMS_SHR of a logon server:

- CLRLEVEL.COM
- CHOICE.COM
- DOSVER.COM
- NETSPEED.COM
- NETSPEED.DAT
- SETLS programs for the processor types you support at your site (see the following Note)
- SMSLS.BAT
- SMSLS.INI

N O T E   The SETLS files need to be renamed. For example, the SETLS32.EXE for Intel X86 processors should be renamed to SETLS32I.EXE. The different versions are located in subdirectories of the LOGON.SRV directory.

By default, the computer is added to the domain containing the logon server. You can use the SMSLS.INI file to control which domain the SMS client is added to. If you are using a master domain model, all client workstations appear in the master domain by default because this is the domain containing the logon servers. You may want to have client workstations appear in resource domains instead of having all client workstations appear in the master domain.

By making an entry of the following form:

```
logondomain = SMSDomain
```

in the [DOMAIN] section of the SMSLS.INI file, you can control the SMS domain that contains particular client workstations. For example, if you want a workstation to appear in the INTERNAL domain even though the user logs on using an account from the GSULLIVAN master domain, you should place the following entry:

```
GSULLIVAN = INTERNAL
```

in the SMSLS.INI file for those users whose workstations belong in the INTERNAL domain.

After you have placed the files listed previously in the logon scripts directory and optionally created appropriate SMSLS.INI files, you are ready to modify user logon scripts. The format for the SMSLS.INI file is covered in Chapter 3 of the *SMS Installation and Configuration Guide*.

To change a user's logon script, follow these steps:

1. Run User Manager for Domains.
2. If the site domain is not the displayed domain, choose User, Select Domain. Select the site domain from the list of domains, or enter the domain name in the Domain box.
3. Scroll down the list of users until you find the user in question. Double-click the user's name. The User Properties dialog box appears.
4. Click Profile. The User Environment Profile dialog box appears (see Figure 43.30).

FIG. 43.30

Use the User Environ-
ment Profile dialog box
to select the logon script
for a user.

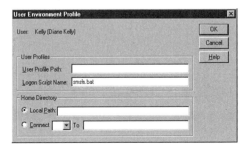

5. Enter the name of the SMS logon script (SMSLS.BAT) in the Logon Script Name box. If the user already has a logon script, you must find the logon script and edit it to include a line calling SMSLS.BAT. Click OK.
6. Close User Manager for Domains.

You also can add a client workstation to the SMS system manually without modifying the user's logon script. This process adds the SMS components to the client workstation and adds the workstation to the SMS system. If the user manually deletes one or more components from the workstation, however, he or she is not automatically added back to the workstation. If the user's logon script executes the SMS logon script, the SMS system is quite resilient at repairing or replacing damaged or missing client files. The logon script modification is, therefore, a slightly preferable method for adding clients.

If you do want to manually add a client workstation without modifying the user's logon script, follow these steps:

1. Connect a drive letter to the SMS_SHR of a logon server. Change the currently logged drive to the new drive letter.
2. Run the SMSLS batch file.

In a LAN Manager or Windows NT environment, you can accomplish this by entering the following commands:

```
NET USE Z: \\logonserver\SMS_SHR
Z:
CALL SMSLS
NET USE Z: /DELETE
```

In a NetWare environment, the procedure is slightly different. You connect a drive letter to the NetWare volume on which the SMS logon server components have been installed. Then change the current directory to the LOGON.SRV directory. Because Z: is usually used by NetWare to map a search drive to the PUBLIC directory, you should pick a different, unused letter. If you are unsure which letters are currently being used, enter the MAP command with no arguments. The following is a series of commands for a NetWare environment using L for a drive letter and assuming that the SMS root directory on the logon server is named SMS:

```
MAP L: \\logonserver\volume
L:
CD \SMS\LOGON.SRV
SMSLS.BAT
```

Using SMS to Inventory Your Computer Network

One of the most powerful and useful capabilities of SMS is to build and maintain an inventory of servers and workstations on your network. SMS client components scan the computer for hardware information including the amount of Random Access Memory (RAM); number and type of processor(s); video display type; disk drive types, sizes, and available free space; network adapter type; and much more. The SMS administrator also can define software packages that should be inventoried on a regular basis. This information is gathered at intervals set by the SMS administrator. A typical schedule would be daily for computer hardware and weekly for software.

A closely related task is the capability to audit software packages. A software inventory looks for a small number of well-defined software packages on a relatively frequent basis. A software audit, on the other hand, scans computers for a relatively large number of potential software packages. Because the number of packages to search for is greater, the audit takes longer and is therefore done less frequently to avoid alienating the user community. Software auditing is discussed in the next section, "Setting Up Auditing."

The SMS system uses the Inventory Agent service to scan servers running LAN Manager and Windows NT. NetWare servers are scanned by the Maintenance Manager service running on the site server. These services scan the servers at intervals controlled by the Hardware Inventory Frequency and the Software Inventory Frequency settings. These settings appear on the Inventory dialog box, which is opened from the Site Properties dialog box. If the settings indicate to scan at every workstation logon, servers are still scanned only once in each 24-hour period.

The inventory process for client workstations begins with a user logging on to the network. Client components on the user's computer scan for hardware and software depending on the inventory interval settings. The scanning process creates a "raw" file that is placed on the logon server in the INVENTORY.BOX directory. The Maintenance Manager service on the site server polls the INVENTORY.BOX directories on all logon servers at regular intervals and moves the raw files to the SITE.SRV\INVENTORY.BOX directory on the site server.

The Inventory Processor processes files that it finds in the site server's inventory box and creates another intermediate file type called a Delta-MIF. The Delta-MIFs created by the Inventory Processor are placed in another directory on the site server. They are then loaded into the site database by the Inventory Data Loader service.

This process obviously takes some time. A common misconception for new SMS administrators is to expect inventory information to show up immediately. The actual time required for a particular computer to be added to the site and inventory information to be processed depends on many factors, including the monitoring frequency and system load settings for the site, the number of computers on the network, and the amount of network activity. Even if the Response setting for site services is set to Fast, the Maintenance Manager's logon server monitor interval is 60 minutes. It is not unusual, therefore, for an hour or more to elapse before computers appear in the site database. See the earlier section, "Site Services Settings," for more information.

Client workstations that have been added to the SMS system automatically begin hardware inventory scanning at the interval specified. To conduct a software inventory, however, the software packages that you want to inventory must be defined for the SMS system. This process is described in the following section.

N O T E   An interesting problem occurs when a mobile user connects to a WAN in various locations using the same portable computer. The question arises, in what location or site should SMS report the computer's inventory information? The SMS system defaults to a rule of three times. If a user logs on to the network at a new site with a portable computer three consecutive times, the computer is moved to the inventory of that site. ▪

Defining Packages for Inventory

The three distinct sets of properties for an SMS Package are as follows:

- ▪ Workstations properties
- ▪ Sharing properties
- ▪ Inventory properties

In this section, you learn about setting Inventory properties for packages to enable the SMS inventory collection components to recognize specific software applications. The other two types of properties are discussed in Chapter 44, "The Role of the SMS Administrator."

▶ **See** "Defining Packages for Software Distribution and Installation," **p. 1518**

To define an inventory package, follow these steps:

1. Start the SMS Administrator program.

2. Open the Packages window, and choose File, New. The Package Properties dialog box appears (see Figure 43.31).

FIG. 43.31

The Package Properties dialog box allows you to define new packages.

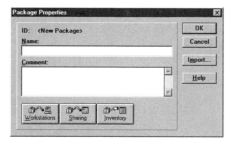

3. Enter a name for the package in the Name box. If the package describes an application, it is usually a good idea to use the name of the application itself as the name of the package.

4. Enter a brief description of the package in the Comments box.

 T I P A package can be one or more files of any type, including data files, although they are most often used to define applications.

5. Click Inventory. The Setup Package for Inventory dialog box appears (see Figure 43.32).

FIG. 43.32

You define package properties for software inventory by using the Setup Package for Inventory dialog box.

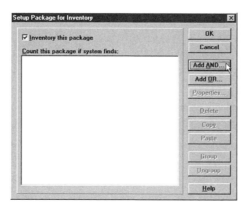

6. Click the Inventory This Package check box. A check mark should appear in the box. You now begin an iterative process of defining the rule(s) used to identify a particular package.

7. Click Add AND. The File Properties dialog box appears, as shown in Figure 43.33.

8. Enter the name of a particular file that is part of this package (for example, EXCEL.EXE). Enter the complete file name with extension. You cannot use wildcard characters.

9. If you want SMS to collect a copy of this file and store it on the site server, click the Collect This File check box. Collecting the file is not necessary if you just want to scan computers to inventory this package.

FIG. 43.33

Use the File Properties
dialog box to describe
a file so that it can
be identified during
inventory processing.

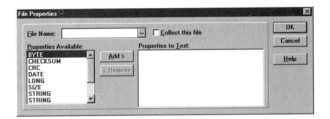

10. Select one of the properties listed in the Properties Available scrolling list box. For example, you might select SIZE if you want to specify the size of the file as an identifying attribute. Click Add, and a dialog box for the specific attribute appears.

11. Enter a value for the attribute selected. For example, enter the size of the file in bytes (characters) if you selected the SIZE attribute. Click OK to close the attribute's dialog box.

12. Repeat steps 10–11 as many times as desired to define attributes for the file specified in the File Name box. When you have entered all attributes for this file, click OK to close the File Properties dialog box.

13. If you have entered all the identifying characteristics you need to identify the package, skip to step 15.

14. If the package includes multiple files, and you want to add one or more additional rules to specify identifying attributes for other files, you can add additional clauses. You can combine these clauses with the original clause using logical AND and OR operators to form a complex expression. Click the Add AND or the Add OR button to insert a logical operator into the Count This Package If System Finds box. Return to step 7.

15. When you have specified all the files and properties you need to uniquely identify this package, click OK. You return to the Package Properties dialog box.

16. Click OK.

SMS now scans for this package, using the rules you defined, whenever software inventory is performed. Packages defined with Workstations properties or Sharing properties do not become active until a job is created. There is no need, however, to create a job to activate the Inventory properties of a package. After the inventory properties have been defined, the package definition is used to inventory this package whenever software inventory is taken.

Viewing Inventory Information

After SMS has started collecting inventory information, you can use the Sites window in the SMS Administrator to view the information for particular computers. The information available is extensive. SMS also keeps track of changes that occur over time by maintaining historical inventory information. The SMS Administrator program can even highlight historical records that are different from the latest inventory information to make it easy to identify elements of the inventory that have changed.

To view the inventory information for a particular computer, follow these steps:

1. Start the SMS Administrator program.

2. Open the Sites window. Choose Tree, Expand All from the menu to completely expand the display to show all sites and domains in the left pane of the window. Select the domain that contains the computer in which you are interested.

3. In the right pane of the Sites window, select the computer. Choose File, Properties. The Personal Computer Properties window appears, as shown in Figure 43.34.

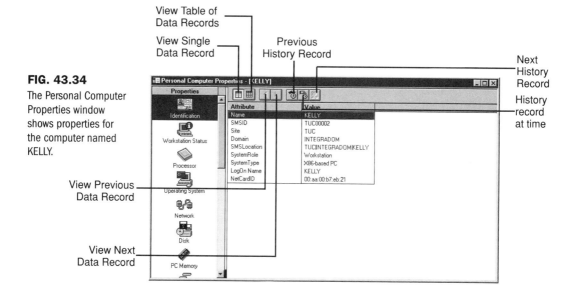

FIG. 43.34
The Personal Computer Properties window shows properties for the computer named KELLY.

View Table of Data Records

View Single Data Record

Previous History Record

Next History Record

History record at time

View Previous Data Record

View Next Data Record

4. This window also has left and right panes. Highlight an item in the left pane, and details regarding that item display in the right pane. The left pane shows the computer's properties. A property in this window might be the computer's disk drives, for example, or the computer's network information. Properties also may include tools such as the Help Desk utilities that are part of the SMS system. Some of the items listed in the Properties pane are specific to particular types of machines and do not appear for all computers.

   Scroll down the Properties pane and select any item you want. Details for that item display in the right pane. If the item has multiple instances, a computer with several disk drives for example, the details for those items display in tabular format in the right pane.

5. To view information on software inventory, scroll down the Properties pane until you see the Packages icon. Click the icon, and information about the packages you have defined with inventory properties displays in the right pane.

6. To view historical information for a particular item, highlight the item in the left (Properties) pane. The current information for that item displays in the right pane. You can step

one record backward or forward by choosing View, Previous History Record, or View, Next History Record from the menu.

7. Alternatively, you can choose View, History Record at Time from the menu. The History dialog box appears. Select the View Historical Data option button. You may enter the date for which you want to view information. The date and time specified appear in the title bar of the Personal Computer Properties window.

   You can select any item in the Properties pane to see the historical information for that group. Any information that differs from that in the current inventory record for a particular group appears in red so that it can be readily identified. When you want to reset the view to current data, choose View, History Record at Time from the menu again. Select the View Current Data option button.

8. To close the Personal Computer Properties window for a computer, click the Control Menu icon at the left end of the title bar and choose Close from the menu.

You can view inventory information in many different ways. You have already learned how to use the SMS Administrator program to see the details of a particular computer's inventory. In an upcoming section, you learn how to use *queries* to find all computers with a certain attribute. For example, you can display all computers that have a 486 processor or all computers that have more than 20M of available disk space. In addition, a utility program called SMSVIEW makes it easier to use other applications to view information in the SMS database. For example, you could use Microsoft Access to create reports on the inventory information. The SMSVIEW utility program is discussed in Appendix A of the *SMS Administrator's Guide*.

Interpreting Inventory Information

Now that you have seen how to view information about a computer's inventory, there are a few additional things you should understand about how the SMS system processes inventory information. A common misconception among people new to SMS is that the inventory information is "live." First-time users of the system often think that the SMS Administrator program connects to the computer in question and polls it for inventory information. Although this is exactly what the SMS Help Desk utilities do, the majority of inventory information is not retrieved directly from the computer workstation.

Understanding Where the Information Is Stored

If you have been following along through all the SMS chapters, you already know that the SMS system uses a SQL Server database to store information about the computers it is managing. This includes the current and historical inventory information that you learned how to view in the preceding section. The SQL Server may be installed on the site server, or it may be installed on a different server to help distribute the workload. An overview of the flow of inventory information from workstation to logon server to SQL Server database was presented earlier in the "Using SMS to Inventory Your Computer Network" section.

What Is Collected?

SMS provides a great deal of information about the computer systems it inventories. There is information about all the following items:

- **Identification.** The unique name and SMS identifier given to this computer along with its site name, domain name, and other identifying attributes.

- **Workstation status.** The date and time of the last inventory update and other status information.

- **Processor.** Number and type of Central Processing Units (CPUs) that the computer has.

- **Operating system.** The name and version number of the operating system.

- **Network.** The name and version number of the networking software the computer is using. This group also includes the transport protocols being run and the IP address (if TCP/IP is being used).

- **Netcard.** The brand of network interface card being used and any pertinent settings such as interrupt, I/O address, DMA usage, and so on.

- **Disk.** The number, type, and size of disk drives in the system, including information about the amount of space used and available.

- **Video.** The type of video hardware in use and, if possible, the resolution of the video display.

- **Mouse.** The type of mouse being used.

- **Packages.** The software found on this computer that matches identifying attributes defined in packages with inventory properties.

- **Audited software.** Software that matches criteria defined in a package rule file and used by the software audit program.

- **Services.** Server-based services, if any, that are installed on this computer and their status (running, paused, or stopped).

- **Environment.** Environment variables, if any, that have been set and their values.

- **IRQ table.** The hardware interrupts being used by this computer.

This list is not comprehensive, and not all of these items are available for every type of computer. It does, however, give you an overview of the type of information and the level of detail that is available. The SMS system may be constrained in what it is able to determine about a particular piece of equipment by the characteristics of the hardware itself. The more current the product, the likelier it is that SMS will be able to accurately identify it and provide detailed information on its attributes. With some older equipment, it is simply impossible to tell exactly what is being scrutinized through an automated scanning process. A good example is the video resolution of a particular system. This can be determined on some equipment, and not on others.

Using DMI (Desktop Management Interface Specification) to Add Information

There is some information that a computer system is never able to scan for automatically. Good examples of this would be the name of the person who usually uses the computer, the person's phone number, or the identifier used to denote the location of the computer in a particular building. The SMS system provides a mechanism to extend the inventory information about the computer to include these types of attributes.

As discussed in Chapter 42, "Preparing for SMS," a group of companies in the information systems business formed an association called the Desktop Management Task Force (DMTF). The DMTF created a standard file format for identifying information called the Management Information File (MIF). By creating a file that adheres to this format, you can cause SMS to include additional information in the inventory database.

You could use any word processor or text editor to create a MIF because it is a standard ASCII text file. There are rules regarding the structure of the file, however, and it may be easier to create a MIF using the utilities provided with SMS for this purpose. There are two such utilities: the SMS MIF Form Generator and the MIF Entry utility. Using the MIF Form Generator, you can create a form that the MIF Entry utility then uses to capture information that you want to add to the inventory. This process can be automated by creating a Run Command on Workstation job to send this utility to an appropriate group of users or everyone on the network. These utilities are documented in Appendix B of the *SMS Administrator's Guide*.

▶ **See** "Run Command on Workstation Jobs," **p. 1525**

Using Queries to View Inventory Information

You have already seen how to view inventory information for one machine at a time. In this section, you learn how to ask the SMS system to display all the computers that match certain criteria. You learn how to formulate a query, submit it to the SMS database, and view the resulting answer that returns. You can create queries and store them for later use, or you can create an *ad hoc query* for immediate execution.

The process for creating each type of queries is similar. You learn how to create and store queries, and how to execute a stored query. Using ad hoc queries is a simplification of this process, which is not covered.

To create a query, follow these steps:

1. Start the SMS Administrator program.

2. Open the Queries window. Choose File, New. The Query Properties dialog box appears (see Figure 43.35).

3. Enter a name for the query in the Query Name text box. Then enter descriptive text in the Comment text box. The name and comment together should describe the query well enough that you can tell what the query is for without having to view the query properties you are about to define.

FIG. 43.35

Use the Query Properties dialog box to define a query that you can apply to the SMS database.

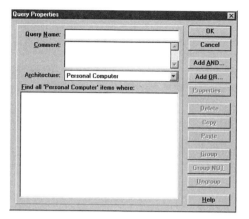

4. Select the architecture appropriate to the items you want to find in the Architecture drop-down list. The default is Personal Computer, which is the architecture you will probably use most often.

5. Click Add AND or Add OR. The Query Expression Properties dialog box appears, as shown in Figure 43.36.

FIG. 43.36

The Query Expression Properties dialog box allows you to create expressions that will be combined to build a query.

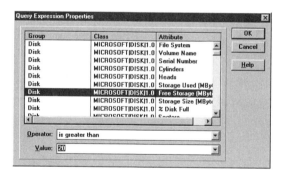

6. Select the attribute you want to add to the query expression from those listed in the list at the top of the dialog box. You may re-sort this list by group, class, or attribute by clicking the heading of that column.

7. Choose an Operator from the drop-down list in the middle of the dialog box.

8. Select a value using the Value drop-down list. You also can type in a value manually if an appropriate value does not appear in the list.

9. Click OK to add this expression to the query you are building.

10. If you have entered all the expressions you need to build your query, skip to step 11.

If you want to add one or more additional expressions to specify identifying attributes for this query, you can add additional clauses. These clauses can be combined with the original clause using logical AND and OR operators to form a complex expression.

Click Add <u>A</u>ND or Add <u>O</u>R to insert a logical operator into the <u>F</u>ind All '*architecture*' Items Where box. The Query Expression Properties dialog box appears again. Return to step 7.

11. When you have specified all the expressions you need for this query, click OK. You return to the Queries window.

To execute a query that you have defined, follow this procedure:

1. Start the SMS Administrator program.

2. Open the Queries window. Choose <u>F</u>ile, Execute Query. The Execute <u>Q</u>uery dialog box appears (see Figure 43.37).

FIG. 43.37
Use the Execute Query dialog box to specify the target sites for a query and to begin its execution.

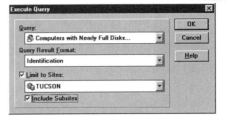

3. Select the query you want to execute from the <u>Q</u>uery drop-down list box.

4. Select the format you want to use to display your query results from the Query Result <u>F</u>ormat drop-down list.

5. If you want, you can limit the sites that the query is applied against. Click the <u>L</u>imit to Sites check box and select the topmost parent site of the subtree of the site hierarchy you want to examine. If you want to include subsites of this parent site, click the <u>I</u>nclude Subsites check box.

6. Click OK. The query executes and displays your results in a Query Results window.

Setting Up Auditing

Although the capability to inventory software applications is useful when you want to carefully watch the usage of a small number of packages, it also is useful to be able to check for the presence of a larger list of applications on an infrequent basis. The Software Audit program allows you to perform exactly this function. Used in conjunction with a Run Command on Workstation job, the Software Audit program can provide important information about your organization's compliance with licensing regulations, track usage patterns for applications, and aid the planning and budgeting process for network growth.

These are the steps you must complete to audit software packages:

1. Define a set of rules to identify the packages you want to audit. SMS includes a utility called FILETOKN.EXE that can find six identifying characteristics of a file that you can use

to uniquely identify a file. After you have found these characteristics, you can follow the process used to create inventory properties for a package to generate a package rule file. (See the earlier section "Defining Packages for Inventory" for more information.)

2. The SMS system creates a package rule file that contains rules for all files for which inventory properties have been defined. This file is stored in the SITE.SRV\MAINCFG. BOX\PKGRULE directory on the site server. You should make a copy of this file in the \PRIMSITE.SRV\AUDIT directory and edit it so that it includes only those packages you want to audit. Alternatively, you may want to use the AUDIT.RUL file provided with SMS as a starting point and add to it.

3. Convert this file to the format used by the Software Audit program using the RUL2CFG. BAT utility provided in the \PRIMSITE.SRV\AUDIT directory. This converts the file and copies it to the \PRIMSITE.SRV\AUDIT\PACKAGE directory.

4. Create a package for software auditing by importing the AUDIT.PDF package definition file. Specify the \PRIMSITE.SRV\AUDIT\PACKAGE directory as the source directory for the package.

5. Create a Run Command on Workstation job to execute the Software Audit program using the rule file you created.

To view the audited software, follow the steps outlined earlier in the section "Viewing Inventory Information." The software audit information appears in the Audited Software group of the Personal Computer Properties window.

▶ **See** "Run Command on Workstation Jobs," **p. 1525**

▶ **See** "Using Package Definition Files (PDFs)," **p. 1534**

From Here...

You have learned a lot about SMS and its inventory and audit capabilities. You learned how to set up your site and establish communications links with other sites. This chapter covered techniques for installing other sites and creating your site hierarchy, as well as the procedures for adding servers and client workstations to your site. Finally, the inventory and audit capabilities of SMS were described.

For related information, refer to the following chapters:

■ For a review of SMS basics, see Chapter 42, "Preparing for SMS."

■ For information on automatically distributing and installing software and using the Help Desk features of SMS, see Chapter 44, "The Role of the SMS Administrator."

■ For information on establishing policies for improved security and specific guidelines for securing your site, your servers, and client workstations, see Chapter 46, "Implementing Real-World Security."

■ For information on developing a proactive approach to avoiding network problems and server outages, see Chapter 48, "Proactive Network Administration."

CHAPTER 44

The Role of the SMS Administrator

by Tim Darby and Don Benage

The role of the Systems Management Server (SMS) administrator is unique. It is often mistakenly assumed to be little more than a glorified software installer. On a large network, this could not be farther from the truth. The SMS administrator certainly needs to understand software installation—it is generally difficult to automate something that you don't already know how to do manually. The successful SMS administrator also needs a strong background in Windows NT network administration and setting up communications links for wide area networks (WANs). In addition, because SMS uses SQL Server to store its site database, the SMS administrator may need to double as the database administrator (DBA).

Of course, in a large network environment where all these skills are required, there is usually a team of individuals working together to support the environment. It is important to recognize, however, that all these skills must be available when SMS administrative tasks are carried out. If you do not possess all these skills yourself, it is prudent to seek assistance from other members of the support team to complete some tasks. You also may find it useful to review the material on Windows NT Server, SQL Server, and other Microsoft BackOffice components provided in other chapters of this book if you have not already done so. In addition, the manuals and online reference materials provided with BackOffice products are valuable resources.

How to define packages to automate software installation

Create packages that you can use to automate the process of distributing and installing computer software. Create packages for applications that will be installed directly on client workstations, or to be installed as a shared, server-based application.

How to create jobs to implement the packages you have defined

Create jobs that activate your packages and initiate their actual distribution and installation. Learn about the different types of jobs and the various options that control their behavior.

How to control access to SMS tools and features

Prevent malicious or accidental use of the powerful capabilities provided by SMS. Explore the features of the SMS Security Manager and learn how to assign various roles to different administrative personnel.

How to use the Help Desk features to control remote workstations

Explore the Help Desk features provided by SMS—Remote Control, Remote Chat, and Remote Reboot. Configure workstations to enable these features and disable remote control of workstations that do not want to be accessed.

Some of the concerns faced by the SMS administrator are as follows:

■ The impact that automated processes have on server performance and network bandwidth, especially over slow links

■ The disruption of normal user computing routines caused by mandatory processes and inventory scanning or auditing

■ Planning the installation of a new software package or update to occur in stages to minimize the possibility of inflicting problems on a large number of users at the same time

■ Trying to create redundancy in key components of the system to avoid single points of failure

In this chapter, you learn some of the more advanced features of SMS. You learn how to automate the process of software distribution and installation. SMS Security is reviewed, as well as accessing SMS from remote locations using dial-up lines. The chapter also explores Help Desk features of SMS and provides procedures for using the Network Monitor protocol-analysis tool. Finally, some techniques for monitoring and troubleshooting SMS are discussed. ■

Defining Packages for Software Distribution and Installation

In Chapter 43, "Implementing SMS," you learned how to create a package and define inventory properties for that package. In this section, you learn how to define properties that tell SMS how to distribute packages and install applications. You can use SMS to distribute any type of information, including data files. It is most often used, however, to distribute and install applications. Applications can be installed directly on client workstations or set up on a server and shared so that users can run them at client workstations over the network. Defining a package is the first step in automating software distribution and installation. The package is not "activated," however, until you create a job using the package and define a schedule and target for its use. See "Creating Jobs for Software Distribution and Installation" later in this chapter.

Creating Package Source Directories

For either type of software installation package, those that will be installed directly on client workstations or those that will be shared from a server-based installation, you must create a *package source directory*. This is nothing more than the location of all the files that make up the package and any installation scripts or programs that are needed. The package source directory can be on the site server or on a shared directory on another server. It can even be on a server that is not included in the SMS site. When you define the properties of the package, the topic discussed in the next two sections, you tell SMS where to find the package source directory. You specify the location relative to the location of the Scheduler service. The Scheduler is on the site server by default. If you have moved the Scheduler, or if the package source directory is not on the site server, you should use a Universal Naming Convention (UNC) name to specify the location of the package source directory.

T I P A UNC name is of the form *servername**sharename*. You can specify additional directories (and subdirectories) if appropriate. For example, you could specify a UNC name such as \\PRIMSRV\DATA\SCHEDULER.

The package source directory should contain all files that are part of the package itself, as well as any setup program and script files that may be used to automate setup. If the installation of the package uses a script processor (such as MTRUN.EXE, the processor for Microsoft Test version 3.0), you can place this utility directly in the package source directory, or in the LOGON.SRV\MSTEST directory on the server. In addition, if the package will be defined using one of the Package Definition Files (PDFs) supplied by Microsoft, described in the "Using Package Definition Files (PDFs)" section later in this chapter, the PDF file itself should be copied to the package source directory.

If you are creating a package source directory for a shared network application, follow the network installation instructions for the application. Depending on the application, you may need to create separate package source directories for different client platforms running different operating systems. Some applications place platform-specific configuration files in the source directory as part of the network installation process and therefore require separate source directories for each platform.

> **CAUTION**
>
> If you are adding Workstation or Sharing properties to a package that has already been defined with other properties, you should proceed carefully. If active jobs use this package, you should not change the name of the package or other properties that might affect the active job. See "Monitoring the Status of Jobs" and "Canceling and Deleting Jobs" later in this chapter for information on how to check the status of an active job and possibly cancel it or remove it from the system.

Run Command on Workstation Packages

On large networks, visiting all the client workstations to install new applications or update existing applications can be very time-consuming and expensive. In some cases, the cost of installing and maintaining the software may exceed the cost of the computer itself! SMS provides some relief by allowing you to define Run Command on Workstation packages that can be distributed and run on client workstations automatically. You can make these commands mandatory, or allow users to decide for themselves whether they want to run the command. The command may be a Setup program for a software application, or a utility such as a virus checker.

To define a Run Command on Workstation package, follow these steps:

1. Start the SMS Administrator program.

2. Open the Packages window. Choose File, New from the menu. The Package Properties dialog box appears.

Part
IX

Ch
44

3. Enter a name for the package in the Name text box. If the package describes an application, it is usually a good idea to use the name of the application itself as the name of the
   package. Enter a brief description of the package in the Comment text box.

4. Click Workstations. The Setup Package for Workstations dialog box appears, as shown in
   Figure 44.1.

FIG. 44.1

The Setup Package for
Workstations dialog box
allows you to define
properties that will
enable this package to
be installed on client
workstations.

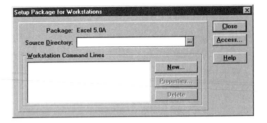

5. Enter the location of the package source directory in the Source Directory text box. See
   "Creating Package Source Directories" earlier in this chapter for more information on
   how to create a package source directory.

6. You are now ready to define one or more command lines that will apply to this package.
   These command lines typically initiate the installation process of a software application,
   but you also can launch a virus check, for example, or other processes. As you define
   command lines, they are listed in the Workstation Command Lines list box. Click New to
   define the first command line. The Command Line Properties dialog box appears (see
   Figure 44.2).

FIG. 44.2

Use the Command Line
Properties dialog box to
define a command line
that can be run on
workstations, manually
or automatically, that
receive this package.

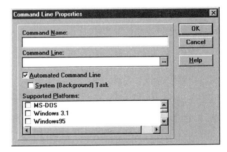

7. Enter a descriptive name for the command in the Command Name text box. For
   example, you might name a command Run Widget Setup Program.

8. Enter the actual command to be executed in the Command Line text box. This command
   must be a batch file or executable program name with optional command-line switches.
   The command will run from the root of the package source directory.

9. Indicate whether input is required from the user after this command executes, by
   checking or clearing the Automated Command Line check box.

10. If the command will run on Windows NT systems without displaying a window or requiring input, check the System (Background) Task check box. This is particularly useful for background tasks that need to run on unattended servers at remote locations or locked machine rooms. SMS includes a Package Command Manager service for Windows NT systems that can automatically execute such packages.

11. Click the appropriate check boxes in the Supported Platforms scrolling list box to indicate the operating systems that will support this command. On client workstations that are running selected operating systems, this package appears in the Package Command Manager application (after you create a job to activate the package). See "Creating Jobs for Software Distribution and Installation" later in this chapter.

12. Choose OK to return to the Setup Package for Workstations dialog box. The new command now appears in the Workstation Command Lines list box. If you are done defining command lines, continue with step 14.

13. You may now add another command line, or edit existing command lines. Click New to add an additional command line, or select a command line in the Workstation Command Lines list box and click Properties. Return to step 7 and continue.

14. Choose Close to return to the Package Properties dialog box. Click OK to update the package's new Workstation properties.

Part
IX

Ch
44

Share on Server Packages

An alternative to distributing packages to be installed directly on client workstations is to install them on servers and share them for access over the network. SMS automates the process of compressing packages and distributing them to sites, decompressing the packages and placing them on distribution servers, sharing the resulting directories, and providing access to selected groups of users. This type of package can be used to define a job that will distribute any type of files, including data files, in addition to networked applications.

After networked applications have been distributed to file servers and shared, users with sufficient permissions can connect to these locations and execute the applications in the same manner they would use for applications installed using conventional methods. You can complement Share on Server packages by creating Program Groups using the SMS Administrator, which automatically causes the creation of Program Manager groups (or Start Menu groups for Windows 95 and Windows NT 4.0) on client workstations, with icons for the shared applications. The Program Group Control components of SMS, which run on client workstations, perform this task based on definitions you have made. See "Creating Program Groups for Shared Applications" later in this chapter.

Sharing applications on servers can simplify the task of upgrading to new versions, because the old application is installed only on file servers, not on dozens or hundreds of workstations. Using shared applications does imply that if the network is down, all users requiring the applications will be unable to do their work; however, with appropriate engineering and redundancy of key components, you can mitigate this risk.

To create a package for sharing applications on servers, follow these steps:

1. Start the SMS Administrator program.

2. Open the Packages window. Choose File, New from the menu. The Package Properties dialog box appears.

3. Enter a name for the package in the Name text box. If the package describes an application, it is usually a good idea to use the name of the application itself as the name of the package. Enter a brief description of the package in the Comment text box.

4. Click Sharing. The Setup Properties for Sharing dialog box appears (see Figure 44.3).

FIG. 44.3

The Setup Package for Sharing dialog box is used to enter properties that define how to set up a shared, server-based application.

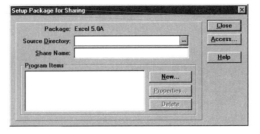

5. Enter the location of the package source directory in the Source Directory text box. See "Creating Package Source Directories" earlier in this chapter for more information on how to create a package source directory.

6. Enter a share name of eight characters or less in the Share Name text box. If you are using NetWare file servers, you must enter a volume name and subdirectory as the share name.

7. Click Access if you want to change the default permissions that will be granted to this network share. By default, Users and Guests are granted Read and Write access. The Access dialog box appears (see Figure 44.4).

FIG. 44.4

Use the Access dialog box to set access permissions for shared applications.

8. Click the check boxes reflecting the permissions you want to assign. Click OK to close the Access dialog box.

N O T E Users in a Windows NT file-server environment refers to the Domain Users global group for Windows NT domains that are part of the target site. Guests refers to the Guests global group. In NetWare environments, Users refers to the default group EVERYONE, and Guests refers to the default user account GUEST. ▪

9. You are now ready to define one or more program items to apply to this package. As you define program items, they are listed in the Program Items list box. Click New to define the first program item. The Program Item Properties dialog box appears (see Figure 44.5).

FIG. 44.5

Use the Program Item Properties dialog box to define the shared program's properties.

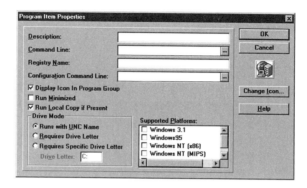

Part
IX
Ch
44

10. Enter a description for the program item in the Description text box. This will appear as the name under an icon in the Program Manager (or on the Start Menu) or when the application is minimized.

11. Enter the command line that will start the application in the Command Line text box. You should specify the file name of the executable or batch file that launches the application.

12. Enter a Registry Name in the text box provided. This name will be used in the Registry of the client computer and should be recognizable to aid potential troubleshooting. If you do not make an entry, the SMS package ID is used, a less than ideal alternative.

 You may want to import some of the PDFs for Microsoft applications provided with SMS to see the Registry names defined for those packages. This may provide additional guidance in determining an appropriate Registry name for your package. See "Using Package Definition Files (PDFs)" later in this chapter for more information.

13. If an application requires a setup or installation routine to be run the first time a client uses this network application, enter the command line used to launch that routine in the Configuration Command Line text box.

14. You will usually want to select the Display Icon in Program Group check box. An exception is the shared Microsoft mini-applications that come with Microsoft Office known as the MSAPPS, or a similar utility package that is always called from another application.

15. Select the Run Minimized check box if you want the application to be minimized immediately after it starts.

16. Select the Run Local Copy if Present check box to cause the Program Group Control function on the client workstation to scan the directories in the local path for a copy of this application before running the networked copy.

17. Select the option button to reflect the type of drive connection required for this application. Some applications don't work well with UNC names, especially older applications. This choice also may be affected by corporate policy. For example, an organization may decide to always use certain letters for particular applications or users' home directories.

18. Click the check boxes to indicate the operating systems that will support this application.

19. If you want, click the Change Icon button to select a different icon to display for this application. The Change Icon dialog box appears (see Figure 44.6). Select the file containing the icon you want to use. Click OK to return to the Program Item Properties dialog box.

FIG. 44.6

The Change Icon dialog box allows you to select an icon that will be used to launch this application from client workstations.

20. Choose OK to return to the Setup Package for Sharing dialog box. The new program item now appears in the Program Items list box. If you are done defining program items, continue with step 22.

21. You may now add another program item or edit existing program items. Click New to add an additional program item, or select a program item in the Program Items list box and click Properties. Return to step 10 and continue.

22. Choose Close to return to the Package Properties dialog box. Click OK to update the package's new Sharing properties.

Now you know how to define packages. Until you create a job to distribute the package, however, it will not be useful. In the next section, you learn how to complete the process by defining jobs to activate your packages.

Creating Jobs for Software Distribution and Installation

After you have defined a package, you are ready to create a job to distribute your package and put it to work. SMS includes several different types of jobs. Some of the jobs in an SMS system are created by SMS services. These are called *system jobs* and require no action on your part. You can create jobs of three types:

■ **Run Command on Workstation.** These jobs compress the contents of the package source directory, send the compressed package to target sites, decompress the package, place it on specified servers, and make the package available to specified clients. The client workstations that are part of the job target see the package appear in the Package Command Manager at the scheduled time.

- **Share Package on Server.** These jobs also compress the package, send it to target sites, decompress the package, and place it on specified servers. The directories are then shared and made available to the specified users. You also can define a Program Group to offer the shared packages to specified users with the Program Group Control utility on client workstations.

- **Remove Package from Server.** These jobs remove both the compressed packages from receiving site servers and the uncompressed packages from shared directories on distribution servers. It does not remove the original package source directory that you created before defining the package.

Part

IX

Ch

44

The first two types of jobs are the mechanism for distributing and installing software. These jobs consist of a package, a target, a schedule, and additional properties specifying actions for SMS to complete. The target for a job can be one or more sites. It also can be the list of machines that are the results of running a query. You can even create a machine group containing arbitrary computers to use as a job target. If you want to use a query or machine group as a job target, it should be created before you define the job.

Run Command on Workstation Jobs

You can use Run Command on Workstation jobs to start executable files or batch files. They can be used to start an application's setup program, or run a command to perform a task such as a virus checker. These jobs are presented to client workstations using the Package Command Manager client utility program. They can be mandatory jobs that must be run, optional jobs that can be run at the user's preference, or jobs that are optional until a certain date at which time they become mandatory.

To create a Run Command on Workstation job, follow these steps:

1. Create a package source directory and define a package with Workstation properties. See "Defining Packages for Software Distribution" earlier in the chapter to review how to do this.

 T I P Be sure that the SMS service account has permission to access the package source directory.

2. Start the SMS Administrator program.

3. Open the Jobs window. Choose File, New from the menu. The Job Properties dialog box appears, as shown in Figure 44.7.

4. Enter descriptive information about the job in the Comment text box. This information is visible only to SMS administrators—it is never exposed in a client utility on a user's desktop. The text used in the Package Command Manager comes from the Package Properties dialog box. You can therefore use this comment to store notes about the job without concern for making it understandable to users.

5. Select Run Command on Workstation from the Job Type drop-down list.

6. Click Details. The Job Details dialog box appears (see Figure 44.8).

FIG. 44.7

The Job Properties dialog box lets you select the type of job, its schedule, and other properties that affect its use.

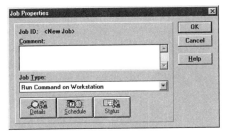

FIG. 44.8

This figure depicts the Job Details dialog box for a Run Command on Workstation job.

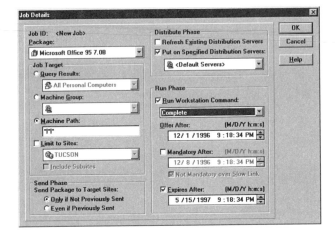

7. Select the package you want to use in the Package drop-down list.

N O T E Only packages with workstation properties defined are displayed in the Package drop-down list. ▪

8. In the Job Target box, you have three option buttons and a check box to specify the clients that should receive this package. Select Query Results if you want to use the list of machines that result from a query. Choose the query in the drop-down list. Select Machine Group if you want to use a predefined group of computers as the job target. Choose the machine group in the appropriate drop-down list. Select Machine Path to specify a path of the form *site:domain:computername*. You can use the * character as a wild card. For example TUC:*:* specifies all computers in all domains at the site with a site code of TUC. TUC:INTERNAL:* specifies all computers in the INTERNAL domain at site TUC.

9. You also can use the Limit to Sites check box and the corresponding drop-down list to select a specific site. Click the Include Subsites box to include subsites of the selected site. You can combine the check boxes with the option boxes in the Job Target box. For example, you can specify all computers that are in a Query result set and are members of a specific site.

TIP If you specify a machine path using a site code (for example, TUC:*:*), the Limit to Sites and Include Subsites check boxes will not have any effect. To use the check boxes, specify a machine path of *:*:*.

10. In the Send Phase box, select the option button to indicate whether the job should be re-sent to sites that have already received it. If you have made changes to a previously sent package, select Even If Previously Sent to overwrite the old copy of the compressed package on the site's default package server with a new one.

11. In the Distribute Phase box, click the Put on Specified Distribution Servers check box and select Default Servers in the drop-down list. Use the Refresh Existing Distribution Servers check box if you make a change to a package and need to update the decom-pressed version of the package on file servers.

12. Finally, make selections in the Run Phase box. If you defined multiple command lines for the package being used, select the command you want to use for this job in the Run Workstation Command drop-down list. If you clear the Run Workstation Command check box, SMS will distribute the package to sites but will not offer a command to client workstations in the Package Command Manager.

13. The next three drop-down list boxes determine when the package will appear on client workstations in the Package Command Manager. If you want to postpone the first date the package will be offered, select the date in the Offer After drop-down list. If the job should be mandatory, either when the package is initially offered or after an initial period of optional execution, click the Mandatory After check box and select a date in the associated drop-down list. If the package is large, it is a good idea to click the Not Mandatory over Slow Link check box. If the job should expire after a certain date, click the Expires After check box and select a date in the associated drop-down list.

14. Click OK to return to the Job Properties dialog box. Click OK to close the Job Properties box. The job will be added to the SMS database, given a unique job ID, and made available for execution when the schedule indicates. You can open this job at a later time and click the Status button to check on its progress. See "Monitoring the Status of Jobs" later in this chapter for more information.

Share Package on Server Jobs

There are a few differences in the Job Details dialog box for this type of job, but Share Package on Server jobs have many similar characteristics to the Run Command on Workstation jobs that you just learned about. They are somewhat easier to define because there is no Run Phase box to indicate when the package should be offered to clients (because the job is just placed on servers). Remember that you can use this type of job to distribute a package of data files, or any other type of files for that matter. If the job you are defining is a networked application, recall that you may want to define a Program Group to automatically build a Program Manager group with icons or Start Menu items for the application on the Windows desktops of selected groups of users. See "Creating Program Groups for Shared Applications" later in the chapter for more information.

To create a Share Package on Server job, follow these steps:

1. Create a package source directory and define a package with Workstation properties. See "Defining Packages for Software Distribution and Installation" earlier in this chapter for more information.

 T I P   Be sure that the SMS service account has permission to access the package source directory.

2. Start the SMS Administrator program.

3. Open the Jobs window. Choose File, New from the menu. The Job Properties dialog box appears (see Figure 44.9).

FIG. 44.9

This figure depicts the Job Properties dialog box being used to define a Share Package on Server job.

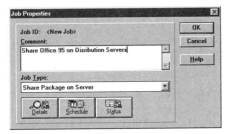

4. Enter descriptive information about the job in the Comment text box. This information is visible only to SMS administrators—it is never exposed in a client utility on a user's desktop. The text used in the Package Command Manager comes from the Package Properties dialog box. You can therefore use this comment to store notes about the job without concern for making it understandable to users.

5. Select Share Package on Server from the Job Type drop-down list.

6. Click Details. The Job Details dialog box appears (see Figure 44.10).

FIG. 44.10

This figure depicts a Job Details dialog box for a Share Package on Server job.

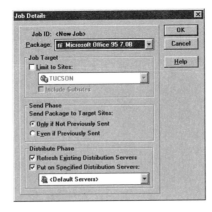

7. Select the package you want to use in the <u>P</u>ackage drop-down list.

N O T E   Only packages with sharing properties defined are displayed in the <u>P</u>ackage drop-down list. ■

8. In the Job Target box, you can use the <u>L</u>imit to Sites check box and the corresponding drop-down list to select a specific site. Click the <u>I</u>nclude Subsites box to include subsites of the selected site.

9. In the Send Phase box, select the option button to indicate whether the job should be re-sent to sites that have already received it. If you have made changes to a previously sent package, select E<u>v</u>en If Previously Sent to overwrite the old copy of the compressed package on the site's default package server with a new one.

10. In the Distribute Phase box, click the Put on Spe<u>c</u>ified Distribution Servers check box and select Default Servers in the drop-down list. Use the Refresh E<u>x</u>isting Distribution Servers check box if you make a change to a package and need to update the decom-pressed version of the package on file servers.

11. Click OK to return to the Job Properties dialog box. Click OK to close the Job Properties box. The job will be added to the SMS database, given a unique job ID, and made available for execution when the schedule indicates. You can open this job at a later time and click the St<u>a</u>tus button to check on its progress. See "Monitoring the Status of Jobs" later in this chapter for more information.

Creating Program Groups for Shared Applications

The Program Group Control utility, which runs on all versions of Windows clients, provides some powerful capabilities. This is another tool that can help the SMS administrator effectively manage the enterprise network. Most of the capabilities it provides work in either a Windows NT Server or NetWare environment. One of the features, however, is only available in environments running Windows NT Server on the network's file servers.

If you are using Windows NT file servers, SMS will leverage the capability of Windows NT to limit the number of users who can connect to a shared resource at one time. SMS includes two utility programs, APPCTL and APPSTART, that connect to one of a group of servers offering a particular shared application and start the application. When the application terminates, the network connection is released. The APPCTL and APPSTART utilities are part of the Program Group Control capability on client workstations. By combining this with the capability to limit connections to a share, you can achieve a limited software-metering function.

In addition, the Program Group Control capability allows you to create Program Manager groups or Start Menu items that will "follow" users if they move from one computer to another. This can be especially useful for support personnel who visit different computers on the net-work and may require a suite of troubleshooting utility programs. It also is useful in industrial environments where a population of users shares a group of machines but doesn't have exclu-sive use of a particular workstation.

Beginning with SMS 1.2, the Program Group Control capability is available to users of all versions of Windows. Shared applications also are accessible by browsing for them in the Network Neighborhood, or by connecting a drive letter to the share; however, it's preferable to make use of the Program Group Control facility.

Program Group Control is dynamic. At regular intervals specified by the client configuration, Program Group Control checks a database to find the program groups that have been defined for a particular user and build program groups in Program Manager (or submenus on the Start Menu). This happens when you initially log on to the network and may be updated throughout the day if you want. The update interval can be set on individual client workstations by an administrator or directly by the user if the default value is unacceptable. The Help Desk features of SMS can be used to set this option for users from a central administrative console if desired. See the section "Remote Control" later in this chapter for more information.

To define program groups for a package, follow these steps:

1. Start the SMS Administrator program.

2. Open the Program Groups window. Choose File, New from the menu. The Program Group Properties dialog box appears (see Figure 44.11).

FIG. 44.11

The Program Group Properties dialog box is used to define SMS Program Groups that provide instructions for client components to dynamically build program groups in the Program Manager on client workstations.

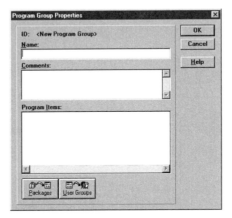

3. Enter a name for the program group in the Name text box. This name appears at the client workstation as the name of the program group in Program Manager on the client's Windows desktop.

4. Enter additional descriptive text to describe the program group in the Comment text box. This text does not appear anywhere on the client's desktop and can therefore be used for administrative notes.

5. Click Packages. The Program Group Packages dialog box appears (see Figure 44.12).

FIG. 44.12

The Program Group
Packages dialog box
enables you to define
the packages to be
included in this SMS
Program Group.

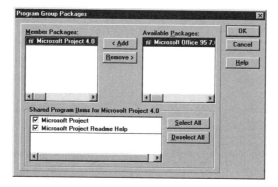

6. Select the package you want to add to this program group from the list of available packages in the list box. Click Add to add the package to the list of packages that are members of this group. The package is added to the Member Packages list.

7. Select the package in the Member Packages list. Any program items that have been shared for this package appear in the Shared Program Items For package list box. You typically want to make sure that all check boxes are selected, but if you want to exclude a shared program item, clear its check box.

8. Repeat steps 6 and 7 multiple times to build a program group that has icons for several different packages. When you have added all the packages to the program group, click OK to return to the Program Group Properties dialog box.

9. Click User Groups to define the groups of users that will be offered this program group. The User Groups dialog box appears (see Figure 44.13).

FIG. 44.13

The User Groups dialog
box allows you to define
the groups of users that
will receive this pro-
gram group (provided
that they are using the
Program Group Control
component on their
workstation).

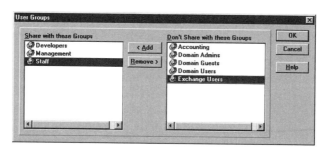

10. All Windows NT global groups, LAN Manager groups, and NetWare server user groups appear in the Don't Share with These Groups list box. This box lists all groups for the current site and all its subsites. Select a user group that should be offered this program group and click Add. The group's name moves to the Share with These Groups list box. Repeat until all the groups who should see this program group on their desktops have been added. Click OK to return to the Program Group Properties dialog box.

11. Click OK to close the Program Group Properties dialog box. The site database is updated, and the program group database is distributed to the appropriate sites. At that time, users who belong to the designated groups and are running Program Group Control on their Windows desktops will have a program group or a Start Menu submenu created dynamically on their desktop.

TROUBLESHOOTING

I am attempting to run an application from an SMS program group and it fails to execute. The program groups you define and assign to user groups are created and displayed regardless of whether the corresponding package has been distributed with a Share on Server job. Check to make sure that the Share on Server job has finished. You may want to make sure that such a job has been completed *before* creating the corresponding program group. See "Monitoring the Status of Jobs" later in this chapter for more information.

Remove Package from Server Jobs

To define a Remove Package from Server job, follow these steps:

1. Start the SMS Administrator program.

2. Open the Jobs window. Choose File, New from the menu. The Job Properties dialog box appears (see Figure 44.14).

FIG. 44.14

The Job Properties dialog box is depicted during the definition of a Remove Package from Server job.

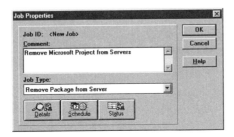

3. Enter descriptive information about the job in the Comment text box. This information is only visible to SMS administrators—it is never exposed in a client utility on a user's desktop. The text used in the Package Command Manager comes from the Package Properties dialog box. You can therefore use this comment to store notes about the job without concern for making it understandable to users.

4. Select Remove Package from Server in the Job Type drop-down list.

5. Click Details. The Job Details dialog box appears (see Figure 44.15).

6. Select the package you want to remove in the Package drop-down list.

FIG. 44.15

This figure shows the Job Details dialog box for a Remove Package from Server job.

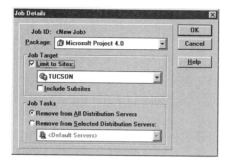

N O T E All packages defined in the site database that you logged onto with SMS Administrator are displayed in the Package drop-down list.

7. In the Job Target box, you can use the Limit to Sites check box and the corresponding drop-down list to select a specific site for package removal. If you want to include all sites, select the central site. Click the Include Subsites box if you also want to include the subsites of the selected site.

8. In the Job Tasks box, select the option button that corresponds to your wishes. You may remove the package from all distribution servers, or only selected servers. If you remove the (uncompressed) package from all distribution servers, the (compressed) package also is removed from the site server at each target site. If you remove the package from only selected servers, the compressed package is left intact at site servers for potential redistribution later.

9. Click OK to return to the Job Properties dialog box. Click OK to close the Job Properties dialog box. The job is added to the SMS database, given a unique job ID, and made available for execution when the schedule indicates. You can open this job at a later time and click the Status button to check on its progress. See the section "Monitoring the Status of Jobs" later in this chapter for more information.

Canceling and Deleting Jobs

The process that SMS follows to complete a job involves multiple steps that occur over a period of time. A particular job may impact many computers at a number of sites. Therefore, exercise care when removing jobs to be sure that you delete the package components from all desired locations.

The simplest case is a pending job or a completed job. You can delete a pending job, and it is removed before the distribution process ever occurs. A completed job can be deleted, but, of course, the components of the job that have already been installed at servers and clients are not removed. You can use a Remove Package from Server job to delete shared packages from site servers and distribution servers. You can use a Run Command on Workstation job to uninstall applications from client workstations for those applications that have an uninstall command.

Active jobs should be canceled before being deleted. This causes a Cancel system job to be initiated that removes the job's instructions from all points where the job's instructions have been distributed. It does not remove components that have already been installed on servers or clients, however. Again, you must use Remove Package from Server jobs and Run Command on Workstation jobs to remove installed components from servers and clients. The steps for checking the status of active jobs are described in the "Monitoring the Status of Jobs" section later in this chapter.

To cancel an active job, follow these steps:

1. Start the SMS Administrator program.
2. Open the Jobs window. Select the job you want to cancel.
3. Choose Edit, Cancel Job from the menu.
4. Click Yes when prompted to confirm that you want to cancel the job.

To delete a job, follow these steps:

1. Start the SMS Administrator program.
2. Open the Jobs window. Select the job you want to delete.
3. Choose Edit, Delete.
4. Click Yes when prompted to confirm that you want to delete the job.

You have now learned how to define packages that can be used to install software on workstations or to set up a shared application on one or more servers. You also learned how to create a job that can "activate" the package and implement it on computers you designate. And you learned how to remove packages and to cancel and delete jobs.

Using Package Definition Files (PDFs)

In addition to operating systems, Microsoft is the developer of some popular applications. Products like Microsoft Office, Word, and Excel are among the best-selling applications available. They also include sophisticated setup programs that offer a variety of installation types, from minimal to complete. These setup programs can generally be customized by modifying a file that controls setup, which usually has an STF extension. You could attempt to create packages for these applications on your own, but SMS includes Package Definition Files (PDFs) to make the job of automatically distributing and installing these applications easier.

Microsoft also has started including PDFs for new applications on the CD-ROM for the application itself. For example, PDFs have been included on the Office 95 and Office 97 CDs (both Professional and Standard Editions) and Word for Windows 95.

Table 44.1 lists many of the applications for which PDFs are available and their associated PDFs.

Table 44.1 Applications with PDFs

Application	PDF
Access V2.0A	`ACS200.PDF`
Excel V5.0A	`EXC50A.PDF`
Office V4.2A (Standard)	`OFF42A.PDF`
Office V4.3A (Professional)	`OFP43_.PDF`
Office 95 V7.0 (Standard)	`OFS95_.PDF`
Office 95 V7.0 (Professional)	`OFP95_.PDF`
Office 95 V7.0A (Standard)	`OFS95A.PDF`
Office 95 V7.0A (Professional)	`OFP95A.PDF`
Office 95 V7.0B (Standard)	`OFS95B.PDF`
Office 95 V7.0B (Professional)	`OFP95B.PDF`
Office 97 V8.0 (Standard)	`OFF97STD.PDF`
Office 97 V8.0 (Professional)	`OFF97PRO.PDF`
Office 97 Mini-applications	`MSAPPS97.PDF`
Office 95 Mini-applications	`MSAPPS32.PDF`
PowerPoint V4.0A	`PPT40A.PDF`
Project V4.0A	`PRJ40_.PDF`
Word for Windows V6.0A	`WWD60A.PDF`
Word for Windows 95	`WRD95.PDF`
Works V3.0	`WRK30A.PDF`

T I P It is a good idea to check the Microsoft Web server (**http://www.microsoft.com**), CompuServe, or the Microsoft Network at regular intervals to see if there are new PDFs, or other updated information or files. For example, a Knowledge Base article from November 1, 1995 (ID Q135084) describes how to correct problems with the Office 95 Standard Edition and Word for Windows 95 PDFs.

Much of the process for creating packages using PDFs is the same process you would follow to create a package for other applications without a PDF. You must still create a package source directory. You can create a directory that includes the files for both Run Command on Workstation and Share Package on Server packages. To create the package source directory for Microsoft Office or one of the individual Office applications (for example, Excel), follow these steps:

1. Create a directory for the application on a server. For example, you might create a directory named EXCEL for Microsoft Excel. Share it with the same name. This becomes the package source directory for the application.

N O T E   Instructions regarding MSAPPS, the shared mini-applications for Office, such as those in steps 2 and 4 should be followed only if you are installing a Microsoft application that uses the mini-applications. This includes Word, Excel, and PowerPoint. The mini-applications are a set of utilities that augment the Office products but cannot run on their own. Word Art and the Equation Editor are examples of mini-applications. These steps are not necessary with applications in general.

2. On the same server, create a directory named MSAPPS for the Microsoft mini-applications shared by all Office applications, and share it with the name MSAPPS. This will be the package source directory for the shared mini-applications.

3. Go to a client workstation, log on to the network with an Administrative account, and connect to the new directories you just created.

4. Perform an administrative install of the application. Specify the network-connected directories as the destination directories for the application and MSAPPS, respectively.

5. After installing the application onto the server, you must copy a special directory, called the SMSPROXY directory, from the SMS\PRIMSITE.SRV\IMPORT.SRC directory on the site server into the package source directory. There is an SMSPROXY directory for each application that has a PDF.

You are now ready to create the package itself. First, you learn how to create packages for both the application and MSAPPS that include Workstation and Sharing properties. Then you create a job to distribute these packages for sharing on network file servers. Finally, to complete the process, you create a Program Group and make it available to the Domain Users group.

To define a package for Microsoft Excel version 5.0a with properties for both workstations and sharing using a PDF, follow these steps:

1. Start the SMS Administrator program.

2. Open the Packages window. Choose File, New from the menu. The Package Properties dialog box appears.

3. Click the Import button. The File Browser dialog box appears.

4. Find and select the PDF for Microsoft Excel—EXC50A.PDF. Click OK to return to the Package Properties dialog box.

5. Click Workstations. The Setup Properties for Workstations dialog box appears.

6. Because you have imported a PDF, many of the entries in this dialog box are already completed. However, you still need to tell SMS where the package source directory you created for Excel (following the instructions at the beginning of this section) is located. Enter the location of the package source directory in the Source Directory text box.

7. Click Close to return to the Package Properties dialog box.

8. Click §haring. The Setup Properties for Sharing dialog box appears.

9. Enter the location of the package source directory for Excel in the Source Directory text box. This should be the same package source directory you used for workstation properties if you followed the directions at the beginning of this section.

10. Click the Access button if you want to change the default permissions that will be granted to this network share. By default, Users and Guests are granted Read and Write access. The Share Access dialog box appears.

11. Click the check boxes reflecting the permissions you want to assign. Click OK to close the Share Access dialog box.

12. Click Close to return to the Package Properties dialog box.

13. Click OK to close the Package Properties dialog box.

14. Choose File, New from the menu. The Package Properties dialog box appears.

15. Click the Import button. The File Browser dialog box appears.

16. Find and select the PDF for the Microsoft mini-applications—MSAPPS PDF. Click OK to return to the Package Properties dialog box.

17. Click Workstations. The Setup Properties for Workstations dialog box appears.

18. Enter the location of the package source directory for MSAPPS in the Source Directory text box.

19. Click Close to return to the Package Properties dialog box.

20. Click §haring. The Setup Properties for Sharing dialog box appears.

21. Enter the location of the package source directory for MSAPPS in the Source Directory text box.

22. Click the Access button if you want to change the default permissions that will be granted to this network share. These permissions should match those you just made for Microsoft Excel. Click OK to close the Share Access dialog box.

23. Click Close to return to the Package Properties dialog box.

24. Click OK to close the Package Properties dialog box.

You can now use this package to create two different kinds of jobs: Run Command on Workstation and Share Package on Server. The following example only shows you how to create a job to share this package on default distribution servers. (See the section "Run Command on Workstation Jobs" earlier in this chapter for information on creating the other type of job.) The example also demonstrates the capability of using drag-and-drop with a package icon to create a job. You drag a package from the Packages window and drop it on the site in which you want to share the package. This opens a job properties window with many of the boxes already properly completed for you. You have already learned how to create jobs using other methods in the section titled "Creating Jobs for Software Distribution and Installation."

To use drag-and-drop to create a Share on Server job with the Excel and MSAPPS packages you just defined, follow these steps:

1. Open both the Packages and Sites windows. If necessary, choose Window, Tile Horizontally from the menu to arrange the windows so that both are visible.

2. Click and hold down the left mouse button on the Excel package in the Packages window. Drag the package onto an appropriate target site in the Sites window and release the mouse button when the site is highlighted, which indicates that it has been selected as a target for the job. The Job Details dialog box appears.

3. As with package definition, many of the boxes are already properly completed. In the Send Phase box, select the Only If Not Previously Sent option button because this is the first time you are sending this package.

4. In the Distribute Phase box, click the Put on Specified Distribution Servers check box and select Default Servers in the drop-down list. Use the Refresh Existing Distribution Servers check box if you make a change to a package and need to update the decompressed version of the package on file servers.

5. Click OK to return to the Job Properties dialog box. Click OK to close the Job Properties box. The job is added to the SMS database, given a unique job ID, and made available for execution when the schedule indicates. You can open this job at a later time and click the Status button to check on its progress.

Follow the same steps to create a job to distribute MSAPPS substituting the MSAPPS package for the Excel package. Then you will be ready to create a program group for Excel and MSAPPS. To do so, follow these steps:

1. Open the Program Groups window. Choose File, New from the menu. The Program Group Properties dialog box appears.

2. Type **Microsoft Excel** in the Name text box. This name appears at the client workstation as the name of the program group in Program Manager (or on the Start Menu) on the client's Windows desktop.

3. If you want, enter additional descriptive text for the program group in the Comment text box.

4. Click the Packages button. The Program Group Packages dialog box appears.

5. Select Excel in the Available Packages box. Click Add to add the package to the list of packages that are members of this group. The packages are added to the Member Packages list box.

6. Select Excel in the Member Packages list box. Make sure that all check boxes are selected.

7. Repeat steps 5 and 6 with MSAPPS. Click OK to return to the Program Group Properties dialog box.

8. Click the User Groups button to define the groups of users that will be offered this program group. The User Groups dialog box appears.

9. Select a user group that should be offered this program group and click the Add button. The group's name moves to the Share with These Groups list box. Repeat until all the

groups that should see this program group on their desktops have been added. Click OK to return to the Program Group Properties dialog box.

10. Click OK to close the Program Group Properties dialog box. The site database is updated, and the program group database is distributed to the appropriate sites. At that time, users who belong to the designated groups and are running Program Group Control on their Windows desktops will have a program group created dynamically on their desktop for Microsoft Excel and the mini-applications.

Monitoring the Status of Jobs

On many occasions, it is appropriate to check the current status of a job. As noted earlier, it is especially important when you are preparing to cancel or delete a job. It also can be useful to help troubleshoot a job that is not yet visible at a particular site. To check the status of a job, follow this procedure:

1. Start the SMS Administrator program.

2. Open the Jobs window. A summary of all defined jobs and their current status appears (see Figure 44.16).

FIG. 44.16
The Jobs window displays a summary status of currently defined jobs.

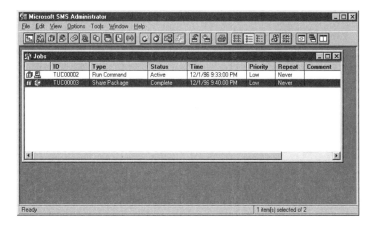

3. If you want to see detailed status information for a job, select the job and choose File, Properties from the menu, or simply double-click the job. The Job Properties dialog box appears.

4. Click the Status button. The Job Status dialog box appears (see Figure 44.17).

5. The job status is displayed for all sites selected as targets of the job. If you want to see the detailed status for a particular site, select the site and click the Details button. The Job Status Details dialog box appears (see Figure 44.18).

FIG. 44.17

The Job Status dialog box provides detailed status information about a job.

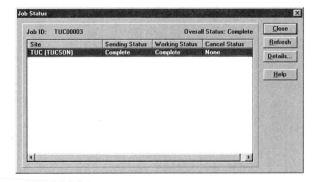

FIG. 44.18

The Job Status Details dialog box provides step-by-step detail on the processing of the job.

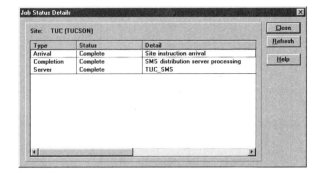

6. This dialog box provides detailed information about the status of the job at this particular site. Click Refresh to update the information displayed if you want to leave the dialog box open and watch the job progress through various stages.

7. Click Close to return to the Job Status dialog box. Click Close again to return to the Jobs window.

You should now have a good grasp of the fundamentals involved in defining packages and jobs, and how they are used to automate the distribution and installation of software. These are powerful capabilities that can help you manage your network and save hours of time for your administrative staff. However, if these tools are maliciously misused, they can cause serious repercussions for the operation of your network. In the next section, you learn how to safeguard these tools and how to set permissions so that only authorized personnel can use them.

Using the SMS Security Manager

The SMS Security Manager allows you to set different access rights for various users. After these rights have been set, users can use the SMS Administrator program to perform the actions for which they have been granted permissions. It is possible, therefore, to divide the different tasks that are required to administer an SMS system among several individuals and use the security features of SMS to prevent unauthorized use of the SMS Administrator program.

By default, users have no access rights to use the SMS Administrator program. SMS security is based on the security provided by SQL Server. By controlling who has access to the SMS database, and tables within that database, you can effectively control the capability to complete various SMS administrative functions. Microsoft SQL Server provides the capability to use different security models—standard, integrated, and mixed. The model you select for your SQL Server affects the SQL Server login ID you use to run the SQL Administrator program.

▶ **See** "Choosing a Security Model," **p. 1164**

Part

IX

Ch

44

Granting Permissions to Specific Users

For a user to be able to use SMS Administrator for administrative tasks, you must create a SQL Server login ID for the user and grant them rights to use the site database. A simple approach for users who use SQL Server only for SMS databases is to assign the site database as their default database. You can create this login ID and set the user's default database to be the site database, using the SQL Enterprise Administrator program. After you have created a login ID and username for the user, you can use the SMS Security Manager to grant specific rights to that person.

N O T E SQL Server uses the terminology *login* ID rather than logon ID. It has the same meaning. ▨

▶ **See** "Creating Login IDs and Usernames," **p. 1172**

To use the SMS Security Manager to grant rights to a specific user, follow this procedure:

1. Start the SMS Security Manager. The SMS Security Manager Login dialog box appears (see Figure 44.19).

FIG. 44.19

The SMS Security Manager Login dialog box verifies that you have sufficient privileges to assign permissions to other users.

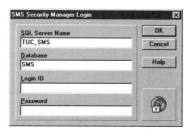

2. Enter the name of the SQL Server being used at this site, the name of the database (usually SMS), a login ID, and password. To administer security for this site, you need a login ID with system administrator (sa) or database owner (dbo) privileges on the site database.

 T I P If you are using Integrated security for your SQL Server, use the Windows NT user ID and leave the Login ID and Password boxes blank.

3. The drop-down list contains all users that have been added to the site database. If the user you want to set privileges for does not appear, add the user's account to the site database using the SQL Enterprise Manager.

4. Select the user whose access rights you want to set from the drop-down list box. If you have added the user since starting the SMS Security Manager, choose Security, Refresh from the menu to update the list box.

5. Select the component for which you want to set rights. From the Security menu, select the setting you want—No Access, View Access, or Full Access. The Proposed Rights in the table should change to reflect your new choices.

6. Choose Security, Save User to save the new settings you have made. The site database is updated.

   ▶ **See** "Understanding Object Ownership and Permissions," **p. 1232**

Understanding Permissions

You can set three different access levels or permissions for a particular user on a given object. The permissions, and a brief explanation of the permission's implications, are as follows:

■ **No Access.** This permission grants a user no capability to view or modify the object in question. For example, if the user was granted No Access for Help Desk, he or she could not activate the Help Desk features in the SMS Administrator. No Access to Jobs would prevent the user from even opening the Jobs window. If you set No Access to Packages, the user could not open the Packages window, or even access packages in job properties dialog boxes or when defining program groups.

■ **View Access.** The user can view the object but cannot create objects of this type or modify existing objects. View Access to Packages would allow the user to see and use packages when defining jobs (if the user had full access to jobs), but the user could not change the characteristics of the package in any way.

■ **Full Access.** The user can view, create, and modify objects of the type in question.

> **CAUTION**
>
> The various objects in the SMS database are highly interrelated. It is logical, therefore, that setting permissions on these objects affects the permissions required for other objects for your settings to operate properly. Refer to Table 6.1, "Security Object Access," in Chapter 6 of the *SMS Administrator's Guide* for detailed information on object access permissions.

Understanding Administrative Roles

To simplify the process of setting rights for SMS administrators, several predefined roles have been created as templates. Appropriate rights to various objects have already been set, with care taken to observe the various object interactions. It may be a good idea to use these templates to set rights for your users.

Templates have been created for the following types of SMS administrative roles:

- Asset Manager
- Job Manager
- Network Monitor
- Software Manager
- Tech Support

To use a template to assign rights to a user, follow these steps:

1. Start the SMS Security Manager. The SMS Security Manager Login dialog box appears.

2. Enter the name of the SQL Server being used at this site, the name of the database (usually SMS), a login ID, and password. To administer security for this site, you need a login ID with system administrator (sa) or database owner (dbo) privileges on the site database.

3. Select the user whose access rights you want to set from the drop-down list.

4. Choose Security, Use Template from the menu. The User Templates dialog box appears (see Figure 44.20).

FIG. 44.20

The SMS Security Manager User Templates dialog box provides the capability to easily choose a predefined role for a user. You can then modify this role if further customization is necessary.

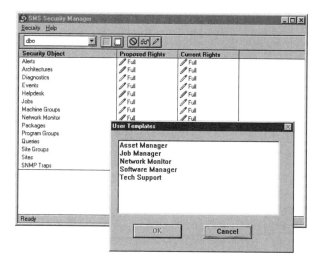

5. Choose the user template you want to copy for the selected user. The Proposed Rights in the table should change to reflect your new choices.

6. Choose Security, Save User to save the new settings you have made. The site database is updated.

With the techniques you have just learned, you can keep unauthorized users from maliciously, or accidentally, using the tools and capabilities of SMS. In the next section, you learn about the capability to use SMS in an environment that includes the Remote Access Service (RAS). Special configuration requirements for SMS are provided. The Remote Access Service is described in detail in Chapter 12, "Implementing Remote Access Service (RAS)."

Using Dial-Up Access to SMS

In a Windows NT Server environment offering RAS, you can connect to the network from a remote location using a modem and standard telephone lines. In general, you can access all network features although the speed of the line does have an impact on some capabilities. This section outlines the things you should be aware of when administering an SMS site that supports RAS access.

The primary thing that is affected by the slower line speeds of a dial-up connection is the delivery of Run Command on Workstation packages. A check box on the Job Details dialog box for Run Command on Workstation jobs allows you to indicate that even mandatory jobs should not be forced over a slow link (refer to Figure 44.8). Before clearing this check box, and thereby forcing mandatory commands over slow links, you should conduct tests to determine the time it takes with a particular package and modem speed. Even relatively modest packages may take an inordinate amount of time to download over a modem and effectively render the network unusable to remote users. Because these users are often traveling, or working after hours from home, the ramifications of this selection should be carefully considered.

The Help Desk features, especially remote control, depend on a reasonably fast link between the computer running the SMS Administrator and the client workstation being remotely controlled. With high-speed modems and the compression offered by RAS, it is possible to perform relatively simple tasks via remote control. A few settings may need to be changed to make this possible. In Chapter 10 in the *SMS Administrator's Guide*, "Remote Troubleshooting," there is a short section titled "Using the Microsoft Remote Access Service," which outlines the settings that may need fine-tuning to perform remote control operations over a dial-up line. Another section of the *SMS Administrator's Guide* you may find helpful is "Specifying Lana Numbers" in Chapter 10.

The Help Desk Remote Diagnostic Capabilities

SMS provides capabilities to aid in diagnosing problems that may occur on client workstations. These features allow you to connect to a client workstation from the SMS Administrator program and remotely control the client workstation. You see the same display that the user is viewing and are able to use your keyboard and mouse to control the remote computer. In addition, you can conduct an interactive "chat" in a double-paned window with users who are not able to use a telephone. You also can reboot the computer remotely.

For these utilities to work, the computers running the SMS Administrator and the client workstation must be running the same transport protocol. The computer to be controlled also must be inventoried in an SMS site. In addition, the Remote Control feature must be enabled at the user workstation. This is a security safeguard to prevent unauthorized viewing of users' workstations. If a user does not want anyone to be able to remotely control their computer, they can simply not enable this feature. If it is enabled by default, the user can run the Help Desk Options program as outlined in the next section and deselect the Allow Remote Control check box. These Remote Control features are available for clients running all versions of Windows. SMS 1.2 added support for Windows NT.

On the client workstation, be sure that the appropriate Remote Control utility is loaded. If you selected Remote Control as a default client component, the remote control utilities should already be loaded. These utilities are Terminate and Stay Resident (TSR) programs. Two TSRs can be used: USERTSR and USERIPX. USERTSR is used in conjunction with a transport that supports NetBIOS (NetBEUI or TCP/IP), and USERIPX is used with the IPX transport.

▶ **See** "Default Client Component Settings," **p. 1484**

Remote Control

To use the Remote Control feature, follow these steps:

1. At the client workstation, start the Help Desk Options utility program. It can be found in the SMS Client program group. The Help Desk Options dialog box appears (see Figure 44.21).

FIG. 44.21
Use the Help Desk Options dialog box to configure the options that should be active on a client workstation.

2. Click the check boxes desired to enable the features you want. For remote control, check Allow Remote Control. You also can select check boxes in the Local Options box to affect the behavior of remote control operations. If you want an audible signal to sound whenever someone is controlling your workstation, for example, click the Audible Signal When Viewed check box.

3. Click Save As Current.

4. At the SMS Administrator console, open the Sites window. Open the site and domain containing the computer you want to control by double-clicking their names in the left pane of the Sites window. Find the computer you want to control and double-click the computer's name in the right pane of the Sites window. The Personal Computer Properties window appears.

5. Scroll down through the list of properties in the left pane of the window until you find the Help Desk icon. Click the Help Desk icon in the left pane, and then click the Remote Control button in the right pane. You will see the message Attempting to locate *computername* in a message box, and possibly the message Trying Additional Protocols. When the computer is found, a viewer window displays (see Figure 44.22).

FIG. 44.22
This figure depicts a computer, which is running Windows 95, being remotely controlled from a Windows NT Server computer with the Help Desk features of the SMS Administrator. The striped border outlines the remote desktop.

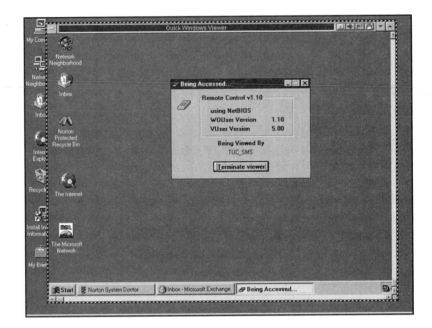

6. You can now use your keyboard or mouse to remotely control the remote computer. When you are finished, close the viewer window and the connection will be broken.

Remote Chat

To use the interactive Remote Chat feature, follow these steps:

1. If the client workstation doesn't allow Remote Chat by default, you must enable this feature. At the client workstation, start the Help Desk Options utility program. It can be found in the SMS Client program group. The Help Desk Options dialog box appears.

2. Click the Allow Chat check box.

3. Click Save As Current.

4. At the SMS Administrator console, open the Sites window. Open the site and domain containing the computer you want to control by double-clicking their names in the left pane of the Sites window. Find the computer you want to control and double-click the computer's name in the right pane of the Sites window. The Personal Computer Properties window appears.

5. Scroll down through the list of properties in the left pane of the window until you find the Help Desk icon. Click the Help Desk icon in the left pane, and then click the Remote Chat button in the right pane. You will see the message Attempting to locate computername in a message box, and possibly the message Trying Additional Protocols. When the computer is found, a double-paned chat window displays (see Figure 44.23).

FIG. 44.23
This figure depicts Remote Chat windows with an interactive discussion taking place.

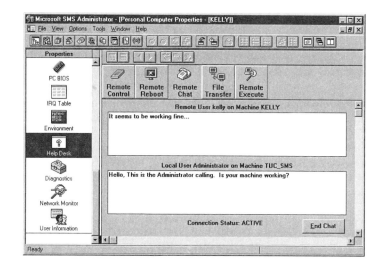

6. Whatever you type in your half of the Chat window displays in the Chat window at the remote computer and vice versa. When you are finished, close the Chat window and the connection will be broken.

Remote Reboot

To use the Remote Reboot feature, follow these steps:

1. If the client workstation doesn't allow remote reboot by default, you must enable this feature. At the client workstation, start the Help Desk Options utility program. It can be found in the SMS Client program group. The Help Desk Options dialog box appears.

2. Click the Allow Remote Reboot check box.

3. Click Save As Current.

4. At the SMS Administrator console, open the Sites window. Open the site and domain containing the computer you want to control by double-clicking their names in the left pane of the Sites window. Find the computer you want to control and double-click the computer's name in the right pane of the sites window. The Personal Computer Properties window appears.

5. Scroll down through the list of properties in the left pane of the window until you find the Help Desk icon. Click the Help Desk icon in the left pane, and then click the Remote

Reboot button in the right pane. You will see the message `Attempting to locate` `computername` in a message box, and possibly the message `Trying Additional` `Protocols`. When the computer is found, you will see the message `Rebooting Remote` `Computer`.

Using the Network Monitor

Every network administrator eventually encounters a situation in which something is not working and yet everything seems to be properly configured. When you have checked all the settings on your servers and clients and things still aren't working, you may want to "see" what is happening "on the wire." That is, you may want to capture and observe the contents of all the network traffic between two or more computers to analyze exactly what is taking place. The Network Monitor utility included with SMS allows you to perform this task. It is similar in many ways to other products that perform protocol analysis of LAN/WAN traffic, although the exact feature sets for these products vary.

In addition to troubleshooting functions, the Network Monitor allows you to *benchmark* your network by recording the values of certain indicators of LAN usage at regular intervals. When you install the Network Monitor, additional objects and counters become available in the Performance Monitor utility included with Windows NT Server and Windows NT Workstation. Although detailed coverage of this utility is beyond the scope of this book, the simple examples presented in this section introduce you to this powerful tool and familiarize you with its capabilities.

Protocol Analysis

To capture and view network traffic with the Network Monitor, follow these steps:

1. Start the Network Monitor. The Capture window appears in the Network Monitor window (see Figure 44.24).

2. Choose Capture, Start from the menu. After a brief pause, you see all the displays in the Capture window being updated to reflect the information that is being captured.

3. When you are ready to view the traffic that you have captured, choose Capture, Stop and View from the menu. The Capture window (with Summary pane maximized) appears (see Figure 44.25). If you choose the Zoom Pane button on the toolbar or double-click any frame in the Summary pane, you'll see the Detail and Hex panes which provide detailed information about the contents of each frame (see Figure 44.26)

FIG. 44.24

The Network Monitor display is shown in this figure with the Capture window open and active.

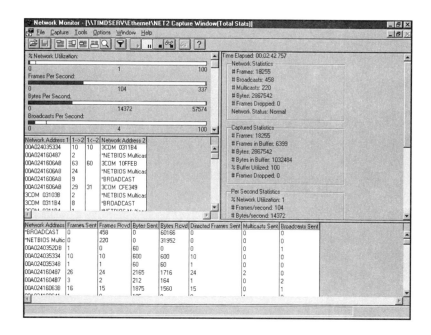

FIG. 44.25

This figure depicts the Network Monitor with the Capture window open.

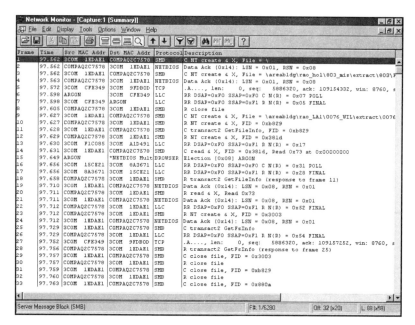

FIG. 44.26

The three panes of the Capture window provide different levels of detail about the makeup of a frame.

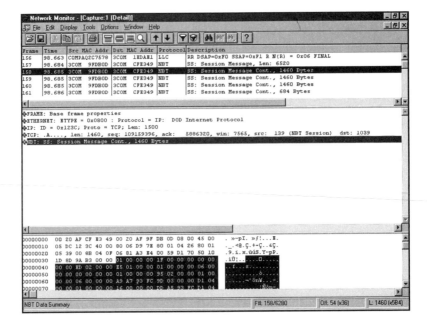

Display Filters On a busy network, Network Monitor will capture thousands of frames in just a few minutes. Sometimes this shotgun approach is needed to help you spot the problem, but most of the time you've got a pretty good idea of what you're looking for and you want to quickly focus on the suspected frames. Display filtering is one feature of Network Monitor that enables you to focus.

A Display Filter allows you to specify frame characteristics such as protocols and addresses that can be applied to a Capture window to eliminate all but the frames that have those characteristics. You build a Display Filter by combining expressions with logical operators. The logical operators (AND, OR, and NOT) appear as nodes and expressions appear as branches from the nodes.

To set up a Display Filter, follow these steps:

1. Choose Display, Filter (or press F8). The Display Filter dialog box appears (see Figure 44.27).

2. The initial Display Filter is interpreted as "frames containing any protocol AND frames from any machine to any machine," which effectively displays all captured frames. To make the filter more restrictive, select either of the default expressions and click the Operator button. A dialog box appears that allows you to edit the expression.

3. To add more expressions or nodes to the filter, first select the appropriate node or expression depending on where you want to insert the new line and click Expression, AND, OR, or NOT from the Add group.

FIG. 44.27

This is the starting point for creating a Display Filter.

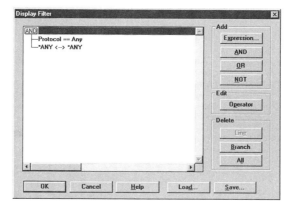

4. To delete any part or all of the filter, click one of the buttons in the Delete group.

5. Figure 44.28 shows a completed Display Filter. This filter will display "any frame that is a broadcast AND is NOT an IP frame OR an SMB frame."

FIG. 44.28

This is a completed Display Filter example.

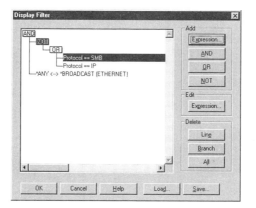

Capture Filters You've just seen how Display Filters can help you separate the wheat from the chaff in a large Capture window. But wouldn't it be better not to capture unnecessary frames in the first place? Network Monitor allocates a fixed size memory buffer for frame capture. If that buffer overflows, you may miss those important frames you really wanted. Capture filtering allows you to make the most of that precious buffer space.

A Capture Filter allows you to specify frame characteristics, such as SAP/ETYPE, addresses, and byte pattern matches, that are applied to frames as they are being captured. Any frames that don't satisfy the filter criteria are discarded. You build a Capture Filter by combining expressions with logical operators as you did with the Display Filter. The logical operators (AND, OR, and NOT) appear as nodes and expressions appear as branches from the nodes.

To set up a Capture Filter, follow these steps:

1. Choose Capture, Filter (or press F8). The Capture Filter dialog box appears (see Figure 44.29).

FIG. 44.29

This is the starting point for creating a Capture Filter.

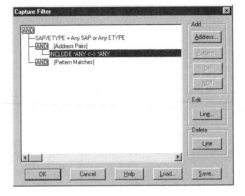

2. The initial Capture Filter is interpreted as "frames containing any protocol AND frames from any machine to any machine AND no pattern matching," which effectively captures all frames. To make the filter more restrictive, select either the SAP/ETYPE line or the INCLUDE *ANY <—> *ANY line and click the Line button. A dialog box appears that allows you to edit each expression. You get only one SAP/ETYPE line, and you can edit it but not remove it.

3. To add more expressions or nodes to the filter, first select the appropriate node or expression, depending on where you want to insert the new line, and then click Address, Pattern, OR, or NOT from the Add group. For Address Pairs, you can add more lines under the AND node, but no logical operators.

4. To delete any line in the filter, click the Line button in the Delete group.

5. Figure 44.30 shows a completed Capture Filter. This filter will capture "only frames that are broadcasts AND IP frames."

FIG. 44.30

This is a completed Capture Filter example.

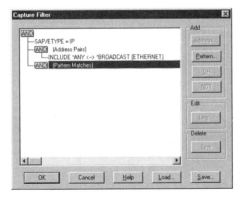

Additional Features

Network Monitor provides a number of easy-to-use features that are quite informative, and you don't have to be a rocket scientist to use them. This section covers the most interesting ones.

Identifying Network Monitor Users   Network Monitor can identify other machines on the network that are running Network Monitor. You can use this feature for tracking down unlicensed copies, but it also lets you know if an unauthorized person is using Network Monitor to snoop on your network. Select Tools, Identify Network Monitor Users, and you get a dialog box that identifies other machines running Network Monitor.

Part

IX

Ch

44

Finding Routers   One very useful feature is the capability to determine which physical addresses represent routers. Network Monitor attempts to do this by performing a capture (if one is not already there) and analyzing the frames containing a specific set of protocols. The protocols it uses exhibit recognizable patterns when traversing a router, and Network Monitor is designed to detect them. First, from the Capture window, choose your capture network (Capture, Networks) if you haven't already. Choose Tools, Find Routers, and you get an intermediate dialog box—Find Network Routers—that allows you to configure some of the parameters that Network Monitor uses to find routers. When you close this dialog box, Network Monitor performs a capture, if necessary, and displays any machines that it thinks are routers.

Resolving Addresses from Names   You can obtain address information about machines on your network by selecting Tools, Resolve Addresses from Name. This brings up a dialog box with a place for you to type in a machine name. Then you click the Run Query button, and Network Monitor attempts to resolve the address of that machine using any or all of the following: DNS, Local Address Database, NetBIOS, SAP, and SMS Remote Database.

Identifying the Heaviest Users of the Network   Wouldn't you like an easy way to determine who is hogging the network? Network Monitor provides a simple way to do this. First, you must perform a capture and then stop and view it. Now choose Tools, Find Top Users, and you get an intermediate dialog box—Find Top Users—that lets you specify certain parameters such as the number of users (the default is ten for both sending and receiving) to list in the output windows. When you click the OK button, Network Monitor analyzes the capture and displays the top ten heaviest senders and receivers.

Performance Monitor

To use the Network Monitor objects and counters in the Performance Monitor, follow these steps:

1. Start the Performance Monitor.

2. Choose Edit, Add to Chart. Select a computer that you want to monitor. This may be the computer you are currently using, or any other computer running Windows NT Server or Windows NT Workstation for which you have appropriate access rights.

3. In the Object drop-down list, select one of the Network Monitor objects. For example, you might select Network Segment.

4. Select one or more of the counters available. For example, you might select Broadcast Frames Received per Second and Total Bytes Received per Second. The following counters are available:

- % Broadcast Frames
- % Multicast Frames
- % Network Utilization
- Broadcast Frames received/second
- Multicast frames received/second
- Total bytes received/second
- Total frames received/second

N O T E   The % Network Utilization counter is particularly useful for charting the level of network activity on a particular network segment. The Broadcast frames received/second is good for charting broadcast activity on a network segment. You can use this if you suspect that excess broadcasts are overwhleming the available bandwidth on a segment.

5. Click Done to view the Chart.

Using Alerts to Monitor SMS

SMS administrators can use the Alerts feature of SMS to automatically detect certain conditions that may be of interest or indicate a potential problem. The conditions are detected using a query, and when those conditions are met, certain actions can be automatically *triggered*. When an alert's trigger condition is met, one or more of the following actions can be set to occur:

- Execute a command
- Send a message to a user or a specific computer
- Enter an event in the SMS event log

To create an alert, follow these steps:

1. Create a query upon whose results the alert will be triggered.

2. Open the Alerts window. Choose File, New from the menu. The Alert Properties dialog box appears (see Figure 44.31).

3. Enter a name for the alert in the Name text box. Enter a comment describing the alert in the Comment text box. Click Query. The Alert Query dialog box appears (see Figure 44.32).

4. Select the query you want to use in the Query drop-down list. If you want to use this alert to monitor only specific sites, select the Limit to Sites check box and choose the site from the drop-down list. If you want to include subsites, click the check box.

FIG. 44.31

The Alert Properties dialog box enables you to define an alert. You can use the buttons provided to select the query that will trigger the alert and the actions that should be taken.

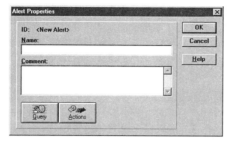

FIG. 44.32

The Alert Query dialog box provides the opportunity to select a query, set how often it runs, select the sites to which it is applied, and the "hit count" that will trigger the alert.

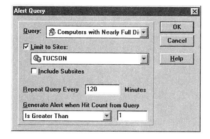

5. Enter an interval for the query to be run on. The default interval is to run the query every 120 minutes.

6. Make a selection from the Generate Alert When Hit Count from Query drop-down list. Enter a number of hits that corresponds to this selection. These two items define the triggering condition for the alert. Click OK to return to the Alert Properties dialog box.

7. Click Actions. The Alert Actions dialog box appears (see Figure 44.33).

FIG. 44.33

Use the Alert Actions dialog box to define the actions that should be taken when the alert is triggered.

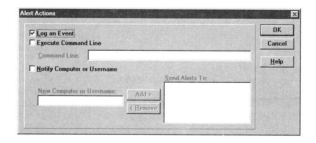

8. Fill out the dialog box to indicate the action that should be taken if an alert is triggered. Click OK to return to the Alert Properties dialog box.

9. Click OK to close the Alert Properties dialog box and activate the new alert.

Using SMS with SNMP Traps

Simple Network Management Protocol (SNMP) is an industry standard protocol for sending and receiving management information to and from network devices. SNMP also has a trap mechanism which enables a device to send an unsolicited packet to a network management computer based on the occurrence of events, such as a cold start, warm start, network link up, network link down, etc.

SMS supports SNMP traps in two complementary ways. First, you can create Trap Filters for each site that tell SMS to watch for and either ignore or record in its database the receipt of specific traps. Second, SMS provides an NT Event to SNMP Trap translator, which enables you to specify for individual Windows NT client machines that specific NT events will be translated and sent out as SNMP traps. To create or edit SNMP Trap Filters for a site, follow this procedure:

1. Start the SMS Administrator program.
2. Open the Sites window.
3. Highlight the primary site name in the left pane of the window by clicking it once.
4. Choose File, Properties. The Site Properties dialog box appears.
5. Click SNMP Traps. The SNMP Traps dialog box appears, as shown in Figure 44.34.

FIG. 44.34

To create or edit an
SNMP Trap Filter for
a site, use the SNMP
Traps dialog box.

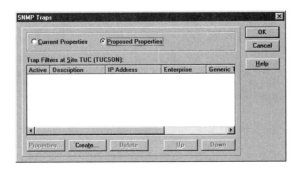

6. Select the Proposed Properties option button.
7. Click the Create button to create a new filter. The SNMP Trap Filter Properties dialog box appears (see Figure 44.35).
8. Enter a descriptive name for the filter in the Description box and then select the criteria to be applied to incoming traps. You can filter on a variety of attributes, including the IP address of the machine that sent the trap, the name of the Windows NT event source, and any or all of the seven traps defined in the SNMP standard. Finally, choose whether to Write to Database or Discard when an incoming trap satisfies the filter criteria.
9. Click OK. Then click Yes when prompted to confirm an update to the site.

FIG. 44.35
The SNMP Trap Filter Properties dialog box provides a variety of criteria you can specify for testing against incoming traps.

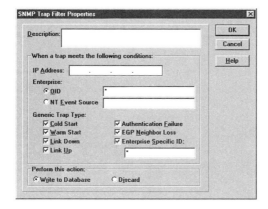

From Here...

In this chapter, you broadened your knowledge of SMS. You learned how to define packages and how to create jobs to activate those packages and begin the process of software distribution and installation. You learned how to use PDF files to simplify the process of using SMS with Microsoft applications. You also discovered how to control the use of SMS by using the SMS Security Manager. In addition, you explored the remote control capabilities provided by SMS and received an introduction to the Network Monitor, a protocol analysis utility included with SMS.

The following chapters cover related topics:

- For information on establishing policies for improved security, and specific guidelines for securing your site, servers, and client workstations, see Chapter 46, "Implementing Real-World Security."

- For information on building custom applications using BackOffice as a foundation, see Chapter 47, "Building BackOffice Applications."

- For information on developing a proactive approach to avoiding network problems and server outages, see Chapter 48, "Proactive Network Administration."

CHAPTER 45

SMS Advanced Topics

by Tim Darby

The preceding chapters have given you a basic understanding of what SMS is, what management activities it can provide and automate, what steps you must perform in order to make things happen, and the issues involved in managing a large network with SMS. As you've seen, SMS is a complex system with many interrelated components. SMS can do a lot for you, but you must have the knowledge and experience to apply the SMS capabilities to your management problems.

System administrators of today's PC LANs face many of the same issues. Rolling out large software installations, generating clear reports for management, and getting the information you really need without resorting to walking around the building with a pad of paper are just a few of these. This chapter explores some of the network management topics that are of interest to system administrators trying to cope with today's LANs and PCs, such as migrating a large user population over to Windows 95.

Learn how to perform software installations

Examine the steps involved in distributing two major software packages (Windows 95 and Office 95) to your users.

Customize the information that SMS collects

Discover how you can add your own specialized inventory data to the standard SMS inventory for each machine on your network.

Customize SMS Reports

Explore the capabilities of the SMS reporting and go beyond it with the bundled Crystal Reports application.

Learn about third-party application integration with SMS

Find out about the level of integration with HP OpenView, a popular network management platform.

Using SMS to Install Windows 95

The installation of Windows 95 involves a number of issues and decisions. You must look at the machines that will be upgraded and decided which ones are capable of receiving and running Windows 95. You need to decide which features of Windows 95 you want to install and whether you want the setup program to query the user or run unattended. Finally, you need to verify whether the installation really succeeded. Good planning is key to the ultimate success of the installation. In addition, a test installation should be performed on a small group of machines so you can discover what problems are likely to occur in your real installation. The following list summarizes the planning steps you should take for a Windows 95 rollout:

1. Study Windows 95 thoroughly.
2. Create a team and write a project plan.
3. Decide on client configurations.
4. Set up a lab to test the rollout.
5. Test the rollout in the lab.
6. Plan a pilot rollout.
7. Conduct the pilot rollout.
8. Finalize the rollout plan.
9. Conduct the full rollout.
10. Provide ongoing support.

 TIP The *SMS Deployment Guide* and the *Windows 95 Resource Kit* are invaluable resources that investigate in great detail the issues and problems involved in rolling out Windows 95 to a large group of users.

The following steps summarize a Windows 95 installation using SMS and will be discussed in more detail in subsequent sections:

1. Run a query to identify the machines that are capable of being upgraded to Windows 95 and build a machine group containing these machines.
2. Run ScanDisk on the machines in the machine group using an SMS job.
3. Create a source directory and share for the Windows 95 installation source files.
4. Create a package and job to install Windows 95.
5. Verify that Windows 95 installed successfully.

Running the Query

Using the SMS query capability, you can determine which client machines are suitable for upgrade to Windows 95. Typical criteria that you'd want to look at are disk space, existing OS, and processor type. Listing 45.1 is an example of a query to determine if a machine is capable of running Windows 95.

Listing 45.1   A Windows 95-Capable Machine Query

```
(
MICROSOFT|DISK|1.0:Free Storage (MByte) is greater than or equal to '80'
AND
MICROSOFT|DISK|1.0:Disk Index is 'C'
)

AND
MICROSOFT|X86_PC_MEMORY|1.0:Total Physical Memory (KByte) is
greater than or equal to '8000'
AND

(
MICROSOFT|PROCESSOR|1.0:Processor Name is like '486'
OR
MICROSOFT|PROCESSOR|1.0:Processor Name is like 'PENTIUM'
)

AND
MICROSOFT|OPERATING_SYSTEM|1.0:Operating System Name is
'MS Windows for Workgroups'
```

This query requests a list of all machines that have at least 80M free disk space, at least 8M RAM, Windows for Workgroups, and a 486 or better. You can build and execute this query in the SMS Administrator program.

▶ **See** "Using Queries to View Inventory Information," **p. 1512**

After the query has been executed, you can add the resulting list of machines to a machine group by selecting the machines you want in the query results window and selecting File, Add to Group in the SMS Administrator. The resulting dialog box is shown in Figure 45.1. You may also want to search for applications and TSRs that are incompatible with Windows 95 on the machines to be upgraded.

FIG. 45.1

The Add to Machine Group dialog box lets you build a target machine group for your Windows 95 installation.

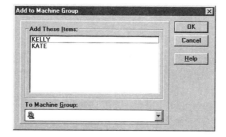

Running ScanDisk

It's a good idea to run ScanDisk before performing the Windows 95 installations in spite of the fact that it is included as part of the Windows 95 setup routine. This allows you to fix problem machines and avoid having ScanDisk present a dialog box that halts an automatic installation.

To do this, simply build a Run Command on Workstation package for the ScanDisk utility and create a job to run on it on each machine. You'll be using version 6.22 of ScanDisk for both Windows 3.x and DOS machines. You'll also want to set switches on the ScanDisk command line as appropriate. The four recommended switches are /AUTOFIX, which performs a check of the disk and repairs it; /NOSUMMARY, which prevents ScanDisk from stopping at summary screens; /ALL, which scans all drives; and /SURFACE, which performs a surface scan.

To build the package for ScanDisk, refer to the steps in the section "Run Command on Workstation Packages" in Chapter 44, along with the following specific instructions:

1. Choose a suitable name for the package (for example, ScanDisk for Win95 Installation).

2. For the source directory, supply the UNC path of the directory that contains the ScanDisk program.

3. For the command name, choose an appropriate name (for example, ScanDisk).

4. For the command line, enter **SCANDISK /ALL /NOSUMMARY /AUTOFIX / SURFACE**.

 T I P   The Microsoft SMS Deployment Guide includes a PDF file for ScanDisk.

The final step is to create a Run Command on Workstation job for your ScanDisk package.

▶ **See** "Run Command on Workstation Jobs," **p. 1525**

Once this job has been created, you can monitor its progress from the SMS Administrator using the Job Status Details dialog box. When the status column for the job changes to Complete, ScanDisk creates the file SCANDISK.LOG in the root directory of the C: drive on each machine. You can examine each machine manually to see the results, but a smarter approach is to make use of the power that SMS provides. You can simply add the file SCANDISK.LOG to the list of files that SMS collects during its normal inventory scan.

▶ **See** "Defining Packages for Inventory," **p. 1506**

Creating the Windows 95 Source Directory

Before you create the package, you must create a source directory and share on a network server and then create the Windows 95 installation source files there. There are a variety of options for creating the source installation files. The simplest option is to use the compressed .CAB files from the Windows 95 CD and the WIN95.INF file from your SMS site server's PRIMSITE.SRV\IMPORT.SRC\ENU directory. The WIN95.INF file is the file the Windows 95 Setup program uses to control the setup process. It is well commented and you can use any text editor to manually change this file to suit your particular installation. Windows 95 also comes with BATCH.EXE, a program that allows you to make a customized MSBATCH.INF file for Windows 95 Setup. To create the source installation files for Windows 95, perform the following steps:

1. Create a source directory and share on a network server for the Windows 95 installation source files.

2. Use BATCH.EXE to create a customized MSBATCH.INF file.

3. Open both MSBATCH.INF and a copy of the WIN95.INF file from your SMS directory. Copy and paste changes from MSBATCH.INF to WIN95.INF.

4. Copy the entire WIN95 directory from the Windows 95 Installation CD and your modified WIN95.INF file to the source directory created in step 1.

N O T E   INFINST and INFGEN are utilities, in addition to BATCH, that you can use to create INF files. NETSETUP is a utility that allows you to create a source directory of decompressed Windows 95 installation source files. These utilities are covered in more detail in the Windows 95 Resource Kit and in the SMS Deployment Guide.

The Windows 95 Package and Job

Part
IX

Ch
45

With the source directory in place, you can build the Windows 95 package. Actually, the work is mostly done for you, since SMS includes a PDF, WIN95.PDF, for Windows 95 installations. You need a Run Command on Workstation package and can create the package by simply importing the WIN95.PDF file in the Package Properties dialog box of SMS Administrator and providing the other package parameters.

▶ **See** "Run Command on Workstation Packages," **p. 1519**

To build the package for installing Windows 95, perform the following steps:

1. Start the SMS Administrator program.

2. Open the Packages window. Choose File, New from the menu. The Package Properties dialog box appears.

3. Click Import. A standard File Selection dialog box appears.

4. Open the file \PRIMSITE.SRV\IMPORT.SRC\ENU\WIN95.PDF on your site server to import the predefined Windows 95 installation package. Importing the PDF file fills in all required properties, except the package source directory.

5. Enter the location of the Windows 95 package source directory you created earlier in the Source Directory text box.

6. Choose Close to return to the Package Properties dialog box. Click OK to update the package's new Workstation properties.

When you examine the command lines in WIN95.PDF, note the programs DOS2W95.EXE, WIN295.EXE, and W95TOW95.EXE. These are helper programs for DOS, Windows 3.x, and Windows 95, respectively, and they are designed to fill in certain values that setup requires, such as username. For Windows 3.x and DOS clients, the helper programs also ensure that the SMS components are upgraded correctly.

N O T E   The Windows 95 Setup command lines in WIN95.PDF use the /IS switch to prevent ScanDisk from running. In other words, the assumption is that you've already run ScanDisk on the target machines before doing the Windows 95 upgrade.

Creating the job is straightforward. You need to build and issue a Run Command on Workstation job that specifies the appropriate command line (depending on the operating system) for each target machine group.

▶ **See** "Run Command on Workstation Jobs," **p. 1525**

To build the job for installing the Windows 95 package, perform the following steps:

1. Start the SMS Administrator program.

2. Open the Jobs window. Choose File, New from the menu. The Job Properties dialog box appears.

3. Enter descriptive information about the job in the Comment text box. This information is visible only to SMS administrators—it is never exposed in a client utility on a user's desktop.

4. Select Run Command on Workstation from the Job Type drop-down list box.

5. Click Details. The Job Details dialog box appears.

6. Select the Windows 95 installation package you just created in the Package drop-down list.

7. In the Job Target box, you have three option buttons and a check box to specify the clients that should receive this package. If you have performed the recommended Windows 95-capable query, select Query Results and choose the query in the drop-down list.

8. You also can select the Limit to Sites check box and the corresponding drop-down list box to select a specific site. Click the Include Subsites box to include subsites of the selected site.

   You can combine the check boxes with the option boxes in the Job Target box. For example, you can specify all computers that are in a Query result set and are members of a specific site.

9. In the Send Phase box, select the option button to indicate whether the job should be resent to sites that have already received it. If you have made changes to a previously sent package, select Even If Previously Sent to overwrite the old copy of the compressed package on the site's default package server with a new one.

10. In the Distribute Phase box, click the Put on Specified Distribution Servers check box and select Default Servers in the drop-down list. Use the Refresh Existing Distribution Servers check box if you make a change to a package and need to update the decompressed version of the package on file servers.

11. Finally, make selections in the Run Phase box. If you have a mix of client operating systems to upgrade, then you'll need to create a separate job for each operating system to be upgraded and select the appropriate command you want to use for each job in the Run Workstation Command drop-down list.

12. The next three drop-down list boxes determine when the package will appear on client workstations in the Package Command Manager.

- If you want to postpone the first date the package will be offered, select the date in the Offer After drop-down list.

- If the job should be mandatory, either when the package is initially offered or after an initial period of optional execution, click the Mandatory After check box and select a date in the associated drop-down list box. If the package is large, it is a good idea to click the Not Mandatory over Slow Link check box.

- If the job should expire after a certain date, click the Expires After check box and select a date in the associated drop-down list.

13. Click OK to return to the Job Properties dialog box. Click OK to close the Job Properties box. The job is added to the SMS database with a unique job ID, and is available for execution when the schedule indicates.

You can open this job at a later time and click the Status button to check on its progress. The status column should eventually change to Complete in the Job Status Details dialog box, indicating that the job has been successfully distributed and executed at each machine.

▶ **See** "Monitoring the Status of Jobs," **p. 1539**

Part
IX
Ch
45

Verifying the Installations

Make sure that the all the target machines have reported their inventory after the Windows 95 upgrade and then perform the "Computers by Operating System" query. There are a variety of reasons why the upgrade may fail, including changes the user made to the system after you ran the Windows 95-capable query or simply that the user manually aborted the installation. There is also the possibility that the machine contained hardware that is compatible with the Windows 95 Setup routine, but not with Windows 95 itself.

Using SMS to Install Microsoft Office 95

The installation of a major software suite like Office 95 requires careful planning. You must look at the machines that will be upgraded and decide which ones have the necessary resources to run Office 95. You must decide whether your users will run Office 95 as shared network applications or locally from their hard drives. You need to decide which features of Office 95 you want to install and if you want the setup program to query the user or run unattended. Good planning is key to the ultimate success of the installation. In addition, a test installation should be performed on a small group of machines so you can discover what problems are likely to occur in your real installation.

The following list summarizes the planning steps you should take for an Office 95 rollout:

1. Study Office 95 thoroughly.
2. Create a team and write project plan.
3. Decide on client configurations.
4. Set up a lab to test the rollout.
5. Test the rollout in the lab.

6. Plan a pilot rollout.

7. Conduct the pilot rollout.

8. Finalize the rollout plan.

9. Conduct the full rollout.

10. Provide ongoing support.

 TIP The *SMS Deployment Guide* and the *Office for Windows 95 Resource Kit* are invaluable resources that investigate in great detail the issues and problems involved in rolling out Office 95 to a large group of users.

The following steps summarize an Office 95 installation using SMS and will be discussed in more detail in subsequent sections:

1. Run a query to identify the machines that are capable of running Office 95 and build a machine group containing these machines.

2. Decide if Office 95 will run as a shared application or be installed on local hard drives.

3. Create a source directory and share for the Office 95 installation source files.

4. Create a package and job to install Office 95.

5. Verify that Office 95 installed successfully.

Running the Query

Using the SMS query capability, you can determine which client machines are suitable for installing Office 95, assuming a local installation. Typical criteria that you'd want to look at are disk and memory resources and, of course, machines that are running Windows 95. The following guidelines will help you to formulate this query:

■ **Memory.** 8M are required to run two Office 95 applications. Allow more than 8M for more than two applications running simultaneously. Wordmail or Access require at least 12M.

 TIP Although these memory requirements will allow you to run the applications as stated, you'll want to have a minimum of 16M RAM to run two or more Office 95 applications or Access 7.0.

■ **Disk Space.** Table 45.1 identifies disk space requirements for various installations of Office 95.

Table 45.1   Disk Space Requirements for Office 95

Installation Type	Office 95 Standard	Office 95 Professional
Compact	28M	40M
Typical	55M	87M

Installation Type	Office 95 Standard	Office 95 Professional
Custom	Up to 89M	Up to 126M

▶ **See** "Using Queries to View Inventory Information," **p. 1512**

Listing 45.2 is an example of a query to determine if a machine is capable of running Office 95.

Listing 45.2 An Office 95-Capable Machine Query

```
(
MICROSOFT¦DISK¦1.0:Free Storage (MByte) is greater than or equal to '87'
AND
MICROSOFT¦DISK¦1.0:Disk Index is 'C'
)

AND
MICROSOFT¦X86_PC_MEMORY¦1.0:Total Physical Memory (KByte) is
greater than or equal to '8000'
AND

(
MICROSOFT¦PROCESSOR¦1.0:Processor Name is like '486'
OR
MICROSOFT¦PROCESSOR¦1.0:Processor Name is like 'PENTIUM'
)

AND
MICROSOFT¦OPERATING_SYSTEM¦1.0:Operating System Name is
'MS Windows 95'
```

Part

IX

Ch

45

Of course, you can specify a variety of other things in your query, depending on what your users will be doing with Office 95. For example, if your users depend on the workgroup features of Office 95, you can specify Microsoft Windows-compatible networking as part of your query.

Shared Application versus Local Application

You can install Office 95 as a network shared application or as a local application on each machine's hard drive. There are tradeoffs associated with either choice. For example, you can save a lot of disk space on each user's machine by creating a shared application, but performance will be slower. The Office 95 Setup program allows you to choose which type of installation you want during the installation process. Since disk space has become inexpensive and plentiful, it's easier to decide in favor of local installation than it was a few years ago. Therefore, this example assumes that type of installation.

Creating the Office 95 Source Directory

Before you create the package, you must create source directories and shares on a network server and create the Office 95 installation source files there. Office 95 requires two installation directories: one for the Office 95 application source files and one for the Microsoft Shared Applications (ClipArt Gallery, MS Draw, Spell Checker, etc.). To create the source installation files for Office 95, perform the following steps:

1. On a network server, create a source directory for the Office 95 source files and share it with an appropriate name (OFFICE95, for example). On the same server (or a different server), create a source directory for the MS Shared Application files and share it with an appropriate name (MSAPPS95, for example).

2. From a PC running Windows 95 or Windows NT 4.0, map a drive letter to each of the shares you just created.

3. From the Office 95 installation media, run SETUP /a. Setup prompts you for the directory locations for the Office 95 files and the MS Shared Application files. Use the drive letters you mapped in step 2.

4. Setup asks you for the type of installation you want: Server (network shared application installation), Local (user's hard drive installation), or User's Choice. Choose Local to create an installation point that will install files to the user's local hard drive.

5. Customize the SETUP.STF file, if your installation requires it. Typically, you modify this file to add or remove components of Office 95 from the installation. This file contains default settings and other parameters that Office 95 Setup uses. You can customize this file by running the Network Installation Wizard from the Office for Windows 95 Resource Kit. This Wizard enables you to change the defaults that Setup uses during installation.

CAUTION

Here are some things to watch out for when performing the administrative installation:

- The source directories must be empty.
- The source directories must be locked to prevent network access by users.
- Check that you have enough space on the server (about 125M for Office 95 Standard and about 155M for Office 95 Professional).
- Disable virus-protection software that might interfere with the normal operation of Setup.
- You must run Setup on a computer running Windows 95 or Windows NT 3.51 or greater.

The Office 95 Package and Job

With the source directory in place, you can build the Office 95 package. SMS conveniently includes several PDFs for various versions of Office 95 and each one includes the installation types Typical, Custom, Compact, Complete, and Uninstall. The following PDFs are included in SMS 1.2:

- Office 95 Professional 7.0: OFP95_.PDF
- Office 95 Professional 7.0a: OFP95A.PDF

■ Office 95 Standard 7.0 and 7.0a: `OFS95_A.PDF`

■ Office 95 Standard and Professional 7.0b: `OF95B.PDF`

You need a Run Command on Workstation package. To create the package, you can simply import the appropriate PDF file in the Package Properties dialog box of SMS Administrator, provide the other package parameters, and you're done.

▶ **See** "Run Command on Workstation Packages," **p. 1519**

To build the package for installing Office 95, perform the following steps:

1. Start the SMS Administrator program.

2. Open the Packages window. Choose File, New from the menu and the Package Properties dialog box appears.

3. Click Import. A standard File Selection dialog box appears.

4. Open the appropriate PDF file (see the list at the start of this section) in the directory `\PRIMSITE.SRV\IMPORT.SRC\ENU\` on your site server to import the predefined Office 95 installation package. Importing the PDF file fills in all required properties, except the package source directory.

5. Enter the location of the Office 95 package source directory you created earlier in the Source Directory text box.

6. Click Close to return to the Package Properties dialog box. Click OK to update the package's new Workstation properties.

N O T E Each PDF file for Office 95 also contains inventory package properties. When you create the package as described here, you are also adding Office 95 to the list of software to be inventoried on each machine. This is useful as a check that the installation succeeded. ■

N O T E The Office 95 PDF files provided with SMS use the `/Q1` (quiet mode) switch on the command lines, which means that the install will not request any user input. ■

Creating the job is also straightforward. You need to build and issue a Run Command on Workstation that specifies the appropriate command line (depending on the type of installation you want) for each target machine group.

▶ **See** "Run Command on Workstation Jobs," **p. 1525**

To build the job for installing the Office 95 package, perform the following steps:

1. Start the SMS Administrator program.

2. Open the Jobs window. Choose File, New from the menu. The Job Properties dialog box appears.

3. Enter descriptive information about the job in the Comment text box. This information is visible only to SMS administrators—it is never exposed in a client utility on a user's desktop.

4. Select Run Command on Workstation from the Job Type drop-down list.

5. Click Details. The Job Details dialog box appears.

6. Select the Office 95 installation package you just created in the Package drop-down list.

7. In the Job Target box, you have three option buttons and a check box to specify the clients that should receive this package. If you have performed the recommended Office 95-capable query, select Query Results and choose the query in the drop-down list.

8. You also can select the Limit to Sites check box and the corresponding drop-down list to specify a specific site. Click the Include Subsites box to include subsites of the selected site.

   You can combine the check boxes with the option boxes in the Job Target box. For example, you can specify all computers that are in a Query result set and are members of a specific site.

9. In the Send Phase box, select the option button to indicate whether the job should be re-sent to sites that have already received it. If you have made changes to a previously sent package, select Even If Previously Sent to overwrite the old copy of the compressed package on the site's default package server with a new one.

10. In the Distribute Phase box, click the Put on Specified Distribution Servers check box and select Default Servers in the drop-down list. Select the Refresh Existing Distribution Servers check box if you make a change to a package and need to update the decompressed version of the package on file servers.

11. Finally, make selections in the Run Phase box. If you have a mix of client operating systems to upgrade, then you'll need to create a separate job for each operating system to be upgraded and select the appropriate command you want to use for each job in the Run Workstation Command drop-down list.

12. The next three drop-down list boxes determine when the package will appear on client workstations in the Package Command Manager.

   - If you want to postpone the first date the package will be offered, select the date in the Offer After drop-down list.

   - If the job should be mandatory, either when the package is initially offered or after an initial period of optional execution, click the Mandatory After check box and select a date in the associated drop-down list. If the package is large, it is a good idea to click the Not Mandatory over Slow Link check box.

   - If the job should expire after a certain date, click the Expires After check box and select a date in the associated drop-down list.

13. Click OK to return to the Job Properties dialog box. Click OK to close the Job Properties box. The job will be added to the SMS database, given a unique job ID, and made available for execution when the schedule indicates.

You can open this job at a later time and click the Status button to check on its progress. The status column should eventually change to Complete in the Job Status Details dialog box, indicating that the job has been successfully distributed and executed at each machine.

▶ **See** "Monitoring the Status of Jobs," **p. 1539**

Verifying the Installation

Make sure that all of the target machines have reported their inventory after the Office 95 upgrade, and then wait a sufficient length of time for all machines to have their software inventory taken by SMS. If you used one of the included PDFs for Office 95, then Office 95 was added to the list of packages to be inventoried and it will be found if the installation was successful.

Customizing the Information Collected by SMS

As you've already seen, SMS collects a great deal of hardware and software information about each machine on your network. In addition to that, SMS uses a predefined form to collect some personal data about each user, such as their name, phone number, location, and so on (see Figure 45.2). An MIF file is the mechanism that SMS uses for reporting all of the information it collects. An MIF file has a specific format that has been defined and standardized by the DMTF working group.

▶ **See** "Exploring Systems Management Server," **p. 1447**

Part

IX

Ch

45

FIG. 45.2

The standard MIF entry form included with SMS, UINFO.XNF, collects personal information about each user. The same MIF entry application shown here is used for any custom XNF files that you create.

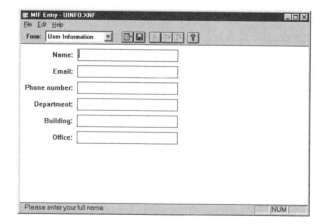

SMS not only supports the standard MIFs, it provides a tool that allows you to create your own MIFs and develop forms with text-entry fields that correspond to the data you're trying to collect. In this way, you can expand the inventory information that SMS collects from each machine to incorporate any type of data you require. Let's take a look at how you go about designing your own MIF form and the mechanics of getting SMS to present that custom form at each client computer.

First, you need to identify the information you want to collect. For this example, let's assume that the administrator wants to include equipment tags in the SMS database.

To create the MIF custom form, perform the following steps:

1. From the Start Menu, select Programs, Systems Management Server, SMS MIF Form Generator. This brings up the MIF Form Generator as shown in Figure 45.3.

FIG. 45.3

You can create a new MIF entry form using the MIF Form Generator.

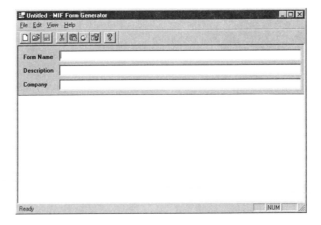

2. Fill in the Form Name, the Description, and the Company name.

3. You build the form by adding fields one at time. To add a field, select Edit, New Field. You'll be asked to select which type of field you want to add. Your choices are Number, Text, and List as shown in Figure 45.4. The first two are self-explanatory. The List type allows you to create a list of predefined choices for the user to select from.

FIG. 45.4

You must choose the data type for each field you add.

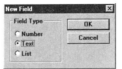

4. Select the Text type to open the Text Item dialog box shown in Figure 45.5.

FIG. 45.5

The Text Item dialog box lets you define the properties of your text-entry field.

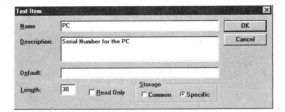

5. Define the following properties for the text-entry field:

- **Name.** The label that appears next to the field on the form
- **Description.** Appears at the bottom of the form window when that field is selected by the user
- **Default.** The value that initially appears in the field
- **Length.** Sets the maximum length of the field
- **Read Only.** Specifies that the field cannot be changed by the user

Choose OK to complete the field properties and return to the MIF Form Generator.

6. Select File, Save As to save the MIF form. By default the MIF form is saved to the X86.BIN, MIPS.BIN, or ALPHA.BIN subdirectory (depending on your architecture) with extension .XNF.

Now that you've created the custom MIF form, the next step is to distribute it to your client machines. You do this the same way you would distribute any other software with SMS. First, you build a package and then you create a Run Command on Workstation job to enable the form to be executed at each user's machine.

▶ **See** "Run Command on Workstation Packages," **p. 1519**
▶ **See** "Run Command on Workstation Jobs," **p. 1525**

To create the package for your MIF form, perform the following steps:

1. Open the SMS Administrator program and open the Packages window.

2. Select the menu commands to create a new package and fill in the blanks as shown in Figure 45.6 using the UNC path to the X86.BIN directory on the site server.

Part **IX** Ch **45**

FIG. 45.6

Use this dialog box to set the source directory that contains your custom MIF form.

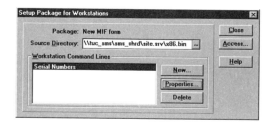

3. Figure 45.7 shows the details of the command Serial Numbers. The command invokes MIFWIN.EXE with the file name of the MIF form we created as the single command-line parameter.

N O T E MIFWIN is for Windows clients. Use MIFDOS for DOS clients and MIFMAC for Mac clients. ▨

FIG. 45.7

Specifying the command line for executing your custom MIF form.

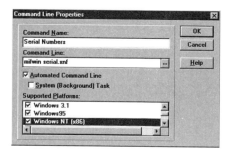

To create the Run Command on Workstation Job for the MIF form, perform the following steps:

1. Open the SMS Administrator program and open the Jobs window.

2. Select the menu commands to create a new job and select the package for the MIF form that we previously created along with any other settings you need as shown in Figure 45.8.

FIG. 45.8

Specifying details of the job for sending out your custom MIF form.

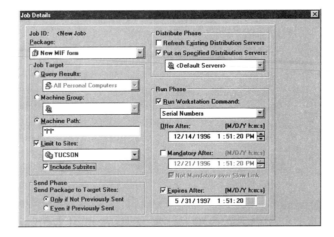

3. Check the status of this job periodically in the SMS Administrator to see when it has completed.

Now that you created the job, it will eventually appear in the Package Command Manager for each machine that you've specified as shown in Figure 45.9.

FIG. 45.9

The Package Command Manager at a user machine has received the new MIF form.

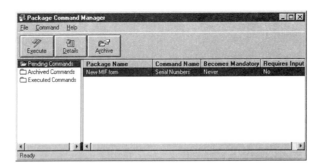

When the user clicks the Execute button to execute the command, the MIF Entry program launches using the MIF form that you created. The user (or perhaps an assistant administrator) can then fill in the fields as shown in Figure 45.10 and select File, Save followed by File, Exit to save the information and exit the program.

FIG. 45.10

Your custom MIF form executes from Package Command Manager.

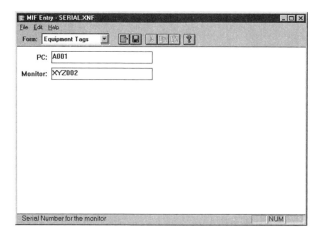

The next time a software inventory is performed on the machine (as set by the SMS Administrator program), the Inventory Agent adds the new MIF file to its regular inventory collection and the group defined by the MIF is added to the client's inventory.

You can verify that this has occurred by opening the SMS Administrator program and opening the Properties window for a machine that has reported the new MIF information. Figure 45.11 shows the new group for the machine KATE.

FIG. 45.11

The Personal Computer properties for this machine show that the new group has been added to the inventory.

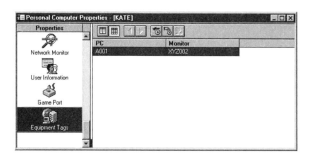

Creating Custom Reports with SMS Information

In Chapter 43, "Implementing SMS," you learn how to perform a query of the SMS database. You can create a report by simply outputting the query results. When you perform a query using the built-in SMS query function, the results are formatted according to the currently selected result format. SMS comes with only one result format, the Identification format, but allows you to easily define your own. By creating your own result formats, you can customize the output of your query to display just the information you really want.

This basic reporting capability is fine for just getting information out quickly, but it doesn't permit very much layout flexibility and it certainly isn't presentation quality. Fortunately, Microsoft has included a version of Crystal Reports that is specifically designed to work with

SMS so you can customize your report layouts as much as you want. In this section, we see how Crystal Reports integrates with SMS, what steps are required in order to get the data you want into Crystal Reports, and how to create a sample report.

Basic SMS Reporting

The basic reporting capability included in the SMS Admninistrator is fine for quick reports, but hardly qualifies as a true report generator. Therefore, you'll see how it works and then move on to the preferred report generation method—Crystal Reports. To see how the basic reporting functions work, first execute a query as described in Chapter 43, "Implementing SMS."

Figure 45.12 shows the results of executing the built-in query "All Personal Computers" with the Identification format.

FIG. 45.12

A simple SMS query that shows the default results format.

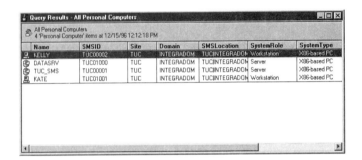

▶ **See** "Using Queries to View Inventory Information," **p. 1512**

As you can see, the Identification format contains all the information contained in the Identification group that is part of each computer's SMS inventory. For many queries, though, you want to get a different set of data on each PC. With the "Computers with Nearly Full Disks" query, for example, it would be useful to have a column that shows the free space remaining on the disk drives. A custom result format allows you to do this. To create a custom result format, follow this procedure:

1. Start the SMS Administrator program.

2. Open the Define Query Results Format window. Choose File, Define Query Result Formats. The Define Query Result Formats dialog box appears (see Figure 45.13).

3. From the Architecture drop-down list, choose the architecture to which your custom results format applies. SMS provides six architectures:

   - JobDetails
   - PackageLocation
   - Personal Computer
   - SMSEvent
   - SNMP Traps
   - UserGroups

FIG. 45.13

The Define Query Result Formats dialog box lets you create your own results formats for each SMS Architecture.

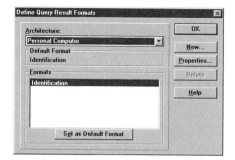

You must specify an architecture both for defining queries and for defining results formats. A results format defined for one architecture cannot be used for another architecture. This dialog box identifies the default results format that will be used with queries for each architecture and allows you to change the default by clicking the Set as Default Format button.

4. Click the New button to create your custom format. The Query Result Format Properties dialog box appears (see Figure 45.14).

FIG. 45.14

The Query Result Format Properties dialog box lets you choose attributes and other properties that determine the format of a query results window.

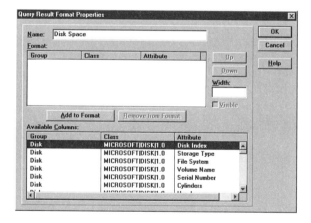

5. Enter a name for the results format in the Name text box.

6. In the Available Columns list, select the attribute you want to include in your results format and click the Add to Format button. The available columns list will be different depending on which architecture you've selected.

7. The attribute you added appears in the Format list. You can change the default width in pixels of the column by using the Width text box, and you can hide the column by clearing the Visible check box.

8. Repeat steps 6 and 7 until you've built the desired custom results format.

9. To further customize the look of your report, you can change the order of the columns.

The top attribute in the Format list will be the far-left column, and the bottom attribute will be the far-right column when the query results are displayed. You can change the order of the columns by selecting an attribute and using the Up and Down buttons to move it.

10. Click OK twice to close both dialogs.

SMS Architectures

An architecture in SMS is a structure for organizing the attributes of any object in the SMS system. The architectures have names that are self-explanatory (for example, JobDetails is for information related to SMS jobs). Each architecture consists of at least one group (the Identification group). A group is a collection of attributes that have something in common. For example, the Personal Computer architecture contains the Processor group, which contains such attributes as Processor Name, Processor Type, and Quantity.

Now when you execute a query for that particular architecture, you can select the custom results format you just created (see Figure 45.15). After you click OK to execute this query, you'll see a report similar to to the one in Figure 45.16.

FIG. 45.15

Executing a query using your custom results format.

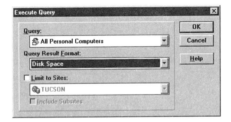

FIG. 45.16

This is the resulting output of an SMS query using a custom results format that focuses on disk attributes. Notice that the report only displays the disk attributes for the disk with the lowest index value (the floppy drive). This points out one of the big limitations with the SMS administrator that can be avoided by using Crystal Reports instead.

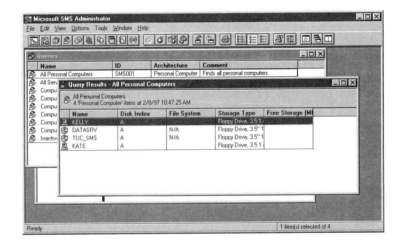

Using Crystal Reports

Crystal Reports is a third-party report writer application that Microsoft has bundled with SMS. This application provides the capability to generate professional-looking reports from data in the SMS database and overcomes the limitations of the basic reporting capabilities built into SMS.

Crystal Reports is a separate application on the BackOffice CD in the SMS12 directory. You must perform the following steps in order to install and use it:

1. Begin the installation of Crystal Reports by running Setup from the directory \SMS12\REPORTS on the BackOffice CD containing SMS. This brings up the initial installation dialog box (see Figure 45.17).

FIG. 45.17
You must choose a directory location for Crystal Reports.

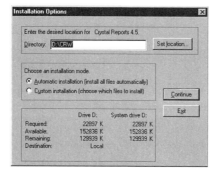

Part
IX
Ch
45

2. Type in the desired Directory location and click Continue. Crystal Reports asks you to decide if you want to run the application from other machines on the network (see Figure 45.18). Click No to run it as a stand-alone application from your workstation.

FIG. 45.18
You can choose to run Crystal Reports only from your workstation or set it up to be accessible from other machines on the network.

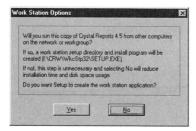

3. Crystal Reports completes the installation and pops up a dialog box to inform you that ODBC has been installed and that you need to run ODBC setup. You'll do that now.

4. From the Start Menu, select Programs, Crystal Reports 4.5, 32-Bit ODBC Setup. This brings up a Welcome dialog box with options to Continue or Exit.

5. Click Continue to continue the installation. This brings up the Install Drivers dialog box (see Figure 45.19). Select SQL Server from the Available ODBC Drivers list and click OK to install it. You may receive a warning that you are about to replace a newer version of the SQL Server ODBC driver with the one from Crystal Reports. You should keep the newer version.

FIG. 45.19

This dialog box installs ODBC drivers for use with Crystal Reports. You need the SQL Server driver to generate reports from your SMS database.

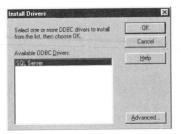

6. ODBC Setup will then copy some files to your disk. You may encounter a warning that the file ODBC32.DLL is in use. Click Ignore to ignore this warning and continue.

7. The next dialog box you'll see is the Data Sources dialog box (see Figure 45.20). Click the Add button to bring up the Add Data Source dialog box (see Figure 45.21).

FIG. 45.20

The Data Sources dialog box lists the installed data sources and enables you to add a data source. You need to add one for your SMS database.

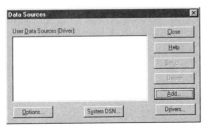

FIG. 45.21

This dialog box provides a selection of ODBC drivers to use for your data source.

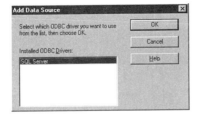

8. Select SQL Server and click OK. This brings up the ODBC SQL Server Setup dialog box. Click the Options button to see the full dialog (see Figure 45.22). The required fields are Data Source Name (SMSData, unless you changed it during SMS installation), Server

(the name of the NT server that hosts your SMS database), and Database Name (SMS, unless you changed it during SMS installation).

FIG. 45.22

The ODBC SQL Server Setup dialog box lets you fill in many parameters for your data source. Data Source Name, Server, and Database Name are all that you need for Crystal Reports.

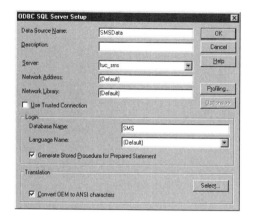

9. Click OK to create the data source. This returns you to the Data Sources dialog box. Click the Close button to exit ODBC Setup.

10. The final procedure is to run the SMSVIEW program. SMSVIEW creates a view of the SMS database and is required because Crystal Reports can't work with the database tables directly. From the Start Menu, select Programs, Systems Management Server, SMS SQL View Generator. This brings up the Create Views dialog box (see Figure 45.23).

FIG. 45.23

The Create Views dialog box allows the SMSVIEW program to log on to your SMS database with administrator privileges.

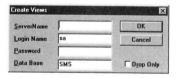

11. Fill in the ServerName (the NT server that hosts your SMS database), Login Name (the database administrator login ID), Password (the database administrator password), and the Data Base (the name of your SMS database) and click OK. You'll get a dialog box informing you that the views were successfully created, if the information you entered is correct.

This completes the setup steps required to use Crystal Reports for SMS.

After you've completed the preceding installation and configuration steps, you're ready to use Crystal Reports. From the Start Menu, select Programs, Crystal Reports 4.5, Crystal Reports 4.5. The application window appears (see Figure 45.24).

FIG. 45.24

This version of the Crystal Reports application is designed specifically to work with SMS.

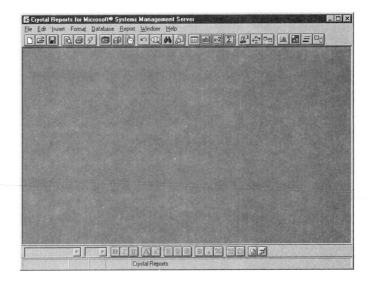

To see how much better a report prepared by Crystal Reports looks, call up one of the predefined reports:

1. From the Crystal Reports menus, choose File, Open, and then choose the report SPACE.RPT.

2. Choose Report, Zoom to zoom in on the report (see Figure 45.25).

FIG. 45.25

The sample report SPACE.RPT shows available space on hard drives.

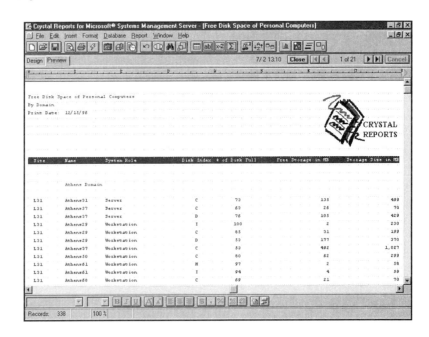

3. The data that appears in the report windows is simply data that was included with the sample report. You can refresh the report to show data from your own SMS database by choosing Report, Refresh Report Data.

Crystal Reports asks you to confirm the refresh and then asks you for the data source name that you created during the ODBC setup portion of the Crystal Reports installation and the administrator ID and password for your SMS database. It then extracts the required data from your SMS database and refreshes the report window (see Figure 45.26).

FIG. 45.26

This is the sample report SPACE.RPT after it has been refreshed to include live data.

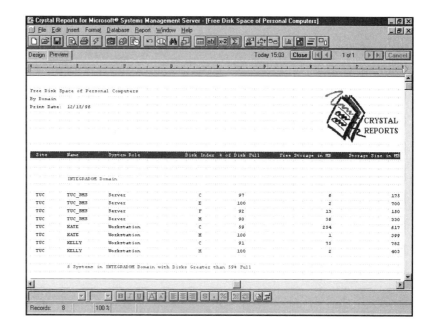

Part

IX

Ch

45

Crystal Reports provides tools that allow you to easily build sophisticated reports. You can insert fields from your SMS database into a report and customize virtually every aspect of your report layout. The online help that comes with Crystal Reports is excellent and includes a tutor to help you create your first report.

T I P An excellent way to learn how reports are constructed is to open the sample reports and examine their layouts in the design view.

Creating your own reports in Crystal Reports is easy thanks to the included Report Creation Wizard. To see how this works, you'll create a report that contains the following information for each PC in an SMS database: Site, Domain, Machine Name, Network Card, Physical Memory, Disk Storage, and Free Disk Space.

To create a custom report in Crystal Reports, perform the following steps:

1. From the Start menu, select _P_rograms, Crystal Reports 4.5 to open Crystal Reports.

2. From the menu bar, choose _F_ile, _N_ew. This brings up the Create New Report Wizard (see Figure 45.27).

FIG. 45.27

The Create New Report dialog box is the starting point for creating a report. It provides a number of predefined report types to choose from and also lets you create a custom report.

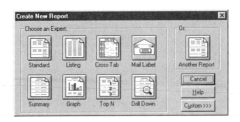

3. Click the Standard report icon. This brings up the Create Report Expert dialog box (see Figure 45.28).

FIG. 45.28

The Create Report Expert dialog box will walk you through the creation of a report from start to finish. It even provides performance enhancement suggestions.

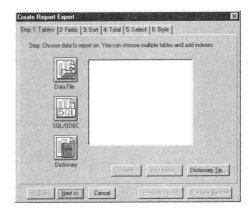

4. Click the SQL/ODBC icon since your report is coming from a SQL Server database. You'll be asked to log on to the server (see Figure 45.29). Choose ODBC SMSData and click OK. This brings up a SQL Server Login dialog box (see Figure 45.30).

FIG. 45.29

The Log On Server dialog box allows you to choose the data source that Crystal Reports will use to access the SMS database. This is usually SMSData.

FIG. 45.30

The SQL Server Login dialog box allows Crystal Reports to log on to your SMS database.

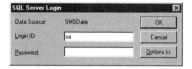

5. Type in the administrator ID and password and click OK. Crystal Reports will connect to your SMS database and bring up the Choose SQL Table dialog box (see Figure 45.31).

FIG. 45.31

The Choose SQL Table dialog box provides you with a list of all the tables and views that are defined for your SMS database. You can select the views that contain the fields you want to have in your report.

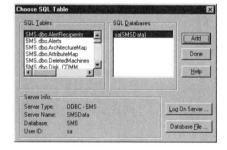

Part
IX

Ch

45

6. Using this dialog box, you can add the views of the SMS database that contain the fields you want to have in your report. Double-click the following views to add them to your report: SMS.dbo.vIdentification, SMS.dbo.vNetcard, SMS.dbo.vPC_Memory, and SMS.dbo.vDisk.

> **CAUTION**
>
> Crystal Reports can only use the views that were generated by SMSVIEW, not the actual database tables. The views are easily identified because their names begin with SMS.dbo.v.

7. Click Done when you are finished adding views. This brings up a graphical view of the views linked by Machine ID (see Figure 45.32). There are a variety of options for you if you are not satisfied with the way your views have been linked, but normally you should accept the automatically generated links.

8. Click Next to continue. This dialog box is where you actually assign fields to your report (see Figure 45.33).

   To add a field, double-click the name of that field in the Database Fields list. For each field you add, you can assign your own column heading using the Column Heading text box. With a field highlighted in the Database Fields list, you can click the Browse Data button and you will get a list of all the data values found in the SMS database table for that particular field.

FIG. 45.32

The Links dialog box shows the views you added and the links that were automatically created by Crystal Reports. You can change the views and the links here.

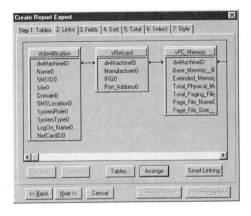

FIG. 45.33

The Fields dialog box provides a list of all the fields contained in the views you've chosen. You can selectively add these fields to your report and customize the heading for each field.

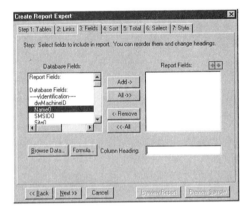

The Formula button allows you to assign one or more formulas to your report. These formulas are logical expressions that consist of field names and comparison operators and they are typically used to limit the the data included in the report to a specific range of values. For example, you can specify that you are only interested in machines with less than 16M of memory by creating a formula. For this example, let's add the following fields and columns:

Column Heading	Field Name
Site	Site0
Domain	Domain0
Name	Name0
Network Card	Manufacturer0
Physical Memory	Total_Physical_Memory__KB0
Disk	Disk_Index0
Storage Size	Storage_Size__MByte_0
Free Space	Free_Storage__MByte_0

9. Click Next to continue. This dialog box allows you to group fields and choose a sort order (see Figure 45.34). You can double-click a field in the Report Fields list to add it to the Group Fields list. Then you pick the sort order in the Order drop-down list. Group the fields by site, then domain, and leave the sort order as ascending (the default).

FIG. 45.34

The Sort dialog box provides a list of all the fields you can add to your report and allows you to select one or more fields by which to group the results of your query.

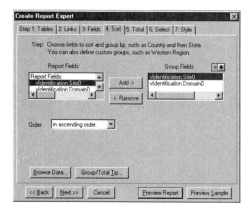

10. Click Next to continue. This dialog box contains a tab for each group you created in the previous screen (see Figure 45.35). The dialog box also assumes that you will be summing numeric fields, so it automatically adds those fields to the Total Fields list. For this example, you don't want totals, so remove all the fields.

FIG. 45.35

The Total tab allows you to specify fields that you want to total for each group.

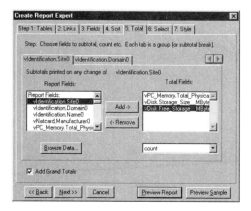

11. Click Next to continue. This dialog box enables you to enhance the speed of report generation by using indexed fields and filter expressions (see Figure 45.36).

For each field in the Report Fields list, you can specify a filter expression that will limit the amount of data that the server returns to you. Be sure to click the Speed Tip button for an explanation of this screen and some other valuable performance tips. We will add our report fields to the Select Fields list, but leave the filter expression at the default of "is any value."

FIG. 45.36

The Select dialog box provides a list of all the fields you've chosen for your report and enables you to create a filter expression for each one. If you can limit the range of values you're interested in, you'll get faster reports.

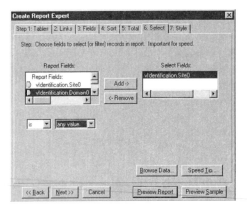

12. Click Next to continue. This dialog box enables you to title your report and choose the report format (see Figure 45.37). Title it "PC Hardware Report" and choose the Leading Break format. Be sure to click the Preview Tip and Disribute Tip buttons for useful information on previewing and distributing your report.

FIG. 45.37

The Style tab allows you to add the finishing touches to your report. You can add a title, select the presentation format, and add a picture.

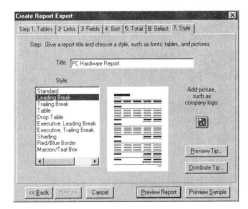

13. Click Preview Report to see the finished report (see Figure 45.38). You'll probably want to make use of Crystal Reports' formatting features to adjust fields and field headings, fonts, etc. You can modify all aspects of the report by selecting the Design tab (see Figure 45.39).

FIG. 45.38

This is a finished report using the Report Creation Wizard. It can now be fine-tuned using the Crystal Reports layout tools and options.

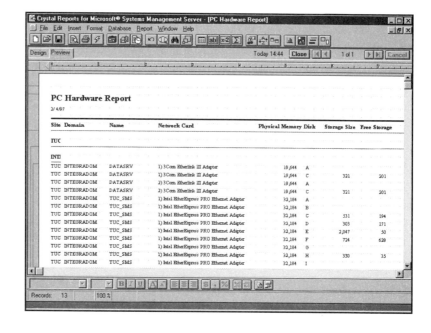

FIG. 45.39

The Design tab provides a view of a report that enables you to add and remove fields, change borders and shading, change the placement of fields, and much more.

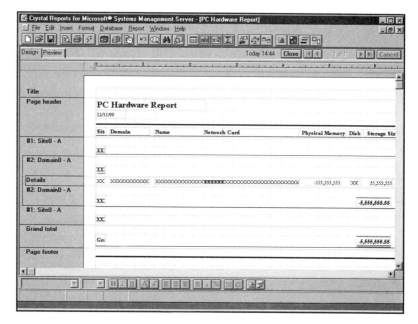

SMS Integration with HP OpenView

SMS is a fine management platform for PC LANs but it undeniably has holes that third-party vendors have rushed to fill. (Table 45.2 lists these vendors.) SMS add-ons and products that directly integrate with SMS are widely available. Digital's POLYCENTER NetView and AssetWORKS, OnDemand Software's WinInstall, Cheyenne Software's InocuLAN, ASI Corporation's AssetPro, BMC Software's PATROL, and Hewlett-Packard's OpenView are all products that are designed to integrate with various parts of SMS. This section describes the level of SMS integration available in one popular network management platform, HP OpenView for Windows Professional Suite.

Table 45.2   Third-Party Products that Work with SMS

ASI Corporation's AssetPRO	AssetPRO: Enterprise Asset Management combines all the features of traditional life cycle asset management with automatic data collection, integrated help desk, and electronic asset procurement. AssetPRO is aimed at assisting MIS in reducing workloads, tracking and identifying hardware and software, issuing asset-responsibility to users, and solving user issues via HelpDesk.
BMC Software's PATROL	PATROL provides automatic alert capabilities for applications, databases, messaging, middleware, operating systems, and other underlying resources. The PATROL data-management family of products automate many of the manual, error-prone steps associated with data management.
Cheyenne Software's InocuLAN	InocuLAN for Windows NT is an anti-virus solution designed to protect your entire network with support for Windows 3.x, Windows 95, DOS, Macintosh, and Windows NT workstations. InocuLAN is fully integrated with SMS.
Digital's POLYCENTER NetView and AssetWORKS	POLYCENTER Manager on NetView for Windows NT is integrated with POLYCENTER AssetWORKS and Microsoft's Systems Management Server. Through the use of bidirectional launch capabilities, these products provide a comprehensive approach to managing enterprise-wide, multivendor hardware, software, and network resources. From POLYCENTER Manager on NetView for Windows NT, the network manager can launch Microsoft's Systems Management Server and POLYCENTER AssetWORKS to display a Systems Management Server property sheet for a network or system object.

POLYCENTER AssetWORKS operates in conjunction with Microsoft's Systems Management Server to provide a broad range of configuration management capabilities for multivendor computer systems across the network. From the Systems Management Server and POLYCENTER AssetWORKS, the network and system manager can launch NetView to find a network object, diagnose it, show its properties, and to graph network traffic.

OnDemand Software's WinINSTALL

WinINSTALL totally automates software distribution and makes quick work of adding new applications or upgrading installed applications to the latest release.

WinINSTALL is tightly integrated with Systems Management Server. It is a simple matter to create System Management Server "Run Command on Workstation" jobs that use the power of Systems Management Server to determine target machines, to distribute files to servers throughout the enterprise, and to launch WinINSTALL as the install process on the user's desktop. This approach combines the strengths of both products to provide an extremely effective network management combination.

Part

IX

Ch

45

HP OpenView is one of the leading network management platforms and its strengths have been in the areas of hub and router management and, of course, management of a variety of HP products. The latest version is clearly moving toward the area of PC management and the integration with SMS is one example of that. This chapter assumes that your organization is already committed to HP OpenView as a network management platform and wants to deploy SMS for PC management.

HP OpenView for Windows is a comprehensive network management platform built around the HP OpenView Workgroup Node Manager. This software suite addresses HP hub, printer, and server management, and also the desktop management issues of hardware and software inventory, software distribution, and software metering. The suite is comprised of the following 12 modules:

- HP OpenView Workgroup Node Manager
- HP AdvanceStack Assistant
- HP JetAdmin
- HP PowerWise Assistant
- HP TopTOOLS
- HP NetServer Assistant

- HP NetMetrix/Win
- HP Exposé from Symantec
- Norton pcANYWHERE from Symantec
- Norton Administrator for Networks from Symantec
- Notify! Connect from Ex Machina, Inc.
- Saber LAN Workstation from McAfee

Of these modules, the one we'll focus on is the HP OpenView Workgroup Node Manager, since this module directly integrates with SMS. From the OpenView Workgroup Node Manager, you can highlight a machine on the network and, if that machine has been inventoried by SMS, you can call up the SMS Properties window for that machine from within OpenView. You also can run the SMS Administrator from within the Workgroup Node Manager. Similarly, in SMS Administrator, you can open the Properties window for a particular machine, and you'll see a new OpenView icon (see Figure 45 .40). When you click this icon, the Workgroup Node Manager window pops up and the icon representing the machine you were viewing in the SMS Administrator is highlighted.

FIG. 45.40

The OpenView icon appears in the Personal Computer Properties for each machine. This icon is a direct link to HP OpenView Workgroup Node Manager.

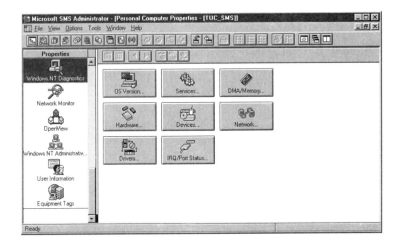

NOTE The OpenView Workgroup Node Manager must be running in order for the OpenView icon to appear in SMS Administrator. However, you don't need to have the SMS Administrator running in order to access the SMS machine properties in the Workgroup Node Manager.

To use these capabilities, you must first install the HP OpenView for Windows Professional Suite on the same machine that you use for the SMS Administrator application. Select OpenView Workgroup Node Manager as one of the components to install. To enable the integration between SMS and OpenView, you also must install the OV/SMS Bridge program. The Setup program for the Bridge is located in the directory \SMS12\SUPPORT\ISV\HP\SETUP on the BackOffice CD.

To install the Bridge for SMS/HP OpenView integration, perform the following steps:

1. Launch the Windows NT Control Panel and double-click the System icon. In the System Properties dialog box, choose the Environment tab and select the Path variable from the list of System Variables (see Figure 45.41).

FIG. 45.41

You must manually edit the Windows NT Path variable in order to run the Bridge program.

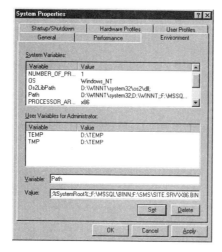

2. Add the path **`<SMS directory>\SITE.SRV\X86.BIN`** to the Windows NT Path variable. Click the Set button and then click OK to accept the change and close the dialog box.

3. From the BackOffice CD that contains SMS, run the program `\SMS12\SUPPORT\ISV\HP\SETUP\SETUP.EXE`. You'll get the introductory dialog box shown in Figure 45.42.

FIG. 45.42

The Bridge program uses a standard Windows setup routine for installation.

4. The next screen prompts you for your SMS directory (see Figure 45.43). Type in the location and click the Continue button.

FIG. 45.43

You must install the Bridge program in the same directory where you installed SMS.

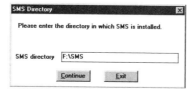

5. The Setup program will then prompt you for your database server name, your SMS database name, the administrator logon ID, and the administrator password. Enter the information and click Continue. Setup will then complete and terminate.

To see how this works, launch the OpenView Workgroup Node Manager. The OpenView Workgroup Node Manager has a Basic Layout function for quickly creating a view of your network and an AutoDiscovery function that can automatically discover network devices after you've configured it with the network addresses of your network segments. Figure 45.44 shows the OpenView Workgroup Node Manager window after a limited AutoDiscovery has been performed.

FIG. 45.44

The HP OpenView Workgroup Node Manager is displaying network machines that have been identified via the AutoDiscovery function.

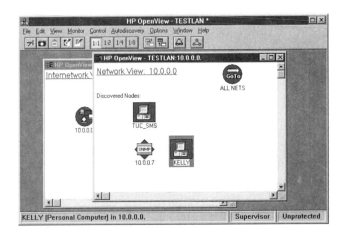

To view the SMS properties for the machine TUC_SMS, select the icon for TUC_SMS, and then choose Monitor, SMS, Properties. The SMS Personal Computer Properties window appears as shown in Figure 45.45. Note that the SMS Administrator is not running at this point. To launch SMS Administrator, choose Monitor, SMS, Run SMS.

FIG. 45.45

You can call up the SMS Personal Computer Properties window from within OpenView Workgroup Node Manager.

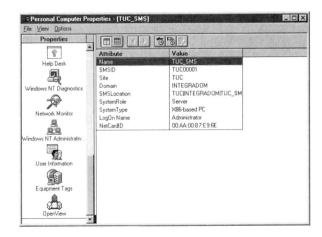

The other integration that OpenView Workgroup Node Manager provides is the monitoring of SNMP traps or Alarms, as OpenView refers to them. SMS 1.2 provides enhanced support for SNMP traps and these can be forwarded to OpenView Workgroup Node Manager and collected in the Alarm Log.

From Here...

In this chapter, you have applied your knowledge of SMS to specific areas that are of interest to many systems administrators. You learned how to roll out two complex software packages, Windows 95 and Office 95, using the SMS software distribution capability. You learned how to customize basic SMS reports and produce even better reports by using the separate Crystal Reports application that comes with SMS. Additionally, you discovered that the basic SMS inventory capability can be expanded to include any data items you like. And you got a look at how one third-party application, HP OpenView, integrates with SMS.

See the following chapters for related information:

- For a review of the SMS basics, see Chapter 42, "Preparing for SMS."
- For information on collecting inventory from machines and executing queries on that information, see Chapter 43, "Implementing SMS."
- For information on automatically distributing and installing software, see Chapter 44, "The Role of the SMS Administrator."

Part

IX

Ch

45

P A R T

X

Applying Microsoft BackOffice Technology

CHAPTER 46

Implementing Real-World Security

by Don Benage

This chapter does not review specific products but discusses certain types of products. Broad coverage is provided rather than in-depth details, for two reasons. First, the details of the systems and products change, but a sound approach will continue to provide a strong measure of security. Second, it is ineffective to get so focused on the details of one area that you overlook another weakness. The adage describing a chain as being only as strong as the weakest link is certainly apt when discussing security. Encrypting a report on your hard disk is less effective if the draft copies you printed and discarded are sitting in a trash bag by the elevator waiting to be removed by a janitor. ▪

Security areas in which you may be vulnerable

Review the potential risks that you should analyze. Find out where your organization may be vulnerable.

Different types of security

Learn about several of the major types of security—physical, network, data, and e-mail. Discover the important elements of each and review some approaches to implementation.

How to secure your servers

Explore the capabilities offered in Windows NT Server that help to provide strong server security. Learn some of the techniques you can use to prevent unauthorized access and what you must do to prevent an intruder from gaining access with an Emergency Repair Disk, an often overlooked danger.

How to secure your workstations

Review a variety of techniques for securing workstations using Windows NT Workstation and Windows 95.

Understanding Your Risks and Security Needs

Security is a topic that many people think they understand, fewer people do understand, and fewer still act on their understanding. As the use of personal computers attached to local area networks (LANs) has grown over the last 15 years from a trickle to a torrent, the security that was implemented for the corporate mainframe locked in the "glass house" is still in place, but the information has escaped. It has been downloaded over LANs, stored on laptop computers, and carried out of the building on floppy disks.

Many organizations underestimate the risks they face and the importance of security. They either have no formal policy or do not enforce the policies they have. There is no regular risk assessment, no audit, no disaster recovery plan. Too often people are assigned an administrator's role on a network just to avoid difficulties with assigning access permissions. Many organizations leasing space in office buildings don't know who has keys to their facilities and what screening, if any, is done when hiring maintenance workers and janitorial staff.

This chapter provides an overview of the field of security and recommends an approach that you can use to evaluate your organization's needs and implement a system that meets your requirements. The needs of different organizations vary widely. Perhaps your organization honestly doesn't need much in the way of security, or perhaps you have already implemented an approach that you feel is adequate. The fact remains that most organizations are more vulnerable than they realize. Although the concepts outlined in this chapter may seem like common sense, in the field of security, it seems that common sense isn't very common.

Good security doesn't necessarily imply a lot of security. Security is best when it is suitable for the environment and people it is intended to protect. Applying heavy-handed, burdensome techniques and policies, especially when they are unwarranted, only cause the members of your organization to resent the measures and work to thwart their effectiveness. This underscores the need for education and training on the topic for all members of the organization. Everyone has an important role in preserving the effectiveness of the security systems you adopt.

Analyzing Your Vulnerability

A good place to start when reviewing your security is to conduct an objective analysis of your vulnerability. What types of people and organizations are vulnerable? The answer is *almost everyone*. Every organization is vulnerable to theft. In addition, if your organization represents a cause there is usually an opposing interest. You may be the target of a campaign to procure your information for the purpose of discrediting your organization or to enhance the efforts to oppose your goals. Organizations seen as establishment empires wielding too much control are vulnerable—just ask the telephone industry. Finally, some organizations make themselves vulnerable precisely by appearing to be an easy target, appearing "weak" in the area of security. It is a little like the law of the jungle.

The next important step is to analyze what you are trying to protect. What assets of your organization are most valuable? An obvious answer is the tangible assets of your organization such as office equipment, furniture, and cash. There also are other less obvious answers. Your information systems contain vital information that is certainly valuable. What is your customer list worth? What about the other information stored on your computers?

If you are a consulting organization, your most valuable asset may be the people you employ. Perhaps a list of every employee with their addresses, and phone numbers, might be the target of a competitor or an unscrupulous placement firm. Clearly, you must provide a satisfactory job experience or your employees will leave anyway. But after analysis you may decide that publishing a master list constitutes an unreasonable vulnerability. This is just one example of the kind of exposed position that can be easily overlooked. If you identify them, however, you can take steps to secure these items.

Where are you vulnerable? How does a security problem arise and where is it executed? Only analysis of your individual needs can determine the appropriate level of security for your organization. A problem at one organization may not be a concern for another. For example, a small, tightly knit group of people may be well served by tight physical security on the premises and little or no security once inside the work environment, even if their security needs are stringent. An entirely different approach is required for environments that require regular access by visitors and part-time employees or full-time contract help.

There are many potential areas of concern starting with the keyboards of your computer systems. Computer systems and networks have been designed to provide easy access to information. One of the most intense areas of research and development has been making computers easier to use and information easier to access and understand. What were once arcane stacks of reports printed on greenbar paper, so difficult to interpret that even people with training could hardly make sense of them, are now reports with pie charts, presentations, and in-house publications that make detailed information easy to comprehend. This is a laudable goal, but it makes the job of a security system all the more difficult.

Most organizations have ineffective network logon security and no local security on their individual systems. The policies for the management of passwords are generally lax or nonexistent. If your organization supports dial-up access to the network, this must receive careful attention because the potential for trouble is great. If part or all of your organization's private network is attached to the Internet, another potential concern exists.

A growing threat also comes from the use of network *sniffers* or protocol analyzers. These once were expensive devices that were inaccessible to the individual without a corporate budget. Now, sophisticated software-only solutions exist, including the Network Monitor provided with Systems Management Server (SMS), a BackOffice component. This type of software can be installed on a computer with a network adapter that can be placed in "promiscuous mode" and virtually *all* network traffic can be captured and saved to disk for later analysis and reconstruction. A high level of knowledge is required to perform some of these tasks, but that is little cause for complacency.

Finally, although the focus of this chapter is on computer-based issues, a comprehensive risk analysis also must include the front door (and the back door) of your facilities. A particularly vulnerable situation arises when an organization leases space in an office building. Frequently, you no longer have control over the distribution of keys to your premises or the people who

Part
X

Ch
46

receive them. Does anyone check to make sure that the janitor who is alone in your office at night isn't a career criminal? Perhaps even more alarming is the threat from the so-called *hacker*. An average high-school student with strong computer skills, a part-time janitorial position, and an overactive imagination could add up to an enormous risk. Should you be concerned about this?

If you are responsible for security at your organization, you can conduct an interesting experiment. Spend the night in a quiet corner at the office reading a good book. Alternatively, make random visits to the office at 11:00 p.m. or 2:30 a.m. You may be shocked at what you discover. All too often the front door that is so carefully locked by your employees as they leave for the day is propped open by a janitor's trash can. The janitor is busy in some area of your suite, or even helping out on another floor of the building, and all your equipment and information is there for the taking.

Another related and very common problem is created when you provide 24-hour access to your facility for employees and have locked offices for officers or managers in the company. The lock on the manager's door provides a false sense of security and can lead the office inhabitant to leave the inside of the office unsecured, believing that the lock on the door provides protection. The problem occurs when the janitorial crew comes into your suite and unlocks every door to provide easy access for the vacuum cleaner and the person emptying the trash. There may be an hour or more during which the doors are standing wide open, and no one is watching while the crew moves on to the next suite and the supervisor eventually comes through to lock up.

The reason that this is all so important is the concept of the *weakest link*. If your approach to security is not comprehensive, if you are not vigilant in all areas of potential attack, your system is open to compromise. The sophisticated, high-technology approaches that are available to safeguard electronic information systems are important and frequently appropriate. But don't forget to lock the back door.

Analyzing Threats to Your Security

So far the discussion has focused on who is vulnerable and where the attack might be directed. To complete the analysis, you must review who might be interested in attacking your organization. Again, some answers are obvious, others are less so.

A topic that surfaces from time to time in the public media is industrial espionage, and for many organizations this threat should be scrutinized. Unscrupulous organizations and individuals may undertake the task of trying to undermine your organization, steal your assets, or destroy your information systems. Although it may seem like fodder for a spy novel, the threat can be real, and it happens more often than people usually suspect.

Perhaps the biggest threat to an organization comes from the inside—the disgruntled employee. Almost every organization employs someone who is unhappy with the situation in which they find themselves and who blames the organization as a whole, or the managerial staff. Theft or destruction of proprietary information may seem like a reasonable way to strike back. This threat is particularly difficult to defend against because the culprits are so difficult to identify, and they come from the ranks of those who must be trusted with access for the organization to be effective.

The threat from hackers has been touched upon already, but it bears additional discussion. This potential threat is greatest for large organizations. The local telephone company, defense contractors, universities, and large corporate entities have been the traditional targets of the hacker community. The growth of interest in the Internet, however, raises the stakes a bit. Any organization providing Internet access for their network, and dial-up access to that network, has become a potential target for someone desiring free access.

A comprehensive plan to provide protection for your assets and information also must include an approach to managing the threat posed by viruses. There are several good references on this topic. The problem and effective approaches to address it are well understood. You also must develop a plan to deal with the threat posed by natural disasters such as fire or flooding. This chapter does not address these topics but mentions them for completeness. Remember, the *weakest link* is the important one.

Weighing Risks and Costs

After you have analyzed the potential for harm and the possible sources of the attack, you must formulate a plan to effectively provide an appropriate level of security. This involves weighing the risks and the costs associated with eliminating them. There will be financial costs, but perhaps even more unpalatable is the loss of freedom and flexibility that may be imposed upon well-meaning and loyal members of the organization who would never do any harm. If you implement even rudimentary security procedures, your employees still will have to bear inconvenience and occasional frustration as they work within the system.

The crux of the dilemma as you seek to balance access and security is this: you can't lock things up so tight that no one can use them. You must strike a balance between access and control. In addition, you must avoid the situation in which the costs associated with your security system, financial and others, are greater than the losses you might sustain without a system in place. If you spend more than you would have saved, you have already become a victim. The rest of the chapter outlines some specific types of security measures and techniques that may be useful in implementing a security system.

Understanding Different Types of Security

Security measures can be categorized into one of several types. Although this list is by no means complete, the main types of security presented in some detail in this section are as follows:

- Physical
- Network
- Data
- E-mail

Part

X

Ch

46

E-mail security is really a special case combining the elements of network security and data security, but it is such an important area that it bears special attention. All these topics have each been the subject of entire books, and you are encouraged to investigate the subject matter more thoroughly. This section provides an overview of some of the most important points and suggests areas that need closer scrutiny. Based on the analysis of your own organization's needs and the ideas you may develop as a result of this survey, you can begin to develop a comprehensive approach.

Ignorance is a mechanism counted on to provide protection in many organizations. People generally believe that if they don't know how to defeat a particular system or security technique, it must be secure. This is particularly true of network security, where people count on the general lack of understanding on the part of users to provide some measure of protection.

Security by ignorance is no security at all. You should not rely on the public's ignorance of a system's features and weaknesses to keep perpetrators at bay. Although some members of the user population may occasionally be unable to access the network even with a valid account and password, you should count on the potential attacker being much more sophisticated and potentially willing to expend large amounts of time and effort to defeat your best efforts at security. Here then is a survey of mechanisms that are effective and should be components of any security system.

Physical Security

Any approach to securing assets and information must start with physical security. As becomes more apparent in the sections ahead, it is almost impossible to prevent someone from accessing the information on a computer system if they can pick it up and take it with them. The reduction in size and weight of computer systems has been a phenomenal achievement, and the computing power and information now packed into some notebook computers is astounding. It is also a huge problem for security systems. Gigabytes of information—years worth of records or entire project files—can now be carried out of the building in a briefcase.

Physical security starts with the obvious. You should control access to your facilities. As already mentioned, this can be particularly difficult if the organization doesn't own the facilities. An important characteristic of such an access control system is that it must be flexible. Most organizations experience turnover in the ranks of employees or members. A locked door is meaningless if a conventional key is provided to a large group of people. When the inevitable happens and someone leaves the organization, it is unreasonable to replace the lock and provide new keys to the group—it just won't happen.

A big improvement is provided by a variety of systems that allow access to facilities to a group of people, each using an individualized "key." Some of these systems use badges or ID cards that store an identifying number or code in the card itself. The ID can be added or deleted from the group that can enter a door on an individual basis. You can even set the time periods that are valid for a particular ID. Some systems offer the capability to log the time, location, and ID used for each access. If an employee is terminated, the corresponding ID is removed from the system, and all other users continue to access the facilities unaffected. These systems can be used at the entrance to the facility, and internally to control access to machine rooms and wiring closets containing network hubs and other sensitive equipment.

Many additional measures can and should be taken to physically secure your facilities, but they are beyond the scope of this book. It is important, however, that you address the issue of physical security carefully. It is the basis on which all other measures depend.

Network Security

The term *network security* refers to measures that are implemented to prevent unauthorized users from logging on to your network or gaining access to server-based resources, whether they intend to destroy information, copy information for illicit purposes, or simply view the information. A sound approach to network security has several key components. Among the most important elements of network security are the following:

- Prudent use and assignment of roles such as administrators, operators, users, and guests
- Developing, implementing, and maintaining a password policy that is balanced to fit the needs of the organization and is neither too cumbersome nor too unconstrained
- Effective use and assignment of permissions, both on shared network resources and local file systems
- The use of auditing and log files to record salient events and track unauthorized attempts at access
- Appropriate safeguards against attack from Internet connections (if any) such as the use of firewalls, proxy servers, bastion hosts, or other techniques to isolate access and regulate the flow of information into and out of the organization's network

Part

X

Ch

46

User Roles on the Network   Windows NT offers a variety of roles that you can assign to users with different levels of default privileges. The roles are implemented as standard groups that are created when the Windows NT Server system is installed. By assigning a user account to one of these groups, the account will automatically be granted various rights to perform specific actions. In addition, you further customize the default roles by assigning additional rights to individual user accounts and groups. The standard groups are visible in Figure 46.1, which depicts the main display from the User Manager for Domains administrative utility.

The most important role on a Windows NT network is that of Domain Admin. Be very careful about assigning this role. You should have only as many Domain Admins as you absolutely need and assign this role only to people whom you really trust. A Domain Admin can completely disable a network in as little as five minutes, or less, and can leave it in a state requiring days to recover, if recovery is indeed possible.

Even a Domain Admin cannot see the password that a particular user has chosen by opening the properties for a user's account. They can, however, change a user's password and then log on as that user, gaining access to anything that the user has privileges for that is not protected by further means. A Domain Admin also can take ownership of any files or directories in the file system and reassign permissions to any group or user including himself.

FIG. 46.1

The User
Manager for
Domains allows
you to assign
account IDs to
specific roles for
network security
purposes.

Standard groups

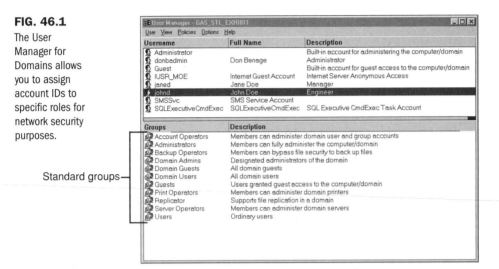

N O T E   All of the elements listed previously are auditable events which leave a record of the actions
in the Event Log *if you have enabled auditing*. This underscores the need for regular review of
audit logs and may suggest the need for a separate auditing person or group that acts independently of
the network administration team. The auditing team does not need to change settings or configuration
details, just review settings and logs to ensure compliance with organizational security standards.

A dishonest Domain Admin could hide its intrusion by disabling auditing and clearing the current audit
logs. However, with a separate auditing team in place (as suggested), any disruption or tampering with
audit logs would be noticed (alerts fired, etc.). In addition, permissions to delete or change files in the
log directory can be denied to Domain Admins. Typically, this would be implemented with the
understanding that for Domain Admins to change audit settings is a terminating offense, which would
be clearly communicated to administrators. Only audit team personnel should manage these files. ■

These capabilities are essential for an administrator to perform needed maintenance and recovery tasks, to help users who have forgotten their passwords, and to recover information in the
event a user is the victim of some calamity or decides to leave the organization. With all this
power, however, it is a role you should use sparingly. Even those who have Domain Admin
accounts should create an additional account with standard user privileges that is used for
everyday needs and use the administrative account only when actually performing administrative tasks to help avoid accidental mishaps.

On a small- to medium-sized network, two Domain Admins should be enough. You must have
at least one backup, even if the majority of work is done by a single individual. You also should
consider assigning a truly secure password to the built-in Administrator account (which is a
member of the Domain Admins group by default), recording it in a sealed document, and storing it offsite in a safe deposit box under the control of a trusted officer of the company. This
extra "insurance" could be especially important if the assigned domain administrators ever
travel together. In the event that an accident occurs, you need to be able to regain access to the
administrative capabilities for your network.

As an alternative to assigning full administrative privileges, you can delegate part of the responsibility for administrative duties by using the *operator* roles. The four groups of operators are as follows:

- Account operators
- Backup operators
- Print operators
- Server operators

Membership in one of these groups confers upon the user the capability to perform specific administrative tasks, such as managing a print queue or making tape backups. Account operators can assist users who have forgotten their passwords and can create new accounts, but they cannot change or create administrator accounts. Using these roles is an effective way to delegate responsibilities for large networks, without placing too much power in the hands of a large group of people.

Another related issue is the use of guest accounts. During installation of a server, a built-in account named Guest and a group named Guests are created. Allowing someone to use the Guest account, or creating an account and making it a member of the Guests group, confers upon the user the capability to log on to the network and possibly to gain access to other resources. Guest accounts can be useful, but you must beware of *privilege creep*—the slow addition of rights and privileges granted to a guest account as the current user becomes a more trusted member of the organization.

The problem with this situation is the difficulty of remembering to reduce or eliminate the extra privileges at a later time. When the current guest leaves and another user eventually begins using the account, the level of privileges assigned may no longer be appropriate. For this reason, some organizations choose not to use guest accounts at all. If a guest user needs greater privileges, especially if they are using the Guest account, it is best to simply create a new account and make them a member of Users, rather than continuing to add additional rights to the Guest account or the Guests group.

Another closely related issue is disabling and eventually removing accounts when employees or members of your organization leave or are terminated. This is a good example of something that sounds like common sense but is often overlooked. In the emotionally charged atmosphere of ending a professional relationship or even an ill-fated trial employment period it is easy to forget to take care of account administration.

N O T E In general, it is a good idea to disable an account for a period of a few weeks or a month, and then to delete it. If there are any questions about the account in the period following the departure regarding access to information or entries in audit logs, they are easier to answer if the account is still defined and can be reactivated and used by an administrator. In addition, you are better able to confirm the value of the underlying security identifier (or SID) associated with the account that may appear in log files.

Part
X

Ch
46

Password Policy A good password policy goes a long way toward securing your network. It is incredible how often this simple capability is overlooked during security implementation. The chief reason it is underutilized is its impact on users. More than any other security provision, users as a group have difficulty with passwords. They forget them; they select bad passwords; they write them down and tape them to the bottom of their chairs; and they generally hate them.

Windows NT Server allows you a good deal of control over the use of passwords. Figure 46.2 depicts the Account Policy dialog box, which you open by choosing Policies, Account from the menu.

FIG. 46.2

Use the Account Policy dialog box to set options that affect the selection and use of passwords in a Windows NT domain.

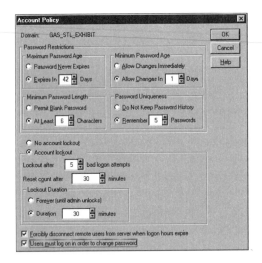

As with security in general, a good password policy is not necessarily a stringent policy. It is one that is set at an appropriate level for the organization in question. Setting all the options on the Account Policy dialog box, as shown in Figure 46.2, will make you a very unpopular person in some organizations. In general, people do not like to have long passwords that they have to change at regular intervals. If you use the aging and history features, people have to invent new passwords and cannot reuse a "favorite" password.

Requiring people to change passwords at regular intervals and forcing a length of at least six characters are almost always good ideas. In fact, all these options have their place and are needed at some organizations. Just be sensitive to the fact that too tight a policy, especially if it is imposed without explaining the rationale behind it and seeking the support of the user community, can have the effect of angering people and causing them to work against you.

Some guidelines for choosing a good password are presented in a Note in Chapter 4, "Enterprise Planning and Implementation," and are repeated here for your convenience:

- A password should be six or more characters long.
- A password should include letters, numbers, and at least one special character such as a dollar sign, asterisk, or exclamation point.

- Do not use a word that can be found in a dictionary, or a word spelled backwards.

- Avoid (like the plague) your favorite color, your dog's name, your birthday, or any similar bit of personal trivia.

- Do not select a password so obscure that you must write it down to remember it.

- Avoid words that beginners think no one else would ever guess (but many people do) such as sex, love, and secret. It is uncanny how often new computer users select a word in this category. If you adhere to the guideline banning words found in a dictionary, these will already be ruled out.

- One way to create good passwords is to alter the spelling of a word by using phonetic spelling, or replacing certain letters with numbers. These tend to be easy to remember, but hard to guess. Some examples are 2ebra&stryps or 4sooth%.

The rationale behind some of these items may be worth explaining. The length of the password is important because it determines the number of possible alternatives an attacker has to try when using a brute force approach to guessing your password. If you have a single-character password, it is clearly much easier to guess than a password that is longer.

What some users don't understand is the fact that so-called "dialer" programs have been employed in the past and are still occasionally employed, to gain access to computer systems. These programs attempt a *brute force logon* and can be effective at gaining access to systems with poor password policies. They typically start with a short list of commonly used passwords and then words from a full dictionary (sometimes forward and backward); then they may go through all possible combinations of characters. With a good password policy, this method is completely ineffectual because of the time required to attempt all possibilities.

Several options in the policy are specifically designed to combat such a brute force attack. Setting a minimum password length of at least six characters helps. Unfortunately, Windows NT Server does not allow you to require the use of special characters, which is another component of a good password. If you allow an unlimited number of failed logon attempts without locking the account (and without logging the events), your system is a prime candidate for a brute force approach. Windows NT Server does allow you to lock the account after a specified number of attempts. Even if you allow the account to reset after an hour, a length of time that shouldn't present too great a hardship for the hapless user, you can dramatically increase the time required to successfully attack with a dialer program. This also provides time to notice the activity in a log file.

Keeping a history of passwords that have been used in the past and setting a minimum password age prevents users from doggedly using the same password for their entire tenure with the organization. Unless you set these options, a stubborn or uninformed user who doesn't understand or approve of the password policy can simply change the password when required by aging and promptly change it right back to its original value.

Using the same password for long periods of time is a bad idea because it increases the likelihood that someone will eventually overhear it, find it written down, or see you enter it on your keyboard. If an intruder learns your password, and you don't ever change it, the intruder can continue to use your account until unusual activity is noticed in a log file or other evidence of tampering is uncovered. This is a weakness that opportunistic attackers have used in the past to gain unauthorized access to systems.

Another password-related feature that is popular with users, due to its convenience, is a potential problem for network (and e-mail) security. Several Microsoft applications and operating systems offer a check box to remember the user's password. This can be particularly dangerous on a laptop computer. It is possible to set up a Windows 95 laptop so that when you double-click an icon, the computer dials the network (using a stored phone number), logs on to the Windows NT domain (using a stored password), and opens a user's mailbox (using another stored password). Needless to say, this presents a security challenge. At a minimum, you should discourage users from using these features. They also should realize that if the computer is lost or stolen, they should immediately inform the administration team so that their account password can be changed.

Windows NT Server and the components of BackOffice allow you to use the same account and password on multiple systems. This is optional with SQL Server, which offers the capability to use a separate password or be authenticated with your Windows NT account ID. SNA Server uses the Windows NT account to control gateway usage, but you usually still need to log on to a host computer using a separate password. The rest of the BackOffice components all make use of the Windows NT account for authentication. This is not necessarily a problem and is again a popular feature with users, but it raises the stakes when choosing and managing your Windows NT account password. It is no longer used just to gain access to the network, but also may provide access to database files, e-mail mailboxes, and other shared resources. The user community should be made aware of this potential danger, and a sound password policy should be implemented and enforced.

Assigning Permissions and Rights   Windows NT Server provides two distinct types of permissions. You can control access to a shared device at the time a user attempts to attach over the network, and you can assign permissions directly to some of the objects that are being used such as file systems or e-mail mailboxes. Both of these capabilities can be useful, and you should evaluate when you should use them individually, or perhaps even combined. For example, when you share a directory on an NTFS file system, you can set permissions for the share itself and set permissions directly on the file system. Setting them in both places provides additional security but may be cumbersome to manage. Using both techniques is a little like wearing two seat belts when driving. The only time the second one is needed is when the first one breaks.

Auditing and the Use of Log Files   The use of auditing and security logs is an important part of the defense system offered by Windows NT Server. If you don't log failed logon attempts, you provide a perpetrator an unlimited amount of time to try to access the system. With enough time, a dedicated attacker will find a weak link in almost any system. It is important, therefore, to detect these attempts quickly and act decisively to stop them.

You can enable auditing in two places using Windows NT Server's administrative utilities: the User Manager for Domains and the File Manager. Both of these methods are described in this section.

To activate auditing of specific system events, follow these steps:

1. Start the User Manager for Domains.

2. Choose Policies, Audit from the menu. The Audit Policy dialog box appears (see Figure 46.3).

FIG. 46.3

Use the Audit Policy dialog box to enable auditing of system events. You can specify logging the success or failure of a variety of important actions.

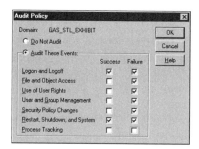

3. Select the option labeled Audit These Events. Then use the check boxes to select the events you want to audit. It is strongly recommended that you audit the failure of Logon and Logoff at a minimum.

4. Click OK to save your changes and close the dialog box.

To enable auditing of specific files and directories, follow these steps:

1. Start the File Manager.

2. Highlight the directory (or file) you want to audit. Choose Security, Auditing from the menu. The Directory Auditing dialog box appears (see Figure 46.4).

FIG. 46.4

This dialog box allows you to enable auditing of specific users' access to directories or files.

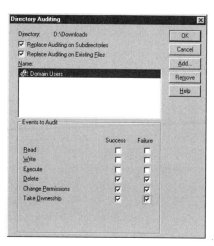

Part

X

Ch

46

3. Click Add. The Add Users and Groups dialog box appears. Select the users whose access you want to audit. If you want to audit all users, select Everyone. Click OK to return to the Directory Auditing dialog box.

4. Check the appropriate boxes in the Events to Audit box.

5. Select the check box to Replace Auditing on Subdirectories if you want these settings to apply to all subdirectories of the current directory. Select Replace Auditing on Existing Files to use these settings on the files in this directory.

6. Click OK to save your changes and close the dialog box.

The individual BackOffice components also contain auditing and logging features.

Controlling the Flow of Information   Many organizations are either attached to the Internet or planning to initiate a connection in the near future. This offers some benefits to the organization, but it also adds some challenges in terms of security. Although the desired outcome of attaching to the Internet is to allow users on your own network to view and retrieve information from servers on the Internet, it also opens the possibility of other users on the Internet viewing and retrieving information from your network. If you implement the security measures available with Windows NT Server and are vigilant in their use, you already have a strong measure of protection against unauthorized access.

In addition to Windows NT Server's security, you can employ other mechanisms that may be warranted. This list summarizes four of the most commonly employed methods and their primary features. You can use these elements individually or together:

- **Screening router.** A router capable of filtering packets based on their source and destination addresses, the type of protocol being used, or other criteria. Only packets that meet the specified criteria are allowed to pass. The rest are discarded.

- **Firewall.** A generic term referring to mechanisms designed to closely regulate the information flowing in and out of an organization's connection to the Internet or other untrusted network. Although this term is used by some to refer to any security mechanism, including screening routers, it is most properly applied to techniques that make use of information available at the upper layers of the Open Systems Interconnection (OSI) reference model, including the application layer. Screening routers operate at the network and transport layers using IP addresses and other lower-level information. Because of the higher quality of information available at the upper layers, a true firewall is potentially more effective and secure. Several commercial firewall products are available including ANS Interlock, Trusted Information Systems (TIS) Gauntlet, and the FireWall-1 Gateway.

- **Proxy servers.** A type of product designed to access the Internet on behalf of client workstations—to act as a *proxy*. These products, some of which are available for Windows NT Server, accept requests for Internet information using the specific protocols designed for Internet services, such as the HyperText Transport Protocol (HTTP). They then pass the request on to the Internet, receive the response, and pass the response to the client. Requests for services using standard file-sharing protocols, such as Server Message Blocks (SMBs), are ignored.

  When used with screening routers, only the packets sent from the proxy server can pass out to the Internet, and only packets addressed to the proxy server can pass back in to the private network. Requests for popular information can sometimes be serviced directly from the proxy server's cache with information recently retrieved for an earlier request.

Proxy server software for Windows NT Server is available from Netscape, Progress Software, and other software companies. Microsoft has announced plans to include proxy server capabilities in a future release of the Internet Information Server.

- **Bastion hosts.** Any system that is a critical component of the organization's network security. You can implement firewall or proxy server software on a bastion host. A bastion host is typically used to act as the only interface between the organization's internal network and an untrusted external network. Because of their role in providing security, they are closely scrutinized, and extensive logging is usually enabled. Like a proxy server, this type of system concentrates access to provide more effective audit capabilities and tighter control. These systems are often implemented on a separate network segment between the organization's private network and the Internet. You also can place a screening router on each side of the bastion host, further protecting access.

Data Security

When you get serious about security, sooner or later you come face to face with the realization that you have to directly secure your information. Either your physical security or your network security will break down, and an attacker will gain access to a server full of your information. Also, most organizations regularly have the need to send a package of information, in electronic form or otherwise, out into the cold cruel world. While en route to its intended recipient, it must fend for itself.

This brings up the topic of data security and very quickly the topic of *encryption*. Although in one sense nearly all security measures are directly or indirectly aimed at protecting data, the focus of this section is on the use of techniques that are applied directly to the data itself for the purpose of security. The history of code making and code breaking is a long one, and the subject is complex. This section provides a glimpse at the possibilities and current state of this rapidly changing field.

The American writer Edgar Allen Poe is credited with a quote frequently repeated in this context: "It may be roundly asserted that human ingenuity cannot concoct a cipher which human ingenuity cannot resolve." Recent breakthroughs in the field of cryptography have offered the tantalizing possibility that, although an "unbreakable code" may not be forthcoming, a code that requires more than a million years of processing time on the fastest known computers to decode may provide suitable security.

N O T E The terms *code* and *decode*, although often used by laymen, have a specific meaning in the field of cryptography. A code is properly a method of disguising a message by substituting an entire word or sentence for another word or sentence based on a code book or other agreed upon method. The use of codes is impractical for general communications because it requires that any word or sentence you want to communicate be included in your code book. The process of applying techniques to arbitrary messages for the purpose of disguising their contents is called *encryption*, and returning the message to its original form is known as *decryption*. ▢

One breakthrough that has had a big impact on the field is the development of *public key systems*. To describe them in very simplified terms, a public key system is based on the development (usually with the aid of sophisticated mathematics) of two related keys. One is kept private; the other made public. These keys have interesting characteristics:

- Possession of the public key does not allow you to calculate the value of the private key.
- A message encrypted with the public key can be decrypted only with the private key and vice versa.

If Suzy wants to send a message to Sam, she can encrypt it with Sam's public key. Only Sam is able to decrypt the message because he is the only one in possession of his private key. Furthermore, Suzy can encrypt a "signature" with her private key, and when Sam receives the message, he can use Suzy's public key to decrypt it. If the "signature" is valid—that is, if decrypting the signature yields some agreed upon value—Suzy must have sent the message because only she has her private key.

To actually implement this concept in the real world requires a number of refinements and supporting techniques. For example, the keys being discussed are generally long sequences of arbitrary characters that are difficult to remember or enter into a computer without error. Some means of managing these keys must be implemented, and yet they must still be kept secure. Also, the algorithms associated with public key systems are generally unsuitable for encrypting large messages or blocks of data due to their relatively slow speeds. Other encryption methods can be employed, and the key to decrypt the message can itself be encrypted with the public key algorithm and transmitted to the recipient.

It is possible to purchase the source code for computer programs that implement many of the encryption algorithms that have been devised. Be aware, however, that implementing your own encryption schemes is a task with many pitfalls. Professionally developed systems take into account many details that are easy to overlook. For example, after your message has been entered into a computer and encrypted for transmission, it is important to completely erase it from any disk systems on your local computer. Often the operating system does not obliterate a file that you've deleted, but simply marks the space as available in the disk's directory. Good encryption systems overwrite the file with Xs or some other suitable value to be sure that they destroy any copies of the unencrypted message.

E-Mail Security

Exchange Server makes use of a public key system and supporting protocols to provide encryption and digital signatures for e-mail users. This capability is provided by Northern Telecom Limited through its Entrust Security Technology, which was licensed by Microsoft. The encryption method employed is known as *CAST*, a block cipher invented by two Canadians that has been shown to be resistant to cryptanalysis. According to the inventors, the name CAST should evoke an image of randomness and refers to the design procedure used for the algorithm, although the four letters in the name also happen to be the initials of the two inventors. At this time there is no known method to break this cipher other than brute force—a task that could take millions of years if a suitable key were chosen.

To use the advanced security features of Exchange Server, you must have a copy of your security file, which has an EPF extension. With this file, and your "remembered password," you (or anyone else with the file and your password) can encrypt and digitally sign your messages. Exchange Server also allows you to store your messages in a personal folder file on your local hard disk or private directory on a server. You can encrypt this file and protect it with an additional password.

▶ **See** "Enabling Advanced Security for Mailboxes," **p. 1080**

A publicly available system that provides encryption and digital signatures, primarily for use with e-mail systems, is known as *PGP—Pretty Good Privacy*. This system is the product of Phil Zimmerman and many collaborators. It has several characteristics that are appealing:

- It is available free of charge on the Internet, or you can purchase in a professionally developed and supported version.

- The source code for the system is publicly available for scrutiny. Cryptographers are justifiably skeptical of systems that rely on the secrecy of their source code for protection. It is just too easy for a dedicated attacker to gain access to the source code. The preferred approach is to build something strong enough that, even with full knowledge of its mechanisms, you cannot break it.

- So far it seems to have held up to dedicated cryptanalytic attacks. As with most systems, it depends on the selection of a suitable key and proper usage.

One of the biggest problems with any public key system is the management and control of public keys. If I want to exchange messages with you, through what mechanism do I originally obtain your public key? How do I know it's from you? Although this isn't too difficult if I know you personally and can arrange a face-to-face meeting, what if we live on opposite sides of the planet? Sometimes it is possible to use a mutually known intermediary, or a trusted corporate entity. This is a difficult problem without any easy answers.

Securing Servers

One of the most important security-related tasks you must perform is to secure your servers. These concentrated repositories of information and processing power are vulnerable to attacks designed to capture data or disrupt operations and destroy information. Windows NT Server provides good support for server security, and if you properly implement it, you can provide reasonable protection for your servers. This section outlines the most important points that you must address.

In terms of basic policies, you should implement dedicated servers in all but the smallest organizations involving only a handful of people. If you have a network involving less than ten people, you may choose to have one of them use the server as a workstation. The natural tendency is to have the most knowledgeable "power user" use the server because it is the most powerful machine. This is the worst possible choice. The power user is likely to use more resources in terms of RAM and processing power, thereby interfering with its use by the rest of the group. The least active user who perhaps runs only a single application at irregular intervals is a much better alternative.

Part
X

Ch
46

If your network is larger than ten people, you should make the investment to deploy dedicated servers. You should lock them up in a secure environment, with access provided to only a small, select group of people. All servers should be plugged into *Uninterruptible Power Supplies* (UPSs) to provide temporary backup power in case of a power outage. Windows NT Server supports the use of UPS devices that send a signal to the server through a serial cable that can cause a message to be broadcast to network users to log off and initiate an orderly shutdown of the server.

Windows NT Server can be made quite secure, but as with all security mechanisms, securing your servers requires care and vigilance. If you are doing everything right, the security you have in place is probably somewhat inconvenient at times. It should not impede the ability of you or the rest of the organization to get the job done, but it may occasionally be somewhat annoying. This is part of the price you pay for protection.

Configuration Details

This section presents some specific steps you should take to make your server more secure. The first step is to implement the NTFS file system. This provides the capability to assign access permissions to the directories and files themselves in addition to the permissions you can apply to the network share. You can format the hard disk with NTFS or convert an existing partition without reformatting during installation. If you have already installed your server software, you can convert your hard disk partitions to NTFS using the CONVERT command.

The default permissions and access rights applied to Windows NT servers provide you with a good start toward a secure server. For example, the capability to log on locally (that is, at the actual console of the server) is limited to the Administrators local group and the various operator groups, as seen in Figure 46.5.

FIG. 46.5

The User Rights Policy dialog box allows you to grant or revoke specific rights to accounts or groups. You can use this facility to customize the default settings granted administrators, operators, and users.

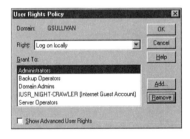

You can modify the list of people allowed to log on locally to server(s) to include or exclude users and groups based on their needs. Many other rights are listed. Most of these, especially the advanced rights, are rarely used.

N O T E If you set the Log On Locally right for the domain with User Manager for Domains, it
controls who can log on to the primary and backup domain controllers. If you set the right
for a single server with User Manager, it applies only to that server.

The need for auditing and the techniques for enabling logging have already been discussed. A
final point regarding logs is to be aware of a technique for breaching security known as *flooding
the log*. Using this technique, perpetrators, aware that their actions are leaving traces in an
event log, perform some unauthorized action. Then, they initiate a series of events designed to
generate massive logging of relatively benign activity such as attempting to gain access to a
resource they are not authorized to use but for which a plausible excuse is available. Depending on the log settings, the actions they initially perform may be overwritten with the less
serious events.

Windows NT provides protection against this technique. You can select log settings that cause
the server to shut down if the log becomes full. Of course, this also is an undesirable outcome,
but it may be the appropriate thing to do if you are trying to catch an elusive attacker. To
change the settings for your security (and other logs), follow these steps:

1. Start the Event Viewer.
2. Choose Log, Log Settings from the menu. The Event Log Settings dialog box appears
   (see Figure 46.6).

FIG. 46.6

Use the Event Log
Settings dialog box to
change the settings for
the three Event Logs—
System, Security, and
Application.

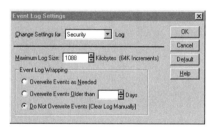

3. Select the log (System, Security, or Application) for which you want to change settings in
   the drop-down list.
4. Select a maximum size for the event log.
5. Select the appropriate option in the Event Log Wrapping box. If security is a chief
   concern, be sure to select Do Not Overwrite Events for the Security log.

N O T E If you indicate that you do not want to overwrite events, Windows NT Server stops when the
log becomes full. It is up to an administrator to regularly archive the log and clear all
events so that this does not happen. The administrator therefore still has the opportunity to review all
logged events, and the flooding technique cannot work. Of course, now the perpetrator has a potential
method to shut down the server, which may be equally serious.

6. Click OK to close the dialog box and register your changes.

Part
X

Ch
46

A useful technique that provides a small additional measure of security is the use of *hidden shares*. When you share a directory on a server, if you add a dollar sign ($) to the end of the sharename, the share does not appear in any browsing applications (such as the File Manager or the Explorer). You should still apply access permissions as though it were a normal share because anyone who has permissions can manually enter the name of the share and connect to it normally. It just prevents people who don't need to know about it from becoming curious and launching an attack to try to gain access.

Finally, an important addition to Windows NT in version 3.5 is the capability to create a custom logon process. This provides logon by the use of an ID card, retinal scan, or other hardware-based system, or to make other specific modifications required by your organization. Being able to modify this first line of defense to best match your requirements is a useful option.

To implement this capability, you must modify a replaceable Dynamic Link Library (DLL), which is called the Graphical Identification and Authentication DLL, also known as GINA. Instructions for performing this modification, and sample code, are provided in the Windows NT Software Development Kit (SDK).

Emergency Repair Disks

Whenever you install a Windows NT operating system, either Server or Workstation, you can create an optional *emergency repair disk* (*ERD*). The ERD contains a copy of the Registry, the hierarchical database that records the configuration settings for the computer. Part of this database is the default account IDs created during installation. As new devices and applications are added and new accounts are defined, the updated Registry can be backed up to tape using the tape backup software provided with Windows NT, or you can use the RDISK utility to up-date the ERD. If a system crash occurs, you then can use the ERD to restore the Registry settings on a repaired or replaced system as part of the recovery process.

▶ **See** "Using the Emergency Repair Disk," **p. 135**

An implication of this recovery mechanism is the capability to use an ERD to gain access to a server. If a perpetrator is given enough time (perhaps less than an hour), an emergency repair disk created on a machine similar to your server, with an entirely different account database, can be restored to your system. After this has been done, the perpetrator can log on using an account and password with administrative privileges for the local machine. He can then use the capability to Take Ownership of files and directories provided on the Security menu in the File Manager, or on the Security tab of the Properties dialog box in the Explorer, to gain access to all the information on the disk subsystems of the computer.

It is important to note that this is not an unplanned back door into the operating system or an accidental error. This is an important safeguard that is required to avoid the potential loss of man-years of effort due to the accidental loss of an administrative password. It does, however, highlight the vital role played by physical security and the potential use of data encryption. You simply cannot allow a server to be stolen, or your information is in grave danger of being com-promised.

Securing Workstations

Workstations are a greater challenge to secure because they cannot be locked up but must be placed throughout the organization on users' desks. Good judgment and balance are critical here to provide reasonable security without frustrating users through unnecessarily heavy-handed approaches. Here are a few points to consider when trying to secure several of Microsoft's desktop operating systems.

Windows NT Workstation

Windows NT Workstation offers mechanisms very similar to those of Windows NT Server. The use of NTFS is still highly recommended. An additional built-in local group called Power Users is created at installation, and this group provides the capability to do most configuration tasks without making a user a full administrator of the local system. If you do not want the user of the workstation to have full administrative control, you have the opportunity to enforce that policy when the workstation joins the domain.

There are two methods to add a workstation to a domain. An administrator can use the Server Manager and add the computer name to the domain in advance. Then the user simply opens the Network icon in the Control Panel, clicks the Change button next to the Domain name, and enters the name of the domain. Because an administrator has already added the workstation to the domain, no further administrative intervention is necessary. An alternative method provides the opportunity to maintain control over the local Administrator's group.

Part
X

Ch
46

Rather than adding the workstation to the domain with Server Manager, you can insist that an administrator physically visit the workstation to complete the operation. This is still done in the Network application of the Control Panel. When the workstation is added to the domain, the person performing the operation must enter a Domain Admin's ID and password. As the machine is added to the domain, the Domain Admins global group is added to the local Administrator's group on the workstation. You then can run the User Manager for the local machine and remove any accounts, including the user's, from the local Administrator's group. The only way to overcome this is to reinstall the operating system, which removes the computer from the domain.

You also can use the User Rights dialog box, in a manner similar to that described earlier in the section "Configuration Details," to determine which accounts can log on locally. In addition, you can remove the rights for all users to Access This Computer From Network. This effectively eliminates the capability to perform peer sharing of resources. For example, the user of a computer with this capability removed cannot share disk directories or printers.

Windows 95

The capability to apply security to the local workstation falls off rather sharply when you select Windows 95 rather than Windows NT Workstation. Although Windows 95 offers many compelling features and is particularly suited to use on laptops because of its strong support for power management, PCMCIA cards, and Plug and Play configuration, its lack of security for the local disk subsystem makes it less attractive.

You can take some positive steps to improve the security offered on Windows 95, however. Tools provided in the Windows 95 resource kit allow you to configure and enforce user profiles that are relatively secure. By specifying that each user of the system use their own profile, you can create an administrative profile that has full rights and a default profile with very few rights. You then provide this profile to any new user that accesses the machine and creates a new profile, something that essentially anyone with physical access can do. You also can create a profile with rights that fall somewhere in the middle, but the default profile must be very strict because it is so easy to access.

This capability is far short of the security features provided on a Windows NT Workstation with NTFS and the rich set of access rights that can be assigned by placing a user in a predefined group or using the User Rights dialog box. Windows 95 does provide a useful level of control, however, and can keep average users from performing unauthorized actions.

From Here...

In this chapter, you learned the basic issues that a security policy must address. You explored various approaches to implementing security and reviewed the potential risks and areas in which your organization may be vulnerable. You also learned specific techniques for improving the security of your servers and your workstations.

For related information, refer to the following chapters:

- For information on the Web server component of BackOffice, Internet Information Server, see Chapter 18, "Building a Web with Internet Information Server (IIS)."

- For information on the e-mail and groupware component of BackOffice, Exchange Server, see Chapter 26, "An Inside Look at Exchange Server."

- For information on the database component of BackOffice, SQL Server, see Chapter 33, "An Inside Look at SQL Server."

- For information on the systems management component of BackOffice, Systems Management Server (SMS), see Chapter 42, "Preparing for SMS."

- For information on creating and using an administrator's "master console," see Chapter 48, "Proactive Network Administration."

CHAPTER 47

Building BackOffice Applications

by Greg Sullivan

The primary purpose of this book is to aid you in your BackOffice implementation. To this end, the majority of the book focuses on "how to" install and administer the BackOffice products.

The primary purpose of this chapter is to aid information systems managers and administrators in understanding what BackOffice means to application development and deployment. Although it is beyond the scope of this book to provide an in-depth look at this topic, it is meaningful to examine some application scenarios. This serves to highlight some of the important aspects of BackOffice with respect to application implementation.

The best way to understand how BackOffice provides a foundation for application implementation is to look at it from the view of application development management and application developers. In this chapter, you see what BackOffice means to developers as they make their decisions about how to build applications. ■

Issues facing today's application developers

Look inside the decisions confronting application developers as they decide how to use BackOffice to build applications.

BackOffice as a platform for application development

Discover why BackOffice is a stable foundation upon which mission-critical applications can be built and deployed, regardless of how the applications are designed.

How BackOffice meets user demand for features and functionality

Learn how you can incorporate BackOffice services into applications you develop.

How BackOffice addresses the technical aspects of developing distributed applications

Relate the common technical problems of today to the world of BackOffice.

How BackOffice products work together to provide advanced functionality

See how BackOffice products work together as a unit to support application development.

Application Development Decisions

Application developers today face a multitude of decisions before they can begin to build applications. In some instances, the technologies and tools used to build applications are specified as a part of the up-front application requirements. In these cases, the technology often drives the need for the solution.

In most cases, however, the conceived application is defined as a result of some business, engineering, or scientific need. Since most applications built today are business applications, the discussion here is focused accordingly. Similar arguments apply to engineering and scientific applications and therefore can be applied to non-business application development, as well.

There are three primary areas of attention at the beginning of each application development cycle:

- Production platform
- Application architecture
- Development tool set

Each of these important aspects of application development is discussed in the following sections.

Production Platform Decisions

The first decision to be made about each application is which platform the application will operate on once it is in production. A subdecision of this is which platform will it be developed and tested on. In most cases it is appropriate to develop and test an application on the same platform it is expected to operate on.

The components of a production platform, in this sense, include the type of network, network hardware, network operating system, server computers, server operating systems, client workstations, and client workstation operating systems. Collectively, these items make up the *production platform*.

Most organizations make production platform decisions separate from individual application platform decisions. Consequently, the production platform is normally specified prior to the commencement of application development. Moreover, it is usually only the operating systems of the network, server, and client workstations that concern application developers. This is because the operating systems appear the same to application developers regardless of the hardware upon which they operate.

Most networks today are based on Ethernet, token ring, or asynchronous transfer mode (ATM) technology. Windows NT Server, as a network operating system, supports each of these network types and many others, as well. Again, however, this is normally of little concern to application developers.

N O T E Production platforms are usually given as an application requirement. BackOffice is one of the most popular production platforms today and has proven itself as an effective development platform, as well. ▪

Windows NT Server, in addition to being a popular network operating system, is also an excellent server operating system. A strength of Windows NT Server as a server operating system is its capability to integrate with other server operating systems such as UNIX.

Application Architecture Decisions

A topic more important to application developers is the architecture of the application. In this sense, application architecture refers to the process model upon which the application is developed. As you saw in Chapter 1, "An Inside Look at BackOffice," there are many process models available with which to build applications.

The most popular process models today are the client-server process model and the I-net process model. In addition to being sound technically, these are, and will continue to be, the predominant process models due to their support from industry vendors and the availability of products such as BackOffice which rely so heavily upon them.

▶ **See** "Understanding Process Models," **p. 23**

One of the beauties of BackOffice is that as an aid to application development, it fully supports both the client-server process model and the I-net process model. This fact about BackOffice makes it a solid foundation upon which to build applications.

Client-Server Process Model   As the client-server process model has increased in popularity and become accepted as a platform upon which mission-critical applications can be deployed, many organizations have begun the transition from host-based process models. Decisions are made to gradually replace, or quickly displace, host-based applications with solutions based on the client-server process model. In other situations, solutions to new problems are based solely on the client-server process model.

▶ **See** "Client-Server Process Model," **p. 24**

The basic premise of client-server as a process model is sound—by accommodating the separation of data, business rules, and user presentation, the client-server process model allows and encourages the effective distribution of processes across the computing enterprise. As such, the client-server process model effectively utilizes the collective processing power of the entire enterprise and, therefore, provides a solid basis for mission-critical applications.

N O T E One of the most common problems in information systems today is that tools, technology, and knowledge are just now catching up to the issues being addressed with the client-server process model. BackOffice is an example of a product that enables the effective use of client-server as a process model for mission-critical application development and deployment. ▪

There are many positive reasons to consider the client-server process model, including the following:

Part

X

Ch

47

■ By definition, the client-server process model takes into account the combined processing power of the enterprise.

■ Client-server is established and widely accepted with many prior experiences to draw upon.

■ Design and development tools for the client-server process model are plentiful, mature, and stable with support from a variety of major vendors.

■ There exists a vast supply of software engineers skilled in application development based on the client-server process model.

■ Numerous application development methodologies have already withstood the test of time.

■ The client-server process model works well within the framework of modern software development techniques, such as object-oriented software engineering.

A few disadvantages of the client-server process model as an application architecture include the following:

■ **Development timelines are often lengthy and laced with hidden delays.** There are many reasons this occurs. In the early years of development based on the client-server process model, this was attributed to the learning curves of the development team. As developers became more experienced, it remained common for development teams to apply obsolete development methodologies to new technologies, such as the client-server process model. This combination often proves dangerous as expectations are inconsistently defined and met. A good example of this is the need for extensive performance-tuning phases in development efforts based on the client-server process model. Performance-tuning is either missing or trivial in many older development methodologies, but extremely important today.

■ **In spite of the purported openness of the client-server process model, platform conversion costs are usually forbidding.** A good example of this is relational database management system (RDBMS). As the client-server process model is open, it stands to reason that converting an application from one RDBMS vendor's product to an RDBMS from another vendor should require little effort. Typically, this is not the case as various vendors exploit aspects of the client-server process model in very different manners. Taking advantage of only the most basic features of an RDBMS makes conversions more reasonable. However, it is rarely the case that vendor-specific features are not utilized.

These issues with development based on the client-server process model have been widely publicized over recent years. Due to the maturity of the client-server process model, these issues are not as dramatic today as they once were.

I-Net Process Model   The I-net process model is still considered, by many, to be leading edge technology. Consequently, it is frequently ignored as an alternative for application architecture. In the history of information technology, it is common for new technologies to exist many years before industries accept them. In fact, the client-server process model so widely used today existed nearly five years before it became a dominant force.

▶ **See** "I-Net Process Model," **p. 25**

The same cannot be said for Internet technologies, however. A consequence of the rush to gain an advantage in the Internet marketplace is that software product cycles (i.e., the time between major version releases) has shortened from one or two years to six months. The major tool vendors have committed their entire organizations to the Internet and its associated business opportunities. A good example of this is the recent publicity Bill Gates has received regarding the "retooling" of the entire Microsoft company to take advantage of opportunities relating to the Internet.

Because so many industry vendors, such as Microsoft, are racing to quickly take advantage of Internet-related business opportunities, there are new tools introduced every week and existing tools are undergoing significant upgrades each month. This is great news for application developers. The downside is that it is now as difficult as ever to stay abreast of ongoing developments. The cost of not staying current can be rather dramatic in a competitive business environment.

Among the many reasons to consider the I-net process model for your application architecture are the following:

■ Applications based on the I-net process model can be built and deployed upon network computers (NCs) as well as personal computers (PCs) for client workstations, with little or no additional effort required to support both types of client workstations. This results in lower overall implementation and support costs.

■ There is much appeal to an association with the Internet which can be an advantage for your customers and even for your development team.

■ The industry momentum is tremendous in that every major vendor has focused almost entirely on the Internet and its related technologies.

■ By taking advantage of the communications capability of the Internet, the I-net process model eliminates most of the communications problems which have long plagued software developers and users.

■ Since all applications based on the I-net process model are accessed by users via Internet browsers there is no need to distribute software to each client PC. This results in significantly reduced implementation costs and ongoing support costs because new software need not be distributed to each user for every application upgrade.

Most of the disadvantages of the I-net process model will be addressed by industry vendors, and the industry in general, over the next few months. Nevertheless, they are listed here as important considerations:

■ Just as in the early days of development with the client-server process model, development costs tend to be higher and expectations are frequently unmet due to the initial learning curve.

Part
X

Ch
47

- Since the predominant Internet technologies for building applications such as Java and Active Server are recent developments, there exists a shortage of software components in the marketplace.

- Development tools centered around Internet technologies are recent and have been rushed to market. It may be several months before they reach a level of maturity acceptable to serious application developers.

- Internet security standards, and other important standards, are only recently being established and are frequently misunderstood.

Choosing a Process Model Today   As with most other difficult development decisions, there is no clear-cut method for determining the most effective application architecture for your application. Given the momentum in the industry and the major vendor commitment to Internet technologies, it seems clear that at some point in the future nearly all application development will be based on the I-net process model.

Even though the I-net process model as an application architecture is gaining momentum and growing in popularity, it remains difficult to make this decision since the development tools to support this application architecture are less mature than client-server development tools. Since the I-net tools lack the maturity of client-server tools, it is common for development costs to be higher and for unknown circumstances to occur. This fear often leads decision makers to fall back on known solutions.

The risk in sticking with client-server tools is that during the development cycle the I-net tools will surpass existing tools in capability and popularity. This seems quite possible given the vendor commitment to Internet technologies. Fortunately, there exists a bit of a middle ground for those unwilling to bear the cost of I-net learning curves today.

Today's applications can usually be broken down into two distinct pieces. One piece is for the ongoing processing of the data which feeds the application. This is commonly referred to as either the transaction processing component of the system or the production system. Second, each application has a reporting element which provides prepackaged reports and the capability to query the data in flexible ways.

▶ **See** "Online Transaction Processing and Online Analytical Processing," **p. 1126**

The middle ground today is to develop the production system using the client-server process model and develop the reporting system (i.e., information distribution) using the I-net process model. In this manner it is possible to gain the benefit of tool maturity in the most critical component of the application—the production system. On the other hand, you can safely distribute information to users through a reporting system built with newer tools designed for the I-net process model.

▶ **See** "The Interactive, Dynamic Web Site," **p. 728**

▶ **See** "Data Warehousing Fundamentals," **p. 1270**

This is not to say that it is wrong to stick entirely with the client-server process model or jump completely into the I-net process model. This middle ground provides the benefit of stability to the core of a system and yet allows development teams to move towards anticipated technologies without putting delivery deadlines at risk.

The chart shown in Table 47.1 highlights the balance between these two process models as application architectures in today's environment. Over time the influencing factors will shift toward the I-net process model simply because of the vendor commitment and the resulting business opportunities.

Table 47.1   Application Architecture Comparison Chart

Influencing Factor	Client-Server	I-Net
Industry acceptance	✓	
Industry momentum		✓
Product maturity	✓	
Development cost	✓	
Maintenance cost		✓
Communications		✓
Software distribution		✓
Vendor support	✓	✓

Development Tool Set Decisions

Once the production platform and application architecture are determined, application developers spend considerable time contemplating which development tools to use for building the application. Most of the popular development tools support BackOffice as an application development environment since BackOffice is one of the most popular production platforms. Nevertheless, there are many important considerations to take into account when selecting development tools, including the following:

■ **Tool maturity.** It is sometimes ironic to speak of tool maturity given the rate of change of technology today. Nevertheless, maturity is an important characteristic of most popular development tools since with maturity comes stability. A stable development tool results in fewer problems during critical elements of the development cycle.

■ **Features and functions.** What are the tool's capabilities and limitations? Not only is it important to look at the current features of a development tool, but also the feature history of the tool. A track record of constant and frequent improvement of the tool is a good indication of the vendor's future commitment to that tool. It is common to select a tool knowing that some future enhancement to the tool will be necessary for your development effort.

■ **Cost of the tool.** Clearly, you must give consideration to the cost of the tool. Pay careful attention to the licensing method employed by the tool vendor. Are there site licenses available, per-seat licenses, run-time licenses, and so on? You also must determine what other tools may be necessary and the costs associated with these additional tools.

■ **Cost of development.** One of the most often discussed aspects of development tool selection is the cost of development. The most powerful tools are typically the most difficult to learn and master. The easiest tools to learn lack the power and flexibility to build efficient and long-living applications. Consequently, there is a tradeoff of development time versus tool capability. It is difficult to make a decision on the front end of a large development effort that will drive up development costs even though the anticipated outcome will be more desirable. This is true because the most significant aspect of the increased cost associated with more sophisticated tools is the time it takes to complete development. In today's business environments, time is the most valuable commodity.

■ **Cost of maintenance.** Similar considerations should be given to the cost of maintenance. This cost is frequently overlooked when selecting development tools even though application maintenance costs normally exceed development costs in the life of a system. As in tool maturity, it is important to test the tool vendor's track record in providing timely and seamless upgrades. Tool upgrades are too often ignored once an application goes into production. This sometimes leads to the untimely termination of an application's existence since support for obsolete tools is difficult to find.

■ **Tool expertise.** Another of the most important considerations is the availability of resources to use the tool. Does your organization possess knowledge and experience with a given tool, or is your organization willing to invest in the training necessary to learn new tools and technologies? A common mistake is to invest in tool training for a tool such as Microsoft Visual C++ without first investing in education in the underlying technology, object-oriented software engineering. Another approach is to "rent" the expertise from contract services firms, a rapidly growing industry. Whether you plan to use internal or external resources for a development effort, it is absolutely critical that abundant human resources are available with knowledge and experience in the tools selected.

■ **Compatibility.** Most development environments today require multiple tools. These tools must all work well together in a convenient manner. It is also important to select tools that work well in the planned development environment, which may indeed be the same as the planned production environment. If not, code transition tools are also a necessity.

■ **Support.** Regardless of the maturity of a tool, there will come a time when support is needed. A thorough understanding of the vendor support and escalation program should be a significant factor in tool selection. It is also helpful to examine the vendor commitment to the tool and make a reasonable assumption about its expected life.

■ **Third-party software components.** The primary job of today's application developers is to assemble individual software components, using development tools, into information system solutions. These software components are developed internally or purchased, or both. Development tools with the most third-party software components available to the general public are usually the most successful tools.

The individual weight these aspects of development tool decisions carry in your environment will vary depending on your situation. It is important to give some weight to each of these areas, as development tools are as important a part of application development as the production platform and the application architecture.

Technical Underpinnings

BackOffice as an application development environment is based on numerous technologies. The manner in which these technologies are applied within and to BackOffice form the technical underpinnings of BackOffice. In order to effectively develop applications using BackOffice, it is necessary to understand these technical underpinnings. This is true whether the application platform, architecture, and development decisions are set prior to development or are determined as a part of building the application. After exploring the underlying technical aspects of application implementation, you will see how BackOffice supports modern-day application development.

Business conditions dictate a majority of the problems these tools and technologies must address. To understand the best way to apply them to the problems, it is necessary to gain some insight into the underlying technical issues. Some of the issues that currently receive the most attention include the following:

- Modern process models
- Remote access
- Internet
- Electronic messaging
- Relational database management systems
- Distributed data
- Host connectivity

These issues comprise a short list of technical characteristics of modern-day applications. This list is not comprehensive. However, it does represent some of the most common issues associated with current application development.

Throughout this book, you have seen how BackOffice is based on these aspects of technology and how it addresses these needs. To better understand how BackOffice supports these concepts in application development, it is meaningful to examine each of these issues at a high level from a developer's perspective.

Part
X

Ch
47

Modern Process Models

Most new applications being developed today are based on the client-server process model. This includes products such as BackOffice, commercial off-the-shelf software, and applications developed by organizations for internal use. Consequently, the client-server process model becomes one of the leading characteristics of today's information systems.

In some ways, this makes it a self-fulfilling characteristic because many decision makers now state as an important requirement that the application be based on the client-server process model. The reasons for its acceptance include the following:

- The client-server process model is truly a solid foundation upon which mission-critical applications can be built, even though it is just a step along the way to fully distributed computing.

- Investments in host-based solutions are reduced each year. These dollars are instead placed into platforms for solutions based on the client-server process model.

- The client-server process model holds the promise of leveraging the investment in computers, because it is designed to effectively utilize all the processors in the enterprise.

- It is more inconvenient to obtain educational services or expert advice on anything other than the client-server process model.

- Industry vendors are investing heavily in products and tools based on the client-server process model. Because these vendors rely on the client-server process model, it becomes a characteristic of computing environments by the nature of the tools employed.

A result of all this is that client-server becomes the process model of choice for most systems being developed today. Some aspect of your information systems will soon, if not already, be based on the client-server process model.

As you have seen in the earlier discussion about application architecture in this chapter, the I-net process model is gaining momentum. Some speculate it may eventually replace the client-server process model altogether. This seems reasonable given the significant shortcomings of the client-server process model that the I-net process model addresses. Furthermore, the I-net process model does so without sacrificing the backbone of client-server systems—the database.

There are many reasons why the I-net process model may overtake the client-server process model in popularity:

- The I-net process model is truly a solid foundation upon which mission-critical applications can be built since it combines the best of the important Internet technologies and the database capabilities of client-server systems.

- Maintenance costs for client-server applications are high due to the cost of managing distributed software. I-net applications eliminate the cost of software distribution since the application is built to run on an intranet or Internet server and users access it from their workstations with only a browser.

- Communication costs are significantly reduced in application development and operation since your intranet or the Internet handles all application communications. Removing this burden from application developers will lead to major cost savings and more stable systems.

■ I-net application deployment presents an opportunity to reduce client workstation costs because you can use NCs in place of PCs. Since NCs cost less than PCs, this may result in significant cost savings if an organization elects to replace PCs with NCs over time.

■ The major vendors in the industry, including Microsoft, are almost entirely focused on the Internet and its related technologies. Consequently, it is likely that future products, education, and expertise will be most available on technologies related to the Internet.

Clearly, Internet technologies influence the path of application developers today as they endeavor to build information systems for any organization. Whether you believe the I-net process model has a future in application development, it is critical you pay attention to its developments and how it is being used in other organizations within your industry and throughout the world.

Remote Access

Computer users often desire to access data from remote locations. There are several reasons why this need exists. One reason is to accommodate those who normally work away from the central office, including remote employees, such as field salespeople.

Another need for remote access to data exists for those who normally work at a single location that is not near the main office. This is true for satellite offices, people who work at home (sometimes referred to as *telecommuters*), or those temporarily assigned to an off-site location.

In all these situations, computer users require remote access to the organization's applications and data. Therefore, remote access becomes an important characteristic for application development.

Internet

With respect to application development, the Internet should be viewed as a worldwide network. On this network you have the capability to do the following:

■ Communicate with everyone else on the Internet

■ Publish information publicly to anyone on the Internet interested in viewing it

These two important aspects of the Internet reflect characteristics to be considered when developing an application.

▶ See "Business Value of the Internet," **p. 503**

The greatest concern regarding the use of the Internet for business transactions is security. Government, industry, and the worldwide academic community continue to work toward resolving security issues to the satisfaction of all. Although it is difficult to imagine that a perfect security scenario will ever exist, it is likely that an effective and durable security system will soon prevail.

As soon as the security concerns are quelled, opportunities to incorporate the Internet into application functionality will rapidly multiply. A wide variety of tools to support this type of development already exist, such as Microsoft's Point-to-Point Tunneling Protocol (PPTP)—its new networking technology that enables remote users to access corporate networks in a

Part
X

Ch

47

secure manner. Regardless, the Internet receives much attention and should be considered an important characteristic of modern-day application development.

▶ **See** "Internet Security Concerns," **p. 760**

Electronic Messaging

One of the most popular new forms of communication is electronic messaging. Usually, this capability is delivered in the form of electronic mail (e-mail). E-mail permits computer users to exchange information at their convenience. It also allows computer users to attach information objects (word processing documents, electronic spreadsheets, and so on) to their message. This provides a convenient means for sending or receiving information.

Organizations that rely on electronic communications are said to have an *e-mail culture*. This is an important attribute of many successful companies today; many companies that have achieved rapid growth rates in short time periods credit electronic messaging as one of the reasons for their success.

As e-mail has become more and more popular, organizations have begun to use electronic messaging as one of the primary forms of communication. For this reason, electronic messaging is considered one of the characteristics of modern-day application development. With each new application, you should give consideration to how the application will integrate with the organization's electronic messaging system. This is especially true now given the many other forms of collaboration available, such as video conferencing.

Relational Database Management Systems

Relational database management systems (RDBMSs) represent the most popular usage of the client-server process models. RDBMS products combine the client-server process model with relational database concepts. This combination, along with many other powerful data management and manipulation features, creates the cornerstone for the majority of application development today. Because RDBMS products are frequently applied to new information systems solutions, they represent, by definition, an important characteristic of application development.

▶ **See** "What Is a Relational Database Management System?," **p. 1110**

It is important to note that RDBMS products are equally as important in applications developed on the I-net process model, as those developed on the client-server process model. Since the major difference between the I-net process model and the client-server process model is on the user interface side of the application, database issues remain the same. It cannot be overemphasized how important it is to give the database similar considerations regardless of which of these two process models you use.

Distributed Data

Many remote users need to store data at their locations. Some of this data exists only at the remote location. In this situation, the remote data is the private data of the remote user and does not need to be copied to a central location.

More likely, however, is that data from the remote user needs to be copied to a central location. It is also likely that data generated in a central location must be copied to one or more remote locations. Yet another scenario exists for remote users in which data is generated in both the remote locations and a central location. The act of combining this data appropriately is challenging.

Two primary issues are associated with distributed data:

- **Replication.** In some situations, the same data must exist in multiple locations. When this need arises, it is important to define one of the locations as the place for data origination because this reduces the opportunity for data-entry error due to double entry. The location of data origination can be assigned the responsibility of notifying other locations of a change to the data. This notification and copying the data to other locations is referred to as *data replication*. Data replication is an important characteristic of modern-day application development that must be carefully planned and executed.

- **Synchronization.** Determining when and how to replicate data is only part of the problem. Another difficult aspect of managing distributed data is resolving conflicts. In a distributed data scenario, it is possible for two locations to change the same element of data during the same time frame. When the database manager then attempts to replicate the data to the other location, each location may lay claim to ownership of the data. However, only one change can be honored. The solution to this problem lies in how changes to the data are *synchronized*. Data synchronization is also a characteristic of applications in today's computing environment.

Of course, there are other problems associated with distributing data across multiple locations, and other scenarios exist in which distributing data is a requirement. For more information on managing distributed data in a BackOffice environment, see Chapter 38, "An Inside Look at Distributed Transaction Coordinator (DTC) and Microsoft Transaction Server (MTS)."

N O T E Data distribution issues are the same regardless of whether the client-server process model or the I-net process model is used to develop an application. ■

Part

X

Ch

47

Host Connectivity

In spite of the proliferation of solutions based on the client-server and I-net process models, many applications built upon the host-based processing model remain in existence. These types of applications are sometimes referred to as *mainframe systems*, or *legacy systems*.

Legacy systems continue to dominate the information systems landscape because so many organizations rely on them for supporting existing business processes. Over time, these systems are being systematically replaced by solutions based on newer process models. In the meantime, however, a characteristic of application development today is the reliance on host-based data. Also, coexistence with legacy systems is an important concern, especially during migratory or transition periods.

Systems built upon newer process models often are dependent on data originating from a host-based application. Data travels between host-based applications and applications built using the client-server process model or I-net process model in two ways:

- **Batch.** Data that flows in this manner between these two application platforms is transmitted in bulk quantity at regularly scheduled intervals. Typically, batch transmissions amount to downloading a file from the host computer (or uploading a file to the host computer) and processing the file on the destination computer. As the data is processed, it is placed into the target database. This type of data exchange requires an occasional connection between the host computer and a server computer.

- **Real-time.** Data that flows in this manner between these two application platforms is transmitted as the applications operate. As soon as data changes in one system, it triggers a change in the other. This type of data flow requires a continuous connection between the host computer and a server computer. The applications must include processes that constantly await the arrival of new data and processes that send data as necessary. Because the flow of data in this situation is on-demand, the interface is referred to as real-time.

To accommodate either type of data flow, it is necessary to be able to connect server computers that store data with host computers. For this reason, host connectivity becomes an important characteristic of modern-day application development.

Programmatic Interfaces

Now that you have been introduced to some of the most common issues facing information systems professionals today, let's look at how BackOffice supports them. The first part of the solution is the BackOffice application services. Each BackOffice product is built upon design strategies based on these concepts. Administrators access these services through administration tools and client interfaces.

The second way BackOffice incorporates these technologies into applications is via programmatic interfaces. Such interfaces, normally referred to as *application programming interfaces* (*APIs*), are simply a means by which an application developer can access the same services available to users and administrators. Often, the available APIs provide access to additional functionality.

As developers work on applications, they frequently encounter situations in which their application requires the services of another application. If the other application provides a programmatic interface such as an API, the developer can "invoke" the service from within his or her application's source code. Although other types of programmatic interfaces are available, this is the most popular method and is fully supported by Microsoft as a part of BackOffice.

The programmatic interfaces needed to develop applications in a BackOffice environment are normally built by Microsoft along with the BackOffice product. However, the API is not normally provided in the product package. Instead, the APIs are bundled in developer tool kits and assorted technical CDs available from Microsoft.

N O T E The APIs important to BackOffice application developers are delivered as extensions to Microsoft's Windows programming interface, Win32. This API is a 32-bit programming interface for developing applications on Windows 95 or Windows NT. As such, it is the broadest API available from Microsoft and is used to develop each of the actual BackOffice products. ■

To understand how developers interact with BackOffice services, you need to be familiar with the available programmatic interfaces. Microsoft provides the following interfaces for BackOffice application developers:

- Win32 API (Win32)
- Internet Server API (ISAPI)
- Messaging API (MAPI)
- Open Database Connectivity API (ODBC)
- System Network Architecture API (SNAPI)

Other programmatic interfaces are available from Microsoft and third-party providers for more specific services. Examples include Microsoft's Telephony API (TAPI) and their recently introduced Speech API (SAPI). You should stay abreast of API availability from Microsoft and other vendors because this is one of the most important ways to take advantage of server application services to improve the functionality of applications developed by your organization.

Figure 47.1 shows how some of the available APIs line up with the individual BackOffice products. Each BackOffice product has at least one programmatic interface, as shown in this figure. Not shown is a programmatic interface for SMS. Although a limited interface is available, it is not yet widely used in application development and, therefore, not covered here.

FIG. 47.1
Each BackOffice product is supported by an underlying programmatic interface.

BackOffice Product	Supporting API
Windows NT Server	Win32
Internet Information Server	ISAPI
Exchange Server	MAPI
SQL Server	ODBC
SNA Server	SNAPI

A brief description of each API follows.

Win32

The largest of all programmatic interfaces available with BackOffice is Win32 and is delivered as a set of dynamic link libraries (DLLs). This API supports the base operating system, Windows NT. It also supports Windows 95. In fact, one of the advantages of building applications using Win32 is that the same interface exists for server applications and client applications because it is available for both operating systems.

Win32 contains several categories of programming interfaces. At the root of Win32 is the windows management capabilities of the base operating system. This includes all the windows control and user interface functions. Win32 is available in C and C++ versions. However, it is far more convenient to use component libraries based on Win32, such as Microsoft Foundation Classes, which is delivered with Visual C++ instead of Win32 itself.

ISAPI

The acceptance of the Internet has led to the need to develop applications that provide services to Internet users. These types of applications are referred to as Internet Server Applications (ISAs). Most ISAs today are built using the Common Gateway Interface (CGI). CGI is an interface for running programs on a World Wide Web (Web) server that are external to the Web server.

The demand for external applications arises out of the need to respond to user actions and choices. As Internet users view information presented to them by a Web site, it is possible the next information presented should be different depending on the choices made by the user or the path taken. In this way, it is desirable to create what is known as a *dynamic Web page*. Chapter 18, "Building a Web with Internet Information Server (IIS)," describes in detail how to use BackOffice to create your own Web.

Dynamic Web pages today are created by execution of a CGI application. This application prepares the subsequent content for the viewer based on the information received from the user. Using CGI applications, however, is a crude way in which to invoke external applications. They typically have to be loaded into memory each time they are invoked and are prone to performance difficulties.

▶ **See** "Using CGI," **p. 572**

The Internet Server API (ISAPI) offers an alternative way to develop CGI applications. Instead of developing stand-alone executables using the CGI approach, an application developer can now build an external application for execution by a Web server using ISAPI. ISAPI allows the applications to be developed in C or C++ and prepares the application as a DLL. Because DLLs have more flexibility in the way they load, they offer many advantages over the CGI approach.

MAPI

The Windows Messaging API (MAPI) is actually a subset of the Win32 API. Given its significance in a BackOffice environment, it deserves special mention. MAPI is available in C, C++, and Visual Basic versions.

MAPI allows application developers to incorporate messaging services directly into applications. It is possible, from within an application, to automatically generate e-mail messages and send them to appropriate addresses. It can be of great convenience to users to have their applications automatically create and send messages with information from the application. A good example of this is an application that alerts a user with an e-mail message or a call to a pager upon the recognition of some undesirable condition. You also can use MAPI to receive messages and manage e-mail.

ODBC

Open database connectivity (ODBC) is the specification prepared by Microsoft that dictates technically how databases will be exposed to applications through a common interface. Microsoft has published ODBC-conformance levels to the industry with the hope that widespread support will result in a consistent interface between applications and databases. It is safe to say that ODBC has been widely accepted, as well as frequently criticized (primarily for performance problems).

The basic premise of ODBC is simple: to provide a consistent manner in which to access data in databases that support ODBC. Because most of the popular database vendors provide ODBC support (in addition to their own access methods), it is important to know what ODBC provides. It allows application developers to access databases using common SQL commands. The major categories of ODBC functions include the following:

- Connecting to a data source
- Obtaining information about the ODBC driver and a data source
- Setting retrieval options
- Preparing SQL requests
- Submitting SQL requests
- Retrieving results and information about the results
- Obtaining information about the data source's system tables
- Terminating a statement or a connection

Applications that support ODBC are assured of having a common interface to a variety of data sources, including databases managed by database management products from other vendors. This is an important characteristic of any application developed in today's information systems.

Part X

Ch 47

SNAPI

The SNA Server component of BackOffice provides connectivity to IBM mainframes and minicomputers. This is an important capability for organizations that maintain large computers in the midst of PC networks. Computer users on these networks also may need access to host-based applications or data.

It is also nice to be able to gain access to host information from within applications developed in the BackOffice environment. To this end, Microsoft provides a System Network Architecture API (SNAPI). With SNAPI, applications can access host information in a variety of ways. Included in SNAPI are interfaces for the following:

- Advanced Program-to-Program Communications (APPC)
- Common Programming Interface for Communications (CPI-C)
- Logical Unit Application (LUA)
- Common Service Verb (CSV)
- High Level Language API (HLLAPI)

All these APIs are included with SNA Server with the exception of EHLLAPI, which is available from third-party vendors.

Business Issues

The aforementioned technologies and programmatic interfaces represent today's most topical aspects of application implementation and development. Again, it is important to understand these technologies and APIs before learning how to build and implement solutions in a BackOffice environment.

Now that you have been adequately introduced to the technical issues, it is time to learn how typical applications rely on them. To demonstrate how these technologies can be incorporated into applications, it is helpful to see how they apply to common business problems. Most applications developed today possess one or more of the following business characteristics:

- Geographically separate locations
- Mainframe transaction systems
- Management reporting
- Remote employees
- Remote customers
- Information publishing

For each of these business characteristics, you will see in the sections to follow which technologies are appropriate to apply toward their resolution. Following each explanation, you learn how BackOffice addresses the application characteristics with the respective technologies and supporting programmatic interfaces.

Geographically Separate Locations

Many organizations maintain offices for personnel in multiple locations. These locations may be within the same city, or they may be spread around the world. Regardless of the distance between the offices, it is often necessary to connect the offices for purposes of transmitting data.

Computers connected within the same physical location are usually connected to the *local area network* (*LAN*). In a LAN, all computers are connected to the same physical cabling system. As the distance between computers grows, it is necessary to use other means (for example, long-distance carriers, microwave, or satellites) to attach computers to the network. The concept of connecting computers to the same network over vast distances is known as *wide area networking* (*WAN*).

Regardless of the number of geographically separate locations your organization has, it likely has one location that is considered the central location, or headquarters. At this location, the WAN is administered, and the majority of network services are provided.

From a technology perspective, BackOffice accommodates this type of networking scenario for three reasons (see Figure 47.2):

■ It is based on the client-server process model.

■ It supports the effective use of the I-net process model.

■ It has the capability to manage distributed data.

FIG. 47.2
The client-server and I-net process models and distributed data capabilities are the BackOffice technical underpinnings that allow it to support geographically separate locations.

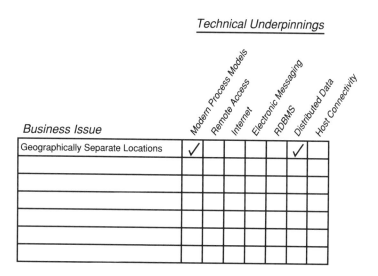

Business Issue	Modern Process Models	Remote Access	Internet	Electronic Messaging	RDBMS	Distributed Data	Host Connectivity
Geographically Separate Locations	✓					✓	

From a developer's point of view, support for geographically separate locations is accommodated through the Win32 and ODBC APIs (see Figure 47.3). With Win32, a developer can build applications that operate on a LAN or WAN, or over a remote connection to the network. Applications can be developed to achieve optimal performance depending on the connection type. ODBC database access is transparent regardless of the user location or connection type.

Part
X

Ch
47

FIG. 47.3
Win32 and ODBC are among the most important APIs needed to support geographically separate locations.

Programmatic Interfaces

Business Issue	Win32	ISAPI	MAPI	ODBC	SNAPI
Geographically Separate Locations	✓			✓	

It should be noted, however, that BackOffice supports geographically separate locations in other ways, as well. In those situations where performance suffers due to the availability of bandwidth, it is appropriate to contemplate supporting remote users with a message-based approach. As such, MAPI may also be an important interface to consider when supporting multiple, remote locations. The message-based approach offers other advantages in that it is more resilient when links are frequently dropped and more flexible when access is available only at certain times.

Several BackOffice products are necessary to fully support geographically separate locations (see Figure 47.4). At a minimum, Windows NT Server is needed to play the role of the network operating system. The remote access service of Windows NT Server also can be used to connect remote users (whether they are internal users, such as remote employees, or external users, such as customers) to the network. Although this is not the only means available to support geographically separate locations, it provides a convenient means for doing so because it is included with Windows NT Server and is easy to use.

FIG. 47.4

Together, Windows NT Server, SQL Server, and Systems Management Server provide the necessary support for geographically separate locations.

Applicable BackOffice Products

Business Issue	Windows NT Server	Internet Information Server	Exchange Server	SQL Server	SNA Server	Systems Management Server
Geographically Separate Locations	✓		✓		✓	

SQL Server can be used to build and manage production databases (transaction systems), as well as data warehouses (reporting databases). Again, these databases can be accessed from any client PC or client NC on the WAN provided that appropriate privileges have been granted. SMS can be used to administer the entire network including those client PCs and client NCs connected to remote LANs.

Figure 47.5 represents a typical BackOffice wide area network. See Chapter 9, "Using TCP/IP with Windows NT Server," for complete coverage of Windows NT Server as a network operating system for a wide area network. This basic network forms the foundation upon which you can develop and deploy applications.

FIG. 47.5

Geographically separate locations are connected as a "network of networks" via a wide area network.

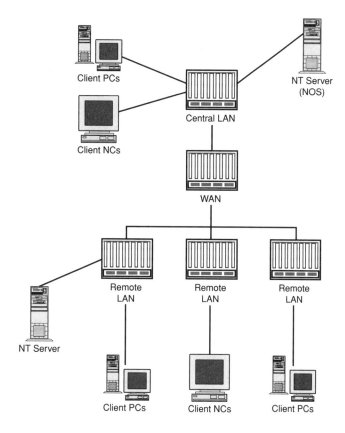

Based on sound technologies, BackOffice provides the capability to support geographically separate locations. This is an important consideration when designing your enterprise network and applications upon which the organization will operate. Regardless of whether you have multiple locations today, you may eventually need to connect to the outside world or allow customers access to your world. For these reasons, it is important to understand how BackOffice supports geographically separate locations.

▶ **See** "Building Your Network," **p. 66**

▶ **See** "Using a LAN or WAN," **p. 110**

▶ **See** "Understanding Dial-Up Access to BackOffice," **p. 114**

Mainframe Transaction Systems

Many information technology experts today advise against further investment into legacy systems. This implies host-based mainframe and minicomputer systems should be maintained and operated at current levels as long as necessary, but that no additional investment should be applied. Instead, new investments should go into applications based on the client-server process model and on the I-net process model.

Part

X

Ch

47

Although this sounds like a simple suggestion, in the real world it is difficult to draw such a clear line between the two process models. In many organizations, host-based transaction systems are the cornerstone of business operations. For years the strength of mainframe and minicomputers has been their capability to process large numbers of transactions in a short period of time. This has led to the proliferation of transaction-oriented systems on mainframes and minicomputers.

BackOffice and similar approaches from other vendors now provide an alternative that permits the successful development and implementation of mission-critical applications based on the client-server process model or the I-net process model. New development tools and development methodologies exist that support this approach to application development and render the mainframe tools seemingly obsolete and inflexible.

Nevertheless, it is common to see new applications based on the client-server process model or the I-net process model be developed in and around existing mainframe transaction systems. Even though the eventual goal may be to replace the mainframe computers with a client-server or I-net computing environment, the transition may take place over several years (sometimes over five to ten years).

These long transitions lead to the need for PCs and NCs on networks to gain access to mainframe applications and data. This concept is commonly referred to as ***host connectivity***. BackOffice provides this important capability (see Figure 47.6).

FIG. 47.6
The host-connectivity capability provided with BackOffice supports application interfaces to mainframe transaction systems.

	Technical Underpinnings						
Business Issue	Modern Process Models	Remote Access	Internet	Electronic Messaging	RDBMS	Distributed Data	Host Connectivity
Mainframe Transaction System							✓

The major distinction between mainframe systems and applications based on the client-server process model or the I-net process model is that mainframe transaction systems typically process large amounts of data in batches at a time; whereas systems rooted in the client-server process model or I-net process model typically process smaller units of data in response to a request. Because these requests are often referred to as "messages," client-server applications and I-net applications are said to be *message-based*.

As developers move from mainframe-based efforts to client-server or I-net design and development, they often experience difficult transitions. Adjusting application design scenarios from batch-oriented solutions to message-based solutions is a challenge overcome only by those who take the time to learn the fundamentals of the client-server and I-net process models.

▶ **See** "Understanding Process Models," **p. 23**

Because Microsoft recognizes that these different types of application scenarios must coexist in today's computing environments, it has provided application developers with a means to support both. The SNAPI programmatic interface provides access to IBM mainframe and minicomputer applications and data from a BackOffice environment (see Figure 47.7).

FIG. 47.7

SNAPI is the programmatic interface that allows BackOffice applications to access mainframe transaction systems.

Programmatic Interfaces

Business Issue	Win32	ISAPI	MAPI	ODBC	SNAPI
Mainframe Transaction Systems					✓

The SNAPI programmatic interface gains access to host systems via the BackOffice product SNA Server (see Figure 47.8). This product also allows users on client PCs and client NCs located throughout the enterprise network to run mainframe applications, provided that they are configured with the appropriate client software. Figure 47.9 shows the role SNA Server plays in the enterprise network.

Part
X

Ch
47

FIG. 47.8

SNA Server is the BackOffice product that supports access to mainframe transaction systems.

Application BackOffice Products

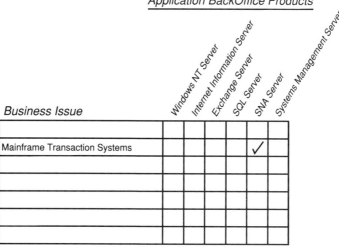

Business Issue	Windows NT Server	Internet Information Server	Exchange Server	SQL Server	SNA Server	Systems Management Server
Mainframe Transaction Systems					✓	

FIG. 47.9
IBM mainframe and
minicomputers are
connected to BackOffice
networks via SNA
Server.

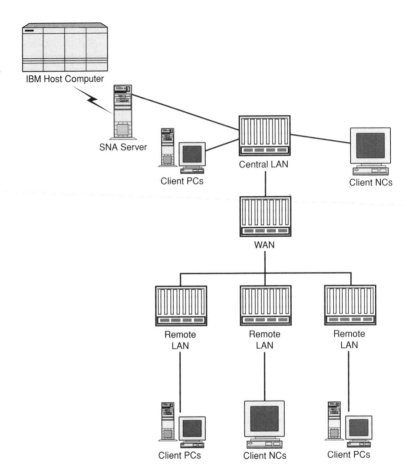

SNA Server is the BackOffice component that provides host connectivity to mainframe transaction systems. This is an important part of application development today and will remain so for many years to come. SNA Server addresses this need from both a user's perspective and a developer's perspective.

Management Reporting

Managers and staff alike constantly request more and better information. The demands placed on them by the organization's stakeholders and by competitive pressures force decisions to be made in shorter and shorter time intervals. This drives the demand for more and better information in the most timely manner possible.

Herein lies the dilemma facing information system professionals today. How can more and better information be delivered in the shortest time possible? The cornerstone of the solution to this problem is a relational database management system (RDBMS). BackOffice provides this important piece to the puzzle (see Figure 47.10)

FIG. 47.10

The capabilities of a relational database management system provide the technical underpinnings necessary to support sophisticated and flexible management reporting.

Technical Underpinnings

Business Issue	Modern Process Models	Remote Access	Internet	Electronic Messaging	RDBMS	Distributed Data	Host Connectivity
Management Reporting					✓		

Many types of reporting requirements must be fulfilled. Some reports are produced and delivered on a regular schedule. Some reports are generated daily, weekly, monthly, or on some other regularly scheduled interval. These reports typically are generated automatically by applications built for this purpose.

From a developer's perspective, these reports are written as a part of the application. In the client-server process model, these reports can be written on the client side or the server side. In the I-net process model, these reports can be delivered to client PCs or client NCs via a browser accessing an internal Web page. There exists a multitude of tools, from Microsoft and other vendors, for creating these reports in either scenario.

Often, management desires an answer to a question more quickly than a developer can prepare a report. In such cases, it is necessary for managers and staff to be able to access the enterprise information. These impromptu requests for information are referred to as *ad hoc queries*.

Regardless of whether the information desired comes from a pre-prepared report or is the result of an ad hoc query, these results are possible only if consistent, convenient access to the information is provided. BackOffice supports such an interface to the RDBMS through the Open Database Connectivity (ODBC) programmatic interface (see Figure 47.11).

Application developers can use ODBC to gain access to data managed by SQL Server for the purpose of preparing reports. Reporting tools also are developed with the capability to access SQL Server data using ODBC. More important, ODBC is a database interface supported by other RDBMS vendors, such as Sybase and Oracle. This allows reports and reporting tools built upon the ODBC programmatic interface to access other databases, as well.

The product that provides the foundation for management reporting in a BackOffice environment is SQL Server (see Figure 47.12). Combined with reporting and query tools for client PCs and sophisticated Web capabilities for client PCs and client NCs, BackOffice permits organizations to fulfill the regularly scheduled reporting requirements, as well as respond to the immediate need for information through ad hoc queries.

Part
X

Ch
47

FIG. 47.11
ODBC is the programmatic interface that forms the foundation of end-user reporting tools.

FIG. 47.12
Combined with client PC reporting and query tools, SQL Server is the BackOffice product that supports management reporting.

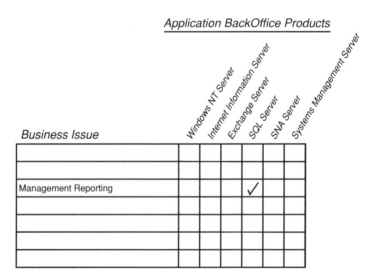

Figure 47.13 depicts how you can use multiple instances of SQL Server. It also shows that SQL Server can be used for multiple purposes. Production databases typically contain the high-volume transaction data necessary to support mission-critical applications. Data for reporting purposes and to support ad hoc queries are stored in data warehouses.

The need for information drives the information systems industry today. BackOffice addresses this need by incorporating a relational database management system and providing convenient access to it for application developers and users. Chapter 37, "Data Warehousing with SQL Server," contains a complete discussion on the data warehousing capabilities of SQL Server.

▶ **See** "Online Transaction Processing and Online Analytical Processing," **p. 1126**

FIG. 47.13
SQL Server can be used to build management reporting databases (data warehouses), as well as enterprise transaction databases (production databases).

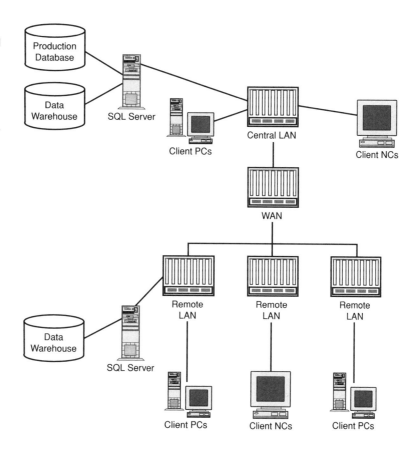

Remote Employees

Many organizations today have employees who perform their jobs from somewhere other than the office. This implies that their PCs cannot physically connect to the network. Often, these people have the greatest demand for information.

One approach is to load their PCs with data when they are in the office and connected to the network. This tends to be a restrictive way to resolve the issue, however, because it often requires frequent visits to the office to ensure accurate information and acceptable performance. Moreover, it may be that the information is too voluminous for a portable PC—not to mention that data may change while the traveler is away from the office. This may result in an inappropriate decision's being made.

Who needs this information while away from the office? Clearly, the most popular example today is field sales personnel. These individuals spend the significant portion of their days calling on customers at the customer sites. While engaged with customers, salespeople need a lot of information to facilitate customer service and be most competitive in the sales environment.

In addition to field sales personnel, many organizations employ people who work from home. Although this trend has not yet achieved widespread acceptance, it is gaining in popularity. Many part-time employees currently work from home on a temporary basis, and many full-time employees anticipate they will in the years to come.

What does all this mean to application developers? Most importantly, it means that applications must be developed to behave well in a remote computing environment. It also means that the organization's network must provide remote access capabilities. BackOffice provides the technical foundation upon which these types of applications can be developed because it is based upon the client-server process model, accommodates the use of the I-net process model, and incorporates remote access capabilities (see Figure 47.14).

FIG. 47.14

The modern process models and remote access capabilities are the BackOffice technical underpinnings that allow it to support remote employees.

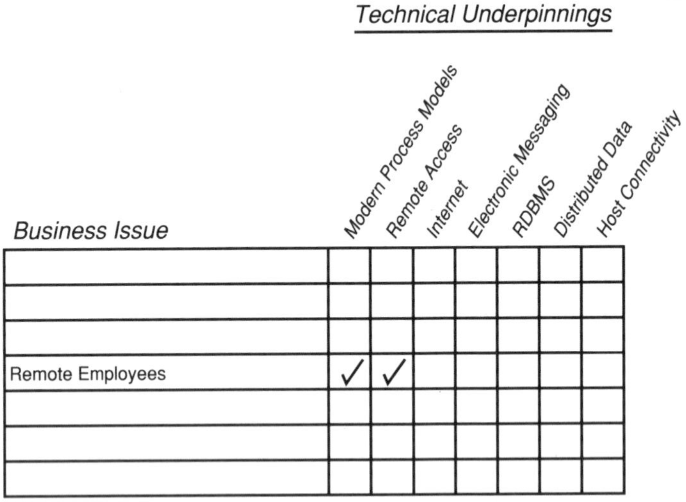

BackOffice provides a comprehensive set of programmatic interfaces for developing applications in a remote usage environment. The programmatic interface provided by Microsoft for this purpose is Win32 (see Figure 47.15). This API includes capabilities to control access to the network from remote PCs, the capability to execute processes in the office (remote procedure calls) to reduce the amount of data transmitted, the capability to reduce bandwidth requirements through message-passing interfaces such as MAPI (included within Win32), and the important capability to build applications based on the client-server process model or the I-net process model due to the availability in Win32 of a network protocol interface such as TCP/IP.

▶ **See** "Understanding Network Protocols," **p. 110**

All these capabilities are built directly in to Windows NT Server (see Figure 47.16). Developers have access to each of these interfaces, and many others, in application development. Microsoft also uses these interfaces to develop such products as the Exchange Server client software. This is a good example of client software that is optimized to operate in a remote environment. Any applications built today should consider to what extent remote operation should be supported.

FIG. 47.15

The Win32 program-matic interface is necessary to build applications for use by remote employees.

Programmatic Interfaces

Business Issue	Win32	ISAPI	MAPI	ODBC	SNAPI
Remote Employees	✓				

FIG. 47.16

The best means available in BackOffice to support remote employees is the remote access service of Windows NT Server.

Applicable BackOffice Products

Business Issue	Windows NT Server	Internet Information Server	Exchange Server	SQL Server	SNA Server	Systems Management Server
Remote Employees	✓					

Part
X

Ch
47

Figure 47.17 depicts how remote employees such as field salespeople connect to the network. They can connect either to the central LAN or a remote LAN—wherever a Windows NT Server exists with the remote access service enabled. See Chapter 12, "Implementing Remote Access Service (RAS)," for a complete description of how to implement this capability.

Remote access to information is quickly becoming one of the most important aspects of modern-day application development. It is important that you understand this need and how BackOffice addresses it. It is imperative that you design your applications with remote access in mind. This absolutely means that the amount of data transmitted to and from the client PC must be minimized, which is a consequence of utilizing the full capabilities of either the client-server process model or the I-net process model.

FIG. 47.17

Remote employees connect to the network via Windows NT Server remote access service.

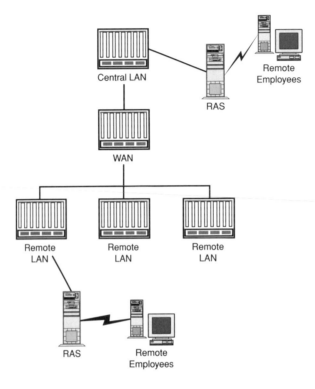

Central LAN

RAS

Remote Employees

WAN

Remote LAN

Remote LAN

Remote LAN

RAS

Remote Employees

Remote Customers

Similar to the situation with remote employees, many organizations have a need to connect their customers, or other interested parties, to their enterprise network. The largest companies demand electronic interfaces to their vendors and suppliers to shorten the amount of time for vital information flow.

To the uninitiated, supporting remote customers may appear to be the same as supporting remote employees. This is true with one major exception—security. Employees demand access to internal information to make decisions about their work. Customers, on the other hand, must be restricted to the information pertinent to the specific transaction at hand.

To allow customers access to your enterprise network, you must, just as for remote employees, base application development on the client-server process model or the I-net process model, as well as the remote access capabilities of BackOffice. In addition, it is important in some situations to give customers access to information via the Internet (see Figure 47.18).

Just as with remote employees, applications built to support remote customers must be based on Win32. Additional interfaces for security also must be exploited within the Win32 programmatic interface. And, because the Internet represents another possibility for accommodating customer access, it may be necessary to incorporate ISAPI into application development (see Figure 47.19).

FIG. 47.18
The modern process models, the remote access service of Windows NT Server, and the Internet together form the technical under-pinnings necessary to support remote customers in a BackOffice environment.

Technical Underpinnings

Business Issue	Modern Process Models	Remote Access	Internet	Electronic Messaging	RDBMS	Distributed Data	Host Connectivity
Remote Customers	✓	✓	✓				

FIG. 47.19
Win32 and ISAPI are the programmatic interfaces necessary to build applications for remote customers.

Programmatic Interfaces

Business Issue	Win32	ISAPI	MAPI	ODBC	SNAPI
Remote Customers	✓	✓			

Part
X
Ch
47

Windows NT Server and Internet Information Server are the BackOffice products that support remote customer access to your enterprise network (see Figure 47.20). Even though the Internet is only recently considered a secure enough environment for some transactions (such as financial transactions), it remains a reasonable means by which to deliver nonsensitive information to customers. Moreover, there is much progress in the Internet community toward putting in place security measures suitable for confidential transactions. For this reason, it is important to evaluate the Internet as a possibility for fulfilling customer information demands.

▶ **See** "Internet Security Concerns," **p. 760**

Figure 47.21 depicts the manner in which remote customers can connect to the organization. If customers connect via the Internet, they can do so through any Internet Service Provider (ISP) using their favorite Internet browser (although it is possible that you may create your Internet information optimized to work best with a given browser). Customers connecting via the remote access service of Windows NT Server must execute applications that you provide and that are optimized to operate on remote PCs.

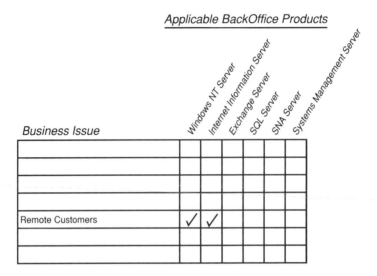

FIG. 47.20

Windows NT Server and
Internet Information
Server are the
BackOffice products
necessary to support
remote customers.

FIG. 47.21

Remote customers
connect to the
enterprise either through
the remote access
service of Windows NT
Server or through the
Internet via the Internet
Information Server.

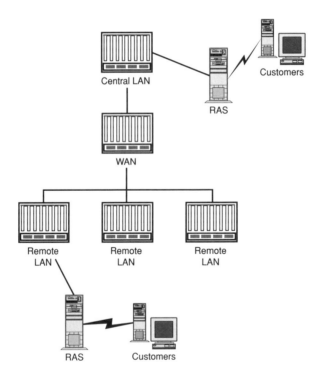

The capability to connect customers and other interested parties to your network may soon,
if not already, be important to your organization. When you are confident that all appropriate
security measures are in place, this capability can yield strategic benefits or competitive advantages. BackOffice provides a thorough means by which to support remote customer access.

Information Publishing

The recent revolution centered on the Internet is largely due to the availability of information on the World Wide Web. Many people spend many hours scouring the Internet with their browser searching for information on a topic of interest. This provides a rich and growing audience for this type of publishing.

Through the Internet, you now have the capability to publish information electronically that is available to the entire Internet community. As the Internet community becomes more closely aligned with the global community, the capability to publish information electronically becomes more important.

The Internet, combined with electronic messaging and the capability to send files to anyone on the Internet, forms the technical foundation upon which information publishing can take place in today's world (see Figure 47.22). The great news for information publishers is that the same technologies and tools used for externally published information can be applied to internally published information. As you have seen, creating a private network for this purpose is commonly referred to as an *intranet*, as a takeoff on the word *Internet*.

▶ **See** "What Is an Intranet?," **p. 515**

FIG. 47.22

The Internet and electronic messaging provide the technical underpinnings necessary to support external and internal information publishing.

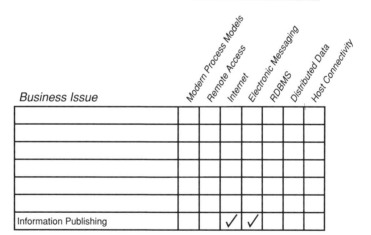

To support application development in this environment, Microsoft provides the ISAPI and MAPI programmatic interfaces (see Figure 47.23). Applications can be designed with Internet integration built in and automatic messaging capabilities. A popular example of how messaging can be incorporated into an application is seen in Microsoft Word. After you prepare a document in Microsoft Word, you can e-mail it to another individual automatically on the BackOffice network, simply by choosing File, Send from the menu.

FIG. 47.23

ISAPI and MAPI are the programmatic interfaces used to build applications in support of both external and internal publishing.

Programmatic Interfaces

Business Issue	Win32	ISAPI	MAPI	ODBC	SNAPI
Information Publishing		✓	✓		

This example illustrates only the simplest form of electronic messaging. As seen in Chapter 26, "An Inside Look at Exchange Server," many other capabilities included with Exchange Server are available. Maintaining document libraries, facilitating document routing, automatic routing of forms, bulletin boards, news flashes, and discussion forums are other examples of how BackOffice supports information publishing with Internet Information Server and Exchange Server (see Figure 47.24).

FIG. 47.24

Internet Information Server and Exchange Server are the BackOffice products that best support information publishing activities.

Applicable BackOffice Products

Business Issue	Windows NT Server	Internet Information Server	Exchange Server	SQL Server	SNA Server	Systems Management Server
Information Publishing		✓	✓			

Figure 47.25 depicts how customers access published information by browsing the Internet and using Exchange Server. Security for the Internet is provided by third-party products known as *Internet firewalls*. These products restrict access to only the information you want to make available to the outside world.

▶ **See** "Security for Your Internet Server," **p. 570**

FIG. 47.25
Customers gain
access to published
information using any
Internet browser or the
Exchange Server client.

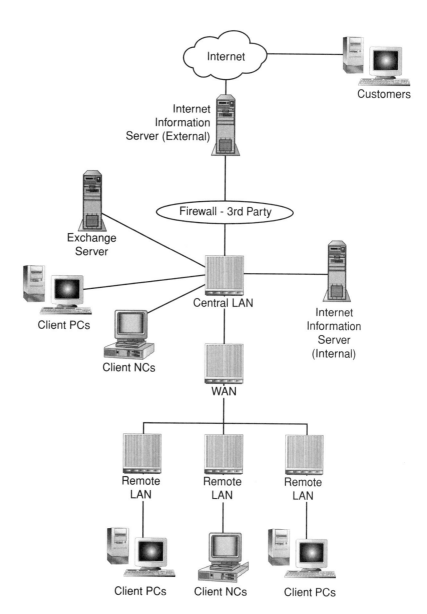

One of the primary purposes for implementing BackOffice in your organization is to facilitate
the seamless flow of meaningful information to the client PCs and client NCs within the organization. The information publishing capabilities of BackOffice make it well suited for this purpose, as well as for publishing public information on the Internet.

Part
X

Ch
47

Entire BackOffice Solution

You have just explored several important topics in the world of today's information systems. You also have seen how BackOffice offers support for these needs and how it applies to real-world situations. Figure 47.26 shows all the business issues discussed previously in this chapter and maps them against the technical aspects of modern-day computing environments.

FIG. 47.26
BackOffice provides thorough coverage of the most important technical underpinnings of modern-day information systems.

Technical Underpinnings

Business Issue	Modern Process Models	Remote Access	Internet	Electronic Messaging	RDBMS	Distributed Data	Host Connectivity
Geographically Separate Locations	✓					✓	
Mainframe Transaction Systems							✓
Management Reporting					✓		
Remote Employees	✓	✓					
Remote Customers	✓	✓	✓				
Information Publishing			✓	✓			

These technical underpinnings are further supported through programmatic interfaces. Figure 47.27 shows, all together, which programmatic interfaces are needed to support the various business issues. You have learned how these APIs are important to application developers and what they mean to them. More important, as a manager or an administrator, you have gained insight of BackOffice from an application developer's perspective.

FIG. 47.27
Each BackOffice product is supported by a programmatic interface so that developers can incorporate BackOffice services into their applications.

Programmatic Interfaces

Business Issue	Win32	ISAPI	MAPI	ODBC	SNAPI
Geographically Separate Locations	✓			✓	
Mainframe Transaction Systems					✓
Management Reporting				✓	
Remote Employees	✓				
Remote Customers	✓	✓			
Information Publishing		✓	✓		

The BackOffice products are designed to work as a unit toward resolving today's business issues. Figure 47.28 shows each BackOffice product and the role it plays in addressing these concerns. Through the scenarios presented earlier in this chapter, you learned that each individual product is built upon a solid technical foundation while fully exploiting the most current technologies.

FIG. 47.28

Together, the BackOffice products satisfy the prevailing business issues.

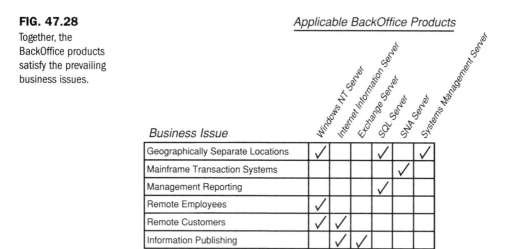

Applicable BackOffice Products

Business Issue	Windows NT Server	Internet Information Server	Exchange Server	SQL Server	SNA Server	Systems Management Server
Geographically Separate Locations	✓			✓		✓
Mainframe Transaction Systems					✓	
Management Reporting				✓		
Remote Employees	✓					
Remote Customers	✓	✓				
Information Publishing		✓	✓			

Finally, bringing all the BackOffice products together in a single enterprise network is shown in Figure 47.29. If you were to overlay the diagrams in all the figures in this chapter, you would find that they exactly match Figure 47.29.

By bringing all this together in building blocks, the intent is to demonstrate how you can use BackOffice as a platform upon which to build and deploy mission-critical applications. Many organizations have already achieved success in so doing, and many more are engaging in BackOffice-based application development each day.

Part
X
Ch
47

FIG. 47.29
An organization can use BackOffice to fulfill the vast majority of its connectivity and user service needs.

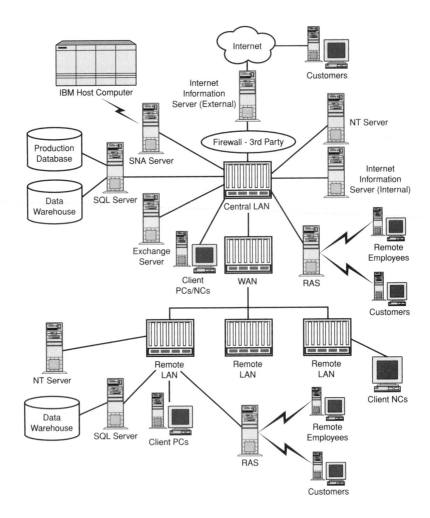

From Here...

In this chapter, you learned that BackOffice is a platform upon which mission-critical applications can be developed and deployed. This was accomplished by first examining the important decisions facing application developers, exploring the technical underpinnings of modern-day application development and deployment, and understanding how BackOffice addresses the application implementation issues. This served to demonstrate the worthiness of BackOffice as a suitable platform upon which mission-critical applications can be defined, constructed, and operated.

Looking ahead, Microsoft has stated publicly their intention is to continue the development of the BackOffice family of server applications. You are encouraged to keep apace with BackOffice product information and published materials; significant advances are anticipated in the months and years to come.

For information related to this chapter, refer to the following:

- To review the foundation upon which BackOffice is built, see Chapter 2, "Characteristics of BackOffice."

- For a thorough examination of the I-Net capabilities of BackOffice, see Chapter 16, "The BackOffice I-Net Toolbox."

- To see how Exchange Server supports today's applications, see Chapter 31, "Exchange Server Advanced Topics."

- To see why SQL Server is a sophisticated tool for developing modern-day applications, see Chapter 37, "Data Warehousing with SQL Server."

- For a practical approach to security, see Chapter 46, "Implementing Real-World Security."

Part

X

Ch

47

CHAPTER 48

Proactive Network Administration

by Don Benage

At this point, you've learned a lot about how to set up servers with BackOffice Family components. You've also learned a number of techniques involving the Windows NT event log, alerting mechanisms, and the Performance Monitor that can help you keep your servers running and respond to errors when they do occur. This chapter is about aggressively working to avoid problems. It will help you to develop an approach to network and server management that will catch most problems before the user community has felt any significant impact. ■

How to manage your network proactively

Learn how to watch key indicators to help uncover problems before they impact the user community. Learn about the various monitoring tools available with Windows NT Server and the BackOffice suite.

How to use Windows NT Performance Monitor

Learn how to use the Performance Monitor to create charts, store information in log files for later analysis, and set alerts on important counters that will reflect the status of your servers and their applications.

How to use SQL Mail and SQL Alerts to receive e-mail or pages when an error occurs

Explore the capabilities of the SQL Server Alert mechanism and the use of SQL Mail to notify operators by e-mail messages or by paging.

Proactive Network Administration—An Approach

Many network administrators find themselves in the role of "firefighter." Each day is spent responding to problems and complaints raised by users. In this type of environment, it is easy to feel overwhelmed, and it is very difficult to seize control of the situation and make positive changes. You are so busy merely keeping up with the demand for immediate short-term fixes that you cannot take actions that provide long-term benefit.

At some point, the firefighting administrator inevitably decides there must be a better way. The following sections address this issue. They describe concrete steps that you can take to gain some control over your network and to see problems while they are still "smoldering," before they have flared up and caused big problems for your user community—and for you.

How to Watch Your Network and Servers

What does it mean to be proactive about network administration and management? Other than waiting for users to tell you a shared resource is not functioning, what can be done to watch your network and servers for the first signs of trouble? Fortunately, the answer is that a lot can be done on a Windows NT Server network to take an aggressive approach toward problem avoidance and identification.

Windows NT Server includes a powerful tool called the *Performance Monitor*. This general-purpose monitoring utility can provide performance information on the core services of Windows NT Server and BackOffice Family components that have been added to a server. Information can be stored in a log file and used to create reports or graphs using tools like Microsoft Excel.

Several BackOffice Family components have their own monitoring tools and utilities as well. For example, Exchange Server includes the capability to establish both Server Monitors and Link Monitors. Server Monitors watch the status of server-based services to ensure that they are still running. Link Monitors are used to "bounce" a special type of message, known as a *ping message* off a remote messaging system at another site. If the return message is not received, the link between your server and the remote site may be down.

▶ **See** "Monitoring Your Site," **p. 1027**

SQL Server has a powerful alerting mechanism that monitors the event log for error conditions. If it detects a specified error condition, it sends an e-mail message to a selected operator or to an e-mail mailbox set up for a pager. With third-party software not included with BackOffice, the pager mailbox can be monitored for incoming messages, and one or more pagers can be contacted with an appropriate message. You can use the tools in SQL Server to define one or more operators and assign responsibility for specific error conditions during selected hours of the day and days of the week. Procedures for using this capability are provided in the "Using SQL Mail and Alerts to Monitor SQL Server" section, later in this chapter.

Systems Management Server (SMS) includes a software-based protocol analyzer capable of capturing the packets sent over the network and displaying them for analysis. In addition to this basic function, it also has a display that shows the level of broadcast and multicast traffic, percent of bandwidth utilization, and other useful statistics. Even if you do not want to engage in sophisticated protocol analysis, this can be a useful tool for monitoring your network. In addition, you can use new counters in the Performance Monitor that are added when you install the Network Monitor. These counters let you use the Performance Monitor to chart, log, or set alerts on network-specific activity not associated with any particular server.

▶ **See** "Using the Network Monitor," **p. 1548**

Windows NT Server also includes an SNMP service that you can use in conjunction with an SNMP console application, such as HP's OpenView or Sun's NetManager, to monitor the status of your servers and other network components. The SNMP service is not covered in this book, but if your organization is already using an SNMP console, you should investigate integrating the Windows NT SNMP monitoring service with your other tools.

How Do You Know There's a Problem?

Despite all the useful tools and utilities that have been discussed already, being able to *automatically* detect if there is a problem is still an issue. Certainly, if you are a trained administrator sitting at the console, logged on to the server as a catastrophic problem occurs, you are likely to receive some error message or other indication that something is amiss. But suppose that the server is locked up in a machine room or wiring closet somewhere, and you are using your computer to run a productivity tool such as Microsoft Word? What concrete events or mechanisms can alert you that a potential problem has occurred?

One of the best indications that you have a problem, which is exploited by the Server Monitor in Exchange Server, occurs when one or more services stop running. Under ordinary circumstances, when you start the services on a server, they start running and just keep going. There are a number of reasons why they might stop, almost all of which represent problems. Any kind of accidental power outage is one obvious source of an unintentional service stoppage. A service also can stop due to a lack of resources on the server, such as disk space or RAM.

If you make sure that all servers have an Uninterruptible Power Supply (UPS), then you will have eliminated most problems caused by accidental power outages. It is still possible, however, that the backup power offered by the UPS is not sufficient to last through an entire power outage. This will cause an orderly shutdown of the server, provided that the UPS settings are configured properly. While this is better than a sudden power outage with no UPS, the fact that services have stopped—even though the situation may be temporary—is a noteworthy event that is sure to affect users. If you can at least be among the first to be aware of the problem, and are already working on fixing it when the phone calls come in, your proactive approach is paying some dividends.

In the case of resource shortages, you should have an opportunity to get an earlier warning. Ideally, an alerting mechanism signals when a resource is in short supply. An event is triggered in the event log when the hard disk space on a server falls below a certain threshold. The event is usually raised while there is still time to do something about it, unless someone is copying massive files to the server's hard disk. This is a good example of an alert that helps identify a general problem that can affect all services and users across the board and should certainly be

Part

X

Ch

48

watched. You can use the Free Megabytes counter on the Logical Disk object to set an alert in the Performance Monitor.

An indication of potential networking problems occurs when e-mail messages are not getting through the path between one server and another, or between a server and a remote messaging system, for example a system on the Internet. This is the principle behind the Link Monitors in Exchange Server, and these can be useful tools even if you do not use Exchange Server for your messaging system. This type of mechanism can detect a downed router, for example.

You also can use counters like the I/O – transactions/second counter of the SQL Server object to watch for sustained performance at a very high rate, which can indicate the need to offload some of the work on an additional system or to provide more processing power on the original system. In addition, if the level falls below expected norms during business hours, you may have a problem. With this type of counter, you need to use judgment to determine whether you have a potential problem, indicated by a sustained value that is out of the expected range, or an aberrant spike value that you can safely disregard.

One type of error that is not detectable with any of the mechanisms available in the Microsoft BackOffice product is a network card or other similar component that has gone bad and is producing bad network packets. Occasionally, a network adapter malfunctions in such a way that it floods the network with malformed packets. The Network Monitor, a software-based protocol analyzer, cannot detect these packets because elements of the protocol stack discard the bad packets. A hardware device capable of detecting these problems is a worthwhile investment. Relatively inexpensive LAN-monitoring devices can augment the upper layer analysis offered by the Network Monitor. This often is a less expensive solution than a dedicated hardware-based protocol analyzer capable of detecting and analyzing problems across the network spectrum.

Establish Benchmark Values

If you want to take a proactive approach to network administration, a good place to start is the establishment of some benchmark values for key statistics and counters. Every network is different and, although some generalizations can be made, you need to find out what constitutes average behavior for your network. This presents an awkward difficulty if your network is already causing trouble. You cannot very well establish norms for your network if it is behaving abnormally. You should first attempt to troubleshoot the problem, using standard troubleshooting techniques, and then after you've resolved the problem, come back to these techniques to help you spot trouble more quickly the next time.

Using the Performance Monitor

A number of tools are available for monitoring the behavior of BackOffice Family components, but by far the most powerful general-purpose monitoring utility is the Windows NT Performance Monitor. This utility was created by a team led by Russ Blake, a key member of the Windows NT development team, who has been involved in the field of operating systems performance measurement and monitoring for over a decade. Performance Monitor was not an afterthought product that was "bolted on" after the operating system was finished. Rather, Windows NT was designed to be easy to monitor, and the Performance Monitor was itself used to help shape the development of the operating system.

The Performance Monitor offers three main capabilities: charting, logging, and alerts. This section discusses procedures for all three functions. A *chart* provides a real-time graph of the item being monitored. It can be presented as a line graph, or as a histogram-style bar chart that changes at the intervals you have specified for plotting new values. You can monitor the local computer or select a computer from over the network to monitor. You then can choose from a number of objects and associated counters that are available to monitor. For example, the Server object offers the Total Bytes per Second counter, which measures the total number of bytes sent or received by the server service on a computer and provides a basic measure of how busy the server is. There are options for the chart, including a legend at the bottom showing the counters being plotted, grid lines, and a value bar showing the maximum, minimum, average, and last value for a counter.

You can create *log files* that capture the values of the same objects available for charting. By placing the information in a log file, you can view the information later using the Chart option with data coming from the log file, or you can export the file in tab- or comma-delimited format and create your own graphs or reports using a tool like Microsoft Excel or Microsoft Access. You can set the interval at which the log records values so you can use a frequent sample interval to watch a counter closely for a short period of important activity, or an infrequent interval, say every 15 minutes, to gather information about a counter throughout the day.

Alerts provide the capability to watch any of the counters available for the value to rise above or fall below a specified threshold value. If an alert is triggered, a program can be run the first time or every time. In addition, you can select options to write an entry in the event log when an alert is fired and/or to send a network message with the content of the alert. You also can set an option that causes the Performance Monitor to switch to the Alert View if an alert is triggered. The alert view displays a report showing up to 1,000 alerts that have been triggered.

An entire manual in the Windows NT Resource Kit is devoted to how to use the Performance Monitor. This manual outlines in detail an approach to performance tuning, a different focus from that presented here. The manual is written by Russ Blake, the designer of the Performance Monitor, and is the authoritative work on the subject. It is worthwhile reading for any Windows NT or BackOffice administrator. This section presents an overview of the Performance Monitor and discusses how you can use it as a tool for proactive server management.

Part
X

Ch
48

Charts

The chart feature of Performance Monitor is used to graph real-time information as it is being gathered, or to display the information that has been recorded in a log file. The live graphing capability is more useful as a troubleshooting or tuning tool than as a component of proactive network administration; however, its role as a display tool for log files is very useful.

To create a chart using Performance Monitor, follow these steps:

1. Start Performance Monitor.

2. Click the View a Chart toolbar button, or choose View, Chart from the menu.

3. Click the Add Counter toolbar button, or choose Edit, Add To Chart from the menu. The Add to Chart dialog box appears (see Figure 48.1).

FIG. 48.1

Use this dialog box to select the computer, object(s), and counter(s) you want to monitor on this chart.

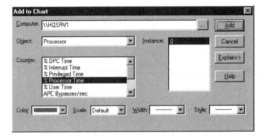

4. If you want to chart the counters from another computer, click the ellipsis button (...) at the right of the Computer text box. The Select Computer dialog box appears (see Figure 48.2).

FIG. 48.2

The Select Computer dialog box lets you select a computer whose object counters you want to view on the selected chart.

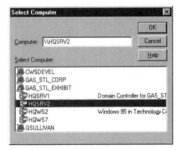

5. You can enter the name of the server you want to monitor in the text box, or browse domains for the server you want in the Select Computer box. If you enter the name manually, be sure to precede the name with a double backslash (\\). Click OK.

6. The Add to Chart dialog box now reflects the computer you selected. Using the Object drop-down list, select an object you want to monitor. After selecting an object, select one or more counters in the Counter list. You can hold down Ctrl and click new counters to add to your selection. Click Add when you are satisfied with your selection(s).

   Almost all servers have some objects, such as the Server object. As products are installed on the server, new objects will appear in the list. For example, when you install SQL Server, approximately eight objects and their associated counters are added to the list of available objects for that server. The exact list depends on the server-based applications you have installed and the installation options you selected.

7. The choices you selected are added to the chart, and the Add to Chart dialog box remains open. You can repeat step 6 as many times as you want to keep adding objects and counters to the chart. Click Done when you have added all the counters you want to view.

8. Charts are most effective if the counters you add all share a similar scale. In other words, if you are viewing one counter whose values vary from 0 to 100, such as a percent counter, and another counter whose values vary from 0 to 10,000, the line representing the percent counter is likely to appear nearly flat. You can use the scale button on the Add to Chart dialog box to change the scale of a particular item. Double-click the item whose scale you want to change in the legend at the bottom of the chart. This opens the Edit Chart Line dialog box (see Figure 48.3).

FIG. 48.3

The Edit Chart Line dialog box allows you to change the scale or appearance of a chart line in a Performance Monitor chart.

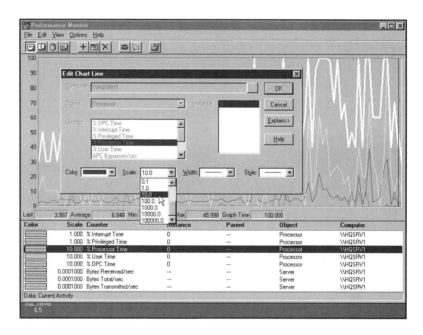

9. When you have added all the counters you want to watch, you can use the highlight feature to help follow a single counter more easily. Highlight one of the counters in the legend at the bottom of the chart and press Ctrl+H. The line corresponding to the counter you selected displays with a wide white line. You can use the mouse or the arrow keys to select a different counter to change the highlighted line.

10. You also can set a number of options that change the appearance of your chart. Select Options, Chart from the menu. The Chart Options dialog box appears (see Figure 48.4).

11. The Chart Options dialog box allows you to add horizontal or vertical grid lines to your chart. You can select the type of chart you want (a graph or a histogram) and the scale of the vertical axis. You also can select whether the legend and value bar should display at the bottom of the chart. Click OK when you are satisfied with your choices.

FIG. 48.4

Use the Chart Options
dialog box to set
options that change the
appearance of the chart
being viewed.

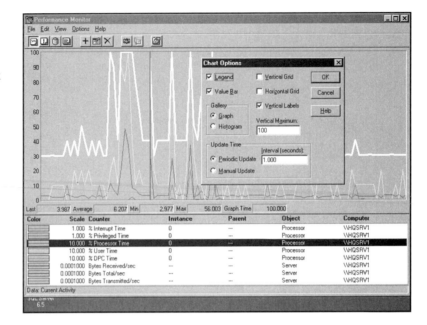

12. You can select other options directly from the Options menu. You can toggle the display
    of several elements on or off using this menu. The menu and title (together), the toolbar,
    and the status bar can be toggled in this manner. You also can toggle the display of the
    menu and title bar by double-clicking in the body of the chart.

13. When you have created a chart whose settings you want to save, you can store the
    settings for the chart in a file. Choose File, Save Chart Settings. In the resulting Perfor-
    mance Monitor Save As dialog box, enter the name of the chart-settings file you want to
    use. The extension for these files is PMC by default.

Logs

Log files are a key element of benchmarking the performance of your servers and your network. By recording the values of selected counters throughout the day and over the course of
weeks or months, you learn what constitutes ordinary behavior on your servers. This in turn is
vital information that can help you set alerts at appropriate levels so you are neither ignoring
an important problem in action, nor being alarmed at a routine spike that will return to normal
with no ill effects.

To log information on the performance of your server for later analysis, follow these steps:

1. Start Performance Monitor.

2. Click the View Output Log File Status toolbar button, or choose View, Log from the
   menu.

3. Click the Add Counter toolbar button, or choose Edit, Add To Log. The Add To Log
   dialog box appears (see Figure 48.5).

FIG. 48.5

The Add To Log dialog box allows you to select the computer and object(s) for which you want to store information in a log file.

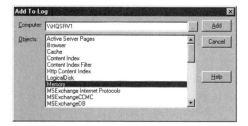

4. If you want to log the counters from another computer, click the ellipsis button (…) at the right of the Computer text box. The Select Computer dialog box appears.

5. You can enter the name of the server you want to monitor in the Select Computer text box, or browse domains for the server you want. If you enter the name manually, be sure to precede the name with a double backslash (\\). Click OK.

6. The Add To Log dialog box now reflects the computer you selected. Using the Objects list, select an object you want to monitor. You can hold down Ctrl and click new objects to add to your selection. Click Add when you are satisfied with your selection(s).

    When you are creating a log, all counters for a particular object are stored. Therefore, you do not have to select the counters you want to log.

7. Your selections are added to the log, and the Add To Log dialog box remains open. You can repeat step 6 as many times as you want to keep adding objects to the log. Click Done when you have added all the objects you want to log.

8. You can set a number of options for the log file you are creating. Choose Options, Log from the menu. The Log Options dialog box appear (see Figure 48.6).

FIG. 48.6

Use the Log Options dialog box to enter a name for the log file you are creating and to set the interval at which counter values are stored in the log file for the objects you've selected.

Part
X

Ch
48

9. The Log Options dialog box allows you to enter a name for the log file. You also can set the interval at which counter values are stored in the log file for the objects you've selected. Most importantly, you can use the Start Log button to begin capturing information. The Status box in the upper right of the window changes from Closed to Collecting, and the file size gradually grows at the interval shown in the Log Interval box.

10. You can select other options directly from the Options menu. You can toggle the display of several elements on or off using this menu. You also can toggle the menu and title (together), the toolbar, and the status bar in this manner. And you can toggle the display of the menu and title bar by double-clicking in the gray area at the top of the log display.

11. When you have set up a log whose settings you want to save, you can store the settings for the log in a file. Select File, Save Log Settings from the menu. In the resulting Performance Monitor Save As dialog box, enter the name of the log-settings file you want to use. The extension for these files is PML by default.

If you want to use Microsoft Excel to graph the information you have already captured in a log file, follow these steps:

1. Start the Performance Monitor.

2. Choose Options, Data From. The Data From dialog box appears (see Figure 48.7).

FIG. 48.7

The Data From dialog box allows you to select the source of information for charting. You can use it to display information that has been saved in a log file.

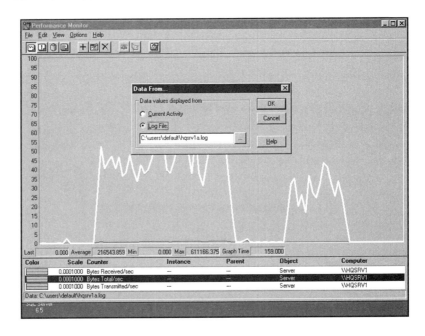

3. Click the ellipsis button (…) to browse for the log file you want to use. When you have selected the file, click OK to close the Data From dialog box.

4. Now you can add counters to the chart in much the same manner as you would if the data were coming from current activity; however, only those objects you saved in the log file will be available. Add the items in which you are interested to the chart.

5. Choose File, Export Chart from the menu. The Performance Monitor–Export As dialog box appears (see Figure 48.8).

FIG. 48.8

You use the Performance Monitor – Export As dialog box to specify the delimiter that will separate values in the export file and the file's name and path.

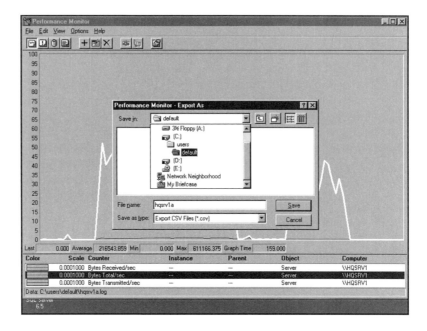

6. Select Export CSV Files in the List Files of Type drop-down list. Use the Drives and Directories controls to select the location in which you want to store the file, and enter a file name. Click OK. This creates the export file. You can close the Performance Monitor until you are ready to use it again.

7. Start Microsoft Excel.

8. Choose File, Open. The Open dialog box appears (see Figure 48.9).

FIG. 48.9

You can use the Open dialog box in Microsoft Excel to open an export file created by the Performance Monitor. Select text files (.CSV) from the Files of Type drop-down list.

Part
X

Ch
48

9. Select Text Files in the Files of Type drop-down list. Use the file-browsing controls to find your export file and highlight it. Click Open.

10. The initial display may be difficult to read if the column widths are too narrow. Position the mouse cursor over the line between columns in the lettered column headers. The cursor changes to a line with arrows pointing in each direction. Double-click the left mouse button to auto-size the column to fit the data.

11. Select the information you want to graph and proceed as you would with any Excel chart. You may need to delete extraneous rows or columns, or copy selected portions of the data to another location on the spreadsheet to create the chart you want (see Figure 48.10).

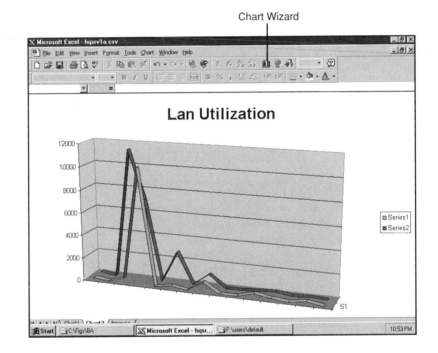

FIG. 48.10

This is an Excel chart created from Performance Monitor information.

12. Save or print the chart as desired. Exit from Excel.

Alerts

Alerts are the primary tool for the administrator interested in proactive network management. After you have gathered information on important counters for your servers over a period of a week, or even a month, you are ready to analyze the information and establish threshold values that indicate abnormal activity. This will not necessarily indicate a problem, but such activity is at least worth further investigation. You must be the judge of how sensitive you want the alerts to be. If you have a mission-critical component that bears close scrutiny, perhaps an occasional false alarm is worthwhile to avoid any possibility of missing a problem. You may even want to set both upper- and lower-threshold values for a few key counters that you expect to fall within a certain range during routine operations.

To set alerts that notify you when a performance monitor counter crosses a threshold value, follow these steps:

1. Start Performance Monitor.

2. Click the View the Alerts toolbar button, or choose View, Alert from the menu.

3. Click the Add Counter toolbar button, or choose Edit, Add To Alert. The Add to Alert dialog box appears (see Figure 48.11).

FIG. 48.11

The Add to Alert dialog box allows you to select a counter and then to enter the threshold value that will trigger an alert.

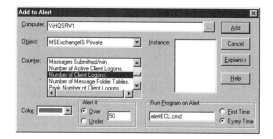

4. If you want to set alerts on counters from another computer, click the ellipsis button (…) at the right of the Computer text box. The Select Computer dialog box appears.

5. You can enter the name of the server you want to monitor in the Select Computer text box, or browse domains for the server you want. If you enter the name manually, be sure to precede the name with a double backslash (\\). Click OK.

6. The Add to Alert dialog box now reflects the computer you selected. Using the Object drop-down list, select an object you want to monitor. After selecting an object, select one of the counters in the Counter list. Then enter the threshold value in the Alert If box that will trigger the alert. Select the Over or Under option button in the Alert If box. Click Add when you are satisfied with your selection(s).

7. Your selections are added to the list of Alerts, and the Add to Alert dialog box remains open. You can repeat step 6 as many times as you want to keep adding alerts to the list. Click Done when you have added all the alerts you want to monitor.

8. You can set a number of options for the alerts you are monitoring. Choose Options, Alert. The Alert Options dialog box appears (see Figure 48.12).

9. When an alert is triggered, Windows NT will check the options you specified in the Alert Options dialog box to determine what action it should take. You can have the Performance Monitor to switch to the Alert view (from a Chart or Log view). An event can be written to the Applications event log if you want, and you also can send a network message to a username from the Windows NT Server account database for your domain.

10. You can select other options directly from the Options menu. You can toggle the display of several elements on or off using this menu. You also can toggle the menu and title (together), the toolbar, and the status bar in this manner. And, you can toggle the display of the menu and title bar by double-clicking in the gray area at the top of the Alert View display.

Part
X

Ch
48

FIG. 48.12
Use the Alert Options dialog box to specify the actions that should occur when an alert is triggered.

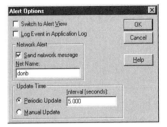

11. When you have set alerts whose settings you want to save, you can store the settings in a file. Choose File, Save Alert Settings. In the resulting Performance Monitor Save As dialog box, enter the name of the alert-settings file you want to use. The extension for these files is PMA by default.

Using SQL Mail and Alerts to Monitor SQL Server

You have already learned how to use the Windows NT Performance Monitor to create alerts on native Windows NT services, such as the Server service, and additional BackOffice Family components that have been added to the server, such as Exchange Server and SQL Server. In this section, you learn how to use the Alerting mechanisms included in SQL Server to send e-mail to an administrator or *operator*, or send e-mail to a pager account that in turn calls a specified beeper. You can set up one or more operators who are responsible for responding to a particular set of alerts at defined times during the week.

Setting Up SQL Mail

For SQL Server to use SQL Mail for sending mail, you must first configure a mailbox for SQL Server to use. Instructions for setting up an Exchange Server mailbox are provided in "Setting Up Recipients" in Chapter 27. You will also need to install the Exchange Client software on the SQL Server (either Outlook or the Exchange Client) and create a profile for the e-mail account you are using. These procedures are covered in Chapter 28 in the sections "Installing Exchange Client Software" and "Creating a User Profile." If you are using a different e-mail product, consult your administrator's manual for instructions on creating an e-mail account and mailbox. It is a good idea to test the new e-mail account manually before configuring SQL Mail.

You can start SQL Mail manually by using the xp_startmail extended stored procedure. It is much easier, and more reliable, to start SQL Mail automatically whenever SQL Server starts. In addition to setting SQL Mail to start automatically, you must also specify the e-mail profile which should be used by SQL Mail. This can be done using the SQL Server Setup program. You can change the configuration for SQL Mail using the SQL Enterprise Manager if you need to do so at a later time.

The first time you set up and test SQL Mail, it is recommended that you log on to the server using the SQL service account that will be used for SQL Mail. This should be the same account that you are using for SQL Server itself, and should be the primary Windows NT account assigned to the e-mail mailbox that is specified in the profile you are using for SQL Mail.

After you have created and tested the mailbox and a complimentary profile, you are ready to use the SQL Server Setup program to configure the use of SQL Mail. To set up SQL Mail, follow these steps:

1. Run the SQL Server Setup program.

2. After the Welcome dialog box, the Microsoft SQL Server Options dialog box appears. Select the option button labeled Set Server Options. Click Continue. The Select Server Options dialog box appears (see Figure 48.13).

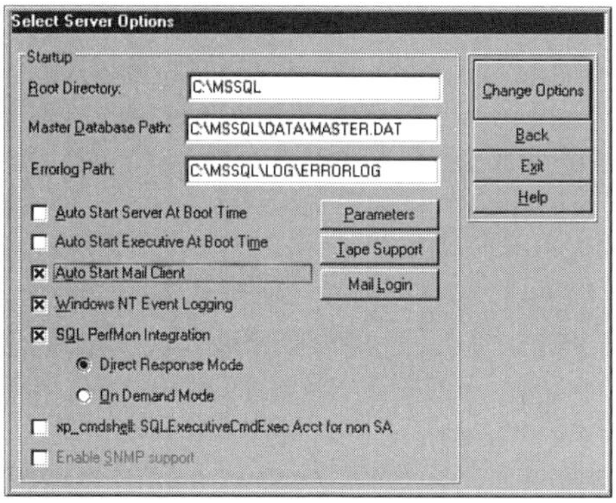

FIG. 48.13

Use the Select Server Options dialog box to select options for SQL Server, such as the Auto Start Mail Client option.

3. Click the check box to Auto Start Mail Client. Then click the Mail Login button. The Exchange Login Configuration dialog box appears (see Figure 48.14).

4. Enter the Profile Name. Click Continue.

5. SQL Server configures the mail client. Click Continue to return to the Select Server Options dialog box. Click Change Options to save your changes and exit SQL Server Setup.

If you need to change the SQL Mail profile at a later time, you can simply select Server, SQL Mail, Configure from the menu in the SQL Enterprise Manager and enter the name of the new profile you want to use. You can also use SQL Enterprise Manager to manually start and stop SQL Mail by right-clicking the SQL Mail icon in the Server Manager window and using the pop-up menu.

Creating User-Defined Error Messages

It is not necessary to create user-defined errors to use alerts; however, it does provide a convenient testing capability. In addition, it offers you the possibility to raise these user-defined errors in your own programs and stored procedures, which can in turn raise alerts. To define your own error message, follow these steps:

1. Start the SQL Enterprise Manager and connect to the SQL Server of your choice.

2. Click the SQL Query Tool toolbar button, or choose Tools, SQL Query Tool.

Part
X

Ch
48

FIG. 48.14

The Exchange Login Configuration dialog box lets you tell SQL Server which e-mail profile (and therefore which e-mail account) to use for SQL Mail tasks.

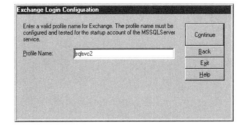

3. Select the master database in the DB drop-down list. Click the Query tab if it is not already selected.

4. User-defined error messages are created with the sp_addmessage system procedure. User-defined messages must begin at error number 50001. You can give your message a severity level of 1 through 25. Only a system administrator can define a message with severity 19 through 25, which should be used very carefully because this level represents a serious error that can shut down SQL Server. An informational message has a severity of level 10. Enter a command something like this (see Figure 48.15):

```
sp_addmessage 50001, 10, 'DataSrv needs attention. Error = 123.'
```

FIG. 48.15

Here the SQL Query Tool is being used to create a user-defined error message.

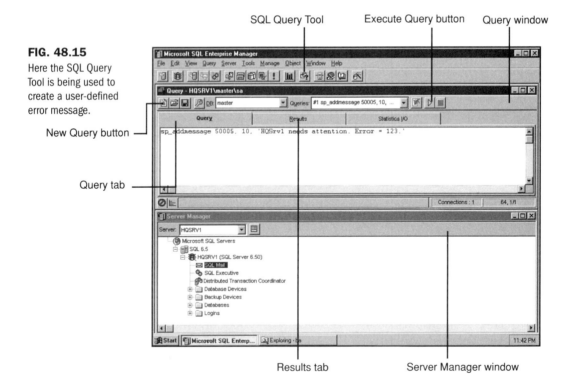

5. Execute the query. You error message is added to the sysmessages table.

6. To test your message, you can use the RAISERROR Transact-SQL statement. You may want to create a stored procedure called test_alert, which you can use to test your newly defined error message and again to test your alert after it is defined in an upcoming section. Enter a procedure similar to the one depicted in Figure 48.16.

FIG. 48.16

This procedure is being defined so that it can be used to test the user-defined error message and alerts.

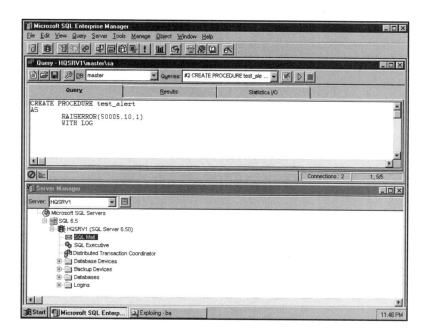

7. Execute the query. You then can open a new query with the New Query toolbar button and simply enter the command **test_alert**. This should cause an entry to be placed in the Applications log on the server if you specified the WITH LOG option when you created the test_alert procedure as it was shown in the example.

8. You are now ready to define Alerts and assign them to operators.

Defining SQL Server Alerts

You can either define alerts first and then create operators and make assignments, or create the operators first and assign alerts as the new alerts are defined. In this example, you first define an alert based on the user-defined error message you have created, then create an operator, and finally assign the responsibility for the newly created alert to that operator. Alerts for more serious system-defined errors are created in exactly the same way. The use of a user-defined message simply facilitates testing the alert because you can raise an error without artificially creating a serious problem.

Part
X

Ch

To define a new SQL Server alert, follow these steps:

1. Start the SQL Enterprise Manager and connect to the SQL Server of your choice.

2. Click the Manage Alerts toolbar button, or choose Server, Alerts from the menu.

3. Click the Alerts tab if it is not already visible. The alerts that have already been defined display. Click the New Alert toolbar button, the one at the far left of the toolbar. The New Alert dialog box appears (see Figure 48.17).

FIG. 48.17

Use the New Alert dialog box to define the properties of a new alert.

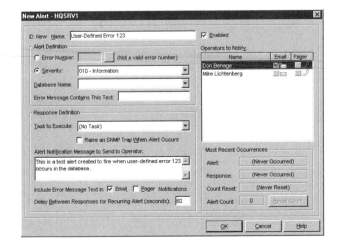

4. Enter a name for the new alert. The name you choose is arbitrary but should be descriptive of the condition that causes it to fire. For the example, you might choose a name like "Demo Alert - Information Only."

5. You can raise the alert based either on a specific error-message number or on a certain severity level. For this example, select the Severity option button and then select 010 Information from the Severity drop-down list.

6. The Database Name and the Error Message Contains String are optional constraints you can use to further narrow the situations that cause this alert to fire. They are not used in this example.

7. In the Response Definition box, you can select a task to be executed by the SQL Executive. In this case, you only use SQL Mail to notify an administrator, but you could define some action to attempt an automatic repair. This, in turn, could send a message based on success or failure. Leave Task To Execute set to (No Task) and enter a message in the box labeled Alert Notification Message To Send To Operator. The message should reflect the nature of the alert.

8. Select the appropriate check boxes to indicate how the message should be sent. You can include the message in an e-mail or pager notification.

N O T E To use pager notification, you need to purchase a third-party software application that can initiate a page based on the receipt of e-mail in a mailbox. Several such packages exist (such as WinBeep or AlphaPage). ■

9. Click OK to define your new alert. You are ready to continue with the next procedure.

Defining SQL Server Operators

Now that you have defined an alert, you must define one or more operators and assign the alert to an operator. To define an operator and assign the alert, follow these steps:

1. If you have not already done so, start the SQL Enterprise Manager and connect to the SQL Server of your choice.

2. Click the Manage Alerts toolbar button, or choose Server, Alerts from the menu.

3. Click the Operators tab if it is not already visible. The operators who have already been defined display. Click the New Operator toolbar button, the fourth button from the left that depicts a hat. The New Operator dialog box appears (see Figure 48.18).

FIG. 48.18

This dialog box allows you to define a new operator, create a schedule for pager responsibilities (if any), and assign alerts.

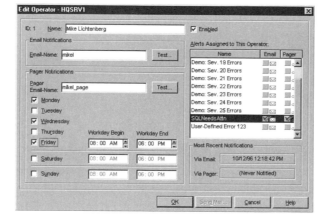

4. Enter a name for the operator. The name does not need to match an e-mail ID or a Windows NT account ID.

5. In the Email Notifications box, enter the e-mail alias that will receive notifications for this alert. This should be the name of a SQL Server administrator, not the name of the SQL Mail account.

6. If you have set up paging software, enter the name of the pager account.

7. Click the Test button for either type of notification and a test message will be sent to the recipient you have defined to ensure they can receive these notifications.

8. For pager notifications only, you can define a schedule during which this operator is "on call." You can define a specific time period for any selected weekdays and separate times for Saturday or Sunday if either or both are selected.

Part
X

Ch
48

9. In the Alerts Assigned To This Operator box at the right of the dialog box, select the type of notification to be sent for each defined alert (if any).

10. When the schedule and the alerts have been selected, click the Send Mail button. This composes a mail message informing the operator of their new responsibilities (see Figure 48.19).

FIG. 48.19

Clicking the Send Mail button creates an e-mail message notifying the operator of the new responsibilities assigned to them.

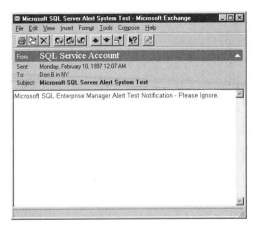

11. Click OK to finish defining the new operator. You can select the Alerts tab again to see check marks in the e-mail or pager columns indicating that the alert has been assigned to at least one operator.

Testing Your SQL Server Alert Definitions

To test your alert and see if the SQL Mail component is working, follow these steps:

1. If you have not already done so, start the SQL Enterprise Manager and connect to the SQL Server on which you defined the alert.

2. Click the SQL Query Tool toolbar button, or choose Tools, SQL Query Tool from the menu.

3. Enter a RAISERROR statement (see Figure 48.20), or simply enter the command **test_alert** if you defined this procedure as described in the section "Creating User-Defined Error Messages" earlier in this chapter. Execute the query. This should cause an entry to be placed in the SQL Server error log and an entry in the Applications event log on the server if you specified the WITH LOG option. It also should cause an e-mail and/or pager notification to be sent to the account(s) you specified in the operator definition.

4. You can view the SQL Server error log in the SQL Enterprise Manager by choosing Server, Error Log from the menu (see Figure 48.20). Start the mail client on an appropriate machine that has a profile created for the operator who should receive the notification messages. Request delivery of new messages, and you should see the notification message from SQL Mail.

FIG. 48.20
The SQL Server Error
Log is reflecting a user-
defined error condition.

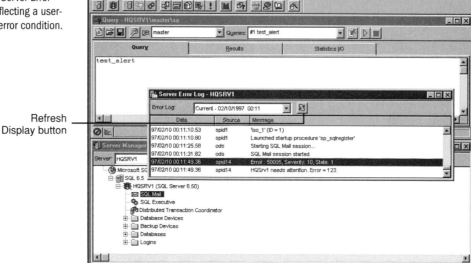

Refresh
Display button

From Here...

In this chapter, you learned some techniques that will allow you to take a proactive approach to network management, rather than react when things go wrong. You learned how to use the Windows NT Performance Monitor and how to use some of the diagnostic aids included with SQL Server to anticipate and respond quickly to error conditions. You can use the same type of approach with all BackOffice Family components to help keep your organization running smoothly.

You are ready! You have learned the basics and then some. Continue to explore the Microsoft BackOffice Family, its tools, and its services. It is a rich set of products that has great depth. The more you investigate, the more ways you will discover to exploit its features and capabilities.

If you would like to review some of the products you have learned about, consult the following chapters:

- For information on using BackOffice on the World Wide Web or an intranet, see Chapter 16, "The BackOffice I-Net Toolbox."

- For information on the e-mail and groupware component of BackOffice, Exchange Server, see Chapter 26, "An Inside Look at Exchange Server."

- For information on the database component of BackOffice, SQL Server, see Chapter 33, "An Inside Look at SQL Server."

- For information on the systems management component of BackOffice, Systems Management Server (SMS), see Chapter 42, "Preparing for SMS."

Part
X

Ch
48

Appendix

SNA Server Preparation Forms

by Jim Marshbank

This appendix provides blank copies of the forms listed here, which are useful in gathering and organizing SNA Server installation planning data (see Figures A.1 through A.16). Use them as necessary to plan and organize your SNA Server installation parameters. The forms included in this appendix are listed on the right. ■

- Server Resources Planning Form
- Server Information Form
- Initial Connection Settings Form
- 802.2 Settings Form
- SDLC Settings Form
- X.25 Settings Form
- Channel Settings Form
- 3270 LUs Form (for Individual LUs)
- 3270 LUs Form (for Ranges of LUs)
- 3270 LU Pools Form
- Users and Groups Form
- Local APPC LUs Form
- Remote APPC LUs Form
- Mode Properties for LU-LU Pairs Form
- CPI-C Properties Form
- 3270 RTM Settings Form

FIG. A.1

Server Resources Planning Form

Server Name: _____
Comment: _____

Installed adapters:

_____
_____
_____

Connections:

_____   _____   _____
_____   _____   _____
_____   _____   _____

Remote system(s) to connect to:

_____   [ ] Host   [ ] Peer   [ ] Downstream
_____   [ ] Host   [ ] Peer   [ ] Downstream
_____   [ ] Host   [ ] Peer   [ ] Downstream
_____   [ ] Host   [ ] Peer   [ ] Downstream
_____   [ ] Host   [ ] Peer   [ ] Downstream

FIG. A.2

App
A

Server Information Form

Server Name: _____ Server Location: _____

Machine manufacturer: _____ Type: [ ] Intel [ ] MIPS [ ] Alpha

Machine model: _____ RAM (megabytes): _____ Speed: _____

Network adapter: Manufacturer: _____ Model: _____

Adapter Manufacturer	Model	Interrupt
_____	_____	_____
_____	_____	_____
_____	_____	_____
_____	_____	

IRQ (interrupt)	Common usage	Usage on this server
3	COM2	_____
4	COM1	_____
5	LPT2 or network	_____
6	Disk controller	_____
7	LPT1 or SCSI adapter	_____

UPS: [ ] Yes (__COM1 __COM2)   [ ] No

Network and version:
[ ] Microsoft networking (named pipes)   [ ] TCP/IP   [ ] AppleTalk
[ ] NetWare®, version _____   [ ] Banyan VINES, version _____

Transport:
[ ] NetBEUI [ ] TCP/IP [ ] IPX/SPX [ ] DECnet™ [ ] RAS [ ] Other

Role: Domain: [ ] Primary controller [ ] Backup controller [ ] Server
          Replication: [ ] Export [ ] Import [ ] Both

SNA server: [ ] Primary [ ] Backup [ ] Member
Installation support: Supports network installation [ ] Yes [ ] No

FIG. A.3

Initial Connection Settings Form

Server Name: _____   Connection Name: _____

Comment: _____

Link Service: _____

Remote End: [ ] Host System
                                                 [ ] Peer System
                                                 [ ] Downstream
Activation: [ ] On Server Startup
                                                 [ ] On Demand
                                                 [ ] By Administrator
Allowed Directions: [ ] Outgoing Calls
                                                 [ ] Incoming Calls

Virtual Circuit Type (X.25 only) :   [ ] Switched   [ ] Permanent

FIG. A.4

802.2 Settings Form

Server Name: _____ Connection Name: _____

Basic Settings

Remote Network Address: _____

Local Node ID: [__ __ __] [__ __ __ __ __]

Remote Node Name:

    Network Name: _____

    Control Point Name: _____

    Remote Node ID: [__ __ __] [__ __ __ __ __]

Connection Activation:

Maximum number of attempts: _____ Delay after failed attempts: _____

Advanced Settings

XID Type: [ ] Format 0   [ ] Format 3

Remote SAP Address: _____   Retry Limit: _____

Max BTU Length: _____   XID Retries: _____

Response (t1) Timeout: _____

Receive ACK (t2) Timeout: _____

Inactivity (ti) Timeout: _____

Receive ACK Threshold: _____ frames.

Unacknowledged Send Limit: _____ frames.

FIG. A.5

SDLC Settings Form

Server Name: _____ Connection Name: _____

Basic Settings

Dial Data: _____

Local Node ID: [__ __ __] [__ __ __ __ __]

Remote Node Name:

  Network Name: _____

  Control Point Name: _____

  Remote Node ID: [__ __ __] [__ __ __ __ __]

Connection Activation:

Maximum number of attempts: _____ Delay after failed attempts: _____

Advanced Settings

XID Type:	Encoding:	Duplex:	Data Rate:
[ ] Format 0	[ ] NRZ	[ ] Half	[ ] Low
[ ] Format 3	[ ] NRZI	[ ] Full	[ ] High

Poll Address: _____ Contact Timeout: _____ x0.1s

Poll Rate: _____ per s Contact Retry Limit: _____

Poll Timeout: _____ x0.1s Idle Timeout: _____ x0.1s

Poll Retry Limit: _____ Idle Retry Limit: _____

Max BTU Length: _____ s

Multidrop Primary: [ ] Yes   [ ] No
Select Standby: [ ] Yes   [ ] No

Switched Connection Establishment Timeout: _____

FIG. A.6

X.25 Settings Form

Server Name: _____ Connection Name: _____

Basic Settings

Remote X.25 Address: _____

Local Node ID: [__ __ __] [__ __ __ __ __]

Remote Node Name:

    Network Name: _____

    Control Point Name: _____

    Remote Node ID: [__ __ __] [__ __ __ __ __]

Connection Activation:
Maximum number of attempts: _____ Delay after failed attempts: _____

Advanced Settings

XID Type: [   ] Format 0   [   ] Format 3

Max BTU Length: _____

Packet Size (PVC only): _____

Window Size (PVC only): _____

PVC Alias (PVC only): _____

Facility Data (SVC only): _____

User Data (SVC only): _____

FIG. A.7

Channel Settings Form

Server Name: _____   Connection Name: _____

Basic Settings

Channel Address: _____

Local Node ID: [__ __ __] [__ __ __ __ __]

Advanced Settings

XID Type: [   ] Format 0   [   ] Format 3

Max BTU Length: _____

FIG. A.8

3270 LUs Form (for Individual LUs)

LU Number: _____ LU Name: _____
Connection: _____ Comment: _____

LU type: [ ] Display   Display Model: [ ] 2 (24x80)
              [ ] Printer   [ ] 3 (32x80)
                                                        [ ] 4 (43x80)
                                                        [ ] 5 (27x132)
                                  Model can be overridden: [ ] Yes [ ] No

- -

LU Number: _____ LU Name: _____
Connection: _____ Comment: _____

LU type: [ ] Display   Display Model: [ ] 2 (24x80)
              [ ] Printer   [ ] 3 (32x80)
                                                        [ ] 4 (43x80)
                                                        [ ] 5 (27x132)
                                  Model can be overridden: [ ] Yes [ ] No

- -

LU Number: _____ LU Name: _____
Connection: _____ Comment: _____

LU type: [ ] Display   Display Model: [ ] 2 (24x80)
              [ ] Printer   [ ] 3 (32x80)
                                                        [ ] 4 (43x80)
                                                        [ ] 5 (27x132)
                                  Model can be overridden: [ ] Yes [ ] No

FIG. A.9

3270 LUs Form (for Ranges of LUs)

Connection: _____
Base LU Name: _____
First LU Number: _____
Number of LUs: _____
LU Numbers: _____
LU Names: _____
Comment: _____
LU type: [ ] Display   Display Model: [ ] 2 (24x80)
              [ ] Printer   [ ] 3 (32x80)
                                                     [ ] 4 (43x80)
                                                     [ ] 5 (27x132)
                                      Model can be overridden: [ ] Yes [ ] No

- -

Connection: _____
Base LU Name: _____
First LU Number: _____
Number of LUs: _____
LU Numbers: _____
LU Names: _____
Comment: _____
LU type: [ ] Display   Display Model: [ ] 2 (24x80)
              [ ] Printer   [ ] 3 (32x80)
                                                     [ ] 4 (43x80)
                                                     [ ] 5 (27x132)
                                      Model can be overridden: [ ] Yes [ ] No

FIG. A.10

3270 LU Pools Form

Pool Name: _____ Comment: _____

Display Model: [ ] 2 (24x80)
                         [ ] 3 (32x80)
                         [ ] 4 (43x80)
                         [ ] 5 (27x132)
Model can be overridden: [ ] Yes [ ] No

LUs in Pool:

_____ _____ _____ _____
_____ _____ _____ _____
_____ _____ _____ _____
_____ _____ _____ _____

· ·

Pool Name: _____ Comment: _____

Display Model: [ ] 2 (24x80)
                         [ ] 3 (32x80)
                         [ ] 4 (43x80)
                         [ ] 5 (27x132)
Model can be overridden: [ ] Yes [ ] No

LUs in Pool:

_____ _____ _____ _____
_____ _____ _____ _____
_____ _____ _____ _____

FIG. A.11

Users and Groups Form

User or Group Name: _____
Domain: _____
Comment: _____
3270 LUs: _____   _____   _____   _____
              _____   _____   _____
Default Local APPC LU: _____
Default Remote APPC LU: _____

- -

User or Group Name: _____
Domain: _____
Comment: _____
3270 LUs: _____   _____   _____   _____
              _____   _____   _____
Default Local APPC LU: _____
Default Remote APPC LU: _____

FIG. A.12

Local APPC LUs Form

Server: _____ LU 6.2 Type: [ ] Independent   [ ] Dependent
LU Alias: _____
Network Name: _____ LU Name: _____
LU Number (Dependent only):   _____
Comment: _____
Enable Automatic Partnering: [ ] Yes [ ] No
Member of Default Outgoing Local APPC LU Pool: [ ] Yes [ ] No
Implicit Incoming Remote LU: _____
Timeout for Starting TPs: _____

Partner LUs: _____   _____   _____
                 _____   _____   _____

- -

Server: _____ LU 6.2 Type: [ ] Independent   [ ] Dependent
LU Alias: _____
Network Name: _____ LU Name: _____
LU Number (Dependent only):   _____
Comment: _____
Enable Automatic Partnering: [ ] Yes [ ] No
Member of Default Outgoing Local APPC LU Pool: [ ] Yes [ ] No
Implicit Incoming Remote LU: _____
Timeout for Starting TPs: _____

Partner LUs: _____   _____   _____
                 _____   _____   _____

FIG. A.13

Remote APPC LUs Form

Connection: _____

LU Alias: _____ LU Name: _____

Network Name: _____ Uninterpreted LU Name: _____

Comment: _____

Supports Parallel Sessions: [ ] Yes [ ] No

Enable Automatic Partnering: [ ] Yes [ ] No

Implicit Incoming Mode: _____

- -

Connection: _____

LU Alias: _____ LU Name: _____

Network Name: _____ Uninterpreted LU Name: _____

Comment: _____

Supports Parallel Sessions: [ ] Yes [ ] No

Enable Automatic Partnering: [ ] Yes [ ] No

Implicit Incoming Mode: _____

- -

Connection: _____

LU Alias: _____ LU Name: _____

Network Name: _____ Uninterpreted LU Name: _____

Comment: _____

Supports Parallel Sessions: [ ] Yes [ ] No

Enable Automatic Partnering: [ ] Yes [ ] No

Implicit Incoming Mode: _____

FIG. A.14

Mode Properties for LU-LU Pairs Form

Mode Name: _____

Comment: _____

LU-LU pairs that will use this mode: _____

Local   Remote
_____   _____
_____   _____
_____   _____
_____   _____

Parallel Session Limit: _____
Minimum Contention Winner Limit: _____
Partner Min Contention Winner Limit: _____
Automatic Activation Limit: _____

Enable Automatic Partnering: [ ] Yes   [ ] No
High Priority Mode: [ ] Yes   [ ] No

Pacing Send Count: _____ Max Send RU Size: _____

Pacing Receive Count: _____ Max Receive RU Size: _____

FIG. A.15

CPI-C Properties Form

Name: _____ Comment: _____
Partner TP Name
Application TP: _____
OR
SNA Service TP (in hex): _____

Partner LU Name
Alias: _____
OR
Fully Qualified: _____

Conversation Security: None   [ ]
                          Same   [ ]
                          Program   [ ]
                                    User ID _____
                                    Password _____
Mode Name: _____

FIG. A.16

3270 RTM Settings Form

RTM Data Sent at: [ ] Counter Overflow   [ ] End of Session
RTM Timers Run Until:
          [ ] First Data Reaches Screen
          [ ] Host Unlocks Keyboard
          [ ] Host Lets User Send

                                        RTM Thresholds
Threshold #1: _____ x0.1s   Threshold #3: _____ x0.1s
Threshold #2: _____ x0.1s   Threshold #4: _____ x0.1s

Index

BackOffice Solutions Don't Stop Here...

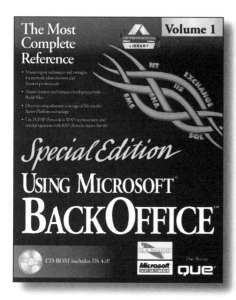

The Most Complete Reference

Volume 1

Special Edition

USING MICROSOFT BACKOFFICE™

CD-ROM includes IIS 4.0!

ISBN: 0-7897-1142-7 • PRICE: $75.00 USA

For more answers to your BackOffice questions, complete your BackOffice set with *Special Edition Using Microsoft BackOffice, Vol 1.*

Discover additional coverage of:

- Internet and intranet implementation
- Internet Information Server with Active Server Pages technology
- Index Server
- Proxy Server
- Content Replication System
- Dial-up access with the Remote Access Service (RAS)
- Using TCP/IP protocols
- Security for all BackOffice products

Volume 1 also includes a power-packed CD-ROM with electronic versions of these Special Edition Using books in Que's BackOffice Library:

- Special Edition Using Commercial Internet System
- Special Edition Using Internet Information Server 2
- Special Edition Using Windows NT Server 4
- Special Edition Using FrontPage 97

Available at your local bookstore!
Or to order call 1-800-772-0477
Or visit us on the Internet at: http://www.quecorp.com

Discover The Power™ Copyright 1997 Macmillan Computer Publishing USA. A Simon & Schuster Company. The Publishing Operation of Viacom Inc.

Complete and Return this Card
for a *FREE* Computer Book Catalog

Thank you for purchasing this book! You have purchased a superior computer book written expressly for your needs. To continue to provide the kind of up-to-date, pertinent coverage you've come to expect from us, we need to hear from you. Please take a minute to complete and return this self-addressed, postage-paid form. In return, we'll send you a free catalog of all our computer books on topics ranging from word processing to programming and the internet.

Mr. ☐   Mrs. ☐   Ms. ☐   Dr. ☐

Name (first) ☐☐☐☐☐☐☐☐☐☐☐☐☐   (M.I.) ☐   (last) ☐☐☐☐☐☐☐☐☐☐☐☐☐☐☐☐☐

Address ☐☐☐☐☐☐☐☐☐☐☐☐☐☐☐☐☐☐☐☐☐☐☐☐☐☐☐☐☐☐☐☐☐

☐☐☐☐☐☐☐☐☐☐☐☐☐☐☐☐☐☐☐☐☐☐☐☐☐☐☐☐☐☐☐☐☐

City ☐☐☐☐☐☐☐☐☐☐☐☐☐☐☐   State ☐☐   Zip ☐☐☐☐☐ ☐☐☐☐

Phone ☐☐☐ ☐☐☐ ☐☐☐☐   Fax ☐☐☐ ☐☐☐ ☐☐☐☐

Company Name ☐☐☐☐☐☐☐☐☐☐☐☐☐☐☐☐☐☐☐☐☐☐☐☐☐☐☐☐☐☐

E-mail address ☐☐☐☐☐☐☐☐☐☐☐☐☐☐☐☐☐☐☐☐☐☐☐☐☐☐☐☐☐☐

1. Please check at least (3) influencing factors for purchasing this book.

Front or back cover information on book .... ☐
Special approach to the content .... ☐
Completeness of content .... ☐
Author's reputation .... ☐
Publisher's reputation .... ☐
Book cover design or layout .... ☐
Index or table of contents of book .... ☐
Price of book .... ☐
Special effects, graphics, illustrations .... ☐
Other (Please specify): _____ ☐

2. How did you first learn about this book?

Saw in Macmillan Computer Publishing catalog .... ☐
Recommended by store personnel .... ☐
Saw the book on bookshelf at store .... ☐
Recommended by a friend .... ☐
Received advertisement in the mail .... ☐
Saw an advertisement in: _____ ☐
Read book review in: _____ ☐
Other (Please specify): _____ ☐

3. How many computer books have you purchased in the last six months?

This book only .... ☐   3 to 5 books .... ☐
2 books .... ☐   More than 5 .... ☐

4. Where did you purchase this book?

Bookstore .... ☐
Computer Store .... ☐
Consumer Electronics Store .... ☐
Department Store .... ☐
Office Club .... ☐
Warehouse Club .... ☐
Mail Order .... ☐
Direct from Publisher .... ☐
Internet site .... ☐
Other (Please specify): _____ ☐

5. How long have you been using a computer?

☐ Less than 6 months   ☐ 6 months to a year
☐ 1 to 3 years   ☐ More than 3 years

6. What is your level of experience with personal computers and with the subject of this book?

	With PCs	With subject of book
New	☐	☐
Casual	☐	☐
Accomplished	☐	☐
Expert	☐	☐

Source Code ISBN: 0-7897-1130-3

7. Which of the following best describes your job title?

Administrative Assistant .... ☐
Coordinator .... ☐
Manager/Supervisor .... ☐
Director .... ☐
Vice President .... ☐
President/CEO/COO .... ☐
Lawyer/Doctor/Medical Professional .... ☐
Teacher/Educator/Trainer .... ☐
Engineer/Technician .... ☐
Consultant .... ☐
Not employed/Student/Retired .... ☐
Other (Please specify): _____ ☐

8. Which of the following best describes the area of the company your job title falls under?

Accounting .... ☐
Engineering .... ☐
Manufacturing .... ☐
Operations .... ☐
Marketing .... ☐
Sales .... ☐
Other (Please specify): _____ ☐

9. What is your age?

Under 20 .... ☐
21-29 .... ☐
30-39 .... ☐
40-49 .... ☐
50-59 .... ☐
60-over .... ☐

10. Are you:

Male .... ☐
Female .... ☐

11. Which computer publications do you read regularly? (Please list)

_____
_____
_____
_____
_____
_____
_____
_____
_____

Comments: _____
_____
_____

Fold here and scotch-tape to mail.

Check out Que® Books on the World Wide Web
http://www.quecorp.com

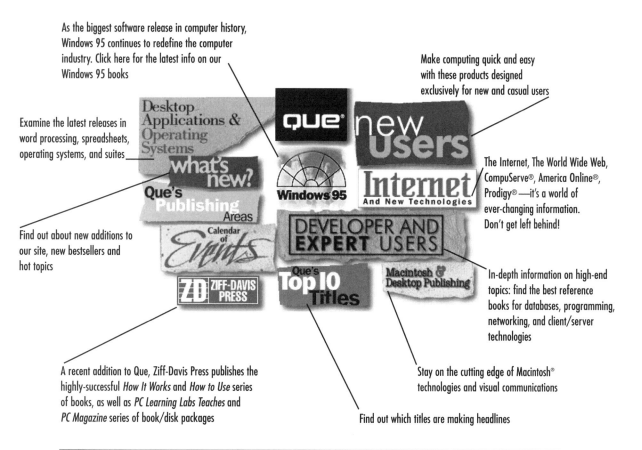

As the biggest software release in computer history, Windows 95 continues to redefine the computer industry. Click here for the latest info on our Windows 95 books

Examine the latest releases in word processing, spreadsheets, operating systems, and suites

Find out about new additions to our site, new bestsellers and hot topics

A recent addition to Que, Ziff-Davis Press publishes the highly-successful *How It Works* and *How to Use* series of books, as well as *PC Learning Labs Teaches* and *PC Magazine* series of book/disk packages

Make computing quick and easy with these products designed exclusively for new and casual users

The Internet, The World Wide Web, CompuServe®, America Online®, Prodigy®—it's a world of ever-changing information. Don't get left behind!

In-depth information on high-end topics: find the best reference books for databases, programming, networking, and client/server technologies

Stay on the cutting edge of Macintosh® technologies and visual communications

Find out which titles are making headlines

With 6 separate publishing groups, Que develops products for many specific market segments and areas of computer technology. Explore our Web Site and you'll find information on best-selling titles, newly published titles, upcoming products, authors, and much more.

- Stay informed on the latest industry trends and products available
- Visit our online bookstore for the latest information and editions
- Download software from Que's library of the best shareware and freeware

Licensing Agreement

By opening this package, you are agreeing to be bound by the following:

The software contained on this CD is, in many cases, copyrighted and all rights are reserved by the individual software developer and/or publisher. You are bound by the individual licensing agreements associated with each piece of software contained on the CD. THIS SOFTWARE IS PROVIDED FREE OF CHARGE, AS IS, AND WITHOUT WARRANTY OF ANY KIND, EITHER EXPRESSED OR IMPLIED, INCLUDING, BUT NOT LIMITED TO, THE IMPLIED WARRANTIES OF MERCHANTABILITY AND FITNESS FOR A PARTICULAR PURPOSE. Neither the book publisher nor its dealers and distributors assumes any liability for any alleged or actual damages arising from the use of this software. (Some states do not allow exclusion of implied warranties, so the exclusion may not apply to you.)